CITIES IN MODERNITY

What made cities 'modern' in the nineteenth and early twentieth centuries? *Cities in Modernity* explores connections between culture, economy and built environment in cities of this period, drawing its evidence principally from London, New York and Toronto. The book discusses both the cultural experience of modernity and the material modernisation of cities – placing special emphasis on their historical geographies, especially the production, representation and use of urban space. The opening chapters present new ways of seeing cities in political and religious discourse, social survey, mapping, art and literature. The book then concentrates on new kinds of public and private spaces, such as apartment buildings, office blocks and department stores, and the networks of communication between them. An important theme throughout is the gendered experience of the new types of environment. The book will appeal to scholars and students of historical geography, urban history and cultural studies.

RICHARD DENNIS is Reader in the Department of Geography, University College London (UCL). He was Associate Editor of the *Journal of Urban History* from 1998 to 2007 and is the author of *English Industrial Cities of the Nineteenth Century: A Social Geography* (1984).

D1470683

Cambridge Studies in Historical Geography 40

Series editors:
ALAN R. H. BAKER, RICHARD DENNIS, DERYCK HOLDSWORTH

Cambridge Studies in Historical Geography encourages exploration of the philosophies, methodologies and techniques of historical geography and publishes the results of new research within all branches of the subject. It endeavours to secure the marriage of traditional scholarship with innovative approaches to problems and to sources, aiming in this way to provide a focus for the discipline and to contribute towards its development. The series is an international forum for publication in historical geography which also promotes contact with workers in cognate disciplines.

For a full list of titles in the series, please see end of book.

CITIES IN MODERNITY

Representations and Productions of Metropolitan Space, 1840–1930

RICHARD DENNIS
University College London

CAMBRIDGE
UNIVERSITY PRESS

CAMBRIDGE UNIVERSITY PRESS
Cambridge, New York, Melbourne, Madrid, Cape Town, Singapore, São Paulo, Delhi

Cambridge University Press
32 Avenue of the Americas, New York, NY 10013-2473, USA

www.cambridge.org
Information on this title: www.cambridge.org/9780521468411

First published 2008

Printed in the United States of America

A catalog record for this publication is available from the British Library.

Library of Congress Cataloging in Publication Data

Dennis, Richard, 1949–
   Cities in modernity : representations and productions of metropolitan
space, 1840–1930 / Richard Dennis.
     p.   cm. – (Cambridge studies in historical geography ; 40)
Includes bibliographical references and index.
ISBN 978-0-521-46470-3 (hardcover) – ISBN 978-0-521-46841-1 (pbk.)
1. Cities and towns – History – 19th century.   2. City planning – History – 19th century.
3. Urban geography – History – 19th century.   4. Cities and towns – History – 20th century.
5. City planning – History – 20th century.   6. Urban geography – History – 20th century.
7. Cities and towns–Case studies.   I. Title.   II. Series.
HT119.D46   2008
307.7609′034 – dc22   2007045454

ISBN   978-0-521-46470-3 hardback
ISBN   978-0-521-46841-1 paperback

Contents

Illustrations

Tables

Preface

This book is both longer and shorter than it ought to be. Shorter in that in aspiring to cover *every* site of significance in modern cities, I am conscious of having omitted much that others would consider absolutely vital: no discussion of the seats and sites of government, discipline and order – city halls, courthouses, jails, police stations, fire stations, hospitals, schools and colleges; nothing on the palaces of modern transportation – the grand railway termini; little on the sites of manufacturing production, or on the popular culture of pubs and bars, music halls and movie houses.

But it is still a longer book than I originally anticipated. Although it deals with the modernity of cities, and modernity has spawned a department-store-full of critical theory over the last thirty years, my emphasis is not primarily theoretical. Whatever else they were, cities in late nineteenth-century Britain and North America were packed full of people, buildings and activity, and I want to convey this crowding and frenetic energy. So my text is deliberately full to overflowing with examples, incidents and asides, as writer and readers pick their way along crowded city streets or wait (im)patiently at the bus stop while a succession of vehicles on other routes pass by. As with any comparison shopping, it takes time and energy to evaluate alternatives; so this book engages in a good deal of browsing the sites and sights of London, New York and Toronto. The 'modern' experiences and environments I discuss are restricted – mostly middle-class, Anglophone, First World, usually through male eyes, even when women are the focus of attention. This is not to deny the importance of all those 'other' modernities – colonial and postcolonial, or however marginalised – but, in this book, I am more interested in the built environment and its experience by self-consciously modern people in the Anglo-American cities I know best.

The book's origins go back to the mid-1980s, when I first developed research interests in model dwellings in London and landlordism in Toronto. Seeking an excuse to continue research in Toronto, I followed Jim Lemon's advice to examine the contested early history of apartment housing in the city, a topic that quickly led in diverse directions, guiding me into fictional, documentary and visual representations of the city, as well as the quantifiable sources with which I was most comfortable. It also led me back to undertake new research on middle-class flats in London, complementing my previous interest in working-class housing. Needing a framework to integrate these different perspectives on the social geography of cities, I was soon directed, initially by Peter Jackson and John Radford, to some of the classics of writing about modernity.

Meanwhile my UCL colleague, Hugh Clout, had invited me to contribute sections on 'Victorian London' to *The Times London History Atlas*, of which he was the academic editor, a task that called for thinking beyond the issues of housing and residential segregation that had dominated my research hitherto. An opportunity to spend a term at Macalester College and the University of Minnesota in fall 1991 allowed me to restructure my UCL course on 'Urban Historical Geography' and to reflect on its relevance for North American students and cities. I also joined with Roger Miller in teaching a graduate seminar in historical geography, picking up on Roger's enthusiasm for urban cultural studies.

Back in London, 'Urban Historical Geography' was soon re-born as 'Cities and Modernity'. The structure of that course provides the framework for this book, focused firstly on new ways of seeing the city and secondly on new spaces within cities and new forms of connection between those spaces. Much of my inspiration lay in the geographer's traditional activity of fieldwork – in this case walking the city. Hence my focus on three cities whose downtowns, at least, I have walked extensively – London, Toronto and New York – supplemented by examples from other cities, including Chicago, Montreal and Melbourne, where I have had the opportunity to explore in the company of local experts.

My debts are numerous. First, to friends and colleagues, who have accommodated, entertained and guided me around their home towns: Jim and Carolyn Lemon, Richard Harris and Carol Town, Larry and Paula Bourne, John and Marilyn Harrison, David and Maureen Carter-Whitney, Peter Goheen, Grif Cunningham and Rusty Shteir, and Rob Lewis in Ontario; Sherry Olson, Michèle Dagenais and Brian Young in Montreal; Roger Miller, David Lanegran and Judy Martin in Minnesota; Martyn Bowden, Michael Conzen, Deryck Holdsworth and David Ward variously scattered around the United States; and Alan Mayne and Jane M. Jacobs (now in Edinburgh) in Melbourne. Back home, Jim Sturgis, the late John Davis, Phil Buckner, Chris Dummitt and Steve Shaw provided encouragement and regular opportunities to discuss Canadian cities; Coral Howells and Ceri Morgan enthusiastically emboldened me to do more than just read novels about place and space; and Michael Hellyer, Vivien Hughes and Jodie Robson offered unfailing institutional support for my Canadian interests. Encouraged by a positive reception for my ventures into Canadian literature, I have edged into American literature, too, thanks to fellow participants in meetings organised by the Nottingham-Birmingham-based 'Three Cities Project', and I have more comprehensively plunged into the world of the English novelist, George Gissing. I am especially grateful to Pierre Coustillas, Bouwe Postmus and John Spiers for their warm welcome and wholehearted support for a geographer among Gissingites.

Among the ranks of archivists and curators, I want particularly to register my thanks to Alex Werner and his colleagues at the Museum of London; to John Sargent and staff of the City of Westminster Archives Centre, especially Hilary Davies and Jill Barber, formerly Education Officer there; to Emma Chambers of the UCL Art Collection, Anne Oxenham and Nick Mann of the UCL Geography Map Library, Jeremy Smith of Guildhall Library, and Heather Creaton, formerly at the Centre for

Metropolitan History; and to Karen Teeple and staff of the City of Toronto Archives. Isobel Watson has pointed me to sources about flats that I should have known about already, and Geoffrey Best, Mona Domosh, Seamus O'Hanlon, Paul Laxton and Gillian Tindall have variously contributed information, advice and encouragement. Among numerous colleagues at UCL and the Institute of Historical Research, I *must* acknowledge Iain Black, Hugh Clout, Martin Daunton (now at Cambridge), Davide Deriu, Claire Dwyer, John Foot, Adrian Forty, Matthew Gandy, Alan Gilbert, David Gilbert, David Green, Tom Gretton, Derek Keene, James Kneale, David Lowenthal, James Moore, Barbara Penner, Hugh Prince, Ann Varley and Peter Wood.

Special thanks to Ceinwen Giles, Research Officer on an ESRC-funded project on Canadian apartment-house tenants; to doctoral students, now Drs Jeremy Stein, Larry Cort, Caroline Bressey and Sarah Glynn; to successive groups of 'Modernity, Space and Place' master's students, especially Bob Ross, Sue Haddrell and Desmond Fitz-Gibbon; and to undergraduates whose coursework and dissertations have provided insights and references I would probably not have discovered for myself, including Josh Holmes, Erin Brooks, Guanming Low and Ting Cheung.

As well as the Economic & Social Research Council, I acknowledge with gratitude the financial assistance of the Government of Canada (Canada Research Awards) and the Foundation for Canadian Studies, the Leverhulme Trust, the Central Research Fund of the University of London, and the Dean's Fund of University College London, who have variously supported research trips and visits to North American and Australasian cities. Richard Harris read most and Michèle Dagenais some of the first draft, but Deryck Holdsworth has read drafts of every chapter that appears here and some that, thanks to his wise advice, do not. Deryck and Alan Baker have always been supportive co-editors of the Cambridge Historical Geography series, and Richard Fisher and, latterly, Michael Watson and Helen Waterhouse, enthusiastic and human faces of the Press. Maps and diagrams have been expertly produced by Miles Irving, Catherine D'Alton, Elanor McBay and Dai Kurebayashi Williams at the Department of Geography, UCL.

Anne-Marie was quickly converted to the delights of Toronto, as was Helen, though Sam was harder to persuade, and Anne-Marie has since been won over to the pleasures of New York. Sadly, both my parents died during the book's lengthy gestation period. Without realising it, they initiated me in the love of London – those early trips from Carshalton into Victoria and a sinister, dark, unredeemed Victoria Street; to Hamley's on Regent Street and Gamage's in Holborn, both renowned for their spectacular model railways, the latter also providing the launch-pad for one of my most haunting childhood experiences – wandering through the overgrown, bombed-out ruins of the City, truly one of modernity's graveyards. I dedicate this book to their memory.

Richard Dennis
UCL and North Harrow
March 2007

A note on vocabulary and units of measurement

I have not attempted to convert monetary terms into present-day equivalents. My British citizens trade in pounds, shillings and pence; my North Americans in dollars and cents, but at very different exchange rates with the pound from those prevailing today. Likewise, they all thought and acted in miles, yards, feet and inches, so those are the units I have used. While I have used English spelling, I have retained American spelling as appropriate in quotations. I have attempted to keep my vocabulary consistent with the places I am discussing: my North Americans ride streetcars and elevators, use sidewalks and pay property taxes; my Londoners make do with trams, lifts and pavements, and pay rates.

1

Building bridges

This is a book about the spaces of 'modern cities' in Britain and North America during the second half of the nineteenth and the first third of the twentieth centuries, a period often identified as quintessentially 'modern' by cultural historians. For a simple working definition of 'modern' I will begin with Marshall Berman's 'dynamic and dialectical modernism' concerned with the 'intimate unity of the modern self and the modern environment'.[1] My interest is in the relationship between the modernisation of environment and society, the introduction of new ways of making sense of a changing world, and the development of new forms of self- and group-consciousness through the experience of modernisation. All these themes are predicated upon a 'shock of the new' – the realisation that now is not the same as then, but that there is an ongoing dialogue between past and present, remaking the past to serve the purposes of the present, the fetishisation of some aspects of the past in an 'invention of tradition', the rejection of other aspects in order to validate the new, but sometimes also the retention of the past as 'other' as a continuing proof of the superiority of the new.[2]

In practice, I will explore, on the one hand, new modes of representing city life, by social commentators, reformers, cartographers, novelists, artists and social scientists, and on the other, the planning, construction and use of new types of space within cities: new streets and public spaces and ways of modernising existing streets and spaces, new forms of residence in suburbs, apartment houses and 'model dwellings', new types of workplace, especially in office buildings, new spaces of consumption and recreation in department stores, exhibition buildings, parks and gardens, and new forms of connections between these segregated, specialised spaces – tramlines, railways above and below ground, pipes, sewers, cables, wires, the infrastructure vital to sustain circulation of people, goods and ideas in the forerunners of today's 'networked cities'.

I want to emphasise the active role of space in stimulating new forms of representation and shaping new identities. Space is not simply a container in which modern life is played out. Rather, the ways we conceptualise and operationalise space are products of political, economic, social and cultural processes. In turn, the organisation of space offers opportunities and constraints for the further development of those processes. For example, new artistic forms – such as the shift 'from realism to the "impression" '[3] – emerged principally in major cities because that is where artists congregated, where an art market developed among a new urban bourgeoisie, where there were new subjects for art, including new sites and viewpoints, where the coincidence of all these things stimulated imagination and innovation – technologically, financially and artistically.[4] Earlier versions of this synergy might be associated with renaissance Florence or early modern Amsterdam,[5] but the scale of stimulation for change was of a different order of magnitude in nineteenth-century London, New York or Paris.

Within modern cities, rationalism – the search for spatial and economic order and efficiency, as embodied in planning, zoning and regulation – made space for pluralism – an increasing diversity of social, ethnic and gendered identities.[6] The development of specialised neighbourhoods did not simply accommodate existing classes, 'races' and sexual identities, but provided spaces in which hybrid identities emerged. To be Irish in 1850s London or Jewish in 1900s Toronto was not the same as to be Irish in Kerry or Jewish in Kovno. Broadway and Fifth Avenue, Times Square and Central Park, Regent Street and Victoria Street, Trafalgar Square and Piccadilly Circus, all offered new public spaces which stimulated new forms of looking and performing. At the scale of individual buildings, too, skyscrapers, department stores and mansion flats were more than containers for new functions and peoples; they offered the possibility (or the threat) of cross-class or cross-gender interaction; they required new ways of thinking about private and public space.

This implies a Lefebvrian view of the production of space, connecting 'representations of space', conceptualisations made by planners, politicians, academic theorists, the discourse of the powerful, telling us how space should and *will* be organised, to 'representational spaces', the spaces of the imagination, of resistance, of carnival, of subversion and appropriation made by the powerless. The third element of Lefebvre's spatial theory – 'spatial practices' – involves the implementation of both sets of visions as far as power allows: actually building an environment of boulevards or tower blocks, or introducing regulations to control land use or manage traffic; or of occupying space, not just symbolically, as in carnival, but in the practices of everyday life, the routine of the journey to work, or of house-hunting, or the 'polite politics' of tactical transgression associated with Michel de Certeau: what people actually do in spaces.[7]

De Certeau is also relevant for the contrast he drew between the panoptic view from above, discerning order at the expense of familiarity with individual actors, and the perceptions of walkers at street level, fully engaged with their immediate surroundings but unable to see beyond them. De Certeau distinguished between 'place' which we map, and 'space' which is actualised through the tour. 'Place' implies stability and an outsider's view, 'space' is about direction, movement, velocity. Space is a 'practiced place'. In Lefebvrian language, place can be associated with representations of space, while space, in Andrew Thacker's reading, is a combination of representational space and spatial practice.[8] This is useful in thinking about forms of representation in fiction, but it can be applied more widely, for example to contrast representations of cities as organisms or networks – as connected spaces – and as mosaics of different places. A recurring theme in cultural analyses of modern cities is the creative tension between increasingly structured and segregated spaces and the opportunities among socially and geographically mobile populations to transgress the boundaries between them.

Representation lays stress on visuality and there is no doubting the significance of spectacle and display in modern cities, the self-consciousness of seeing and being seen that connected citizen and government, individual and crowd, performer and audience. Reacting against an overemphasis on representation, Patrick Joyce, in his introduction to *The Rule of Freedom*, claims to be less interested in 'the idea of a static and monolithic social *order*' and more concerned with 'the idea of social *ordering* as a fluid, open and many-stranded activity'. Consequently he focuses on 'questions of *agency*' – how things work – rather than representation – 'what things *mean*'.[9] Joyce's focus is on issues of governmentality and performance. But the language of representation is not incompatible with that of performance. Our knowledge of historical performance necessarily depends on representations in contemporary media or on our 'reading' of archaeological, architectural and environmental 'traces'; and the effectiveness of a 'rule of freedom' depends on citizens perceiving – representing to themselves – the disciplines of improvement and technology in ways intended by their instigators.

Nigel Thrift wants to dispose altogether of the language of modernity, which he sees as reductive and ahistorical. The 'shock of the new' cannot be confined to changes in politics, science and technology in the wake of an eighteenth-century enlightenment. 'Time-space compression' has gone on for millennia; the sense of alienation and 'placelessness' associated with modern cities is merely a reflection of people's inexperience with new places which, in time, come to be just as personal communities as the supposedly pre-modern places they left behind. Thrift is particularly concerned that portmanteau terms like 'modernity', 'capitalism' and 'imperialism' imply an inevitability about processes which, in reality, were tentative and uncertain, which could have turned out differently. Rather, we should focus on difference, on individual agency, on performance, on knowledge, on the interaction between rationality and irrationality.[10]

My intention in this book is not to add to the weight of social and cultural theory of modernity. I will continue to use 'modernity' as a form of 'historical shorthand',[11] acknowledging Thrift's caveats but also the self-evident truth that in Britain and North America and most other 'western' nations the nineteenth century witnessed urban growth, immigration and cultural diversity, and technological change on an unprecedented scale. But modernity for me is also a method, enshrined in Berman's dialectic between modernisation and identity, or Harvey's Marxist–humanist analyses of the experience of urban capitalism.[12] I aim to build bridges connecting cultural and economic interpretations of urbanisation, and between qualitative and quantitative modes of analysis, abstract theory and the wealth of often untheorised or differently theorised empirical studies of nineteenth- and early twentieth-century cities. To this end, I will devote most of this introductory chapter to the stories of three bridges, whose histories embody the range of arguments I want to make about the order, the ordering, the experience and the performance of cities at the end of the nineteenth and beginning of the twentieth centuries.

Three bridges: Brooklyn Bridge, Tower Bridge, and Bloor Street Viaduct

Brooklyn Bridge

In 1995, as she prepared to move after nearly sixty years in the same house, my mother uncovered a slim picture book – *New York Illustrated* – price 25 cents, undated but apparently published around the end of World War I: the title-page illustration depicted the temporary 'Arch of Victory' erected at Fifth Avenue and 24th Street (Madison Square) to celebrate the end of the war.[13] Facing this, the inside cover included scenes of 'Old New York', pointedly emphasising the extraordinary and never-ceasing transformation of the city over the preceding century. The message was reinforced by the captions accompanying these picturesque illustrations: 'This old wooden house stood no later than 1849 at a spot on 45th Street, near 5th Avenue. This has now become the most fashionable section of the city, famous for its costly residences and the millionaires that occupy them.' A sketch of City Hall noted that it 'was built in 1812 at the spot which was then the City limit. No one then ever thought the city would extend 16 miles north of that point. Skyscrapers have since taken the place of 2 and 3-story structures . . .' After this celebration of modernity through its 'other', most of the booklet's illustrations recorded the landmarks of new New York – the Statue of Liberty, the Woolworth Building, and a host of then-prominent office buildings and hotels, some either artists' impressions or heavily doctored photographs. One illustration – and only one – depicted immigrant New York, exoticising Chinatown as a place of otherness: 'Chinatown, with its crooked streets, its houses with subterranean communications, its joss houses, its secret societies and organizations, is still a problem to the New York Police. . . . It is a curious sight at night, and attracts a big crowd of visitors.' As intriguing as the caption's emphasis on the spectacle of deviance is the provenance of the illustration, derived from a photograph by Arnold Genthe which the Museum of Modern Art confidently identifies as 'Street of Gamblers (Chinatown, San Francisco)' and dates to the 1890s.[14] Evidently, the factual accuracy of the illustration was secondary in importance compared to the evocation of a counter-modern other at the heart of the modern city.

However, it is the cover illustration of *New York Illustrated* which most attracted me. This illustration, in colour, depicted Brooklyn Bridge as a gateway to the cornucopia of opportunities represented by the skyline, rising behind the Manhattan tower of the bridge as viewed from the top of the Brooklyn tower. The central span, viewed end-on, provides a ceremonial avenue into the city, and the twin arches of the tower at the Manhattan end are both gatehouse and victory arch – welcoming but also regulating the pilgrim's entry to the promised land (Figure 1.1).

The building of Brooklyn Bridge was a heroic undertaking. There were plans for a bridge across the East River from early in the nineteenth century. As shipping increased, there was conflict between ferries crossing the river east–west and ocean-going vessels moving north–south. A bridge would stimulate a rise in property values in Brooklyn, encouraging more workers in downtown Manhattan to make their homes there; but it would need to allow unimpeded passage for river traffic. Hence the idea for a high-level suspension bridge. John Augustus Roebling, who had already built suspension bridges and aqueducts in Pittsburgh, Niagara, and

Figure 1.1. Brooklyn Bridge, from the Cover of *New York Illustrated* (c.1919) (Author's Collection).

along the Delaware & Hudson Canal, first put forward proposals for a bridge across the East River in the mid-1850s, but it was not until 1867 that a bridge company was officially chartered.[15] Roebling envisaged that New York would soon overtake London as the centre of world trade and that his bridge would need to be supplemented by further connections between Manhattan and Brooklyn, including tunnels under the East River. In practice, the first subway tunnel was opened in 1909, by which time the Williamsburg and Manhattan Bridges had also been completed.[16]

Eventually begun in 1869, but not completed until 1883, construction of the Brooklyn Bridge proceeded despite the early death of its designer, fatally injured when a ferry collided with the jetty from which he was surveying the site for one of the towers. About twenty navvies also died during the building work, mainly those working long periods in caissons (compressed air chambers) beneath the riverbed, attempting to find bedrock on which to anchor the two towers. Washington Roebling, who took over from his father, himself fell victim to 'the bends' (decompression sickness) while supervising work in one of the caissons, and from 1872 onwards was obliged to direct operations from his invalid's bed in a house on Brooklyn Heights. The bridge was celebrated as a technological marvel, an eighth wonder of the world, 'more wonderful than the Pyramids'.[17] Moreover, the Pyramids had been built by slave labour whereas Brooklyn Bridge was 'a monument to the skill of a free people'.[18] With a main span of 1595 feet, it was the longest suspension bridge in the world, efficiently segregating different categories of traffic: outer lanes for road traffic, middle lanes for a cable-operated, later electric, railway, and an elevated pedestrian boardwalk. The latter was envisaged not only as a walk for commuters, many of whom in fact proved to be in too much hurry not to use public transport, but also as a healthy promenade, a downtown equivalent of Central Park.[19]

When erected in 1875, the towers of the bridge, each 277 feet in height, were the tallest non-religious buildings in the city, allowing photographers such as Joshua Beal to produce panoramic views hitherto possible only from the less secure vantage point of a hot air balloon (Figure 1.2).[20] New Yorkers could start to make sense of their city from above, much as de Certeau discussed, yet without resorting to flights of fancy. In the ease of access (if not to the towers then at least to the boardwalk, itself high enough to offer a view over and into what was still a low-rise city in the early 1880s), there was also a sense of democratisation: everybody (or, at least, everybody who could afford the one-cent toll) could survey and make sense of the city.

Brooklyn Bridge straddled not just the East River but, in its lengthy approaches, several blocks of eighteenth- and nineteenth-century counting-houses and warehouses on and behind the waterfront. The modern city was superseding and surpassing the old mercantile city. The practical reason was to provide a gentle approach for pedestrians, horse-drawn vehicles and cable cars, but the effect was to deposit those who crossed the bridge right in the heart of the city, City Hall to the right and a proto-skyscraper, the 260-feet high Tribune Building, to the left. During the decades following the opening of the bridge, this area became the core of modern Manhattan, flanked by additional newspaper head offices to the south, massive new municipal buildings to the north, and the 792-foot Woolworth Building closing off the view to the west.

It is not just for its technological modernity, its segregation of users, or its contribution to efficient circulation that Brooklyn Bridge merits its place in this introduction. It also quickly assumed the status of an icon. The combination of Gothic arches and immensely strong steel cables embodied the integration of old and new, tradition and modernity, just as many pre-World War I skyscrapers combined steel frame, electric elevators and lighting with curtain walls decked out with Gothic detail, crenellations, grotesque gargoyles and other medieval affectations. Such a hybrid of Gothic and

Figure 1.2. Brooklyn Bridge Under Construction with a View over Lower Manhattan (c.1880). By kind permission of Royal & SunAlliance Insurance Group plc; Guildhall Library, City of London Ms 31522/285.

modern was not to everyone's liking. The contemporary architectural critic, Montgomery Schuyler, 'admired the engineering but deplored the art'. He praised the steel superstructure as an honest marriage of form and function, but thought that the Gothic towers disguised rather than emphasised the structural elements of the bridge.[21]

Brooklyn Bridge may have provided a link for commuters from Brooklyn to Lower Manhattan, but in spirit, it was a bridge from the Old to the New World. It was sketched, painted and eulogised endlessly in literature and film. Most artists celebrated it as gateway to Manhattan, or exaggerated its elegant curvature to imply a kind of balletic movement, an exuberant take-off into the modern world.[22] But a few representations depicted the vertical cables as prison bars, the city seen through a wire mesh and under storm clouds.[23] Brooklyn Bridge could be a place for romantic meetings but also the ideal location for suicide: a consummation of the individual's new-found freedom, or of the city's potential for alienation. As an example of 'absolute stability' created out of an 'aggregation of unstable elements', of conflict translated into harmony, the bridge was a parable of what America could become, a moral as well as a mystical symbol.[24] In 1923, the year after publication of T. S. Eliot's *The Waste Land*, Hart Crane began to write his epic poem, *The Bridge* (1930). In *The Waste Land*, the crowd that flowed over London Bridge was a procession of the dead; but Crane wanted to celebrate life in his use of Brooklyn Bridge. In the same vein, Lewis Mumford, the eminent American urbanist, confessed to a transcendental vision while crossing the bridge in the 1920s. Setting off from Brooklyn late on a blustery March afternoon, but with enough light in the sky for the Manhattan skyscrapers to appear in silhouette against a setting sun, Mumford claimed to sense his whole life laid out before him, and to be conscious of 'the power and glory of the present world'. So, to quote Alan Trachtenberg, the bridge provided 'a roadway for traffic below and a structure for poets above'.[25]

More commercially, but often as imaginatively, Brooklyn Bridge was used to sell everything from beer to Vaseline, boots to 'Pinkham's Vegetable Compound'. Most appropriately, an advertisement featuring a side-on view of the Brooklyn Bridge, emphasising the strength in elegance of the suspension cables, asked 'Have you a Singer sewing machine?'[26] Singer's own headquarters, at Broadway and Liberty Street, not far from the Manhattan end of the bridge, a 47-storey, 612-feet high, dome-topped tower, completed in 1908 and, briefly, the world's tallest building, was itself as important symbolically as commercially, an unmistakable shape for a company logo, and a popular subject for painters and photographers (Figure 1.3).[27]

Back in 1883, the *Brooklyn Daily Eagle* had sought to position the opening of the bridge in the context of world geography and history. The paper noted how the bridge provided an incentive to unite the two sides of the East River administratively and politically in a single city, just as 'it is London on both sides of the Thames and Paris on both sides of the Seine'.[28] Opening Day, 24 May 1883, coincided with both Queen Victoria's birthday and the crowning of Tsar Alexander III in Moscow. The spontaneous celebrations of a 'free people' in Brooklyn were contrasted with the orchestrated celebrations of imperial subjects. Festive displays in the city's shop windows plundered the classics for quotations applicable to the bridge: 'Here's metal more attractive' (Hamlet); 'We extol ancient things, regardless of our times' (Tacitus).[29] With no hint of irony, or recognition of the fate that ultimately befell the cities to which it alluded, a leading Brooklyn department store proclaimed that 'Babylon had her hanging garden, Egypt her pyramid, Athens her Acropolis, Rome her Athenaeum; so Brooklyn has her Bridge'.[30]

Yet Opening Day proved a highly contested occasion: Irish labourers protested at the choice of Queen Victoria's birthday, Brooklyn's Common Council *directed* its citizens to take a day's holiday whether they wanted to or not, no construction workers were invited to the official opening, and the general public were not allowed onto the bridge until midnight, and then only on payment of the toll. Haw concludes that 'Rereading the opening day from a historical distance, we find little in the way of democratic practice or public support. Instead, we discover a tightly controlled municipal event characterized by segregation and omission.'[31] There could be few better illustrations of the tensions between disciplinary and liberating dimensions to modernity.

Figure 1.3. Singer Building, Lower Manhattan, from *New York Illustrated* (c.1919) (Author's Collection).

Figure 1.4. Tower Bridge in 1894: 'View looking north-west, with bascules up for ships to pass'. *Illustrated London News*, 30 June 1894, p. 817. Senate House Library, University of London.

Tower Bridge

London's Tower Bridge may seem more like tourist kitsch than modern icon. Yet, in its more vulgar way, it too embodies the integration of tradition and modernity (Figure 1.4). The need for a river crossing downstream from London Bridge, but which still allowed ocean-going vessels passage to wharves facing and adjacent to the Custom House, such as Hay's Wharf and Billingsgate (London's fish market), became more acute during the course of the nineteenth century. London Bridge had been rebuilt in 1831, but mid-nineteenth-century prints show it intensely congested with commuters, travelling between south London suburbs and the City, entangled with carts moving both everyday goods and cargoes to and from the docks and riverside wharves.[32] Two pedestrian tunnels had been constructed under the Thames, completed in 1843 and 1869. Like the Brooklyn Bridge, the Brunels' Thames Tunnel – between Wapping and Rotherhithe – suffered a succession of engineering and financial crises during a 20-year construction period. It had been intended for vehicular traffic, but there were insufficient funds to build ramps at each end, so it catered solely to pedestrians until, as the novelty of a lengthy underground promenade wore off, it was converted to a railway tunnel in the 1860s. The Tower Subway, opened in 1869 between Tower Hill and Bermondsey, was more speedily and efficiently constructed, a successful trial for James Greathead's tunnelling shield which was subsequently used to construct London's tube network; but it was a tiny bore (only seven feet in diameter) of limited capacity. Originally intended to carry a cable-operated tramway, it was soon converted to pedestrian use.[33] Both tunnels therefore allowed workers, whether City clerks or dock labourers, to cross the Thames, but at the cost of a penny or halfpenny toll; and neither solved the problem of moving freight around the capital, especially between south-east London and the East End.

A succession of imaginative, often ludicrously impracticable plans through the 1870s and early 1880s culminated in an act of parliament in 1885, authorising the construction of a bascule bridge with an opening span allowing a clear width of 200 feet, headroom of 135 feet, and to be in a Gothic style compatible with the neighbouring Tower of London.[34] The architect, Sir Horace Jones, had been Architect and Surveyor to the City of London Corporation since 1864, much more of an establishment figure than the Roeblings in New York. He was partnered by the engineer, John Wolfe Barry, son of the architect Charles Barry, whose other sons had also become architects. Between them, the Barry family designed some prominent Gothic and Italianate London buildings, including the Houses of Parliament, Dulwich College and the Charing Cross Hotel. Tower Bridge was promoted by the City of London, through the Bridge House Estates Trust, a medieval foundation established to collect tolls and rents from users of the original shop-lined London Bridge. Brooklyn Bridge had begun as a private enterprise, dependent on the investment of stockholders, but had passed into public ownership when financial crisis compelled the Cities of New York and Brooklyn, hitherto entitled to a minority holding, 'to buy out the private stockholders, and become the sole owners of the work';[35] but Tower Bridge was dependent on public finance from the outset, albeit from a secure, historical source of income which did not require levying new charges on tax- or rate-payers. Construction began in 1886 and the bridge was opened in 1894, though Jones, like John Roebling, died even before completion of the foundations.

The mock medievalism, described by *The Builder* as 'somewhat after the manner of Scottish Castellated Gothic', was not universally admired. The combination of steel frame and masonry cladding emulated early skyscraper construction even more closely than in the Brooklyn Bridge. Barry acknowledged that 'some purists will say that the lamp of truth has been sadly neglected in this combination of materials'. True to his expectations, the *Building News* called the bridge a sham, 'as no real art can tolerate a casing', and *The Builder* refused to include illustrations of 'the so-called architecture', concentrating its attention on 'the only part of the structure that is worth anything, viz., the constructive steelwork'. Less architecturally concerned critics were more enthusiastic, although embarrassment at the bridge's apparently anti-modern disguise continued through the twentieth century.[36]

Irrespective of the requirement that Tower Bridge fit in with the adjacent architecture of the Tower of London, it is unsurprising that such a heroic structure should be cloaked in Gothic dress. Not only the Houses of Parliament (1837–1860), but many other prominent London buildings were erected in a form of Gothic: for example, the Midland Hotel at St Pancras, the grandest of London's railway hotels (1868–1872); the Royal Courts of Justice on the Strand (1871–1882); and the head offices of the Prudential Assurance Company, which pioneered life insurance for the ordinary working classes, on Holborn (1879).[37] Each, it should be noted, was associated with a different aspect of modern life: rail travel and the associated need to cater to the consumption of well-off people on the move; legislation to regulate increasingly complex commercial and social life; and the extension to the mass of the population of security in the face of change. Tower Bridge was a late arrival on the scene of Gothic modernity, but in good company nonetheless.

Yet if the bridge itself was of dubious stylistic modernity, in its geographical context it catered and contributed to a modernising metropolis. The growth of major cities involved segregation and specialisation, the assignment of different land uses to different areas: a place for everything and everything in its place. It was zoning (as in New York after 1916) and town planning (in Britain after 1909) which formalised this economically efficient use of land. But geographical specialisation involved huge increases in the movement of people, commodities, essential services and information, between residences, workplaces, warehouses, shops, power stations, waterworks, sewage works, and places of worship, entertainment and social interaction. For example, as the City of London, the square mile around St Paul's and the Bank of England, concentrated on office employment to the exclusion of housing, so the residential population declined – from 112,000 in 1861 to 27,000 in 1901 and only 14,000 in 1921 – while employment increased. By the turn of the century, the City's daytime population was 360,000. Fewer employees lived within walking distance of their work. The system of employment in the docks also meant that dock labourers needed to be flexible, to travel to wherever work was available.[38] So London needed a good circulation; to become a 'networked city', and Tower Bridge is one very obvious expression of that process.

In 1800 there were only three bridges spanning the Thames below Battersea: London Bridge, and two eighteenth-century bridges – Westminster and Blackfriars. By 1894, there were ten road bridges, four railway bridges, two railway tunnels, a pedestrian tunnel, and a road tunnel under construction. By 1914, three more underground railway tunnels, another road tunnel, and another pedestrian tunnel had been added. The Tower Subway, no longer needed as a foot tunnel, was converted to carry water mains. At the same time, new streets, sewers and railway lines were being cut through, over and under the congested inner city. From the late 1850s into the 1870s Sir Joseph Bazalgette's scheme for intercepting sewers, diverting waste away from the polluted Thames towards downstream pumping stations and sewage works, the building of the first underground lines – essentially today's Circle Line – and the reclamation of parts of the Thames to form the Embankment, involved massive short-term pain for the sake of long-term benefit.[39] From Regent Street in the 1820s by way of New Oxford Street in the 1840s, to Victoria Street in the early 1850s, Holborn Viaduct in the late 1860s, Charing Cross Road and Shaftesbury Avenue in the 1880s, and culminating in Kingsway and the Aldwych, opened in 1905, new streets not only enhanced circulation but also provided an excuse for slum clearance and redevelopment to 'improve' rateable values.[40] Redevelopment was not as ruthless or as geometrically satisfying as in Haussmann's Paris, but it substantially changed the face and the structure of London.

Yet the river remained a vital element in London's transport system. Bridges upstream of London Bridge were improved for navigation by enlarging their central spans. For example, Vauxhall Bridge, opened in 1816 as the first iron bridge across the Thames, was reduced from nine arches to seven arches in 1881, and replaced by a new five-arch steel bridge between 1895 and 1906.[41] Around 45 per cent of London's trade was now handled by docks downstream of Tower Bridge, but this left more than half to be dealt with at riverside wharves, including those upstream of the Tower. Hence the need for either a high-level bridge or a bridge that opened to allow vessels through. In its first year of operation, Tower Bridge was raised for river traffic 6,160 times, equivalent to 17 times daily. Between these hourly road closures, it was also crossed by 60,000 pedestrians and 8,000 horse-drawn vehicles daily.[42]

Like Brooklyn Bridge, Tower Bridge offered a high-level vantage point from which to observe the developing metropolis. When the bascules were raised to allow shipping to pass through, pedestrians could climb the towers (206 steps) or take a hydraulic lift but, in practice, the time this took was longer than the time the bridge remained closed to traffic. The walkways were so little used that they were closed to the public in 1910, and it was only with the bridge's renovation in 1982 and its reinvention as the 'Tower Bridge Experience' that they became the observation decks originally envisaged.[43]

Tower Bridge was free to users from the outset, unlike the tunnels (discussed above) and other nineteenth-century road bridges (Vauxhall, Waterloo, Southwark, Lambeth), which all began life as toll bridges. In this respect it reflected a wider freedom of movement in late Victorian London. A Metropolitan Anti-Bridge-Toll Association had been formed in 1839, but it took until the late 1870s before tolls were removed from bridges in central London. Meanwhile, a Toll Reform Association agitated for the removal of toll-bars from turnpike roads leading into the metropolis. In 1864–1865, 140 toll-bars were removed. But there were still more than 200 privately erected bars and gates restricting access to streets in mid-Victorian London. The eventual removal of most of these, including more than sixty in the early 1890s, reflected the resolve of the newly created London County Council (LCC), the democratically elected municipal government which replaced the much less powerful Metropolitan Board of Works (MBW), the indirectly elected body which had been responsible for building new streets and main sewers since 1855.[44] However, neither the MBW nor the LCC had any authority within the old City of London, where the Corporation of the City remained supreme.

Although Tower Bridge was owned by the City Corporation, it was located outside the City. We might even interpret Tower Bridge as a declaration of the City of London's continuing authority in the face of more modern forms of government all around. Nevertheless, co-operation between the different authorities was also necessary. The approaches to the bridge were the responsibility of the MBW and, after 1888, the LCC. The northern approach could be squeezed in along the line of the Tower Ditch, between the Tower of London and the warehouses adjoining St Katharine's Dock. However, it was necessary to make road improvements farther north, where Mansell Street was widened and extended to provide a direct link between Whitechapel Road and Tower Bridge Approach. South of the bridge there had been a wall of warehouses lining the river, backed by narrow streets of cottages such as Freeman's Lane. In their place, a new road, Tower Bridge Road, was constructed. By 1894, this extended only as far south as Tooley Street, itself a MBW improvement of the early 1880s lined by block dwellings ostentatiously known as Devon Mansions, but subsequently Tower Bridge Road was extended south through Bermondsey to link up with the main road to Dover, thereby creating a new arterial route between the Channel ports and the London Docks. In the process, space was found for other elements of modern city life. Where the Ordnance Survey map of 1894 depicted a newly created desert at the junction of Tooley Street, Queen

Elizabeth Street and Tower Bridge Road, the 1914 edition showed the same intersection colonised by a row of new shops with flats over, and a bank, a new public
house, police station, Tower Bridge Police Court, a new Congregational Church and
adjacent Sunday School and, at the apex of the junction, a statue and new public
lavatories (Figure 1.5).[45]

Tower Bridge may not have been popular with architects and aesthetes, but it
quickly assumed the status of an icon, not only for London, but for the British Empire,
featured on countless souvenirs, or used as an opening shot to establish location in
numerous films.[46] In an advertisement for Pearce Duff Lemonade Crystals, the towers
and connecting high-level span were each constituted by a box of the said crystals,
while Owbridge's Lung Tonic, 'a tower of strength', was promoted by depicting each
tower as a giant bottle of tonic, the decorations and crenellations represented by
additional miniature bottles![47] Just as Brooklyn Bridge represented New York to
the world, so Tower Bridge symbolised London. Both bridges were envisaged as
gateways, but whereas Brooklyn Bridge was usually portrayed end-on (as in *New
York Illustrated*) or obliquely, so that both Gothic arches were visible, providing a
gateway to Manhattan, Tower Bridge was (and is) most frequently depicted side-
on, from mid-stream, with the bascules raised: an open bridge allowing people and
goods to flow in and out between London and the World. The bascules might even be
interpreted as raised arms, saluting or welcoming those who passed through. Yet, in
reality, even in its early days, and certainly in recent years, the normal experience of
Tower Bridge is with the bascules lowered, a drawbridge allowing traffic to flow across
the bridge, but a portcullis regulating entry to the city, a new kind of gate or bar.

Bloor Street Viaduct, Toronto

Toronto's Prince Edward Viaduct, more commonly known as the Don Valley Viaduct
or the Bloor Street Viaduct, may be a less dramatic and certainly less well known
feature than either the Brooklyn Bridge or Tower Bridge, but it too constituted a vital
link in the modernisation of its city and demonstrates the marriage of technology
and myth-making. The population of Toronto doubled between 1900 and 1913, from
200,000 to 400,000, but physical expansion of the built-up area to the north-east was
limited by the Don Valley. Bloor Street, the principal west-east artery through the city,
turned into a polite residential backwater east of Yonge Street, the main north–south
route, and stopped altogether when it reached Sherbourne Street, where further
progress east was limited first by the deeply incised Rosedale Ravine and, beyond
that, the broader but equally deep Don Valley. The marginal status of this part of
the city was reflected in the pattern of nineteenth-century land uses: St. James's and
Necropolis Cemeteries, Riverdale Park and, across the valley, brickworks, a paper
mill and the Don Jail (Figure 1.6).[48]

A succession of privately and publicly commissioned plans were drawn up from
1905 onwards, most envisaging a diagonal boulevard extending north-east from
downtown to Broadview Avenue on the far side of the Don Valley, but without
specifying quite how the Don was to be bridged. Not only radial boulevards but also
parkways along the valley bottoms (of the Don to the east and the Humber to the
west of the city) reflected the spirit of then fashionable 'city beautiful' planning.[49]

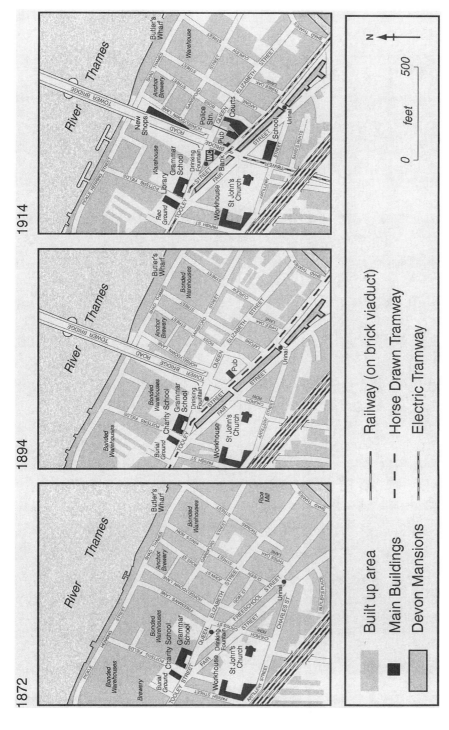

Figure 1.5. The Impact of Tower Bridge on its Environs: Tooley Street and the South End of Tower Bridge. Based on 1:2500 O. S. Maps, 1872, 1894, 1914.

15

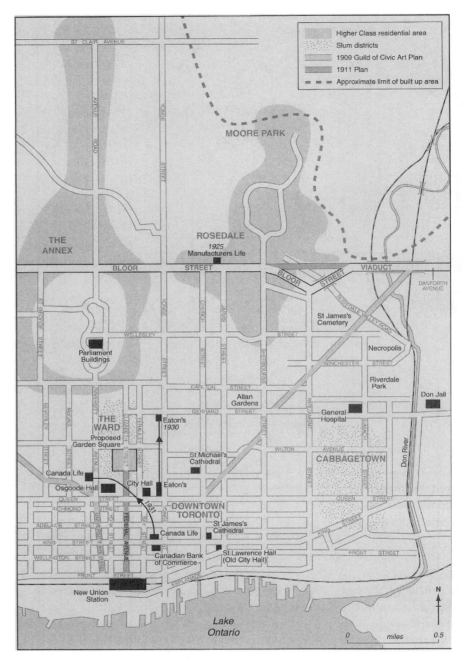

Figure 1.6. The Bloor Street Viaduct and Downtown Toronto, 1900–1930.

There were also discussions about the need for a subway system, emulating those being introduced into American cities. But it proved hard enough to persuade the city's taxpayers to approve plans for trunk sewers and associated sewage works, let alone vote to pay for less vital projects such as subways and boulevards. In 1910, a Civic Improvement Committee was established, R. C. Harris was appointed to take charge of public works in the city, and a firm of New York City consulting engineers

Figure 1.7. Bloor Street Viaduct Under Construction in July 1917. City of Toronto Archives, Series 372, Sub-Series 10, Item 841.

recommended the building of both a subway and a viaduct across the Don Valley, but it was not until 1913 that the viaduct was finally approved by taxpayers, at the fourth attempt in successive years.[50]

By this time, the idea of a radial boulevard had been abandoned. Toronto was rapidly expanding northwards, away from the lakeshore, and the old downtown, around the intersection of King and Yonge Streets, was no longer the only destination for commuters and shoppers from the suburbs. In place of a starburst of radials, it seemed more logical to extend Bloor Street due east to connect with Danforth Avenue on the far side of the Don Valley. A dead-straight east–west street had obvious modernist appeal, but following this logic meant straddling Rosedale Ravine, a local beauty spot that also functioned as a kind of moat protecting the exclusive elite district of Rosedale from lower middle- and working-class areas to the south. In the end a compromise was agreed, diverting Bloor Street around the southern edge of the ravine, thereby creating a three-stage project, altogether a mile in length: an embankment carrying the road parallel to the ravine, a short concrete bridge across the ravine, and the viaduct itself, centred on five steel-framed arches encased in reinforced concrete, one third of a mile long and 125 feet above the Don River (Figure 1.7).[51]

Plans for the subway were shelved, although the recommendation of the New York consultants that a second deck be built into the viaduct, beneath the roadway, was implemented, making the eventual construction of the subway (in 1966) that much easier.[52] Ironically, by the time construction of the viaduct started, the growth bubble had burst: 1913 and subsequent years were a period of economic retrenchment, and labour and materials continued to be in short supply throughout World War I.

Nevertheless, work on the bridge went ahead, and it was opened to the public in October 1918, overshadowed even in the local press by reports from Europe of the impending end of the war and by the 'Spanish flu' pandemic that had just reached the city. On opening day the chief engineer for the project, Thomas Taylor, was himself confined to bed with the flu.[53] There are shades of Washington Roebling's much more permanent confinement to bed, not only during the opening, but through the preceding years of construction of Brooklyn Bridge.

Despite the advice of the city's medical officer, discouraging people from meeting in crowds or spending too long in public gatherings, several hundred did attend the low-key opening ceremony, and it was estimated that over 2000 vehicles used the viaduct on opening day (a Friday). The following Monday, the Toronto press reported on the thousands of vehicles and pedestrians using the bridge during the weekend. For a brief time, at least, the viaduct fulfilled the same role as the boardwalk across Brooklyn Bridge, as a promenade for healthy relaxation.[54]

Just as Brooklyn Bridge can be viewed as a bridge between old and new worlds, so too, Bloor Street Viaduct may be interpreted as reflecting Toronto and Canada's changing place in the world. The design, construction and planning of the viaduct were all rooted in New World forms of government – a Board of Control (an 'inner sanctum' of a handful of full-time politicians who controlled the city), taxpayers' referenda, city beautiful planning and New York consultants. In all these respects, Toronto was an American city. Yet *The Canadian Engineer* claimed the viaduct as 'one of the largest . . . in the British Empire'; and when the whole scheme, including the approach road along the ravine edge, was completed in August 1919, it was officially named in honour of Prince Edward (the future Edward VIII), then on a visit to the city.[55]

Like Brooklyn and Tower Bridges, Bloor Street Viaduct contributed an essential link in the making of a networked city. As a route for electric streetcars, it allowed the opening up of new suburbs and increased choice for commuters. Newspapers reported on its immediate use by 'express wagons, furniture vans, bread vans and quick delivery rigs of all kinds'. It was used by ambulances carrying patients stricken with the flu, by funeral corteges, and by worshippers riding the streetcar to attend a memorial service downtown. It had implications for neighbouring patterns of land use, converting Bloor Street East into a through route and stimulating trade along Danforth Avenue, the retail strip east of the viaduct.[56]

Unlike the two more famous bridges, Bloor Street Viaduct cannot be said to have symbolised Toronto to itself, let alone to the world. It was rarely the subject of fine art or popular advertising.[57] In literature, several Toronto writers, including Hugh Hood and Margaret Atwood, identified the city's narrow ravines (like Rosedale Ravine) and the fragile insecure bridges that crossed them, as elements of wild nature and potential sites of horror disrupting the ordered life of a disciplined, modern metropolis.[58] But in 1987, another Toronto-based writer, Michael Ondaatje, employed the viaduct as a key component in his novel, *In the Skin of a Lion*, mixing fact and fiction in a story in which the bridge is built by immigrant-anarchists and a nun is swept off the half-built bridge only to be caught in free-fall by a Macedonian 'daredevil' bridge builder, thus setting in motion a chain of events which ends twenty years later in the near destruction of Commissioner Harris's greatest project, the waterworks (now the R. C. Harris Filtration Plant) at the eastern boundary of the city. Ondaatje describes the waterworks as a 'palace of purification'; it has the potential to cancel out the dark, death-filled waters of the ravines with life-giving, clear, unpolluted water, only provided that it can avoid the human threat of disorder posed by the anarchists.[59]

All of this is an elaborate fantasy on Ondaatje's part, except that it is grounded in the very real history of the construction of these great public works in early twentieth-century Toronto, and in the record of their construction by the city's official photographer, Arthur S. Goss, preserved in thousands of photographs in the City Archives.[60] For Ondaatje, the bridge is a miracle of the imagination – 'The bridge goes up in a dream' – and a place for myth-making: a lone figure on a bicycle breaks through the police barriers to beat the official car across the bridge at its opening and, the night before that:

the workers had arrived and brushed away officials who guarded the bridge in preparation for the ceremonies the next day, moved with their own flickering lights – their candles for the bridge dead – like a wave of civilization, a net of summer insects over the valley.[61]

In reality, residents *had* appropriated the bridge for their own crossings before the official opening day; and one of Goss's photographs records an almost empty bridge, devoid of any traffic except a lone cyclist who just creeps into the far left of the frame, presumably by accident. Moreover, the dramatic scene of the nun's fall from the unfinished bridge, dated by Ondaatje as occurring on 'an April night in 1917' can also be matched to a photograph by Goss showing the unfinished viaduct minus its central span, but replete with steel scaffolding and a travelling crane, and dated 12 April 1917.[62]

In various ways the bridge was a place of unheeded authority. In Ondaatje's novel, the nuns trespassed on the bridge (by accident), and Harris's authority was subverted by the immigrant labourers working under him; and in real life, local residents protested at barriers intended to stop them from using the bridge before its official opening and ignored the medical officer's advice to stay at home during the flu epidemic. In the novel, the bridge was also a place of liberation and of new beginnings, for the rescued nun, resurrected as actress, mother and lover, and for her rescuer, whose respectable proprietorship of an East End bakery provides cover for his sponsorship of anarchist attacks on the city's infrastructure and establishment. Liberation and new beginnings operated in reality, too, for thousands of Torontonians who bought their own homes in new suburbs off Danforth Avenue during the 1920s. Lastly, the bridge was a place of stark inequality: the labourers who had already risked their lives escaping from the Balkans at the outbreak of war, crossing the Atlantic in filthy, overcrowded cargo vessels, now risked their lives again suspended from the half-built bridge while sections of pipe, steelwork, timber and 'arm-thick wires' swung crazily free, liable to slice in two anybody who misjudged their movement; and all for a dollar an hour. For less skilled workers on the surface of the bridge, the pay was only 40 cents. Harris's tweed coat 'cost more than the combined weeks' salaries of five bridge workers'.[63]

All three bridges represent the hopes and fears of modernity, its opportunities and its threats. Variously, they required the mobilisation of local government, of the latest engineering techniques and the latest building materials, of skilled labour, of capital. Variously, they offered new opportunities for those engaged in their construction, for those who used them to move more easily between Manhattan and Brooklyn, the City and south-east London, downtown Toronto and its new suburbs, and for those who invested in the development of newly accessible areas or who sought to structure their cities in new forms. They also symbolised the marriage of old and new, and the imagined ability of modern society to triumph over nature, to make progress, to effect improvement.

But bridges also highlighted some of the anxieties of modern urban living. They might bring different peoples and activities *too* close together. Noting the anxieties experienced by Russian immigrants living in the Lower East Side close to the Brooklyn Bridge in the 1900s, Richard Haw concludes that 'The bridge represents an environment of hostility and estrangement: a barrier, not a passageway'.[64] A fear of crossing bridges was also one of the symptoms of agoraphobia.[65] While new bridges allowed most citizens to break down boundaries and make new connections, for a minority they induced physical symptoms of dizziness, vertigo and palpitations, and stimulated desires to throw themselves over the parapet; and for others, suffering economic and social as well as psychological problems of urban life, bridges provided the opportunity to commit suicide. George Cruikshank depicted 'the poor girl, homeless, friendless, deserted, and gin-mad', leaping from London Bridge into the Thames as the final plate of 'The Drunkard's Children' (1848); Bud Korpenning (in Dos Passos' *Manhattan Transfer*) is but the best known literary suicide to utilise Brooklyn Bridge; and after accounting for more than 480 deaths in eighty-five years, Bloor Street Viaduct was at last clothed in a 'luminous veil' to deter or, if necessary, catch those who attempt suicide.[66]

Our knowledge of the construction of these bridges is also a product of modernity. In his novel, Ondaatje observed that 'There are over 4,000 photographs from various angles of the bridge in its time-lapse evolution', and he reinforces the relevance of this later in the book by having one of his characters sitting in the public library reading old newspaper reports of the viaduct's opening.[67] Ken Burns' documentary film of Brooklyn Bridge likewise depended on the photographs, prints, plans, newspaper reports, letters, diaries, artworks, feature films and cartoons onto which he grafted the reminiscences and observations of present-day commentators. The 'Tower Bridge Experience' trades on a similar range of contemporary sources.

Three cities: London, New York and Toronto

In the chapters that follow, I draw many of my examples from the three cities that I have already introduced through their bridges. London features prominently in every chapter. It is the city where I have lived and worked for most of my life and which I know best. Examples from New York and Toronto also appear throughout the book, along with occasional references to other actual or aspiring metropolises, such as Chicago and Montreal, particularly where published studies are the best available on their topics and suggest processes and experiences relevant to my overall argument.

Irrespective of convenience, London and New York choose themselves. London already had a population of two and a half million in 1851, the year when it played host to the Great Exhibition, and in which, according to most commentators, the 'urban' population of England and Wales first exceeded the 'rural' population. London's population continued to increase at around 20 per cent per decade until the beginning of the twentieth century, when the population of the administrative County of London – what we now consider Inner London – started to decrease. Thereafter, growth was concentrated in suburban districts which remained administratively outside London (although within certain jurisdictions such as the Metropolitan Police District) until the replacement of the London County Council by the Greater London Council in 1964. By 1930, London's population exceeded eight million, almost exactly divided between the County of London and the built-up area beyond county boundaries (Tables 1.1, 1.2).[68]

New York's population was only 700,000 in 1850, but by 1930, seven million people lived within Greater New York (the five boroughs of Manhattan, the Bronx, Brooklyn, Queens and Staten Island, which had been constituted as Greater New York in 1898). When it was created, Greater New York more nearly matched the New York metropolitan area than was the case in London, where the LCC area was substantially underbounded from the outset, but it still excluded commuter areas of Long Island and New Jersey. New York's population growth rates exceeded London's in every decade – unsurprisingly, given the lower base from which the city grew – but especially in the period 1900–1930, when New York's absolute levels of increase exceeded London's.[69]

Toronto may seem a curious third choice and there is, of course, a degree of personal bias in the selection, reflecting the locale of much of my own archival research over the past twenty years. In population terms, it was only a baby: Toronto's population in 1930 was little more than New York's in 1850 but, building from such a modest base, its growth rates, especially in the 1880s and during the decade to 1913, signified some acute problems in adjusting to big-city status. To the city's own historian, Toronto was a 'nearly national metropolis' in the early twentieth century.[70] The 'shock of the new' was profound in a city experiencing a transition from 'provincial' to 'metropolitan'. But Toronto was also going through a transition from 'British' to 'North American'. In the nineteenth century, it was a British city on North American soil, 'Victorian' if not 'hyper-Victorian', white, loyal to the British crown, reproducing the social formation of its Scots and Irish settler population in its Presbyterianism and moral order. By the late twentieth century, Toronto was often cited as a successful example of multiculturalism, a 'city that works', with a well-developed welfare state, apparently in contrast to its near neighbours to the south, cities like Buffalo, Cleveland, Detroit, not to mention New York or Chicago, which evidently were 'not working' in the 1970s and 1980s. Yet, in the intervening decades, between 1900 and 1950, Toronto became a characteristically 'North American' city, its continuing flow of British immigrants supplemented by large southern and eastern European populations, and its development attributable more to American planners, architects and financiers than to Britain.[71] This shift from 'British' to 'North American' in governance and aesthetics runs in parallel with a continuing espousal of modernity which Toronto shares with London as well as New York.

Of the other cities mentioned above, Chicago grew from virtually nothing in 1830 to over two million by 1910. By 1930, Chicago's population was approaching 3.4 million, or nearly 4.7 million in the wider metropolitan area including suburbs beyond city limits. Devastated by fire in 1871, Chicago's subsequent development entailed almost as many signs of world-city status as New York's. It was Chicago where the steel frame was first employed and the word 'skyscraper' first coined, Chicago that

Table 1.1. *Population of New York, London and Toronto, 1850–1950 (all figures in thousands)*

Date*	New York			London			Toronto		
	Manhattan	Rest of Greater New York	Total	County of London	Rest of Greater London	Total	City of Toronto	Rest of Metropolitan Toronto	Total
1850–1	516	181	696	2363	289	2652	31		
1860–1	814	361	1175	2808	380	3188	45		
1870–1	942	536	1478	3261	579	3841	56		
1880–1	1165	747	1912	3830	883	4713	86		
1890–1	1441	1066	2507	4228	1344	5572	181		
1900–1	1850	1587	3437	4536	1971	6507	208		
1910–1	2332	2435	4767	4522	2639	7160	377	33	410
1920–1	2284	3336	5620	4485	2902	7387	522	90	611
1930–1	1867	5063	6930	4397	3713	8110	631	187	818
1940–1	1889	5565	7455	4013	4602	8615	667	242	910
1950–1	1960	5932	7892	3348	4846	8194	676	442	1117

* Figures for New York from decennial censuses in 1850, 1860 . . . ; for London and Toronto from censuses in 1851, 1861 . . . except that in the absence of a census in London in 1941, estimated figures for 1939 have been used.

Sources: K. Jackson (ed), *Encyclopedia of New York City*, pp. 920–923; J. M. S. Careless, *Toronto to 1918*, pp. 200–201; J. T. Lemon, *Toronto Since 1918*, p. 194; B. Weinreb and C. Hibbert, *The London Encyclopaedia*, pp. 612–614.

Table 1.2. *Population Percentage Growth Rates per Decade for New York, London and Toronto, 1850–1950*

Decade	New York			London			Toronto		
	Manhattan	Rest of Greater New York	Total	County of London	Rest of Greater London	Total	City of Toronto	Rest of Metropolitan Toronto	Total
1850–60	58	100	69	19	32	20	46		
1860–70	16	48	26	16	52	21	25		
1870–80	24	39	29	17	53	23	54		
1880–90	24	43	31	10	52	18	110		
1890–1900	28	49	37	7	47	17	15		
1900–10	26	53	39	0	34	10	81		
1910–20	–2	37	18	–1	10	3	39	169	49
1920–30	–18	52	23	–2	28	10	21	108	34
1930–40	1	10	8	–9	24	6	6	30	11
1940–50	4	7	6	–17	5	–5	1	82	23

Source: Table 1.

23

accommodated its country's celebration of the four-hundredth anniversary of Colum-bus' 'discovery' of America, the Columbian Exposition of 1893. Chicago was the home to Hull House, the social reform programme established by Jane Addams in emulation of London's Toynbee Hall, soon to be copied in settlement houses and women's movements throughout North America; and in the early twentieth century it spawned the Chicago School whose ideas continue to influence urban geography, anthropology, sociology and economics a century later.[72]

Throughout the period covered in this book, Montreal's population exceeded that of Toronto. In 1871, Montreal's population of 115,000 was almost double that of Toronto. In 1931, Montreal was about 200,000 ahead. Despite its majority, predomi-nantly working-class, Francophone population, Montreal qualifies as an Anglophone city in terms of access to political and business power: the owners and managers of new industries in Quebec 'were not French Canadians, but English-Canadian, Amer-ican, and British capitalists'.[73] Montreal housed the headquarters for various national organisations, such as the Canadian Pacific Railway and the Royal Bank of Canada. It also led Toronto 'in the sphere of international banking and stock exchange activ-ity'. Yet, as early as 1911, Toronto company headquarters controlled more branch businesses than did Montreal headquarters,[74] and by the late twentieth century the two cities had changed places, demographically as well as in financial status.

A similar jockeying for position had earlier affected the fortunes of Australia's leading cities. Melbourne was famously treated by Asa Briggs as one of his 'Victorian cities', running a couple of decades ahead of Toronto until the early twentieth century. The city's population increased from 23,000 in 1850 to 268,000 in 1881 and 473,000 in 1891, more than double that of Toronto, and about 80,000 ahead of its rival, Sydney. Attracting epithets such as 'marvellous Melbourne' and 'the Chicago of the South', Melbourne was the go-ahead, American-style metropolis, contrasting with Sydney where people appeared to be less assertive. But the city's boom through the 1880s collapsed into a prolonged depression in the 1890s when banks failed, wool prices fell and Melburnians retreated into a life of thrift, austerity and sober respectability. Through the twentieth century Melbourne was the more 'British', class-conscious and conservative while Sydney took over as Australia's New York.[75] Although I rarely refer explicitly to either Australian city in what follows, many of the arguments I deploy about modernisation and the representation and performance of modernity are applicable to them.[76]

What unites all these cities is not only the rapidity of their growth at different times during this pivotal period of modernity, but also their actual or potential metropoli-tanism. As Davison notes of Melbourne, so it was true that each of these cities pos-sessed an 'overwhelming hegemony in its region, a complex internal economy and characteristically metropolitan ethos'.[77] Although they were all centres of industrial production, they were not only industrial cities, but places with major administrative, commercial, financial, intellectual, artistic and recreational functions. London, New York, Chicago and Melbourne all hosted major international exhibitions. Toronto's annual Industrial Exhibition, begun in 1879, was a more provincial affair, at least until its transformation into the Canadian National Exhibition in 1904. Montreal had to wait until the World Fair (Expo) of 1967 for a truly international display, although it had its own 'Crystal Palace' for local exhibitions as early as 1866.[78]

Unlike industrial cities dominated in spirit as well as in number by relatively regularly and securely employed working classes, the cities featured in this book were home to both professional, business and intellectual elites and armies of the casually employed 'underclass', thereby accommodating a diversity of urban experience which was compounded by the diverse origins of their inhabitants. In 1910, more than 40 per cent of New Yorkers were foreign-born.[79] New York's black population increased from 60,000 in 1900 (less than 2 per cent of the city's population) to over 300,000 by 1930. The Irish-born declined from 8 per cent in 1900, when as many as 22 per cent of New Yorkers claimed to be 'Irish' (whether by birth or descent) to 3.2 per cent in 1930. During the same period, the Italian-born population increased from 4.2 per cent to 6.4 per cent. By 1930, 17 per cent of New Yorkers claimed to be 'Italian'.[80]

In 1911, almost as large a proportion of Torontonians as New Yorkers had been born outside their country of residence: 38 per cent; although in Toronto the local politics of race distinguished between 'foreign-born' (9 per cent) and 'British-born' (29 per cent) who were not regarded as 'foreign', for example in discussions of the city's social problems. By 1931, the British-born had slipped to 25 per cent, but the non-British foreign-born now made up another eighth of the city's population. In terms of religious diversity, Toronto's 7 per cent Jewish and 14 per cent Catholic in 1931 lagged well behind New York, where the Jewish population peaked at nearly 30 per cent of the total population in 1920.[81] In 1901, London accommodated 60,000 Catholics born in Ireland, another 375,000 Catholics of Irish descent (making a total Catholic proportion of about 6.7 per cent), 135,000 Jews (2.1 per cent), mostly recently arrived as refugees from pogroms in eastern Europe, and smaller groups of Italian-, German-, Czech-, Asian- and African-born, cumulatively comprising several tens of thousands.[82]

All these cities, therefore, embraced a degree of ethnic and cultural pluralism which, as I noted at the beginning of this chapter, was an important counterpart to spatial and economic order and efficiency in the construction of nineteenth- and early twentieth-century modernity. To Ward and Zunz, rational planning (perhaps validating as much as regulating an economically rational capitalist system of land use) made space for diversity, assigning different ethnic and cultural minorities their own, albeit unequal, spaces.[83] 'Deviant' behaviour was much more likely to be tolerated if it could be managed out of sight of the majority. Diversity was both the catalyst and the consequence of the modern metropolis.

My selection of evidence from different cities is not made with the intention of eliciting differences between them explainable by some form of economic or political determinism, for example by invoking their different histories of immigration, different urban politics, or different modes of providing public services. Rather, their common experience of modernity overrides the detail of public or private ownership of utilities, of implicit rather than explicit graft or corruption in municipal government, of greater or lesser proportions of non-Anglophone inhabitants. The point of overlaying examples from different cities is to accumulate broadly similar responses to the ambiguities of modernity, irrespective of local variation.

Modernity may seem an inappropriate concept to apply to late nineteenth- and early twentieth-century London, given the emphasis in British history on narratives of industrial decline and faltering imperialism. Certainly, the modernisation of British society took place in the context of relative political, economic and social stability, compared to continental and American modernities associated with revolution or disruptive demographic and social change.[84] Nonetheless, while the response of British, American and continental nation-states may have varied, the challenges, opportunities and risks of new scientific theories, new technologies, new media, new gender roles, new work practices and new forms of governance were similar for ordinary citizens in major cities in all these places.

Some comments on time and method

As in the histories of Brooklyn Bridge, Tower Bridge and the Bloor Street Viaduct so, throughout this book, my interest extends from the mid-nineteenth century forward into the inter-war years, but peaking in the last quarter of the nineteenth and the first two decades of the twentieth centuries. This corresponds to the end of the second and the beginning of the third of three phases into which the history of modernity is often divided (1500–1789, 1789–1900 and post–1900).[85] Berman argues that before the late eighteenth century, awareness of modernity was restricted to scientific and business elites. By 1900, at least in the developed world, the idea of modernity was losing its capacity to give meaning to people's lives; being modern was something you took for granted. Moreover, in Britain and much of Europe, faith in the improving power of technology was rudely challenged by the horrors of World War I, which could hardly be justified as an extension of the *creative* destruction characteristic of economic and environmental modernisation in nineteenth-century cities. In North America a decade later, the Wall Street Crash and the Great Depression provided a different kind of challenge to assumptions of perpetual economic progress and individual betterment. The early twentieth century also saw the emergence of literary and artistic modernism as a *critique* of the metanarrative of progress and order that culminated in the totalitarianism of state communism and national socialism. The further we venture into the twentieth century, the more ambiguous and contradictory the concept of modernity appears.

Consider, for example, the apparent contradiction between 'calculability' (the search for certainty and exactness, nothing left to chance) and 'fortuitousness' (randomness, risk-taking, chance) that David Frisby discusses.[86] Does the embrace of both 'calculability' and 'fortuitousness' under the banner of modernity reflect alternative responses to the same external stimuli, just as some people revel in the diversity, hybridity and unpredictability of city life while others retreat into internally homogeneous gated communities? Or are they contradictory only to outsiders like ourselves, mindful of the social discipline that underlies individual decisions perceived by those who made them as freely chosen, or bemused by the spatial chaos that appears to follow from countless acts of individual rationality? Or are they counter-responses: literary and artistic spaces of representation that celebrate risk and chance defying the straitjacket of authoritarian representations of space? The challenge of working with the concept of modernity is that it forces us to make sense of the messiness.

London, along with other European capitals, was not only 'modern' in the nineteenth and early twentieth centuries; it was also an 'imperial city'. Sites within London such as Bank Junction, St Paul's Cathedral, Whitehall, the Mall and Trafalgar Square, were variously depicted as 'Heart of the Empire'. Successive international exhibitions were associated with empire, culminating in the British Empire Exhibition staged at Wembley in north-west London in 1924. Driver and Gilbert have emphasised the range of imperial sites in the landscape of London: not only Whitehall, and the Mall, and Museumland in South Kensington, all planned, self-consciously imperial landscapes, but also the Strand, home to high commissions, colonial offices and stores catering to the needs of visitors to and from the outposts of empire; the Docks, handling the trade of empire, outgoing cargoes of troops and settlers as well as incoming cargoes of raw materials and foodstuffs; and the suburbs, gardens planted with exotic species, street and house names charting the progress of colonial settlement and military campaigns.[87]

Toronto, too, was a kind of imperial city. Just as its viaduct was compared to other engineering marvels of the British Empire, so its successive skyscrapers through the 1910s and 1920s, modest by American standards, could nonetheless be announced as 'tallest in the Empire'. Royal visits, such as that by the Prince of Wales in 1860, and annual parades on Victoria Day (commemorating Queen Victoria's birthday, 24 May) and Dominion Day (1 July), were key events in the city's calendar, often demonstrating the contested nature of the city's public spaces.[88] Among the city's many nicknames – 'Hogtown', 'City of Churches', 'Toronto the Good' – the most complimentary was 'Queen City', implying an allegiance to Queen and Empire as much as its superiority to other Canadian cities.[89]

The 'American Empire' is a more contentious and mostly late twentieth-century concept, but New York was known as the 'Empire City' from at least the 1820s and by the mid-nineteenth century, 'empire' was used in the names of many New York businesses and institutions. As David Scobey notes, the word was used to invoke not only mercantile power but also moral and political leadership. 'Empire' rarely carried any negative connotations of unjustified expansionism; an imperial New York not only conferred the blessings of cultural and economic progress on its citizens but also spread civilisation to those with whom it communicated.[90]

A historical geography of imperial cities would place more emphasis on ethnicity, national identity and colonial relations than I do by focusing on modernity. Nonetheless, the unravelling of modernity in the twentieth century is paralleled by the unravelling of imperialism. Jonathan Schneer has noted the anti-imperial discourse that emerged in London at the start of the twentieth century; Iain Black suggests that the bombastic architecture of early twentieth-century banks and head offices in the City of London was an attempt to bolster confidence in the continuing efficacy of imperial business; and the Wembley exhibition may be interpreted as a propaganda exercise promoting the same message more broadly. There was anti-imperialism in New York, too, and everywhere the awareness that empires did not last for ever.[91]

The period 1840–1930 was not an unchanging slab of modernity, therefore, and my start and end dates are not cast in stone. The period merits attention precisely because it covers a transition in values and experiences in the context of economic change and technological innovation.

I have already laid bare something of my method in the vignettes of Brooklyn and Tower Bridges and the Bloor Street Viaduct. Given the range of my interests, this is mostly a work of synthesis. The literature of continental modernity is full of references to the figures of the flâneur, the ragpicker, the collector, the prostitute, the journalist and the detective. In essence, these professions embrace my own: collecting, observing, inferring, exploring empirical material in new contexts and from new vantage points. In *Imagining the Modern City*, James Donald discusses the conceit of imagining himself as 'a Man About Town'.[92] Sitting in record offices working my way through microfilm after microfilm of census records, I could easily be mistaken for yet another family historian. My conceit is that whereas *they* are researching their own genealogies, *I* am probing other people's histories! Researching, writing and reading are themselves kinds of performance; and the assembly of a persuasive narrative is a far from innocent form of choreography.

In the chapters that follow, I begin with three chapters exploring different modes of representation, arguing for the existence of parallels between developments in artistic and documentary spheres, in art and literature on the one hand, and in social survey on the other. First I contrast the association of 'progress' and 'modernity' with popular late twentieth- and twenty-first-century perceptions of 'Victorian' as far from progressive. Next I consider a variety of metaphors – drawn from nature, from exploration and from the Bible – which contemporaries used to make sense of their cities. A chapter on new ways of measuring, surveying and mapping city populations connects with Foucauldian ideas on governmentality but also hints at parallels with trends in the representation of cities in novels and painting, themes that are pursued in more detail in Chapter 4 which particularly focuses on writers' and artists' conceptualisations of how space was organised and how space worked.

Chapters in the second half of the book address the production of new kinds of space, as planned, imagined, used and contested. The range of spaces is not intended to be exhaustive. I focus more on domestic and residential space than on work spaces. There is a rapidly expanding literature on the concept of 'home', though most of it reflects present-day concerns with homeownership, the home as a place for imparting and expressing self-identity, and a locale for domestic production, reproduction and consumption. All these themes are important, but so is the positioning of domestic space in a wider economic and geographical context. I will consider three principal locales and types of new residential environment: the suburb, including working-class as well as middle-class suburbs; the working-class 'block dwelling', often provided by philanthropic agencies or limited dividend housing companies but also, in Britain, by local councils; and the middle- and upper middle-class apartment or mansion flat, a controversial form of housing in many late nineteenth-century cities, which provides a window onto a great many other aspects of modern life related to privacy, gender relations and the family. With regard to workplaces, I restrict my attention to the new, late nineteenth-century space of the office as more metropolitan in character than the space of the factory, and to the store, where it is necessary to consider who worked there as well as who shopped there, the perspective that has received most attention in recent studies of the cultural history of consumption. Home, work and consumption also need to be situated in the context of public space, especially the changing design and use of streets. Three chapters provide such a context, the first two focusing on reform and use of streets, the last examining some of the connections – through the provision of public utilities and communications systems – which facilitated the efficient working of modern, networked cities.

2

The idea of progress

It is hard to separate the concept of modernity from ideas about 'progress'. In this chapter I begin by examining perceptions of late nineteenth- and early twentieth-century urbanism, and how we reconcile ideas of progress with other, less positive, images of 'Victorian cities'. In the second half of the chapter, I will focus on nineteenth-century ideas about progress, and how they meshed with more ambivalent and even negative representations of city life that drew on analogies between cities and natural organisms, between the exploration of unknown lands and 'social exploration' of 'unknown' cities, and between modern and ancient, especially biblical, civilisations.

'Modern cities' and 'Victorian cities'

The late nineteenth century in both North America and Britain was full of 'progressive' movements. In the United States, 'progressivism' signified the application of science to the management of society. Reacting to the corruption of big business working in league with machine politics, as well as to the problems presented by urbanisation and immigration, progressivism built on earlier reform movements that had focused on helping individuals to help themselves, and on a 'social gospel' movement that stressed service to others as a practical demonstration of Christian faith. Concentrating on reformers' attitudes to urban problems, we can identify three phases: firstly, in the mid-nineteenth century, when the blame for slums and poverty was attributed to individual slum dwellers who needed to be reformed personally and individually; secondly, later in the century, an age of 'scientific philanthropy' where more emphasis was placed on reforming the environment in which the poor lived; and thirdly, a 'progressive' phase from the 1890s into the twentieth century, where responsibility for urban problems was extended to embrace central government, business corporations and the suburban rich. One stimulus for progressivism was the economic depression in North America in the 1890s, which demonstrated that the problem of poverty went far deeper than individual indiscipline or environmental determinism. Progressivism was not at first a matter of party politics; rather it signified the possibility of management and regulation by 'experts' who were 'above

politics'. Progressives saw it as government's responsibility to regulate private business, especially activities that impinged on people's daily lives, such as the provision
of utilities, public transport and housing; and to protect workers and the poor from
exploitation in housing and job markets. They also ventured into the field of social
control in their support for legislation on issues of moral purity, prohibition, and
eugenics. Their emphasis on regulation and scientific management rather than self-
help aligns progressivism with modernist thinking; but the conjunction of science
and racism indicates the thin line between social democratic and totalitarian forms
of modernism.[1]

In Britain, the London County Council was controlled from its first election in 1889
until 1907 by a 'Progressive' alliance of Liberals and socialists, committed to improving the lot of the working classes through welfare provision, public housing, direct
labour schemes and the control of public utilities. There were equally 'progressive'
administrations in Glasgow and Liverpool. The Metropolitan Board of Works, which
the LCC replaced, was not as blatantly corrupt as Boss Tweed's control of Tammany
Hall in New York in the 1860s and early 1870s, but it was certainly inefficient and
undemocratic in the mode of election of its members.[2]

It is easy enough to equate 'progressive' and 'modern', but how do we fit 'Victorian'
into the equation when 'progressive' regulation is so often contrasted with, and
seen as a reaction to, 'Victorian' laissez-faire? In the 1980s British prime minister
Margaret Thatcher proudly celebrated and called for a reapplication in her own
age of 'Victorian values', by which she meant values of thrift, temperance, self-help,
enterprise, philanthropy, civic pride, and above all 'family values'. But her opponents
associated 'Victorian values' with inequality, patriarchy, colonialism, exploitation
and hypocrisy, at most a veneer of respectability. To Neil Kinnock, then leader of the
opposition Labour Party, 'Victorian Values' meant 'cruelty, misery, drudgery, squalor
and ignorance'. Neither protagonist in this debate would have equated 'Victorian'
with 'modern'.[3]

The literary critic, D. J. Taylor, offers us a way out of this apparent contradiction.
In an essay marking the centenary in 2001 of Queen Victoria's death he pointed to
the awkwardness with which the twenty-first century views the nineteenth. His essay
was headed with three mock-dictionary definitions, neatly juxtaposing 'Victoria',
'Victorian' – 'once used to describe a golden age; now primarily a term of abuse' –
and 'victim' – 'one that is subjected to oppression, hardship, or mistreatment'. Yet,
as he pointed out, 'much of what we value in the early 21st century, most of the
cement that binds our lives together, can be tracked back to a grounding in the
Victorian rock'; and he catalogued a long list of scientific, technological and political
innovations, all of which, 'if they were not invented by the Victorians, received their
greatest impetus in the period 1840–1900'.[4]

For a British historical geographer to apply the term 'Victorian' to the United States
may seem the rashest kind of neo-colonialism. But numerous American historians
have no such scruples, typically associating the term with Victorian gothic architecture and Victorian attitudes to home, family and sexuality. Popularly, in organisations such as the 'Victorian Society in America', the tone is celebratory.[5] The subtext
seems to be Englishness, a romantic nostalgia for a time before progressivism, mass
immigration and mass culture. This is not a conception of 'Victorian' that would be

comfortable with 'modernity'. Yet Thomas J. Schlereth portrays 'Victorian America' as advancing rapidly along the road to modernity, enthusiastically surveying transformation and innovation in a society that was constantly on the move. Asserting that the Victorian period ended not with Queen Victoria's death but with the onset of World War I, he uses 'Victorian America' to cover the years between the 1876 Centennial Exposition in Philadelphia and the 1915 Panama-Pacific Exposition in San Francisco, but he does not question the appropriateness of applying the term 'Victorian' to American society in the first place.[6] Regardless of the 1900s and 1910s, what was 'Victorian' about American cities *before* 1901?

Schlereth ends by acknowledging the paradoxes at the heart of 'Victorian' society: an obsession with rationality and measurement combined with a fascination for mystery and fantasy and, 'most paradoxical of all', a belief in 'rugged individualists espousing traditional values' played out in a bureaucratic and institutional context that encouraged conformity and homogeneity.[7] This sounds close to Berman's observation that 'To be modern is to live a life of paradox and contradiction . . . to be both revolutionary and conservative' in the face of 'immense bureaucratic organizations'.[8] Victorian cities were not yet modernist, but they were modern. Environmentally, too, if we envisage Victorian cities as both improved and decayed, full of new sewers, avenues, railway stations, hotels, stores and public buildings, all bathed in fog which could be beautiful (to Whistler or Monet, for example) at the same time as it was both mysterious (to Dickens and Conan Doyle) and deadly (to those who inhaled it), and juxtaposed with rickety and labyrinthine slums, degrading workhouses and exploitative sweat-shops, we approach a cultural definition of modernity: the 'shock of the new' and the necessity for a tangible – preferably picturesque – past constraining opportunities for 'creative destruction'.[9]

As Taylor also pointed out, 'there were at least three Victorian eras' (in Britain) – up until the Great Exhibition of 1851, 'an infinitely drawn out, late-Victorian twilight' and, between them, a 'middle stretch during which what we now regard as quintessential forms of "Victorian" self-expression, and concealment, began to establish themselves'.[10] The historical geographer, David Ward, has also applied a three-phase model, associating different social and spatial structures with successive periods of mercantile, industrial (or entrepreneurial) and corporate capitalism, and with different scales of urban system – the regional (prior to the railway age), the national (when inter-regional communications facilitated movements of people, materials and ideas, and specialisation developed among different cities) and the international or global (when investment, too, became internationally mobile). Restricting his attention to the second and third phases, Ward also discerned a shift in the representation of urban space: from cities with distinctive middle-class sectors accommodating a tiny minority of the population, and relatively undifferentiated working-class districts in which a destitute (and self-selective?) minority was concentrated in 'rookeries'; to cities in which a zonal pattern of social class predominated, in which upward social mobility was associated with suburbanisation, but a substantial and worrying 'residuum' was permanently stranded in inner-city slums (Figure 2.1).[11]

Extending this spatial and economic model, an early nineteenth-century 'age of improvement' and a twentieth-century 'progressive age' may be envisaged as

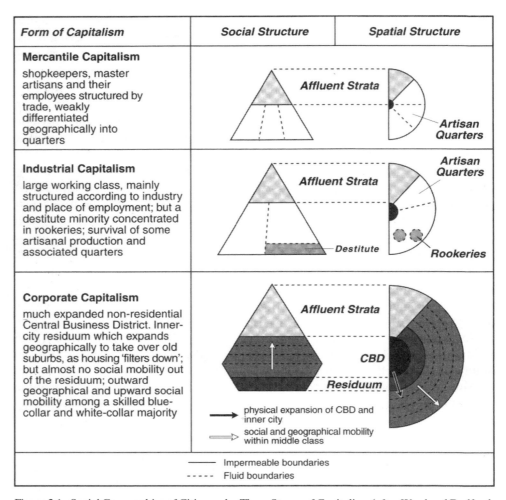

Form of Capitalism	Social Structure	Spatial Structure
Mercantile Capitalism shopkeepers, master artisans and their employees structured by trade, weakly differentiated geographically into quarters		
Industrial Capitalism large working class, mainly structured according to industry and place of employment; but a destitute minority concentrated in rookeries; survival of some artisanal production and associated quarters		
Corporate Capitalism much expanded non-residential Central Business District. Inner-city residuum which expands geographically to take over old suburbs, as housing 'filters down'; but almost no social mobility out of the residuum; outward geographical and upward social mobility among a skilled blue-collar and white-collar majority		

Figure 2.1. Social Geographies of Cities under Three Stages of Capitalism (after Ward and Radford, 1983) (originally published in B. Graham and C. Nash, eds, *Modern Historical Geographies* (Harlow, 2000), p. 219, reproduced by permission of Pearson Education Ltd).

book-ends for a mid-Victorian period which, in the twentieth century, was variously regarded by planners and historians as either an abyss of neglect and indifference, sharply differentiated from preceding and following periods, or, more optimistically, as the tentative origins of the twentieth-century welfare state. According to the former view, Victorian cities were 'chasmic', not only in chronological terms, but also socially: in Disraeli's view of the 'two nations', an unbridgeable chasm separated the poor from the rich; half a century later, Jack London in *The People of the Abyss* and Charles Masterman in *From the Abyss* indicated the impossibility of climbing out of the abyss in which so many of the working classes found themselves.[12] From a chasmic perspective, even the modest improvements that the Victorians attempted, such as model dwellings for the poor, proved to be counterproductive, as the impetus to improvement succumbed to pressures of rational calculation and laissez-faire economics. Charity organisation societies in both London and New York proved to be means of regulating and dehumanising charity. Even model dwellings turned out to be 'built-in slums'.[13]

This chasmic view of nineteenth-century cities was especially popular with early visionaries of town planning, including Patrick Geddes, Thomas Sharp and Lewis Mumford. Indeed, it was necessary for them to portray the Victorian era as one of social failure in order to justify their own agendas for the recovery of urbanity and for interventionist social engineering in the form of garden cities, inner-city reconstruction and new towns. Writing at the outbreak of World War II, Sharp constructed a chronology of urbanisation in which 'Right up till a hundred years ago there was a remarkably strong and virile town tradition in England' exemplified by London which 'as late as seventy-five or a hundred years ago, was a supremely civilised city'. But during the nineteenth century, 'there came the degradation of the town: utter black and hopeless degradation . . . The town should be an object of love and loyalty. The Victorian town was an object of indifference at best, of hatred and loathing at worst.' Nor could the Victorians be excused because of the rapidity and enormous scale of urban growth with which they were confronted. Rather than constitute a problem, such changes should have been claimed as an opportunity. In Sharp's view it was easier to plan well when you were laying out whole new towns or districts than when engaged on piecemeal renewal or accretion.[14]

Mumford, too, denigrated 'the rising philistines who built the nineteenth-century city', overwhelming the urbanity of Georgian planning in cities such as Bath and Edinburgh and forgetting the very nature and purpose of what cities should be. In Mumford's view, the 'magnification of all the dimensions of life, through emotional communion, rational communication, technological mastery, and above all, dramatic representation, has been the supreme office of the city in history'. But in the nineteenth century, a laissez-faire ideology, the promotion of mindless speculation, contempt for nature, and 'indifference to the elementary necessities of hygiene or amenity' produced 'the most degraded urban environment the world had yet seen'. Nor was Mumford's condemnation confined to British cities: new industrial cities in early twentieth-century America also attracted his disgust. The only redeeming feature was that 'in the end the disease stimulated the antibodies needed to overcome it'. Not that he was all that impressed with the solutions: the minimum standards introduced in housing by-laws were a 'final proof' of degradation.[15]

Contrasting with the chasmic view is a 'whiggish' interpretation of Victorian cities, which stressed the progress made by nineteenth-century reformers, recognising the unprecedented problems with which they were faced. After all, they had no recent experience of large-scale urbanisation on which to draw. Theirs was pre-eminently 'the age of great cities' (to use the title of a book by Robert Vaughan, a leading commentator on the new urban culture).[16] In the circumstances, they should be congratulated for what they *did* achieve, not castigated for what they failed to do. The emphasis, then, was on *progress* and *reform*, on the idea of *improvement*. And the perspective was looking backwards, from the present into the past. In this way, Victorian Britons were seen as founders of the welfare state, as if they already had the objectives of a National Health Service or Unemployment Benefit in mind when they opened the first poor law infirmaries or built new workhouses. According to this view, even the middle decades of the century were not ones of neglect, but of debate and experiment – a positive and heroic view of a Victorian heyday.[17]

According to which perspective we favour, so the research we do will vary. Those who adopt a chasmic view concentrate on urban problems, on slums and rookeries, and on the pathological consequences of urban living, such as disease and crime. Those of a whiggish disposition are more likely to concentrate on solutions, such as council housing and garden cities, and on institutional responses – the history of public health and town planning. Whereas the first type of history may be 'from below', exploring the experiences of ordinary people who were the recipients of, or resistant to, political regulation and social policy, whig histories more often concentrate on history 'from above' and on the formulation of policy.

I referred earlier to David Ward's discussion of three phases in the diagnosis of the 'slum problem' in American cities between 1840 and the 1920s. It is worth elaborating these phases here and considering the relevance of this chronology to British and Canadian cities. In the first phase, diagnosis was moral. Poverty was blamed on the idleness or profligacy of poor people. It was assumed that 'the pig made the sty' (poor families were to blame for the appalling environment in which they lived), so the only solutions were through personal (probably religious) salvation, through a district system of dealing with poor relief, so that personal and paternalistic relationships could be developed between donors (whether charitable individuals or the agents of government relief) and recipients, or through isolation, attempting to reform offenders (prostitutes in lock hospitals, criminals in prison, juveniles in residential schools, paupers in workhouses) away from the rest of the population. Even if reform failed, at least the influence of the depraved would have been removed. In a second phase, 'scientific philanthropy', more attention was paid to classifying the poor, differentiating between deserving and undeserving. Classification was central to the project of modernity. So, too, was the focus on improving the environment (following the argument that 'the sty made the pig'), providing sanitary housing, clean water and drains, whether by public regulation of private companies (e.g. by-laws regulating housing standards), or by encouraging limited-dividend housing companies and trusts. Finally, in a third phase associated with political progressivism around the turn of the century, the analysis of poverty became much more complex, subject to multivariate analysis, and sympathetic to structural explanations, recognising that the problems of slums lay not in the slums themselves, but in the nature of labour and housing markets in which slum-dwellers operated.[18]

Ward developed his analysis in an American context, but it is possible to fit different movements in Canada and Britain into his model. For example, the settlement movement associated in America with Hull House in Chicago and other settlements and mission houses in Boston, New York and Philadelphia had begun with Toynbee Hall, established in the East End of London in 1883; but it was also central to the Canadian 'social gospel' movement led by J. S. Woodsworth from All Nations' Mission in the immigrant North End of Winnipeg in the 1900s.[19] Among detailed social surveys, Charles Booth's poverty survey in London continued from the mid-1880s until 1900, but there were also numerous surveys of American cities, such as Pittsburgh and Washington. The establishment of a 'Bureau of Municipal Research' in Toronto during the 1910s was just one Canadian imitation of similar agencies in cities across the Great Lakes.[20]

Ward acknowledged that his categorisation was not perfect. There were pioneer 'structuralists' in the mid-nineteenth century (consider Engels' analysis of *The Condition of the Working Class* first published in 1845), and there are always people anxious to blame the disadvantaged for their plight; but it reflected the broad trend in attitudes to urban problems through the latter decades of the nineteenth and into the twentieth century. Yet Ward was not primarily concerned with analysing the twentieth-century historiography of nineteenth-century cities; he was more interested in categorising the diversity of contemporary (nineteenth-century) attitudes. As such, his study provides a link to the rest of this chapter, in which I will explore the language and especially the metaphors employed by nineteenth-century observers to describe their own cities.

But, to summarise my argument so far, it is that we think about the same period very differently according to the language we use. The language of 'modernity' implies something different from the language of 'Victorian'. Yet Victorian cities *were* modern cities. Modernisation does not entail just material progress. It also involves conceptual modernisation – new representations of space and society, focused on collectivities of structures, classes and areas rather than the particularities of individuals. Just as 'modern' required the construction of its 'other', the 'ancient' or 'traditional', so 'progress' required the construction of 'poverty'. Of course, there had always been poor people, even 'the poor', and 'poverty' as a word describing the condition of 'being poor' had been in common use in medieval society; but the language of poverty-classes and of being 'in poverty' acquired new significance once there were parliamentary investigations and social reformers to worry about poverty, surveys to identify poverty areas and label them as 'slums', and an ideology that associated physical poverty with moral poverty.

Visualising progress

It is not only twentieth- and twenty-first-century commentators, looking back, who hold differing views about nineteenth-century cities. Contemporaries also subscribed to a range of positive and negative views, variously expressed in a rich language of urban description, and also in the way that buildings were represented pictorially.

When the first Peabody Buildings (model dwellings for working-class families) were opened in Spitalfields in London's East End early in 1864, one contemporary illustration stressed the progressive nature of the block, portraying it like the bow of a ship ploughing through the waves (Figure 2.2). The message was that here was something innovative, quite unlike previous schemes for housing the poor. But the same building was represented by the *Illustrated London News*, in anticipation of its imminent completion, and in *Reynolds's Miscellany* as much more traditional, but perhaps also more solid: a building you could trust. The building was domesticated by the inclusion of everyday traffic and activities – street vendors, a boot-black in the *Illustrated London News*, a child playing with a hoop in *Reynolds's Miscellany*. There was less emphasis on its angularity, as if the building was a conventional four-square block (which it is not).[21] Likewise, when new luxury flats – Oxford and

Figure 2.2. Contrasting Contemporary Images of the first Peabody Buildings, erected in Spitalfields, London in 1864: (1) As 'progressive' and 'disciplined'. © British Library Board. All Rights Reserved; (2) As 'respectable' and 'polite'. *Illustrated London News*, 18 July 1863, p. 73. Senate House Library, University of London.

Cambridge Mansions – were erected near Edgware Road station in 1881–1882, an illustration in *The Builder* emphasised their ornate qualities as an external sign of luxury, but overall portrayed the block quite conservatively, as if it was little different from a row of town houses. In 1880s London, middle-class flats were still a controversial novelty. They could not be depicted as too unconventional. By the 1900s the block was rapidly getting out-of-date – it did not have lifts, or telephones in every suite, like the latest Edwardian blocks. If agents were to let it successfully, they had to emphasise that it was still a progressive and fashionable address. Hence, a photograph in a publicity brochure which focused on its angularity, adopting a low vantage point, similar to the first illustration of Peabody Buildings.[22] Of course, these sets of illustrations reveal some problems of making an interpretation a century or more later. Maybe an image of 'progress' is evidence that the buildings were not really so progressive and had to be made so. But it is an image that constantly recurred in late nineteenth- and early twentieth-century illustrations, especially of skyscraper offices, hotels and apartment buildings in North American cities.

The Flatiron Building, erected in New York in 1902 at the intersection of Broadway and Fifth Avenue, was frequently likened to the bow of an ocean liner. The *Brooklyn Daily Eagle* (21 November 1902) described it as 'an enormous steamship, plowing its way up through seas of buildings and dashing aside a foam of traffic', while other early observers called it 'a glorious white ship', 'a gigantic galleon sailing majestically into a shadowy harbour' or, by night, 'a ghostly ship that never reaches port and never changes course'.[23] Paintings such as John Sloan's 'Dust Storm, Fifth Avenue' (1906) (Figure 2.3), and photographs by Alfred Stieglitz and Edward Steichen portrayed the Flatiron Building as other-worldly, as much nature as culture, overwhelming, on an unstoppable voyage of progress. But they implied, thereby, that progress might not be such an undeniable good, threatening the habits and lifestyles of ordinary New Yorkers, such as those caught in the dust storm in the foreground of Sloan's picture. The Flatiron was part of nature, albeit an out-of-place nature; skyscrapers and the streets between them were often referred to as mountains, cliffs and canyons. Sloan's Flatiron was as super-natural as the dust storm it helped to generate.

Figure 2.3. John Sloan (1871–1951), 'Dust Storm, Fifth Avenue' (1906). Oil on canvas (55.9 × 68.6 cm). The Metropolitan Museum of Art, George A. Hearn Fund, 1921 (21.41.2). Image © The Metropolitan Museum of Art.

While most publicity shots of buildings like the Flatiron or the Times Building (on a similar sharp-angled junction at the intersection of Broadway and Seventh Avenue at the south end of Times Square) were unambiguously celebratory, fine-art representations of 'progress' were more ambivalent.[24] The same ambivalence was also true of contemporary commentators connecting urbanisation to 'progress'. As Andrew Lees has argued, only a minority of nineteenth- and early twentieth-century commentators on urbanism were unambiguously pro- or anti-city life. Most were neither 'city haters' nor 'city lovers' but 'saw the urban world as a complex mixture of both good and evil . . . a superabundance of both dangers and opportunities'.[25] What they shared was a propensity to employ a variety of metaphors and analogies in their attempts to understand the form and processes of urbanisation.

City as natural system

Underlying much of their language was the idea that the city either constituted a natural system or at least could be better understood by drawing parallels with nature or with the human body. Graeme Davison observes that 'From Aristotle's *Politics* to the Chicago School and beyond, social theorists have likened cities to bodies or organisms; dissected them into constituent organs, such as "heart", "lungs" and "arteries"; and charted their growth and decay'.[26] Yet there was a paradox here. Cities might be associated with civilisation, with human endeavour, nature transformed, but the ways in which cities functioned seemed to parallel the workings of natural systems. Perhaps cities were to be envisaged as freaks of nature – nature gone wrong. There were numerous allusions to 'monster cities', where 'monster' referred to more than their unprecedented size.

To George Augustus Sala (1859) 'the monster London' was a giant by turns asleep or at work, 'in his mad noonday rages, and in his sparse moments of unquiet repose'.[27] Yet Sala's stance was one of horrified fascination at the diversity of the city rather than moral condemnation of its excesses. For W. T. Stead (1885), editor of the *Pall Mall Gazette*, in his crusade against moral evil, 'the London Minotaur' was devouring the sacrifice of innocent maidens unwittingly lured into prostitution.[28] Even Henry James (1888) described London as 'like a mighty ogress who devours human flesh'; although James qualified this apparent condemnation by noting that 'the ogress herself is human'.[29] We should also note James' persistent gendering of London as feminine in contrast to Sala's pantomime male monster. A few pages farther on in his essay, James switched from cannibalistic ogress to 'strangely mingled monster', 'strangely mingled' in the clumsy, accidental juxtaposition of rich and poor, making for a monster whose uncoordinated body was growing out of control: 'And as the monster grows and grows for ever, she departs more and more . . . from the ideal of a convenient society, a society in which intimacy is possible' tending instead toward 'the momentary concussion of a million of atoms', heralding an unpredictable but potentially explosive future.[30] New York, too, was a 'monstrous organism', laced together 'by the ceaseless play of an enormous system of steam-shuttles or electric bobbins', James' metaphor for the movements of countless ferries and tugs, constantly glinting and whistling in the waters around and between the geographical constituents that made up the early twentieth-century city. James' New York monster was a dehumanised technological mutant: 'some colossal set of clockworks, some steel-souled machine-room of brandished arms and hammering fists and opening and closing jaws', its parts subject 'to certain, to fantastic, to merciless multiplication'.[31] This was a vision not unlike the monstrous 'moloch' of a machine at the heart of Fritz Lang's classic film, 'Metropolis' (1927).[32]

The physical expansion of cities was also described using less disturbing metaphors from nature, but the implication was still that the process lay beyond human control. London's growth was likened to a flood, or a rising tide.[33] To the imagery of tidal erosion employed by the antiquarian, W. J. Loftie, E. M. Forster added corrosion, writing in *Howards End* thirty years after Loftie, that 'the city herself, emblematic of their lives, rose and fell in a continual flux, while her shallows washed more widely against the hills of Surrey and over the fields of Hertfordshire'. From the perspective of still-rural Howards End, Helen Schlegel observes '"London's creeping." She pointed over the meadow – over eight or nine meadows, but at the end of them was a red rust.'[34] To Ford Madox Ford, too, London's presence was evidenced by its impact on nature: 'Viewed from a distance it is a cloud on the horizon. From the dark, further side of the hills at night, above the inky sky line of heather, of pine tops, of elms, one may see on the sky a brooding and sinister glow. That is London – manifesting itself on the clouds.' London was also defined by its pollution: 'we may say that London begins where tree trunks commence to be black'.[35] Gail Cunningham summarises a range of representations of urban expansion by Conan Doyle and H. G. Wells, noting that 'all these images exclude human agency . . . The dominant images are of alien forces breaking natural or historic bounds.'[36]

Victorian commentators had also made more positive analogies between the functioning of cities and the human body. St Paul's image of the church as the body of Christ, comprised of different but equally important parts, whose health depended on their functioning in harmony with one another, cannot have been far from the minds of urban essayists, many of whom, like James Boone in London, Robert Vaughan, first in London and later in Manchester, and Amory D. Mayo in New York, were ordained ministers.[37] In the centuries following Harvey's discoveries of the circulation of the blood, the need for good circulation was applied to both nations and cities.[38] To James Boone (1844), arguing for the importance of Christianity in cities, London was 'the heart to which and from which the life-blood circulates through every artery and vein of the entire body'. Mixing his metaphors, he concluded: 'let London become thoroughly irreligious, and there will come a dry rot into the whole fabric of our greatness'.[39] Writing in 1883, shortly after the opening of Brooklyn Bridge had enhanced circulation in metropolitan New York, William Conant declared the metropolis to be the nation's heart 'whose vital pulsations gather and redistribute the vital currency from and to the remotest veinlets'.[40] Within cities, too, streets could be regarded as arteries and veins, carrying traffic to and from the heart. Charles Masterman employed this imagery to describe patterns of working-class commuting: 'as if propelled by the systole and diastole of some mighty unseen heart, the wave of humanity from north, east and south rolls daily in and out of London'.[41]

But what if the heart or its arteries became diseased or ceased to function efficiently? Just as early nineteenth-century physicians attributed fevers to problems of circulation when the blood became 'overcharged with the products of decomposed organic matter'[42] for which one solution was blood-letting, so urban problems were blamed on an oversaturated infrastructure that required improved sanitation, ventilation and the opening-up of new spaces and new routes. Faced with the spread of slums in New York, 'the hearts and limbs of the city will sooner or later suffer, as surely as the vitals of the human system must suffer by the poisoning or disease of the smallest vehicle'.[43] Writing in 1898, Josiah Strong updated St Paul's reference to the parts of the body to the scientific language of cells and organisms: 'every organism is composed of numberless living cells which freely give their lives for the good of the organism'. But American cities were diseased because some 'cells' were 'introducing selfishness and disorder into the social organism'.[44]

Ideas of circulation applied not only to the city but to the nation, and not only to physical motion – the circulation of air through the spaces between buildings, or of traffic along roads, or of waste through sewers – but also to less tangible matter. Wealth circulated through the Bank of England, 'the heart of active capital'; ideas and information through the penny post and the telegraph but also through 'circulating libraries'. David Trotter has traced the genealogy of circulation from eighteenth-century political economy, in which 'circulation, not production, is the vital principle', to Dickens' novels, where stagnation, decay and overflow so often interrupt the circulation of love and happiness.[45]

By the mid-nineteenth century, the consequences of bad circulation in the human body were recognised as not only fevers but strokes, caused by blood clots. More pervasive arteriosclerosis as a cause of heart attacks was not widely understood until after World War I, and by-pass surgery to replace malfunctioning arteries is an innovation of the late 1960s, so it would be inappropriate to draw too close parallels between heart surgery and street improvements. Nevertheless, the Victorians were aware that arteries could become obstructed, or simply prove inadequate channels of circulation and that, in the same way, streets could be unable to cope with increased densities of traffic as cities grew ever bigger.[46]

The language of surgery could also be applied to slum clearance, eliminating the 'black spots' (literally black on Charles Booth's poverty maps) in much the same way that a cancerous growth was to be cut out of the body. At the beginning of the nineteenth century William Cobbett had famously described London as 'The Great Wen', simultaneously sucking life (in-migrants, investment) out of the rest of the nation while corrupting the surrounding countryside physically (through the expansion of the built-up area and the impact on agriculture) and morally (by spreading metropolitan values and lifestyle), and similar sentiments continued into the twentieth century in theories of urban degeneration (again both physical and moral), and even in a political economy which commended the 'breeding' of labourers in the countryside, where food and housing was cheap, before exporting them to work in cities where they would die of ill-health as soon as their useful working life was over.[47]

Despite using a language of choked arteries, contemporaries were less anxious about heart disease than about respiratory illnesses. In an age of 'consumption' (tuberculosis) concern for fresh air and ventilation could be expressed at every scale. The idea of parks as well as wide new boulevards functioning as a city's lungs was commonplace.[48] The American novelist and social explorer, Jack London, was taken to see 'one of London's lungs': Spitalfields Gardens. Finding it smaller than his own domestic garden, devoid of flowers, and full – in mid-afternoon – of sleeping homeless men and women (sleeping during the day because they were denied access at night), he was not impressed: '"A lung of London," I said; "nay, an abscess, a great putrescent sore."'[49]

Michel Foucault argued that the early nineteenth century saw a shift in the conception and classification of disease from one based on appearances to an anatomical approach in which specific illnesses were associated with specific locations in the body. Space also assumed a new importance in terms of treatment, with 'the birth of the clinic', where treatment could be more specialised, based on close and continuous observation *into* as well as *at* the body, and where the discipline of observation could be imparted to future practitioners. Similar ideas of classification and isolation were also applied to the treatment of lunatics, paupers and criminals in asylums, workhouses and prisons, removed from the community and subject to the panoptic eye of constant surveillance. All these practices applied to individuals' bodies stimulated new ways of conceptualising and analysing diseases on the body of the city, leading to the birth of sanitary science.[50]

Sanitary improvement was just one strand in an elaborate language of improvement or 'ameliorism' – making things better. Programmes of sanitary improvement were inseparable from programmes of moral improvement. But the mechanics of improvement depended on the particular concept of environmental influence to which reformers adhered. Were diseases spread by contagion, or by miasmas, invisible gases given off by excrement, rotting organic matter, or even the sweaty, perspiring human body? Later in the nineteenth century there developed a water-borne theory of the spread of infectious diseases and, eventually, a germ theory. But in the early and middle decades of the century the debate was pitched between contagionists and miasmatists.

The former demanded policies of isolation and quarantine – forms of spatial regulation – whereas the latter favoured sanitation and ventilation, opening up closed spaces where stagnant air might accumulate, blowing the miasmas away, or flushing away the excrement that exuded miasmatic gases. Both theories prompted a concern with density and overcrowding. Too many people meant too much contagion, but also too much waste. So there was a consensus that densities should be reduced. Beyond that, contagionists wanted to isolate the victims or carriers of diseases; miasmatists wanted to wash the diseases away.

But the same arguments about contagion and miasma were extended to moral health. Immorality was contagious. In Britain, policies of isolation included workhouses to isolate the idle – hence the emphasis in Poor Law Reforms on indoor relief, inside the workhouse, which proved quite impracticable to implement in many urban settings; on separate confinement to isolate criminals from one another inside prisons that already isolated them from the outside world; on asylums for the containment and treatment of lunatics and lock hospitals for the physical treatment and moral reform of prostitutes.[51] Model dwellings to protect the respectable poor from the residuum were a form of inverse isolation, reflecting the widespread anxiety that hitherto law-abiding artisans were being led astray by criminal neighbours. In *The Bitter Cry of Outcast London* (1883), Andrew Mearns, a Congregationalist minister, observed how often the 'family of an honest working man [was] compelled to take refuge in a thieves' kitchen.... There can be no question that numbers of habitual criminals would never have become such, had they not by force of circumstances been packed together in these slums with those who were hardened in crime.'[52]

There were also policies to eliminate 'moral miasmas': slum clearance and the construction of new streets would not get rid of just the physical characteristics of slums, but also their moral (dis)order. Slum clearance proposals, such as the London County Council's pioneering scheme transforming the 'Nichol', a labyrinth of crooked alleys and mean cottages, into the Boundary Street Estate of straight avenues and block dwellings, cited the crime rate as justification for the scheme.[53] Mearns' *Bitter Cry* also pointed to the connection between overcrowding, incest and irreligion. Consider, too, the title of George Godwin's *Town Swamps and Social Bridges* (1859). Godwin was editor of *The Builder*, but his argument was more about moral reform than sanitary reform. Morality was to be produced through better housing. The very phrase 'town swamps' was suggestive of miasmatic theory – with the slums exuding a kind of poisonous marsh gas, or acting as quagmires which sucked the poor under.[54]

Exploring the city

It was a short journey from metaphors of natural organisms to the language of exploration. Towards the end of Jack London's *The People of the Abyss* is an extraordinary chapter, 'A Vision of the Night', in which the author recounted a late-night walk from Spitalfields to the Docks:

I may say that I saw a nightmare, a fearful slime that quickened the pavement with life, a mess of unmentionable obscenity that put into eclipse the 'nightly horror' of Piccadilly and the Strand. It was a menagerie of garmented bipeds that looked something like humans and more like beasts... these males looked at me, sharply, hungrily, gutter-wolves that they were, and I was afraid of their hands, of their naked hands, as one may be afraid of the paws of a gorilla. They reminded me of gorillas. Their bodies were small, ill-shaped, and squat.... They are a new species, a breed of city savages. The streets and houses, alleys and courts, are their hunting grounds. As valley and mountain are to the natural savage, street and building are valley and mountain to them. The slum is their jungle, and they live and prey in the jungle.[55]

This was a 'human zoo' as much as a jungle, for the male savages – the muggers of their day – along with female prostitutes and their pimps, who also inhabited these streets, were under the watchful eye of the police, 'brass-buttoned keepers [who] kept order among them when they snarled too fiercely'. London's vision was intended as warning to the rich, 'the dear soft people... of the West End', whose hypocrisy, engaging in minor acts of charity while supporting an economic system that drove down wages and immiserised millions of their fellow citizens, he constantly attacked.[56] But in this vision, the West End was outside the jungle. By contrast, in the novel by London's friend, Upton Sinclair, *The Jungle* (1906), it was the whole city of Chicago, not only the stockyards, packinghouses and frame cottages of the south side, but also the Gold Coast mansions north of the downtown 'Loop', that constituted a jungle.[57] At both scales – the slum and the city – the rule of the jungle was the survival of the fittest, but the criteria for fitness differed: physical strength, quick-wittedness and gang membership in the slum, as depicted in another classic of East End literature, Arthur Morrison's *A Child of the Jago* (1894); economic and political power at the scale of the city, as represented by the corruption of machine politics and dishonest employers in Chicago.[58] Andrew Lees observed that Darwinism led to an interpretation of individual suffering as an essential prerequisite for the advancement of society. It was argued by laissez-faire liberals that the problems of the city brought out the best in people.[59] But London and Sinclair seemed to indicate the potential for a reversion to savagery, cloaked in civility on the part of the bourgeoisie, exposed in the raw among the poorest and most marginalised.

Jack London had ventured into 'the abyss' of London's East End disguised as an American seaman down on his luck. He was not the only social explorer to dress down in the hope of gaining acceptance amongst the poor.[60] But most 'explorers' were more imperious in their investigations of 'how the other half lived'.[61] Just as explorers were exploring 'darkest Africa', so social explorers were charting 'darkest England'. In 1861 John Shaw noted the juxtaposition of Oxford Street shops to back-street slums whose inhabitants were comparable to 'the wildest colony of savages, transplanted by an act of conjuration from the centre of Africa'.[62] But as society became increasingly segregated, most of the middle classes never went anywhere near the slums. So, it was suggested, they knew as little about the East End and East Enders as they knew about African or Polynesian tribes. The same was true in New York, where the Reverend Walter Rauschenbusch described 'a new literature of exploration. Darkest Africa and the polar regions are becoming familiar; but we now have intrepid men and women who plunge for a time into the life of the lower classes and return to write books about this unknown race.'[63] Rauschenbusch's choice of words – intrepid, plunge, return, unknown – perfectly illustrates Alan Mayne's argument about 'the drama of performance' intrinsic to representations emphasising the otherness and elsewhereness of slums: 'the recurring representation of slumland as a hidden world; of visitors as bands of explorers among foreign tribes in unmapped territories'.[64]

So social exploration required as much forward planning as mounting a colonial expedition. Jack London began his 'descent' with a visit to Thomas Cook's, the travel agents, 'pathfinders and trail-clearers, living sign-posts to all the world, and bestowers of first aid to bewildered travellers':

unhesitatingly and instantly, with ease and celerity, could you send me to Darkest Africa or Innermost Thibet, but to the East End of London, barely a stone's throw distant from Ludgate Circus, you know not the way!

The travel-agent clerk excused his company's inability to help:

'We are not accustomed to taking travellers to the East End; we receive no call to take them there, and we know nothing whatsoever about the place at all.'[65]

London was not the only commentator to use the word 'abyss'. So did Charles Masterman, Cambridge-educated and subsequently Liberal MP, in *From the Abyss* (1902), based on his experiences sharing a flat in a working-class tenement block in Camberwell in south London. Jack London's abyss was one from which escape was almost impossible, except there was the terrifying prospect that one day, rather like a prehistoric monster from a 'lost world', the 'savages' might emerge to destroy the comfortable world of the West End. The same imagery, but translated from East End – West End into a multi-level world of subterranean drones and an above-surface decadent elite, had already been used by H. G. Wells in *The Time Machine* (1895) and was subsequently employed by Fritz Lang in *Metropolis*. Wells projected the contemporary class structure into a distant future when two polarised classes had evolved into separate species. The Eloi in the Upperworld had become so accustomed to a utopian abundance that they had lost the ability to do anything for themselves; they lived like flower-children among the ruins. The Morlocks (from the same root as 'moloch') in the Underworld were the descendants of an exploited working class; they still had some understanding of machinery and it seems that, almost out of habit, they continued to provide some necessities of life for the Eloi, but they also preyed upon them, emerging from the Underworld under cover of night. Wells pointed up the connections with the present: the 'tendency to utilize underground space for the less ornamental purposes of civilization' including subways, underground workrooms and restaurants. 'Even now, does not an East-end worker live in such artificial conditions as practically to be cut off from the natural surface of the earth?'[66] Indeed, Wells spent part of his own childhood at Uppark, a minor stately home in West Sussex where his mother was housekeeper, and where 'the servants moved unseen by the masters through a labyrinth of underground tunnels', an existence which had outraged the young Wells.[67]

In describing London's East End, Jack London preferred the title 'City of Degradation' to 'City of Dreadful Monotony', the designation he attributed to 'well-fed, optimistic sight-seers, who look over the surface of things and are merely shocked by the intolerable sameness and meanness of it all'.[68] In making this criticism, he no doubt had in mind Masterman, whose abyss was more like an ocean, or an innumerable grey, eerily silent mass, inexorably spreading, like Loftie's and Forster's tide. Masterman hinted at the potential for a political uprising, but the general tendency of his writing was to emphasise the meaningless and powerless monotony of life in his abyss.

Yet *From the Abyss* merits discussion on several counts. First, given the emphasis in theories of modernity on the development of self-identity, it is worth noting Masterman's reference to 'the creeping into conscious existence' of the population of the Abyss. Second, and in the light of interest in the 'uncanny' in modernity, emphasising the essential pairing of transparency and opacity, 'home' and the 'unhomely', strangeness and familiarity, for citizens who also find themselves to be strangers, it is surely more than coincidence that Masterman regarded the denizens of his abyss as 'a weird and uncanny people', living in 'a silence that becomes the more weird and uncanny with the increasing immensity of our number'.[69] These people were strangers in their own city, uncannily silent because of their disengagement from processes of political and religious education or decision-making. Third, Masterman foreshadowed the language of urban ecology in his account of the inner-city's invasion of the suburbs. The elaborate form of his ecological analogies in some ways paralleled Wells' prophecies of future decay. Masterman likened the growth of London's population to luxuriant tropical vegetation springing up wherever there was a nook or ledge that would sustain life. Like Wells, he discerned two layers of population:

Tall trees insolently rise to heaven . . . Below are all forms of life driven under, forced to adapt themselves to unnatural surroundings, distorted into repulsive, twisted, grotesque forms of existence; each seemingly prepared for any monstrous change if only it can preserve its life and propagate its kind.

But he foresaw a future where

the torrent of life has overreached itself; the struggle has become too terrific; the vitality is gradually dying. And then, as the whole mass festers in all the gorgeous, wonderful beauty of decay, comes the mangrove – dark-leafed, dank, slippery, unlovely, sign and symbol of the inevitable end. And with the mangrove the black-marsh and the reeking, pestilential mud.[70]

We are back in the swamps of Godwin's moral decay, headed for the post-human, end-of-the-world seashore on which Wells' time-traveller at last alighted.[71]

To many Victorians, confident of the superiority of their culture and reliant on the superiority of their technology, the logical consequence of exploration was colonisation. For General William Booth, founder of the Salvation Army, colonisation and conversion of the East End was as vital as colonisation and Christianisation of the

Empire. So, in the wake of H. M. Stanley's *In Darkest Africa*, Booth produced *In Darkest England and the Way Out* (1890).[72] But General Booth's crusade was relevant to North American as much as British cities. His Salvation Army, developing since the 1860s but first known by this title in 1878, was exported to New York in 1880, promoting similar social programmes to those in London, even sponsoring farm colonies in the west of the United States equivalent to the overseas farm colonies advocated by Booth as a solution to the problems of the East End.[73]

Quoting extensively from Stanley, Booth emphasised the darkness, impenetrability and apparent endlessness of the Congo forest that Stanley had traversed. This was a place 'where the rays of the sun never penetrate', where human beings were 'dwarfed into pygmies and brutalised into cannibals' and whose inhabitants could not imagine that there was a world beyond the forest. So Booth argued his way through a thicket of allusions to his inevitable conclusion: 'As there is a darkest Africa is there not also a darkest England?' Each was characterised by 'its monotonous darkness, its malaria and its gloom, its dwarfish de-humanized inhabitants, the slavery to which they are subjected, their privations and their misery'.[74]

But Booth went beyond the conventional Victorian evangelical focus on drunkenness, idleness and sexual immorality, making a resounding condemnation too of 'firms which reduce sweating to a fine art, who systematically and deliberately defraud the workman of his pay, who grind the faces of the poor, and who rob the widow and the orphan, and who for a pretence make great professions of public-spirit and philanthropy'. He invited his readers: 'Read the House of Lords' Report on the Sweating System, and ask if any African slave system ... reveals more misery.'[75] He believed in progress as much as salvation: 'there is a light beyond'. His rescue plan included conventional missionary virtues, like settlement houses, temperance and self-help, but also a return to rural life and the involvement of the poor in the colonisation process. One solution to metropolitan problems lay in the farm colonies of Australasia, Canada and South Africa, a classic, colonial 'spatial fix' but also reflective of an English (and Jeffersonian American) anti-urban stance, emphasising the need for small-scale, knowable communities and the intrinsic desirability of being close to nature.[76]

Other social explorers drew more practically from the method of anthropological exploration rather than imperial conquest of distant lands. Henry Mayhew, whose 'letters' on London's poor, based on interview as much as observation, appeared first in the *Morning Chronicle* in 1849, but continued in book form through the 1850s and 1860s, defined himself as an 'ethnologist', and referenced the work of contemporary anthropologist, James Prichard, on 'wandering tribes'. Deborah Nord has argued against too literal interpretations of Mayhew's use of this term as a form of racism. His use of the word 'tribe' was not intended as a euphemism for 'species', as if the poor were a physiologically defined 'race apart'. Rather, his reference to Prichard indicated his acceptance of the ethnologist's belief that 'There is essentially one race, and all variations among humankind can be attributed to *differences in external conditions* and to the different influences that derive from these conditions'. So Mayhew took a detailed interest in the cultural norms and behaviour of the street-sellers, costermongers, labourers whose case histories he presented in successive volumes of *London Labour and the London Poor*, in order to demonstrate not their 'apartness' from more respectable society, but their adaptation to circumstances. All 'races' were on the same upward path of progress.[77]

Biblical cities

However scientific their beliefs (and sometimes because of them) most social commentators resorted to apocalyptic language somewhere in their writings.[78] So the slums of London and New York, and sometimes entire cities, were portrayed as 'city of dreadful night', 'nether world' or 'inferno'. Edward Bellamy, in his utopian *Looking Backward* (1888), imagined the South Cove tenement district of Boston from the perspective of the year 2000, describing it as an 'Inferno' inhabited by a 'great multitude of strangled souls' whose bodies were 'living sepulchres'.[79] Five years later, Benjamin Flower's *Civilization's Inferno* also focused on Boston's slums as the product of the sins of capitalism and the source of potential unrest and plague.[80] James and Daniel Shepp's illustrated guide to New York (1894) referred to the Bowery as 'the vestibule of Pandemonium'.[81] In describing the noise and chaos of the street, they conformed to the modern definition of pandemonium as uproar and confusion; but in capitalising the word, they alluded to Milton's *Paradise Lost* where Pandemonium was the place of all demons, 'the infernal regions'.[82] And in commenting on its great width – 'one of the widest avenues in the city', 'unlike most streets that are the abode of the "under-world"' – they hinted at Jesus' reference to the wide gate and broad road that lead to destruction.[83]

The image of the city as an inferno or as Hades was reinforced by the onset of industrialisation. Blast furnaces, mill chimneys, and the associated sounds and smells of industry encouraged apocalyptic visions of cities, blood-red and afire. Alternatively, contemporaries saw the same things as awesome, part of the drama of progress rather than auguries of Armageddon. Urban boosters celebrated parallels with great civilisations in the past. Manchester was a modern Athens, while Americans had no scruples about bestowing ancient classical names on their new cities: Ithaca, Rome, Syracuse, Troy, Utica, without venturing outside a small part of upstate New York. Neo-classical architecture recalled the virtues of Athens, Rome and Alexandria. Alternatively, imitations of Venetian or Florentine architecture invoked the renaissance age of merchant trading, providing cultural legitimacy to upstart industrial and commercial cities.

But the most pervasive allusion among contemporary commentators was to Babylon, a city that was remade in the imagination as Bible knowledge declined and archaeological research developed. Until the early twentieth century even the most sceptical or atheistic writers employed, and assumed an understanding by their readers of, an armoury of biblical references. Jack London quoted at length from 1 Samuel and Job in *The People of the Abyss*. H. G. Wells not only named the Morlocks after Moloch, the Ammonite god to whom references are scattered through the Bible from Leviticus onwards, but also derived the name of the Eloi, the helpless inhabitants of the Upperworld, from Christ's cry on the cross: 'Eloi, Eloi, lama sabachthani? which is, being interpreted, My God, my God, why hast thou forsaken me?'[84] Wells' *War of the Worlds* is also riddled with biblical allusions: a recent annotated edition identifies quotations from the books of Genesis, Exodus, Judges, II Kings, Psalms,

Matthew, and Revelation.[85] So it is unsurprising that many, more devout, authors drew on the prolific biblical references to Babylon in trying to make sense of their own cities.

'Babylon' evoked a whole series of, predominantly negative, images. Firstly, Babylon as Babel (from which we also get 'babble') – the story of the Tower of Babel, in which the peoples of the earth resolved: 'let us build us a city and a tower, whose top may reach unto heaven; and let us make us a name'.[86] This desire for self-aggrandisement, challenging God's omnipotence and trusting in their own strength, causes God to confound their language, so that they no longer understand one another and are forced to abandon building. The city as Babel was, therefore, a place of confusion, but also of arrogance and rebellion.

Secondly, Babylon appears regularly in the prophecies of Isaiah and Jeremiah as a magnificent, but wicked and corrupt city. At the end of the New Testament, John's vision of the fall of Babylon includes a lengthy inventory of the city's spectacular wealth, extending from 'merchandise of gold, and silver, and precious stones, and of pearls, and fine linen' to 'horses, and chariots, and slaves, and souls of men'.[87] In Babylon, everything was for sale; everything had its price. Its disdain for the sacred was epitomised in King Belshazzar's use of sacred gold and silver vessels from the temple at Jerusalem for a purely secular orgiastic feast.[88]

The satisfying, but also fearful, thing about Babylon was that it got its just desserts. As Belshazzar drinks from the sacred vessels, he sees the 'writing on the wall' signifying God's judgment on his regime. 'In that night was Belshazzar the king slain.'[89] Likewise, in Revelation, 'Babylon the great is fallen'.[90] So references to Babylon were also warnings that modern cities were destined for eventual destruction. Sir Richard Phillips, writing in 1811, opined: 'great cities contain in their very greatness, the seeds of premature and rapid decay. . . . Ninevah, Babylon, Antioch, and Thebes are become heaps of ruins, tolerable only to reptiles and wild beasts. Rome, Delhi, and Alexandria, are partaking the same inevitable fate; and London must some time, from similar causes, succumb under the destiny of every thing human.' Even earlier, William Cowper had compared London to 'Babylon of old'. London was just as opulent as Babylon ever was, but 'this Queen of cities, that so fair / May yet be foul, so witty, yet not wise'.[91]

This image of Babylon was also brought home to early nineteenth-century observers by two massive panoramic paintings by John Martin: *The Fall of Babylon* (1819) and *Belshazzar's Feast* (1820). These paintings were widely exhibited and copied, and even explained through the publication of interpretative guides. *Belshazzar's Feast* was reproduced in an enlarged 2,000 square-foot version at the British Diorama in Oxford Street in 1833. The original had first been exhibited at the British Institution in 1820, where it had to be railed off to protect it from enthusiastic viewers. Then it was displayed in a shop in the Strand, where visitors could buy a descriptive booklet and key to the painting. Arrows and numbers on a diagram of the painting indicated points of interest, such as 'the writing on the wall', the 'brazen serpent', 'Daniel interpreting the writing' and 'Belshazzar dropping his cup'. Martin himself made several versions of the painting; and the diorama version – not by Martin, but by Hippolyte Sebron, who worked with Daguerre – was also exhibited on Broadway in New York.[92]

In Gustave Doré's and Blanche Jerrold's *London: A Pilgrimage* (1872), a book that has powerfully shaped subsequent perceptions of the Victorian city as teeming with life – and death – and invariably full of foreboding, Doré's final full-page illustration, entitled 'The New Zealander', depicts a future London, in ruins and deserted save for a lone figure, the visitor from the farthest reaches of empire, surveying the devastation from a rock overlooking the Thames (Figure 2.4). Lynda Nead discusses Doré's illustration, and the texts imagining ruined London with which Jerrold would have been familiar, as the coda to her own book on *Victorian Babylon*, in which she argues that 'The dystopic vision of the ruins of Victorian Babylon was not just a figure of the possible distant future, it was a cipher for the experience and condition of modernity itself'.[93] If modernity was to be defined by and required constant reminders of its 'other', the evidence of progress necessitated constant reference back not only to the continued presence of poverty but also to the imminence of collapse.

Nearly twenty years after Doré's vision, William Morris envisaged a future when 'London . . . the modern Babylon of civilization' had disappeared, proving 'more like ancient Babylon now than the "modern Babylon" of the nineteenth century was'.[94] Morris, however, saw its replacement by a communitarian utopia, less an urban New Jerusalem than a revival of medieval villages and small towns, but without the oppression of unequal feudal society. Morris's arts-and-crafts socialism, like General Booth's muscular Christianity, reflected a pervasive anti-urbanism characteristic of both an English pastoral tradition and the general tenor of Old Testament scriptures: the first biblical city was built by Cain after he had killed his brother Abel; the cities of Sodom and Gomorrah were so wicked that God had to destroy them; Jonah was sent by God to preach to the wicked people of Nineveh – and then was upset when they repented so that God did not destroy Nineveh after all. All these and many other biblical references no doubt reflect the perspectives of an initially nomadic and subsequently rural Israelite people, first confronted and then neighboured by threatening city-states, but they served to colour the attitudes of early Victorian social commentators and historians, especially those with an academic training in theology.[95]

Babylon was also a place of slavery, exile or banishment: 'By the rivers of Babylon, there we sat down, yea, we wept, when we remembered Zion. . . . How shall we sing the Lord's song in a strange land?'[96] In the nineteenth century, Babylon was the place of enslavement to the machine, and to the market. It was not really 'home' for the army of migrants from the countryside, forced by changes in the rural economy to seek urban employment. If the nineteenth-century industrial city could be interpreted as a kind of Babylon, so could some colonial outposts to which administrators felt they were being banished in the early twentieth century. Canberra, newly created capital of Australia, but still a town of only a few thousand, mostly civil servants and their families, and with few attractions, was likened to a 'bush Babylon' in the 1920s. So, to the English artist and writer Wyndham Lewis, as late as 1940, was the Canadian city of Toronto, not because it was especially sinful or spectacular – in fact, Toronto had a reputation for temperance and dull conformity – but because it seemed so remote, an urban wilderness and a place of (in Lewis' case, self-imposed) exile.[97]

Figure 2.4. Gustave Doré (1832–1883), 'The New Zealander', from G. Doré and B. Jerrold, *London: A Pilgrimage* (London, 1872).

When Charlotte Brontë's heroine, Lucy Snowe, arrived in London for the first time, 'late, on a dark, raw, and rainy evening', she found 'a Babylon and a wilderness'. But next morning, as the sun broke through the fog, the same environment became exciting, liberating, pleasurable.[98] And so, as the century wore on, to less austere, worldlier writers, 'Babylon' seemed a more attractive prospect. Henry James, arriving in London in conditions similar to those that welcomed Lucy Snowe, found it a 'murky modern Babylon', whereas Paris was a 'vast bright Babylon'.[99] By the late 1920s, to the young liberal Catholic Canadian novelist, Morley Callaghan, fresh from Toronto, Paris was the 'lovely Babylonian capital'.[100]

Despite these more nuanced views of London, Paris and New York as 'modern Babylons', less sympathetic views also persisted. In *Howards End* (1910), E. M. Forster referred disparagingly to 'Babylonian flats', ostentatious and vulgarly decorated blocks of mansion flats which were displacing a more cultured but less profitable environment of town houses.[101] The spectres of not only Babylon but other ancient cities – Nineveh, Athens, Rome, Constantinople – also continued to loom over New York in John Dos Passos' *Manhattan Transfer* (1925). Marc Brosseau notes that the 'little symphonic poem' that alludes to all these cities, and which appears twice – in Chapter 2 of First Section and Chapter 7 of Second Section – 'portends a very bleak future for this arrogant city: babelization . . . and destruction'.[102] Fire is a recurring theme through the novel; babelisation is conveyed through its disconnected, fragmentary and multivocal structure; and destruction comes in the harangue of a deranged tramp in the last chapter of the book:

'Do you know how long God took to destroy the tower of Babel, folks? Seven minutes. Do you know how long the Lord God took to destroy Babylon and Nineveh? Seven minutes. There's more wickedness in one block in New York City than there was in a square mile in Nineveh, and how long do you think the Lord God of Sabboath will take to destroy New York City an Brooklyn an the Bronx? Seven seconds. Seven seconds.'[103]

If Babylon, especially in the nineteenth century, signified corruption, exploitation, alienation, and likely destruction, Jerusalem denoted the hope of heaven on earth, as in Blake's vision of building Jerusalem in England's green and pleasant land. Although the Bible is full of man-made cities in rejection of God, it also portrays Heaven as a city – first in Ezekiel 40 and later, more emphatically, in Revelation 21 – the vision of 'the holy city, new Jerusalem, coming down out of heaven from God'.[104] It would have been ridiculous to apply that title to any existing metropolis – the most ardent city booster could not fail to acknowledge the deficiencies and injustices of modern cities – but reduced to material dimensions, the heavenly Zion was echoed in countless plans for ideal cities and new towns – from James Silk Buckingham's 'Victoria' (1849) by way of Benjamin Richardson's 'Hygeia' (1876) to Ebenezer Howard's 'Garden Cities of Tomorrow' (1902) and Le Corbusier's 'Ville Radieuse' (1933).[105] Like the biblical New Jerusalem, they were invariably regular and symmetrical in plan, clearly bounded, separate from the 'natural world' of sin and death, or disease and no drains. So a spiritual concept came down to earth, as plans for drains and clean water, discipline and order, a continuing parallel between physical and moral goodness. In North America, similar connections were made in Daniel Burnham's 'White City' in the form of the Chicago Exposition, a New Jerusalem bathed in white light, and in subsequent visions of the 'City Beautiful'. But there were also more literal new Jerusalems thanks to the presence of so many Jews for whom even 'the dense Yiddish quarter' of New York constituted a 'city of redemption' compared to the 'foul, stifling Ghettos of other remembered cities' from which they had fled in eastern Europe.[106]

Conclusion

Summarising nineteenth-century images of Babylon and Jerusalem, John Short sees them as describing different perceptions of rural and urban. The city as Babylon was part of a worldview which celebrated the order, harmony and sheltered existence of rural life, which the city rudely disrupted. The city as Jerusalem rescued us from the idiocy and the stultifying repression of rural life.[107] But by the early twentieth century, these polarities were less secure. The modern city was increasingly to be seen as simultaneously Babylon *and* Jerusalem: a city of licence (and potential disorder) was also a city of individual liberty; a city of toil was also a city of opportunity for self-betterment; one person's disorganisation (represented by the rule of the mob in Short's analysis) was another person's community.

Returning from Paris to Toronto, Morley Callaghan produced a succession of novels with biblical titles (*Such Is My Beloved* (1934), *They Shall Inherit the Earth* (1935), *More Joy in Heaven* (1937)), focused on the plight of the economically or socially marginalised, and often inverting the conventional 'moral geography' of respectable, law-abiding, God-fearing suburbia and immoral, hell-bound inner city. Callaghan's suburbanites, business elites and church leaders are hypocritical, concerned with keeping up appearances, sexually repressed; but the despised and marginalised inhabitants of inner-city lodging houses, and the slum priests who admit to their doubts and failings while they show compassion to the poor, are the more 'blessed'. Callaghan's city was a sanctified Babylon, a practical Jerusalem which offered opportunities for good – for forgiveness, reconciliation, self-sacrifice – just because it was such a dangerous, threatening and unjust place.[108]

Metaphors and analogies prove resistant to change. 'Progress' may no longer be part of the vocabulary of cultural historians, but it is still the language of governments and development agencies. We still 'explore', we still demonise 'slums', 'ghettos' and 'inner cities', we still (and increasingly, in an age of sustainability) think about cities as natural systems, and we still imagine the apocalypse played out in the ruins of major cities, especially in the face of new freaks of nature and culture, whether asteroid strikes or supervolcanic eruptions, or the man-made monsters of sea-level rise, extreme weather or global terrorism.

But it is the dilemma of reconciling licence and order, liberty and responsibility that lay at the heart of the planning and regulation of modern cities – allowing diversity without disorder, encouraging self-help without exploitation, making citizens who exercised their freedom with due regard for their neighbours and for the common good, producing top-down representations of space that translated into responsible spatial practices. Key to such a project were questions of survey and surveillance, which are central to my next chapter.

3

Surveying the city

Modern societies demanded ever more detailed information about their populations, resources and activities. Governments required information in order to plan,
regulate and tax. Businesses desired information on potential investments and customers. Lawyers, landlords, tenants and homeowners sought information about rights
to property. Residents turned to information about retailers, tradesmen and the
providers of services. Tourists and travellers looked for information about the places
they were visiting. Information became a marketable commodity and, as for other
commodities, markets were created where none had previously existed. Hence the
proliferation through the nineteenth century of censuses, surveys, maps, tax records,
credit ratings, directories and guidebooks.

Information is central to the minimisation of risk, and the management of risk has
been a central theme in studies of modernity. City-dwellers needed education and
information – on environmental hazards, for example – if they were to act as rational, self-governing individuals who conformed to tenets of liberal governmentality.
Liberal government itself involved the art of 'rule from a distance'. Governing cities
as much as governing colonies required mapping and delimiting territory and enumerating the people and resources it contained. Matthew Hannah emphasises three
moments in a cycle of social control: observation, normalising judgment, and enforcement or regulation. Observation by central and local government included practices
of census-taking and mapping, organised by 'grids of specification' to define objects
of interest such as race, gender, class, age, nationality or spatial units, such as the
real grids on which many cities were laid out. None of this was value-free: judgment
informed observation as much as observation invited judgment. The third moment in
the cycle is the consequence of judgment, regulation, which could be either 'support-
ive/fostering' (e.g. the introduction of compulsory education) or 'restrictive/coercive'
(e.g. controls on immigration). What emerges is the absence of any clear distinction
between laissez-faire liberalism and interventionist progressivism: the social regulation for which observation through census-taking or Ordnance Survey mapping was
the prerequisite was intended as a 'rule of freedom'. Moreover, at the same time as
government officials classified people into 'native' or 'foreign', 'male' or 'female',
'black' or 'white', 'master' or 'servant', labels which at least implicitly appeared to
value some more highly than others, so – in Patrick Joyce's argument – by counting

and mapping *everybody*, giving each piece of information equal weight in a statistical aggregate, censuses and Ordnance Survey maps implied that the 'common person-hood' of those surveyed mattered more than their differences.[1]

Nevertheless, even if – like Joyce and Hannah – we treat censuses, surveys and maps as performances of governmentality, we must also consider them as representations of the spaces and peoples that were being surveyed. Every survey, every map, every source of statistical data was also a form of representation of modern life, as selective, as ideologically grounded, as subject to individual interpretation, as more obviously 'subjective' sources such as novels and paintings. So the purpose of this chapter is to examine the proliferation of new forms of measurement in the nineteenth and early twentieth centuries as evidence of both the practice of governmentality and the representation of space in modern cities.

The demand for information might originate in the metropole, but frequently it was directed at the hitherto ungovernable periphery, whether geographically dis-tant in 'darkest Africa' or an internally unexplored 'darkest England'. The western American frontier of uncharted 'Indian territory' was matched by the Lower East Side, where 'the other half' lived.[2] The British government's desire to know Ireland prompted a Survey Act of 1825 which specified what boundaries should be shown on Ordnance Survey (O.S.) maps of Ireland, and gave its surveyors rights of access to private property. In 1841 the same rights of survey were extended to the British mainland.[3] The subsequent production of maps at scales of 6 inches, 25 inches and 60 inches to the mile led to their use as the base maps on which social, economic and sanitary indicators could be overlain. Draft versions of Charles Booth's poverty maps were plotted on 25 inch O.S. maps, although the published versions used as their base the 'library maps' of London produced by Stanford's, one of the leading private map-making firms.[4] Stanford's map, at a scale of 6 inches to the mile, had first appeared in 1862, adding enormous detail to the 'skeleton survey' that had been produced by the Ordnance Survey in 1848, which had shown little more than the outline of streets.[5] In this way we can see state-sponsored surveys facilitating if not collaborating with the production of privately generated but publicly available sources of information such as Stanford's maps and Booth's survey. Indeed, we should not forget that maps and panoramas, surveys and reports, were sources of entertainment and education as well as instruments of power. Just like novels and pictures, maps and surveys told stories.

The panoramic city

The ability to see the city from above – whether from the top of a tall building such as the dome of St Paul's Cathedral or the tower of a New York newspaper office, or from a hot-air balloon – stimulated a fashion for panoramas, ideally 360 degree views, displayed in specially constructed buildings where viewers stood on a central platform surrounded by painted canvas. In London, the first permanent exhibition building was the Panorama, Leicester Square, which existed from 1793 until 1863. On the edge of Regent's Park, itself a very modern residential and leisure space in the 1820s, the Colosseum, erected between 1824 and 1829, was designed to accommodate Thomas Hornor's panorama of London, painted from sketches he had made from a temporary hut precariously fixed to the dome of St Paul's when it was undergoing repairs in 1820. Visitors to the Colosseum were able to enjoy the spectacle rather more safely, travelling to a viewing platform in the 'Ascending Room', London's first hydraulic lift. They could then continue to the top of the Colosseum's own dome, to compare the painted view from St Paul's with their own 'real' view from above Regent's Park.[6]

Early panoramas were advertised as educational, their proprietors stressing the accuracy of their representations. As novelty palled, so they relied more on gimmickry. In the Colosseum, 'London by Day' was replaced each evening by 'London by Night'. Later, it was taken on a tour of American cities. More elaborate 'dioramas' (and a London Diorama was erected shortly before, and only yards from, the Regent's Park Colosseum) created the illusion of movement: pictures or viewing platforms might rotate, clouds and lighting effects came and went.[7]

Meanwhile, artists in New York were also active in depicting panoramic views – from the steeple of the city's own St Paul's, from Trinity Church farther downtown, from the Latting Observatory far uptown (a timber and iron tower, north of 42nd Street, erected in 1853 in conjunction with the New York version of the Crystal Palace, but destroyed by fire only three years later) or, more conventionally, from Brooklyn Heights across the East River or New Jersey across the Hudson.[8] New York's own Colosseum, run by impresario P. T. Barnum, offered the chance to see more spectacular and larger scale panoramas and, as in London, to emerge onto the roof to get a real panoramic view.[9]

Painted panoramas were soon superseded by photographic versions. In Toronto, the City Council commissioned a series of photographs in 1856, including three panoramas making up an almost-360 degree view from the roof of a downtown hotel, to demonstrate the extent to which their city had developed, physically and architecturally. The portfolio was part of the case they made to the Colonial Office in London, arguing that Toronto should be the capital of Canada.[10] Multiple plate panoramas, a succession of photographs which butted onto one another to create a continuous vista, became popular in the 1870s, exemplified by Muybridge's panoramas of San Francisco, taken in 1877–1878. New York, more densely developed, was less easy to encompass, although Joshua Beal managed a partial panorama from the Brooklyn-side tower of Brooklyn Bridge, still under construction in 1876.[11] The first edition of Moses King's *Handbook of New York City* (1892) included ten photographs adding up to a complete panorama from the dome of the recently completed New York World Building, then the city's tallest building, while *New York Illustrated* (c. 1919) featured skylines of both Manhattan riverfronts and views east and south from the top of the Woolworth Building, the new tallest building.[12]

Another type of panorama, closer in form to the map, was the bird's-eye view, implying the ability to see *into* the city's streets and buildings, and to make connections that might not be so obvious from ground level, the logic of aerial representation discussed by Michel de Certeau as 'the concept city' in contrast to 'the textured city' experienced from street level.[13] The invention of the hot-air balloon in the 1780s gave credibility to aerial views that had previously only been imagined. Through the nineteenth century, artists created 'balloon views' and journalists recounted the experience of flying over their cities. At Cremorne Pleasure Gardens in west London, balloon flights were a regular part of the entertainment.[14] Ingenious artists imagined views from ever higher altitudes, such as John Bachmann's circular 'fish-eye' view of 'New York and Environs' (1859), depicting the whole of Manhattan Island and Brooklyn from the perspective of a bird flying high above Staten Island.[15] In the following year J. W. Black published the first bird's-eye *photograph* of an American city, an 'Aerial View of Boston', seen from a balloon 1200 feet above the city.[16]

All of these representations were primarily for popular education, entertainment or decoration, but the connection between bird's-eye views and surveillance was more obvious in the camera obscura installed in the Outlook Tower, adjacent to Edinburgh Castle, from which the pioneering social planner and ecologist, Patrick Geddes, could study his surroundings in magnified detail.[17] Here we are closer to de Certeau's vision that the view from above makes the city known and therefore governable, what James Donald calls 'the city of benign surveillance and spatial penetration'.[18] Early bird's-eye views, such as John Henry Banks' 'Baloon View of London' (1851),[19] were still most often from an oblique angle, attempting to encompass a whole city – from above, just a little higher than in a panorama from a tower or church steeple, but from one side. But the true bird's-eye view was closer to the perpendicular and thus closer to the image presented by a flat map. Whereas the panorama implied a single viewpoint 'from which the appearance of the city slowly unfolds in a kind of narrative circuit', in the geometric map 'the city is abstracted into free space and constructed space' and 'there is no specific viewpoint'.[20]

Mapping knowledge

It was a short but significant step from pictorial representations to cartographic images which offered information about the character or use of buildings and streets. Sanitary reform prompted 'health maps' which plotted the incidence of infectious diseases or deaths from particular causes, sometimes overlain on other distributions, such as the extent of drainage or street cleansing, or the quality of housing, to indicate an ecological correlation and infer the causation of diseases such as cholera and typhus. Following on the heels of cholera and sanitary maps of Leeds, in 1848 Hector Gavin produced a similar map of sanitary conditions in Bethnal Green, east London, and in 1867 the *Report of the Medical Officer of the Privy Council* contained printed cholera maps of the whole of London.[21] One reason why the Ordnance Survey began mapping towns at the scale of 5 feet to the mile (1:1056) was to respond to demands from the Royal Commission on Large Towns and Populous Districts (1844–1845) and, in London, the Metropolitan Sanitary Commissioners, newly appointed in 1847. Even this scale proved inadequate to show all the necessary details of water and gas pipes and sewers, and between 1848 and 1852, many towns in the north of England were surveyed at the scale of 10 feet to the mile (1:528), mainly with subsidies provided by local authorities. After 1855, a further 440 town plans were prepared at the scale of 1:500.[22]

In Britain, another *legal* stimulus to large-scale mapping, reflecting increasing concern for property rights, was the Land Registration Act (1862), which led to the establishment of a Land Registry. Maps at the scale of 1:2500 were regarded as an essential base for the plotting of property boundaries.[23] But they never marked the extent or ownership of particular pieces of property. Some things, notably the interior layout of private dwellings, factories and warehouses, were too private to mark on publicly available maps, but the ground-floor layouts of publicly accessible buildings – workhouses, prisons, hospitals, schools, churches, and even the Bank of England – *were* represented on O.S. 1:1056 maps published in the 1870s. Joyce observes that following this initial flood of public information, later editions of large-scale O.S. maps revealed progressively less about these increasingly private public places. On the other hand, once large-scale maps had been produced, revealing the narrowness or twistedness of streets and the disorderly layout of districts, they acted as an invitation to councillors, engineers and planners to imagine their redevelopment. Just as census officials enumerated all persons equally, but judged them unequally, so O.S. maps implied that all spaces were equally important, but not all equally desirable.[24]

Perhaps the most elaborate form of geographical information system in the nineteenth century was the insurance atlas: in Britain and Canada, Charles E. Goad, and in the United States, the Sanborn Map Company, produced extraordinarily detailed maps for issue to insurance companies who could thereby assess both the risk of fire (what building materials were used: wood, stone, brick, concrete, etc; and what inflammable products – especially chemicals and textiles – did buildings contain?) and the prospects of extinguishing a fire once started (how tall were buildings – how easy to project a jet of water at a fire high up a skyscraper; and where were water mains and fire hydrants located?) (Figure 3.1). In this way, insurers could decide terms and premiums for the policies they issued.[25]

Sanborn's produced such maps from 1867 until 1961, initially straying beyond the boundaries of the United States into Canada. Charles Goad commenced business in 1875, mapping the town of Levis, across the St Lawrence from Quebec City. He subsequently took over and updated Sanborn's maps of Canadian cities and in 1885 established a British branch. Within two years, fifteen English, Scottish and Irish city centres had been mapped, all at a scale of 11 feet to the mile (1:480). In Canada, by 1910, approximately 1,300 urban places of all sizes had been mapped, central areas at 1:600, suburban districts at 1:1200.

Given the limited number of customers for the maps – a handful of property insurance companies and central and local government agencies – and the high cost of production, Goad and Sanborn were anxious to restrict access to the information they contained only to companies whose subscriptions entitled them to copies. Informal copying and tracing was not allowed. In effect, companies leased the atlases from the mapmakers, and were obliged to return them if they ceased to subscribe. As new buildings were erected or old ones modified or redeveloped, subscribers would return their atlases to the map companies, so that patches could be glued over the changed portions of their maps. Eventually, a completely new edition of the atlas would be issued. In passing we might note that this process of patching can be both useful and frustrating for historical researchers using these atlases today: on the one hand, we can see a record of successive changes in the built environment of the city; on the other, it is not always obvious when a particular change was made or to what date a map refers – dates inscribed in the top corners of maps usually refer to the time when the original surveys were undertaken, without any of the later additions and alterations.

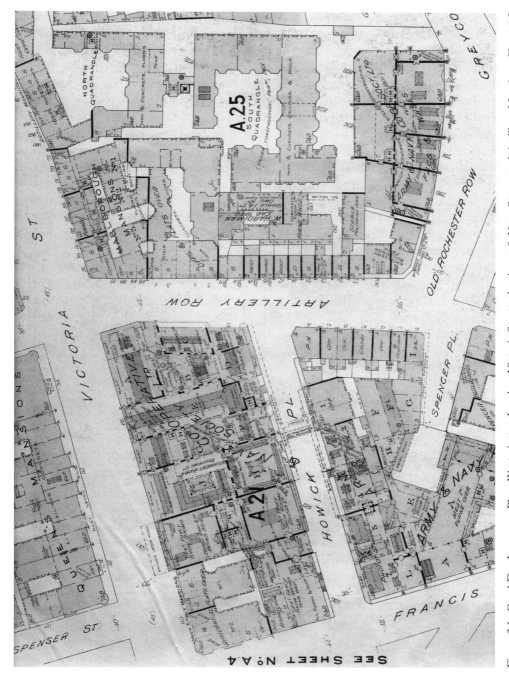

Figure 3.1. Goad Fire Insurance Plan, Westminster, London: Victoria Street, the Army & Navy Stores and Artillery Mansions. Sheet A5 (1901). City of Westminster Archives Centre.

In their time, the maps embodied the modernist desire for complete knowledge, and the value that was placed on privileged access to information. Today, they offer scope for the application of the latest computer mapping technology. As pre-computerised forms of geographical information system, the maps lend themselves to digitisation and conversion to three-dimensional images.[26] For example, using information on building heights contained on fire insurance maps of New York, Deryck Holdsworth reconstructed the visual appearance of lower Manhattan as new skyscrapers were erected at the end of the nineteenth and beginning of the twentieth centuries. It is possible to view the city from different angles, to recreate the experience of contemporaries whether viewing the city from a distance (rather like Beal's panorama from Brooklyn) or positioning oneself in the heart of Broadway or Wall Street, and to examine the impact of introducing each new building. More quantitatively, information contained on the maps can be used to calculate the relative significance of different land uses, plot-ratios, and other measures of the changing intensity of urban land use.[27]

The growth of tourism, and the expanded size of cities, increased the demand for privately produced street maps from visitors and residents alike. For the Great Exhibition in London in 1851, a variety of illustrated maps included novelties such as a bilingual (French and English) 'New Distance Map of London', overlain with half-mile equilateral triangles which allowed users to calculate cab fares and avoid being overcharged by unscrupulous cabmen. John Tallis & Co., already well-known for strip maps showing the elevations and names of shops along major thoroughfares such as Regent Street, produced a hand-coloured map fringed by 49 views of prominent buildings; and there was also a map printed on a glove, obviating the necessity of *carrying* and having to *consult* a map overtly, actions which marked the user as a stranger, and thereby liable to all the dangers that befall the less-than-streetwise.[28] Designed to be worn on a lady's right hand, the map (Figure 3.2) included major railway termini at which visitors to the Exhibition might be expected to arrive, while Hyde Park and the exhibition buildings were located on the wearer's fingertips; but the glove's most useful application – as an aid to shopping – is indicated by the way that Oxford Street and Holborn extended along the length of the index finger into the palm of the hand.[29]

Three years later, H. G. Collins introduced an *Illustrated Atlas of London with 7,000 References*, to be used on the street 'without notice', but the idea appears not to have caught on: Collins was soon bankrupt and his business passed into the hands of Stanford's. The atlas was still rather too bulky for the average coat pocket and it was not until the 1880s that truly pocket atlases of London, forerunners of today's *A to Z* (one of the largest independent map-publishing companies in the U.K.), became popular.[30]

The ability to map and to photograph were also products of technological change, as much in the ability to mass produce the results as to undertake the necessary surveys or take, develop and print photographs. While there continues to be a sense in which maps and photographs were works of art, both media came to be treated more as working documents, recording useful facts. Yet as Brian Harley so clearly demonstrated, and as some of the foregoing illustrations have shown, no map (or photograph) is ever so innocent.[31] As the 'artistic' element declined, the role of

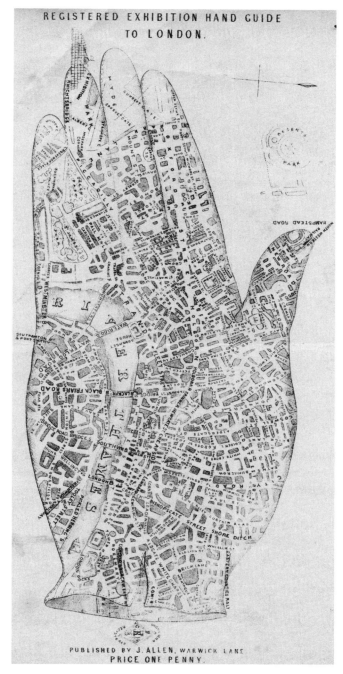

Figure 3.2. Registered Exhibition Hand Guide to London (Glove Map): Published by J. Allen, Warwick Lane (1851), after a registered design by George Shove. Lithograph (23.1 × 13.1 cm). Guildhall Library, City of London Pr. Gp. 5.

maps and photographs as propaganda increased. Alongside Charles Booth's poverty maps (to be considered later in this chapter) were more overtly campaigning maps, such as the National Temperance League's 'Modern Plague of London' (c. 1884), overprinting a street map with garish red dots to denote where alcohol was for sale, and printing the dots sufficiently large not only to be visible but so that they coalesced to present parts of the West End as drowning in a sea of alcohol! Booth himself produced a more sober set of drink maps, distinguishing between on- and off-licences, charting the differences between landscapes of street-corner beerhouses in working-class neighbourhoods and grandiose 'gin palaces' on main thoroughfares and in the West End.[32]

Among similar campaigning maps in North America, one example must suffice: a series of maps of Toronto produced in 1918 by the Bureau of Municipal Research, a citizens' lobby group, which showed the distributions of venereal diseases, 'feeble-mindedness' and juvenile delinquents, attempting to argue thereby that (some kinds of) immigrants were responsible for a physical degeneration of the city's population.[33]

Nearly half a century after the 'Modern Plague', in 1933, the first version of Harry Beck's map of the London Underground network reshaped the way in which Londoners and visitors viewed the metropolis, expanding City and West End relative to suburbia, and plotting railway lines and the course of the Thames (the map's only 'topographical' feature) as a fluent succession of horizontals, diagonals and verticals. Beck's map not only implied that central London was too big to be walkable, but also encouraged suburban sprawl by including such distant locations as Hounslow, Uxbridge, Rickmansworth, Watford and Cockfosters within its boundaries, thereby suggesting their nearness to the centre. Moreover, by exaggerating north and west at the expense of east and south-east London, Beck emphasised the middle-classness of London, the opposite message to Booth's poverty map or Masterman's *From the Abyss* of thirty years earlier.[34]

Photography and social reform

Photographs were increasingly employed as evidence of the benefits of good government or of the need for reform, much like sanitary mapping half a century before. John Tagg notes the parallels between Robert Baker's sanitary maps of Leeds in the 1830s and 1840s and photographs of slum housing commissioned by the city's Medical Officer of Health in the 1890s. Both aimed 'to describe a situation meticulously, to grasp it, to control it'. The photographs were 'a means both of record and publicity'.[35] The same could be said of the partnership between Toronto's official photographer, Arthur Goss, and the city's Medical Health Officer, Charles Hastings, although Goss's slum photographs, taken in 1911, occasionally featured local residents whereas Cameron's pictures of Leeds' courts and yards, made ten to fifteen years earlier, were invariably devoid of human life.[36] Of course, photographic technology had improved – shorter time exposures, safer flashlighting – yet the limitations of his equipment had not prevented the most famous of reform photographers, Jacob Riis, from including numerous inhabitants of New York slums in his depictions of *How the Other Half Lives* as early as 1890.

In early Victorian England, one way of popularising or advocating reform had been to dress it up as a novel: think of the various 'condition of England' novels by Dickens, Disraeli and Mrs Gaskell. The only illustrations were line engravings. By the time Henry Mayhew published his interviews with street-people in *London Labour and the London Poor* photography was available to record their portraits, but it was still not economically viable to publish photographs in books priced to attract a mass readership. Even John Thomson's *Street Life in London* (1877), thirty-seven photographs illustrating the lives of people who made their living on the streets of the city, including cabmen, flower sellers, shoe-blacks, street musicians, a variety of stallholders and – a reflexively postmodern touch – itinerant photographers, was more coffee-table art than sociological analysis, and with long time exposures, stiff poses were the order of the day, even outdoors. Meanwhile, for illustrating books such as Mayhew's, photographs continued to be converted, usually crudely simplified, into engravings.[37]

The conversion process offered scope for 'idealisation' – making the illustration conform to the moral being preached by the author by emphasising, or even adding, details in the published engravings. Peter Hales cites an example in Helen Campbell's *Darkness and Daylight* (1897), a typical New York moral reform tract, in which an illustration of a drunk lying asleep on the sidewalk was idealised by the insertion of an 'ill-drawn infant'. There was no escaping the implication that the drunk was the child's irresponsible father, yet the child had not appeared in the original photograph![38]

By the time of Campbell's book, Jacob Riis had been photographing slum scenes, including tenement interiors, for nearly a decade. As a crime reporter for the *New York Tribune*, Riis's beat took in the Lower East Side. Riis took a genuine interest in the community where he worked, and began to write articles about 'slum life'. By the late 1880s, photographic technology had advanced sufficiently to permit dry plates at speeds as fast as 1/30 second. Some crude (and quite dangerous, explosive) forms of flashlighting were also possible, permitting indoor shots. On reading about the feasibility of flash photography in 1887, but before he had taken up photography for himself, Riis collaborated with three amateur photographers to form a 'raiding party', visiting Lower East Side tenements to take indoor photographs of the buildings and their inhabitants. Early the following year, Riis acquired a camera of his own and began to take pictures which he made into lantern slides. Nevertheless, it is clear that many of the illustrations he used in lectures and books were taken by one of his 'raiding' partners, Richard Hoe Lawrence. They can be attributed to Riis in the same sense that the look of a film is attributed to its director as much as to its cinematographer. Having assembled his illustrations, Riis travelled round church halls in suburban New York, giving lectures on 'The Other Half, How It Lives and Dies in New York', which he later converted into his first book, *How the Other Half Lives* (1890).[39]

The costs of reproducing photographs meant that of forty-three illustrations included in the first edition of *How the Other Half Lives*, only seventeen were reproduced as half-tone photo-engravings. The remainder still had to be converted into wood engravings, in the course of which, though more subtly than in Campbell's book, some changes were made to emphasise particular aspects of the pictures. Some of Riis's photographs were very artfully contrived, for example looking from a low angle into the corner of a room, thereby exaggerating the extent of chaos and overcrowding; or shooting slightly off the horizontal, again giving the impression of instability and disorder. The dazed expression of some of his subjects perhaps reflects

Figure 3.3. Richard Hoe Lawrence, 'Bandits' Roost, 59½ Mulberry Street' (c. 1890). Museum of the City of New York. The Jacob A. Riis Collection (Riis #101).

their response to the explosive flashgun; and captions, while sometimes straightforwardly informative – 'Bohemian Cigarmakers at Work in Their Tenement' – could also be manipulative. For example, 'Sewing and Starving in an Elizabeth Street Attic' shows two women sewing in a bare, but apparently clean and tidy room. Only the caption makes us interpret the picture as one of poverty and overcrowding.[40]

A more complex case was 'Bandits' Roost' (Figure 3.3), depicting a blind alley off Mulberry Street, in the block known as 'The Bend', subsequently razed to create

Mulberry (now Columbus) Park. Riis and his colleagues (the photograph was almost certainly taken by Lawrence) are on the outside looking into the alley, along which several men are ranged, some perched on balcony railings (thereby confirming the 'roost' of the title), others staring, apparently menacingly, at the camera. Other residents lean out of windows, and the view is closed off by laundry hanging to dry across the end of the alley. The message seems to be 'keep out', yet the photograph had obviously been posed, presumably with the co-operation of the inhabitants.[41] Maren Stange suggests that many of Riis's photographs drew on imagery with which his readers and viewers were already familiar from artists' magazine illustrations, while David Leviatin differentiates between posed photographs, which invited pity, sympathy and even guilt on the part of middle-class viewers, and candid, apparently spontaneous pictures which evoked terror, too, as if we had lost our way and stumbled upon the scene by accident.[42] But some images, including 'Bandits' Roost', defy this simple classification. The text of *How the Other Half Lives* described Bandits' Roost as one of the most notorious Italian back-alleys, implying that this was the accepted name for the alley, not simply Riis's invention in order to evoke a social and moral distance between viewer and viewed.[43] Yet his chapter on 'The Bend' also contained some of the 'humorous or adventuresome anecdotes' which, according to Stange, 'imposed a reassuring order on content whose "crime and misery" might otherwise overwhelm'.[44] As Douglas Tallack comments in discussing two other Riis photographs of Mulberry Bend, of 'Bottle Alley' and 'Baxter Street Alley', 'Had the other half been pictured as wholly other, completely untouchable, then this would have been counterproductive to Riis's efforts to raise funds from philanthropic sources.' Nonetheless, the buildings and their inhabitants were objectified, 'constructed by the detached authority of one-point perspective'. Riis and, by extension, the viewers of his photographs were placed to control access to the scene, and to determine a kind of ordered disorder.[45]

Whereas Riis's subjects were at least aware that they were the object of his gaze, Paul Strand, best known for his modernist, semi-abstract compositions of patterns in the built environment, opted 'to photograph people in the streets without their being conscious of his activity'.[46] For a series of pictures in Lower Manhattan in 1916, beginning at Five Points, at the south-west corner of Mulberry Park, Strand employed a camera with a hidden lens, so that he could photograph people on the streets while appearing to be pointing in another direction. The results certainly captured the weariness and emotions of people going about their business, but we may be uneasy at the way in which these images were captured.

Strand's method was akin to that of private detectives, employing hand-held cameras such as the 'Detective Angle Graphic' of 1901, which enabled them to record intimate scenes by stealth. Writing about British photographers' use of detective cameras, Lynda Nead notes the class bias running through debates about the violation of personal privacy: 'The working classes were generally regarded as a cast of picturesque types who could not possibly object to being photographed unless they were being deliberately awkward.' Indeed, they were assumed 'only too pleased to be "took" in a picture they can never have the pleasure of looking upon'.[47] Street photography thus acquired the same connotations of power, surveillance and self-presentation that characterised censuses and social surveys. We can only speculate

whether pedestrians altered their behaviour in anticipation that they might be photographed, a veritable triumph of governmentality. Still photography, potentially
freezing unseemly antics for posterity, often provoked a different response from cin-
ematography, where the equipment was too ungainly to be hidden and the novelty
of seeing one's own body in motion invited an element of self-conscious playing up
to the camera.[48]

Maria Morris Hambourg defends Strand's deception, arguing that 'We lose our
indifference and distance before the immediacy of these pictures', and notes that,
like Lewis Hine, 'Strand was collecting the hard evidence of poverty among diverse
cultures that crowded together in America's metropolis'.[49] Hine had been employed
in the Pittsburgh Survey (1907–1909) to provide illustrations, which were not simply
accompaniments to statistical results, but central to the argument for reform being
propounded by the survey's organisers. Subsequently, Hine became the best-known
American photographer of work and working-class home life, combining documentary and aesthetic approaches to photography. His work, and that of the Pittsburgh
Survey, described by Hales as 'a brilliant holistic attempt to draw photography and
social thought into a new symbiosis and to generate from it the next stage of urban
utopianism', provides the link to the four sections that make up the second half of
this chapter, focused on systematic survey as a source of knowledge about the social
geography of cities.[50]

Censuses

I will focus firstly on the activities of the central state, especially in the taking of
regular censuses; secondly on the growth of social survey, usually stimulated by the
desire for reform; thirdly on the local state, in its tax-raising role, enumerating people
and property liable for tax, and in its regulatory role, issuing permits for building
or licences to allow trading; and fourthly on the role of business, compiling and
exploiting annually updated city directories, but also demanding and subject to the
production of detailed information on the creditworthiness of firms, another aspect
of risk assessment in a modern economy.

All these sources of information constitute contemporary representations of the
structure and form of past cities, although much of the data would not have been
accessible to many people at the time. Nonetheless, summary results of censuses and
social surveys were widely disseminated through the journals of statistical societies,
published evidence to government inquiries (such as British Royal Commissions
and Select Committee reports), reform tracts, and the pages of both periodical and
daily presses. In North American cities, where statistical data were often employed
in the service of boosterism – to demonstrate how rapidly a city was growing, or how
quickly living standards, levels of employment and housing conditions were improving – both privately compiled city directories and municipal publications included
statistical summaries to show, for example, how the proportion of homeowners in
the population or the assessed value of property was increasing, year by year.

The first official U.S. census was taken in 1790, the first British census in 1801. Initially, both were little more than head or family counts and there was no requirement
for enumerators to issue census schedules to be completed by each household. In the

United States, the census was one instrument in the setting up of a new democratic nation state: an accurate population count underlay the apportionment of representatives in Congress and the liability of constituents to direct taxation.[51] In Britain, one catalyst to census-taking was the war with Revolutionary France which, combined with bad harvests, provoked a Malthusian crisis of population in excess of the food supply.[52] Population enumeration was one way of establishing the need for food, the size of the agricultural population available to produce it, and the population eligible for military service.

In neither country was the census initially suited to providing information on the internal structure of towns and cities. The assignment of street numbers to particular addresses was still rudimentary so that, even if enumerators did collect information systematically house-by-house, they rarely matched individual households to precise locations. Throughout the nineteenth century, American census enumerators' schedules lacked space in which to enter the street number or name; assiduous enumerators scribbled this information in the margin or wherever they could find room. Another indication that the census was not yet a truly 'modern' – impersonal, confidential and purportedly objective – survey lay in the recruitment of enumerators who were local to the districts they enumerated, usually respected figures of authority such as schoolmasters and local government officials, who knew the people they were counting and could supply or correct information on behalf of those reluctant to respond or inclined to mislead. Compare this with present-day expectations that enumerators should not deal with people they already know for fear of breaching confidentiality.

The transition to a modern census began in both countries around 1840. Statistical societies – in London and Manchester by 1834; and in America, the founding of the American Statistical Association in Boston in 1839 – lobbied their national governments to implement more elaborate household censuses, commented on the results, and conducted their own private house-to-house surveys.[53] The American census expanded substantially in 1850 with the creation of a Census Board and schedules designed to collect information on individuals rather than households, although it was not until 1902 that a permanent Bureau of the Census was established. In Britain in 1840, the census became the responsibility of the General Register Office, originally established a few years earlier to oversee the registration of births, marriages and deaths. The collection of more accurate information on ages, occupations and birthplaces related in part to a desire to calculate age- or class-specific fertility and mortality rates, which could then be used to improve the practices of friendly societies paying sickness and death benefits, by varying subscriptions on the basis of subscribers' life expectancy, essentially the same problem that faces the pensions industry today. So, from 1841 in embryo, and from 1851 more fully, census schedules demanded information on the name, age, sex, marital status, occupation, birthplace, disability (e.g. whether blind, deaf or dumb) of every individual, and their relationship to the 'head' of their 'household'.[54]

The centrality of these latter terms – 'head' and 'household' – indicates the ambiguity and ideologically-laden nature of the enterprise, especially when applied to urban populations who lived in tenements and lodging houses rather than neatly defined single-family dwellings and whose 'households' rarely corresponded to simple nuclear families comprised of a resident male 'head of household', his wife and children. A series of illustrations, entitled 'Taking the Census', published in the *Illustrated Times* in April, 1861, revealed the dilemmas of the enumerators. One illustration showed the enumerator at the door of a substantial London town-house. Inside an obviously middle-class establishment, 'paterfamilias' was shown seated at table, pen in hand with the members of his family arranged around him: there is no doubting who was the 'head' of this 'household'. But another illustration depicted an enumerator standing in 'a Gray's Inn-lane tenement' (just south of King's Cross), completing the form himself on behalf of illiterate or semi-literate residents, having to decide just who was to be designated 'head' and who was related to whom among a disparate group of children and adults. Finally, enumerators had to track down and classify the homeless, camped in St. James's Park or huddled in the arches of the Adelphi, a labyrinth of cellars between the Strand and the pre-Embankment Thames.[55]

There were other sources of uncertainty: did people know how old they were or where they had been born, especially adults whose birth predated compulsory civil registration; how was 'women's work' to be treated, or the occupations of any who had more than one source of employment?[56]

To the British census's family values and masculine gaze in its treatment of 'households', the American census added stratification by 'color'. From 1870, 'colors' could be differentiated into 'white', 'black', 'mulatto', 'Chinese' and 'Indian'; by 1890 additional categories included 'quadroon', 'octoroon' and 'Japanese'.[57] The British census omitted questions on 'race', 'ethnicity' or 'colour' until 1991 (when a similarly ambiguous, part-colour, part-origins classification was introduced), prompting inferences on the part of researchers and policy-makers, for example on whether 'Irish-born' could be equated with 'Irish'.[58] The black population of Victorian London is even harder to uncover, short of linking institutional photographs or textual records (associated with entry into prisons, hospitals, orphanages or appearances in court, all biased towards 'outsiders').[59] Hannah notes the philosophy of Francis A. Walker, superintendent of the 1870 and 1880 U.S. censuses, that statistics could eliminate ambiguity but make room for complexity. In this spirit, Walker created 'foreignness' as a social category, asking respondents to declare not only their own place of birth, but also whether each of their parents was 'of foreign birth'. Having created this synthetic category of the 'foreign', he then mapped its distribution (in his *Statistical Atlas of the United States* (1874)), inferring its association with mortality from various diseases by visually comparing their spatial distributions. In effect, he was seeking a 'factual' justification for immigration restrictions by implying that the 'foreign' population was the cause of physical, mental and moral degeneration.[60]

The spatial building blocks for the census were enumeration districts, intended to be manageable by one enumerator, but rarely having any social coherence. Maps of district boundaries are hard to find but, in the British census, each enumerator's book was prefaced by a verbal description of the territorial limits of the enumerator's responsibilities.[61] Where street numbers were not introduced until late in the nineteenth century, or subject to frequent revision as infilling occurred, it may still be possible to assign households to particular dwellings by retracing the enumerator's walk on contemporary large-scale maps, noting particularly where side streets, yards and alleys, and prominent named buildings, such as pubs, were recorded in the enumerator's book.[62]

In British cities, enumeration districts were supposed to comprise approximately 200 households, small enough for enumerators to collect all the completed schedules on the day following census night. In 1901 the General Register Office instructed local registrars that the population of each district should not exceed 1,500. In practice, almost one in ten districts contained more than 1,500 inhabitants. Faced with such large districts, and with the likelihood of multi-occupancy of tenements and lodgings, and the use of ostensibly non-residential buildings for residential purposes, it is surprising that enumerators missed as few inhabitants as they did, probably only about 2 per cent of the population.[63]

The problem of under-enumeration was worse in rapidly changing North American cities. The maximum population of U.S. enumeration districts was reduced from 20,000 in 1870 to 4,000 in 1880, still far too large to be canvassed in a single day, even in a compact urban district. Given the difficulty of finding and contacting pioneer families in remote frontier and wilderness areas, enumerators were allowed four months to complete their work in 1870, reduced to one month in 1880, but still plenty of time for many people to have moved house at least once and to be counted either more than once or, more likely, not at all. In theory, the U.S. census asked enumerators to count persons according to their place of abode on the first day of June in each census year; in practice, collecting this information two or three months later was an invitation to forget about transients, lodgers and others outside of stable nuclear families.

Municipal governments had an interest in maximising the size of their populations, to exaggerate their cities' importance and rates of growth: in 1870 both Philadelphia and New York City and, in 1871, following the Canadian census of that year, Montreal, protested that the census had undercounted their populations. In the case of Montreal, a recount in 1872 raised the population from 107,225 to 118,000, still far below the 150,000 predicted by local newspapers (and, of course, many of the extra 10,000 may have arrived during the time between the two counts). In the two U.S. cities, recounts revealed under-enumeration of no more than 2.5 per cent, although it is likely that *both* counts fell short of the 'true' population: more recent research comparing names in the two enumerations of Philadelphia concluded that only 82 per cent of households listed in the first count were re-enumerated five months later, and it seems unlikely that all the others had died or moved out of the city.[64] Other attempts to calculate rates of under-enumeration, comparing successive census records with other nominative lists, have estimated that as many as 15 per cent of adults were omitted from mid-nineteenth-century American censuses, with worst coverage in cities, especially those, like New York, experiencing rapid growth, and among poor and marginal groups such as blacks and foreign-born boarders. In Boston, for example, estimates of under-enumeration range between 11 per cent and 14 per cent for the censuses from 1850 to 1880.[65]

Whatever our reservations about their accuracy and completeness, censuses provide vast amounts of information about named individuals which, with the growth of urban history since the 1950s, has been plotted geographically, subjected to ecological or individual correlation, for example between birthplace, occupational status, family size, servant-keeping, and a host of other statistical indices that can be derived from the enumerators' books, or used in record linkage, for example to connect information on individuals named in the census with further information about the same individuals in directories, tax rolls, church membership records, registers of births, marriages and deaths, and other, less common, nominal lists.[66] But, at the time the data were gathered, they were accessible only in aggregate form, in published census reports and accompanying tables. Results were never published for individual enumeration districts, so it has only been since manuscript returns were made available for research (after 100 years in Britain, 70 years in the United States) that it has been possible to map the social geography of cities at this scale. We now know more about the internal social morphology of Victorian cities than contemporaries ever did. Frustratingly, we also know more about the period up to 1901 (in Britain) or 1930 (in the United States) than about later decades, for which the original returns are still subject to confidentiality agreements.

Even for the nineteenth century, we are bound by the limited range of questions that the census asked. Only in 1891 did the British census start to gather data on overcrowding; at the same time the U.S. census started to collect information on homeownership, but equivalent data were not collected in the Canadian census until 1921 and in the British census until 1961.[67] For all the British censuses open to inspection under the 100-year confidentiality rule, therefore, the relationship between housing tenure and 'social status' (measured, for example, in terms of occupation or the employment of domestic servants) can be examined only by linking census data to information in rate-books which, erratically, recorded names of owners and occupiers of dwellings, and their rateable value, which provides a crude indication of housing quality.[68]

Nor, until 2001, did the British census inquire about individuals' religion, although in 1851 a religious census was conducted through places of worship, inquiring into the capacity of churches and Sunday schools, the regular level of attendance and the actual attendance on 'Census Sunday'. The motive was the fear that church-building was not keeping up with urbanisation, that there was insufficient capacity to allow everybody to attend services of worship in new residential districts; but also the suspicion that even where there were sufficient churches, levels of attendance were lower than they had been in rural communities, that urbanisation was associated with secularisation. There was also interest in the apparently declining role of the established Church of England relative to new nonconformist 'sects' and to Roman Catholicism. On the ground, all these concerns were reflected in the desire of ministers of religion to maximise attendance, by specially encouraging worshippers to attend on Census Sunday, providing reasons why attendance was less than usual, for example by alluding to unseasonably bad weather, or by falsifying returns or simply refusing to co-operate, on the grounds that if there was no information, no damaging conclusions could be drawn.[69]

These examples point to the limits of surveillance in a liberal society: there were some areas of life which governments chose not to probe, and others where the statistics present too neat a picture of a society which was not as ordered or compartmentalised as officials might have preferred. Patrick Joyce makes the vital point that 'governmentality depended upon reaching a balance which involved not only knowing the governed but *not* knowing them as well . . . knowing enough not to have to know more. What it [the liberal state] knew, or sought to know, was vital to it, but of equal importance was securing the trust of citizens by not attempting to know too much.'[70]

Censuses and large-scale maps alike imposed a false appearance of stability on what were economically and culturally unstable cities and city-spaces. Nor did cross-sectional surveys like censuses capture the diurnal rhythms of society. The census enumerated where people *slept* on one particular night, not necessarily where they normally slept, and not where, or with whom, they spent their working or leisure time. A modern, classificatory instrument yielded a society in its own image. Meanwhile, other surveys were being undertaken, privately initiated, that specifically targeted the social and geographical spaces of society presumed to be the most disordered.

The growth of social survey

In Britain systematic door-to-door surveys began with the activities of the London and Manchester Statistical Societies in the 1830s, but reached their maturity in Charles Booth's massive survey of London life and labour in the 1880s and 1890s.[71] Booth had presented a paper to the Royal Statistical Society in May 1886, based on analysis of occupational data in the 1881 census. But by then he had decided that the census could never answer the questions he had about the extent and causes of poverty. The catalyst for embarking on his own survey was the Trafalgar Square riots of February 1886. In response, the Mansion House Enquiry into the causes of and solutions to poverty and distress in London had proved disappointing, both in its lack of any serious factual basis and in the predictability of its recommendations. Booth initially doubted whether the situation was as black as often claimed, including the assertion made by the radical socialist, H. M. Hyndman, that a quarter of the population of London lived in poverty. He also felt that sensationalist tracts, like Mearns' *The Bitter Cry of Outcast London*, misrepresented the situation, playing on readers' emotions by citing extreme cases, yet obscuring the true extent and character of working-class poverty. In Christian Topalov's words, 'Booth wanted to transform the representation of the city, just as the tales of the explorers had given way to the maps of the administrators of the Empire'.[72]

Booth did not employ researchers who interviewed individual households. Rather, he drew on the knowledge of School Board Officers, whose responsibility it was to ensure that children of school age attended school as required under the 1870 Education Act. His method was to interview these officials after they had finished their regular work and, in effect, to walk down one street at a time, asking them who lived in each house and what they knew of their circumstances. Their responses were recorded in hundreds of notebooks, which now constitute the Booth Archive at the London School of Economics. Booth's survey purported to be about all Londoners, but in practice the School Board Officers did not know much about middle-class families, who might send their children to private schools or who almost certainly did not need persuading of the value of education, nor about households that lacked children. Even this method proved too time-consuming; house-by-house records were produced for East London, Central London and Battersea, but the rest of London was recorded only street-by-street.

Life and Labour of the People in London eventually ran to seventeen volumes, including not only a 'Poverty' series, with separate volumes on different parts of London, but also sets of volumes on 'Industry' and 'Religious Influences'.[73] In these cases, Booth and his assistants followed a more typical interviewing procedure, talking to a local elite of employers, clergy, schoolteachers and settlement-house workers. Several of Booth's assistants became well-known social investigators in their own right, including Hubert Llewellyn Smith, who subsequently edited a 'New Survey' of London life and labour,[74] and Beatrice Potter, a cousin of Booth's, who wrote several sections of *Life and Labour* including substantial essays on docks, tailoring and Jews, and who later married the leading Fabian, Sidney Webb, with whom she wrote numerous social and political books during the first forty years of the twentieth century. Her involvement illustrates the connections between the supposedly objective survey and humanitarian concerns; she was also working as rent collector and 'lady visitor' in Katharine Buildings, an estate of block dwellings in Cartwright Street (near St Katharine's Dock), owned by the East End Dwellings Company, a limited-dividend philanthropic housing company. Another of Booth's female – and, in this case, feminist – researchers was Clara Collet, who contributed an essay on women's work. Collet was subsequently employed as Senior Investigator in the Labour Department at the Board of Trade. In the 1890s she became a very close friend of the novelist George Gissing.[75] Intriguingly, in the first edition of *Life and Labour* (1889) Booth had commended Gissing's novel, *Demos* (1886). Booth was as dismissive of most novels as he was of sensationalist social explorers, but he conceded that 'Something may be gleaned from a few books, such for instance as "Demos"'. Gissing read both the first two volumes of Booth's survey with sufficient interest to record them in his diary and letters, and when he discovered the reference to himself he proudly passed the news on to his sister.[76] The parallels between Booth's scientific method and Gissing's socially and geographically precise storytelling illustrate my argument that social survey and social realism in literature and art were both products of modern mentalities, combining panoramic and intimate ways of seeing society, from above and from within.

Despite Booth's claims to objectivity, and to refrain from moral judgements, moralism permeated his work. Consider, first, how he classified the population into eight classes, labelled A to H. Topalov suggests that 'To classify the population was not just a simple matter of statistics, but a strategic operation'.[77] First, he needed to establish a 'poverty line' distinguishing the poor (A–D) from the better-paid and regularly employed working classes (E–F); secondly, he distinguished the problem of disorder (associated with class A, who were 'savage, semi-criminal') from poverty (B–D); and thirdly, he separated the deserving poor (C–D) who suffered the low wages and insecure employment that were endemic in the London labour market from the undeserving (class B) who were 'shiftless, hand-to-mouth, pleasure loving, and always poor'. What Booth was doing was reformulating old impressions (the idea of the 'savage' outcast residuum, the contrast between 'deserving' and 'undeserving') as new scientifically demonstrated certainties. While it was shocking that 30.7 per cent of Londoners were assigned to classes A–D (i.e. substantially more than

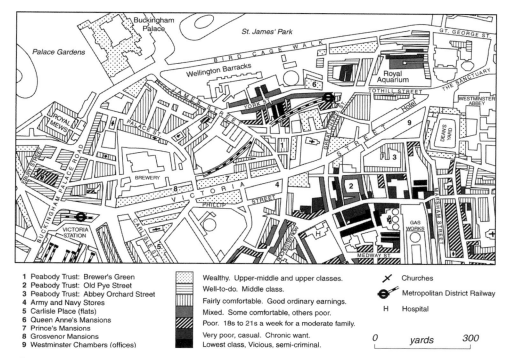

Figure 3.4. Charles Booth's Descriptive Map of London Poverty (1889): Victoria Street.

1 Peabody Trust: Brewer's Green
2 Peabody Trust: Old Pye Street
3 Peabody Trust: Abbey Orchard Street
4 Army and Navy Stores
5 Carlisle Place (flats)
6 Queen Anne's Mansions
7 Prince's Mansions
8 Grosvenor Mansions
9 Westminster Chambers (offices)

Wealthy. Upper-middle and upper classes.
Well-to-do. Middle class.
Fairly comfortable. Good ordinary earnings.
Mixed. Some comfortable, others poor.
Poor. 18s to 21s a week for a moderate family.
Very poor, casual. Chronic want.
Lowest class, Vicious, semi-criminal.

✗ Churches
⊖ Metropolitan District Railway
H Hospital

0   yards   300

the quarter claimed by Hyndman), the hard core of poverty was restricted to the 1.2 per cent in class A and 8.4 per cent in class B.

Secondly, consider Booth's mapping of poverty, which Topalov suggests 'owed something both to "slumming", in its attention to social types, and to the panorama in its global vision of the city'.[78] 'Slumming' was the middle-class practice of visiting the slums, whether on charitable business or in search of 'low life'. As Sam Warner has observed, 'to slum' did not mean to live in a slum, but to visit one. 'Slum' was a middle-class perception imposed on a working-class district.[79] Booth's street-by-street mapping, in which each street was coloured in one of seven colours to indicate its situation on the poverty scale, especially drew attention to the poorest areas, by colouring them black. They were, on the map at least, 'black spots' (Figure 3.4). This was the view from the railway viaduct, to which we will return in the final chapter, the middle classes identifying the slums from a safe distance and an elevated situation. At the other extreme, the wealthiest areas were portrayed in gold. So London assumed a tonal form which it is difficult to imagine in any other way: the gold and red of the West End, with occasional specks of blue and black where Dickensian 'rookeries' still survived or where mews premises had been taken over by the very poor, but contrasted with the greyness of most suburban districts and the blue-black darkness of much of the East End. Imagine changing the colour code, painting the rich black and the East End gold: a familiar city instantly rendered unknown.

The published versions of Booth's maps contained seven colours, indicating a slight mismatch with the eight poverty classes into which he assigned individual households. More critically, however, the maps were of streets, not of households.

On early versions of the maps, there was scope for colouring streets a mixture of two colours to reflect a degree of social mix, but still the unit of mapping was the street. This tended to reinforce the image of London as a segregated city. In particular, it served to define 'slums' as areas, and to suggest that the problem of poverty was amenable to an environmental solution: slum clearance.

If slums were areas, then boundaries could be drawn around the problem. The implication was that areas outside 'slums', streets painted grey or pink, did not have families in need. Booth was not the creator of the 'slum', nor the instigator of 'slum clearance' – in London the Metropolitan Board of Works had already begun designating whole areas for clearance and redevelopment under the terms of the Cross Act, passed in 1875.[80] But Booth's map reinforced and gave legitimacy to the operations of local government in designating slum clearance districts, a legitimacy that was reinforced with the creation of the London County Council in 1888 and the passage of a Housing of the Working Classes Act in 1890, which widened the powers available to local authorities to erect and manage council housing. Indeed, Topalov emphasises the significance that 'the boundaries of Booth's inquiry coincided with those of the Metropolitan Board of Works' and then, 'while Booth's work was at its height' with the boundaries of the newly established London County Council. He argues that the map allowed for a unitary vision of rich and poor areas as part of the same city, subject to the same government. Countering the image of growing residential segregation, the implication was that rich areas had some responsibility for the existence and improvement of poor areas, legitimating one of the aims of those who had argued for the creation of the LCC, that it would allow the transfer of funds through a rate equalisation programme, whereby West Enders could expect to pay to alleviate the suffering of East Enders. Topalov concludes, 'When the L.C.C. began work, in 1889, Booth's map was in its in-tray'.[81]

The first edition of Booth's poverty map was revised ten years later, but without recourse to the labour-intensive method of house-by-house reports from School Board Officers. Instead, Booth's assistants walked the streets in the company of local police officers, who offered their knowledge of the neighbourhood population and discussed whether a change of colour was merited. The notebooks they compiled emphasised the importance of street life – the cleanliness and politeness of children on the streets – and the interface of public and private – the experience of police in dealing with domestic disputes and crimes – rather than the incomes and material conditions of local inhabitants, again subverting the idea that the maps were based on an objective, statistical measurement of poverty.[82]

Other mapping exercises followed. For example, when Russell and Lewis published their study of Jewish London (1900), George Arkell – one of Booth's assistants – produced a coloured map of Jewish East London, plotting the percentage of Jewish households street by street, just like the poverty maps.[83] And the methodology spread beyond Britain, as social reformers from overseas visited London and as the poverty map was taken on tour as a spectacle in its own right – first at East End settlement houses (Toynbee Hall and Oxford House), later at the Paris Exhibition of 1900.[84]

An 1895 survey of the neighbourhood around Hull House, the Chicago settlement house established by Jane Addams, included a wage map that used the same colour scheme as Booth's. The area surveyed was much smaller, only one ward of the city, but wages were mapped by *household*. The same was true of a map of 'nationalities', depicting a patchwork of fifteen different groups, although a degree of segregation was evident, for example in the concentration of Italians on particular blocks.[85] W. E. B. Du Bois' study of the 7th Ward in Philadelphia (1897), a pioneering study of black Philadelphians by a black academic, plotted both the distribution of 'negro inhabitants' and their 'social condition', using language very similar to Booth's: Du Bois' 'Grade 1' were 'The "Middle Classes" and those above'; 'Grade 4' were 'Vicious and Criminal Classes'. Like the Hull House maps, Du Bois' depicted the character- istics of households rather than whole streets, but covered only one ward, and only the black population within that ward.[86]

North American social surveys were associated with the 'scientific philanthropy' and 'progressive' phases in the understanding of social problems discussed in Chap- ter 2. Jane Addams, the daughter of a prosperous Illinois businessman, had visited Toynbee Hall in 1888. Back in Chicago, she moved into a mansion in the city's 19th Ward and established Hull House in 1889. The object of Hull House was 'to pro- vide a center for a higher civic and social life; to institute and maintain educational and philanthropic enterprises, and to investigate and improve the conditions in the industrial districts of Chicago'.[87] In practice, this meant very practical things like running a kindergarten, baby-care, preparing the dead for burial, nursing the sick, educating girls and mothers in 'home-making', and providing an adult education programme including drama, debating and literature. There was also a research pro- gramme, illustrated by the publication in 1895 of *Hull House Maps and Papers*, which included investigations on slum life by the middle-class inmates, such as the maps just mentioned. Yet in her introduction to the book, Addams was uncomfortable about the research side and quick to emphasise that most of the work at Hull House was devoted 'not towards sociological investigation, but to constructive work'.[88] The regime did not suit everybody. As a student in the mid-1890s the future Canadian Lib- eral Prime Minister, Mackenzie King, had signed on at Hull House while undertaking graduate work at the University of Chicago. But he lasted only a few weeks, feeling uncomfortable at the degree of interaction and practical work that was expected of him. On his return to Canada, he quickly plunged into research on housing and labour conditions in downtown Toronto, but adopting the arms-length approach of interviewing employers and officials rather than ordinary workers and residents.[89]

Philip Mackintosh invokes the concept of the 'domestic public' in discussing the motivations and methods of middle-class reforming women in turn-of-the-century Toronto, engaged in social survey in the spirit of Jane Addams. He argues that they felt obliged to scrutinise public space, investigating districts and activities considered far from safe or polite, in order to gather evidence supportive of their campaigns for municipal reforms which would protect the values of domestic family environments, thereby articulating connections between public and private space. He refers to the Toronto Local Council of Women's 'creation of a city-as-parlour' and their criticism of male councillors and city officials for their neglect of 'civic housekeeping'.[90]

Elsewhere in Canada more conventional survey methods were exemplified in Herbert Ames' *The City Below the Hill* (1897).[91] Ames was a Montreal business- man, from the same mould as Charles Booth; director first of a successful family boot and shoe manufacturers and later of a leading Canadian insurance company, and subsequently entering politics as a city alderman and Conservative member of parliament. In 1896 he sponsored a house-to-house survey of a substantial, predominantly working-class sector of Montreal, literally 'below the hill', close to the St Lawrence and the Lachine Canal, in comparison to the elite who lived, in Ames' words, in 'the city above the hill'. There is the implication that the elite looked down upon the working classes, socially as well as topographically.[92] Ames' focus was on tabulating and mapping the information he collected on employment, income, family structure, housing conditions and costs, 'nationalities' (whether of 'British', Irish or French origin), religion (whether Roman Catholic, Protestant, Jewish or 'Pagan'), mortality rates and environmental conditions (how many churches, schools, saloons and 'liquor grocers' in each section of the city). Unlike Booth, he provided little in the way of structural analysis or recommendations for political action, merely a call to business philanthropy, exemplified in his own promotion of a limited-dividend housing scheme, Diamond Court. A subsequent evaluation of Ames concluded that 'his pursuit of statistical truth became an end in itself. . . . Too often he lost sight of his goal in a welter of figures and calculations'.[93] In this respect, his study foreshadowed a more general demise of the survey movement during the inter-war years.

For all their similarities, there were also significant differences between reform-inspired surveys on either side of the Atlantic. Notwithstanding the press attention given to Booth's maps, the North Americans were generally more adept at raising public consciousness, using models, photographs and mass-produced booklets to advertise their results. In Britain, settlement houses had a direct line to government; their predominantly male inmates usually stayed only for a few years, between graduating from Oxbridge and taking up a seat in parliament, joining the government or securing a senior civil service post, where they could be trusted to draw upon their personal experiences in implementing or administering social policy. In the United States, there was not the same establishment route into government; participation in higher education was greater, especially among women, for whom settlement-house work and social research became life-long careers.[94] It was more important to mobilise public opinion to lobby those in power.

For example, a Charity Organization Society exhibition in 1900 to promote tenement housing reform in New York featured about 1100 photographs, maps, charts and diagrams, but also six elaborate architectural models, including four of entire blocks of housing, depicting how little open space existed in a typical, grossly overcrowded section of the Lower East Side, and how much more overcrowded conditions could be while keeping to the current law (Figure 3.5). Forty-seven maps of the city's tenement districts were displayed, including disease maps (showing the distributions of infectious diseases) and charity maps (of the distributions of applicants for charitable relief), implying that if housing conditions were improved, residents would be not only healthier but also less dependent on hand-outs from the rich. Held in rooms in midtown Manhattan, the exhibition was intended to appeal to the city's middle classes, who may never have ventured into the Lower East Side. Visitors were encouraged to wander through the exhibition much as the more adventurous might wander through real slums, discovering the facts for themselves. Captions were minimal, suggesting that exhibits depicted the generality of conditions, not specific and unique circumstances. Ten thousand visitors attended over two weeks. The following year,

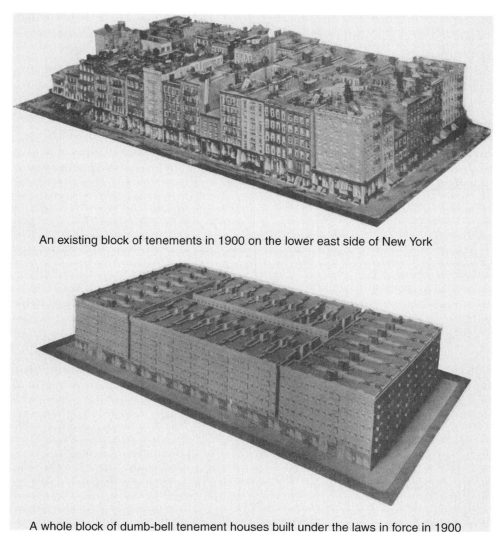

An existing block of tenements in 1900 on the lower east side of New York

A whole block of dumb-bell tenement houses built under the laws in force in 1900

Figure 3.5. Models exhibited at the Tenement House Exhibition, New York (1900), from R. W. DeForest and L. Veiller, *The Tenement House Problem* (New York, 1903).

a new Tenement House Act was passed, acceding to virtually all the proposals made by Lawrence Veiller, the exhibition's organiser, who soon found himself appointed to important state and federal commissions dealing with housing and planning.[95]

Further exhibitions followed, for example in New York and Pittsburgh in 1908 and Springfield, Illinois in 1914. In 1918 the Russell Sage Foundation, which had sponsored the Pittsburgh Survey, published *The ABC of Exhibit Planning*.[96] But despite the proliferation of surveys and exhibitions, their impact was on the wane. Faith was placed in 'the correcting power of facts'.[97] Yet as Dickens had implied, in his caricature of Mr Gradgrind in *Hard Times*, written soon after the beginnings of the statistical movement in Britain, you can have too many facts. As the newly radical David Harvey argued in rejecting liberal-hearted human geography as practised in the early 1970s, the collection of more and more facts about injustice and inequality simply served as a substitute for action.[98] Ultimately, surveys *delayed* reform. In the Depression, one critic called them the 'great American fact finding farce'.[99]

It should be clear by now that social survey, mapping and exhibitions were critical elements in the logic of governmentality: in the provision of information which governments could use to govern; in revealing opportunities for reform, for example through the patterns revealed by maps; and in educating citizens to accept the need for regulation. But surveys were also spatial practices in a Lefebvrian sense, operationalising representations of urban space based on preconceived ideas about the causes of poverty and bad housing, the responsibilities of business and philanthropy and the limits to acceptable state intervention.

Municipal records

The *consequences* of local government intervention and regulation included yet more varieties of data collection, for example in assessing the value of property in order to levy local taxes, or in granting building permits and licences to trade. Although these records were not designed for purposes of representation, they completed the circle of Hannah's 'cycle of social control': the products of regulation which then become units of observation in a new round of decision-making.[100] In the aggregate, these data would not normally have been accessible to contemporaries other than city officials. Yet municipal authorities *did* publish their own analyses of some assessment data. For example, annual increases in population, or rates of homeownership, or of the assessed value of property were all used to chart the health and growth of a city's economy, and sometimes to demonstrate differences between wards within a city. In Toronto, statistics from a religious census of each ward were included in the Assessment Commissioner's Annual Report in December 1914. Some of these data also found their way into city directories and newspaper articles.[101] Citizens' lobby groups might also be granted access to data; the official-sounding but unofficial Bureau of Municipal Research in Toronto published maps and graphs of changing land values based on city assessment records.[102] In a similar fashion, building and architecture journals published aggregate statistics derived from the estimated values of buildings for which permits were granted.[103]

Buildings were not the only objects of municipal licensing. On and off licences for the sale of alcohol, entertainment licences for music halls and theatres, the regulation of noxious activities such as laundries, slaughterhouses and, in the twentieth century, petrol filling stations, and especially the control of street trading all generated revenue, statistics and reports and controversies in the local press.

All these forms of information provide the raw material for research by later generations of social scientists, but we need to pay attention to the circumstances in which the data were collected. For example, British rate-books, recording the rateable values of real property for the purpose of calculating 'rates' (the forerunner of today's 'council tax'), contained columns in which the names of both owners and occupiers could be listed. In the residential suburbs of the northern industrial town of Huddersfield, names were invariably listed in both columns, making it possible to calculate levels of homeownership (where the names were the same in both columns) and the scale of landlordism (counting up the number of properties assigned to the same owner).[104] But among the mansion blocks, model dwellings and tenements of Westminster, it was rare for officials to complete both columns: all that really concerned them was that the rates were paid and, except in *very* low-value property, payment was the responsibility of the occupier, not the owner. Recognising this crude functionality of the record may then lead us to question the veracity of other information: why bother to update information on 'owners' if it was not immediately needed? Moreover, how do we interpret cases where the same person was listed as 'occupier' of numerous properties? Presumably they were absentee tenants, subletting or 'farming' their property out room by room to the real 'occupiers'.[105]

In annually revised Toronto assessment records which appear like mini-censuses, listing the age, occupation, religion and number of residents associated with each 'occupier', can we trust the accuracy of much of this information? The assessed values of land, 'improvements' (buildings) and, at certain dates, different forms of personal income that were liable to local taxation were, presumably, recorded assiduously, as were the designations 'P' for public school and 'S' for separate school to indicate which School Board the occupier wished to support with their taxes (in general, 'P' coincided with Protestant and 'S' with Catholic). But there seems little reason why the assessors should have worried about getting the other information exactly right. Nor, in the case of building permits, was there any guarantee that the granting of a permit would result in the erection of a building. The problem, of course, is that we use these data for purposes very different from those for which they were intended. As with the census, but even more so, the representations we make are constrained not only by the questions they asked but also by the reasons why they asked them and the answers they deemed acceptable.

Selling information

Not all surveys were either state-sponsored or reformist in character. As noted at the beginning of this chapter, there was also a market for commercial information – not only fire insurance atlases, discussed earlier, but also printed 'reference books' (and detailed manuscript reports) updated every six months by firms such as R. G. Dun & Co. (later Dun & Bradstreet), estimating the value of businesses, their security and creditworthiness.[106]

But the most commonplace, widely available information was contained in city directories. Peter Atkins notes that the earliest London directory was Samuel Lee's *A Collection of the Names of the Merchants Living in and about the City of London* (1677).[107] The date is critical, as Cynthia Wall has discussed, for in the aftermath of the Great Fire, consumers needed directions to tell them where businesses had relocated.[108] Thereafter, trade directories – the equivalent of today's *Yellow Pages* – were published almost annually, recording the names of businesses in alphabetical order, but also classified according to the kind of trade or service they offered. As the size of a city's middle and upper class increased, so there was a need to publish court directories, recording the names and addresses of the fashionable, and sometimes, the hours when they were 'at home' to receive visitors. In London, Boyle's *Fashionable Court Guide* was published regularly from 1792 until 1925, and other court guides rivalled it from the early nineteenth century, some surviving until the outbreak of World War II. Specialist guides to the professions, such as doctors and lawyers, were also produced. By the mid-nineteenth century, stimulated both by the Penny Post and the need to provide precise addresses in cities where individual dwellings were no longer distinguishable from one another, street directories recorded householders and businesses in street order. Thus by the 1880s Kelly's *Post Office Directory* ran to several thousand pages, annually revised, with separate sections for central and inner London, and for suburban London, with businesses classified by trade and in alphabetical order, with lists of members of the professions, also in alphabetical order, with a street directory, numerous other sections recording important information about local government, schools, churches, etc, and hundreds of pages of illustrated advertisements.[109]

Yet, compared to many North American city directories, this was still a modest effort. British directories rarely listed the occupations of householders unless they were self-employed tradesmen operating from home; they rarely recorded more than one occupier per dwelling (thereby omitting all women other than spinsters and widows who headed their own households); and they failed to list the residents of poorer parts of cities who were neither the object of canvassing by businesses in search of customers nor the users of the directory themselves in search of businesses they wished to patronise.

In Toronto and many North American cities, the number of entries in a directory was a sign of a city's virility; hence the need to demonstrate year-on-year growth, either by enumerating genuine new blood or by increasing the coverage of the existing population. Perhaps also reflecting a less class-conscious society, poor districts were canvassed as well as middle-class streets; and working women, including living-at-home daughters were included. In Toronto, Might's Directories listed not only occupations, but often also the names of employers, making it possible to reconstruct the journey to work for many among the population in the late nineteenth and early twentieth centuries.[110] The only employed adults to escape the net were the occupants of lodging houses and apartment hotels, too transient to merit inclusion; and some of these were listed where their employers provided directory compilers with lists of employees. Some inter-war directories identified homeowners (presumably it was useful for businesses to know who was responsible for the upkeep of their own homes, or who owned property on which to secure loans), or who had a telephone at home.

We can, of course, question the reliability of directories. How did canvassers obtain information, especially if householders were out whenever they called? The proprietors of directory companies made attempts to check that their employees were not making up entries; but it was difficult to ensure that respondents provided correct information about their absent neighbours. All directories contain typographical errors, misspellings, and incorrect initials which become evident as soon as record linkage is attempted. Perhaps the greatest problem was the time it took to compile or revise a directory. Whereas, at least in theory, by the end of the nineteenth century the census involved an army of officials enumerating the population at a specific moment – census night – directories took months to compile. Consequently, many people who moved house might appear at both old and new addresses, while others would appear at neither; or a canvass of employers would yield a different address for an employee than the one returned by the door-to-door survey of residents.

Conclusion

In this chapter I have been illustrating the modernist impulse to survey, measure, classify, regulate and inform, to produce inventories of buildings, peoples and activities. The reasons for compiling all this information were various: to enhance business and make its conduct more efficient; to demonstrate the inadequacy of existing conditions as a prelude to reform; to facilitate taxation which financed urban improvement as well as the provision of ongoing services; and, more instrumentally, to empower government and business to exercise influence and control. The products of all this information gathering were the representations of cities in maps and surveys, in published census reports and the commentaries that accompanied them, in reformist tracts, in local government reports and in boosterist guides like the texts that prefaced city directories. But, as I have hinted especially in the later sections of this chapter, we can also make our representations using these surveys as resources amenable to our own modernist techniques of classification and spatial analysis. Just as we can recognise the situatedness of a work of art, but still draw on its content as evidence of *what* was perceived, so we can recognise the power relations, the partiality and the socially constructed nature of statistical surveys, but still analyse their content as evidence of one reality of the structure and conditions of modern cities. Moreover, as I show in the following chapter, the same panoptic and regulatory tendencies that were evident in nineteenth-century surveys also characterised some nineteenth-century novels and paintings; and the same more analytical, fragmentary, almost de-constructionist tendencies of twentieth-century social analysis can also be discerned in the modernist novels and art of the early twentieth century.

4

Writing and picturing the city

Why, and how, should urban historians and geographers make use of literary and artistic sources in reconstructing and interpreting the modernity of nineteenth- and early twentieth-century cities, especially given the profusion of statistical and documentary sources surveyed in the previous two chapters? Are we interested in art and literature primarily as evidence of ideology and values, attitudes to cities and perceptions of city life, regardless of the factual accuracy or typicality of what was being portrayed? Or, at the other extreme, should we treat textual and visual sources as surrogate social science, plugging the gaps which contemporary sociologists and political economists failed to investigate, and representing 'reality' as factually as the maps and censuses discussed in Chapter 3? Unsurprisingly, I want to have my cake and eat it too! – using the 'content' of artistic production to generate new questions with which to interrogate the social scientific record, or to answer questions of motive, mechanism or implication raised by spatial-temporal patterns generated by statistical analysis; but remaining sensitive to the conditions under which different forms of art were produced, to the positionality of the producers, to their changing values, and to changes in ways of seeing and of translating experience into art.

In practice, the dividing line between social science and artistic invention has been constantly transgressed by writers who combined careers as novelists and journalists, or artists who survived by working as newspaper and magazine illustrators. Henry James was a distinguished travel writer, Jack London was best known as a writer of adventure fiction, but features in this book for his documentary investigation in *The People of the Abyss*, Morley Callaghan began his writing career as a junior reporter for the *Toronto Star*, where a more senior journalist was Ernest Hemingway. Even George Gissing, whose best known novel, *New Grub Street* (1891), charted the plight of impoverished authors who refused to prostitute their talent by writing slick and superficial pieces for popular magazines, began his literary career by writing stories about English life for the *Chicago Tribune*, and later wrote vignettes of types of Londoner for magazines edited by Jerome K. Jerome; and his technique involved serious research – exploring localities on foot and attending public meetings just like contemporaries working with Charles Booth, and trawling through newspapers for odd facts and stories which he might employ in new combinations.[1]

Most of New York's Ashcan artists started out as newspaper illustrators. But over time, as a more corporate press relied increasingly on syndicated material, eliminating the need for so many local items and illustrations, and as the reproduction of photographs in newspapers replaced artists' impressions, they concentrated on fine art. Artists such as John Sloan and George Bellows also turned to work as illustrators and cartoonists for political magazines such as *The Masses*. To make ends meet, Edward Hopper churned out commercial art and narrative illustrations for trade journals such as *Hotel Management*. Another prominent New York artist, Joseph Stella, best known for his modernist representations of Brooklyn Bridge and the New York skyline, had earlier worked on the Pittsburgh Survey, sketching 'social types'.[2]

Changing genres, changing attitudes, changing cities

The personal experience of many writers and artists as 'ordinary' city dwellers implies that we can treat their works as expressions of everyday spatial practice, as representations grounded in a material 'reality'. Yet they were also conceptually informed, related to how their creators thought the city should be represented – realistically, impressionistically, expressionistically, abstractly. How do conceptual shifts relate to 'real' changes in built form, economy, social structure and technology? Typically, accounts of literary and artistic evolution describe a trend from social realism to modernist abstraction in which authors/artists shifted from being narrators/outside observers, looking down on and even orchestrating their creation, much like de Certeau's panopticist, to becoming part of the action, limiting their knowledge and vision to what was knowable and visible to their characters or expressing only what they felt to be true to their own experience.[3] Peter Keating contrasts 'a particular kind of nineteenth-century vision, the drive towards comprehension and cohesion', characteristic of novels written 'from above', with twentieth-century totalising novels, where the view was from below.[4] While it was physically easier to view the twentieth-century built environment from above – as far as the eye could see from atop the Woolworth Building or, later, the Empire State Building – writers were no longer confident that they could make sense of the whole, from above or from a distance: 'There is no longer any position *outside* the city from which it can be viewed as a coherent whole.'[5]

Where Dickens and Gissing shared a sociological vision with Booth in which, even when they descended into the city streets they did so as social explorers, and a conception of city structure that runs from Engels in 1840s Manchester to Burgess in 1920s Chicago, modernist writers such as James Joyce and John Dos Passos were more like *participant* observers, artfully limiting their knowledge to that of their fictional protagonists.

Emily Gilbert has explored parallels between Theodore Dreiser's and Upton Sinclair's novels set in Chicago and the sociological writings of Park and Burgess a generation later. She argues that the novelists' *point of view* was invariably that of *narrator*, distanced from the action, not as remote as Dickens, more like a literary *flâneur*, on the street, part of the crowd, yet also estranged from it. Likewise, the Chicago ecologists appeared simultaneously horrified and fascinated in their mostly arms-length accounts of 'Little Italy' or 'The Ghetto', 'The Gang', or 'The Gold Coast'. Both novelists and ecologists were flâneurs in their 'understanding of the city as spectacle, in which one was both removed from and yet master of the world'.[6]

We can make similar points looking at the panoramic art of nineteenth- and early twentieth-century artists, from Frith, Ritchie and Levin painting in mid-nineteenth-century London to the grittier, but still socially exploratory work by Ashcan artists in early twentieth-century New York.[7] There are political differences: the New Yorkers were more sympathetic to the plight of the people they depicted on the streets of the Lower East Side even if they were still different from them socially and politically, whereas painters like Frith were primarily concerned with entertaining middle-class gallery-goers. But they were all depicting 'other people'.

By contrast, in modernist literature and art it is not a 'natural' or 'real' city that is being represented, but a subjective city of sensations to be experienced, internalised in the protagonist's mind. To Raymond Williams, 'in a way there is no longer a city, there is only a man walking through it. . . . The substantial reality, the living variety of the city, is in the walker's mind'.[8] Malcolm Bradbury contrasted 'the "real" city' depicted by Zola and Dreiser, 'that materially dominant environment of sweat-shops and hotels, shop-windows and expectation', with 'the "unreal" city' of modernism, a 'theatre of licence and fantasy, strange selfhoods in strange juxtapositions'.[9] This 'unreal city' is evident not only in writers such as Virginia Woolf, John Dos Passos and the 'imagist' poets of the 1920s, but in artists such as John Marin and Max Weber in New York and especially in continental expressionists such as Kirchner and Munch.[10]

At issue here is how we integrate stylistic and conceptual changes in representation with substantive changes in the attributes of cities, and with changes in attitudes to urbanisation and urbanism. Not only in polemical works, such as those discussed in Chapter 2, but in everyday storytelling, too, there has been a morality of landscape, expressed, for example, in eighteenth-century literature where pastoral innocence was cheated or corrupted and virtue besmirched by metropolitan duplicity. Yet by the twentieth century the contrast between town and country had changed: now the city was associated with vitality and alertness, the country with ignorance and routine.[11]

Activating the contrast meant not just praising one and denouncing the other, but contrasting fears and opportunities: burgeoning worries about loss of identity, alienation and brute indifference in fast growing metropolises set against the awareness that urban life brought opportunities for self-advancement. Williams identified an urban way of seeing that belonged to the street: people passing, colliding, speaking *at* or *past* but not *to* others, concerned to express their own identity and to define themselves relative to impersonal others. Individuals became self-conscious to the point of self-obsession, oblivious of any sense of collective consciousness. In country novels, communities were transparent, but individuals – or, at least, working-class individuals – were submerged in the 'knowable community'; in city novels, communities were opaque and experienced only through the minds and thoughts of individuals. Hence, noted Williams, the paradox that in the very places with the greatest potential for collective consciousness – the great cities where people were described as 'classes' or 'masses' – there was 'an absence of common feeling, an excessive subjectivity'.[12]

Modern cities and modern culture

Whether or not writers and artists depicted city life in their work, there was a close relationship between the growth of big cities and the rise of the novel and the painting as bourgeois cultural forms.[13] To Malcolm Bradbury, the city was both the natural habitat of writers and critics – notwithstanding their frequently claimed abhorrence of all things urban – and the natural setting for the modern novel:

Here are the essential literary institutions: publishers, patrons, libraries, museums, bookshops, theatres, magazines. Here, too, are the intensities of cultural friction, and the frontiers of experience: the pressures, the novelties, the debates, the leisure, the money, the rapid change of personnel, the influx of visitors, the noise of many languages, the vivid trade in ideas and styles, the chance for artistic specialization.[14]

And here, too, among newly literate and affluent artisans, clerks, teachers and the rest of the urban lower middle classes was the market for inexpensive editions of adventures, romances, detective stories, and more serious prose and poetry. Just as the painting by impressionists of the parks and boulevards of modern Paris, or by Camden Town artists of the terraces, squares and music halls of inner London, depended on both the restructuring of the environment to provide the subject matter for their paintings and the restructuring of society to provide their clients, so the novels of writers like Gissing, Wells and Dreiser required both the settings and the market that the big cities offered. Slums, suburbs and apartments, offices, department stores and workrooms, streets, parks, theatres and railway stations were their locales rather than country houses and village squares; and an expanding middle class had both time to read and money to afford fiction. Middle-class men (and, increasingly, their unmarried young adult daughters) faced lengthy journeys to work by train or tram between suburbs and City, for which reading a book (or a newspaper) was the perfect solution to the embarrassment of intimacy with strangers. No wonder that W. H. Smith could build an empire out of station bookstalls, and that the phrase 'railway literature' quickly became a 'catchphrase for cheap popular fiction'.[15] Or, isolated in a suburban home, married women had time for reading and a preference for light fiction over the weighty classical and morally uplifting tomes recommended by their forebears. Stories were published in serial form in weekly or monthly magazines; and three-decker novels, borrowed a volume at a time from commercial circulating libraries, gave way over time to one-volume editions, forerunners of today's paperbacks, cheap enough to purchase outright. To Bradbury, 'one might argue that the unutterable contingency of the modern city has much to do with the rise of that most realistic, loose and pragmatic of literary forms, the novel': contingency in the plots of novels, but also contingency – or its avoidance – in the lives of readers.[16]

While increasing numbers of 'ordinary' urbanites could afford to buy or borrow novels, few would have had the opportunity to view new paintings at first hand. Art historians describe the unprecedented numbers who attended modern art shows in the 1900s. In New York an exhibition of 'Eight Independent Painters' (including artists subsequently labelled as 'Ashcan', such as Robert Henri and John Sloan) attracted up to 300 visitors an hour on opening day in 1908. Two years later, a crowd of 2,000 attempted to gain entrance to the opening of an 'Exhibition of Independent

Figure 4.1. William Powell Frith (1819–1909), 'The Railway Station' (1862). Oil on canvas (116.7 × 256.4 cm). © Royal Holloway and Bedford New College, Surrey, UK / The Bridgeman Art Library.

Artists' timed to coincide with the National Academy's Spring Exhibition. As many as 300,000 attended the International Exhibition of Modern Art (better known as the Armory show, after its New York venue), at which leading modernist European painters exhibited alongside American art, when it toured New York, Chicago and Boston in 1913. Still more attended exhibitions of (mainly more conservative) art at international exhibitions such as the Chicago Columbian Exposition in 1893 or the Paris Exhibition of 1900. But the numbers are still tiny compared to the populations of major world cities at the time.[17]

Nonetheless, there were important changes associated with the display and marketing of art during the later nineteenth century. A few works of art – like the panoramas discussed in Chapter 3 – were attractions in their own right. Frith's 'The Railway Station' (1862) (Figure 4.1) was the subject of single-picture exhibitions in galleries in London's Haymarket (in the West End), where it was seen by more than 21,000 people in seven weeks, and Cornhill (in the City), before going on national and continental tours.[18] And artists, like other craft workers, were switching from 'custom manufacture' ('made-to-measure' for a particular client who had commissioned the work in advance) to 'speculative painting', for purchase by as yet unknown clients seeing the finished work on display. Increasingly, such clients might be buying the painting not for its immediate 'use value' (because they liked looking at it), but as an investment in its future 'exchange value' (because they thought that this artist's works would be more highly valued in the future). As art became more of a business, so artists' studios were differentiated from commercial galleries, part of the specialisation and segregation process intrinsic to urban modernity. By the early twentieth century, major department stores offered original works for sale in their own art departments. A now-familiar painting by Robert Gagen of the Toronto waterfront backed by skyscrapers as seen from out in the harbour, entitled 'Temples of Commerce' (1914), originally failed to find a buyer, but eventually – and appropriately given its title – sold through Eaton's department store, one of the city's greatest cathedrals of commerce.[19] Another fêted representation of modernising Toronto,

Bell-Smith's 'Lights of a City Street' (1894) (Figure 6.5), continues to be part of the art collection owned and exhibited by The Bay, Queen Street (formerly Simpson's) department store.[20]

Methods of reproducing works of art en masse also became important – not so much the long-standing techniques of woodcut, etching, engraving, lithography, mezzotint, drypoint, but their application to mass production in newspapers and illustrated magazines. Two aspects of this are critical. First, the establishment of illustrated magazines such as, in London, the *Illustrated London News* (1842), *Illustrated Times* (1855) and *Graphic* (1869), and in New York, *Harper's Monthly* (1850) and *Weekly* (1857) and *Leslie's Illustrated Newspaper* (1855) created a demand for high-quality illustrations, often with some social or documentary content.[21] In William Dean Howells' *A Hazard of New Fortunes* (1890), itself first published in serial form in *Harper's Weekly* during 1889, the reason for Basil March's move from Boston to New York is to take up the editorship of a new magazine, called 'Every Other Week', and several of the characters in the novel are artists who contribute illustrations to the magazine. For its first issue in December 1869, the *Graphic* commissioned Luke Fildes to produce 'Houseless and Hungry', depicting the queue of homeless outside a London workhouse. The illustration appeared accompanied by an extensive commentary which explained that 'The figures in the picture before us are portraits of real people who received the necessary order for admission on a recent evening, and whose names and last sleeping-place are all entered in the police-books'.[22] Five years later, Fildes converted his illustration into a large-scale oil painting, 'Applicants for Admission to a Casual Ward'.[23] Art was thereby conscripted to the cause of political education.

Second, the publication of cruder, more rapidly executed impressions of dramatic news stories such as fires and accidents provided employment to illustrators who aspired to higher forms of art in their spare time. In 1892, more than a thousand illustrators were employed by American newspapers and magazines, providing 10,000 illustrations every week.[24] Robert Henri and his followers who made up the Ashcan School began as illustrators for newspapers in Philadelphia. John Sloan worked first for the *Philadelphia Inquirer*, then the *Philadelphia Press*, and briefly in 1898 for the *New York Herald*.[25]

So, just as major cities attracted authors, they also attracted artists, even though most artists ignored urban scenes in favour of more pastoral or wilderness subjects for their paintings. The domed Reading Room of the British Museum not only enfolded the products of literary culture but also accommodated a range of users who exploited its resources in different ways: academics and scholars (like Karl Marx) researching their latest treatises in history or philosophy; editors of literary magazines (Alfred Yule in Gissing's *New Grub Street* (1891)); their assistants condemned to working in a literary mill grinding them down as both the products and the operatives of a kind of cultural production line (Yule's daughter, Marian); writers of serious fiction seeking warmth as well as inspiration (like Gissing himself, as well as Reardon and Biffen, two struggling novelists in *New Grub Street*); and less high-minded writers ready to turn their hand to any kind of writing that pays (Gissing's Jasper Milvain, who, in Adrian Poole's words, 'raids the reading-room for smatterings of knowledge to flavour his facile concoctions').[26]

Victorian novels offer a similar picture of the emerging art world. In Amy Levy's *The Romance of a Shop* (1888) the well-bred but impoverished Lorimer sisters run a photography business on Baker Street through which they meet Frank Jermyn, who 'works chiefly in black and white for the illustrated papers', notably 'The Woodcut', and is dispatched on an assignment to central Africa, making illustrations of a colonial war in the company of Mr Steele, illustrator for the rival 'The Photogravure'. Jermyn shares a studio in York Place with Mr Oakley, 'a middle-aged bohemian', but is also familiar with Sidney Darrell, whom he describes as 'brilliant', 'sensational', 'a great swell', and who paints and then proposes eloping with the most sylph-like (aesthetically fashionable, but also sickly consumptive) of the sisters. Darrell has a smart house in St John's Wood and the reputation to fill a New Bond Street gallery all by himself. Another key character, Lord Watergate, of Sussex Place, Regent's Park, represents the connoisseur, the wealthy patron and collector on whom the burgeoning art market depends. By the end of the novel, Jermyn has married one of the sisters and he and his new wife have both 'succumbed to the modern practice of specializing': she concentrates on photographing young children, an occupation compatible with raising her own children, while he has 'permanently abandoned the paint-brush for the needle'.[27]

The relevance of art and literature to urban history and geography

Invoking Gissing and Levy as illustrations of literary and artistic metropolitan culture returns us to the central question: what can novels and paintings tell us about contemporaries' experience and understanding of the cities they depicted, and how should twenty-first century urbanists make use of such 'sources' about past cities? Do writers and artists stand as articulate spokespersons, reflecting or exemplifying more widely held attitudes? Or are they individuals of such heightened consciousness that they not only express what the rest of us fail to articulate, but also think what we fail to think? Most city-dwellers were not like Gissing or Whistler or Sickert. We cannot simply infer that novelists and painters *must* have reflected the attitudes of a wider society, just because they were parts of that society. We also need to ask whether novelists had an effect: did they convert readers, and, on occasions, policy-makers to their way of thinking? Were ordinary people persuaded to see cities through artists' eyes?

People read Dickens and were influenced in their attitudes to slums or workhouses or the legal system; they read Disraeli's 'condition of England' novels and gained relatively painlessly what few of them would have bothered with had it meant wading through thousands of pages of select committee reports on sanitary conditions and factory communities. More immediately influential was Upton Sinclair's novel about Chicago, *The Jungle* (1906), which was credited with inspiring legal reforms on food-processing and hygiene – the passage of the Pure Food and Drug Act (1906) – following his exposé of the appalling conditions that pertained in slaughterhouses and meat-packing plants on the city's south side. In the longer term, cities of the imagination became more real than real cities. Victorian London *is* Dickens' London or Doré's London; we are surprised, and sceptical of our data, if the evidence of archival research contradicts what we have imagined through reading Dickens' novels or viewing Doré's illustrations. So the interpretations of cities made by historians and historical geographers now, even those ostensibly based on 'factual' materials like censuses and social surveys, depend in part on those practitioners' awareness of contemporary art and literature. Of course, in a *market* for culture, novelists and artists had an increasingly reflexive relationship with consumers. They wrote not only what they were moved to write, but also what the market expected of them. They painted what would sell. Consider the young French fauvist, André Derain, dispatched to London in 1906 by his Paris dealer, Ambroise Vollard, to make paintings, especially along the Thames, that would contrast with but also cash in on the popularity of Monet's series paintings of Waterloo Bridge, Charing Cross Bridge and the Houses of Parliament, made just a few years previously.[28] However distinctive Derain's vision of a rainbow-coloured metropolis, it originated as a commercial venture.

We should also beware of assuming that authors and painters always represented contemporary scenes of which they were immediate eye-witnesses. Ideas and images were refined and re-worked, often far from the places to which they referred. Gissing's final novel, *Will Warburton* (1905), set in Chelsea and Fulham, was written in south-west France; James Joyce never visited Dublin after 1912 and wrote *Ulysses* (1922) in Trieste; Edith Wharton had long been resident in France when she wrote her powerful critique of elite New York society, *The Age of Innocence* (1920). Morley Callaghan was living in Paris on an extended honeymoon, socialising with Scott Fitzgerald and Ernest Hemingway, when he wrote one of his most Toronto-imbued novels, *It's Never Over* (1930). Many of these novels were also set in time far removed from their date of composition. *The Age of Innocence*, published in 1920, was mostly set in the 1870s. Dickens' novels, too, often reflected the London of his youth in the 1820s and 1830s, when he lived in Camden and worked in Covent Garden and Chancery Lane, rather than the 1840s-1860s when most were written.[29] Joyce used a 1904 street directory of Dublin and checked topographical details with his aunt who was still living in the city.[30] Monet's paintings of the Thames were begun in rooms in the Savoy Hotel or from the terrace of St Thomas' Hospital, but worked into their final form over the following years in his studio in Giverny; Derain took little more than his sketchbooks back to Paris to work on his London paintings.[31] One of Walter Sickert's best-known paintings of a London music-hall, 'Gatti's Hungerford Palace of Varieties', previously dated to 1888, is now known not to have been painted until about 1903.[32] It is assumed to be a copy of a painting now lost, but we cannot know for certain how closely the copy resembles the original, or why Sickert should have chosen to repaint the scene fifteen years on. The point is that these were places seen from afar, constructions of memory or research. We should not assume they are factual records.

Yet, in practice, as Marc Brosseau has argued, historical-geographical interpretation of fiction has often rested on 'an instrumental conception of literature', which assumes its factual accuracy and effectively denies its imaginative status.[33] The focus has been on the 'literal meaning of landscape',[34] with researchers anxious to check that authors had really 'been there'; or that they really did belong to the social milieus they described. In Brosseau's view, most researchers have treated novels as *sources* to answer existing historical or geographical questions rather than as new and different ways of seeing which generate their own questions.[35]

Brosseau's own recipe for a more fruitful dialogue between geography and literature focuses less on the topographical detail and more on the topography of the text
itself – its structure, composition, narrative modes, varieties of language and style. He
suggests that we have become too accustomed to thinking of landscape or city as text;
instead we should think of the text itself as a kind of city. This strategy can certainly
work for readings of modernist novels such as Joyce's *Ulysses*, Woolf's *Mrs Dalloway*
or Dos Passos' *Manhattan Transfer*, where there are dramatic shifts of language and
style from one section to the next, where there is no omniscient narrator making
sense of the drama, and where the onus is on the reader to discern the relationship between successive scenes and characters. In the particular case of *Manhattan
Transfer* Brosseau argues that while it shares some of the same themes with contemporary sociology – such as its critique of capitalism, and its focus on alienation
and anomie in the modern city – the novel's 'particular composition, montage and
syntax . . . explore them through a very different logic and representational mode'.
It is the fact that the novel is *not* a social survey that makes it worth our attention.[36]

Panopticism and synopticism

Whether they imagined the metropolis as a mosaic of, or a struggle among, different social classes, as a network of connections, or as a kaleidoscope of individual
diversity, most nineteenth-century authors and artists adhered to a *panoptic* vision
in which they were all-seeing and all-knowing. There was no doubting the *authority*
of the vision: readers and viewers were expected to accept the same metanarrative
that underlay authorial understanding. Between 1854 and 1862, William Powell Frith
produced three large paintings, of 'Life at the Seaside (Ramsgate Sands)', 'Derby
Day' (the scene on Epsom Downs where London's most popular horse race was
(and is) run), and 'The Railway Station', depicting passengers and their well-wishers
on the platform at Paddington, the London terminus of the Great Western Railway,
before the departure of a mainline train (Figure 4.1). Of the three settings, the first
two were not metropolitan in location, but metropolitan in character: the metropolis
at play at activities which attracted all social classes. The third was a site of transition, comings and goings, again allowing the possibility of diverse characters who
would not normally be found in company with one another. Frith's paintings were
to be read like Victorian novels (or at least as connected series of short stories); the
trained reader/viewer could construct the narrative from the expressions, juxtaposition, deportment and dress of the characters.[37]

Yet for all its 'eyewitness' qualities, 'The Railway Station' is more than simply
a panoramic snapshot. Frith included himself in both 'Ramsgate Sands' and 'The
Railway Station', implying that he was enthusiastic participant as well as authoritative
observer of London society.[38] The clothes worn by his workingmen were too clean
and unworn, and his passengers too smartly dressed to be embarking on a real train
journey: either they were 'ideal types' or Frith was acceding to the expectations of his
middle-class viewers, who wanted spectacle, not social realism. Two newsboys selling
papers hint at the immediacy of the information age, and at parallels between the
'montage of incidents on the canvas' and 'the assembly of items on the typeset page';
and the arrest of a fraudster by plain-clothes detectives on the right-hand margin of

the painting is framed by a newspaper being read by a passenger already seated on the train: in the next edition the arrest will be in the news![39]

Frith was not the only Victorian painter to depict the range of contemporary social structure in a single canvas. John Ritchie's 'A Summer Day in Hyde Park' (1858) and 'A Winter's Day in St. James's Park' (1858) also assembled large casts in precisely delineated locations at precisely specified times. 'A Summer Day' portrays the north-east corner of the Serpentine, Hyde Park's artificial lake, with Connaught Place, Marble Arch and Park Lane in the background. The cast includes a gentleman reading the latest news about the Indian Mutiny and a couple up from the country, their unfamiliarity with the metropolis indicated by a map of London lying at their feet. 'A Winter's Day' looks to our eyes like the stage set for a Dickensian musical – young men, rich and poor, jauntily raising their hats, having fun, skating – but the painting is also notable for the presence centre-stage of a small black boy, smartly dressed – a groom in a St. James's household? – sliding on the ice in the midst of (perhaps, tripped up by) a group of less respectable youths.[40] The black population of London in 1858 was not numerous, but neither was it non-existent, and there had long been a fashion for black servants. Another black figure, this time a blind beggar, appears in Phoebus Levin's painting of Covent Garden Market (1864), depicting the scene at 5 a.m. when the cast included male market porters hard at work, market gardeners up from the suburbs to sell their produce to wholesalers, female flower sellers, shopkeepers choosing what to buy, and a variety of public-house patrons.[41] Unlike Frith's scenes, in Ritchie's and Levin's paintings, the artist (and, by extension, the viewer) was outside the frame, whether a flâneurial bystander or a theatrical director choreographing the scene on stage. But in all these mid-Victorian scenes we can choose to interpret the image symbolically, as representative of the structure of metropolitan society were it possible to assemble the whole population together as if in a school photograph, or literally, as depicting a particular occasion in the station, the park or the market. Either way, we can use the content of the images to raise questions we might otherwise overlook: how common were black servants, or beggars, in mid-Victorian London; how widespread was the circulation of maps or newspapers; who went to the Derby, or took their holidays in Ramsgate?

A more complex and explicitly didactic Victorian street scene was Ford Madox Brown's 'Work' (1852–65), set in Heath Street, Hampstead, close to Brown's own home, depicting navvies hard at work excavating the street (Figure 4.2). The picture also includes representatives of the leisured classes (who do not need to work), philanthropic workers (a lady distributing evangelical tracts), street-traders (selling flowers and oranges), sandwich-board men, various idlers (sleeping tramps, ragged children), and 'brain-workers', the intellectuals Thomas Carlyle and F. D. Maurice, founder of the Working Men's College, where the artist taught, and which is advertised in a poster attached to the wall in the left foreground of the picture.[42] In effect, Brown was painting Henry Mayhew's classification of the population into those that will work, those that cannot work, those that will not work, and those that need not work.[43] And while Brown's intellectuals may have admired – and expressed a desire to 'improve' – the hard-working labourers on Heath Street, it is unlikely that there was much meaningful interaction or communication between the classes.

Figure 4.2. Ford Madox Brown (1821–1893), Preliminary study for 'Work' (1863) (1852–1865). Oil on canvas (137 × 197.3 cm). © Manchester Art Gallery, UK / The Bridgeman Art Library.

Heath Street is a real location in Hampstead yet, as in some of the Frith and Ritchie paintings, there is just too much happening for us to accept it as a credible representation of everyday life. The artist might have witnessed each of the participants and activities in this place at some time or other, but not all at the same time! Writing about George Bellows' painting, 'New York' (1911), which provides a panoramic view of Manhattan much like a stage set, with a cast of thousands going about their business in front of a backscene of the city skyline, Douglas Tallack observes that it is almost, but not quite, a real location – Union Square. But Bellows amalgamated elements from the square with other buildings to its north and south, and he 're-routed' the 'green and yellow Broadway trolleys, the red cars of Third Avenue and the Sixth Avenue elevated railway' to make a more comprehensive statement about the diversity of New York life:

These familiar signs of New York life come together in *New York*; that is, in the space of the painting rather than in the space of the city. Bellows' effort to create a typical New York street scene might be said to have produced an excess of signification commensurate with the meaning of 'New York' (then and since), but beyond what any one city site could generate. . . . The lack of literality . . . suggests that George Bellows is painting a need to know more than could actually be seen.[44]

Reverting to Ford Madox Brown's 'Work', we can reach the same conclusion – 'an excess of signification . . . beyond what any one city site could generate' – except that Brown was choosing to collapse time where Bellows collapsed space.

Brown's painting is in a pre-Raphaelite tradition of moral education through art. But later nineteenth-century artists were less inclined to preach so overtly. One response to moral didacticism was the retreat into 'art for art's sake'. Whistler responded to Ruskin's criticism of his 'Falling Rocket' nocturne, which represented a fireworks display at Cremorne Gardens, itself a site of amoral modern leisure, by emphasising that artists should 'seek and find the beautiful in all conditions and in all times', focusing on the aesthetics rather than the morality of landscape.[45] By contrast, Ruskin's disapproval of Cremorne as a place, as a site of duplicity and adulterous liaisons, informed his judgment that it was an unsuitable subject for fine art. The route through Whistler led to Sickert's matter-of-fact art of the bedroom and the music-hall, and parallels in Gissing's and Dreiser's non-judgmental litera-ture. Indeed, writing in the context of American fiction, Philip Fisher identifies a shift from 'victim narratives' in nineteenth-century literary naturalism to 'narratives of bohemian freedom', from accounts of suffering to catalogues of pleasure, from the city as a machine for indifference and destruction to the city as an opportunity for adventure.[46] And this applies whether the outsider is rich or poor, middle-class or working-class. In American fiction, Dreiser's *Sister Carrie* (1900) may mark the beginning of this shift. The central character is an outsider, Carrie, newly arrived in the city (Chicago), just like Oliver Twist in London sixty years before, but the focus has shifted from *problems* to *opportunities*. Whereas Oliver's experiences were a plot on which Dickens could hang a critique of the Poor Law, Dreiser had no equivalent axe to grind in *Sister Carrie*. This shift occurred, *not* because problems had been solved, but because there had been a change in perspective. The 'city as problem' novel derived from a perception that was rural, small-town, pro-family, anti-urban. But by the twentieth century the urban way of life had become the norm: 'A new norm of the temporary, of free-wheeling individualism, of the search for experience and excitement, of the dreamer and the artist' had taken over.[47] Less ebulliently, similar shifts were at work in Gissing. Here, the shift was more from *problems* to *constraints*. The poor will always be with us; cities will always be places of alienation and exploitation, so there is little point in conceptualising these phe-nomena as problems, better to see how individuals make (or fail to make) sense of their lives given the constraints of their status and situation. But in both cases, the concept of an external (God-given or society-accepted) moral authority had vanished.

Another response to urban life was to make a different kind of moral lesson, informed by radical political rather than establishment values. This route led to the political critiques evident in George Bellows' art and Jack London's and Upton Sinclair's socialist literature or to the Christian socialism modestly espoused by William Dean Howells and, in its Catholic social tradition, by Morley Callaghan in 1930s Toronto. Bellows' acerbic 'Why don't they all go to the country for vacation?', published in *The Masses* in 1913, bears comparison with William Hogarth's intensely moral portrayals of eighteenth-century London, such as 'Beer Street' and 'Gin Lane' and the series narrating 'The Rake's Progress' and, especially, 'Industry and Idleness'.[48] Bellows depicted a New York tenement landscape teeming with people: the street is crammed with peddlers, children playing leapfrog, fighting, screaming, women wearily nursing babies or just sitting exhausted at the foot of the stairs; a streetcar is somewhat optimistically trying to make its way through the crowd; but there are more people on balconies, looking out of windows, tumbling down fire escapes, and the evidence of yet more is provided by the signs – 'Room for Rent',

Figure 4.3. George Bellows (1882–1925), 'Why Don't They Go to the Country for Vacation?' (1913). Transfer lithograph (63.5 × 57.2 cm). Los Angeles County Museum of Art, Los Angeles County Fund (60.43.1). Photograph © 2006 Museum Associates/LACMA.

'Hot Soup' – and the lines of washing strung across the street (Figure 4.3). Snyder and Zurier comment that this last feature emphasises 'that these peoples have no secrets from us': there is no private space.[49] The noise and humidity are palpable. Bellows produced a painting of the same scene, less pointedly entitled 'Cliff Dwellers', more decorous and (slightly) less crowded than his drawing in *The Masses*. Indeed, to one art historian, 'There is no mass here, but rather a collection of lively, picturesque individuals; nor is this a slum, but rather a sort of urban village.'[50] A similar distinction between politicised illustrations for socialist magazines like *The Masses* and depoliticised, if still satirical, picturesque oil paintings also typifies the work of other Ashcan artists, especially John Sloan.

Howells wrote *A Hazard of New Fortunes* (1890), a mostly genial story about a couple moving from Boston (old urbanism) to New York (new metropolitanism) shortly after the Haymarket Massacre in Chicago in 1886, when a bomb killed eight policemen and, subsequently, 'in an atmosphere of brutal mob hysteria' four anarchists were hanged and another committed suicide.[51] Howells was appalled by this descent of American society into class warfare and eye-for-an-eye revenge and used his novel as a warning against the futility of violence. In *The Jungle* (1906), Sinclair preached a cruder version of salvation through socialism. His central character, Jurgis Rudkus, is a Lithuanian immigrant newly arrived in Chicago, whose progress through the city depends on a succession of unlikely events and coincidences. The novel is an excuse to introduce readers to the variety of horrors facing new immigrants – awful working conditions in stockyards and slaughterhouses, the duplicity of real estate sharks, the corruption of the meat packing industry and of Chicago city politics, the plight of hobos, the self-indulgence of the idle rich in the 'Gold Coast', leading at last to Jurgis realising the need for a Socialist solution to the city's ills.

Less well known, certainly in Britain, Morley Callaghan's minimalist novels, often written in the baldest language, what the Canadian critic George Woodcock called his 'styleless style', closer to the clinical lines of modernist architecture than to the word-play and experimentation of modern literature, were also intensely *moral* novels, reflecting his own Catholic upbringing and, in the 1930s, the influence of the Catholic humanist philosopher, Jacques Maritain.[52] But even in his pre-Depression and pre-Maritain novels, Callaghan demonstrated not only a fierce antipathy to hypocrisy and injustice, but also an awareness of the need for compassion and reconciliation. He provides good examples of the construction of a moral geography that critiques conventional social geographies, and of the mobilisation of space as a symbolic landscape. In several novels, Callaghan made reference to the spire of the Catholic cathedral in downtown Toronto, variously interpreted according to the mood of his characters: as a symbol of truth, goodness and salvation – the cross of Christ held high in the midst of a corrupt society; or as a sign of exploitation and rape, as the institutional church lined up with big business to suppress, or make money out of the sufferings of, the poor. Callaghan was also interested in the micro-geography of light and dark places, and the juxtaposition of childhood innocence, represented by school playgrounds, next door to the tragedy of adulthood, contained in seedy rooming-houses and cheap apartments. His obsession with the symbolism of darkness and light means that, as in cinematic 'film noir', his city is best observed at night: as revealed by its lighted avenues, illuminated electric signs, and buildings – such as apartment houses – that are known by patterns of lighted windows seen from a distance. The lights represent a range of emotions and experiences: as indications of real people going about their lives and relationships, as stimuli for nostalgia or regret, as invitations to go inside. There are also contrasts between the inconstancy of flashing signs, the security of more predictable patterns of street and house lights, and the revelatory 'natural' light of sunrise and sunset.[53]

Callaghan's plots highlight features of their city that most Torontonians would have preferred to ignore; certainly they run counter to images of 'Toronto the Good', the 'city of churches' or the 'city of homes' more customarily used to market Toronto. Reversing the conventional moral geography of his time, Callaghan found more 'community' and more sense of 'home' in down-market, inner-city apartments and rooming houses than in unwelcoming, privatised suburbs or superficially smart but inwardly cold and alienating luxury apartment buildings. So he created a 'moral geography' of Toronto very different from the geographies we could construct from census returns or contemporary social surveys.

Dickens' viewpoint was not simply panoptic – the novelist as all-knowing and all-determining. It was also synoptic, 'structured upon the need to establish the inter-relatedness of city life, the urgent need to recognize the connections that *do* exist and *must* be traced between superficially disparate elements'.[54] But in the decades after Dickens there are other, less determinative paths to synopticism. Frith may have been depicting a modern society, but his panoramic perspective, freezing the action artifi-cially, was 'anathema to the modernist spirit'.[55] His version of Paddington Station is challenged by Sidney Starr's a quarter-century later, reviewed by the *Sunday Times* in 1886 as 'cosmopolitan'. Starr's painting contains some *potential* stories – a middle-class lady approached by a flower-seller, a girl with a dog in conversation with a porter, a boy kneeling to inspect a rabbit in a wooden cage, a line of cabs await-ing the arrival of an approaching train – but nothing is resolved. Richard Thomson comments on 'the abandonment of a stage-like setting for an open, "chanced upon" space; the placement of figures close to the surface to make the spectator feel part of the picture's fiction; the dismissal of the sentimental anecdotes required in paintings of the previous generation . . . in favour of banal, momentary conjunctions'.[56] We are invited to walk *through* the scene rather than *past* it.

Following on from Bellows' 'New York', there are countless post-expressionist and abstract paintings that go by similar titles – for example, paintings by John Marin, Joseph Stella, Max Weber, Abraham Walkowitz and Stuart Davis among others, leading to the ultimate abstraction of the grid city in the art of Piet Mondrian – which, like Bellows' painting, demonstrate 'a desire to know more than can actually be seen'.[57] Tallack hints at this in commenting on another of Bellows' paintings of New York, 'Blue Morning' (1909), one of a series depicting the construction of Pennsylvania Station, where Bellows assumed a viewpoint which would have been inaccessible in reality, suspended in mid-air at a point where there was no window overlooking the scene. Only in this way could the artist depict building and labourers, both within the frame provided by the superstructure of the Ninth Avenue El, and thereby offer not only a pleasing composition but a comment on the relationship between people and planning (represented by the construction project but also by the grid frame of the picture mirroring the Manhattan grid). Tallack jumps from this example to the theoretical point that 'there is no one place from which to see modernity'.[58] Dickens and Frith's confidence that theirs is *the* vision of Victorian society is replaced by a multiplicity of alternating perspectives, sometimes competing for attention on the same canvas. Perhaps the best literary example of this synoptic universalism is to be seen in Dos Passos' *Manhattan Transfer*.

Synopticism exemplified: Dos Passos' *Manhattan Transfer*

Although some characters have 'starring' roles in *Manhattan Transfer*, the overall effect is of a kaleidoscope of incidents and plot lines, some of which never connect.

What unites them is their common setting in New York. The novel is divided into three sections. There is little explicit chronology, especially in First Section, which spans the longest time period, roughly 1892 to 1910, and only by noting occasional references to 'real' events, most often alluded to in newspaper headlines that attract characters' attention – 'MORTON SIGNS THE GREATER NEW YORK BILL COMPLETES THE ACT MAKING NEW YORK WORLD'S SECOND METROPOLIS' (1896) or 'JAPS THROWN BACK FROM MUKDEN' (1904) – can readers reconstruct the chronology.[59] Second Section is more obviously focused on the period leading up to and during the first few months of World War I, and Third Section on the aftermath of war – characters returning from Europe, prohibition, and the post-war economic crisis. Each section is subdivided into chapters, with titles such as 'Ferryslip', 'Metropolis', 'Dollars', 'Tracks' and 'Steamroller' (the titles of the five chapters in Section One). Within each chapter there is a multiplicity of scenes, some only a paragraph, others running for several pages. Altogether, we can enumerate 137 scenes in the course of the 350-page book.

Successive scenes may depict dramatic contrasts, mirroring the city's social heterogeneity and gross inequalities; they may involve completely different characters; or they may be linked by one character moving between contrasting environments. Occasionally, contrasting social realities meet in the same scene: the down-and-out Bud Korpenning is promised a dollar by a lady living on 53rd Street if he will shift a load of coal from the street in front of her house to her back yard; but when he has completed the task, and complains at being given only a quarter, she accuses him of 'Such ingratitude'.[60] Later, the last in a chapter of departures, Bud commits suicide by leaping off the Brooklyn Bridge. As Brosseau notes, 'The social critique, the interpretation of the city's social injustice, is not "literally" or "transitively" *expressed* as it would be in a sociological text: it is the contrasted montage that shows the injustices bred by the modern city. In other words, the social critique is "exemplified" within the textual form.'[61]

Yet the novel is not quite as disorientating or unconventional as this might suggest. While there is no authorial interpretation, there are hints of Dos Passos's sympathies, as in several anti-capitalist 'speeches' put into the mouths of, usually minor, characters. There are some recurring motifs: the fire witnessed by Ellen's father down the street from their 110th Street apartment, the fire in an apartment adjacent to Mme Rigaud's 8th Avenue delicatessen, the fire started in his 200th Street apartment accidentally by the drunken Stan Emery that kills him, the garment factory fire that severely burns Anna Cohen, are all symbolic of the hell-fire that will surely one day overwhelm all Manhattan;[62] the distractions which lead to serious traffic accidents for Gus McNeil and Phil Sandbourne, and the steady stream of ocean liners arriving – with new immigrants and returning soldiers – and departing – with deported communists and failed businessmen – all reflect a more structural restlessness than the frequent personal mobility that characterises Gissing's London.

While many characters appear only once, and we are left to speculate about the identity of others, twelve characters each appear in at least seven scenes, with Ellen in as many as forty, from the first, in which, unnamed, she is born, through scenes in which she is growing up in the company of her father, Ed Thatcher, to subsequent liaisons, marriages and divorces as she makes her name on the New York stage. In her social and geographical mobility, as well as her career on stage, she is not so different from Dreiser's *Sister Carrie*.

Moreover, as Philip Fisher has argued, there are other parallels between Dreiser's novel and *Manhattan Transfer*.[63] In the second half of *Sister Carrie*, Carrie and her lover, Hurstwood, have run away from Chicago to New York. In Chicago she had been the poor mistress to his affluent, urbane manager. But in New York he sinks down into unemployment, the rooming house and, ultimately, suicide, while Carrie becomes an actress, leaves him and makes her way to stardom in the New York theatre. Dreiser juxtaposes chapters telling their respective but by now disconnected stories. Dos Passos extends this pattern of juxtaposition. Chapter titles such as 'Rollercoaster' and 'Revolving Doors' indicate the ups and downs and the transiency of success and happiness in a city that bore 'The Burthen of Nineveh', a tendency to (self) destruction. *Manhattan Transfer* is strewn with the wreckage of business failures, marriage failures, arsonists and suicides.

Alluding to 'the novel as newspaper and gallery of voices', Fisher compares the fragmentation of stories in *Manhattan Transfer* to the apparently random arrangement of items in a newspaper, what he calls 'mere side-by-sideness'.[64] Newspaper stories can take on new meanings according to the order in which we choose to read them, or the order in which they are arranged on the page. Is there a 'right' order in which we should read a newspaper; is there only one order in which Dos Passos could have presented the fragments that make up *Manhattan Transfer*, especially where different fragments are *taking place*, chronologically, *at the same time*? All of which points to the need for re-reading. As one critic commented on *Ulysses*, 'Joyce cannot be read – he can only be reread'.[65] Individual fragments make sense only after you have seen the whole, and can piece together the *spatial* relations between different events. Brosseau concludes with the injunction: '"Read me again, and do it spatially".'[66] The analogy of a newspaper is one of which Dos Passos was all too conscious. Not only do readers learn to situate the action through the headlines of newspapers, but internally to the novel, unconnected characters learn about one another's stories through reading them in the paper, or construct fantasy newspaper stories about their own lives; and Jimmy Herf, the most prominent male character, is a junior reporter on a New York daily paper.

We might also consider this technique of juxtaposition as a forerunner of modern film-making, cutting often between a variety of parallel and occasionally intersecting story lines. But this only goes to emphasise the artfulness of the enterprise. Newspapers have editors, films have directors, and novels – however lacking in authorial commentary – have authors. Coincidence (or its absence) and contingency are as carefully plotted as in *Bleak House*. What differentiates *Manhattan Transfer* from an earlier generation of epic novels is the illusion of randomness, the acceptance of 'causelessness'[67] and the plurality of voices.

The fragmented text also mirrors the multiple identities of characters and even of the places through which they move. As she progresses through New York society, the principal character changes her name from plain Ellen to theatrical Elaine to intellectually respectable Helena. One of the more sympathetically painted characters, 'Congo Jake', originally from Bordeaux, working his way round the world as a ship's cook, is called 'Congo' 'because I have curly hair an dark like a nigger' and

'Jake' because 'when I work in America . . . guy ask me How you feel Congo? And I say Jake . . . so dey call me Congo Jake'.[68] But later, making a living as an upmarket bootlegger, he calls himself 'Marquis Des Coulommiers'; and finally, established in a luxury apartment on Park Avenue, he has become (or regained his original identity as?) 'Armand Duval'. Both Ellen and Congo remake their identities in response to the opportunities the city offers.

Places, too, accommodate a variety of identities. Central Park offers a space for childhood fantasy for Ellen growing up on the Upper West Side; a place for young men to pick up pretty girls, for Sunday afternoon strolls, for evening romance, for 4 a.m. carriage rides between champagne and breakfast; and a view for appropriation from the roof gardens of luxury apartments and hotels. Broadway is where Jimmy Herf as a young boy goes shopping for candy, where Bud finds a dead-end job washing up in a lunchroom kitchen, where an 'old man in the checked cap sits on the brownstone stoop with his face in his hands . . . sobbing through his fingers in a sour reek of gin', ignored or giggled at by the passing crowds. It is also where, in 'a small room the shape of a shoebox', 'the changing glow of electric signs' reflected on the ceiling, Anna, a young dressmaker from the Lower East Side, has sex with a buyer; and where George Baldwin, a highly respected lawyer, keeps a prostitute-dancer in a private apartment. Farther downtown, Broadway denotes the businessmen's club, where 'the wealthiest and the most successful men in the country eat lunch'. It is where, by night, Ellen, in love with Stan, 'watched faces, fruit in store-windows, cans of vegetables, jars of olives, redhotpokerplants in a florist's, newspapers, electric signs drifting by', but where, at 5 a.m., returning home, bitterly cold, from his newspaper office, Jimmy knows there wouldn't be anywhere he could get a drink.[69] So, although there are clearly 'specialist spaces' – the Jewish Lower East Side, Lower Manhattan, Park and Fifth Avenues – there are also these spaces which assume different identities at different times or as they are experienced by different characters.

Ecological novels

What of novels that focus on the details of such 'specialist' or at least small-scale spaces? Keating, following the American critic Blanche H. Gelfant, identified a type of novel labelled 'ecological', centred on one small geographical area of the city – a neighbourhood, a street or just a house and its various occupants.[70] In Arnold Bennett's *Riceyman Steps* (1923), the setting is a district of grey streets in inner London – Regency and early Victorian terraces along King's Cross Road, between King's Cross and Clerkenwell. The area had seen better days, but had gone to seed by the beginning of the twentieth century, much like the middle-aged secondhand bookseller around whom the novel revolves. Much the same district also featured in George Gissing's *The Nether World* (1889), which ranges from the artisanal respectability of Sidney Kirkwood's home in Tysoe Street, Clerkenwell to the poverty of the Hewetts' tran- siency through slum tenancies, lodgings and the Farringdon Road model dwellings. John Goode notes that 'more than thirty streets and eight public buildings which actually exist are named' and most of them are within a district no more than half- a-mile square.[71] Arthur Morrison's *Child of the Jago* (1896) took an even smaller canvas, recreating the 'Nichol', a real East End slum, as the lightly fictionalised 'Jago'.

The 'Nichol' was the subject of a major slum clearance and redevelopment scheme undertaken by the newly formed London County Council during the 1890s, leading to the creation of the Boundary Street estate of five-storey blocks of flats arranged around a central 'circus' and bandstand. Similarly, Morrison's 'Jago' is also subject to redevelopment. Morrison was critical of a scheme which produced impressive new buildings, but simply displaced and intensified the poverty of criminalised former residents. All these examples are set in working-class neighbourhoods of London, indicative of the limited mobility and territorially defined community of the poor – what Raymond Williams termed the 'mutuality of the oppressed'[72] – though other, more middle-class metropolitan novels are also predominantly confined to a particular district, but look outwards to the rest of the city, reflecting the wider horizons and greater mobility of the more affluent. Gissing's *In the Year of Jubilee* (1894) centres on the lives of a group of young adults in the south London suburb of Camberwell, yet much of the novel takes them beyond Camberwell to the rest of London and on holiday in Devon.

The extreme version of the ecological novel focused on just one building – Arnold Bennett's *Imperial Palace* (1930) (a grand hotel) or, straying into the mid-twentieth century, Wyndham Lewis' *Self Condemned* (1954) (a Canadian apartment-hotel), or Kurt Weill's opera, *Streetscene* (a New York tenement), first performed in 1947, but based on a 1929 stage play by Elmer Rice, who used as a model a tenement building on West 65th Street. In each case, the building is either a device to bring together different characters and their intersecting stories, or is used to symbolise the state of the city or society as a whole. In Lewis' novel for example, the corruption, chaos, dilapidation and ultimate destruction by fire of the Hotel Blundell mirror the corruption and collapse of the world's economic and political systems prior to World War II. In Weill's opera, each suite is occupied by a family from a different ethnic group – Jews, Italians, Germans, Irish, and Swedes, and a black janitor – encapsulating the problems and the potential of the city's 'melting pot' in a single building. In effect, these examples illustrate the use by realist authors of synecdoche, where a part of something stands for the whole: newcomers are new *faces*, factory workers are reduced to *hands*, civilisations to institutions.

Paintings such as Bellows' 'Cliff-Dwellers' and other Ashcan representations of slum life in New York's Lower East Side, such as George Luks' 'Hester Street' (1905) or Everett Shinn's 'Cross Streets of New York' (1899), could also be categorised as 'ecological', but the critical issue which raises such stories and artworks above the anecdotal or particular lies in their ability to stand for something greater, either because, as in Wyndham Lewis' and Arnold Bennett's novels, the setting constitutes a microcosm of the city as a whole, even of the world, or because, as in Gissing's novels, the place and the protagonists are integrated into and explained by what is going on elsewhere. This is perfectly exemplified in the paintings made of Toronto streets and houses by the Canadian artist, Lawren Harris, subsequently fêted for his central role in the 'Group of Seven' who shaped Canadian landscape painting in their depictions of 'wilderness' and 'the true north' in the inter-war years.

Returning to Toronto from Berlin in 1908, Harris began to paint 'anonymous, ordinary, and clearly city houses', often face-on views of row housing, especially middle-class terraces that had declined into slums, but also working-class shacks on the urban fringe.[73] Harris's own home environment was 'elegant and easy'; his

Figure 4.4. Lawren S. Harris (1885–1970), 'Houses, Chestnut Street' (1919). Oil on canvas (81.7 × 97.2 cm). Gift of Joan F. Pelly, Edward D. Fraser, John C. Fraser, Charles L. Fraser, 1985. The Robert McLaughlin Gallery, Oshawa, Canada. Photography: Tom Moore.

family were leading manufacturers of agricultural machinery, and he lived in a succession of comfortable houses in elite areas of Toronto.[74] We can interpret Harris's paintings as examples of 'psychic landscape'. The industrial city had been the creation of the middle-class bourgeoisie – people like Harris's father – but it quickly proved 'inhospitable to bourgeois culture', triggering a flight to new suburbs, and leaving behind houses and neighbourhoods from which the middle classes were now alienated. Harris himself did not like industrial cities, as witness his own poetry and his later championing of a landscape art that expressed Canadian identity in 'the true north'. So, for him, 'old houses, the shells of an ebbing urban culture, were an appropriate image to embody the paradox of the new city and the bourgeoisie's ambivalence towards it'.[75] These houses presented expressionless, flat façades to the viewer. It was difficult to know if there was life within, but the suspicion was that these places were no longer *homes*.

It was also important that these were not just any old houses. Harris's sketches and paintings were of particular streets and buildings: 'Old Houses, Wellington Street' (1910), 'Houses, Richmond Street' (1911), 'Houses, Chestnut Street' (1919) (Figure 4.4). They are like portraits of people who had once been somebody – ex-VIPs or people who were suffering from a chronic degenerative condition, who can no longer relate to their former friends and family. Harris's house paintings predate Edward

Hopper's equally enigmatic representations of New York streets, tenements, apartments and hotel lobbies, but in Hopper it is the artist/viewer who seems detached and alienated from the built environment whereas in Harris's paintings there is more sense of loss or regret.[76]

Ecological novels, and neighbourhood paintings like Harris's, where the setting symbolises or connects to a much greater whole are, therefore, synoptic without laying claim to literal panopticism. The term 'ecological' here relates to the social or human ecology of the Chicago School, but it also prompts a brief diversion into the representation of 'nature' in the metropolis. In Chapter 2 I discussed some aspects of the conceptualisation of the city as a natural system. Here I want to consider the role of nature *in* the city, the culture *of* nature.

Nature and culture

I have already alluded to paintings of the Thames: representations of London's river by Turner, Whistler, Monet and Derain are just the best known examples among countless artists, many from Europe and North America, who were attracted to depict the interaction of nature and culture in scenes that celebrated the metropolis's diverse moods under changing characteristics of weather, light and pollution.[77] Their paintings concentrated on 'natural' effects of sunlight through haze, fog or twilight, yet it was not only the smoke pollution of factory chimneys, lead works, coal-fired power stations, railway locomotives and domestic fires that was man-made. By the 1870s the Thames was an embanked and many-bridged river. This not only affected the built environment of the Chelsea, Victoria and Albert Embankments, of Westminster Bridge (rebuilt in 1860), old Battersea Bridge (dismantled and replaced in the 1880s), Charing Cross, Blackfriars and Cannon Street Railway Bridges, all of which feature prominently in Whistler's, Monet's and Derain's art, but also the physical characteristics of the river itself – its depth, velocity of flow and tendency to meander. Modernisation of the built environment also provided some of the vantage points from which artists worked: Monet painted the Houses of Parliament from the terrace of St Thomas's Hospital, newly located opposite parliament in 1870 following its displacement from the vicinity of London Bridge by the building of the South Eastern Railway's Charing Cross extension; and Monet and Whistler both occupied rooms in the Savoy Hotel (built 1885–1889) from which they could look down on Waterloo and Charing Cross Bridges.

Paintings of London's parks – for example, Monet's paintings of Hyde Park and Green Park in 1871 – show them as an escape from the city. Indeed, the city is hardly to be seen thanks to London's low-rise skyline. Eric Shanes contrasts the informality and irregularity of London's parks with the formality and regulations associated with open spaces in the centre of Paris;[78] but we should also note the differences between London and New York where most public open spaces were relatively small squares, such as Washington or Gramercy squares, or awkward intersections where Broadway cut across the grid at an angle, for example at Union and Madison squares. Each square was laid out with formal paths and gardens and hemmed in by buildings that were already 5–10 storeys high when Childe Hassam began to paint them in impressionist style in the 1880s. Although much larger in area, Central Park too was far from natural, involving massive reconstruction of nature in the creation of lakes, glades, lawns and rocky viewpoints. It was also bordered by high-rise luxury apartments and hotels.

To Wanda Corn, American impressionists imported an artistic language based on the painting of nature, marrying French impressionism to the American sublime practised by landscape painters such as Church and Bierstadt who celebrated an awesome and overwhelming nature of snow-capped mountain peaks, lushly vegetated slopes and crystal-clear streams. So, in New York, skyscrapers became cliffs or mountain ranges and streets became canyons. The city was, if not an urban wilderness, a frontier ripe for colonisation. Corn suggests that these depictions in the snow or at twilight denoted strategies of both resistance and accommodation: 'Marrying nature and skyscrapers was a way of learning how to describe what was novel by using terms that were timeworn and familiar.' Depicting the skyscraper in subdued lighting when its manmade details were least decipherable was a 'strategy of accommodation' as well as 'lingering romanticism'; but it thereby subverted the tendency to Babylonian self-aggrandisement.[79] In essence, these buildings were the product of natural materials, reshaped by human ingenuity into steel and reinforced concrete, but still bearing a family likeness to the mountains and cliffs from which they had been hewn.

American impressionism idealised the landscape, playing down the contested nature of the built environment. By the time Childe Hassam painted it, Union Square was much rougher than his pastel colours suggested: it was no longer the centre of fashionable middle-class society, which was moving north to the Upper West Side in the face of commercial invasion. The square was less a place to promenade than a venue for radical political protests.[80] Hassam's art tended to reduce the spaces of the city to sights of spectacle, a landscape to be admired under diverse climatic conditions rather than a site of struggle; even the severity of winter seems benign. Some of Alfred Stieglitz's early photographs of New York skyscrapers, such as 'The "Flat-iron"' (1903), erased almost all traces of human occupancy, using soft-focus to present the building as a 'natural' form, flattened and eerily devoid of substance. Yet Shapiro's conclusion is that Stieglitz and his contemporaries, Edward Steichen and Alvin Langdon Coburn, 'humanized the new skyscrapers by capturing Impressionist climatic effects', making an accommodation with modernism much as Corn suggested.[81] However, later in the 1900s Stieglitz rejected soft-focus in favour of more sharply geometric, objective, so-called 'straight' photography, a more modernist art, influenced by European futurist and cubist movements.

Among the most interesting representations of nature in New York are those of Maurice Prendergast, who reversed the naturalisation of the city by metropolitanising nature in his post-Impressionist views of Central Park. Prendergast had visited Paris in the early 1890s, sketching and painting the ordered nature of the Luxembourg Garden and other open spaces characterised by severely vertical, closely cropped urban trees, gravel paths and park benches.[82] In 'Central Park' (originally 1908–1910?) (Figure 4.5) he depicted parallel horizontal layers of pedestrians, people sitting on park benches, horse-riders, trees, and horse-drawn carriages, with vertical tree trunks and the uprightness of the people converting a park which was supposed to imitate nature into a space that imitated and extended the grid of the New York

Figure 4.5. Maurice Prendergast (1858–1924), 'Central Park' (c.1914–1915). Oil on canvas (52.7 × 68.6 cm). The Metropolitan Museum of Art, George A. Hearn Fund, 1950 (50.25). Image © The Metropolitan Museum of Art.

streets. This inversion was reinforced by his use of clearly defined patches of colour contradicting the pastel elisions of nature. Of course, there were many more conventional, impressionist or romantic depictions of Central Park as an escape from the rigid discipline of the city grid, though the dress and deportment of park users in these pictures never leaves any room for doubt that this is a metropolitan scene. But where William Glackens and John Sloan depict city types enjoying nature, Prendergast's technique implies that the people are part of nature, albeit a nature that has been disciplined to metropolitan rhythms.[83]

City in film

The flashbacks, cross-cutting between scenes, and avoidance of authorial narrative employed by Dos Passos were all devices associated with film, and by the time *Manhattan Transfer* was published, the role of popular storyteller of city life was already passing from artist and novelist to filmmaker. I noted earlier that Dickens and Doré provide the prism through which we view Victorian London. In the same way it may be argued that we view twentieth-century cities through their depictions in film; to Jean Baudrillard, 'the American city seems to have stepped right out of the movies'.[84] Yet a closer examination suggests that in the first thirty-five years of its existence, the silent film era from 1895 to the late 1920s, cinema produced little in the way of original interpretations of city life. The only pre-World War II films discussed by Nezar AlSayyad in his *Cinematic Urbanism* are the semi-documentary 'Berlin: Symphony of a City' (1927), Fritz Lang's science-fiction dystopia 'Metropolis' (1927) and Charlie Chaplin's critique of the gospel of efficiency and automation, 'Modern Times' (1936).[85] Colin McArthur suggests that most early films, if they bothered to portray the city at all, were structured around crude dichotomies of city v. country or metropolis v. small town, little different from the binaries discussed by Raymond Williams in the context of literature.[86] A few films, mostly musicals from the 1930s such as 'Broadway Melody' (1929) and '42nd Street' (1933), celebrated the opportunities of the big city, usually New York; and one notable silent film, King Vidor's 'The Crowd' (1928), recognised the tension between the city as site of alienation and impersonality and as site of romance and excitement.[87]

In their representation of the urban mosaic, most big-city films concentrated on the extremes of 'high society' and 'low life' with little in between. McArthur refers to Hollywood's 'London discourse', perpetuating into the mid-twentieth century images of London derived from Dickens, Sherlock Holmes and Jack the Ripper. Of course, there were technical problems of making films on location, and these were, at least briefly, accentuated when 'talking pictures' were introduced. In the silent film era it had been relatively easy to mix footage from different origins, combining a drama shot in the studio with stock documentary footage of city streets and skylines, but after about 1928 audiences expected a seamless integration of sound and pictures which discouraged exterior scenes. The one new and specifically urban genre was the gangster film. The gangster was perceived as a creation of the big city, and the city was his natural habitat.[88]

There were also documentary films, and especially films concerned with housing reform and the planning of future cities, and, until they were squeezed out by the enhanced financial demands of sound recording, art films which elaborated on themes already depicted in modern art and photography, best represented by Ruttmann's 'Berlin: Symphony of a City', Vertov's 'Man with a Movie Camera' (1929, filmed in a variety of Soviet cities) and, much shorter but made by two established artists, photographer Paul Strand and precisionist painter Charles Sheeler, 'Manhatta' (1920). Inspired by, and interspersed with intertitles from Walt Whitman's poem, 'Leaves of Grass', 'Manhatta' features dramatic shots of vessels in New York Harbour, the city skyline and views looking vertically down from skyscrapers to the streets and elevated trains far below. Eight years later, 'The Crowd' employed very similar footage, along with advanced techniques of superimposing different shots of moving traffic and pedestrians, and some startlingly surreal and expressionist scenes to imply both the ephemerality and the stresses of city life.[89]

As important, therefore, as the *content* of early films was the experience of film-going. Short films were initially included as 'turns' in vaudeville (in North America) and music hall (in Britain). Leo Charney notes that cubism, jazz, film and vaudeville were all 'arts of fragmentation' but that the disjunctures between items were a way of diverting audiences from their anxieties: chaos was constructed and ordered.[90] Early film artfully mirrored and reinforced Georg Simmel's analysis of metropolitan experience as a clash of diverse and cumulatively discordant sensations. In Stephen Kern's words, 'The cinema reproduced the mechanization, jerkiness, and rush of modern times'.[91] John Sloan built on precedents by Walter Sickert and Spencer Gore in London and Everett Shinn in New York of painting music-hall and theatre audiences to present images of cinemagoers individually absorbed or distracted by on-screen drama, whether happily joining in with the crowd, consciously standing out from those around them, or (as so often in Edward Hopper's art) alone and anxious.[92] In King Vidor's film, 'The Crowd', the closing shot is of John Sims, the archetypal American, born 4 July 1900, who has tried and failed to make his way apart from the crowd, apparently laughing contentedly along with the rest of a cinema audience. It is almost as dispiriting a resolution of the dilemmas of city life as had he succeeded in committing suicide by jumping in front of an oncoming express train a few minutes' earlier in the film.

The representation of spatial practice

I have concentrated in this chapter on changing forms of representing city life, changing attitudes to the city, and different scales of representation, from urban-rural polarisation to the neighbourhood or the individual building, both as a site for storytelling and as a microcosm of the city as a whole. I want to conclude by considering further the concept of (urban) space as 'practised place' and analysing how novelists (and to a lesser degree, artists) set space to work. How did they exploit the geometric as well as cultural and political characteristics of space and place, rather than simply treating location as an empty stage on which their stories were performed?

Franco Moretti identifies connections between space and style, and between space and plot in nineteenth-century novels. For example, when characters reach the margins of an author's experience, probably a geographical border, 'figurality' – the use of metaphor – increases; you have to use metaphors to write interestingly about places you (or your characters) don't know. Moreover, the reason for sending characters across boundaries is usually to enact some decisive event in the plot.[93] So we might explore the relationship between the language of the text and the spaces and activities in which the protagonists are engaged. Moretti's basic argument is that making maps of novels can change the way we read them, revealing themes and arguments never made explicit in the text. For Moretti, 'Space is not the "outside" of narrative, then, but an internal force, that shapes it from within . . . *what* happens depends a lot on *where* it happens.' He is also interested in why novels so often mix real and imaginary locations: whether some kinds of events work better in real spaces while others 'prefer' fictional spaces. By comparison with Jane Austen, whose happy endings seem to demand unreal spaces, more pessimistic authors seem more reliant on real locations.[94]

We can consider realist novels by George Gissing in the light of Moretti's question. Gissing's first published novel, *Workers in the Dawn* (1880), begins in Whitecross Street, just outside the northern boundary of the City of London, and more particularly in Adam and Eve Court, 'a narrow, loathsome alley', a real alley condemned and cleared by the Metropolitan Board of Works just at the time Gissing was writing. But the scene then switches to 'Bloomford', an idyllic country parish 'in one of the pleasantest of the southern counties'.[95] In London, Gissing's characters nearly always occupy real streets and buildings. Outside of London, and especially in settings of

comic excess, such as Whitsand, the site of Luckworth Crewe's speculative and out-
landish advertising ventures in *In The Year of Jubilee* (1894), or of carefree idyll,
most notably, in *The Whirlpool* (1897), in 'Greystone', 'the midland town which was
missed by the steam highroad, and so preserves much of the beauty and tranquillity
of days gone by', Gissing resorts to imaginary locations.[96] 'Bloomford' and 'Greystone' are both places of childhood reminiscence, too good to be true; 'Whitsand'
with its caves, 'lighted with electricity, and painted all round with advertisements of
the most artistic kind'[97] beggars belief, at least to the anti-commercial Gissing; but
Adam and Eve Court is so awful it could not be invented.

    Writing about geographies in literary modernism – from E. M. Forster by way of
James Joyce and Virginia Woolf to Jean Rhys – Andrew Thacker especially wants to
clarify the use of the terms 'place' and 'space'.[98] 'Place' is typically associated with
being, indwelling, and the concept of 'sense of place'. 'Space', which quantitative
geographers once thought of as little more than abstract geometry – the friction of
distance, the spatial coordinates of one location relative to another – is now conceived
as socially produced, not just a spatial container and never empty, but implying
history, change, becoming. Thacker invokes Michel de Certeau's distinction between
'place' which we map, and 'space' which is actualised through the tour. Place implies
stability, space is about direction, movement, velocity. Space is a 'practiced place'.[99]
A map is equivalent to 'a discourse that lists where sites are located'; a tour 'describes
a location through a set of actions'.[100]

    In practice, it is hard to find city descriptions that are solely 'map-like'. Thacker's
own example is a piece of scene-setting by Thomas Hardy; another example might
be Wells'/Ponderevo's description of Bladesover at the beginning of *Tono-Bungay*
(1909).[101] Both are rural: places with history and natural history and, however subject
to evolutionary change, texturally as well as textually distinct from city districts where
even the most descriptive of passages employ active narrators whom we accompany
on their explorations. Good examples here are Gissing's descriptions of Whitecross
Street in the opening pages of *Workers in the Dawn*, and of Caledonian Road, north
of King's Cross, in *Thyrza* (1887).[102] In each case the reader is treated as a fellow
social explorer and the 'discovery' of the area parallels the explorations of Charles
Booth's assistants as they accompanied police officers on their beat in revising the
poverty map in the late 1890s. At the other extreme are 'tours' through or past rather
than into urban neighbourhoods, as in *Mrs Dalloway* where we learn about Bond
Street or Whitehall as characters cross streets, look in shop windows, follow strangers,
their physical journeys all the while stimulating memories of emotional and psychological journeys; or in *Manhattan Transfer*, where Dos Passos sent his characters on
elaborate journeys across Manhattan: for example, from Maiden Lane up Broadway, west along West 4th Street, past Washington Square, over Sixth Avenue, to
253 West 4th.[103]

    It may be objected that most readers of Gissing's or Dos Passos' novels would not
know the locations they depicted, even when they were spelt out explicitly in the
text. If you could enjoy their work without having an *A to Z* to hand, does this local
geography matter? The point is that it mattered to the authors. Locating characters
and events geographically helped to locate them socially and symbolically, and the
discipline of physical space and the time it took to move between locations was as

critical for writers as it was for the real-life counterparts of Inspector Bucket or Sherlock Holmes in determining the limits of possible behaviour.

In subsequent chapters of this book I make use of novels and artworks, not simply to confirm or flesh out the results of my own and others' archival research, but also to explore how pedestrians, commuters, residents, shoppers and office workers experienced and exploited new city spaces. Realist and modernist writers alike were constrained by the same attributes of places and spaces. They used 'topographical space' to signify the physical and social surroundings in which their stories were set. Here, space was still primarily a container for plot, but could also function symbolically. For example, in Chapter 7, I discuss the kinds of houses in which Gissing placed his characters in *In The Year of Jubilee*. At the end of the novel, Nancy, the principal female character, moves from Camberwell to Harrow. In Camberwell everything is sham; hypocrisy rules. In Harrow, Nancy's home is 'in a byway which has no charm but that of quietness' and the small house in which she lodges had been built 'not long ago, yet at a time when small houses were constructed with some regard for soundness and durability' – very different from Gissing's assessment of houses in Camberwell.[104] Clearly, the setting tells us something about Nancy's desire to get away from the lifestyle, the space as well as the place that was Camberwell. But it is also critical that Harrow was physically distant: in the farthest reaches of Middlesex, north-west of London, about as far from Camberwell as you could go without leaving London altogether (Figure 4.6). Physical distance signified cultural distance.

In other novels, physical distance implies time, and time is crucial in setting limits to which the plot must conform but also opportunities that the author and his characters can exploit. Physical distance is especially important in Gissing's *The Whirlpool* in the location of Cyrus Redgrave's bungalow in Wimbledon. A bungalow, even more than a flat, implied a bohemian, even cosmopolitan lifestyle in 1890s London.[105] Not only was Wimbledon an authentic location for a nouveau riche bungalow, but Gissing could also exploit its location relative to Pinner (the next suburb out from Harrow in north-west London), the home of Alma and her husband Harvey Rolfe, and Oxford & Cambridge Mansions, a fashionable block of flats close to Edgware Road underground station, where Hugh and Sibyl Carnaby reside. Alma first visits the bungalow following an afternoon concert in Putney, accompanying the aptly named Mrs Strangeways by carriage to Wimbledon and then back to her house in Porchester Terrace, Bayswater, for dinner. She is back in Pinner by 11 p.m., a detour from Putney sufficiently brief that she has no trouble in hiding it from her husband. Yet Wimbledon was far enough out of London for all kinds of plot development to take place in the time it took for a round trip. Hugh Carnaby leaves home in Oxford & Cambridge Mansions at 11 a.m., transacts business 'in town', then stops for lunch in the Strand, where he happens upon Alma, lunching alone. He takes a cab to Waterloo, intending to travel to Weymouth where his mother-in-law is gravely ill; but in the station bookstall he has a second coincidental meeting, with his ex-housekeeper who is now working for Redgrave. Changing his plans, he travels with her by cab to Wimbledon and then returns home about 6 p.m. Meanwhile, his wife, Sibyl, has received and responded to a telegram and set off to visit her dying mother, while Alma, thinking that Hugh is out of the way en route to Weymouth, has paid a

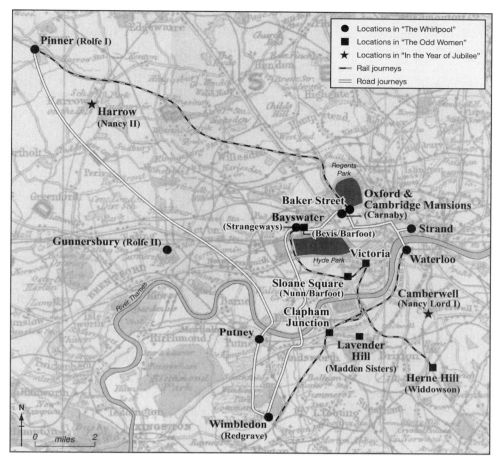

Figure 4.6. The London of George Gissing: Sites and Journeys in *The Odd Women* (1893), *In The Year of Jubilee* (1894) and *The Whirlpool* (1897).

fruitless visit to the Mansions, hoping to see Sibyl on her own. Both Hugh and Alma still have time, independently of one another, to make further trips to Wimbledon in the early evening. There, the denouement depends upon the micro-geography of the bungalow and its surrounding garden.[106]

As Lynne Hapgood notes of Monica's ever more frenetic movements between Herne Hill, Lavender Hill, Victoria and Chelsea in another of Gissing's best known novels, *The Odd Women* (1893), his plots can be driven by the railway timetable. Space becomes time: 'Gissing used the time taken, the time wasted, the time required as the trains shunt Monica from place to place as the logic of the plot.' Yet space is also more than time: 'The fixed relationships of Lavender Hill and Chelsea, for instance, are easily negotiated by foot, train or hansom, but the ideological distances are far harder to negotiate.'[107] Monica's spinster sisters, old before their time, live close to Clapham Junction which, in terms of space syntax, would have been one of the most highly connected places in the world, yet they hardly ever leave home.[108]

Like many Victorian novels both these examples trade in coincidences (or, sometimes, the denial of coincidences that readers anticipate). They raise the question of where people meet, whether by convenient accident or by design, and especially where those who have little private space of their own find public spaces where they can be private in public, a theme I return to in Chapter 6. In Howells' *A Hazard of New Fortunes* (1890), the spaces of the Manhattan grid offer opportunities for coincidental meetings at key intersections: in front of Brentano's bookstore in Union Square, where the idealistic Conrad Dryfoos bumps into the angelic Miss Vance, who, through her words encouraging him as a peacemaker, effectively sends him to his death, caught in the crossfire between police or strikers at another, unspecified intersection on a West Side streetcar line; or in the middle of Fifth Avenue, where Conrad's father's carriage almost runs down Basil March.[109]

A less innocent set of meetings in public space are those contrived by Bob Hewett and Clem Peckover in *The Nether World* (1889). They meet by chance, after a long absence, walking along High Holborn, and adjourn to the British Museum. Subsequently, they arrange to meet at an Italian pastry shop on Old Street and on the Thames Embankment between Waterloo Bridge and Temple Pier.[110] None of these venues is more than a mile from Clerkenwell, where most characters in the novel live, move and interact, but they are culturally and economically remote: out of the way places beyond the everyday space of residents of the nether world, places where Bob and Clem can be private in public. Likewise Clara Hewett meets Mr Scawthorne, a scheming solicitor's clerk who lives in lodgings in Chelsea (much as Gissing himself lived in rooms there from 1882 to 1884), in the anonymous surroundings of Waterloo Station:

a convenient rendezvous; its irregular form provides many corners of retirement, out-of-the-way recesses where talk can be carried on in something like privacy. The noise of an engine getting up steam, the rattle of cabs and porters' barrows, the tread and voices of a multitude of people made fitting accompaniment to a dialogue which in every word presupposed the corruptions and miseries of a centre of modern life.[111]

Space syntax, investigating how people move around in and make use of space, operates not only at the scale of streets, but also within buildings and within rooms. In *A Hazard of New Fortunes*, Howells describes the layout of Basil and Isabel's New York flat: we learn that it is on the eighth floor and has six rooms, entered through a 'gangway' that the building's superintendent referred to as a 'private hall', and comprising a 'drawing-room' and a 'succession of chambers stretching rearward to the kitchen'. This is a typical deep but narrow New York flat of the 1880s.[112] But that is all we are told; we don't learn how the March family, their guests and servants move around and make use of the different spaces within their flat. By contrast, Gissing sets his characters' residential spaces to work; his rooms are active players (Figure 4.7).

In *The Whirlpool*, Redgrave's bungalow resembles a flat in having all its rooms on one floor, allowing a fluidity of movement between public and private spaces denied to those whose homes were arranged vertically. But unlike flats, bungalows also had multiple entrances and exits, affording scope for secret visits and sudden escapes. As his housekeeper observes: 'You remember that his rooms have French windows – a convenient arrangement. The front door may be locked and bolted, but people come and go for all that.'[113]

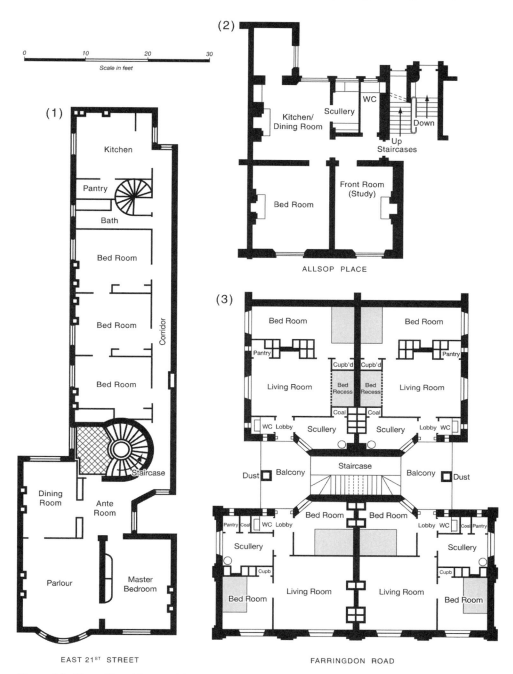

Figure 4.7. Three Novel Spaces: Floor Plans of Flats in New York and London: (1) New York flat at 21 E 21st Street, similar to Howells' description of the Marches' flat in *A Hazard of New Fortunes* (from *American Architect and Building News*, 4 May 1878); (2) flat in Cornwall Mansions, London, similar to Gissing's description of the Reardons' flat in *New Grub Street* (from Drainage Plans, Westminster Archives Centre); (3) flats in Farringdon Road Buildings, London, the setting of the Eagles-Hewett flat in *The Nether World* (from *The Builder*, December 1874).

Edwin and Amy Reardon's flat in *New Grub Street* and the Hewetts' flat in *The Nether World* are both three-room flats, like Gissing's own flat in Cornwall Residences. But where Gissing was generally the sole occupant of his flat there were two adult Reardons and a baby in theirs; and in the Hewetts' model dwelling in Farringdon Road Buildings there were seven people in all: Mr and Mrs Eagles, an older couple who were the official tenants, plus John Hewett, his three children from his second wife, and Clara, his older daughter from his first marriage. Yet the Reardons thought themselves overcrowded, whereas the Eagles and Hewetts were, for the most part, contented with their accommodation. In each case, the layout of the flat was critical for what happened subsequently. As an impoverished author Edwin Reardon worked from home, requisitioning the front room for a study. His wife was then obliged to receive visitors in the kitchen-cum-dining-room-cum-parlour: 'and then the servant [a teenage girl who came each day, not a resident domestic] had to be disposed of by sending her into the bedroom to take care of Willie. Privacy, in the strict sense, was impossible, for the servant might listen at the door (one room led out of the other) to all the conversation that went on.'[114] No wonder Amy found the situation unbearable and decamped to her mother's comfortable middle-class villa.

For the Hewetts, social life was lived on the balcony – a part public/part private space – or in the courtyard-cum-playground between each pair of blocks, or in the community space of the street or the pub. Home was only for sleeping and eating. The Eagles squeezed into one room, 'so encumbered with furniture that not more than eight or ten square feet of floor can have been available for movement'. John and his young son slept in the second (middle) room, where the family also took their meals, and the two young Hewett girls occupied the third. When Clara returned home, ashamed of the scars produced by a rival throwing acid in her face, she had to share with her much younger sisters, although her father phrased things the other way round: 'Clara – shall you mind Amy and Annie comin' to sleep here?' In practice, Clara stayed in the third room most of the time: 'Of necessity she had made the acquaintance of Mrs Eagles, but they scarcely saw more of each other than if they had lived in different tenements on the same staircase.'[115] From the isolation of this third room on the top floor of a five-storey block, Clara looks out on the 'modern deformity' of a built environment, disfigured as drastically as her own body by clearance and redevelopment, and unsurprisingly contemplates suicide.[116]

As these examples illustrate, space was not *determinative* of action, but it set limits to what was possible and it interacted with individuals' circumstances and emotions. The apartments and lodgings occupied by Gissing's characters were the same kinds of rooms which Spencer Gore depicted with some sympathy and at least acceptance, if not optimism, in his views painted between 1909 and 1913 of and from his successive lodgings in Mornington Crescent and Houghton Place in Camden Town.[117] Meanwhile, Gore's colleague, Walter Sickert, used very similar spaces to accommodate, at best, lower middle-class boredom, as in 'Ennui' (1914), and at worst, in paintings of drab rooms with reclining female nudes but fully clothed, apparently despairing, men, intimations of rape or violent death (for example in 'Dawn, Camden Town', 'What Shall We Do for the Rent?' and 'L'Affaire de Camden Town', all painted in 1909).[118] Gore and Sickert may have seen different possibilities in these sparsely furnished lodgings, but for both of them space mattered.

Figure 4.8. John Sloan (1871–1951), 'Night Windows' (1910). Etching (24 × 32.2 cm). Whitney Museum of American Art, New York; Purchase 31.832.

Finally, consider the parallels and differences with some of John Sloan's New York pictures, glimpsed from the rear window of his apartment on West 23rd Street. In 'Three A. M.' (1909) two women, possibly prostitutes, are shown chatting while one fries sausages. In 'Night Windows' (1910), one woman reaches out of her window to the washing line, while her neighbour is framed in her open window, undressing (Figure 4.8). In 'The Woman's Page', one of a series of etchings on 'New York City Life' (1905–1906), a working-class woman is absorbed in a newspaper opened at the fashion and fantasy of 'A Page for Women', oblivious of the surrounding chaos: washboard, drying washing draped everywhere, her young son playing on the bed with a cat.[119] All these and more, especially among Sloan's etchings, demonstrated a coincidence of intimacy with anonymity in city life. To Sloan's biographer, many of these 'views-from-the-back-window...push their way into private space, ask us to be interested in what we are taught as polite people to overlook, make the private manifestly public'.[120] But, unlike Sickert's paintings, Sloan's pictures rarely suggest a sense of alienation. His unselfconscious women appear quite at home in their tenement rooms. Although we may be uncomfortable at the voyeurism, we can celebrate the activities that were depicted. Jerusalem was breaking in.

Entr'acte

In this and the preceding chapters I have discussed the representation of modern and modernising cities by political and theological ideologues, by social explorers, census makers and takers, insurance and tax assessors, directory compilers, surveyors, photographers, artists and novelists, considering their attitudes to and understanding of urbanisation as a physical process and urbanism as a way of life. How did they represent the physical structure and functioning of cities at a variety of scales, from the citywide to the room? My presentation has been informed by, but not ruled by, theoretical constructions of the 'production of space' and 'spatial practice', emphasising how the spaces of the city were more than simply empty containers accommodating social and cultural processes. In the chapters that follow, I draw on all the kinds of sources discussed so far in order to focus on a selection of sites of metropolitan modernity – streets, homes, sites of work, of consumption and of communication. My method lays emphasis on the juxtaposition of unlikely neighbours – a modernist novel alongside an insurance atlas, a mortgage register next to a painting. Each chapter exemplifies the argument about 'building bridges' with which I began the book.

5

Improving streets

How can streets be thought of as a 'modern' innovation? My argument in this and the following chapter will focus on the impact of new technologies and new lifestyles on the streets that accommodated them; on the new and often conflicting uses to which streets were put – as instruments of sanitary and moral improvement; as sites for property speculation and economic improvement; as arteries; as sites for commerce (in the street as well as in the buildings that border it); as spaces for social interaction, display and spectacle; as elements in the public sphere where public opinion could be expressed. Some or all of these activities might be contained within streets on greenfield sites, but new or redeveloped streets carved out of the existing built-up area more obviously demonstrated the potential for 'creative destruction' – the reasons for their construction and direction involved the destruction of undesirable, archaic or anachronistic elements of the old urban morphology.

As I argued in earlier chapters, modernisation was not a straightforward replacement of the old by the new. It also involved a revaluation and conservation of certain parts of the old, its reinterpretation as 'traditional' or 'picturesque', as a counterpoint to the truly modern, a material history lesson. Neither the process of modernisation nor the resultant modern forms and processes went uncontested. Streets were both the object of contestation and sites of resistance where alternative cultural and political viewpoints could be expressed. Streets were also a convenient level of generality in which novelists could set their stories – sufficiently specific to denote a social context, but usually sufficiently vague to avoid identifying real people. When George Gissing situated a character in a flat on London's Victoria Street, he was immediately indicating her status and lifestyle. On the other hand, there were hundreds of real flats on Victoria Street; he could not be accused of basing his character on any one. Drawing on de Certeau's contrasting viewpoints, streets could be observed from above, as by planners, social commentators or panoramic novelists, bringing order out of chaos, or they could be experienced by pedestrians, passengers and drivers, reacting to each new sensation. Councillors, aldermen, planners and other city officials might conspire to regulate behaviour on the streets, either directly by legislation or indirectly by social engineering; citizens would respond by adjusting their behaviour or developing forms of resistance. Streets could be sites for more or less dramatic acts of transgression, 'tactics' in de Certeau's terminology. Regulation could have unforeseen consequences.[1]

The reasons for regulation might be purely managerial, reacting to specific problems of traffic congestion or crime, for example, but we might also conceptualise the regulation of urban life in general and the streets in particular in the context of liberal governmentality, Patrick Joyce's 'rule of freedom'.[2] How could inhabitants be converted into citizens who could be trusted to use their freedom rationally and responsibly? Chris Otter has explored the relationship between vision and civility in late Victorian cities, arguing that certain socio-sensual environments were thought to preclude 'the self-government necessary for liberalism as a technology of rule to operate'. Consequently, liberal society 'needed to be built and maintained – wide streets, slum demolition, sewerage and street lighting were all attempts materially to assemble spaces where ruling through freedom could be made possible and visible'. This perspective extends an instrumentalist argument about slum clearance, street improvements and regulation as forms of surveillance and social control onto a new plane in which citizens 'freely formed a new relationship with their senses' as a result of material environmental improvement in which 'sight, movement and civility were privileged', resulting in the pursuit of right liberal values. As illustrations of his argument, Otter discusses attempts to improve air quality – a difficult line to argue, since factory smoke was so often taken as evidence of prosperity and full employment – and the introduction of plate glass – important in the context of street-life not only for enhancing visibility and facilitating shop window displays, but also as noise insulation: 'Plate-glass formed an ample barrier against sound waves. Thus, silent meditation was encouraged, both inside public spaces and into the public from the private.' This leads to his final example – of attempts to control noise, 'recrafting the street into a space where the visual could assume primacy', particularly by producing quieter road surfaces, using wood or asphalt rather than macadam or granite blocks.[3] So Joyce's and Otter's argument takes us from some quite abstract theorising about laissez-faire society to some literally 'down-to-earth' processes in the making of streets.

Another overarching framework is provided by debates about the changing relationship between private space and public space, and the value placed upon public space. Is public space to be defined as 'publicly owned', vested in central or local government in a democratic state, excluding such spaces as pleasure grounds and shopping arcades to which the public have access, but only subject to privately determined rules and regulations, perhaps including the payment of an admission fee? In this case, public space is reduced to public streets, squares, parks and common land. Or is public space defined, not in terms of property but in terms of use? In this case, some popular commercial spaces might be regarded as public, while some publicly owned spaces, such as public parks, might in practice be treated as the private preserve of a subset of the population who effectively monopolise their use.[4] Or is public space to be treated as a component of the 'public sphere': the 'realm of our social life in which something approaching *public opinion* can be formed'?[5] Following this argument, Goheen defines public space as where citizens' 'collective rights to performance and speech are entrenched'.[6] In practice, my interest in this chapter includes some of the privately owned spaces that border on public streets and give them their character, while in the next chapter I focus more directly on questions of rights and performance.

In the context of changing attitudes to working-class domestic space, Martin Daunton argued that the nineteenth century witnessed a transition from a 'promiscuous' to an 'encapsulated' use of space and from a 'cellular' urban morphology to an 'open' structure.[7] In the old arrangement, working-class families shared washing and toilet facilities and lived in dwellings ranged round courts – communal, semi-private spaces which outsiders would be deterred from entering except on business. Alternatively, through streets would be treated as shared, almost private, space by hanging washing across the street or by children using the street as a playground in defiance of any through traffic. By the end of the nineteenth century most newly-built dwellings were self-contained. Even if the toilet was outside, in the backyard, it was private to the householder's family. But the street was now invariably public space, publicly maintained and policed, open to anybody who chose to traverse it. Equivalent changes characterised middle-class environments. Townhouses facing onto communal gardens (semi-private) and located in urban estates where gatekeepers regulated access to the (semi-public) streets gave way to suburban villas surrounded by their own private gardens but generally set on public streets. Wolfgang Schivelbusch argues that, until the nineteenth century, there was no distinction drawn between interior and exterior light in and around the middle-class home. Paintings of bourgeois domesticity by seventeenth-century Dutch artists such as de Hooch show a seamless integration of interior and exterior, as light streams through windows and open doors and along passageways. But from the nineteenth century, artificial gas or electric light was differentiated from outdoor light, whether natural sunlight or artificial street lighting. Outside light shining into the room from the street represented an invasion of the private by the public sphere, prompting more use of curtains, especially lace and net curtains, to keep the public out. Schivelbusch also notes the irony that the sources of indoor light – private power corporations or public utility agencies – were anything but private to the household.[8]

The question then arose as to whether this clearer demarcation between the private and the public led to a devaluation of public space, its conversion into empty space, for which citizens abdicated responsibility: waste space as far as sociability was concerned. According to this argument, the public activities of the street were absorbed into new privately owned or carefully regulated 'public' spaces such as shopping arcades, public halls or amusement parks. Some publicly owned spaces, such as parks, were incorporated into the private sphere, redefined as safely domestic for middle-class women and children hitherto restricted to the more obviously domestic space of the private home. Public streets lost their publicness: streets designed for vehicular traffic became less conducive to social functions; and 'the public' became too diverse, made up of too many 'other' people for any group or for the population as a whole to feel 'at home' on the streets.[9]

My focus in this chapter will be on the streets of London, though there will also be occasional excursions elsewhere. By comparison with the restructuring of Paris under Baron Haussmann, or the 'ringstrasse' in Vienna, London's nineteenth-century street improvements are often regarded as modest and fragmentary. Yet consider the following, partial list (see also Figure 5.1):

Regent Street, 1816–24	Albert Embankment, 1869*
King William Street, 1829–35	Queen Victoria Street, 1871*
Farringdon Road, 1845–6	Chelsea Embankment, 1874*
Commercial Street, Whitechapel, 1845–58	Northumberland Avenue, 1876*
New Oxford Street, 1847	Clerkenwell Road & Theobalds Road, 1878*
Victoria Street, 1851	Tooley Street, 1882*
Garrick Street, 1861*	Shaftesbury Avenue, 1886*
Burdett Road, 1862*	Charing Cross Road, 1887*
Southwark Street, 1864*	Rosebery Avenue, 1892**
Holborn Viaduct, 1864–9	Tower Bridge Approaches, 1899**
Victoria Embankment, 1870*	Kingsway-Aldwych, 1905**

* completed by the Metropolitan Board of Works
** completed by the London County Council

Many other streets were straightened and widened; but those listed above involved large-scale slum clearance or land reclamation. They functioned as acts of social engineering, displacing, redistributing and segregating poor from rich; they relieved traffic congestion and thereby stimulated further traffic growth; by facilitating an increase in the speed of traffic they partitioned the areas through which they passed and changed the relationship between 'traffic' and pedestrians; and they created opportunities for new economic development (improved rateable values, street frontages) and for new forms of sociability.[10]

The Metropolitan Board of Works claimed to have constructed nearly 16 miles of new streets between 1855 and 1888 (including just over three miles of Thames embankments), and in the following ten years the London County Council added

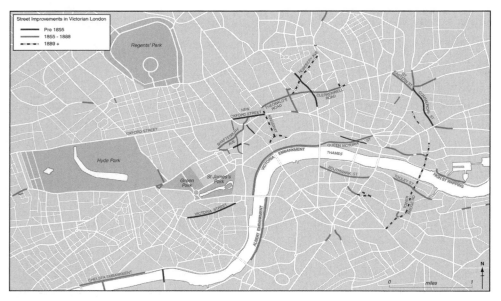

Figure 5.1. Street Improvements in Victorian London.

nearly four more miles. Heroic (and expensive) though many of these undertakings were, carved through densely occupied central and inner-city neighbourhoods, they pale into insignificance by comparison with the building of new suburban streets. In 1889 the total length of streets in London was nearly 2000 miles, and 30 miles of new streets were being added annually.[11]

New streets were also being laid out in the expansion of other cities into suburbia, in the extension of street grids north from Lower Manhattan and away from the Toronto Lakeshore, and in the reclamation of waterfronts extending Manhattan south into New York Harbour and Toronto south into Lake Ontario, more gradual but larger-scale reclamations than those effected by the building of Thames embankments in London. And even in these relatively 'new' cities, there was scope for re-ordering streets within the existing built-up area. In Toronto, minor improvements in the 1910s, eliminating critical 'jogs' in a not-quite-rectangular grid, were accompanied by just as critical name changes: the east-west artery of St Patrick Street, Agnes Street and Wilton Street became one continuous Dundas Street, and St Patrick's name was transferred to a minor north-south street that intersected the old St Patrick's Street. Likewise, Bay Street was extended north along the line of Terauley Street, whose name was reassigned to an adjacent east-west street. Name changes – and resistance to changes – were often attempts to reconstruct the reputation of areas, to expunge memories associated with crime, disease or poverty, or to assert 'ownership' or control.[12] The renaming of Agnes Street as Dundas Street effectively removed it from 'The Ward', then Toronto's most conspicuous slum and 'ethnic' district, giving the street a purposeful, colonial name which differentiated it from the more domestic names attached to adjacent streets – other personal names such as Elizabeth, Louisa and Alice Streets, or names which implied a going-nowhere rootedness such as Elm and Chestnut Streets.[13]

Earlier, Toronto's University Avenue had been fashioned from a carriage drive that ran along the backs of the houses on Simcoe Street, thereby reversing the orientation of their successors. In 1905, 1909 and 1911 there were also grand plans for diagonals radiating from downtown and, in the last of these plans, for a monumental boulevard, Federal Avenue, running north from a new Union railway station to a city square and public gardens which, more probably by design than coincidence, would have involved demolishing much of 'The Ward'. All these proposals imitated then fashionable 'City Beautiful' plans, such as those by Cass Gilbert for Chicago. In practice, none of these major downtown improvements was ever realised, although University Avenue was extended south to Union Station, somewhat west of the line of the proposed Federal Avenue, but not until 1929 (Figure 1.6).[14]

In New York, the generous dimensions of the grid established by the Commissioners' Plan of 1811 left comparatively little scope for new streets. Carriageways were widened to accommodate more traffic, but mostly at the expense of sidewalks, trees and the front gardens of existing houses. Some buildings were demolished in street widening schemes but the pace of 'creative destruction' – replacing old buildings with new – was so fast in many parts of Manhattan that the intervention of municipal authority had little additional effect. As in Toronto, there were plans – in 1899, 1904 and 1907 – for diagonal boulevards and new public squares. Ideas for a diagonal avenue connecting the new Pennsylvania Station (opened in 1910 at Seventh

Avenue and 33rd Street) and the New York Public Library (Fifth Avenue and 42nd Street) were quickly abandoned. Also in 1910 Mayor Gaynor proposed a new avenue between and paralleling Fifth and Sixth Avenues. But the only major modifications to the pattern of north-south avenues to be implemented were extensions southwards of Sixth and Seventh Avenues in the 1920s, where the north-south orientation of the Commissioners' Grid collided with a discordant street pattern in Greenwich Village. Other new streets were the approaches to tunnels under and bridges over the East River, the construction of Park Avenue over the top of the railroad tracks into Grand Central Station, and some early parkways, where the aim was still to provide separate strips for walkers, riders/cyclists and carriages/motor vehicles, for example along Riverside Drive, laid out between 1872 and 1902, overlooking the Hudson. By comparison, later parkways were reserved solely for free-flowing private motor traffic. But the sanctity of private property and the width of streets, even between the tenements of the Lower East Side, meant that there was little slum clearance before 1930, and what there was, for example at Mulberry Bend in the 1890s, did not involve a reorganisation of the street pattern, merely the insertion of public parks in the place of the worst tenement blocks.[15]

Overall, there was a more exclusive objective of reducing traffic congestion in the provision of new streets in New York and Toronto, whereas in London, most street improvements had multiple objectives from the outset. But all streets, new or old, experienced changes in the ways they were used and regulated, and changes in the buildings that bordered them. I will explore these changes using London's Victoria Street as my starting point.

Victoria Street

Victoria Street now extends south-west from Westminster Abbey to Victoria Station (Figure 5.2).[16] But when the street was laid out, in 1850, there were no plans for a major railway terminus at Victoria. One purpose of the new street was to improve connections between the part of the West End around Whitehall and newly developing middle-class suburbs in Pimlico and Belgravia. The existing streets running south-west from Westminster – Tothill Street and York Street – were narrow and congested with commercial traffic and traders. If speculative building, much of it in the hands of London's first really 'modern' building firm – run by Thomas Cubitt – was to be sustained, a more stylish and commodious approach was necessary. It was also in the 1820s and 1830s that Buckingham House, hitherto a relatively modest stately home, was converted into the monarch's principal London residence, Buckingham Palace. There was some concern that the district immediately to its south-east was not a sufficiently salubrious neighbour for a royal palace. Again, the solution was thought to be a new street which would stimulate upgrading of the area. Several plans were made during the 1830s and 1840s envisaging not only a new street but grand terraces, squares and crescents in the area between the street and St. James's Park.

Cubitt's interest was in building terraces of townhouses for single occupancy by well-off families. But Victoria Street itself provided long, if relatively shallow, frontages ideally suited to a different kind of residential development – the building

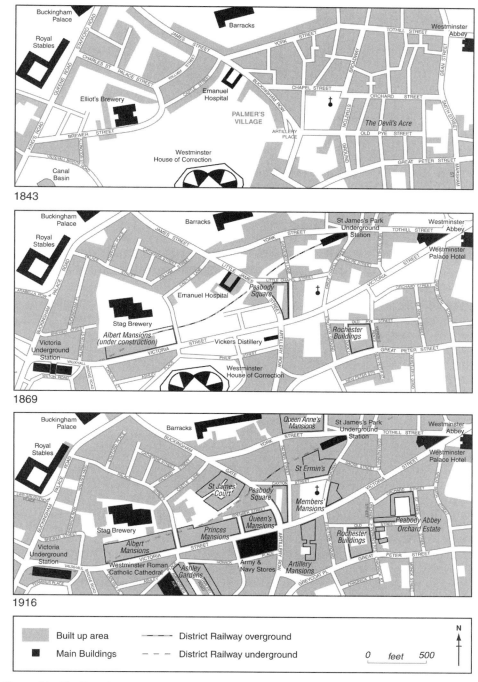

Figure 5.2. The Development of Victoria Street, 1840–1916. Based on B. R. Davies' map, 1843, and 1:2500 O. S. Maps, 1869 and 1916.

of blocks of mansion flats – pieds à terre for businessmen and members of parliament with family homes in the country, and serviced accommodation for bachelors and visitors who required something more than a hotel room. In fact, the building plots bordering the new street were slow to attract developers. Maps from the late 1860s show wide open spaces between occasional blocks of flats or offices. But by the 1890s, a succession of blocks of luxury flats had been erected along the street, including Grosvenor Mansions, Albert Mansions, Prince's Mansions, Queen's Mansions, and Artillery Mansions, with more mansion flats on the adjacent streets – Carlisle Mansions, Morpeth Mansions, Cardinal Mansions and, from 1890 onwards, the spectacular bulk of Ashley Gardens around the site soon to be occupied by a new Roman Catholic Cathedral.

Victoria Street's reputation remained uncertain, not quite respectable. George Gissing positioned the wealthy, young widow, Mrs Luke Widdowson, in a flat on Victoria Street, where she indulged her 'taste for modern exuberance in domestic adornment':

a handsome widow of only eight-and-thirty, she resolved that her wealth should pave the way for her to a titled alliance.... her flat in Victoria Street attracted a heterogeneous cluster of pleasure-seekers and fortune-hunters, among them one or two vagrant members of the younger aristocracy. She lived at the utmost pace compatible with technical virtue.[17]

Ashley Gardens was sufficiently fashionable to feature in a play by George Bernard Shaw, entitled *The Philanderer* (1893), which opens with the stage direction: 'A lady and gentleman are making love to one another in the drawing room of a flat in Ashley Gardens in the Victoria district of London. It is past ten at night.' A postmodern touch is added by the fact that Shaw's leading lady, the actress Mrs Patrick Campbell, really did live in a flat in Ashley Gardens.[18] Inspector Cousins of the nearby Rochester Row Police Station thought there were 'more kept than married women' to be found in Ashley Gardens. Cousins had dealt with 'several cases of one kind or another in queer *ménages* that he has found there' and 'had evidence that second establishments are not uncommon in Ashley Gardens'. In another block, just north of Victoria Street, 'Many of the occupants appear to be of a dubious character not only kept women but some prostitutes living here and that they are "well-dressed" is all that you can say for them.'[19]

Just as bohemian as Mrs Patrick Campbell, Sir Arthur Sullivan (composer of the music for the Gilbert & Sullivan 'Savoy operas') lived first in Albert Mansions, and then, from 1881 until his death in 1900, in a lavishly furnished flat in Queen's Mansions, 'filled with bric-a-brac from all over the world – Persian carpets, silk wall hangings and tapestries, oriental lamps and lanterns, antique Egyptian screens, divans, palms and other potted plants and a parrot'. He was also a domestic telephone subscriber at least as early as 1883, at a time when very few private households had their own phones.[20]

Around the corner from Queen's Mansions was St. James's Court (1896–1905), where the central courtyard includes a spectacular terracotta frieze – scenes from Shakespearean stories – while the entrances to individual staircases are guarded by female 'atlantes'. St. James's Court comprised eight linked blocks of flats with mock medieval names such as 'Minster House', 'Prior's House', 'Falconer's House' and 'Almoner's House', a knowing way of invoking the past in order to distance oneself from it. Both St. James's Court and Artillery Mansions (1895), on Victoria Street itself, also boast elaborate cast-iron fountains in their courtyards.[21]

It is worth emphasising that none of these buildings was on a greenfield site. Artillery Mansions replaced the Artillery Brewery, which in turn derived its name from the pre-modern urban-fringe use of the site for military exercises and target practice. St. James's Court replaced Emanuel Hospital and School – almshouses dating from 1602, the school from 1738 – which moved to Wandsworth, the new south London urban fringe – in 1883. This was a fairly common move on the part of charitable and educational institutions, originally founded on an earlier urban fringe and subsequently migrating to a new fringe belt, financing the move and the construction of new buildings from the sale of the by-now valuable central site. Elsewhere in the same area, the Tate Gallery (now Tate Britain) was erected on the site of Millbank Prison and Westminster Cathedral occupies the site of the Westminster House of Correction, a women's prison that had closed in 1877.

While it was acceptable to live on the ground floor in blocks of flats arranged around courtyards, or on purely residential side-streets, few tenants of flats on Victoria Street itself wanted to live on the ground floor, a window pane away from a busy, noisy street; so street-level premises were let out as shops or offices. According to Charles Booth's researchers, by 1899 there was 'hardly any block of Mansions in which either offices or shop frontages are not creeping in. The latter change is very common, it being the natural transition in such an important thoroughfare as Victoria St.'[22] In time the street also accommodated some larger stores, including the Army & Navy Stores, established in 1871 as a co-operative store for military officers and their families, and taking over a building erected less than a decade before to accommodate a distillery. Membership was at first restricted to army and navy officers, including non-commissioned officers, and their families, to peers and privy councillors, and to a variety of government and colonial officials: 'the sinews of Empire in a single mailing list'.[23] By the mid-1880s there were more than 15,000 shareholders, nearly 5,000 life members and 17,500 annual subscribers.[24] T. H. S. Escott described the impact of the store on the street: 'rows of carriages and cabs, two or three deep' drawn up in front of the store:

Every kind of vehicle that can be bought or hired in London is here – from the open barouche or closed brougham, with their thoroughbred horses, to the carriage jobbed by the month, or let out by the hour, as well as the hansom or four-wheeler. Footmen, grooms and pages are stationed at the doors, through which there pass ladies and gentlemen – some on the point of transacting their business, others having completed their purchases, which are carried by servants to the purchasers' carriages.

The establishment is not only an emporium, but a lounge, a place of gossip and pleasure as well as of business. . . . The place, in fact, discharges not a few of the purposes of a club for ladies and gentlemen; it gratifies the prevailing passion for combining pleasure and business, and gives the customers of the store the satisfaction of knowing that at the same time they meet their friends they are getting their wares – whether it be an ormolu clock or a jar of pickles – at a cheaper rate and of a better quality than they could elsewhere.[25]

It was not until 1918 that the store officially opened its doors to the general public, and not until 1922 that it acquired a street frontage with plate-glass windows that made it look more like a department store than a private club. But its impact on Victoria Street and the surrounding area was substantial, in part because it contributed to, as well as drawing upon, the street's colonial and imperial character. Colonial servants and military officers on leave or retired were disproportionately represented among the area's residents; and in the streets behind the store, warehouses stocked goods that were distributed around the Empire in response to orders from the store's mail order catalogues, and garment factories made and altered many of the items of clothing stocked in the store.

The store also offered a choice of two eating-places – the Nelson and Wellington Rooms. In Virginia Woolf's *Mrs Dalloway* (1925, set on a single day in 1923), Elizabeth (the Dalloways' daughter) and Miss Kilman (her dowdy lower middle-class tutor) took tea in the cafeteria of the Army & Navy Stores. Miss Kilman displayed a childlike passion for cake – 'sugared cakes', 'the pink one', 'chocolate éclair' – clear evidence of her inferior status. When she finally got up to leave, 'she lost her way, and was hemmed in by trunks specially prepared for taking to India; next got among the accouchement sets and baby linen; through all the commodities of the world, perishable and permanent, hams, drugs, flowers, stationery, variously smelling, now sweet, now sour, she lurched.'[26]

This treasure chest of commodities was also displayed cartographically on the insurance atlases of the period, on which materials especially liable to combustion were highlighted. In 1901 the Goad insurance plan for the store indicated 'general fancy show rooms' on the ground floor, 'toys' and 'drugs' in different parts of the basement, 'grocery and provisions' and more 'drugs' on the first floor, then 'drapery', 'books' and 'trunks', ending with 'tailoring' on the fifth floor. Most of the fourth floor was occupied by 'refreshment rooms' (Figure 3.1). Miss Kilman's route, from refreshments past trunks, drapery, grocery and drugs, indicates that very little can have changed in the layout of the store between 1901 and the 1920s, despite the changes to its façade and its clientele. At the rear a subway led beneath Howick Place to the warehouses and workshops along Francis Street. The 1901 plan showed buildings containing 'photo studio', 'gunsmith', 'boots', 'bedding', 'furniture', 'meat' and 'wines and spirits'. A revision of the Goad plan in 1928 marked additional subways under Howick Place and some new departments, such as 'motor car showrooms' and 'jewel workshops'.

Some flats were occupied as offices – by engineers, architects, philanthropic societies: professional men who valued close contact with parliament and government, and whose presence further reinforced the area's links with empire. At the Parliament Square end of the street, Westminster Chambers provided a whole block of small office suites, and the 130-bedroom Westminster Palace Hotel (1861) was one of the first hotels *not* directly associated with travel, in the way that coaching inns had been and railway hotels continued to be. The architects inspected more than thirty hotels in continental Europe before producing their plans which included lifts, 'ample space for business meetings, and separate "gentlemen's and ladies' coffee rooms"'.[27] Several members of Parliament used the hotel as their London home, and Blanchard Jerrold and Gustave Doré were based there while writing and illustrating

London: A Pilgrimage.[28] At the other end of the street, adjacent to Victoria Station, the Grosvenor Hotel (1860) more directly provided for the needs of travellers and newly arrived visitors to London. *The Builder* observed that the hotel was 'almost a little town under one roof'.[29] On the ground floor were private sitting rooms, a large dining room and separate ladies' and gentlemen's coffee rooms, the latter adjoining a smoking room. There was a lift for passengers and luggage, leading to two storeys of family suites, each with its own drawing room and dining room, and several floors of regular bedrooms. There was a bathroom on every floor, except the topmost one, which was intended for servants. In fact, the structure of the hotel offered a cross-section through Victorian society, from the opulence of the lower floors, through middle-class respectability to the servants in the garret.

I have already noted in passing that Victoria Station was not part of the original rationale for Victoria Street. The station occupied the basin of the Grosvenor Canal, a short waterway running into the Thames, that had been convenient for bringing in foodstuffs and, especially, building materials during the construction of Pimlico and Belgravia, but which was little used by the 1850s. Its route provided a convenient entry into the West End, without the need for large-scale demolition of existing buildings. But once the station was functioning, it changed the character of the area, attracting commercial premises, eating houses, and some cheap and less respectable hotels – another form of marginality to add to the cultural bohemianism of mansion flats and the religious marginality of the new catholic cathedral, begun in 1895 only a few minutes' walk from Westminster Abbey, the symbolic centre of the established church. Revising Charles Booth's Poverty Survey in 1898–1899, Booth's assistants accompanied local police officers on walks through their areas. The Victoria end of Vauxhall Bridge Road had 'gone down a good deal since [Inspector Cousins] came, and now has a bad reputation; many of the houses, both those with apartments and those that call themselves hotels, are houses of accommodation; the women who use them mostly live away, many of them in Pimlico, but a certain number of "flash women" are living in the Road.'[30] A painting by the Camden Town artist, Charles Ginner, 'Victoria Station, The Sunlit Square' (1913), looking out from the shadows cast by the railway station, suggests the slightly seedy world of the private detective or the prostitute watching for a client. In the background are mansion flats between Vauxhall Bridge Road and Carlisle Place, and beyond them, the campanile of Westminster Cathedral (Figure 5.3). In fact, the station was really two stations, side-by-side, the West End termini of both the London, Brighton & South Coast Railway and the London, Chatham & Dover Railway. Although the stations were refronted in 1908–1909, it was only in 1924 (following the amalgamation of the companies into the Southern Railway) that a hole was knocked in the wall between them. In Oscar Wilde's *The Importance of Being Earnest* (1895), Jack Worthing recounts that as a baby he was found in 'a somewhat large, black leather hand-bag' that had been deposited in the left-luggage office of Victoria Station. He adds, 'the Brighton line', partly to confirm how he got his surname – Worthing was a destination for LB&SCR trains and the gentleman who found him had a ticket to Worthing – but also to emphasise his respectability: the LC&DR was a much more ramshackle affair, constantly on the verge of bankruptcy, and its station offices were correspondingly more modest than those of the Brighton company.

Figure 5.3. Charles Ginner (1878–1952), 'Sunlit Square, Victoria Station' (1913). Oil on canvas. ©
Atkinson Art Gallery, Southport, Lancashire, UK / The Bridgeman Art Library. Reproduced by
kind permission of Sefton MBC Leisure Services Department, Arts and Cultural Services, Atkinson
Art Gallery.

None of this impresses Lady Bracknell, from whose exalted perspective 'the line is
immaterial'.[31]

The building of the station also turned Victoria Street into a busy thoroughfare,
well served by the early 1900s by an 'excellent motor bus service'[32] and paralleled
by the underground Metropolitan District Railway (opened in 1868), but also full
of strangers making their way into central London. Yet a photograph taken in 1899
suggests a fairly relaxed atmosphere (Figure 5.4). In the windows of the ground floor
flat nearest the camera there is a poster soliciting 'Voluntary Contributions', there
are advertisements for 'suites to let', and there are horse buses, cabs and carters' vans,
but not so many to make crossing the street difficult. There are few pedestrians on
the pavement in front of Prince's Mansions, rather more close to the photographer,
such as the fashionably dressed man with stick and straw hat. Architectural critics
complained that the buildings were too high for the width of the street. Nevertheless,
the street was perhaps the nearest that London came to a Haussmannesque Parisian
boulevard. One can imagine a Pissarro or a Caillebotte discreetly observing passers-
by on the street from the vantage point of an upper-floor balcony;[33] but the street

Figure 5.4. Bedford Lemere, 'Victoria Street' (1899). BL 15472A. Reproduced by permission of English Heritage NMR.

was not wide enough, nor did London mores and by-laws allow for pavement cafes and the self-conscious flâneurs they attracted in Paris.

Traffic

By the 1920s, however, we can envisage a busier, more agitated street. Richard Sennett argues that as travel through the city streets became a faster and more comfortable experience – no more being bounced about on cobbled streets, but the smoothness of a pneumatic tyre on an asphalt surface; no more exposure to the elements on an open top deck or squeezed among strangers of diverse origins and status in the tiny confines of a horse-bus, but a comfortably padded seat insulated from the noise and the weather by a plate-glass window – so travellers were distanced from the areas through which they passed. Either they ignored these areas altogether, their heads buried in books or newspapers, or they viewed them as scenery, urban spectacle, safe behind the window, much as Wolfgang Schivelbusch has suggested of the railway journey as a new way of seeing.[34] 'Public transport' provided a space in which you could be private in public, the interests of passengers divorced from, even opposed to those of pedestrians. If traffic was to flow swiftly and smoothly, people trying to cross the road were a nuisance.

Knowing how to cross the road without, as yet, the aid of traffic lights or pedestrian crossings became a key urban skill. Marshall Berman discusses Baudelaire's poem, 'The Loss of a Halo' (1865): 'I was crossing the boulevard, in a great hurry, in the midst of a moving chaos, with death galloping at me from every side.' But, in contrast to Sennett's emphasis on the anti-communitarian tendencies in the new individualism of the passenger and the pedestrian, Berman stresses the liberating potential of becoming streetwise: 'A man who knows how to move in and around and through the traffic can go anywhere, down any of the endless urban corridors where traffic itself is free to go.' Berman sees the chaos of traffic on the boulevard as 'a perfect symbol of capitalism's inner contradictions: rationality in each individual capitalist unit leading to anarchic irrationality in the social system that brings all these units together'.[35]

A film of London's Cheapside (the heart of the City, near the Bank of England, the symbolic heart of capitalism) in 1903 depicts just such rational chaos of unregulated traffic, compounded by an extraordinary degree of pedestrian indiscipline, as walkers weave in and out of the traffic. Another film, of Seven Sisters Road in North London in 1898, shows pedestrians recklessly making their way around the blind side of trams to board them in the middle of the street.[36] One consequence of the growth of traffic unmatched by changes in pedestrian behaviour was a massively increasing number of traffic deaths and accidents. In 1872, 2677 persons were injured on the streets of London; in 1900, 7730. In 1906, 222 persons died and 15,851 were injured; in 1913, there were 625 deaths and 25,822 injuries. Seven people died in separate incidents in the space of six weeks while trying to cross the junction of Gray's Inn Road and Theobald's Road.[37]

None of this may be apparent in the decorous turn-of-the-century scene on Victoria Street, but we need move forward only a few years to E. M. Forster's *Howards End* (1910):

And month by month the roads smelt more strongly of petrol, and were more difficult to cross, and human beings heard each other speak with greater difficulty, breathed less of the air, and saw less of the sky. . . . In the streets of the city she [Margaret Schlegel] noted for the first time the architecture of hurry, and heard the language of hurry on the mouths of its inhabitants – clipped words, formless sentences, potted expressions of approval or disgust.[38]

Advance another decade to *Mrs Dalloway* and a scene that demonstrates both the dangers of rampant traffic and the freedom available to the streetwise who have learnt another urban skill, knowing how to board the bus 'calmly and competently'.[39] We are back on Victoria Street, where, after her visit with Miss Kilman to the Army & Navy Stores, Elizabeth waits for a bus to take her up Whitehall and along the Strand:

Buses swooped, settled, were off – garish caravans, glistening with red and yellow varnish. But which should she get on to? She had no preferences. Of course, she would not push her way. . . . Suddenly Elizabeth stepped forward and most competently boarded the omnibus, in front of everybody. She took a seat on top. The impetuous creature – a pirate – started forward, sprang away; she had to hold the rail to steady herself, for a pirate it was, reckless, unscrupulous, bearing down ruthlessly, circumventing dangerously, boldly snatching a passenger, or ignoring a passenger, squeezing eel-like and arrogant in between, and then rushing insolently all sails spread up Whitehall.[40]

Elizabeth presumably normally saw London in the company of her parents or their servants, through the windows of a cab rather than amid the social heterogeneity of the top deck of a London bus. The trip took her into unfamiliar territory, neither Westminster, which was her father's domain, nor Bond Street, the luxury shopping street favoured by her mother, but the legal district around the Strand.[41] Deborah Nord implies that this indicates the new arena for the public woman in the twentieth century, neither domestically tied to her husband's territory, nor frivolously consumerist, but independently career-focused.[42]

For the moment, however, I want to stay on the bus. Woolf describes a scene of unregulated liberalism, which in real life had been provoked by the inability of the principal bus operator, the London General Omnibus Company, to meet growing demand. In response, a variety of independent or 'pirate' companies provided duplicate services on popular routes: 'Street accidents soared as drivers raced one another to be the first at a crowded bus stop.'[43] It is clear that Woolf had captured a very particular moment in London's history. London buses carried more passengers than the railways after 1921, and more passengers than the trams after 1923. Post-war materials shortages meant that independent operators were unable to acquire their own buses until 1922. By the end of 1923 there were 159 independent buses on the London streets and by 1925, 556 independent buses (compared to about 4500 buses owned by London General and its associates). But the passing of the London Traffic Act in 1924 introduced regulation of routes and, during the later 1920s, the LGOC was able to take over many of its new rivals.[44] So *Mrs Dalloway*, published in 1925 and set in 1923, precisely captures this moment of competition on the city's streets.

Victoria Street had witnessed another phase of innovation in public transport some sixty years earlier. In 1861 it had been one of three sites chosen by the American, George F. Train, to demonstrate the utility of street tramways, which were already widespread in American cities. However, there were objections that the rails, which stood proud of the street, interfered with ordinary horse-drawn carriages, and all three routes were closed within a few months.[45] When tramways with rails flush with the road surface were at last introduced to London in 1870, they were banned from most of the City and West End. A line ran south-east from Victoria along Vauxhall Bridge Road, but Victoria Street was left prey to the more flexible, but sometimes more anarchic buses just described. A principal form of regulation of tramways in British cities was the Tramways Act (1870) which gave local authorities the right to acquire private tramways operating in their areas once twenty-one years had elapsed from the time when the tramway had first been authorised. In many British cities, where tramways were first constructed during the 1870s, this meant that nearly twenty-one years had elapsed by the time that electrification became feasible in the 1890s; but electrification required massive capital investment – in electricity generation, substations, overhead wires and new rolling stock – to which companies were reluctant to commit themselves, uncertain whether they were about to lose their franchise. In practice, many municipalities exercised the right to take over the running of the trams themselves.[46] In outer London, municipally-owned electric tramways were established by councils in East Ham and Croydon in 1901 and in other, mainly East London suburbs, by 1906. The London County Council exercised its powers of compulsory purchase to acquire horse-tramway companies inside county boundaries, leasing back operation to the private companies while it finalised its plans for electrification, which began in 1903. The transport historian Robert J. Harley argues that the costs of electrification were 'completely beyond the financial capabilities of most of the metropolitan horse tramway companies. Realistically, only the County Council had the wherewithal to instigate and complete such a vast civil engineering scheme.'[47] By 1918, municipal operators in London catered for 647 million passenger journeys (523 million on the LCC's own tramways), while private companies registered 164 million journeys.

Similar legislation in Toronto, allowing the council to assign operating leases for fixed terms, with the right to take over the running of the system itself at the end of the term, had other significant consequences. Here, the franchise passed in 1891 from the Toronto Street Railway Company, which had operated horse-drawn cars, to the Toronto Railway Company, which was granted a 30-year franchise on the understanding that the system would be electrified, ticket prices reduced, and free transfers introduced, allowing passengers to change cars without having to incur a second fare. The system was duly electrified between 1892 and 1894.[48] As in London, new forms of public transport, in conjunction with increased road traffic more generally, necessitated changes in the behaviour of passengers and pedestrians. Horse trams 'had travelled at little more than a brisk jogging pace, between four and seven miles per hour, allowing passengers to board or disembark with little fear of injury even while the tram was moving. Furthermore, horses were living creatures, responsive to the human voice.'[49] The new electric cars ran twice as fast, with less noise (except for the gong sounded to warn of their approach). Their speed and much larger size and weight, meant that they took longer to stop in an emergency. And they adhered more precisely to an advertised timetable, demanding a new time discipline on the part of potential passengers. In essence, pedestrians had to pay more attention and learn to judge time and space more exactly.

The increasing conflict between traffic and pedestrians on city streets was further accentuated by the growth of motorised traffic – in North America following Henry Ford's introduction of the Model T in 1908; in Britain more slowly during the 1920s. From the car driver's viewpoint, two very familiar problems quickly took root: too much traffic caused congestion, reduced speeds and increased journey times; and parking either required off-street facilities such as 'parking apartments' (early forms of multi-storey car park) or reduced the width of city streets available for driving by 33–50 per cent. One way to regulate traffic, on the assumption that more orderly lanes and flows of traffic would also move more quickly, was the introduction of traffic lights.[50]

If we return to London's Victoria Street, we need go no further than the far side of Parliament Square, at Victoria Street's eastern end, to encounter London's (and probably the world's) first road traffic signal – a set of semaphore arms (rather like railway semaphore signals, with red and green gas lights for night-time visibility) – erected in 1868. Like the first trams on Victoria Street, it was not a success and lasted only a few months. Thereafter, traffic regulation was the responsibility of traffic constables, of whom by 1872 there were 176 full-time, supplemented by 230 more in rush hours. It was not until 1926 that the first electric traffic lights were installed in London, at Piccadilly Circus.[51] In the United States there were semaphore traffic signals in Toledo in 1908 and the first, permanent, manually controlled, red-green traffic light in Cleveland in 1914. The first automatic lights (i.e. not controlled by a strategically placed police officer, who both chose when to operate the lights and ensured that drivers obeyed them) were introduced in the early 1920s. New York had 98 automatic lights in 1926, 3484 by 1928.[52] Toronto's first automatic traffic lights were installed at Bloor and Yonge Streets in August 1925 and on Yonge Street between King and Queen Streets by March 1927.[53] James Winter comments that to the laissez-faire Victorians, the street had been a site of equality, 'a democratic island in a sea of privilege and stratified authority'; but regulation promoted inequality, by elevating some people's rights over those of others.[54] In New York, there was no doubting whose interests the system served: on Fifth Avenue 'the lights were topped with small statues of Mercury, the Greek god of speed'. Moreover, it proved easier for motorists than pedestrians to accept control: 'Pedestrians had a more difficult time adapting to the new automatic lights because they faced a new regulation of an old behavior, a more demanding adjustment than facing new rules for new behaviors (like driving).'[55]

Street lighting

The perfection of the traffic signal was just one application of electric light, a technology that had come of age during the 1880s. However, we must beware of exaggerating the significance of electric lighting: many of the claims made for it – that it would reduce crime and make the streets safe for ordinary citizens, and that it allowed the 'colonisation of the night', for example by allowing shops to stay open later – had also been made for gas lighting fifty years earlier. Lynda Nead notes that in London 'public gas lighting extended the hours of social life in the city' but also 'magnified the symbolic significance' of sites of darkness such as the river and the central London parks.[56] West End shops stayed open until at least 8 p.m., suburban shops even later, and the Early Closing Movement, founded in 1842 to campaign for time off for shop workers, blamed gas lighting for the late hours. The attractions of night-time shopping were not just convenience, but related to the *idea* and the *experience* of shopping at night. The same activity, the same commodities and the same public spaces took on new meanings by night. After the Early Closing Movement succeeded in closing shops early, in the 1860s, the streets seemed darker and more dangerous than they had done before there had been any gas lighting. Gas turned the streets into a form of theatrical spectacle, but it also enabled the theatre to dramatise the street. For example, the climax of Boucicault's play, *The Streets of London* (1864), featured a spectacular scene of Charing Cross at midnight.[57] Even those who had not yet ventured onto the streets at night could gain the experience during an afternoon in the safety of the theatre!

Nevertheless, there were important differences between gas and electricity, in the quantity and quality of light. Nead argues that gaslight 'created patches of light interspersed with pools of darkness. Gas seemed to have the power equally to create illumination and to cast shadow.'[58] Whereas gas created oases of light in the dark, electricity abolished the darkness. So gaslight almost *created* the menacing environment of mid-nineteenth-century cities: a flickering light sufficient to encourage citizens to go out, but insufficient to expose what might be lurking in the shadows. On the other hand, electric light could be so powerful that it interfered with citizens' awareness and enjoyment of natural light, such as starscapes and sunsets. Photographs such as Edward Steichen's nocturne of the Flatiron in New York (1904) became less possible by about 1910 because the city was so much brighter at night.[59]

In fact, the night-time experience of public space was shaped as much by the lighting of major buildings that lined the streets as by the street lights themselves. It was electricity that created the night-time skyline. In the 1880s, major buildings would have been barely visible on moonless nights; the streets would have been gaslit, but there were no lights in office buildings after the end of the working day. Irrespective of cost, gas lighting was too unsafe to be left unattended all night. By the 1910s, skyscrapers stood out against the night sky, a blaze of electric lights. In 1907 the Singer Building, then the world's tallest building, became the first skyscraper to be lit at night, a spectacle trumped by the opening ceremony in 1913 for the Woolworth Building, the new 'tallest building', which involved the U.S. President, Woodrow Wilson, pressing a button in Washington, 236 miles away, to switch on 80,000 light bulbs throughout the new building. The upper storeys of both buildings were also soon illuminated by floodlighting.[60] The lighting of skyscrapers was designed to make them look even higher than they were, reflecting the development of verticality as an aim of American commercial architecture, in contrast to the horizontal monumentality of civic buildings that stressed security and trustworthiness rather than assertive power.[61] The phenomenon of a downtown filled with light, horizontal as well as vertical, was all the more impressive because, until after World War I, few residential streets and even fewer private residences were lit with electricity. The contrast was far greater in New York than in European cities. Not only did New York have tall buildings to create an illuminated skyline, but overall the city consumed five times as many kilowatts of electricity per inhabitant on lighting than Berlin or London.

The qualities of different forms of gas and electric light made for very different experiences on the street. Nead suggests that gas 'articulated social difference . . . its flame took on the human attributes of its user', and she contrasts contemporary descriptions of 'the over-cultivated gaslights' of Moses and Son, a firm of London tailors and outfitters, whose shops were criticised for their over-bright gas chandeliers, with 'the raw, unmediated flame of the street butcher' who unscrewed the burners of his gas pipes to create 'great tongues of flame'.[62] More usually, gaslight was described as grey and wavering. It consumed oxygen, raised temperatures uncomfortably, and gave off a mixture of ammonia, sulphur and carbon dioxide, which discoloured paintings and furnishings indoors and left a sooty residue outdoors. However, none of this was worth observing while the only rivals to gas were candles and oil lamps. It was only the availability of electricity that made commentators aware of the deficiencies of gas.[63] According to its context, it could signify modernity and metropolitan improvement or the flames of hell and urban degeneration. In contemporary guides such as George G. Foster's *New York by Gas-Light* (1859) or James D. McCabe's *New York by Sunlight and Gaslight* (1882), gas lighting was synonymous with, at best the theatre, restaurant and bar, at worst crime, gambling and prostitution.

The earliest form of electric light – arc lighting – also flickered, but gave a very bright, harsh and unadjustable glare. If the supply system used alternating current there was a loud humming sound and considerable heat was generated, making arc lighting unsuitable for prolonged use in confined indoor spaces. Early arc lamps also required daily 'trimming' although subsequent technological improvements produced arc lamps which provided up to 350 hours of use. Streets such as New York's Bowery, which had seemed rather seedy under gaslight, took on at least a superficial air of brilliance – 'The air seems supersaturated with electricity, flashing and crackling on every hand' – an atmosphere reinforced by the electrification in 1902 of the elevated railway that straddled each side of the street. Incandescent electric light, introduced by Edison in the early 1880s, was clear and white, but at first seemed less bright to eyes grown accustomed to arc lighting. Initially, incandescent lighting was mainly used indoors, and it was only in the 1900s and 1910s that it started to be used extensively for street lighting.[64]

Gas lighting of the streets had been introduced in London, following a trial in Pall Mall in 1807, and in Manhattan in the mid-1820s. In both cities, despite the argument that gas lighting reduced street crime, there was opposition from residents who feared explosions, especially because gas works were often in the midst of residential areas. For example, in London, the Gas-Light and Coke Company, incorporated in 1812, established its gasworks in Great Peter Street, just east of Victoria Street.[65] An explosion at the London Gaslight Company works in Nine Elms, just south of the Thames, in 1865 not only killed nine men in the gasworks but also substantially damaged houses in the neighbourhood.[66] Nevertheless, progress in installing gas street-lights was impressive: by 1880 there were a million gas lamps on London streets. There was also a small army of lamp-lighters, 380-strong by the 1840s.[67] In New York there were only 384 gas street lights in 1835, and it was not until 1851 that there were more gas lamps than oil lamps. Even in 1892 there were only 27,000 gas street lights in New York.[68]

Electric lighting in London was first experimented with on Westminster Bridge in 1858, but it was not until the late 1870s that arc lighting was applied more widely and permanently – along the Embankment and in public places such as theatres and railway stations (including Victoria Station in 1880).[69] In North America, Philadelphia, Cleveland and San Francisco all had some arc lighting on the streets in 1879. In New York, Brush Electric was authorised in 1881 to erect street lights along Broadway and Fifth Avenue, from 14th to 34th Streets. But arc lighting was too bright, and too expensive, to warrant its general application. Merchants and residents on Fifth Avenue also objected to the unsightly overhead wires connecting the lamps, and the street soon reverted to 'the gloom of gas'.[70] Gaslight, which only a few years earlier had been 'dazzlingly white', 'as bright as day', was now regarded as 'a twilight glow'.[71] It was the invention of the vacuum filament lamp (the incandescent light bulb) by Swan and Edison that stimulated the widespread adoption of electric lighting, though during the 1880s and 1890s, many of the applications were local and indoor. For example, in 1883 the Grosvenor Gallery in London's New Bond Street, celebrated for its exhibitions of 'aesthetic' art, such as Whistler's nocturnes, which must have been especially susceptible to discoloration from coal-gas soot, installed its own electricity generator, quickly expanding its operations in response to requests from neighbouring businesses. The gallery's private operations turned into the London Electricity Supply Company in 1887 with a new power station beside the Thames in Deptford two years later. Another early supplier was the Kensington Court Electricity Company (1886), established to provide electric lighting for an upper middle-class housing scheme – a mixture of Queen Anne-style townhouses and blocks of luxury flats – but subsequently expanding into other parts of West London. These companies functioned under licence in a similar way to private tramway companies: the Electricity Lighting Act (1882) gave them rights to dig up streets or install overhead cables in specified areas, but allowed local authorities to buy them out after 21 (later extended to 42) years. The result was a multiplicity of local companies, supplying electricity in different forms at different voltages.[72] The same was true in New York: while Edison used direct current, Westinghouse employed alternating current, which was initially thought to be more dangerous but allowed electricity to be transmitted over much longer distances from the generating plant.[73]

Toronto began to experiment with electric street lights in 1881 and in 1884 the City Council voted to divide the street lighting contract between gas and electricity. In 1882 the Toronto Industrial Exhibition (the forerunner of the Canadian National Exhibition, and far more leisure-oriented and 'popular' than its name implied) was lit by electricity, allowing the fair to continue each evening until 10 p.m. instead of closing at sunset.[74] By 1893, New York City boasted 1,500 electric arc street lights and, by the turn of the century, nearly 17,000 electric street lamps. Toronto had more than 2,100 arc lamps by 1901, and 18,000 single incandescent lights plus 500 cluster lights by 1911, but many European cities continued to rely on gas lighting. Berlin, for example, had fewer than 700 electric street lights in 1903. By 1913, there were 19,520 arc lamps, 18,000 incandescent lamps, and 46,500 gas lamps on the streets of New York.[75] In the United Kingdom as a whole, gas still retained 92 per cent of the market for urban lighting in 1900 whereas in the United States, where gas had never been so dominant, 41 per cent of urban lighting employed gas in 1900.[76] As these figures imply, conversion from gas lighting to arc electric lighting and from arc to incandescent lighting was a very slow process, and much of the light that illuminated city streets came not from 'street lighting' per se but from indoor incandescent lamps in shops and offices and, from the 1890s, from the proliferation of electric signs and giant advertisements. Conversion to new lighting technologies was an economic decision: not only whether it was more economical to install and operate electric lights, but also whether the consequence would be to attract more people onto city streets at night, generating more income from retail sales and recreational spending. Did lighting raise property values or attract private investment? It took until the second half of the twentieth century before some street lights were converted from gas, meanwhile perpetuating an urban geography of light differentiating between brightly lit, dimly lit and unlit streets.

As with other innovations, electric lighting was not regarded as an unmitigated blessing. There was opposition from established interests (gas companies) but also from moralists. One Toronto clergyman denounced the electric motor as an instrument of evil which threatened to 'release girls from honest toil to wander the streets and fall prey to the wiles of Satan': he presumably wished to continue to confine women to the domestic sphere, and perceived electric lighting, by making the streets safer for women, as a means of liberating them from this confinement.[77]

So how did electric lighting change the use of the streets? Firstly, it was argued that it made the streets safer – for everybody, but especially for women. Everywhere, it was claimed that 'a light is as good as a policeman',[78] a late nineteenth-century version of present-day arguments in favour of closed-circuit television. But if lighting was to prevent crime and immoral behaviour, it had to be the right kind of light. 'Bright lights' might be conducive to immorality, attracting excitable crowds and gullible victims to Times Square or Piccadilly Circus. Visiting New York in 1907, Maxim Gorky thought that visitors to the Coney Island amusement parks had their consciousness 'withered by the intense glow' of the lights.[79] Moreover, the question of safety had become more critical in the wake of suburbanisation, which had led to the abandonment of downtown neighbourhoods by the middle classes. Areas of Lower Manhattan or the City of London which ceased to accommodate night-time residents became more threatening for the handful of people who remained or found themselves stranded after working late in the office. Better street lighting was the antidote to functional segregation.

It can also be argued that the brightness of the new electric lights made the unlit places even darker, and increased fear of the 'city of dreadful night'. This applied at the scale of individual shadows, where lights might be too infrequently spaced to illuminate every corner and alley, as well as to the contrast between well-lit downtowns and ill-lit or unlit suburbs and slums; and by floodlighting particular buildings, others might be obscured – in Jakle's phrase, landscapes could be 'visually edited'.[80] David Nye comments that lights erased 'unattractive areas and cast everything unsightly into an impenetrable darkness. If by day poor or unsightly sections called out for social reform, by night the city was a purified world of light, simplified into a spectacular pattern, interspersed with now-unimportant blanks.'[81] As with so many other aspects of modernity, the introduction of electric light accentuated patterns of differentiation and segregation between the lit and the unlit, the safe and the unsafe, the haves and the have-nots.

And yet, electric light was celebrated as a 'colonisation of the night' to be enjoyed, or suffered, by all social classes. 'Natural' rhythms of long summer evenings and winter darkness could be ignored and a new uniformity of routine introduced. If gas had allowed the extension of shopping hours, arc lighting offered even more ways of enjoying the night. A floodlit football match at Toronto's Jarvis Street Athletic Grounds in 1885 ended with victory by Toronto over New York, 2–1![82] At Coney Island 'electric bathing' by arc lamps preceded the exploitation of electricity to power the chain of amusement parks that were established from 1897 onwards. These amusement parks often copied or acquired exhibits first used in world's fairs such as the Chicago World Columbian Exposition of 1893. Such exhibitions used electricity on a grand scale – searchlights at the Chicago fair consumed three times as much electricity as was used to light the city's streets – and commentators stressed that visitors were missing out if they failed to attend at night.[83] Not only could shops stay open later, but shop window displays could safely remain illuminated even when stores were closed and unattended. Window-shopping became a new reason for visiting downtowns at night. Marshall Field's store in Chicago installed electric lights in 1882 and a generation later, Field's erstwhile manager, Gordon Selfridge, opened his

Figure 5.5. 'Selfridge's by Night' (1909). Reproduced by permission of Selfridges and the History of Advertising Trust.

purpose-built store on London's Oxford Street, celebrating its illuminated window displays in spectacular advertising (Figure 5.5).[84]

Theatres, vaudeville (music) halls, cinemas and even churches used electric lighting to draw attention to themselves.[85] Neither Piccadilly Circus nor Times Square was worth a second glance as an architectural attraction, but their illuminated advertisements created a new form of architecture. In the former, some businesses, such as the Monico Restaurant, had modest illuminated signs advertising themselves by as early as 1893, but by 1910 electric signs advertising products unconnected with the buildings to which they were attached had been erected: 'Bovril' and 'Schweppes', followed by 'Perrier' and, in photographs just after World War I, for cigarettes and newspapers. Despite the LCC's opposition, it was powerless to prevent their erection.[86] In New

York, the first giant electric sign was erected on the roof of a building on Broadway just south of Madison Square. The Municipal Art League complained at the subsequent commercial degradation of the environment and there were proposals for non-commercial electric art on Broadway. Fifth Avenue merchants agreed to ban large illuminated signs, but the city's 1916 Zoning Law confirmed the legitimacy of giant signs (up to 75 feet high on fireproof buildings) downtown. In Times Square some relatively low-rise business premises, not worth redeveloping until land values increased, proved ideal for illuminated signs mounted on the roof – at just the right level for viewing from the street. Perversely, therefore, it was the marginal, low-grade, low-value built environment which made the square ideal for electrical architecture and, at least in the short term, it was more profitable for property owners to rent out space for signs than to redevelop their land. In seven years prior to 1924, the Wrigley Company spent more than $700,000 in renting space at Times Square for a sign advertising Spearmint chewing gum.[87]

David Nasaw opened his essay on 'Cities of Light, Landscapes of Pleasure' by interweaving references to Theodore Dreiser's realist novel, *Sister Carrie*, and Frank Baum's childhood fantasy, *The Wizard of Oz*, both published in 1900. He noted that Carrie, on visiting downtown Chicago, was 'dazzled by the brilliancy of the wonderful city', words that Baum used to describe Dorothy's reactions to Oz.[88] Electricity also weaves its way through the New York sections of *Sister Carrie*. When Carrie accompanies her new friend, the upwardly mobile Mrs Vance, to Sherry's restaurant at Fifth Avenue and 28th Street, she observes the incandescent lights: 'the reflection of their glow in polished glasses, and the shine of gilt upon the walls combined into one tone of light which it required minutes of complacent observation to separate and take particular note of'.[89] Their dinner party includes Mrs Vance's cousin, Mr Ames, who is 'connected with an electrical company'.[90] Some years later (in the mid-1890s), Ames is revealed as having invented 'a new kind of light'. At the mention of his name, Carrie's eyes 'lighten clearly' and Mrs Vance describes him as 'as bright as he can be'.[91] When Ames and Carrie meet again, his talk is of exploiting one's natural powers: 'Every person according to his light.'[92] Meanwhile, Carrie's erstwhile lover, Hurstwood, who has exhausted his powers, sees her name 'blazing, in incandescent fire', up in lights at the theatre where she now has a starring role, but when he tries to see her in person, he is turned back at the stage door.[93] For him she is now merely a spectacle.

The connection between electricity and spectacle is also reflected in the increasing use of words like 'electrifying' or 'highly charged' to mean 'exciting'. Electric light not only enhanced theatrical 'shows'; often it *was* the show. Or the street became a stage-show in its own right: visiting the 'Great White Way' (Broadway through the department store and theatre districts) could be as entertaining as visiting a Broadway show.[94] Schivelbusch refers to 'the illuminated window as stage, the street as theatre and the passers-by as audience – this is the scene of big-city night life'. The brightly lit street assumed the character of 'an interior out of doors', the surrounding darkness equivalent to the walls and ceiling bounding a lit interior or stage set.[95]

Electric lighting was supposed to make the streets safer, but initially it had the opposite effect. Just as pedestrians had to learn how to adjust to automobiles and traffic lights so, more generally, both pedestrians and motorists had to adjust to the stimuli of the illuminated night – not to be distracted by flashing advertisements, illuminated shop windows or the glare of oncoming lights. The provision of electric headlamps on motor vehicles encouraged motorists to drive faster. So the balance of power shifted in favour of car drivers. We can speculate that this shift was more pronounced in North American cities than in Britain, where rates of car ownership lagged behind. Nevertheless, the trend towards different kinds of streets – streets for traffic separate from streets for sociability – was reinforced.

Electric lighting was just one aspect of the electrification of the street. I have already referred to electric trams/streetcars. Publicly displayed electric clocks contributed to the new emphasis on time discipline; the electric telegraph, telephone and telex machine (to which I will return in the final chapter) not only contributed to the visual landscape of the street – telegraph and telephone wires or underground cables and public call boxes – but also, indirectly, generated the 'ticker-tape' (the output of telex machines) used to festoon political and celebratory parades through city streets.[96]

Technology and street furniture

But some technological innovations impeded the progress of traffic and pedestrians. New technology offered more scope for street furniture: drinking fountains, lamp standards, public toilets, police and telephone call boxes, clock towers, postboxes. But they all cluttered up the pavement (or the road), creating obstacles to the smooth circulation of people and, indirectly, by reducing the efficiency of movement, of money. The 1869 1:1056 Ordnance Survey plan marked a drinking fountain in the middle of Vauxhall Bridge Road just south of the junction with Victoria Street, a cabstand outside the new Metropolitan District Railway underground station, and an octagonal urinal *in the middle* of the intersection of five roads. By 1894 the drinking fountain had been displaced to a new, but still middle-of-the-street, location, closer to the underground station; and by 1916 there was a new, underground, public lavatory in the middle of the Vauxhall Bridge Road junction, next to the 'Little Ben' clock tower which had been erected in 1892. The maps also indicated less obvious items: two 'standpipes', lampposts in the middle of the street, and several 'pillar letter boxes' along the length of Victoria Street.

Cast-iron urinals and more elaborate underground public conveniences were constructed from the 1880s, though facilities for ladies lagged behind those for men, and their provision offers an intriguing measure of the acceptability of women into the public space of the street. William Taylor traces the provision of 'comfort stations' on the streets of New York at the beginning of the twentieth century. In most places, for most of the nineteenth century, the only 'public' toilets apart from those in hotels and department stores were situated in bars. But, as today, many who used such facilities also felt obliged to buy a drink at the bar. A survey in St Louis in 1908 estimated that more than 30 per cent of saloon-bar trade originated with customers who had entered the bar in order to use the toilet facilities. So the campaign for public toilets was part of a moral crusade as well as the provision of a public good. Nor was the morality simply a matter of temperance. The links between saloons and 'boss politics' meant that gullible or easily influenced patrons might end up as servants of corrupt political dynasties (much as happened to Jurgis Rudkus, the immigrant worker in Upton Sinclair's *The Jungle*). So it was important to install public toilets in working-class districts and market halls as well as on upmarket retail streets. Taylor notes that the committees that advocated lavatories and public baths were often the same as those that debated rapid transit. In their minds they imagined a public that was both mobile and embodied.[97]

By 1907, New York had built eight 'comfort stations'. In eleven months during 1907–1908, they were patronised by more than 8 million men, but only 1.27 million women. By the early 1920s, the ratio of male to female users had dropped to about 3:1, the continuing disparity probably reflecting the lack of sufficient facilities for women rather than any lack of demand. By comparison with British cities, American cities lagged behind in this field of public utility: in 1895, for example, Philadelphia had five public toilets while the slightly smaller city of Liverpool had more than 200.[98]

But even this provision was not regarded as an unmitigated blessing. In Melbourne, for example, the first men's urinals were erected in 1859, discharging directly into the street gutter below. But by the end of the nineteenth century such above-ground public urinals upset nearby property owners (presumably for their effect on property values as much as hygiene since, by then, many urinals had been connected to the city's sewerage system). Melbourne's first underground toilets – and the first of the city's public toilets to make provision for women – were opened in 1902.[99] In London, a Ladies' Sanitary Association had been set up in the 1850s, prompting a report by the Medical Officer for Paddington in 1879 emphasising that women's need for public toilets was even greater than men's, and that women were tempted into unnecessary purchases (not, in this instance, in bars but in restaurants, milliners' and confectioners') just so that they could use the toilets.[100] The Châlet Company, a private concern, had built women's lavatories in provincial cities, and in Bethnal Green (East London) and Ludgate Circus (in the City) in 1882, but claimed that elsewhere in London their plans had been opposed by local Vestry Boards (London's local government authorities).

By 1900 St Pancras Vestry had provided at least seven public conveniences for men, but only two for women. Opponents to the provision of female toilets in the heart of Camden Town claimed they would be a traffic hazard and cause a reduction in property values; but, in Barbara Penner's reading, the central, albeit unspoken, issues involved class and sexuality. Middle-class women were thought (by a male vestry) to have no need of public toilets in a suburban locality, as Camden then was: they could use facilities in their own homes, or in restaurants. The provision of a women's convenience would encourage locally employed factory girls to linger in public space, to their moral detriment.[101] In Bayswater, too, plans for public toilets (men's as well as women's) met with objections from local residents who argued that they would attract strangers and act as magnets for prostitution.[102]

New streets and old slums

Public toilets, drinking fountains and water troughs were part of nineteenth-century *scientific* and *sanitary* discourse about improvements in public health. For all its impact on property values and its accommodation of new kinds of traffic, new technology, new buildings and new lifestyles, Victoria Street had also been planned as an exercise in sanitary and moral engineering, a space of destruction as well as construction. Questioned on his choice of route, the architect James Pennethorne explained that, more important than 'the means of local communication, or of architectural ornament or development' was 'the sanatory question': 'My object has only been to ascertain how best to improve the condition of the inhabitants of Westminster by improving the buildings, the levels, and the sewers, and by opening communications through the most crowded parts.'[103] Early illustrations of the street under construction show it as a causeway raised several feet above the low-lying, badly-drained, unhealthy area that lay between Westminster (in medieval times, Thorney *Island*) and Belgravia. Writing in 1850 Thomas Beames noted that a 'considerable portion of the "City of Westminster" lies under high-water mark'. Palmer's Village, for example, lay 12½ inches below high water.[104] Not only was the street intended to act as the stimulus to drain the area, but also it was routed to necessitate the demolition of slum property – a classic example of George Godwin's message about 'town swamps and social bridges'. The street was designed with a slight angle roughly half-way along its length. In this way it could be routed through a disreputable area known as the Devil's Acre.

In similar fashion to Victoria Street, New Oxford Street sliced through the St Giles' rookery, and at the beginning of the twentieth century, Kingsway and the Aldwych targeted disreputable slum areas such as Clare Market and Holywell Street. In practice, as Engels noted of Manchester, slums were not eliminated, but displaced;[105] and the reduction in the quantity of low-rent property and its replacement by high-rent shops and flats often served to worsen living conditions for those who had occupied the slums. The Bishop of London told the House of Lords that five thousand persons had been displaced by the building of Victoria Street, three-quarters of whom moved into already overcrowded districts south of the Thames, while the remainder crowded into existing houses in Westminster. Reporting this information, the journalist, John Hollingshead, added his own gloss:

The diseased heart was divided in half – one part was pushed on one side, and the other part on the other, and the world was asked to look upon a new reformation. A great city, a leprous district, is not to be purified in this manner by a Diet of contractors; and the chief result has been to cause more huddling together. While the nightmare street of unlet palaces was waiting for more capital to fill its yawning gulf, and a few more residents to warm its hollow chambers into life, the landlords of the slums were raising their rents; and thieves, prostitutes, labourers, and working women were packed in a smaller compass.[106]

The transformation of the Devil's Acre was also hinted at in Gustave Doré's stylised illustration of the area in 1871 (Figure 5.6). A courtyard of mean, pinched low-lying houses lay in the rear of slightly more substantial houses (with tall chimneys) that fronted onto Old Pye Street. Yet while the density of occupancy must have been horrendous within this cluster of houses, there was open, waste ground in the left foreground of the picture. This was part of the 'cordon sanitaire' which had been cleared on either side of Victoria Street during its construction and remained undeveloped until the 1880s. Hollingshead had described the yards at the back of the houses in Pye Street as containing 'little mountains of ashes and vegetable refuse'

Figure 5.6. Gustave Doré (1832–1883), 'The Devil's Acre', from G. Doré and B. Jerrold, *London: A Pilgrimage* (London, 1872).

and 'the hilly playgrounds for this hopeful colony' which were the sites adjacent to Victoria Street, 'down by the arches of the roadway' (indicating that, where exposed, the road still ran several feet above the surface of the surrounding area).[107] Density was not to be measured in persons per acre, but in persons per room. The Devil's Acre was contrasted in Doré's illustration with the bulk of Rochester Buildings on the far side of Old Pye Street, the earliest philanthropic housing project in the area, erected by William Gibbs in 1862 and sold by his widow to the Peabody Trust in 1877. Jerrold's text accompanying the illustration also emphasised the proximity of Westminster Abbey, and the way that the slums had become more visible since the construction of Victoria Street: 'The solemn and venerable is at the elbow of the sordid and woe-begone. By the noble Abbey is the ignoble Devil's Acre, hideous where it lies now in the sunlight!'[108] On the one hand Doré and Jerrold were making the point that misery was to be found only yards from the heart of the Establishment; on the other, that a solution was at hand in the form of philanthropic housing. Of course, this was also a very convenient slum for them to depict; as I have already noted their base was in the Westminster Palace Hotel, itself no more than 2–300 yards away.

Census enumerators' books for 1851 indicate the character of common lodging houses on Old Pye Street, the heart of the surviving Devil's Acre. On one page of the census the twenty entries included five 'beggars', two 'beggar bricklayers', one 'labourer beggar', one 'needlewoman beggar', one 'hawker', one 'labourer brick-layer', and one 'errand boy'. Fifteen of the twenty were initially entered as 'birthplace: n.k. [not known]', but 'n.k.' was later crossed out and replaced with 'Ireland'. The enumerator annotated the page: 'I have shown these N.Ks. to Mr Keith [presumably his superior] and he does not consider it wrong to have taken them as Irish.' – a neat example of the assumption and inference that lies behind what we too often take to be statistical 'truth'. On the same street forty years later, when the 'Irish' rookery had at last been replaced by Peabody Buildings, almost everybody was in regular employment and almost nobody was 'Irish'.[109]

As Engels had also noted in 1840s Manchester, poverty was now hidden, out-of-sight and out-of-smell behind the new main-street façades.[110] This is illustrated on the first (1889) edition of Charles Booth's poverty map. For all its suspect sexual morality, Victoria Street was coloured gold, the 'best' category in Booth's survey. Model dwellings erected by the Peabody Trust on side-streets just off of Victoria Street were coloured pink or grey, the colours of modest respectability, just the right side of the poverty line. But there were also areas of blue and black – slums that had proved resistant to reform or into which the poorest had retreated (Figure 3.4).[111] In the Booth notebooks, Vandon Street (between Victoria Street and St. James's Park) was listed as '"very low class"; some rough girls skipping in the roadway were described by [Police Inspector] Cousins as "a fair sample" of the people living on this spot'. By contrast, the notebooks enumerated the Peabody estate only a hundred yards away, 'in the courts of which the numbers of clean and healthy children were noticeable'. On the other (south) side of Victoria Street, Booth's investigators reported on Chadwick Street: '2 and 3 storey houses; black and grimy; open doors, dirty children and bad-faced women; all the normal signs of physical neglect and moral degradation'. Inspector Cousins 'appeared to think that thieving and prostitution were the chief occupations of the people'. Whenever they passed the public house on the corner of Great Peter Street and Chadwick Street, there were 'groups of vulgar, fat, slatternly, lowest standard women gossiping round, some doubtlessly from Chadwick St itself'.[112]

Apart from the casual assumption of guilt – 'some doubtlessly from Chadwick St itself' – perhaps the most intriguing phrase in this description is 'open doors'. Leaving your front door open was not a sign of sociability or confidence in your neighbours, but of promiscuity. And if you invited a promiscuous use of your own physical space, *doubtless* you were also promiscuous with your and other people's bodies and possessions. More generally, deportment and behaviour on the street were assumed to signify the existence of 'slums' and slum populations. Back in 1861 Hollingshead had commented on Pye Street that

A child, dirty and nearly naked, was hanging out of one of the old-fashioned casement windows; and in the summer time it is no unusual thing to see about fifty coarse women exhibiting themselves in the same manner. . . . Short-haired young men, with showy handkerchiefs round their neck, and tight corduroy trousers, were standing at most of the doors, looking pretty sharply about them from under the peaks of their caps. A fiddler was playing a dancing tune to a mixed assembly of thieves and prostitutes, and a morning ball was being arranged on both sides of the pavement.[113]

This passage, implying that the inhabitants were doing the wrong things – 'hanging out', 'exhibiting themselves', 'standing', 'dancing' – in the wrong way – 'showy', 'tight', 'pretty sharply', 'under the peaks of their caps' – in the wrong place – 'on both sides of the pavement' – at the wrong time – 'morning' – illustrates Joyce's and Otter's argument about visuality and liberal reform just as clearly as any description of the decaying environment.

It is an inference not restricted to London. In Toronto, British sanitary inspectors and reformers regarded 'The Ward' as a slum in part because they could not come to terms with how eastern and southern European immigrants treated the streets. Harney and Troper refer to a 'pre-urban approach to the use of city space . . . a tendency . . . to lose sight of the distinction between public and private property'. This was apparent, for example, in appropriating lanes and sidewalks to store or display junk, old iron, bottles or foodstuffs, or simply in spending time 'hanging out' on street corners in discussion, or playing cards or dice, or sleeping outside on verandahs on hot summer nights.[114]

The same was true of the Lower East Side in New York, where the overcrowding was not restricted to the human population. In Howells' description of a street through which Basil and Isabel March, his middle-class protagonists, are driven accidentally while house-hunting in New York, 'the roadways and sidewalks and doorsteps *swarmed* with children; women's heads seemed to show at *every* window'. The shops were '*abounding* in cabbages' and 'ash barrels *lined* the sidewalks and garbage heaps *filled* the gutters'. The impact was not only visual but aural and olfactory: a peddler 'mixed his cry with the joyous screams and shouts of the children and the scolding and gossiping voices of the women' but 'It was to the nose that the street made one of its strongest appeals, and Mrs March pulled up her window of the coupe.'[115] Every sense told the Marches they were out of place. If they had been tourists, or even if they had been established in their own permanent home in another part of Manhattan, they could have viewed the scene voyeuristically or picturesquely, as a kind of stage set for their entertainment, much as travellers now viewed the scene through the windows of the train or the bus. But at this point in the story the Marches are still insecure transients, house-hunting; they have an uncomfortable affinity with people so different from themselves yet also so similar in their provisional and uncertain marginal status as (im)migrants.

In each city, noise was both a way of identifying slums, particularly if it was unintelligible to the hearer, and a proper subject for regulation. In New York a ban on street cries was introduced in 1908,[116] a measure linked to attempts to regulate street trading (see Chapter 6). Much earlier, but just as unsuccessful, was legislation in London in 1864 for the 'Better Regulation of Street Music Within the Metropolis'.[117] The residents of fashionable areas particularly complained about street cries and street musicians whose disruption of peace and quiet was for commercial ends. But the sounds of sociability among working-class citizens could be equally disturbing to middle-class commentators. An article in *Saturday Night* in 1905 described an early evening stroll through 'The Ward' in Toronto. The British Canadian walkers passed hundreds of children, 'screeching at play; fighting at ball; rolling in the dry garbage of the street; promiscuous, happy and unwashed'. Next they encountered 'a score of women, some busy, others gossiping in Yiddish or Russian . . . while the bearded men folk stood about in groups jabbering near the alleyways'. Finally, in 'the Italian precinct', 'The street was even more noisy here. The men smoking in groups talked faster; the women laughed more; the children were even more animated, and from sundry windows came the noise of disgruntled accordions.'[118] Not only was this extrovert behaviour contrary to British moderation, but there is a suggestion, explicit in contemporary debates about eugenics, that exuberance signified fecundity: the take-over of hitherto British Toronto by fast-growing 'others'.

The implication of these *male* reports of unintelligible noise is that liberal governmentality needed to involve aural as well as visual regulation. Ellen Ross notes that *female* visitors to slums were more likely to listen than to look, to eavesdrop on conversations, to draw their conclusions about the need for reform from the *content* rather than simply the *sound* of slum dwellers' speech. She argues that 'Urban poverty, when "heard", appears less exotic and dangerous than when it is "seen": more human, familiar and pathetic.'[119] For present purposes, her interpretation has to be qualified by the fact that most male observations were outdoors, on the street, while most female conversations were indoors, in domestic settings. It was extremely difficult for middle-class women to dress down in order to mix unobtrusively on working-class streets in the way that male explorers like Jack London could do. Men who dressed down achieved anonymity as part of the crowd, no longer fearful that they would attract attention as potential targets for robbery or assault. Women who dressed down subjected themselves to sexual harassment that working-class women were usually able to take in their stride. The exception that proves the rule was Olive Malvery, an Anglo-Indian journalist whose excursions onto the London streets in 1904–1905, disguised as a tramp, gypsy flower girl or organ grinder, were as interesting as experiments in visual identity as for what they revealed about the lives of real women tramps or street traders.[120]

The streets so far

Focusing in part on London's Victoria Street and its environs, I have discussed the role of streets in accommodating new land uses and providing sites for the introduction of new technologies, and I have also alluded to streets as instruments of slum clearance, diverting to consider representations of life on the streets of slum districts, representations which constituted part of the case for why new streets were necessary. The consequences of new technology including new forms of sanitation, transport and lighting were felt not only on the streets in which they were introduced, where they stimulated competition between different users, most obviously between pedestrians and vehicular traffic, and led to new pressures for functional segregation and specialisation, but also in areas of cities that were denied these innovations, that were made relatively more or less accessible, more or less attractive, more or less safe.

In London, the scale of residential segregation around new streets such as Victoria Street was still what we might think of as 'pre-modern', front street-back street. The very poorest, who depended on begging (or stealing), street-selling, and casual labour – on building sites, for example – could not afford to move far from the sites of possible earnings; and the very rich followed a labour-intensive lifestyle which required an army of service workers – builders, cabinetmakers, upholsterers, painters, plumbers, gas fitters, coachmen, ostlers, gardeners, cleaners, cooks, messengers, errand boys, newspaper vendors, butchers, bakers, grocers and greengrocers, fishmongers, delivery boys, dressmakers, tailors, haberdashers, laundresses ... – few of whom were *resident* domestic servants living in the homes of the rich. Hence the functional attraction of blocks of model dwellings, separate from but close to the blocks of mansion flats. But in cities rapidly increasing in population, including through immigration, this functional convenience was also a cause of discomfort for the rich. The relationship of rich households to most of the poor who lived nearby was not the personal or paternalistic one of employer or customer, but an anxiety at the proximity of an anonymous and transient urban mass. One consequence was a desire on the part of the elite for new forms of regulation and a change in the publicness of street life. If the planning and construction of streets corresponded to Lefebvre's 'representations of space' and their implementation through the spatial practices of new technologies, street *life* involved thinking about streets as 'spaces of representation' worked out in the spatial practices of various kinds of 'street people', including the flâneur/ flâneuse, the prostitute, the demonstrator, the rioter, as well as less marginal, more routine occupiers of the streets. It is to the relationship between regulation, performance and resistance that I turn in the next chapter.

6

Public spaces – practised places

In Chapter 5 I suggested that the question 'who (or what) were streets for?' increasingly centred on the competing demands of traffic and pedestrians. One form of mediation was the introduction of traffic regulation; another was the gradual acquisition of new skills and forms of behaviour – how to cross the road, how to catch the bus, how to drive safely. But modernisation of the streets prompted other kinds of competition and conflict triggering demands for regulation and stimulating new ways of behaving in and using public space. Among issues that demand particular attention are the gendering of street life and the right to access and occupy public space.

Regulating access

I ended Chapter 5 by noting a fear on the part of the better-off, especially those whose wealth was vested in property, whether as owner-occupiers or long-term tenants, that public streets were becoming too public – anybody, any class, sex, occupation, ethnicity, had free access to public space. If the 'wrong' kinds of people were on the streets of one's neighbourhood, both one's privacy and, potentially, the value of one's property, might be threatened; so, it might be argued, outsiders should not be provided with excuses to intrude on spaces that local residents regarded as at least semi-private – private to themselves, their neighbours and people they invited in. In eighteenth- and nineteenth-century London the solution to this problem was the private street, demarcated by gates and bars, and policed by gatekeepers. There were private bars on each of the streets leading north out of King's Road into Belgravia, and other bars on streets on the north and west sides of the area. Similarly, there were bars on several roads at the margins of the Duke of Bedford's estate in Bloomsbury. These were rarely completely secure 'gated communities' to which access was *impossible* without a key or the approval of the gatekeeper. Rather, the aim was to exclude through traffic and to deter casual interlopers. In Belgravia, local residents insisted on the maintenance of the bars, which had been erected by Thomas Cubitt, the developer, but the ground landlord, the Marquis of Westminster, was sympathetic to the interests of the general public and inclined to dismantle them. In Bloomsbury, residents and estate managers concurred on the need to defend the neighbourhood.[1]

Atkins calculates that there were never fewer than 200 barriers across streets in London between 1867 and 1897. Most were located in the West End, around the edges of the great aristocratic estates, but there were also increasing numbers in better-off suburbs such as Hammersmith, Camberwell and Sydenham. There were no barriers in the East End, and few in the rest of east or south-east London, except for Woolwich (which was a focus of lower middle-class and 'artisan elite' residence with a higher rate of homeownership than other parts of suburbia).[2] But increasing antagonism to such elitist control of space prompted campaigns for the removal of gates and bars by the last quarter of the century. Local vestries – especially St Pancras Vestry in the case of the Bedford estate – were often in the forefront of reform, claiming to represent public opinion in challenging bastions of privilege. As in so many areas of urban management in London, however, it required the creation of the London County Council before action was taken. Acts of parliament in 1890 and 1893 disposed of 63 bars, and the London Building Act in 1894 forbad the erection of any new barriers.[3]

These actions may appear to run contrary to what I have been arguing: they allowed outsiders in rather than keeping them out; they constituted a challenge to elite privilege. However, they matched the modernist project inasmuch as removal of bars resulted in a clearer distinction between 'public' and 'private' space, with fewer ambiguous, semi-private or semi-public spaces in between. And they were accompanied by stricter building regulations, and the introduction of 'town planning' legislation in Britain and of 'zoning' in North America, to ensure a homogeneity of use and quality within neighbourhoods which generally worked to maximise property values. Moreover, they paralleled a withdrawal of elite groups from single-family dwellings fronting on central-city streets, either moving out to remote suburbs, putting distance between themselves and 'others', or moving into blocks of luxury apartments, reinstating the street barrier in the form of a concierge or early form of entryphone. It has taken another hundred years before the revival of 'gated communities' in British cities, mostly in the context of a return to inner-city living by highly paid professional and business people, but again prompted by fear of strangers. In North American cities, where (apart from in Manhattan) there have always been much higher rates of private homeownership, triggering a defence of property values as well as privacy, there has been a more continuous history of deed restrictions, zoning regulations and gated communities, reflecting too the lower priority attached to public space outside of commercial downtowns.

Regulating trade

Another area of regulation in which the state became increasingly active was the control of street trading. Here we can return, at least briefly, to Victoria Street. Henry Mayhew recorded 119 costers 'usually attending' the street market at 'Tothill-street and Broadway'. This was by no means London's largest street market – Mayhew counted 300 costers in New Cut, just south of the Thames near Waterloo, another 300 in the Brill, just north of Euston Road, and 258 in Whitechapel – but it was an important surviving remnant of a market that had been disrupted by the building of Victoria Street.[4] Street 'improvements' targeted commercial disorder as much as residential disorder. One part of this market, on the south side of Victoria Street, adjacent to the Devil's Acre, survives in Strutton Ground, which Booth's researchers described as 'a busy street; Liptons and the Home and Colonial have shops; a street market towards end of the week'.[5]

The presence of two of the leading 'multiple' grocery chains – Liptons and Home and Colonial – hints at the symbiotic relationship between fixed shop retailing and street trading. Provided that they were offering different commodities or services, the relationship could be seen as positive. For example, boot-blacks or newspaper vendors positioned outside department stores could be judged to be providing useful services. On the other hand, greengrocers selling from barrows in the street had few overheads and might be able to undercut greengrocers in fixed shops who were paying both rents and local property taxes. Other street trades might be regarded as undesirable, deterring customers from visiting fixed shops; for example, fishmongers' or butchers' stalls outside clothing stores. One of the most intriguing debates – exemplified by Andrew Brown-May in his discussion of street trade in late nineteenth-century Melbourne – concerned the licensing of late-night coffee-stalls. Opponents argued that street-corner coffee-stalls attracted all kinds of undesirable characters including prostitutes and petty thieves who would prey on gullible citizens as they made their way home late at night, tired and perhaps the worse for drink. Defenders of coffee-stalls claimed they provided sources of light at street corners – and, as I discussed earlier, 'a light is as good as a policeman' – and their proprietors functioned as a reassuring presence on otherwise empty streets. Moreover, coffee was surely a commendable alternative to alcohol, both for those on their way home and for those who worked through the night such as postmen, market porters and newspaper workers. In Melbourne, the negative view prevailed; late-night coffee-stalls were closed down: 'By the early 1920s the subjugation of night in the city was almost complete.' The consequence was streets that were orderly, but effectively dead.[6]

A problem for late nineteenth- and early twentieth-century urban managers was their inability to distinguish between disorder and diversity, their assumption that any violation of their ideal of public order necessarily equated with anarchy. Hence their unease: with the noise of street traders' cries; with the smells of street markets and the waste that was left behind; with the hours of operation (including late at night and on Sundays, which offended Victorian evangelical regard for the sanctity of the Sabbath), which tended to lengthen as increasing numbers of the poor turned to hawking goods in the street or door-to-door during economic downturns as a last resort against the workhouse; with the congestion created by stalls in the public street and crowds using the pavement for browsing rather than purposeful walking; and with the opportunities for crime (both pickpockets working the crowds and fraudulent traders using dishonest weights or adulterating foodstuffs). When Whiteley's department store turned upper middle-class Bayswater from a residential idyll into a bustling commercial district, there were accusations that it was attracting pickpockets and female flower sellers, turning the neighbourhood into a street market; but street markets were coded working-class (the nearest middle-class equivalent was the covered bazaar or arcade), so what was initially intended as a middle-class amenity was thought to be undermining the area's middle-class character.[7]

There was a potential contradiction, too, in attitudes to hawking or the use of barrows or 'pushcarts', where the trader was required to keep moving, and street trade where costermongers sold their wares from a fixed market stall (i.e. they had a pre-scribed spot and stayed in the same place all day). The latter was easier to regulate through the issue of licences, but also conflicted with the function of streets as sites of circulation and mobility. Daniel Bluestone charted the proliferation of street-trading in New York's Lower East Side, as poor Italian and Jewish immigrants provided both the customers and the proprietors of businesses operated from pushcarts.[8] Bluestone identified four phases in the city's efforts to regulate pushcarts. Initially, fixed stalls in street markets were declared illegal. Traders were not allowed to stay at the same spot for more than a few minutes. Dissatisfaction with this arrangement led, in 1906, to the establishment of the Mayor's Pushcart Commission, chaired by the leading tenement-house reformer, Lawrence Veiller. The commission recommended divid-ing the city into two kinds of areas, granting 'roving licenses' in unrestricted districts, where peddlers could operate anywhere and could travel from street to street, but only 'stationary stands' in crowded districts, where licensees were restricted to a par-ticular spot, their numbers would be limited to four to a corner, and licences would be auctioned annually to the highest bidders. In effect this was a reversal of the pre-vious policy. One objective was to control congestion; but another was to eliminate the 'padrone system' of powerful middlemen organising and charging their compa-triots and engaging in an illegal trade in licences.[9] However, the recommendations were never implemented and, meanwhile, congestion worsened, in part because the enforcement of the existing regulations varied from area to area. In some parts of the city, pushcart peddlers were assiduously moved on; in others, including the Lower East Side, street markets continued to flourish.

Bluestone's second phase began in 1913, when markets were allowed in designated areas – underneath the approaches to bridges across the East River, on city-owned land which was effectively wasteland. In effect, markets were marginalised. Then, with food shortages and rising prices during World War I, the vital role of cheap markets was acknowledged and street markets were permitted on designated streets. Now it was itinerant traders who were excluded, fixed stalls that were permitted, much as Veiller had recommended a decade earlier. Finally, in the inter-war period there was an attempt to move markets off the streets and into enclosed market buildings, an assertion of modernist principles of functional segregation. In this vision, the street was no place for trade.

Several strands weave their way through this history. For immigrant communities not much concerned with the need to keep streets clear for through traffic, street markets were vital *social* spaces. Secondly, there were constant fears of competi-tion between street traders and fixed stores with higher overheads. The effect of street trade was to depress property values, especially but not only on the streets where the markets were located. It was also argued that traffic congestion would depress the city's economy as a whole, and so reduce property values and the city's income from property taxes. But there was also an awareness that markets could be picturesque, imparting an 'air of foreign life which is so interesting to the traveler, lending an element of gaiety and charm to the scene which is otherwise lacking'.[10] It might be thought that street markets could survive as modernity's 'other', highlight-ing the virtues of the truly modern by comparison with the quaint but antiquated, much as Lynda Nead has argued for the case of Holywell Street in mid-Victorian

London.[11] But by the 1930s this argument no longer applied. Pushcart traders came to be regarded as little better than beggars. When New York staged its World's Fair in 1938, pressures to clean up the streets, to give the impression of a spotless, stream-lined, modern metropolis, swept aside any lingering nostalgia. The self-confident modernism of the 1930s no longer needed the reassurance of its own modernity that the coexistence of the 'not modern' had offered.

Back in the nineteenth century, the licensing of street trade had been tolerated for the revenue which accrued to the local state and the knowledge which was thereby accumulated on who the traders were. In Melbourne licences were granted prefer-entially to the elderly and the disabled as a substitute for poor relief. But even there, and then, problems were encountered with traders who were so disabled as to cause visual offence to passers-by, and whose presence was thought incompatible with the image of a 'modern' (and, by implication, perfect, unblemished) city that councillors wished to promote: 'The street stall was not only incompatible with unhindered circu-lation, but its keeper, the cripple or the blind man, the war veteran or the immigrant, was visually and socially incompatible with a definition of respectable public space.'[12]

Regulating bodies

The street traders and street markets I have discussed so far were, at least, deal-ing in household commodities – food, clothing, pots and pans, and the like. But streets were also the place for trading in sex. Christine Stansell and Timothy Gilfoyle have each discussed places of prostitution in nineteenth-century New York, describ-ing a shift from its concentration in a few bawdy houses in poor districts of Lower Manhattan into major public streets like Broadway, then moving north to Longacre Square (renamed Times Square in 1904), then taking advantage of the combination of telephony with the private apartment to adopt a more discreet and more scattered presence through the apartment blocks of the city.[13] Gilfoyle mapped the distribu-tion of 'houses of prostitution' in Manhattan from the 1820s through to the 1910s and enumerated the principal 'sex districts' at the beginning and end of his period. Activ-ities on the streets – the presence of streetwalkers soliciting for custom – were easy to describe in shocked, probably exaggerated language, but off-street businesses – brothels and bawdy houses – were easier to map. Perhaps the most interesting aspect of this activity for consideration here concerns the 'appropriation' of streets. Where brothels were interspersed among 'ordinary' houses and businesses, who controlled the public space of the streets? For example, one observer described Sixth Avenue as 'the Haymarket of New York', implying that here – as in London's Haymar-ket – prostitutes dominated the street: 'Observers repeatedly noted how prostitutes rarely conducted themselves "with the outward propriety" they did on Broadway.'[14] Around Longacre Square, queues of 'eager young men' spilled out onto the street outside the most popular brothels and 42nd Street was 'thick with streetwalkers'. Farther west, on 40th Street in the 'African Tenderloin', 'colored women walk up and down the street, blocking the passage of white men and boys, and in some cases force them into the gutter', or snatching men's hats, luring the men into the hallways of tenements to reclaim them! Other streets, although 'infested by several houses of ill fame', were 'outwardly quiet'.[15]

Time of day was just as critical as space. 'Even Fifth Avenue changed at nightfall. During the 1880s, one resident insisted that after dark the avenue from Washington Square to Fourteenth Street was "not fit for any lady to pass, being a perfect rendezvous for fast women and tramps".'[16] In the same way, London's Regent Street was generally respectable during the day, but no place for a lady on her own in the evening.[17] As for the top of Haymarket, 'It is always an offensive place to pass, even in the daytime; but at night it is absolutely hideous, with its sparring snobs, and flashing satins, and sporting gents, and painted cheeks, and brandy-sparkling eyes, and bad tobacco, and hoarse horse-laughs, and local indecency'.[18] Cremorne Gardens, pleasure gardens by the Thames in Chelsea, was a polite venue for families with children during the day, but took on a louche atmosphere by night as a place where men took their mistresses or met with prostitutes. This was a place where the flickering, shadowy, uncertain gaslight was associated in the moral improver's mind with degeneration rather than progress.[19]

In 1877 Cremorne eventually succumbed, as much to the operations of the real estate market, as its geographical marginality was eroded by the expansion of the built-up area, as to the attacks of moral reformers. The case for the defence of Cremorne accepted that respectable and unrespectable could coexist in the same place without the former suffering the effects of 'moral contagion'. Philip Howell argues that Cremorne constituted 'a commingling of public and private space which served to subvert the bourgeois's ideal world of public and private spheres readily demarcating vice from virtue', and that its defenders demonstrated 'a sort of pragmatic moralism concerned not to suppress licentiousness but to manage it as best possible'.[20] By the late 1870s, however, Cremorne's novelty value had waned and the pressure for redevelopment was irresistible.

We can insert the case of Cremorne into wider debates about the regulation of prostitution in nineteenth-century London. The Contagious Diseases Acts (1864–1886) had introduced a form of spatial regulation, whereby prostitution was permitted in towns with important military and naval bases, subject to the registration, regular medical inspection and, if found to be carriers of sexually transmitted diseases, incarceration of prostitutes. It was a form of regulation intended to protect the armed forces from disease while acknowledging the inevitability of a trade in sexual services. The defence of Cremorne was similar. 'Men about town' mixed with women 'on the town'. Cremorne's commingling was excused as a necessary sop to assertive male sexuality. The contemporary reformer, William Acton, sensitively discussed issues of individual liberty, the right of the state to impose traditional forms of morality, and the public health risks associated with prostitution, and came to the conclusion that the Contagious Diseases Acts should be extended to London, not because he wished to condone prostitution, but because he recognised its inevitability and wished to mitigate its worst effects. In practice the opposite occurred: the acts were repealed and Britain reverted to suppression rather than regulation.

Howell argues that 'regulation was fundamentally an exercise in *spatial* order', defining prostitution as a 'public' problem: soliciting in public places introduced disorder into public space.[21] So regulation was intended to remove prostitutes from the streets and enclose them in specified spaces of sexual exchange (almost as street trading was to be removed from the streets and enclosed in covered markets). Regulated

prostitutional space became an extension of private space. Likewise, to its defenders, Cremorne could be regarded as private space (which, in a sense, it was: it was
privately owned and charged an admission fee). But whereas it was easy to tell who
was engaged in retail trade – in selling foodstuffs or household commodities on the
street – it was harder to discern who was offering sexual services for sale. If, in regulated spaces under the Contagious Diseases Act, 'women could be apprehended in
public purely on suspicion of being unregistered or diseased prostitutes, or both, so
that regulation clearly impacted on *every* woman's rights to inhabit public space',[22]
in unregulated space, too, 'respectable' women could be subject to arrest simply for
being in the wrong place at the wrong time, giving the impression that they might be
soliciting.

A similar story can be told about the regulation of homosexual activity. In Britain
legislation in 1885 criminalised all 'acts of gross indecency', whether 'in public or
private', while the 1898 Vagrancy Law Amendment Act heightened the significance
of behaviour that was not explicitly sexual, but was popularly associated with sexual
'deviancy', such as cross-dressing or men's use of make-up, in places that already
had a reputation as pick-up sites, such as Piccadilly Circus and Haymarket. In practice, it was very difficult for the police to justify raids on private property, so they
concentrated surveillance on public places where they expected to find men looking
for same-sex partners – in parks, public lavatories and West End leisure spaces. Yet
none of these spaces was exclusively gay space, nor was it possible to divide the population into a neat modernist classification of 'homosexual' and 'heterosexual'. To
Matt Cook, 'homosexuality was woven into the fabric of urban culture . . . There was
neither an entirely discernible figure nor a separate territory'.[23]

Middle-class men could afford the privacy of commercialised spaces such as bars,
night clubs or Turkish baths, or of their own West End bachelor flats. Working-class
men, living with parents or occupying rooms in cheap boarding houses policed by
inquisitive landladies, were obliged to seek privacy in public space, making them
much more vulnerable to arrest. But this also applied to *all* kinds of sexual activity
among working-class youths who had no truly private space of their own where they
lived. Matt Houlbrook concludes that 'in the 1920s [queer] men's use of parks and
streets mirrored that of young men and women of the working class', and he cites
statistics for offences committed on Hampstead Heath during eighteen months in
1918–1919: of 71 couples prosecuted for 'indecency', only two were same-sex couples;
the others were heterosexual couples for whom the heath was presumably the most
private space available to them.[24]

There is no doubting the association of homosexual or queer culture with big-city
life. For George Chauncey, New York's 'immense size and complexity set it apart
from all other urban areas', facilitating the growth of a specialised gay subculture,
both informal and commercialised, which helped to explain the city's allure to gay
migrants.[25] Coming to London, too, was a journey in self-realisation: 'London is both
a symbolic and experiential rupture, a productive space that generates and stabilizes
a new form of selfhood and way of life.'[26] On these grounds, we might doubt whether
Toronto had the critical mass to sustain a specialist gay subculture before the city's
population boom of the 1900s, but by 1913 a city judge could make the exaggerated
claim that 'indecency' in Toronto 'was as bad as Canal Street, New York'.[27]

Popular representations in the press and fiction situated gay Toronto in middle-class areas such as Rosedale and Avenue Road Hill, or in rooming-house districts immediately east of Yonge Street, inhabited by predominantly 'British' lower middle-class clerks and shop assistants.[28] Hugh Garner's novel, *Cabbagetown*, recounts the experiences of a teenager growing up in Toronto's East End during the Depression. Garner's semi-autobiographical hero, Ken Tilling, twice encounters Toronto's homosexual culture, each time in the private space of apartment housing: in a house divided into flats near Carlton Street (just east of Yonge), occupied by the urbane but idle Clarence Gurney, 'whose athletic body was running to seed' rather like the neighbourhood in which he lived; and in a modern purpose-built apartment in the much more fashionable 'north-central section of town' (Avenue Road), at a party hosted by 'an old dyke', an identity rarely encountered in Cabbagetown.[29] Yet Steven Maynard shows that, contrary to these middle-class stereotypes, there were numerous working-class immigrants living in East End neighbourhoods around Cabbagetown in the inter-war years who engaged in homosexual activity.[30] But they may not have thought of themselves as 'homosexual' and their behaviour leaves a trace only because, as among working-class Londoners, it necessarily occurred in parks and back alleys, whereas middle-class 'bohemians' had no need to appropriate public space for sexual purposes.

Spaces of representation

In Walter Benjamin's exploration of modernity three archetypal figures of the streets are the flâneur (invariably male), the prostitute (female) and the rag-picker. Early feminist scholarship, wedded to the concept of 'separate spheres', which confined middle-class women to the domestic sphere while their husbands, fathers and brothers occupied the public sphere, concluded that there was no possibility of a female flâneuse in nineteenth-century cities.[31] Flâneurs were male observers, objectifying unaccompanied women, who might return the look but, unless they were prostitutes, were not in a position to do their own independent looking. However, recent interpretations have emphasised that the flâneur was not such a secure figure. His natural habitat was not the boulevards of Haussmann's Paris but the arcades that were in process of destruction, 'public spaces that yet offered the privileges of the private: familiarity, comfort and authority'.[32] So the flâneur was an identity in crisis, 'caught up in the violent dislocations that characterised urbanisation', a nineteenth-century forerunner of more recent economic and sexual crises of masculinity.[33] Deborah Parsons suggests a tension in Benjamin's writing between the flâneur as 'bourgeois or vagrant, authoritative or marginal, within or detached from the city crowd, masculine, feminine or androgynous'.[34] On the one hand, we may conceive of *him* as static, detached, knowledgeable and authoritative, not a 'distracted, dawdling, dandy'[35] but an expert observer – the author of some of Lefebvre's representations of space. On the other, we may imagine a more mobile but marginal figure, a collector of urban knowledge, more scavenger than master-planner, resisting respectable conceptions of urban behaviour – making his (or her?) space of representation. Benjamin himself was a collector, 'a Baudelaire-inspired rag-picker' making 'a collage out of fragments of urban myth'.[36] If we embrace this latter model under the umbrella of flânerie, then there is scope to reinstate female shoppers, tourists, philanthropists as well as prosti-tutes as potential female flâneurs. To those outside feminist cultural studies this may seem like a purely definitional argument – we can redefine the word to make it mean what we want it to mean.[37] Nevertheless, it highlights the importance of reassessing the place of women, revising the 'separate spheres' argument, and acknowledging the agency of women in the public spaces of nineteenth-century cities.

For Lynda Nead in 2000, 'the assumption still remains that the only way to write middle-class women into histories of modernity is by looking at the private sphere, or the history of shopping'.[38] Even in Elizabeth Wilson's celebratory *The Sphinx in the City*, middle-class women are restricted to spaces such as parks and department stores which constituted extensions of the domestic sphere rather than breaks with it.[39] Only working-class women appear free to go where they want to, and they, of course, are constrained economically. So what can we add about other female presences on the city streets?

The female flâneur?

One of the best known literary examples of the independent young woman alone on the city streets is Lucy Snowe in Charlotte Brontë's *Villette* (published in 1853, but set in 'a time gone by', before the onset of the railway age). Lucy spent barely a day in London, but in that time she took lodgings in an old inn near St Paul's Cathedral, visited a bookshop in Paternoster Row, climbed to the dome of St Paul's, and explored the Strand and Cornhill. She expressed a sense of freedom, elation and excitement: 'to walk alone in London seemed of itself an adventure'. But Lucy was less knowing flâneuse than innocent abroad, fortunate to escape as lightly as she did. She found it hard to understand the London accents of cabmen; the chambermaid, 'a pattern of town prettiness and smartness', in 'spruce attire', addressed her with 'mincing glibness'; and in almost every financial transaction – paying the porter who carried her trunk, tipping the elderly waiter at her inn, and settling with the waterman who conveyed her down the Thames to the boat by which she left London – she was cheated: 'but I consoled myself with the reflection, "It is the price of experience."'[40]

However unusual Lucy Snowe may have been in the time the novel was set, by the time it was published the profuse contemporary debates on how women should behave on the streets of London demonstrate that the issue was no longer *whether* young women could ever venture out, unchaperoned, but how, when and where that was acceptable. Much of the evidence against the 'separate spheres' model comes from a reading against the grain of newspaper articles, crime reports, letters to the editor, etiquette guides, cartoons and magazine illustrations, which cumulatively provide strong evidence of the place of independent or unaccompanied women on city streets, and not only in feminised spaces that were effectively an extension of the domestic sphere, such as parks, art galleries and department stores.

Nead discusses a lithograph from the 1860s which shows a fashionably dressed woman being approached by an earnest young clergyman offering her a 'good little book', presumably a tract or a Bible. The 'Lady' responds: 'Bless me, Sir, you're mistaken. I am not a social evil, I am only waiting for a bus.' We might be tempted to interpret this print as warning young women against venturing on the streets for

Figure 6.1. 'Club House, Fifth Avenue and Fifteenth Street, New York', from *New York Illustrated News*, 7 February 1863. Negative number 70511. Collection of The New-York Historical Society.

fear that they might be taken for prostitutes by somebody worse than a clergyman. Reading against the grain, however, Nead concludes that the picture offers 'visual confirmation that respectable women did routinely walk around the city on their own'. We are supposed to laugh at the clergyman's earnest enthusiasm and naivety, not condemn the woman's recklessness.[41]

We might compare this image from London with 'Club House, Fifth Avenue and Fifteenth Street', an illustration published in the *New-York Illustrated News* in February 1863 (Figure 6.1).[42] The picture depicts several fashionably dressed women, either alone or in the company of a child or a male companion, but all purposefully going about their business on the street, while subject to the gaze of a group of effete young men peering out from the windows of the Manhattan Club. Mona Domosh explains that there is a complicated political subtext to this image – one of the men is given the title of an English aristocrat, the club was a centre for upper-class Democrats and, in the context of the American Civil War, Europhile Democrats were not to be trusted.[43] Although the men are doing the looking, they are behind glass – specimens for *our* inspection – and they are indoors, in the domestic sphere, while the female passers-by are in the public sphere. The men are 'out of place', idling away their time when they should be at work. They are behaving 'like women'. Implicitly, therefore, the critique of the men seems to depend on the reader's acceptance that women's place *is* in the home, not on the street like the women in the picture. Or, is the picture indifferent to women – is it acceptable for them to be in either domestic or public space – while asserting that men *should* be in public? Domosh notes that the article accompanying the illustration is addressed to women – 'Mesdames! take your revenge . . .' Whatever our interpretation, we can safely conclude, firstly, that women were expected to be reading the newspaper, partaking of information circulating in the public sphere, and secondly, that women were to be seen on Fifth Avenue on a weekday, on their own or with one another as well as in the company of men.

Correspondents contributing to a debate in *The Times* in 1862 recognised that women on their own risked being bothered by men, but advised minimising the risk by not encouraging men's attention – don't saunter or pause too long in front of shop windows, don't dress provocatively, don't return male glances; but some also acknowledged that young single women positively enjoyed the excitement of flirtation where the public nature of the space provided reasonable assurance of safety.[44] For example, Nead also discusses letters written in the 1850s by the teenage Amelia Roper describing excursions into central London from her home in Walthamstow in the city's north-east suburbs. She was not travelling unaccompanied, but in her account of one visit, to the Olympic Theatre, just off Drury Lane, 'an area notorious for its poverty, drunkenness and immorality', and close to Holywell Street, a narrow, picturesque, half-timbered street dedicated by the mid-nineteenth century to the sale of politically radical and sexually explicit literature, and perceived by its denigrators as modernity's 'other', Roper excitedly lapsed into working-class and sexual slang, 'a revealing combination of naivety and swagger'. In another letter, she debated with herself whether to accept a lift offered by a gentleman in a passing carriage. The surprise is not that she declined the offer, but that she declared that if she had been in the company of the girlfriend to whom she was writing, she would have taken the risk and accepted. Nead concludes that 'her visits to town enabled her to play with and explore different feminine identities'.[45]

By the 1890s, far more middle-class women were confidently exploring London's West End, some of them now employed as teachers, nurses, typists and shop assistants. Erica Rappaport focuses on women who were shoppers or tourists or who shared political and cultural interests. She identifies the institutions that catered for their physical and social needs, including women's clubs and restaurants, noting how the earliest clubs, founded in the 1860s and 1870s, combined women's needs for relaxation and sociability while shopping in the West End with political and feminist concerns. Most clubs for women were in or near the principal shopping streets – Regent Street, Oxford Street, Bond Street. But as their numbers increased, so popular accounts of them laid less stress on politics, converting clubland 'from a feminist into a feminine space'.[46] A new wave of women's clubs welcomed male guests, and some male clubs also started to accommodate female visitors. As the rationale for women-only clubs dissipated, so their role was taken over by suites of rooms, still called 'clubs', set aside by leading department stores, and by restaurants and tea-rooms which catered either exclusively or predominantly to women. Rappaport concludes that women 'both gained and lost' from this shift to purely commercial provision for their bodily needs: 'In the clubhouse, shoppers interacted with workers, listened to or participated in debates, and became involved in . . . a wider public sphere' but in patronising purely commercial facilities, 'female participation in public life and club culture was relegated to the sphere of consumption'.[47]

This is a cautionary tale on several counts. First, it warns against equating 'public space' and 'public sphere' – women were increasingly visible in the city's streets and other public spaces, but it does not follow that they were also more engaged in political and social debate in the 1890s than they had been twenty years earlier. Secondly, it warns against a simple model of 'progress' with respect to women's occupation of public space. Rather, certain kinds of space, notably shopping spaces, were being 'domesticated' – regarded as an extension of the private sphere – while other, potentially more emancipatory spaces, such as debating clubs, were marginalised. Feminised space (space designed for women such as the interiors of department stores) was not the same as feminist space (space not only designed but controlled by women). Thirdly, it implies that, for all its technological modernity, the department store was less than fully 'modern' in restricting middle-class women to the role of shoppers and denying them roles with more agency in shaping the future structure of either consumption or urban society.

These observations suggest that it is possible to exaggerate the extent of 'transgression' or of acts of 'polite politics' by women prior to the 1900s. Most women were in public on men's terms, and where those terms had been relaxed during the nineteenth century, it was usually to the benefit of the urban economy (which was controlled by men), stimulating new forms and levels of consumption, creating new sources of labour, and accelerating the circulation of money capital.

Nonetheless, there were undoubtedly more women, alone or in the company of other women, on the streets of the West End (or on Broadway and Fifth Avenue) by the 1900s than there had been in the 1850s. But the sorry fates of two literary examples on the streets of New York, Lily Bart and Ellen Olenska (in Edith Wharton's *The House of Mirth* and *The Age of Innocence*), indicate that tactical transgressions could prove counterproductive.[48] Carrie Meeber (by now 'Mrs Wheeler') also takes to the New York streets under the tutelage of her neighbour, Mrs Vance. They process down Broadway from 34th Street to Madison Square, the latter 'stunningly arrayed in a dark blue walking dress, with a nobby hat to match', her ensemble complemented by 'trinkets of gold, an elegant green leather purse, set with her initials' and 'a fancy handkerchief exceedingly rich in design'. None of this was exceptional given the context, in which women and men all paraded in the 'very best' or the 'very latest' fashions. Women were certainly the objects of male gaze, but they were also expected to do their share of looking at others of both sexes: 'To stare seemed the proper and natural thing. Carrie found herself stared at and ogled.'[49] However, one might argue that there was too much emotional investment, certainly on Carrie's part, for her to qualify as *flâneuse*. The essence of flânerie was surely a sense of detachment.

Rappaport, who adopts a looser definition of flânerie, less tied to Baudelaire and Benjamin, is happy to argue that, in London, ladies' magazines such as the *Queen* and *The Lady*, and Lady Guides, who physically escorted female visitors around the city, 'created the *flâneuse*'.[50] Commencing publication in 1861, the *Queen* 'fashioned its readers as urban spectators and ramblers', presenting London as a great exhibition akin to *the* Great Exhibition.[51] As with the shift from women's clubs to department stores with facilities for women, so there was a tendency for the magazines to become less political over time, to concentrate increasingly on domestic and consumer issues. Columns entitled 'A Day's Shopping' comprised narratives which organised the city for visitors from the suburbs or farther afield, tours in which readers accompanied the narrator through a succession of metropolitan spaces, learning the relationship of one site to another – how far it was from Oxford Street to Knightsbridge or to the National

Gallery – and which shops were appropriate for different purchases. Shopping was about knowledge, but it also required skill and confidence. Some narratives took on an ethnographic, investigatory form, shopping equivalents to the social explorations of slums discussed in earlier chapters. One subject where advice was critical was in persuading women to use public transport, not only what was available, but how to conduct oneself in a crowded bus or train. In the 1890s 'Society ladies and young women who ventured to the top of a 'bus or traveled alone in a hansom cab were thought to be "fast" . . . a woman who rode public transportation was also in danger of making a spectacle of herself'.[52] There was a residue of this attitude in Elizabeth Dalloway's daring to catch the pirate bus on Victoria Street thirty years later.[53] Riding the bus or the suburban train was another way in which women could adopt the perspective of the flâneur, observing but not participating in the life of areas through which they passed.[54]

The culmination of these guides to shopping was the Lady Guide Association, formed at the end of 1888, when many women needed reassurance that city streets were safe from Jack the Ripper and his ilk. The association employed middle-class women to guide less confident visitors around the city but, like women's clubs, it had a limited life.[55] By the beginning of the twentieth century, such direct guidance was no longer necessary. But another consequence of the association's programme was to imbue the women it employed as guides with skills which would equip them for other forms of professional employment. In this respect, it resembled the fictional secretarial college described by George Gissing in *The Odd Women* (1893), preparing women for a life of financial self-sufficiency.

Gissing's women

Many of Gissing's female characters lead independent lives, confident in their knowledge of the city's geography and use of its public transport. In *The Odd Women*, female characters move around the metropolis freely, apparently undeterred by their constant subjection to the male gaze of potential suitors and jealous husbands. From her home in the South London suburb of Herne Hill, newly wed Monica Widdowson traverses the city alone, visiting sisters in Battersea, a former room-mate near Regent's Park, a prospective lover in Bayswater, the Royal Academy art exhibition in Burlington House, and Mary Barfoot and Rhoda Nunn, two feminist-minded women living in Chelsea, who run the secretarial college in Great Portland Street which Monica had attended prior to her marriage. Monica is a frequent passenger on the London, Chatham & Dover Railway into Victoria, and thence on the Metropolitan District underground to Sloane Square, Bayswater and Great Portland Street (Figure 4.6). On one occasion, she encounters Everard Barfoot, Mary's cousin, as they are both entering Sloane Square station. They engage in conversation on the train – alone together in a first-class carriage, an ideal situation for practising privacy in public. Barfoot deliberately goes to the Royal Academy exhibition the following week in the hope that he will see her there, which he does, though on this occasion she has been followed by her extremely protective husband. On another occasion, Barfoot encounters Rhoda on her own in the gardens of Chelsea Hospital – 'In this part of the gardens there were only a few nursemaids and children; it would have been a capital place and time for improving his intimacy with the remarkable woman.'[56] Even in such domesticated public places, single women could not escape the male gaze, but at least they were no longer likely to be alone or unable to resist male advances.

Early in the novel, Monica's sister, Virginia, sets out to walk alone – past Battersea Park, over Chelsea Bridge, through Victoria and Charing Cross – to the Strand, where she wished to visit the secondhand bookshops. Virginia exemplifies the kind of woman who, moralists claimed, would be corrupted by the pornographic prints displayed in windows of bookshops in nearby Holywell Street. She emerges unsullied by pornography – the object of her quest is a book by the Anglo-Catholic churchman, John Keble – but on her way home she succumbs to another secret vice, solitary drinking, in the bar at Charing Cross Station.[57]

These women have no need of a guidebook or a Guide, and they stray beyond the public-domestic arena (which would, perhaps, include both Burlington House and Chelsea Gardens) to places like Holywell Street and the railway station bar which would not have been on a Guide's itinerary. Monica's confidence no doubt stems from her previous lives as trainee typist in Great Portland Street and, before that, as shop-girl in a draper's on Walworth Road (inner south-east London), sharing a dormitory over the shop with five other girls, of whom none are 'ladies' and at least one moonlights as a prostitute. Her experience straddles the class divide between working-class girls whose lives are necessarily led on the street – they have nowhere else to go when they are not working – and 'ladies,' such as her unmentioned neighbours in Herne Hill, who, if their husbands were anything like Monica's, would never have been allowed out alone. When, after visiting Miss Nunn and Miss Barfoot in Chelsea, Monica proposes to her husband that she pays a visit to her ex-room-mate while he goes home, their exchange pithily exemplifies the clash of contemporary attitudes:

> '. . . I can't have you going about alone at night.'
> 'Why not?' answered Monica, with a just perceptible note of
>   irritation. 'Are you afraid I shall be robbed or murdered?'
> 'Nonsense. But you mustn't be alone.'
> 'Didn't I always use to be alone?'
> He made an angry gesture.[58]

For all their determination, Gissing's 'odd women' cannot really be thought of as flâneuses. They know their way about the streets of London, but their journeys are always purposeful. Melinda Harvey argues that 'The flâneuse is strikingly absent from accounts of the metropolis because women's walking has characteristically never lacked vigilance or design'.[59] Women have always been traversing city streets, but always for a reason, with a fixed destination in mind. For Harvey it is the *mode* of walking that is important. Elaborating on this point, we might suggest that the critical issue is *agency*. Purposeful pedestrians are only agents to the extent that they can exercise a completely free choice of destination and few of us face no constraints over where to work, shop or live. But the archetype flâneur was not sauntering to work or choosing to take a more interesting route home: he was not on his way anywhere; and he was exercising his agency unpredictably, deciding from moment to moment where to go next. Few women had this degree of freedom.[60]

Of all Gissing's female characters, the most striking example of a woman discovering her independence on the streets of the city, an 1880s fictional version of Amelia Roper, is Nancy Lord in *In The Year of Jubilee*. On the occasion of Queen Victoria's Golden Jubilee in June 1887, a royal procession during the day was complemented by an informal celebration during the evening on the streets of the West End. Gissing disdained 'the daylight proceedings' but enthusiastically reported on the evening's festivities:

The Jubilee was amazing. At night, all the great streets were packed from side to side with a clearly divided double current of people, – all vehicles being forbidden. You walked at the rate of a funeral horse from top of Bond Street to the Bank – by way of Pall Mall, Strand, etc. Such a concourse of people I never saw.[61]

Seven years later, he incorporated his experience into *In The Year of Jubilee*, in which the 23-year old Nancy sets off from her home in Camberwell, much against her father's will, in the company of her brother, her best friend (Jessica) and the earnest Samuel Barmby, her father's young business partner, 'to walk about the streets after dark, and see the crowds and the illuminations'. Pressed by the more timid Jessica, Nancy emphasises: 'I should like to walk about all night, as lots of people will' and even to go into public-houses; 'Why not? I should like to. It's horrible to be tied up as we are; we're not children. Why can't we go about as men do?'[62]

The first part of the evening's adventure involves catching the horse-tram from Camberwell Green to its terminus at the south end of Westminster Bridge. Their preference was to sit on the open top deck of the tram but 'A throng of far more resolute and more sinewy people swept them aside, and seized every vacant place on the top of the vehicle'. They have to struggle even to find space inside. 'In an ordinary mood, Nancy would have resented this hustling of her person by the profane public; as it was, she half enjoyed the tumult, and looked forward to get more of it along the packed streets . . . ' Their fellow passengers include a woman who talks loudly about the 'Prince of Wiles', a sure sign that Gissing, who abhorred vernacular language, wants us to think of her as common and vulgar, and 'a working-man, overtaken with liquor' who gets into an argument with other passengers: 'thereupon, retort of insult, challenge to combat, clamour from many throats, deep and shrill'. Here, then, is a collision of social classes, ages, genders, and attitudes that might be considered the very essence of public space, yet its impact is to coarsen those who might have been expected to be moderating influences: 'Nancy laughed, and would rather have enjoyed it if the men had fought.'[63]

Alighting at the terminus, Barmby leads his party across Westminster Bridge, declaring 'We can't be wrong in making for Trafalgar Square', but Nancy has resolved to break away on her own, 'to mingle with the limitless crowd as one of its units, borne in whatever direction'. She waits for the cover of twilight, by which time she, Barmby and Jessica are in Pall Mall. As Barmby starts to lecture the women on the gentlemen's clubs there, Nancy seizes the opportunity to disappear into the slow-moving crowd.[64] She became one among thousands, anonymous – she 'forgot her identity, lost sight of herself as an individual' – subject to the same 'levelling-down' that she had experienced on the tram, no different from 'any shop-girl let loose'. But, like Amelia Roper or Olive Malvery, she was also very self-aware, 'experimenting with risky, metropolitan feminine identities'.[65] Nancy's behaviour also exemplifies Georg Simmel's observations on the metropolis and mental life: a distantiation, deflection or dissociation which 'assures the individual of a type and degree of personal freedom', while 'in the dense crowds of the metropolis . . . the bodily closeness and lack of space make intellectual distance really perceivable'.[66] Various men in the crowd attempt to chat her up, but she retains her sense of middle-class decorum sufficiently to send them packing and resolves instead to keep a rendezvous with Luckworth Crewe, another rather vulgar character who Nancy knows through mutual acquaintances, a young man obsessed with every money-making venture, yet a character for whom his creator had a surprisingly soft spot: 'his manner had no polish, but a genuine heartiness which would have atoned for many defects'. Crewe becomes Nancy's gallant protector when 'A band of roisterers, linked arm in arm, were trying to break up the orderly march of thousands into a chaotic fight' and other women around them were fainting and shrieking hysterically, though Nancy continues to insist 'I like it. It's good fun.'[67]

Even in this all-too-public space, Nancy was able to be private, in her thoughts and in her own encounters and conversations with others. The self-assurance the evening offered was one that she carried into other situations through the rest of the novel. We should also note that the new identities that the fictional Nancy Lord and the real Amelia Roper were experimenting with were old, taken-for-granted identities on the part of young working-class women. As I have already indicated, the debate about women in public space has focused almost exclusively on middle-class women and prostitutes rather than working-class women whose lives had always been more public, employed in clothing factories and workshops, shopping in street markets, finding recreation in the street, the local public-house or the mission-hall, subject to the surveillance and public reporting of social investigators and their accompanying police and school board officers, but rarely known to us through their own voices. The relationship between the classes is also central to nearly all the examples I have discussed above – the fear or the thrill of mixing with, or being mistaken for, women of a different class – while the playing out of gendered family relationships – protective husbands/fathers and independently minded wives/daughters or lone, truly independent women such as Lucy Snowe – also shapes attitudes to the spaces of the city. We might also note the distinction between a suburban or ex-urban mixture of fear and excitement, as exemplified by the real Amelia Roper and the fictional Nancy Lord and Lucy Snowe, and the matter-of-fact engagement with urban space that characterised most of the characters in *The Odd Women*, whose daily routine was in inner or central city.

Women on women in public space

While we need not doubt Gissing's skill in writing authoritatively and, apparently, authentically about women's experiences, we may still feel obliged to test his observations against those of women writers. However much research Gissing conducted into the places and occasions in which he set his characters, he could not research the consciousness of his female protagonists quite so personally. There is a close relationship between walking the city and writing the city. Melinda Harvey observes

that 'Walking is a cogent metaphor for (and, one might venture, an enjoyable eva-
sion of) the act of writing itself. The flâneur, like the writer, selects, (dis)orders,
and forges narratives out of an infinite mass of detail while reading and adding to
that detail.'[68] So, given the paucity of flâneuses, it is unsurprising that so few women
authors in the nineteenth century used city streets as settings for their work. Deborah
Parsons comments that representations of 'new women' as specifically urban figures
were mainly in works by men. Writers who were themselves 'new women' 'rarely
concentrated on the city as a subject for their fiction, unless in terms of its interior
spaces, notably the enclosure of the Victorian drawing-room'. She suggests that this
bias reflects women's 'continued sense of social restraint in urban space'.[69] Deborah
Nord devotes two chapters of her book to writing by 'new women', but most of them
were social investigators such as Beatrice Potter (later Webb) and Clara Collet,
who both worked with Charles Booth.[70] Their reports focus on working conditions
and home life more than on the streets. Reviewing the handful of women writers
who set stories, poems and journalism in public space, Sally Ledger discusses Ella
Hepworth Dixon's *The Story of a Modern Woman* (1894), Nord reviews the work
of Margaret Harkness, especially her novels *A City Girl* (1887) and *Out of Work*
(1888), and both Nord and Parsons make a case for the rediscovery of Amy Levy,
whose novel *The Romance of a Shop* (1888) is most relevant here.[71] By the early
twentieth century there are many more and better known women authors for whom
the streets of London are central to their work, notably Virginia Woolf and Dorothy
Richardson; but I will restrict myself here to some brief comments on Levy and
Harkness.

Amy Levy was 'one of the first women writers to consistently adopt the perspective of a female writer-observer or *flâneur*'.[72] In *The Romance of a Shop*, Gertrude
Lorimer traverses London alone on the top of a bus and, at least once, by underground train after seeing off her sister, Lucy, at Paddington Station, and she has 'a
secret, childish love for the gas-lit street, for the sight of the hurrying people, the
lamps, the hansom cabs, flickering in and out of the yellow haze'.[73] Like Gissing's
Edwin Reardon (in *New Grub Street*) Gertrude and Lucy make frequent walks, sometimes together, sometimes alone, in Regent's Park, where they are likely to encounter
male artist-flâneurs like Sidney Darrell and Frank Jermyn.[74] They set up a photography business in Baker Street, 'appropriating in a modern and commercial form
the capturing look of the male artist',[75] and Gertrude takes the business sufficiently
seriously to undertake a course of photographic reading at the British Museum. Yet
she is as frequently to be found looking out from the window of her flat, anxiously
observing the passing traffic. There were still limits to female flânerie. In her essay
on 'Women and Club Life', published in the same year as *The Romance of a Shop*
(1888), Levy commented that 'the *flâneuse* of St. James's Street, latch-key in pocket
and eye-glasses on nose, remains a creature of the imagination'.[76]

Margaret Harkness also felt herself constrained, to the extent that she chose a male
pseudonym – John Law – for her novels of working-class life. Her political-religious
stance as socialist *and* supporter of the Salvation Army is reflected in her focus on
class relations: an East End girl seduced by a West End armchair socialist in *A City
Girl*, and the juxtaposition of unemployment riots and the celebration of Empire
in *Out of Work*.[77] Like Monica in *The Odd Women*, Nelly in *A City Girl* traverses

the city confidently and, mostly, unselfconsciously. She is most at ease in her own neighbourhood around 'Charlotte's Buildings' (a thinly disguised rendering of the real Katharine Buildings, erected by the East End Dwellings Company in 1884, where Harkness's cousin, Beatrice Potter, was a 'lady rent collector') and in Petticoat Lane market. She also makes trips confidently enough on her own by steamer to Kew and by train from Mansion House to West Kensington (where her seducer lives), although she panics when she loses her return ticket and has no idea which way to walk to get home. Both Nelly and Monica were, at heart, working-class, Nelly obviously so but Monica, too, during her time as a shop-girl, had learnt the urban skills of a working-class girl. We have already seen how middle-class Nancy Lord longed for the streetwise freedom of a shop-girl. It appears that the only way for a middle-class woman to be at ease on the streets of late Victorian London was to become working-class (though, in so doing, she would sacrifice the respect and independence associated with being an 'odd woman').

In all the situations I have discussed, fictional and documentary, it is relevant to consider not only how people *used* the streets, but how their behaviour contributed to the making of place and how place shaped imagination and memory as well as behaviour. The logic of Domosh's interpretation of de Certeau's argument about 'tactics' and 'polite politics' is that spaces are remade by the cumulative effect of countless shoppers, prostitutes, 'new women' and shop-girls silently and undemonstratively occupying them. The interaction between mind and urban environment is exemplified by another visit to *Mrs Dalloway*.

The structure of Woolf's novel comprises a succession of walks through London by different characters. As they pass each other on the street, or in the park, or as their attention is drawn to the same external stimulus – the striking of the hour, the appearance of an aeroplane, signwriting in the sky above the city – so the narrative passes from one character to another. But most of the narrative is taken up, not with what they are doing, or in simply describing where they are, but with what they are thinking, and especially the memories aroused in them. At the beginning of the novel, as Mrs Dalloway makes her way from her home in the vicinity of Dean's Yard, close by Westminster Abbey, across Victoria Street, through the silence of St. James's Park to the hurried elegance of Piccadilly and Bond Street, there is a constant interaction between the experiences of the streets and the memories rushing through her head: these are thoughts in place, which would be thought differently in some other place. Some thoughts are very obviously place-related. As she crosses Victoria Street, she reflects on the foolishness but also the thrill of 'the bellow and the uproar; the carriages, motor cars, omnibuses, vans, sandwich men shuffling and swinging; brass bands; barrel organs'.[78] But at the same time, she is led to think about the impossibility of controlling street life – such as the presence of alcoholic tramps – through Acts of Parliament and, as she listens to the silence before Big Ben strikes the hour, about the state of her heart, 'affected, they said, by influenza'.[79] Other thoughts derive not from the environment but from her business for the day – preparing for a party that evening and anticipating the return from India of her former lover, Peter Walsh – but still they are recast by the places she passes: the houses on Piccadilly, the books on display in the window of Hatchards' bookshop, the glove shop in Bond Street which reminds her of her uncle.

The most sustained example of this interaction not only illustrates a case of flânerie or an 'urban ramble', but also implies another dimension to the uneasy relationship between metropole and empire. It also returns us to the reality that, for all the writing about women in public space, most people on the streets were men. Peter Walsh, aged 53 but introduced by Woolf as 'elderly', from 'a respectable Anglo-Indian family which for at least three generations had administered the affairs of a continent', and just returned from India, walks across the West End from Mrs Dalloway's house to Regent's Park. He began by looking through 'the plate-glass window of a motor-car manufacturer in Victoria Street', then 'marched up Whitehall', though not so quickly that he could keep up with a real marching column of 'Boys in uniform, carrying guns', on their way back from laying a wreath at the Cenotaph, the World War I memorial in the middle of Whitehall, which had been dedicated on Remembrance Day, 1920, while Walsh had still been in India. The use of the streets for acts of commemoration, especially as conduits for processions, is one to which I will return shortly. Meanwhile, Walsh is pausing among the statues in Trafalgar Square, meditating on 'the strangeness of standing alone, alive, unknown, at half-past eleven in Trafalgar Square',[80] experiencing the classic urban paradox of freedom and anonymity. But his route up Whitehall, and the fact that it is in Trafalgar Square that he feels free – and young again – among the ghosts of the past, the statues of generals associated with imperial campaigns, are no accidents. As Barbara Penner observes, 'The spaces through which he passes represent and glorify imperial state power, arousing pride and a sense of belonging in Walsh, almost despite himself'.[81]

Walsh spots a young woman, whom he decides to follow, substituting an obsession with her idealised form and dress for his previous interest in shop-window displays, imagining her identity and exchanges between them, all the way up Haymarket, across Piccadilly, up Regent Street, across Oxford Street, to a side-street off Great Portland Street, where she turns into a house – 'one of those flat red houses with hanging flower-baskets of vague impropriety. It was over.'[82] Walsh has behaved like the stereotypical flâneur, objectifying the stranger, 'fetishizing her clothes and accessories in a way that equates her with the articles for sale in shop windows' and, in the reference to 'vague impropriety', justifying his failure to make contact by writing her off as a prostitute.[83] Penner argues that the two halves of this urban ramble are indivisible: 'It is clearly no coincidence that this sexual pursuit takes place just after Walsh has been contemplating the most potent symbols of Britain's military might.'[84] Colonial power relations are matched by gender power relations. Both are in crisis.

Apart from this last example, I have chosen to concentrate on women, because they were most obviously making new claims and negotiating the transition from absence to presence to acceptance (of themselves as well as by men) in public space. But the case of Peter Walsh returns us to the initial argument of feminist historians that there was also a crisis in the role of men in public space, prompted not only by the burgeoning emancipation of women, but also by other social and technological changes: deskilling and the substitution of mass production (often using female labour) for craft work; overseas competition (especially as the British economy faced competition from Germany and the United States); imperial decline; bureaucratisation and the beginnings of a shift towards a meritocracy and higher rates of social mobility; and continuing immigration and urbanisation. Of course, many of these changes primarily related to London and other British cities, and might be interpreted as opportunities rather than threats in most cities and among most social classes. The point is that the experience of public space was changing for everybody.

The appropriation of space

The Jubilee crowd appropriating the space of Trafalgar Square and nearby upper middle-class streets like Pall Mall, trespassing on the spaces of the establishment, was primarily a working-class crowd with middle-class hangers-on. Normally, 'slumming' involved West Enders spending time exploring the East End, but on this occasion West Enders could enjoy the cultural *frisson* of slumming without leaving their own territory. There were other cross-class, communal celebrations at times of national rejoicing, such as the Queen's Diamond Jubilee (1897), the Relief of Mafeking (during the Boer War, 1900), the Armistice (at the end of World War I, 1918), and annual New Year's Eve celebrations. But there were also occasions, including some only months before and after the Jubilee, when working-class crowds appropriated Trafalgar Square and Pall Mall in a much more violent fashion.

Trafalgar Square contrasts with New York's Times Square as a scene of New Year's Eve festivities, or with Union Square as a venue for political rallies, in its deliberate creation as a site of national and imperial authority; in Rodney Mace's choice phrase, 'somewhere that will impress the neighbours and overawe the country cousins'.[85] Trafalgar Square was laid out to be looked at, but only occasionally to be used. As well as Nelson's Column, erected in 1843, flanked by Landseer's lions, added in 1867, and a variety of establishment statuary – George IV on horseback (1843) and Generals Napier (1856), Havelock (1858) and Gordon (1888), the last-named removed in 1953 to Victoria Embankment – the square included other impediments to the congregation of crowds, such as two ornamental fountains situated between Nelson's Column and the steps up to the National Gallery. In 1841, when the square was still being planned, the government's First Commissioner of Woods, Forests and Land Revenues (responsible for property owned by the Crown, such as royal parks) expressed his concern that 'evils of a generally objectionable character may be anticipated from leaving open so large a space in this particular quarter of the Metropolis'.[86] He feared the assembly of revolutionary mobs, as in Paris, but also the take-over of the square by crowds of homeless or the general disorder and encouragement to petty crime that the gathering of large numbers of people together might engender. Later in the century there were suggestions that one large lake would provide a more effective barrier to crowd formation, and during World War I there were plans to erect a large single-storey building over much of the square, ostensibly to help with the war effort, but interpreted by Mace as a way to prevent public meetings critical of the war from occupying the symbolic 'heart of Empire'.[87]

In November 1887, responding to violent demonstrations in 1886 and 1887, the Metropolitan Police Commissioner banned all public meetings from using Trafalgar Square; and when the ban was lifted by the incoming Liberal administration in 1892, it was replaced by restrictive regulations which allowed the government to decide which meetings could go ahead. Yet despite, perhaps because of, these attempts to keep Trafalgar Square under state control, it has always been associated more with acts of popular protest than official ceremonial. The attempt to reserve the square for official and approved occasions could even have been a stimulus to protest. The square became a prize of enormous symbolic value.

Trafalgar Square shared with Hyde Park, another site of mass demonstration and free speech, the uncertain status of being Crown land. The symbolism of appropriating such spaces for the expression of *public* opinion and, historically, usually working-class public opinion, partook of the spirit of carnival, the world-turned-upside-down, class relations inverted.[88] It was enhanced in these two spaces by the fact that the area between them, through which demonstrators would march, comprised the elite shopping areas of Regent Street and Piccadilly, full of commodities the working classes could never hope to afford, and the gentlemen's clubs of Pall Mall and St. James's, the seat of the establishment at leisure. Unsurprisingly, protests that got out of hand ended in stone-throwing, breaking windows and overturning carriages, and occasional looting in the elite areas between the two sites. It was the fear that the West End was unsafe for its 'rightful' occupants, for the pursuit of commerce and the attraction of tourists, as much as any political threat that led to the prohibition of demonstrations.

In 1855, denied the use of Trafalgar Square, meetings were held in Hyde Park to protest against a Sunday Trading Bill which forbad nearly all Sunday trading in London, a bill which was interpreted as middle-class sabbatarians, who had plenty of time to shop on any day of the week, denying not only working-class shoppers from taking advantage of their one day off work, but also shopkeepers from choosing to open on a day when they could expect to do good business. This was a temporal regulation of trade which shared many of the characteristics of its spatial regulation already discussed. It coincided with another recently enacted bill which limited the hours when drinking places could open on Sundays. A popular protest over Sunday observance became a political protest when the police attempted to ban a second demonstration. At issue was whether the park was private property, owned by the Crown, or public property, where anybody had the right to meet and speak. The authorities claimed the former, the protestors the latter. The second demonstration degenerated into chaos when the police arrested some speakers and demonstrators, effectively ambushing the latter at various points across the park. The police were accused of violence, but were exonerated by a Royal Commission of Inquiry which was more worried about 'lads and young men' who used the protest as an excuse to make trouble, and 'thieves, pickpockets and other reckless and disorderly persons, bent on plunder and mischief, and seeking to effect their purposes under the shield of popular excitement'. A further demonstration, in October 1855, protesting at the price of bread, called for workingmen to meet in 'Our Park': evidently, the effect of trying to suppress popular assembly was to alert the populace to their democratic property rights in a constitutional monarchy.[89]

This issue re-emerged in 1886 in the context of an unemployment demonstration in Trafalgar Square which involved both a Conservative-inspired 'fair-trade' group, claiming that workers needed protection from the exigencies of free trade, and a counter demonstration by the Social Democratic Federation. The latter agreed to defuse the situation by leading an orderly march to Hyde Park, but en route the procession degenerated, possibly in response to abuse from the members of clubs in Pall Mall. In the words of *The Times*, 'the West End was for a couple of hours in the hands of the Mob',[90] and the proceedings were christened 'Black Monday'. Over the following days, there was a classic moral panic, helped by the thickest of London fogs, as rumours circulated that first one mob, then another, was about to take over the streets. When economic conditions worsened in 1887, Trafalgar Square was occupied each night by more than two hundred homeless unemployed men. There are no comments in the historical literature on how the unemployed commingled with the Jubilee celebrants in June 1887,[91] but by October four hundred men were sleeping rough in the square, and in November the Police Commissioner prohibited all meetings there. A demonstration in support of the right to free assembly was called for Sunday 13 November, but huge numbers of police intercepted contingents of marchers from Clerkenwell, a popular site of working-class assembly, in St Martin's Lane, north of the square. Groups from south London attempted to march over Westminster Bridge, but were beaten back by police at the north end of the bridge; and groups from west London got no farther than Haymarket. In Trafalgar Square itself, two of the leading speakers were arrested, and the square cleared by Life Guards cavalry and Grenadier Guards, a notable escalation of events in bringing in armed forces to supplement the police.[92]

The following Sunday, when Trafalgar Square was defended by several thousand police officers – so many, in fact, that there were complaints that the suburbs were left unprotected from crime – a peaceful protest meeting was held in Hyde Park, but some demonstrators decided to walk to the square, where they were met by a charge of mounted police. One demonstrator died from his injuries. In a subsequent parliamentary debate, the question of who 'owned' Trafalgar Square figured prominently, as it had done in the case of Hyde Park thirty years earlier. Liberals argued that the square did not fall within the jurisdiction of the Royal Parks Act of 1872; that it had been 'created by public money for public accommodation'; and that the Home Secretary's authority to 'regulate' processions and meetings did not mean that he could prohibit them altogether. The Conservative government reasserted that the square was 'private' property held in trust by the Queen.[93]

After the introduction of new restrictions in 1892, the square accommodated countless legal demonstrations, including suffragette meetings in 1906 and 1908, and unemployment rallies through the 1920s; but demonstrations were refused permission if they were scheduled for weekdays, when they would disrupt West End business, or if they were deemed unpatriotic, such as anti-war protests in the midst of war. Mace concludes that successive governments were happy to allow radicals to 'let off steam', on the grounds that they were only dangerous if suppressed.[94] As long as the appropriation of space was *merely* symbolic, and no more than the brief inversion of carnival, there was no threat to the status quo. During the nineteenth and early twentieth centuries London never experienced the extreme street violence of, for example, Paris in 1848 or 1871 or the Draft Riots in New York in 1863.[95] It is the symbolism of space, and the way that space was being consciously manipulated, that makes these really quite minor incidents of continuing interest to geographers. The protests in London were *about* public space as well as taking place *in* public space.

Processing through space

In his work on nineteenth-century Canadian cities Peter Goheen has focused on contestation over public space, paying particular attention to processions of various kinds – labour demonstrations, royal visits, funeral processions, anniversary celebrations – moving *through* space as well as simply occupying it. It is worth noting the sheer number of parades and demonstrations. In Toronto in 1855 there were at least twenty-two major events in the streets, five of which involved rioting. Most processions were annual events – marking St Patrick's Day or the Queen's Birthday, for example – but some celebrated special occasions, such as news of victories in the Crimean War.[96] Space was important in at least two ways: what route through the city streets was followed, and how was the parade ordered – who led the way, who marched with whom, who brought up the rear?

Labour marches, to demand higher pay or better working conditions, involved co-operation among different groups of workers expressing solidarity with one another, following routes which combined stops outside workplaces where employers had already made concessions, to raise marchers' morale and offer thanks, with visits to those of less sympathetic employers, to threaten by force of numbers.[97] But workers also needed to lay claim to their city's centre, both as a symbolic act of occupation and to advertise their cause to fellow citizens. The working classes could occupy elite spaces only temporarily. For relatively powerless groups, like the unemployed or suffragettes in London, or manual workers in Manhattan or Toronto, or the members of ethno-religious fraternities, their marches 'constituted . . . a demand for recognition and a reversal of their usual invisibility'.[98] To John Berger, such demonstrations 'interrupt the regular life of the streets they march through . . . not yet having the power to occupy them permanently, they transform them into a temporary stage on which they dramatise the power they lack'.[99] But they are plagued by the paradox that, in Mah's words, such public performances by the powerless 'always undo themselves' because they 'end up proclaiming their own identity, their own particularity'.[100] They seldom persuade onlookers that they share a common cause, that their protests involve universal claims.

From a starting point of greater power, the middle classes could more easily 'render their social particularity invisible and therefore make viable claims to universality'.[101] In Toronto, their orchestration of celebratory processions such as the annual celebration of Queen Victoria's birthday, the visit of the Prince of Wales in 1860, or the week-long series of parades to mark the semi-centennial in 1884 of the incorporation of the City of Toronto, attempted to stress shared civic values, and to stifle dissident voices. The Queen's birthday celebrations involved speeches by political representatives, businessmen, professionals and academics but none by leaders of religious denominations. In a city which took religion very seriously, any speech by a religious leader was more likely to divide than to unite the community. In 1860, at the behest of the Prince, the Orange Order was excluded from the official procession, and in 1884 the organising committee excluded groups 'whose membership was based on inherited divisions of religion and ethnicity'.[102] On both of these special occasions, the aim was not only to promote but to portray a sense of civic community which would have the effect of raising the city's profile among outsiders; and that in turn would be good for (middle-class) business. The Prince's visit was generously reported back in Britain by full-page illustrations in the *Illustrated London News*.

Like working-class demonstrations, the routes of these processions concentrated on main streets downtown, 'those to which were attached the highest symbolic value ... where the public economic, social and political life of the city was focused and where the inhabitants most regularly "rubbed shoulders"'.[103] But unlike the classless solidarity implied by Labour Day parades, most processions organised by the middle classes were predicated on a hierarchical structure of society in which each man (and most marches appear to have been exclusively male) knew his place. In the procession to welcome the Prince of Wales those in 'the humblest positions' – such as members of the 'Loyal United Coloured Society', 'The Native Canadians' and various fraternal associations – headed the parade, 'as remote in space and status from the Prince as possible'. Next came members of professions, and city and county office-holders, culminating in the Mayor. Closest to the Prince and his entourage were members of parliament and the Governor-General.[104]

There was a similarly orderly hierarchical structure in the funeral procession for the politician, Thomas D'Arcy McGee, in Montreal in April, 1868 following his assassination. McGee was an Irish Catholic, who had played a major role in bringing about Canadian Confederation in 1867. It was important for his funeral cortège to visit both St Patrick's Cathedral, the city's principal English-language Catholic church, where requiem mass was conducted, and the Notre-Dame Basilica in the heart of downtown Montreal, where many more mourners could be accommodated, but to avoid passing through French Catholic residential districts where McGee had been unpopular.[105]

Choice of both route and religious destination were also critical in perhaps the two most significant official processions through the streets of late nineteenth-century London, marking Queen Victoria's Golden and Diamond Jubilees in 1887 and 1897 (Figure 6.2). The 1887 procession was limited to the West End, as the Queen processed from Buckingham Palace to Westminster Abbey by way of Piccadilly, Trafalgar Square and Victoria Embankment, returning along Whitehall and Pall Mall. This was almost exclusively elite territory, taking in aristocratic mansions that lined Piccadilly, the gentlemen's clubs of St. James's Street and Pall Mall, and fashionable hotels recently opened on newly constructed Northumberland Avenue. Clubland was also normally an exclusively male preserve. *The Times* noted how the men's clubs opened their doors to lady guests, providing them with privileged viewpoints from balconies and specially erected stands. The working classes, by contrast, mostly viewed the procession from ground level, especially from Piccadilly Circus, where 'the number of people assembled ... could not have been less than 20,000 ... doubtless containing a large proportion of the rougher element', and Trafalgar Square, which 'was literally black with spectators, mostly of the poorer classes'.[106]

Ten years later the Diamond Jubilee was celebrated with a far more elaborate procession over a much longer route – from Buckingham Palace to St Paul's Cathedral, then on through the City and over London Bridge before looping back through the working-class suburbs of south London.[107] Whereas Westminster Abbey might be seen as the monarch's church, St Paul's belonged to the city and the nation. Where

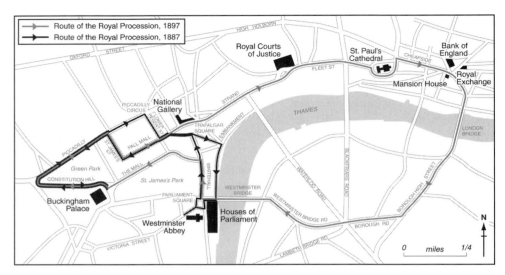

Figure 6.2. Routes Through London followed by Queen Victoria's Golden and Diamond Jubilee Processions, 1887 and 1897.

the working classes had come to the monarch in 1887, encapsulated in *The Times'* observation that 'Immigration from the east-end to the west commenced at a very early hour', in 1897 the monarch was persuaded to go to her subjects.

In 1887 guests from overseas included numerous Indian princes, the Queen of Hawaii and royalty from Persia, Siam and Japan, but most of the visiting dignitaries were European heads of state, members of Victoria's own extended family, and the military presence was quite modest. In 1897, the European cousins were not invited; instead, troops from Britain's colonies and dependencies escorted the prime ministers of the Empire's eleven self-governing colonies over the first stage of the route and then peeled off to form a guard of honour whom the Queen reviewed as she journeyed up Ludgate Hill to St Paul's.[108] *The Times* had recognised an imperial dimension in 1887, concluding that the procession represented, among other things, 'the breadth and width of an unparalleled empire'.[109] But in 1897 it was Empire as much as Empress, and the masculine values of militant imperialism that were being celebrated.

In Montreal in 1868, a procession of about 10,000 mourners had been observed by an estimated 100,000 spectators, as many people as lived in the entire city.[110] In London, even in 1887 it was estimated that two million spectators turned out.[111] McGee's funeral cortège had paused on one of Montreal's most crowded streets so that a leading photographer could record the scene for posterity and for those who had not been present. In London in 1897, the procession was recorded not only in photographs (reproduced, for example, in the *Illustrated London News*), and by newspaper illustrators, with papers vying with one another for the most spectacular images (Figure 6.3), but also on film.[112] These were carefully organised media events where the right use of public space was critical to their effect: performances for all time and space.

DAILY MAIL, LONDON, WEDNESDAY, JUNE 23, 1897.

THE DIAMOND JUBILEE PROCESSION.

VIEWED FROM THE BALL OF ST PAUL'S CATHEDRAL.

By kind and special permission one of the "Daily Mail" artists was enabled to sketch the Diamond Jubilee Procession from the most dominating point in all London—the Ball of St. Paul's. The result appears above, what is, we believe, the largest news illustration ever printed by any daily paper in this country. The drawing was actually completed on the spot, with the exception of the corner showing St. Paul's illuminated, which was added at our own office after nightfall. The X indicates the spot from which the other and larger portion of the drawing was made.

Figure 6.3. View from the Ball of St Paul's of Queen Victoria's Diamond Jubilee Procession, 22 June 1897, from *Daily Mail*, 23 June 1897. Guildhall Library, City of London, C22/2.

Laying claim to leisure space

One of Gissing's most graphic vignettes, 'Io Saturnalia!,' a chapter in *The Nether World* describes a Bank Holiday excursion to Crystal Palace – the south London park and exhibition site – by a rowdy group of youths from the inner-city slums of Clerkenwell. Their day comprised a combination of cheap music and dancing, vulgar sports, a funfair, and alcohol in abundance: one long *shriek*. Like social explorers visiting slums, Gissing made as much of aural disharmony as of visual disorder. On the journey there, they were accompanied in the train by a youth with a concertina; disembarking, they made their way through the pedestrian tunnel that linked the station to the famous glass and iron buildings, 'with many a loud expression of mockery, with hee-hawing laughter, with coarse jokes'. More 'raucous voices' touted for custom in the funfair; even in the tea-rooms 'the uproar of voices was deafening', punctuated by 'shrieks of female laughter'. As darkness fell, dancing migrated to the outdoor terraces, where 'the yell, the cat-call, the ear-rending whistle' were complemented by a bass accompaniment of 'myriad-footed tramp, tramp along the wooden flooring'. Finally, after a firework display, when 'all the reeking multitude utters a huge "Oh" of idiot admiration', Gissing's excursionists fought their way back onto the train: 'We smoke and sing at the same time; we quarrel and make love – the latter in somewhat primitive fashion; we roll about with the rolling of the train; we nod into hoggish sleep.'[113]

Gissing had visited the Crystal Palace on a Bank Holiday as part of his research for *The Nether World*.[114] No doubt he exaggerated the bestiality of the occasion for comic effect. Nonetheless, this must have been a pretty frightening incursion from the perspective of the middle-class residents who inhabited the streets around the Crystal Palace and the respectable visitors who attended classical concerts, strolled in the gardens, and inspected the sculpture and antiquities on display in the exhibition halls. The French impressionist, Camille Pissarro, who lived near the Crystal Palace from December 1870 to June 1871, made several paintings of the surrounding streets and houses. Either they appear semi-rural, such as 'Fox Hill, Upper Norwood', or they exude middle-class respectability. In 'The Avenue, Sydenham' family groups with small children enjoy the tranquillity of a mildly sunny day, while one private carriage occupies the roadway.[115] 'Crystal Palace' depicts the street outside the exhibition buildings (Figure 6.4). This is a busier scene, but still a collection of individual family groups, father and son, a baby in a pushchair, and a few slow-moving carriages; nothing like a crowd, and unlikely to raise more than a whisper. Hardest of all to reconcile with Gissing's bank holiday excess is 'Lordship Lane Station', where Pissarro depicted a straggle of villas and terraces running down the hill on either side of the station, from which a train is slowly advancing towards the viewer. The front-on viewpoint is similar to Turner's dramatic 'Rain, Steam and Speed' (1844), but unlike Turner's revolutionary express, this train 'is of a different ilk . . . suggesting not speed but a gentle chug through the suburbs'.[116] Yet this polite, inoffensive engine is on the same line – Holborn Viaduct to Crystal Palace – that Gissing's day trippers patronised only eight years later.[117] This must have been an appropriation of space, however temporary, which struck horror into regular commuters.

Figure 6.4. Camille Pissarro (1830–1903), 'The Crystal Palace' (1871). Oil on canvas (47.2 x 73.5 cm). Gift of Mr and Mrs B. E. Bensinger, 1972.1164, The Art Institute of Chicago. Photography © The Art Institute of Chicago.

It was not only exhibition sites like the Crystal Palace and pleasure grounds like Cremorne Gardens that provided 'public' spaces contested by different classes. Similar conflicts were evident in the management of truly public (i.e. municipally owned and managed) parks. Residents of Victoria Street could enjoy the open spaces of royal parks, such as St. James's and Green Parks, but the nineteenth century also witnessed the creation of large new public parks, such as Battersea Park and Victoria Park in London and, of course, Central Park in New York. Park life was hedged around with both written and unwritten regulations. In theory, the poor had access on terms dictated by the rich, and most parks, because of their locations in either established middle-class areas or areas that became middle-class because of the attractions that the parks offered, were more conveniently situated for the rich than the poor. Parks, like churches, were intended for all the people; but if too many poor people turned up, they might be made to feel uncomfortable.[118] Victoria Park, on the then outer margins of London's East End, may have been an exception, in part because plans for substantial middle-class villas and terraces overlooking the park were never fully realised. Consequently, the park incorporated working-class activities such as public speaking, by political and trades union activists as well as all shades of religious and anti-religious preachers, and a men's bathing lake (claimed to accommodate 25,000 early-morning nude male bathers) as well as a more conventional ornamental lake.[119] In *Out of Work*, Jos and his apprehensive girlfriend, Polly, 'a pretty Methodist', visit Victoria Park, where Polly is worried by the band, 'playing secular music on a Sunday afternoon' and thinks the opinions of soapbox orators 'downright wicked'. Harkness is anxious to stress the class distinctions within the East End – 'the uninitiated must be pardoned for their ignorance in confounding together shop-keepers, artisans, labourers, and casuals. The initiated are aware how wide is the step which separates these people one from another' – but there was still no denying the overwhelmingly working-class patronage of Victoria Park: 'No West End face is to be seen there, no well-dressed man or woman; only workers bent on enjoying their one day of relaxation.'[120]

The battle for control of New York's Central Park took a variety of forms. Firstly, there was the decision of the Republican-controlled State government, supported by the city's elite, to appropriate land currently occupied by the shanties and pig-geries of poor black, Irish and German families living on what, in 1856, were still the northern margins of the city. Later, in 1870, control passed back to the City and to Democrats who ran the city council. The park's designers, Frederick Law Olmsted and Calvert Vaux, envisaged a polite, aesthetically attractive, 'natural' landscape, as different as possible from the city that abutted it. To Blackmar and Rosenzweig it was 'a controlled public space which, unlike the streets, required parlor manners'; to Matthew Gandy, the park was 'never intended as a forum for political debate and the promotion of discursive interaction between strangers. It was rather an enlargement of the private sphere through the extension of nineteenth-century conceptions of bourgeois domesticity into a public arena.'[121]

A special police force ensured no walking on the grass, no group picnics, no gam-bling, no adult sports, and on Sundays almost nothing at all apart from promenad-ing. There was to be nothing of popular street culture in the park. Unsurprisingly, this limited the park's popularity among the city's working classes, including ethnic minorities, whose only free time was on Sundays, when they wished to participate in communal activities, such as picnics and organised games. Moreover, most people who lived nearby were the middle classes, starting to colonise the Upper East and West Sides during the 1860s, while most working-class citizens lived beyond easy walking distance, and there was as yet no elevated railway to facilitate journeys from downtown. Blackmar and Rosenzweig note that in the 1860s 'more than half the park's visitors arrived in carriages', yet only three per cent of New Yorkers owned a carriage.[122] Even so, there were less elitist crowds for band concerts and ice skat-ing, and there was no guarantee that all the rules would be followed or enforced. During the 1870s and 1880s some rules were relaxed, Sunday concerts were allowed from 1884, the elevated railway increased accessibility and the natural growth of the city meant that more working-class families lived in areas close to the park, such as Harlem. Newspapers reported frequent ball games on the grass and business vehicles on the carriage drives, both contrary to regulations, and the takeover of benches in the park by 'tramps and other unpleasant people'.[123] The establishment of a zoo, contrary to the wishes of nearby Fifth Avenue residents, and the zoo's increasing association with Barnum's circus, added to the popularity of the park for working-class children. Guidebooks now enumerated its commercial attractions as much as its pleasing landscape.

Visiting the park became a more urban experience: more crowded with more diverse types of people; but it was not a site for social mixing across classes. As Prendergast's paintings of the park (discussed in Chapter 4) illustrated, carriages were segregated from horses, and both were segregated from pedestrians; and different parts of the park attracted different social groups. When Henry James visited Central Park in 1904, he emphasised how it 'had to have something for everybody, since everybody arrives famished', but he also observed that, despite the residential proximity of the elite on Fifth and Madison Avenues, the park was now in the possession of recent immigrant groups, evidenced by 'the cheerful hum of that babel of tongues established in the vernal Park'. Central Park, then, experienced occasional 'invasions' for events popular with working-class groups, but it also underwent a form of social ecological succession as the poor (but never the poorest) and 'the alien' proportionally displaced the white Anglo-Saxon Protestant establishment as its main users.[124]

Concluding images

In 1894 Frederick Bell-Smith produced his painting of downtown Toronto, 'Lights of a City Street', looking east along King Street across its intersection with Yonge Street (Figure 6.5). Many of the themes that I have discussed in this and the previous chapter are represented in Bell-Smith's painting. These were not new streets in 1894 but they were experiencing constant destruction and redevelopment, as Gad and Holdsworth have shown in their history of King Street.[125] During the 1880s and 1890s, on a quarter-mile long section of the street either side of Yonge, three major retail stores and nine new office buildings were erected, including the Janes Building (1892), the five-storey block of offices with shops on the ground floor that appears in the top left of Bell-Smith's painting. In the distance (just to the left of the spire) can be seen the dome of the Lewis Rice store (1890), and in the right foreground the lower floors of the five-storey Dominion Bank (1879).[126] As the painting also shows, King Street by 1894 was characterised by modern technology, modern consumerism, modern media and modern people. The first permanent electricity generator in Toronto was installed by J. J. Wright early in 1881 'near the northeast corner of King and Yonge streets'. A rival supplier set up four arc lights at the intersection later the same year, and three years later, Wright's Toronto Electric Light Company installed fifty lamps on King, Queen and Yonge Streets.[127] In the painting, there are lights in the shop windows on the far side of the crossroads and electric streetcars (less than two years old when Bell-Smith painted his picture) displaying their use of electrical energy in multiple ways: a trolley pole sparks on the overhead wire, a streetcar headlight illuminates the wet surface of the street, and the clerestory and interior of the cars are also lit. A chain of electricity poles extends along King Street, from this perspective challenging the height of the Anglican cathedral spire and providing a visual reminder that City Engineer Rust's request to place wires underground, for both safety and aesthetic reasons, had as yet fallen on deaf ears.[128] An electric clock displays the time, just before five in the evening, reminding us of the importance of accurate timekeeping. Newspaper boys compete for custom proffering the evening editions of the city's papers. Toronto had five evening papers; and the need for, and feasibility of, evening editions reflects the constant updating of news, especially stock market prices, made possible by the electric telegraph and the telephone. On or hanging from the sides of buildings are advertisements for 'Equitable Life Assurance', 'Grand Trunk' (one of

Figure 6.5. F. M. Bell-Smith (1846–1923), 'Lights of a City Street' (1894). Oil on canvas. From the Hudson's Bay Company Corporate Collection, used with permission of Hudson's Bay Company.

the principal Canadian railway companies), 'Cunard Line' (transatlantic steamships) and a variety of jewellers, furriers and carpet manufacturers. Bicycles were another recent innovation: safety bicycles, with two equal sized wheels, were introduced only at the end of the 1880s; pneumatic tyres replaced solid tyres after 1888; but it was only during the 1890s that the bicycle became 'a light, fast, and robust machine' and cycling became popular among women.[129]

There are numerous women in Bell-Smith's painting: elderly, young and fashionably dressed, and children among them. One policeman walks towards us and the gaggle of newspaper boys, while the traffic is regulated by another police officer in the middle of the road junction. Pedestrian discipline still leaves something to be desired, at least in the case of a mother and child crossing the street, apparently on a diagonal.[130] Fleming argues that the people in this picture are 'trolley people, already at home in a world more regimented, efficient and punctual than the old world of horse trams'.[131] They also display traits of being 'private in public'. Nobody pays much attention to the man playing a tin whistle on the right of the picture, and there is little eye contact among pedestrians. The elegant gentleman walking towards us raises his hat to the woman he is about to pass, but his companion with the umbrella looks straight ahead, and the woman's daughter is more interested in the streetcar.[132]

Although it is not evident in the painting, King Street was also a principal processional route through the city, whether for special occasions like the Prince of Wales' visit or for regular events like Dominion Day and Orange Order parades.[133] By the 1890s, as banks and offices displaced retailing, King Street's popularity for parading began to wane but the opening in 1903 of the luxurious King Edward Hotel on the south side just east of Yonge provided a new focal point for celebratory processions. In 1911 the connection of Toronto's now municipally controlled power commission to hydro-electric power from Niagara Falls was marked by a procession of marchers 'between lines of white-coated street cleaners holding torches' from the hotel, along King Street and up Bay Street to City Hall. In the execution of this one ritual, many of the improving and modernising functions of the street were enacted: from a private improvement (the hotel) to a public institution (city hall, completed in 1899), along a symbolically cleansed and lit thoroughfare, performing a spectacle for all to see (a crowd of between 30,000 and 50,000).[134]

The differences between mid-nineteenth-century streets and those of the inter-war period are highlighted by a comparison of Gustave Doré's 'Ludgate Hill – A Block in the Street' (1872) (Figure 6.6) and C. R. W. Nevinson's 'Amongst the Nerves of the World' (1930) (Figure 6.7). Both depicted the view from Fleet Street across Ludgate Circus and up Ludgate Hill to St Paul's Cathedral, though Nevinson's viewpoint was from higher up and farther back along Fleet Street. Doré portrayed a scene of total gridlock and indiscipline, every man (sic) for himself, in which horse-drawn traffic competed for space with man-drawn barrows and a flock of sheep. One way in which nineteenth-century artists emphasised the disjunctures of modernisation was to juxtapose animals being driven to market with evidence of the new, such as model dwellings or, in this case, the proliferation of advertisement hoardings – for newspapers ('Daily News', 'Standard', 'Lloyd's News – sale over half a million – one penny') and for the London, Chatham and Dover Railway, whose destinations included the Crystal Palace, advertised on the arch of the viaduct, across which one of the company's trains is making its way.[135] In fact, the steam train is one constant in both illustrations, providing commuters with a way of leapfrogging the congestion of the city streets, as Doré also showed in 'Over London By Rail' (discussed in Chapter 12). By the time Nevinson made his painting, the Southern Railway was well on the way to completing electrification of its suburban network such as the service into Holborn Viaduct depicted here. Equally, by the time Doré drew 'A Block in the Street', the telegraph wires that provide the title for Nevinson's painting had been in place for two decades.

Doré's street seems pre-modern, partly because of the artist's style, yet it contains several modern elements in addition to the train and the hoardings: gas lighting, double-deck horse buses carrying advertising for Bryant & May patent safety matches, and a five-storey commercial building with decorative cornice on the left-hand edge of his picture. We might also note two obelisks, protected by iron railings – another sign of modern sensibilities towards the old and preservation-worthy. On the other hand, the traffic is in chaos, there is an approximation of keeping to the left, but nobody is attempting to direct the traffic. Critically, there is no segregation between different types of traffic: buses and cabs vie for space with a hearse, a brewer's dray, several overladen carts, costermongers dragging barrows of vegetables, and a flock of sheep. The pavement is equally congested. There are a few women on the pavement, but none seated on the top deck of either bus. Of course this is a caricature, but images of gridlocked streets appear so often in illustrations from the 1860s and 1870s that they cannot be so very far from reality.[136]

Figure 6.6. Gustave Doré (1832–1883), 'Ludgate Hill – A Block in the Street', from G. Doré and B. Jerrold, *London: A Pilgrimage* (London, 1872).

Nearly sixty years on, 'Amongst the Nerves of the World' is among the most modernist in style of Nevinson's London paintings. The telegraph wires 'slice up the sky' and the signs – advertising 'NEWS', 'DAILY', 'PAPERS' – 'disengage from their buildings to float autonomously on the picture plane'. This is a modest version of the Futurist style that attracted the young Nevinson before World War I. The wires and the signs are both 'real' elements in the scene, but they also 'give agitation and energy to the composition', symbolically differentiating between the free-floating

Figure 6.7. C. R. W. Nevinson (1889–1946), 'Amongst the Nerves of the World' (c.1930). Tempera on canvas (76.5 x 50.5 cm). © Museum of London, UK (30.167) / The Bridgeman Art Library.

transmission of information across space and the all-too-literal columns of traffic on the street below.[137]

The traffic is not gridlocked. It is moving, slowly and patiently, in an orderly fashion. There are a few pedestrians dodging the traffic to cross the street, but for the most part there are separate files of pedestrians, parked cars, buses and other motorised transport. There is also a continuous flow of buses on the cross street (Farringdon Street), but from the order elsewhere, we can assume that the intersection is under the control of a traffic policeman.[138] The buses are up-to-date: buses with covered tops had been introduced only in 1925.[139] There is no sign of the railing-encumbered obelisks. Modernity no longer needed picturesque props.

As I have argued in this and the preceding chapter, streets were destinations in themselves. As sites for interaction, display and demonstration, they were prime examples of 'practised places', whether appropriated for the exclusive use of one group or function or shared by a range of users and activities, for each of whom they held different meanings. But streets were also – and increasingly – arteries, connecting diverse specialised functional areas and segregated residential districts. I will return to the issue of connection in the final chapter, but next I want to examine some of the new kinds of building associated with specialisation and segregation.

7

Building suburbia

'Suburbia' is a modern word, only in common use since the 1890s. But the adjective, 'suburban', had been used as early as the 1620s and by early in the nineteenth century was being applied to signify 'characteristics that are regarded as belonging especially to life in the suburbs of a city', usually derogatory. 'Suburb', 'those residential parts belonging to a town or city that lie immediately outside and adjacent to its walls or boundaries', can be traced back to the 1380s.[1] In pre-modern times, suburbs were places 'below' the cities with which they were associated, 'sub-urban', often literally so in walled, medieval towns set on high ground for reasons of defence and health. 'Sub-urbs' could also be conceived as not quite urban – socially, culturally, politically and certainly physically marginal. John Archer argues that the relations between suburbs and cities paralleled those between colonies and metropoles; suburbs and colonies were places from which to import goods that could not be produced centrally, and to which to export whoever and whatever was undesirable. He suggests that during the eighteenth century relations between suburbs and cities changed from hierarchical to contrapositional. Rather than suburbs being merely subordinate to cities, they came to be seen as oppositional, more nature than culture, rural than urban, female than male, private than public.[2]

This polarisation, usually condemnatory of suburban life, continued in assessments made by intellectual commentators through the twentieth century, especially as suburbs changed from being retreats for the wealthy, as they had been during the late eighteenth and early nineteenth centuries, to becoming homes to the mass of new lower middle-class families by the beginning of the twentieth century.[3] In *The War of the Worlds* (1898), H. G. Wells, himself the occupant of 'a small resolute semi-detached villa with a minute greenhouse' in Woking, south-west of London, fantasised the desolation of the metropolis by invading Martians, beginning with the destruction of suburbia.[4] Gail Cunningham notes that Wells offered a 'litany of south London suburban locations' each of which is laid waste by the advancing Martians – from Woking to Weybridge to Putney, the reverse of the invasion whereby speculative builders throughout the nineteenth century had been destroying the countryside around London.[5] The suburban landscape is smothered in fast-growing weed, a 'red swamp' of fast-growing vegetation which the Martians inadvertently bring with them from Mars, not so different from the 'red rust' which signified London's invasion of

the countryside in E. M. Forster's *Howards End* (1910).[6] From his hideout on Putney Hill in the heart of middle-class suburbia a survivor castigates the decadence
of humankind, personified in 'the sort of people that lived in these houses, and all
those damn little clerks that used to live down that way . . . They haven't any spirit in
them – no proud dreams and no proud lusts . . . Lives insured and a bit invested for
fear of accidents.'[7]

But Wells was not as wholeheartedly down on suburbia as his fictional creation. By
the end of *The War of the Worlds* suburbia was being reclaimed and rebuilt. Other
commentators, however, offered less nuanced critiques of suburbs as monotonous,
boring, uncultured, places from which anyone with ambition or imagination would
wish to escape. The Dean of St Paul's Cathedral condemned what he called 'bunga-
loid' growth (although, a generation earlier, the first bungalows around London had
been at the cutting edge of a modernist lifestyle, more likely to attract condemnation for their association with bohemianism, cosmopolitanism and sexual transgression, than for their bland uniformity or lack of cultural identity); artists and writers
from George Cruikshank and George Gissing in the nineteenth century to Osbert
Lancaster and George Orwell in the 1930s lampooned suburban architecture and
suburban mores; planners such as Thomas Sharp attacked unplanned sprawl and
ribbon development.[8]

Yet for most citizens, a home of their own in suburbia was a positive goal. A less
acerbic genre of writing about suburbs – to be enjoyed *by* suburban residents, perhaps
as they commuted by train to and from work in central London or as they relaxed
at home in the evening – simply ignored (or, in Lynne Hapgood's interpretation,
deliberately repressed any awareness of) wider economic and social realities, such as
suburbia's dependence on the excesses of imperialism or capitalism or the poverty of
the slums that lay between City and suburbs, emphasising instead the separateness
of a closed, depoliticised, suburban world in which traditional moral values went
unquestioned.[9] Variously self-satisfied or gently ironic in their celebration of suburban domesticity, authors such as Arthur Conan Doyle[10] and William Pett Ridge
provided 'a popular means of imaginative insulation of suburb from city' in which
'family and marital love, neighbourliness, and individualism replace economics as
the logic of this ideal world'. Hapgood invokes further parallels with colonialism,
but now, in contrast to the suburb as exploited colony, she portrays suburbanites as
pioneer settlers, 'like the Pilgrim Fathers taking with them to new lands the traditional values they wished to conserve'.[11] John Hartley adopts a more structural view,
seeing suburban settlers as pawns caught up in the business of imperial expansion.
For him, suburbia was a solution to 'the problem of what to do with large numbers of
white-collar workers needed for petty control functions and professional, technical
and clerical labour in the imperial capital'. At the same time as providing physical
shelter for this new class of labour, suburbia accommodated 'a positive/progressive
value system which put privacy, comfort, family life, self-development and stability
above the attractions of urban or collective culture'.[12]

I am writing this chapter at home, a 1930s semi-detached house in North Harrow,
in the suburbs of north-west London. However much I aspire (beyond the means of a
middle-ranking university teacher!) to live somewhere more 'stylish', more 'cultured'
or more 'urban', the advantages of suburbia are indisputable – friendly, but not too

friendly, neighbours; a relatively safe and clean environment; a five-minute walk to local shops and railway station (along a road grandly entitled 'Imperial Drive'). Paul Oliver enumerates the people who would have been my neighbours in 1930s North Harrow: 'insurance agent, railway clerk, builder, accountant, solicitor, commercial traveller, hairdresser, Marine sergeant, stockbroker, bank teller, theatre box-office manager, LMS railway inspector, schoolteacher, post-office clerk, and several "civil servants", or people with "jobs in the City"'.[13] Although this list encompasses quite a wide social range, it mostly comprises the inter-war equivalents of the lower middle-class suburbanites of the late nineteenth century, epitomised in the character of Charles Pooter, the city clerk who is the fictional author of *The Diary of a Nobody*.[14]

The address of Pooter's home – 'The Laurels', Brickfield Terrace, Holloway – neatly summarises London suburbia of the 1890s: the desire to be close to nature, to have a garden of one's own, and the reality of an urban production line of small houses. Its location, backing onto the railway, indicated the dependence on commuting, an arm's-length relationship with the modern economy denoted by Pooter's affirmation that 'After my work in the City, I like to be at home'. But the railway was also a threat to the suburb's future stability. Pooter worries about the noise and constant vibration from passing trains which causes his garden wall to crack.[15] More critically, steadily cheapening public transport threatened the social stability of suburbia, first allowing families like the Pooters to move into districts previously restricted to a superior middle class, then prompting the slide of inner suburbs like Holloway into working-class multi-occupancy while the next generation of Pooters moved out to semi-detached suburbs like North Harrow. In this process of invasion and succession, a war of the classes if not quite a war of the worlds, 'new suburbanites . . . successfully transformed themselves into the very class which had sought to confine or prescribe their identity'.[16]

The concept of invasion and succession was embedded in E. W. Burgess's ecological model of the growth of the city, based on his observations of early twentieth-century Chicago.[17] So it should not surprise us to find North American equivalents to *The Diary of a Nobody*, lampooning suburban culture, such as Henry Cuyler Bunner's *The Suburban Sage* (1896).[18] Exploitative developers and jerry-builders were also exposed, for example in Upton Sinclair's *The Jungle*.[19] And as in Britain, there were attacks on the supposedly characterless form of inter-war, lower middle-class suburbs, mainly from critics who thought themselves superior, because of their architectural education or urban sophistication. Christine Frederick, the author of *Selling Mrs Consumer* (1929), promoted suburban homeownership as part of her sales pitch for new domestic technology, but argued that 'for more sophisticated and individual types' (such as herself) suburban life was 'a snare and a delusion'.[20] Yet these were exceptional voices, with limited authority, in contrast to the widespread celebration of individualism and private property as foundational values shared by most social and ethnic groups. In Britain, by comparison, the views of landed and intellectual elites, who looked down on the aspirations of the new middle classes to acquire what they had always had and took for granted, were taken more seriously.

The literature on suburbia suggests some other differences between suburbs, through time as well as across national cultures: between nineteenth-century 'street-car suburbs' and the estates laid out by 'community builders' in 1920s America,[21] or between British Victorian suburbs of terraced houses, as many as forty houses per acre on a grid pattern, and semi-detached suburbia in which crescents and culs-de-sac disrupted any regular geometry and densities rarely exceeded the twelve houses per acre recommended by the Tudor Walters Report of 1918.[22]

In Britain, working-class suburbs were mostly built by semi-philanthropic, limited-dividend companies or, from the 1890s, by local authorities; suburbs for working-class North Americans more often involved self-help owner-building or cheap speculative building. In British suburbs – and especially in London – a minority, even among the middle classes, owned their own homes, and it was not until the inter-war years that owner-occupation became the predominant tenure of new suburbanites. In North America, except on Manhattan Island, suburban living sooner came to be equated with homeownership, for blue-collar workers as much as for the middle classes. In Britain, most building for the middle classes was undertaken by speculative builders, erecting houses to a limited menu of variations in style and detailing for clients as yet unknown. In North America, it was more common for subdividers to partition vacant land into individual lots, to be sold to potential homeowners who would then either build their own homes or commission contract builders to erect the homes of their choice. In Britain, mortgage lending was institutionalised in the establishment of building societies, many of which targeted the lower middle classes, first as investors but, by the 1920s, as borrowers; in North America, building and loan companies were less significant but there was a complex system of private mortgages, arranged by lawyers, and vendor-take-back mortgages offered by those selling land or houses as a way of oiling the wheels of property transactions. In Britain (and in Canada), public transport was either owned municipally or, at the very least, subject to municipal regulation through a franchise system, granting private companies the rights to provide services for a specified period, and transport companies were not normally allowed to acquire or retain land for speculative development. In the United States, there was more competition between rival private providers of mass transit, and more explicit and intimate financial links connected the providers of public transport to the providers of new housing.[23]

While all these generalisations are broadly true, they conceal a more complex reality, which it is one purpose of this and the following chapter to interrogate. But another objective is to integrate these topics in a discourse of modernity. Suburbs were 'modern' in at least three ways. Firstly, they offered sites for new social relations – between men and women, parents and children, servants and their employers, and between neighbours – and new lifestyles, focused on home and garden, including a developing male domesticity concerned with gardening, the automobile, and, by the mid-twentieth century, the cult of do-it-yourself. Suburbs were also associated with new ideas about privacy, property, respectability and community, and they were places of more exclusive and certainly larger-scale residential and land-use segregation than had existed in smaller, more compact, densely developed central cities.

Secondly, suburbs were sites for new technology, dependent on new forms of transportation and communications, and on the provision of new infrastructure, such as water and gas pipes, sewers and electricity cables which, in turn, allowed the use of new domestic appliances. Suburban residents relied on buses, trams, commuter trains, bicycles and, in the twentieth century, automobiles, to travel to work, to shop, to worship, to places of entertainment and, in neighbourhoods usually much less densely populated than inner-city districts, to visit friends. They made abundant use of mail services such as the 'penny post' in Britain, which promised several deliveries daily, allowing an exchange of correspondence not unlike today's text messages and emails; they sent and received telegrams in huge numbers, including communicating between home and work by telegraph, and, from its introduction in the late 1870s, they increasingly made use of the telephone. At home, they employed washing machines, vacuum cleaners and refrigerators indoors, and lawnmowers outdoors, if not dispensing entirely with the manual labour of servants certainly reducing their previous dependence upon them.

So the suburb embodied modernity culturally and technologically, but also economically. In David Harvey's model of the 'urbanization of capital', one solution to crises of overaccumulation and a declining rate of profit for industrial capital is to invest in new products and stimulate new markets, often through a 'spatial fix', switching investment from one site to another, one component in the increasing mobility of capital.[24] If colonisation and world trade were large-scale spatial fixes, suburbanisation was an important solution closer to home, offering a new market for the construction industry (in building the suburbs), for financial services (in financing both house construction and house purchase), and for consumer goods industries (in furnishing and equipping new houses).

We need, therefore, to think about suburbs as sites of production (of the built environment, as well as the domestic work of the household), of reproduction (including 'social reproduction' of new generations inheriting and inculcated with their parents' values and social class), and of consumption. And, as I have already indicated in references to H. G. Wells and others, we also need to consider the production and consumption of different imaginative representations of suburbia.

To many of their residents, suburbs were imagined as the antithesis of modernity, sites of refuge from modern business and cosmopolitan diversity, places where 'family values' and 'traditional' architectural styles were celebrated. Yet the desire for such self-conscious retreats was itself part of modernity, a need expressed by new social classes eager to establish their still uncertain status by putting down roots, occupying their own 'castles on the ground'.[25]

This and the next chapter focus principally on London and Toronto. This chapter examines issues of production: building, finance and structural forces promoting residential differentiation. The following chapter discusses how suburbs were owned, consumed and experienced. In both London and the largest American cities, the demand for access to central locations, raising land values and generating traffic congestion and pollution, overcrowding, multi-occupancy and expansion upwards, soon stimulated middle-class flight to new suburbs. In smaller cities, such as Toronto, however much conditions were represented locally as resembling those in London or New York, there was less pressure on land and correspondingly lower land values. It was easier for families to acquire their own homes, and easier for working-class families in particular to combine homeownership on the margins of the city with employment downtown. So we might expect different geographies of suburbanisation in cities differentiated by size as much as by nationality.

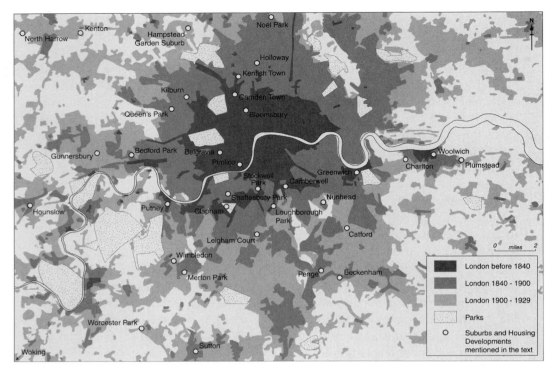

Figure 7.1. London's Suburbs, 1830–1930.

The production of middle-class suburbs

Although pre-modern suburbs were often marginal spaces, socially as well as geo-graphically, the first consciously modern suburbs were for the rich. City merchants retained pieds à terre over or behind their counting-houses, purchasing suburban homes for their families to which they would retreat at weekends. Robert Fishman argues that there were key changes in attitudes to family, children, class and the physical and moral messiness of urban life that stimulated suburbanisation among the bourgeoisie of late eighteenth-century London.[26] He notes the paradox that 'the extremely unequal cities of the eighteenth century tolerated a great measure of close physical contact between rich and poor; whereas the more "equal" cities of the nineteenth and twentieth centuries were increasingly zoned to eliminate such contacts'.[27] Early modern suburbia was a 'collective creation', but it was 'improvised not designed';[28] not *planned* by powerful ground landlords or estate developers but a spontaneous coalescence among groups of like-minded families, exemplified by the case of Clapham in south London (Figure 7.1), associated with the revival of evangelicalism in the 1790s. Yet suburbs like Clapham could not develop on com-pletely 'virgin' sites: they had to be squeezed in among agricultural villages and less appetising urban-fringe land uses, such as the noxious industries that had earlier been excluded from central cities.[29]

So, from the middle decades of the nineteenth century, planned suburbs associated with specific designers and architects were more explicitly intended as retreats, not only from the excesses of metropolitan life but from the randomness of the urban fringe: places like Llewellyn Park, across the Hudson from New York; Riverside, outside Chicago; and Bedford Park in west London.

Laid out in the 1850s, Llewellyn Park was a romantic retreat from the modern metropolis, but itself intrinsically modern: a gated community incorporating and reshaping nature for the benefit of its elite residents. Riverside, designed by Olmsted for the Riverside Improvement Company, involved an even greater manipulation of nature; it was also more obviously at heart a modern property speculation: the company went bankrupt in 1874, but the suburb survived. Bedford Park, London's first 'garden suburb', developed by Jonathan Carr in west London between 1875 and 1883, was associated with the 'arts and crafts' movement, and accommodated a distinctly 'arty' population.[30]

As transport technology improved, as real wages increased and hours of work reduced, so suburbia became accessible to a wider range of social groups. Moreover, the expansion of business stimulated the growth of a lower middle class of junior managers, clerks, commercial travellers and public officials, eager to emulate the suburban exodus of their employers. Classic studies of suburbanisation, such as H. J. Dyos' *Victorian Suburb*, focused on Camberwell in south London, and Sam Bass Warner's *Streetcar Suburbs*, charting the growth of Roxbury, West Roxbury and Dorchester in south-west Boston, demonstrated the expansion of lower middle-class suburbia in the second half of the nineteenth century.[31] In New York, equivalent single-family row housing was colonising Harlem and less central parts of Brooklyn. By the 1920s, when the characteristic form of lower middle-class housing in London had become the suburban semi-detached, the corresponding suburban frontier in New York had moved out into Queens.[32]

For each successive suburbanising class, two geographical possibilities were available: the development of socially mixed suburbs, or a strict segregation of classes within suburbia. For all the advocacy of the former by utopian and communitarian visionaries, the practical modernity of the latter invariably won out. Planned communities such as Hampstead Garden Suburb, begun in 1907 as a suburban microcosm of Ebenezer Howard's ideas for garden cities, intended to accommodate a mix of all social classes, quickly became exclusively middle-class;[33] more haphazard developments usually deteriorated to the neighbourhood's lowest common denominator, as middle-class family villas were converted to multiple occupancy. Of course, there were disadvantages associated with strict spatial segregation. Faced with a mounting 'servant problem', middle-class families were less likely to employ resident domestic servants, more dependent on non-resident charwomen and gardeners; and they continued to patronise local tradesmen and artisans. Every middle-class suburb needed a respectable and useful working class within walking or cycling distance.

But suburbanisation was first and foremost a question of status – lower middle-class families establishing their newly gained respectability, elite families defending their superior status. And a critical indicator of status, in large, impersonal metropolises, was where you lived. George Gissing was careful to locate his characters in specific neighbourhoods of London, often in particular streets, in part as an aid to his own imagination: once he knew where they lived, he knew what they would think and how they would behave. In *In The Year of Jubilee*, set in suburban south London, each location contributes to our understanding of characters' circumstances and values.

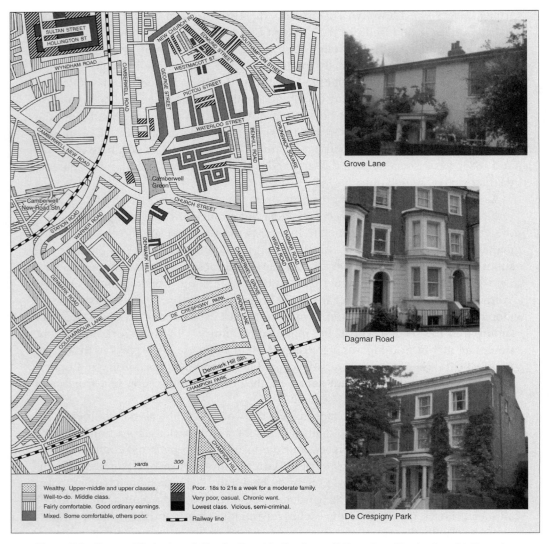

Figure 7.2. George Gissing's and Charles Booth's Camberwell. Based on Charles Booth's Descriptive Map of London Poverty (1889), with author's photographs of houses in streets described in Gissing's *In The Year of Jubilee* (1894).

Nancy Lord lives with her father in Grove Lane, part of the old, dignified, slightly ramshackle eighteenth-century Camberwell that was being overwhelmed by the vulgarity of new money, represented by the Peacheys' pretentious villa in De Crespigny Park (Figure 7.2). When the dull but worthy Samuel Barmby becomes a partner in a local business, he moves to Dagmar Road, 'a new and most respectable house, with bay windows rising from the half-sunk basement to the second storey'. It was critical for his sense of achievement that the bay extended over *both* main storeys. Meanwhile, Mr Vawdrey, a wealthy City investor, occupies a secluded mansion on Champion Hill, half-a-mile uphill and farther out of London than the other characters. It might seem that I am demonstrating the heterogeneity, not the homogeneity, of Victorian suburbs, but social equality is always relative and always about scale. On Charles Booth's poverty map, all these addresses fell into the top two of Booth's eight categories and, within Camberwell, the social distinctions between one group of streets and another were as critical as, at another scale, the more widely recognised differences between London's East End and West End.[34]

The only imaginary address among the principal characters in Gissing's novel is the new house to which Mr Morgan, a debt-collector, and his family move, situated in 'Merton Avenue, Something-or-other Park', damp, ill-built: 'From cellar floor to chimney-pot, no square inch of honest or trustworthy workmanship.' The irony was that something resembling a real park – the gardens of an old mansion – had been destroyed to make way for the new estate.[35]

There were many 'parks' that resembled Gissing's: Loughborough Park and Stockwell Park were closest to Camberwell (and close to Gissing's own rooms in Brixton), but Clapham Park was only another mile away, and Merton Park, five miles to the south-west, was being developed at the time that Gissing was writing his novel.[36] Labelling an area as a 'park' was an obvious marketing ploy, implying both community – the enclosure of an aristocratic park – and status. Whatever an intellectual critic like Gissing thought, a small house in a 'park' was the aspiration of countless lower middle-class families.

Segregation within suburbia also extended to segregation in the journey to work. The high cost of riding by horse-bus or train initially restricted commuting to the middle classes. In London, some developers and railway companies offered free season tickets as an incentive to persuade customers to purchase suburban land or housing, but imposed restrictions to ensure the 'right' class of passenger. For example, the London and North-Western Railway announced in 1853 that it would offer free first-class passes for eleven years to 'persons who would build houses worth not less than 50*l*. per ann.' (in practice, the passes were for the *occupiers* of the new houses) in the vicinity of stations north of London. Most stations served free-standing towns in the Chilterns, but Harrow and Pinner (now Hatch End) were sufficiently close to London to attract daily commuters. Houses to let at £50 per annum would mostly have been substantial detached villas for the well-off business and professional classes; but the train service was still not very convenient for any but the most leisurely commuters. In practice, only 208 house passes had been issued by 1867 when the offer was discontinued.[37]

In the 1850s the single fare between Harrow and Euston (11.5 miles) was a shilling third-class (and two shillings and sixpence first-class), far beyond the resources of skilled artisans earning twenty-five to thirty shillings per week. However, when the Great Eastern Railway proposed to extend its line from Bishopsgate to Liverpool Street, a little closer to City offices, government demanded the introduction of cheap fares for workmen as a quid pro quo for the displacement of more than a thousand persons from their homes. Similar obligations were imposed on several other railway companies at roughly the same time – the mid-1860s – and one or two companies voluntarily introduced workmen's trains in advance of legislation. The Great Eastern's extension was too short for the company to recoup the costs (over £2,000,000 for less than a mile) by raising fares. Instead, they anticipated substantial growth in the numbers of 'suburban gentlemen' who would use the railway. In reality, the company found itself catering for 20,000 new commuters travelling on early morning workmen's trains at a daily rate of 2d. return, whose presence discouraged potential first-class passengers from travelling on the same lines. The company's general manager claimed that speculative building stimulated by cheap fares had 'utterly destroyed the neighbourhood for ordinary passenger traffic'.[38]

It might appear, therefore, that the introduction of cheap fares on some lines but not others led to increasing suburban residential segregation, differentiating between suburbs according to the mix of fare classes on offer on each line. However, east London was already predominantly working-class in character, and the requirement to provide cheap fares merely reinforced an existing tendency. Moreover, railway companies to the south and east of London had always been more inclined to encourage suburban traffic than those to the north and west, for which the potential for long-distance mainline traffic – to Birmingham, Liverpool, Manchester, Glasgow, Bristol, Wales and the West Country – was much greater. On the Great Western and London and North-Western Railways, suburban traffic, apart from the handful of first-class passengers, was an irritation and an inconvenience; on the Great Eastern and London, Chatham & Dover Railways, it was an economic necessity.

John Kellett observed that 'Altering the rail services to make, for example, the fare for the seven miles from Waterloo station to Wimbledon equal the fare for the seven miles from Liverpool Street station to Tottenham would not have made the working man and his family any more welcome in Wimbledon', nor would a fare reduction remotely have compensated for the difference in house rents or have encouraged builders to erect cheaper dwellings. Indeed, covenants incorporated into sales contracts for land in middle-class suburbs, such as Wimbledon, frequently forbad the construction of houses below a value of, say, £1000, at a time when working-class terraced houses were valued at below £300.[39]

The use of restrictive covenants by ground landlords and developers had a long history, but it had mostly been confined to property developed on long (usually 99-year) leases. Developer-builders would erect (or contract with others to erect) houses which, at the termination of the lease, would revert to the ground landlord. The object on the part of landowners was to ensure that the houses their descendants acquired at the end of the lease enhanced the value of their estate. Consequently, they were anxious to include covenants specifying the materials to be used in construction, the minimum value of houses to be erected, and the range of non-residential uses that were prohibited. However, there was no point in specifying high-quality, high-value dwellings for which there would be no demand. So some landed estates also introduced their own forms of zoning, developing different parts of their property for different markets. The Marquis (later Duke) of Westminster had more modest clients in mind in developing Pimlico from those he could attract to Belgravia. When, in the 1880s, the leases fell due on his Mayfair estate, which abutted Oxford Street, it made sense to insert a kind of cordon sanitaire, a buffer zone of superior model dwellings, which could accommodate the tradesmen and artisans on whom the rich depended, and which would protect the heart of Mayfair from the evils of commercialisation or multiple occupancy that might otherwise spread through streets close to Oxford Street.[40]

This model of estate development, employing covenants and informal zoning, was replicated in cities in nineteenth-century North America, although mostly by attaching restrictions to land that was sold freehold. It continued into the twentieth century, including restrictions placed on the 'race' of prospective residents. Deed restrictions routinely excluded Blacks, Jews and Chinese from estates intended for middle-class white families.[41] More informally, real estate agents and housing land-lords might decline to sell or let property to certain groups. When, in 1929, the agent responsible for letting property in a high-class Toronto garden suburb proposed offer-ing a vacant house to a couple who 'from appearances . . . are of Jewish descent' he received an instantaneous reply from the company that owned the estate: 'we long since adopted the policy of not accepting any Jewish tenants'.[42] In the climate of popular anti-Semitism then current, even if the owners themselves were not anti-Semitic, they feared their existing tenants were: offering a house to a Jewish family might lead to other tenants giving notice that they would not renew their leases. If this seems shocking, we might reflect that it is not so different from the attitudes of many present-day NIMBY (Not In My Back Yard) opponents of neighbourhood change, or of homeowners who in the early twentieth century lobbied local governments to introduce 'residential restrictions' prohibiting a range of undesirable land uses from their areas: no apartment buildings, no petrol stations, no (Chinese) laundries. The fear was that any of these activities would reduce local property values or make property harder to sell or let.[43]

It was not enough to ensure that people different from oneself were denied the opportunity to live next door. They might even be prohibited from passing through the neighbourhood, prefiguring today's 'gated communities'. Perpetuating the tra-dition of gates and bars that characterised many middle-class estates in London's West End in the mid-nineteenth century (see above, Chapter 6), the privatisation of suburbia was designed not only to protect private estates from intruders but, in extreme cases, to prevent any contact between adjacent areas of public and private housing or of black and white communities. In 1927, for example, a private developer constructed a concrete wall across a road which would otherwise have allowed ten-ants on the London County Council's Downham estate (in the suburbs of south-east London) to pass through an adjacent area of middle-class housing. The developer's fear, evidently endorsed by the people to whom he sold his houses since the wall survived for nearly twenty years, was that his (and their) property would depreciate in value, sullied by the 'negative externality' of the people next door.[44]

These extreme cases reflect a wider truth: that social segregation was built into every stage of financing, building and marketing suburban estates, especially where they were destined for owner-occupation. It was easier to borrow money to finance housebuilding, easier to attract prospective buyers, and easier for those buyers to obtain mortgages where all the parties were confident that neighbours would share the same attitudes to maintaining and decorating their property, the same pride in gardening, the same respect for privacy, the same 'culture'. On the other hand, resi-dential differentiation by class and 'race' was less likely where most dwellings were rented on weekly or monthly terms, which made it easier for ecological change to occur (frequently occurring vacancies offered opportunities for an incoming group to gain a foothold), where freehold land was held in small parcels, or where build-ing firms erected only a few houses at a time. So, as both rates of homeownership and the average size of building firms increased over time, we might expect increas-ing levels of residential differentiation. And, given higher rates of homeownership in North America, and in the absence of any obvious differences in the relative size of suburban housebuilding projects on either side of the Atlantic, we would expect higher levels of residential differentiation in North American than in British suburbs.

Speculative building

Any kind of statistical analysis is fraught with difficulties in defining the term 'builder'. In London, district surveyors' returns recorded the names of 'owners' and 'builders'. H. J. Dyos defined *speculative* builders as people whose names appeared as both 'owner' and 'builder' in the District Surveyors' Returns. They were building (or arranging with contractors who would do the physical building) *for* themselves. In the context of Victorian London, where few people built in order to become owner-occupiers, Dyos could reasonably assume that once they had erected the houses, they would either let them or sell them, in each case to persons unknown at the time building commenced. The same logic was less applicable in North America, where prospective owner-occupiers were more likely to purchase a vacant lot and then arrange for a contractor to erect a home to their specifications. At the bottom end of the market, owners might provide their own physical labour, similar to the builders of 'self-help housing' in less developed countries today. In both kinds of custom-building, the name of the 'owner' on the building permit was the same as that of the 'builder'. Even where building was clearly 'speculative', the 'builders' included many whose own jobs were outside the building industry and who relied on contractors to undertake every aspect of construction. Nevertheless, some statistical analysis is valuable inasmuch as it will demonstrate the average scale of development: were houses being built one at a time, or were whole streets of dozens or even hundreds of houses being authorised by a single permit; and was a different 'builder' responsible for each project, or were the same names associated with numerous permits or entries in the surveyors' returns?

Most builders had limited capital resources and could afford to build only a few dwellings at a time. In the south London suburb of Camberwell between 1878 and 1880, 416 firms erected a total of 5,670 houses, an average of 4.5 houses per builder per annum, and few streets were developed by only one or two builders. On many roads it took forty or fifty years before all plots were built on. Dyos concluded that devel-opment was 'markedly heterogeneous'.[45] But although the building personnel may have been heterogeneous, most of the dwellings they produced were, in aggregate, variations on a common theme: three-storey terraces in the north of Camberwell, developed before 1880; two-storey terraces and semi-detached pairs in areas farther from central London, developed later. Many small builders operated in the context of large estate developments; whatever personal details they incorporated into their houses, they still had to conform to covenants laid down by estate landowners and developers. Moreover, while 52 per cent of firms each built no more than six houses, between them, they accounted for fewer than one in eight of all new dwellings. A mere fifteen firms (3.6 per cent) erected 1,781 houses, nearly one-third of the total.

Figures for the whole County of London also show a trend towards larger firms by the end of the century: across London, the average number of houses per builder increased from 5.4 in 1872 to 11.6 in 1899, when 59 per cent of builders erected six or fewer houses, compared to 75 per cent in 1872. The biggest seventeen firms together built 2,136 houses (30 per cent of the total) in 1899, of which the largest of all, Watts of Catford, erected over 400 houses across south-east London.[46]

Another large-scale builder in south London, Edward Yates, built over 2,500 houses in the course of a 35-year career. Even for Yates, however, individual schemes were mostly quite small: his largest project, the Waverley Park estate in Nunhead, eventually comprised 742 terraced houses on 50 acres of land, but even this was only a tiny island of just ten streets in the sea of south London suburbia. It was likely, therefore, that a builder's efforts to erect good-quality housing would sometimes be frustrated by jerry-building or industrial development on a neighbouring estate over which he had no control. For most speculative builders the ideal was to sell their finished houses as soon as possible, thereby realising money capital that could be used to finance the purchase of further land and materials: they built to sell and build again. Yet Yates retained ownership of most of the houses he built: in 1905 he owned 2,345 houses, mostly let at £30–40 per annum. To survive so long without financial disaster while operating almost entirely speculatively, like 90 per cent of builders in Victorian London, Yates was both extraordinarily skilful and extraordinarily lucky. In the 1870s he had boasted that his houses were rarely unlet, yet on his death in 1907, more than 300 of his Waverley Park houses were empty.[47] Both housebuilding and landlordism were financially precarious activities.

By the 1930s there were more examples of building firms of the scale of Watts or Yates operating in London's new suburbs; several had originated in Scotland or in Lancashire, and several moved into speculative housebuilding from other forms of construction and contracting, such as civil engineering, which experienced a downturn with the onset of the Depression.[48] Unlike North America, where there was a collapse of all kinds of building during the 1930s, there was still scope to expand residential construction in much of England. As the costs of labour and materials declined, and as interest rates fell, skilled manual and junior non-manual workers who retained their jobs found that at last they could afford a home of their own.

Even where small, locally based builders were involved, their patchwork quilt added up to architecturally and socially homogeneous tracts of residential development, disrupted only by pre-existing villages standing like islands in a sea of semi-detached suburbia, by sites for new shops, schools, churches and cinemas, and by the occasional, often locally opposed, council housing estate (such as the Downham Estate, mentioned earlier). In North Harrow and the adjacent suburb of Pinner, for example, there were numerous local building firms – Cutler's (who built the author's house) worked in over fifty streets, Nash's on more than twenty, Gullett's on twelve – but they rarely built all the houses on one road; on one street of around one hundred houses, eighteen builders were involved.[49] But while there were superficial differences between their houses, they were mostly variations on the same theme – seven or eight-room detached and semi-detached houses priced at between £850 and £1350.

The result was a relatively homogeneous suburban landscape designed for a broad range of 'middling' households, from well-paid skilled manual workers to junior professionals, committed to shared values that prioritised home and family. To insiders, differences between the 'Monk's House' which offered heavy oak timbering, the 'Sunshine House' which had some superficial modernist streamlining, and the steep gables on the 'Honeymoon Cottage' which mimicked rural cottages while reducing the floor area to allow a price affordable by newlyweds, added texture to areas perceived by outsiders as monotonous.[50]

In North American suburbs, the balance of housing provision was different from the overwhelming dominance of speculative building around London, but not as different as is sometimes implied. Richard Harris identifies three types of builder – custom-builders (building on contract to the wishes of particular clients), owner-builders (building their own homes) and speculative builders – acknowledging that the latter 'seem to have expanded their operations most effectively during boom periods such as the 1920s, when demand was strong and the risks of building on spec were minimized'.[51] Speculative builders were probably most active in the largest cities, where demand appeared limitless and where high land values prompted the building of duplexes and triplexes, row housing or, at the very least, houses on narrow lots that allowed little scope for individual expression. In Toronto speculative building was both cyclical – concentrated in the 1880s, the early 1910s and the 1920s – and geographically uneven, avoiding unserviced and inaccessible areas. Harris estimates that prior to World War I speculative builders were responsible for about 25 per cent of new homes (compared to 90 per cent in London). After the war, the proportion probably increased, geographically concentrated towards the edge of the built-up area, but within city limits.[52] Around U.S. cities, too, in the late nineteenth century, 'the majority of moderate-cost suburban houses were built on speculation, not for a particular family'.[53]

Nevertheless, speculative builders were less important in America than Britain. Less speculative building implied more small-scale 'builders'. In Montreal, between 1868 and 1877, 2,000 builders erected 6,000 homes; half of these builders constructed no more than two houses. In Boston, Sam Warner tracked building permits for 22,500 new dwellings, erected between 1870 and 1900 by 9,000 individual 'builders', an average of 2.5 houses per builder. The majority erected only one dwelling. Among a random sample of builders, nearly 30 per cent could not be traced in Boston street directories; another third were listed as engaged in trade, manufacturing or the professions; only 30 per cent were employed in 'building and construction'. At the top of the pyramid 122 builders, of whom 71 per cent listed their occupations as 'building and construction', erected 5,350 houses, or 23 per cent of the total, 44 houses each. However, Warner did not report how many separate projects made up these totals; and the largest builder, responsible for 328 dwellings over the 30-year period, was clearly not in the same league as Watts or Yates in London.[54]

In Hamilton, an industrial city west of Toronto, the annual average number of dwellings per builder increased from 2.5 in 1873, to 4.5 in 1881, to a peak of 10.2 in the boom year of 1913; but in recession business contracted dramatically: only 1.3 dwellings per builder in 1897. In contrast to Warner, who claimed that in Boston 'from the extreme individualism of agency in the building process came great uniformity

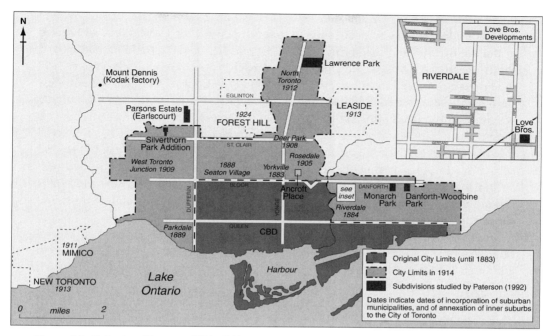

Figure 7.3. Suburban Toronto, 1880–1930, showing locations mentioned in the text. Inset shows streets developed by Love Bros Ltd in Riverdale, 1905–1910.

of behaviour', Doucet and Weaver discerned 'very ragged streetscapes' in Hamilton. Some lots remained vacant for decades; not only were neighbouring houses erected by different builders but houses from the 1850s or 1860s were frequently found next door to houses built twenty or thirty years later.[55]

But 'uniformity' or 'raggedness' depends on the observer's expectations and on the scale of analysis. Housing and population were usually homogeneous at the scale of street blocks, and residential differentiation increased in scale into the twentieth century, particularly under the auspices of 'community builders' who acquired, improved (by installing services) and subdivided large tracts of the urban fringe, which they disposed of to small builders, subject to strict covenants and regulations governing what could be built and for whom.[56]

A Toronto example can serve to illustrate the fragmented, yet concentrated spatial pattern of building by one firm which, in aggregate, helped to produce a relatively homogeneous suburban landscape. Between June 1905 and October 1910, Love Bros Ltd featured as 'owner' on no fewer than 106 residential building permits. In total this added up to 428 dwellings.[57] The largest number of dwellings authorised on one permit was 24, and only six permits were for at least 10 dwellings; no fewer than forty permits were for a single detached dwelling or a single pair of semi-detached houses. Yet the geographical coverage of Love Bros' building was highly concentrated: only eleven permits were for dwellings on the west side of the city; almost all the rest, including all the largest, were for houses within a mile of the firm's offices and yard near the corner of Pape Avenue and Gerrard Street on the east side of the city (Figure 7.3). It is impossible to plot the sequence of building precisely since many permits were given the same geographical description: 'near Logan Avenue on north side Withrow Avenue' applied to seven permits for 33 dwellings authorised in the fall of 1906 and the spring of 1907. By the fall of 1907, building had moved south one block, to 'near Logan Avenue on Riverdale Avenue'. And from 1908 the firm concentrated its efforts on Wolfrey and Dearbourne Avenues and Fairview Boulevard, interspersing detached and semi-detached houses. Details on building permits do not match information in subsequent assessment rolls precisely, but it is clear that the firm was responsible for almost all the forty-eight houses on the north side of Wolfrey Avenue, all estimated to cost between $1800 and $3000, but spread across five building permits issued over twelve months. Over the entire five-year period, more than half their houses had a permit value of between $1000 and $1600. Fewer than one in eight was valued at $3000 or more. This was an architecturally and socially homogeneous advance across the fields of east Toronto.[58]

More modest dwellings, on a much larger scale, characterised the best known of nineteenth-century American builder-developers, S. E. Gross, who specialised in building cheap frame houses in the suburbs of Chicago, beyond the fire limits which demarcated where buildings had to be constructed in brick in order to reduce the risks of fire. By 1882 Gross had laid out 40,000 house lots around the city and in 1889 it was claimed that nearly 8,000 workers had become homeowners by purchasing houses from him. Gross advertised in German as well as English, targeting recent immigrants, asking for only a small deposit, and promising low monthly mortgage repayments.[59] Gross presented himself as public-spirited, helping the honest work-ingman to own his own home. In retrospect, we can see that he was not quite so altruistic. Like many grander developers, he combined land speculation with busi-ness interests in streetcar and electric railway companies, promoting his own town, Grossdale, located just west of Riverside. But he defaulted on paying property taxes on the lots he had not yet sold, thereby threatening the provision of services to those who had already purchased lots and built their own homes.[60]

Other developers were even less scrupulous than Gross. In *The Jungle* Upton Sinclair described the scam which deprives Jurgis Rudkus and his family, recently arrived from Lithuania, of their home on the south side of Chicago. Jurgis works in the stockyards and on his way to work one day is given a brightly coloured advertisement showing an apparently new two-storey home bedecked in the iconography of happy family life. 'Why pay rent? Why not own your own home?' was rendered in Polish, Lithuanian and German, and the words of 'Home, Sweet Home', too, were translated into Polish. The advertisement promised a home with four rooms and a basement for $1500: $300 down and $12 per month for 100 months. The reality was rather less attractive. The basement was unfinished, the attic unboarded, the street outside unpaved and unlit. Nor was the house as new as it appeared in the advertisement. Four previous immigrant families – German, Irish, Bohemian, Polish – had set out to buy the house over the preceding fifteen years. It turns out that $12 per month was not a mortgage payment but a monthly rent – a contract for deed where the purchasers acquired ownership only if they succeeded in making all one hundred monthly payments on time. In a normal mortgage, if they defaulted and the mortgagee foreclosed, they would at least have recovered the equity they had invested up to that point. But, in this case, if they fell behind with the rent, almost inevitable at some time for labourers in the volatile economy of late nineteenth-century Chicago, they faced eviction and lost everything.[61]

Owner-building

As well as artisans buying cottages there were others who built their own homes. One reason for working-class families migrating to the New World was the hope of becoming their own landlord, an aspiration that could be fulfilled in at least some older East Coast cities, such as Philadelphia and Baltimore, and certainly in cities around the Great Lakes and farther west. Land was cheap and plentiful; building materials (mainly timber) were also cheap and balloon-frame construction with timber and nails required little skill. Consequently, many immigrants moved direct to suburbs, including British immigrants in Toronto, and German, Polish and Scandinavian immigrants in Detroit and Milwaukee.[62]

Working-class homeownership was also encouraged by lower levels of taxation in suburbia. North American suburbs were often separate municipalities, with their own by-laws (usually less restrictive than central cities, e.g., with less strict fire regulations), and their own levels of taxation and, correspondingly, service provision. So working-class households might sacrifice some city services by moving to the suburbs – the roads might not be paved or lit, they might have to depend on cesspits rather than mains sewers – but, in return, they got low taxes and a permissive regime allowing them to build what and how they wanted. For example, housing construction began in 1909 in North Earlscourt, a working-class suburb of Toronto that lay beyond city boundaries in the mostly rural York Township; but it was not until 1918 that any building regulations were introduced, 1919 before mains water was connected, 1925 before sewers were constructed, and 1926 before roads were surfaced with tarmac.[63]

The very remoteness of districts like Earlscourt also worked to the advantage of working-class settlers. The Toronto Railway Company was awarded a 30-year franchise to operate the city's streetcar services in 1891 but, as the City annexed surrounding districts during the 1890s and 1900s, the company refused to extend streetcar service to these still thinly populated areas. Local newspapers complained that this intensified congestion in the central city and encouraged the development of apartment housing.[64] The effect would be to force up rents and land prices in the existing built-up area. Eventually, the City decided to construct its own set of suburban lines – three disconnected routes united under the banner of the Toronto Civic Railways – but even this solution was unsatisfactory. Commuters had to transfer from one system to the other at interchange points in North and East Toronto; and they had to pay two fares to get downtown.[65] But another consequence was to discourage speculative builders from erecting middle-class housing in the newly annexed districts, depressing land values relative to the serviced areas, and making it possible for workingmen to afford lots on which they built their own homes. In a perverse way, therefore, the lack of public transport could stimulate working-class suburbanisation just as could the provision of cheap fares.

A series of advertisements for the 'Nairn and Parsons' Estate', part of Earlscourt, in the *Toronto Evening Telegram* during May 1909, neatly illustrates both the ideology and the mechanisms behind self-building. Land cost between $3 and $8 per front foot, implying an outlay of as little as $100 for a home lot. Payments of $10 down and $5 per month thereafter compared with rents of $15–20 per month for small working-class houses in the inner city. As the first advertisement (7 May) advised:

Rent Payers – Why Pay Profits to a Landlord? This is Our Plan: Choose a Home Lot – Pay Down $10.00 and then get possession immediately – Build a little place until you are able (with saved rent money) to enlarge it. If you can't build, put up a tent for the summer. What you save in rent builds you a little house in the fall. Then build larger next year. The payments are only $5 monthly.

In subsequent weeks the message was elaborated:

Want An Investment or a Home – Which? You Can Get Both in the Purchase of a Building Lot in the Nairn & Parsons' Estate . . . no matter how simple the first structure of your home may be, in few years all settlers will have enlarged and beautified their dwellings (14 May 1909).

Do You Want to Make Some Money? Invest a Few Dollars Out of Your Wages in Active Real Estate: Investors Have Their Eyes on It; Homeseekers are Delighted With It (21 May 1909).

In other words, self-building was not just a way of finding somewhere to live but also an incorporation into a middle-class way of life, concerned as much for future exchange value as current use value. Aspirations to middle-class values were also reflected in the layout of streets, 'on the Rosedale Plan'. Rosedale was one of Toronto's most exclusive suburbs. What 'the Rosedale plan' meant in Earlscourt was 'rolling, picturesque ground – many fine trees scattered over it . . . some of the streets are in charming crescents and ovals, others in straightaway, dignified boulevards'. But whereas Rosedale was protected by strict residential restrictions, there were no such restrictions in Earlscourt (Figure 7.4).

While there is plentiful evidence from contemporary newspapers describing the process of owner-building around North American cities, Harris employed assessment rolls to estimate its extent quantitatively. He distinguished between speculative building, denoted by pairs or rows of similarly valued dwellings, and owner-built dwellings, which were usually, at least to start with, assessed for lower values than most speculatively-built dwellings, but were also – like custom-built dwellings at the top of the market – one-off creations. In assessment records, therefore, it is likely that owner-built dwellings will have had low values *and* values different from their neighbours. Harris identified a 'self-built threshold' of around $600 for dwellings built between 1901 and 1907, rising to $1000 for those completed between 1908 and 1913. On this basis, 29 per cent of new houses in the earlier period, and 37 per cent in the later period – about a quarter of new homes within city limits but nearly 90 per cent beyond city limits – were owner-built.[66] Of course, there were exceptions to Harris' thresholds: some very cheap houses were erected by builders speculatively – one row of roughcast dwellings built by Love Bros in 1906 cost only $625 per house to build, far less than the cost of some owner-built homes, especially those purchased in kit form by mail-order or from local timber merchants.[67] The buyers of such kits may have hired local contractors to assemble them, or they may have done the job themselves, probably with the help of friends. Indeed, the term 'owner-builder' should not be interpreted as implying that all construction was undertaken

Figure 7.4. Self-built Housing in Toronto Suburbs: 'House in Earlscourt', 23 January 1914. City of Toronto Archives, Series 372, Sub-Series 52, Item 270.

by the family who intended to occupy the house. In practice, building was frequently done co-operatively, and reciprocally, among groups of families, in what were termed 'building bees', often after work on Saturday afternoons.

Spatial structure and social structure

Whether houses were genuinely 'owner-built' or erected by enterprising speculative builders targeting blue-collar households, the results were similar. Until about 1900, Toronto suburbs were more middle-class than the central city: Harris estimates that about 40 per cent of employed residents living in the City of Toronto had white-collar jobs (owners, managers, professional or clerical), compared to about 60 per cent of residents living in suburban municipalities. But by 1907, the suburbs were more working-class than the city. In 1913, only 5 per cent of householders in North Earlscourt were white-collar; in the suburban districts more generally, the proportion was 20 per cent; but in the city it was 39 per cent. Through the inter-war decades the proportion of city residents who were white-collar remained around 40–50 per cent, while the number of suburban residents in white-collar occupations rose steadily until, by 1950, the suburbs were again more middle-class than the central city.[68] Part of the reason for the change was simply the increasing proportion of the total population in white-collar occupations; but working-class suburban homeowners were also especially hard hit by the Depression, defaulting on loans or forced to sell their homes, move in with friends or family or return to renting rooms in inner-city slums.

The spatial structure of early twentieth-century Toronto, with working-class suburbs and a more middle-class central city, runs counter to Burgess's concentric zone model, but it conforms to Todd Gardner's aggregate statistical analysis of American cities. Gardner found that in the early twentieth century small cities were more likely to have lower-income suburbs (where 'suburbs' were defined according to American custom as separate political entities), while the largest cities were structured as Burgess described. By the 1940s, perhaps because even small cities like Toronto had grown in area and population to acquire more 'metropolitan' housing and traffic problems, but also because of the overall growth of the middle classes, the Burgess model had become much more generally appropriate.[69]

Two other characteristics of North American suburbanisation contributed to its distinctive social geography: annexation and industrialisation. Most suburbs began life as separate administrative areas beyond city limits. Annexation commonly occurred when rural townships were unable to satisfy residents' demands for better services such as more reliable water supply or connections to mains drainage. Central cities might also bid to take over previously independent suburbs simply as a form of urban aggrandisement, to keep ahead of rivals in league tables of city size, population and property valuation.[70] But annexation was not an inevitable process; it might be resisted by wealthy suburbanites who did not want to foot the bill for solving central-city problems, or rejected by city residents who feared that annexing fledgling suburbs would cost them more than they stood to gain. The City of Toronto annexed numerous suburban districts from 1883 onwards, including Riverdale (where Love Bros were based) in 1884 and Deer Park, a leafy middle-class district north of the city centre, in 1908; but Forest Hill, another middle-class suburb, just west of Deer Park, remained independent of the City until 1967 (Figure 7.3).[71] The important point here is that independence at the time of initial development facilitated the growth of specialist suburbs, some poor and unserviced, some exclusive with stringent local regulations reinforced by private restrictive covenants, and some geared to attract manufacturing and service industries by offering tax exemptions and 'bonuses' to employers who chose to locate there.

In the early twentieth century industrial suburbs were especially associated with new assembly-line industries, attracted to low-tax, greenfield sites, with good access to main roads and railways, and putting into practice principles of scientific management expounded by Frederick Taylor and Henry Ford. Research by Robert Lewis on Montreal and Chicago, and by Richard Harris on Toronto, has pointed to the longevity and ubiquity of industrial suburbanisation, well established by World War I, and not only associated with specialist 'model settlements' such as Pullman, outside Chicago, or Saltaire, outside Bradford in England, that feature prominently in histories of planning.[72] In Toronto, firms such as Canada Packers (meat processors) and Willys-Overland (automobiles) located in 'The Junction', a district where rival railway lines crossed on the north-west outskirts of the late nineteenth-century city. 'The Junction' began to develop in the 1880s, but it was not annexed to the city until 1909, and even then it retained its industrial and immigrant character. In the early twentieth century, other engineering companies, automobile and tyre manufacturers moved to districts like New Toronto, west of the city on Lake Ontario, and Leaside, to the north-east, both incorporated as separate municipalities in 1913. Kodak moved their Toronto factory from downtown to Mount Dennis, on the north-west edge of the city, in 1917. At the time of the plant's relocation, most Kodak workers lived close to downtown, but within a few years the majority had moved out to, or had been replaced by workers who lived in, nearby suburbs.[73]

Social housing in suburbia

In densely settled Britain there was little opportunity for owner-building on the edge of fast growing cities.[74] Nonetheless, working-class suburbanisation was advocated as an antidote to fears of demoralisation and degeneration among the inner-city poor. Both Charles Booth and William Booth proposed twin policies of decentralisation and emigration; yet again, suburbanisation and colonisation were linked.[75]

Around London the only ways of facilitating working-class suburbanisation were through philanthropic or state-sponsored provision. Between 1866 and 1868, the Metropolitan Association for Improving the Dwellings of the Industrious Classes, a 'five per cent company' (limiting its return to investors to a maximum of five per cent per annum) which mainly constructed 'block dwellings' in central and inner London, experimented with a cottage estate in Penge, then on the south-east fringe of the metropolis. Pairs of semi-detached cottages were each provided with gardens where artisans could cultivate their own vegetables during the evenings and weekends. The first occupants were workingmen and their families from central London, and the success of the scheme depended on new rail links, especially the completion of direct lines into both the West End, in 1863, and the City, in 1864. The London, Chatham & Dover Railway charged tenants a special concessionary fare of two shillings a week.[76]

More extensive in scale, if less overtly philanthropic, were estates erected by the Artizans', Labourers' and General Dwellings Company: Shaftesbury Park in Battersea (begun in 1872) (named after the pioneer housing reformer, Lord Shaftesbury), Queen's Park in Kensal Green (1877), and Noel Park in Wood Green (1881), later supplemented by Leigham Court in Streatham (1894). By 1895 the company had erected 5000 dwellings on its first three suburban estates, accommodating mostly skilled working-class and lower middle-class families, along with 1500 working-class flats in central London. The style of architecture – more 'cottagey' than most speculatively built suburban housing, with gables and porches (Figure 7.5), sometimes more baronial (corner houses with small towers or turrets, decorated crests with interlaced company initials) – implied both an established social order, but also the popular idea that 'an Englishman's home is his castle', values that were reinforced by naming the estates as 'parks'. Although there was provision for residents to purchase their homes on long leasehold, in practice almost everybody rented from the company.[77]

The Artizans' estates, each convenient for suburban rail services, to take advantage of workmen's fares under the Cheap Trains Act of 1883, were followed by a first group of London County Council cottage estates, built between 1903 and 1914 at White Hart Lane (Tottenham), Totterdown (Tooting), Norbury, and Old Oak (Acton). The Housing of the Working Classes Act (1890) gave local authorities the right to purchase greenfield sites for new council estates, and a further act in 1900 allowed the LCC to acquire land outside its county boundary. Totterdown and Old Oak were inside the boundary, but Norbury and White Hart Lane were outside. Fares of one penny each way were available on the council's electric trams between Tooting and

Figure 7.5. Barfett Street, Artizans', Labourers and General Dwellings Company Estate, Queen's Park, London, 1910. Postcard: WCA00134 (P138 Barfett Street (001a)), City of Westminster Archives Centre.

central London, provided that the journey *to* work was completed before 8 a.m.; and the two out-county estates were served by Metropolitan Electric and Croydon Corporation tramways as far as the LCC boundary (though not at quite such cheap fares).[78] There was no central state subsidy for housing, although the council could use part of its rates income (property taxes) to finance the schemes. After 1919, however, central government introduced subsidies for council housing. The Addison Act (1919) responded to Lloyd George's exhortation to build 'homes fit for heroes', but soon proved financially unsustainable. Subsequent acts reduced the level of subsidy, allowing the construction of more modest, but much more extensive areas of council housing. The LCC laid out cottage estates at Becontree (to the east), Downham (south-east), St Helier (south), Roehampton (south-west) and Watling (north-west), each effectively a new town in its own right (Figure 7.6). Becontree's 26,000 dwellings at one time accommodated 120,000 people. Smaller suburban estates were constructed by local councils to meet purely local housing needs.[79]

In North America, few working-class suburbs were provided by public or 'social' landlords. The Toronto Housing Company was founded in 1912 with the intention of housing the 'average workingman of modest means' while returning a modest profit to investors. The company erected two estates of 2- and 3-storey flats, gabled and half-timbered and set around communal gardens, in inner suburbs east of downtown. But few working-class families could afford to rent the flats. Manual workers – skilled and unskilled – comprised 42 per cent of tenants in 1914–1916, but only 17 per cent by 1923. Meanwhile, single working women, usually sharing with other women, made up between 15 and 20 per cent of householders in the company's flats, at a time when

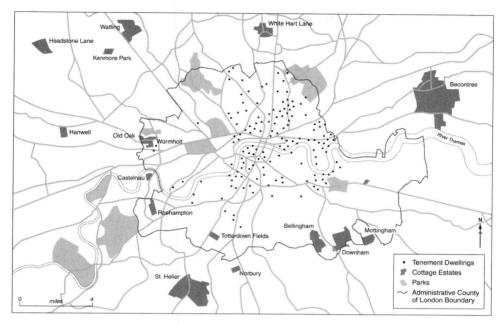

Figure 7.6. London County Council Housing Estates in Inter-War London.

women of all kinds (including widows) comprised only about 10 per cent of all the household heads in Toronto. In another scheme, in 1919–1920, intended to provide houses for sale to 'men and women of limited means', the municipally promoted but business-dominated Toronto Housing Commission built 236 semi-detached homes in the City's near suburbs, in districts well served by public transport and with 20-year mortgages at below-market interest rates. Even so, the commission found it hard to attract working-class buyers. Despite the intention to 'cater exclusively to the workingman', nearly half of the houses were sold to managers, professionals or clerks.[80] However wide this social range, it did not correspond with the aims of the Housing Commission.

Financing suburbia

Upton Sinclair's morality tale of rents and mortgages in *The Jungle* directs our attention to the financial arrangements which underpinned suburban development and house purchase. What was modern about the ways in which all this suburban development was financed? How did builders finance their purchase of vacant lots? How did private landlords and owner-occupiers pay for their houses?

In Britain the building society movement had originated in the establishment of *terminating* societies, in which investors and borrowers were the same individuals, each saving so much per month until the society's assets were sufficient to allow each member to buy a house, at which point the society would be wound up. But by the late nineteenth century, terminating societies had given way to *permanent* societies, in which investors and borrowers were different groups with different expectations (at its crudest, investors want high interest rates; borrowers want low rates), and which required full-time accountants and clerks to run the business. As societies were bureaucratised, so they came to be dominated by the legally and arithmetically articulate middle classes, ceasing to embody principles of working-class self-help and active member involvement. In 1913 only about 9 per cent of British building society funds were held by working-class investors.[81] The collapse of the Liberator Building Society in 1892, which had fraudulently inflated the value of its assets (mainly undeveloped land) in order to attract small investors with the carrot of high interest rates, led to major reforms in the regulation of the building society movement, as well as the requirement that the accounts of public companies should be audited by professionally qualified auditors.[82] One new regulation – that societies could pay interest to investors net of tax at only half the normal tax rate – was a great attraction for taxpayers, but no incentive for those who earned less than £150 per annum (virtually all the working class), who did not pay tax anyway. It seemed, therefore, to reinforce the middle-classness of building societies.

If investors were mainly middle-class, so were borrowers, drawn especially from the petty bourgeoisie and lower middle classes: either builders, borrowing to finance their next speculation, or landlords, acquiring property to rent, making their money out of the difference between rental income and mortgage outgoings. Edward Yates borrowed from five different building societies to finance his operations in south London in the late 1860s, although later in his career he relied on private loans arranged through solicitors, clergymen, widows and spinsters, and estate executors and trustees.[83] But building society borrowers also included upwardly mobile shopkeepers, clerks and teachers, groups for whom homeownership was a potent status symbol. In the south-east London suburbs of Greenwich, Woolwich, Plumstead and Charlton, populated by a combination of lower middle-class commuters, tradesmen and an 'artisan elite' employed in and around the Royal Arsenal and associated military institutions, rates of homeownership were already above average in the late nineteenth century.[84] London's first building society had been founded in Greenwich in 1809, and the Woolwich, subsequently one of the largest sources of finance for house purchase in Britain, started life as the Woolwich Equitable Building Society in 1847.[85]

In *The Diary of a Nobody*, Mr Pooter's acquisition of the deeds of 'The Laurels', which he had hitherto rented, provides an almost orgasmic conclusion to the book! For his superiors, owner-occupation was of little consequence compared to the *type* and *location* of their home and the quality of its furnishings; for his inferiors, owner-occupation was an unattainable fantasy. In Pooter's case, he is indebted to his employer who buys the house for him as a reward for faithful service.[86] But other Pooters proved attractive recipients of building society mortgages, especially during trade depressions in the 1890s and again, much more extensively, in the 1930s. Capital that in periods of economic growth was invested in manufacturing was now being deposited with the societies, yet landlords were not seeking new loans to expand their property portfolios: they could not find tenants or charge rents high enough to make a profit, even on the houses they already owned. The building societies therefore needed to find new types of borrowers. This was possible in Britain because the underlying rate of owner-occupation was still so low. Even in periods of depression, and especially in London, there were enough people in full-time employment who could take advantage of the slump in house prices and building costs to become homeowners. In North America, where the Great Depression was more severe and owner-occupation already encompassed poor households who could barely afford homeownership even in the best of times, there was little scope for this change in strategy on the part of institutional lenders.[87]

In the United States, building and loan associations (BLAs) flourished in Philadelphia from the 1830s. They were less numerous and less successful in Manhattan and Brooklyn, but by 1893 there were 1.5 million members of BLAs across the country.[88] BLAs were perceived as supportive of core American values – elevating neighbourhood and a geographical definition of community over a community of class. Even where most members were working-class, as in Philadelphia, they exploited the BLAs as vehicles of social mobility, 'an escape into property ownership', rather than of class consciousness.[89]

In the nineteenth century, nearly all mortgages were short-term, fixed-interest, so-called 'balloon mortgages' where the only interim repayments were of interest, and the entire loan was repaid at the end of the term, typically after only three to five years. Building and loan associations gradually developed long-term amortised loans (where each repayment is a combination of interest and principal), which were thought to encourage working-class ownership, partly because they avoided the budgeting problem of being faced periodically with the obligation to repay all the principal at once or negotiate a new loan, and partly because in this way, the risk to the mortgagee was reduced and it was feasible to lend a higher proportion of the value of the house. This in turn obviated the need for second and third mortgages, which had previously been ubiquitous. Under this system, a first mortgage for no more than 50–60 per cent of the purchase price would have priority for repayment if the mortgagor defaulted. Second mortgages, usually for about 10–15 per cent, would therefore be charged at higher interest rates because of the greater risk that mortgagees would be unable to recoup their loans. In the Toronto abstracts of deeds and mortgages, it was quite common for institutional mortgages (offered by trust companies and insurance companies as well as building societies), often negotiated after private loans and therefore legally second mortgages, to be redefined as first mortgages, to take precedence over the chronologically earlier loans in any disputes over repayment. All such negotiations of course required the services of lawyers, thereby raising the costs of house purchase still higher.

Mortgages were also commonly bought and sold, whether between private individuals or insurance companies. In some respects, there are more similarities between today's complex money markets and those of a century ago, when compared to a period of streamlined modernity in the years after World War II when lending was dominated by a handful of big institutions offering standard financial products.

Undoubtedly, lending by building societies, building and loan associations, insurance companies and trust companies assumed increasing importance during the early twentieth century, but more so in Britain than in North America. In Britain, new lending by building societies totalled £7 million in 1918, £32 million in 1923, £75 million in 1929 and £103 million in 1933. Alan Jackson states that over 75 per cent of new houses in inter-war suburban London were bought with a building society mortgage. In Canada, the value of mortgages held by life insurance companies increased from

$13.2 million in 1890 to $125.7 million in 1920. Nevertheless, in Canada all institutional sources together accounted for less than half the total value of mortgages, even
during the first half of the twentieth century; and many property sales entailed no
mortgage whatsoever.[90]

In early twentieth-century Toronto, nearly half of all transactions involved no formal borrowing at all – whether an institutional loan, a private mortgage (arranged
with solicitors who were entitled to manage funds deposited with them, for example
by widows or estate trustees) or a vendor-take-back mortgage (whereby the vendor
facilitated the transaction by lending to the buyer). Working with Land Registry
records, which list all legal instruments, such as transfers of title and mortgages, associated with each plot of land, Ross Paterson examined mortgage arrangements in five
developments in the period, 1911–1941.[91] His study included owner-built housing on
the Parsons Estate in Earlscourt, the slightly superior but still solidly working-class
Silverthorn Park Addition, two middle-ranking estates of speculative development
east of downtown, and one upmarket estate, Lawrence Park, in North Toronto (Figure 7.3). Focusing first on 'housing production' (buying the lot and building the
house), he found that no mortgage of any kind was involved in 49 per cent out of
more than a thousand transactions. Of course, it is still possible that builders borrowed informally, or on the security of something other than property (and it should
be noted that between 1872 and 1954 Canadian chartered banks were not permitted
to make loans secured on real estate[92]), but it seems certain that many transactions
were cash deals. Nearly one in five transactions involved a legally registered but private mortgage. Another 17 per cent were vendor-take-back mortgages, and less than
15 per cent were 'institutional'. The latter were most common on the Lawrence Park
estate, and almost unknown among owner-builders.

'Housing consumption' (buying completed houses) was more likely to involve
a mortgage, but very few first mortgages, nearly all restricted to the higher-value
estates, were institutional. In nearly 45 per cent of cases financing was through a
vendor-take-back mortgage. I suspect that this exaggerates the importance of vendor-
take-back mortgages. Paterson notes that 23 per cent of 'second and subsequent
mortgages' were with institutions, but only 7 per cent were vendor-take-back.[93] My
own research, focused primarily on the construction and ownership of *apartment
houses*, which generally involved much larger sums of money than the average single-
family dwelling, and concentrating on a smaller sample of buildings, but tracing *all*
the transactions involving these buildings from construction (between 1900 and 1930)
until after World War II, suggests that many vendor-take-back mortgages took the
form of bridging loans, to be replaced by institutional mortgages within a few months.

Not only owner-occupiers but also private landlords depended on these diverse
sources of financing. Most landlords made their money out of the difference between
rental income and loan repayments. The complex financial arrangements of landlords are evident when we examine probate records associated with the settlement of their estates. When Jacob Singer, one of Toronto's leading private landlords, died in 1911, he owned 226 freehold and 57 leasehold dwellings. He was
the mortgagee (lender) of 17 mortgages, cumulatively valued at $37,000; but he
was also the mortgagor (borrower) of 51 mortgages, on which he owed $312,000.
These included 24 institutional mortgages, averaging more than $4300 each, with

such institutions as Toronto General Trusts Corporation, Union Trust Company, Toronto Mortgage Company, Canada Permanent Mortgage Corporation, Excelsior Life Insurance Company; 7 mortgages, averaging $15,300 each, with estate trustees and executors; and 30 mortgages, averaging $3600 each, with private individuals.[94] Singer was exceptional in the scale of his activities but not in the diversity of his financing. Other private landlords, particularly those who took out second mortgages in order to release capital to expand their property holdings, found themselves in negative equity when property values declined during the Depression. One, who apparently committed suicide in 1938, owned or part-owned 17 houses with a value of $61,550 on which there were outstanding mortgage debts of $52,451. Several of his houses were recorded as having a nominal value of $1, since the mortgage exceeded the current valuation of the property.[95]

These examples may suggest distinctly pre-modern forms of financing construction and house purchase. Rather, we should see the finance system as *flexible*, responsive to the needs of every circumstance, with private mortgages operating alongside the emergence of a modern building society movement. Moreover, all forms of mortgage finance had the decidedly modern consequence of reinforcing social and ethnic segregation. Lenders wished to minimise risks, to ensure that property did not depreciate during the course of their loan, so they favoured new, suburban homes over existing inner-city dwellings, and socially and ethnically homogeneous areas where zoning or deed restrictions minimised the likelihood of 'invasion' and devaluation. Amendments to laws on foreclosure, making it harder for mortgagees to repossess properties as soon as mortgagors defaulted, also served to disadvantage rather than protect marginal owner-occupiers, by making mortgagees more cautious in advancing loans in the first place.[96] Some types of area, property and people were regarded as low-risk, and attracted credit, which helped to maintain their status; others were assessed as too risky to warrant lending, leading to their further marginalisation and decline: a self-fulfilling prophecy.

In a variety of ways, therefore, trends in suburbanisation conformed with Lefebvre's view of the increasing dominance of abstract space, commodification and bureaucratisation. Spatial practices of regulation and zoning and the spatial implications of financial practices conspired to produce more extensive tracts of socially and architecturally homogeneous suburbs, although outcomes might vary according to city size, as reflected in differences between the spatial structure of Toronto and larger cities. Nor were the consumers of suburbia innocent bystanders as they sought to express status and to find security in the face of continuing growth and change.

8

Consuming suburbia

Once built, suburbia still had to be sold and occupied. The marketing of new houses might entail no more than small ads in local newspapers, but more elaborate publicity was necessary to sell a suburban lifestyle. Complementing countless volumes on domestic architecture and economy, more specific information on particular suburbs was provided by books such as W. S. Clarke's *The Suburban Homes of London* (1881), forerunner of early twentieth-century guides such as *Where to Live Round London* and, from 1915, the Metropolitan Railway's annual *Metro-Land*. But whereas the latter included photographs and advertisements for new estates, Clarke's book contained only one illustration – a fold-out map of London – and as much antiquarian history as information on new housing. Its aim was to give new suburbanites a sense of belonging, an identity rooted in local history.[1]

By the 1900s new householders were recruited to publicise their own suburbs through the medium of commercial postcards, displaying what seem now like very ordinary and unexceptional residential streets, but which were intended for newly-installed residents to send to their friends: the suburban equivalent of 'wish you were here' seaside cards.[2] But the new century also ushered in more commercial advertising. London's *Evening News* carried its first illustrated advertisements for new suburban houses during 1905, while from 1906 onwards several railway companies began to produce illustrated guides to the areas they served.[3] By the 1920s, there were weekly pages of 'display ads' in national and local papers, featuring perspective drawings, elevations and floor plans, and regularly updated guides including advertisements from builders alongside tables of practical information, detailing (in the case of *Metro-Land*) season ticket rates, travelling times, local rates (taxes), the cost of utilities (water, gas, electricity), height above sea level and nature of the subsoil. By the 1930s, adverts had become more diverse typographically, more imaginative, more 'arty', no longer confined to the discipline of ordered columns of newsprint.[4]

Builders such as John Laing and Son and T. F. Nash, both active in north-west London, produced copiously illustrated brochures, and solicited interest in their products by building show houses displayed at the Ideal Home Exhibition, held annually from 1908, and also on central London sites where they would be seen by city workers.[5] They wooed prospective buyers with free travel and limousine pick-up from the nearest station, a practice already common in Toronto twenty years earlier. For buyers accustomed to paying rent weekly or monthly, advertisements reinterpreted house prices in terms of weekly mortgage repayments, costed as if they were everyday items in suburban chain-stores like Woolworth's or Marks & Spencer: £1–1–11 per week for substantial three-bedroom semis in Kenton (north-west London), as little as 10/11 for a Wates house in Worcester Park (south-west London).[6] More genteel ads stressed the attractions of a suburban lifestyle – good health, your own garden, relaxed chats with friendly neighbours, 'happy homes'.[7]

Happiness was also central to the marketing of American suburbs.[8] However, here the most prominent advertisements featured vacant lots on new subdivisions rather than finished houses. In addition to differences in the price of lots and in the severity of residential restrictions, different clienteles were attracted through the typography and language of marketing. Compare two advertisements which appeared in the same Toronto newspaper, the *Evening Telegram*, in the same year (1912). 'Cedar Vale' was marketed as 'The Most Beautiful Suburb in Canada'. Well-dressed people were depicted conversing together, standing in front of elaborate, ornamental gates. In the background, horses and a modern automobile traversed a tree-lined avenue. The estate was described in a delicate typeface, the small font accommodating detailed information on the 'Boulevards and Gardens' and 'The Magnificent Ravine'. In combination with some strict residential restrictions, this added up to a 1912 version of a twenty-first-century 'gated community'.[9] By comparison, an advertisement for 'Silverthorn Park Addition' used a heavier typeface and fewer words, and stressed value for money: 'Fine big lots at very low prices. . . . The building restrictions are very moderate, and the terms easy.' Accessibility to workplaces was also key: Silverthorn Park was 'right in the heart of the factory district', 'the most convenient place for the workingman to build his home'. In the centre of the advertisement, watched by his plainly dressed wife and daughter, a workingman was setting down his home (rather like a 'Monopoly' house or a plastic model) in a heart-shaped subdivision surrounded by factory chimneys emitting plumes of smoke that formed a black canopy to the advertisement (Figure 8.1)! There were no worries about environmental pollution – smoke was the sign of full order-books and full employment, which would reassure workingmen that they could keep up repayments on their new homes.

Another advertisement, in *The Toronto Sunday World* just under two years later, featured a further extension to Silverthorn Park: Silverthorn Grove.[10] The advert bombarded readers with testimonials and sworn affidavits, claiming that, with '200 Happy Families' already, and two hundred more expected over the summer, 'This is a real live, humming community, of the best type of English-speaking citizens'. At a time of growing immigration from southern and eastern Europe, 'English-speaking' was almost certainly a euphemism for 'British'.[11] There may not have been any legal restrictions on 'race', but those without British ancestry were clearly less welcome. The emphasis was on families building their own homes, yet entrepreneurship was also condoned: 'Thomas Hatton has already completed one house, and is now starting another one. Mr Hatton says he can complete a house in from one to three weeks in his spare time.' It was acceptable for workingmen to buy land in order to build houses for sale or rent, but not to buy land and leave it vacant. This appears to be the meaning of the bold-print announcement: 'We Don't Want Speculators – we want Home Builders and Investors.'

Figure 8.1. Advertisement for Silverthorn Park Addition, *Toronto Evening Telegram*, 23 August 1912.

Silverthorn Park was barely two miles from Cedar Vale but they were worlds apart. There was no sign of black smoke drifting across the gardens and ravine at Cedar Vale, and no chance that the residents of Silverthorn Park would be allowed through the ornamental gates unless they had come as plumbers or charwomen to service the homes of the rich. Yet both developments were advertised in the same newspaper, perhaps an indication that, while there were the same income inequalities in Toronto as in London, society was not divided so intensely on the basis of *class*. And at both extremes of income, vacant lots rather than finished houses were on offer.

Between these extremes, however, speculative builders promoted their homes aggressively and ingeniously. Love Bros' advertisements stressed 'beautiful rooms' in the 'most beautiful and desirable section in Riverdale; free from noise and smoke'. At least one hundred were 'completely furnished homes', each equipped with its own piano as an additional incentive to prospective buyers. They also insisted that their homes were intended for owner-occupation, not for renting by private landlords.[12]

Suburbanisation and homeownership

In the nineteenth century, homeownership was not the self-evidently desirable tenure that it is taken to be today. Many wealthy households who could have afforded to own their own homes chose to rent, even though they might own other people's homes. Place mattered more than tenure. In Clarke's guide to suburban London in the 1880s, there were few indications that middle-class residents might want to own

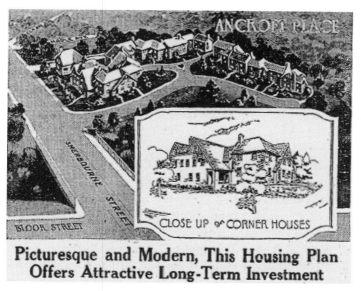

**Picturesque and Modern, This Housing Plan
Offers Attractive Long-Term Investment**

Figure 8.2. Advertisement for Ancroft Place, *Toronto Globe*, 6 October 1926.

their homes: the prices quoted were invariably annual rents. References to property for sale related mainly to building society schemes aimed at skilled artisans. In Beckenham (Figure 7.1), the Birkbeck Building Society offered 800 freehold parcels of land at £40 each, suitable for 'comfortable cottages', of which 'probably half . . . will be occupied by owners'. In nearby Selhurst, houses erected by the Temperance Building Society were 'inhabited to a great extent by incipient owners, subscribers to the society'.[13]

Often perceived as female space, suburbia was probably favoured more by men than women in nineteenth-century America. While both sexes agreed on the centrality of family life, for middle-class American women domestic responsibilities could be combined with increasingly public lives by continuing to live centrally, probably in rented accommodation, and relying on resident servants to do the bulk of domestic work, thereby releasing their mistresses to engage in the social and cultural life of the city. It was their husbands who favoured suburbia, partly so that they could separate their public and private lives, and partly for fear that a burgeoning feminism was threatening family life in the city. Margaret Marsh represents the growth of family-centred suburbs in nineteenth-century North America as a broadening of the evangelical impulse that Fishman held responsible for middle-class suburbanisation around late eighteenth-century London: insulating women and children from the evils of city life at the same time as maintaining a virtuous male presence in metropolitan politics and business. But the *place* of suburbia was more important to middle-class men than the tenure of homeownership.[14]

As late as the 1920s there were some new upper middle-class suburbs of single-family dwellings specifically intended for renting. Ancroft Place, a miniature garden suburb of twenty-one houses, was laid out in South Rosedale, Toronto, in 1926–1927, and was maintained as high-class rental housing by the same owners until its sale in 1972 (Figure 8.2). Each house had its own integral garage, and was centrally heated from a communal plant; kitchens were all-electric. The houses were 'attached', unlike the detached houses characteristic of much of Rosedale, but privacy and individuality were maintained by arranging clusters of dwellings so that no house overlooked any other. They were advertised as 'Picturesque and Modern'. Ancroft Place catered to families who did not want the maintenance responsibilities of ownership, but did not want to live in an apartment block; who expected to stay in the city for only a limited time, for example as diplomats or branch managers of American businesses; or who had moved to the city at short notice and had not yet found somewhere to buy. Tenants included a mixture of company presidents, lawyers, brokers, senior managers and clergymen. Designed for a mobile, consumption-oriented, professional and business class, Ancroft Place was evidence that homeownership was not the only path to *modern* housing.[15]

Nevertheless, by the early twentieth century, homeownership rates were much higher in North America than in Britain, and especially among the skilled working and lower middle classes. In Minneapolis, Detroit and Toronto, more than 40 per cent of dwellings were owner-occupied by 1910. In Chicago and Philadelphia, the rate exceeded 25 per cent. Montreal, Boston and Brooklyn had rates of between 15 and 20 per cent. Only in Manhattan (3 per cent) was homeownership less common than the best estimate of 10 per cent for England and Wales as a whole (with London closer to the figure for Manhattan) (Table 8.1).[16]

During the Depression, rates of owner-occupation declined in North American cities. Even in the nineteenth century, many homes had been owner-occupied when first built, but prospective owner-occupiers were not keen to buy 'secondhand' houses so, when the original owners moved, either they retained ownership, finding tenants to occupy their old home, or they sold, but more often to a landlord than to an owner-occupier. Of 112 houses owner-occupied in 1890 on Ulster, Borden and Lippincott Streets in the west end of Toronto, 67 had new occupants by 1900: 20 were now tenanted but with the same owner, 36 were tenanted with new owners, and only 11 had passed to new owner-occupiers. Overall, the homeownership rate in this increasingly 'mature' suburb declined from 36 per cent in 1890 to 27 per cent in 1900.[17] On Wolfrey Avenue in the city's eastern suburbs, of 41 houses on the street that were owner-occupied in 1909, eight were tenanted by 1914. A similar shift characterised owner-built areas like Earlscourt, where a study completed in 1920 found that the level of owner-occupation had decreased from 71.5 per cent in 1909 to only 39.5 per cent in 1918.[18] These changes were mostly the result of *upward* mobility, the original residents moving on to bigger and better homes; but in the Depression there was a more widespread decline in owner-occupancy. During boom periods, the transfer of existing homes from owner-occupied to rented was more than compensated by the rate of construction of new homes for owner-occupancy. But in depression, few new homes of any kind were built, so the overall tendency was a shift from owner-occupancy to renting. In urban Canada, homeownership peaked at 49 per cent in 1921, declining to 41 per cent by 1941; in urban areas in the United States, home-ownership declined from 44 per cent in 1931 to 38 per cent in 1941. There had been similar, if less dramatic, declines during the smaller depression of the 1890s.[19] In both the 1890s and the 1930s, many of the new landlords were financial institutions, reluctantly acquiring properties when mortgagors defaulted on their repayments.

Table 8.1. *Homeownership rates in North American and British cities*

(i) Percentage Dwellings Owner-occupied in Selected US and Canadian Cities					
Area	1890	1900	1910	1920	1930
Urban US	33	33	35	38	44
New York	6	6	12	13	20
Manhattan			3	2	3
Brooklyn	19	18	18	19	26
Queens			35	37	45
Philadelphia	23	22	27	40	51
Haddonfield (suburb of Phil'a)		40	53		
Overbrook Farms (suburb of Phil'a)		c.60	58		
Boston	18	19	17	19	26
Chicago	29	25	26	27	31
Urban Canada	29	27	45	49	46
Toronto	29	27	48	60	52
Montreal		11		16	17

(ii) Percentage Dwellings Owner-occupied in Selected British Cities		
Area	1900	1938
England and Wales	c.10	c.35
Birmingham	1*	24
Glasgow	12*	
Cardiff	10 (1884) – 7 (1914)	
Surbiton (London suburb)		74

Notes:

Figures for New York are for Manhattan and the Bronx in 1890 and 1900, and for Greater New York, 1910–1930.

Figures for Birmingham and Glasgow marked * are % property owner-occupied *by rateable value*.

All dates are approximate (based on US censuses in 1890, 1900, etc; Canadian censuses in 1891, 1901, etc; and other data from case studies based on locally available assessment records and rate-books).

Sources:

R. G. Barrows, 'Beyond the tenement', *Journal of Urban History* 9 (1983), 416.

M. Daunton, 'House-ownership from rate books', *Urban History Yearbook* (1976), 21–27.

M. Daunton, 'Cities of homes and cities of tenements', *Journal of Urban History* 14 (1988), 304.

R. Harris, *Unplanned Suburbs* (Baltimore, 1996), p. 138.

R. Harris and C. Hamnett, 'The myth of the promised land', *Annals of the Association of American Geographers* 77 (1987), 177–178.

M. Marsh, *Suburban Lives* (New Brunswick NJ, 1990), pp. 97–99, 107.

M. Swenarton and S. Taylor, 'The scale and nature of the growth of owner-occupation in Britain between the wars', *Economic History Review* 38 (1985), 387.

Disinvestment by small-scale landlords during economic booms and acquisitions by large-scale landlords during depressions imply an overall concentration in the ownership of rental property and a less personal, more bureaucratic, arguably more modern set of property relations between owners and tenants.

We need to consider the political agenda underlying the growth of homeownership on both sides of the Atlantic through the twentieth century – the repeated references after 1917 to owner-occupation as a bulwark against Bolshevism, the assumption that in a 'property-owning democracy' the most important property is one's own home. Homeownership was portrayed as more grown-up, more responsible and more moral than renting. Homeownership of a single-family dwelling implied a concern for bringing up children, investing in the future. So, alongside the advertising of particular lots and homes for sale there were also more general advertising campaigns, promoting cities as 'cities of homes' and homeownership as a civic virtue.

The American housing reformer, Lawrence Veiller, referred to Philadelphia's 'reputation as the City of Homes' but the epithet was applied to any city in which most residents lived in single-family dwellings. As late as 1930, more than 90 per cent of dwellings in Philadelphia accommodated only one family, compared to 70 per cent in Queens, New York, 52 per cent in Chicago, and 25 per cent in Manhattan. Interestingly, only 22 per cent of Philadelphia's dwellings were owner-occupied in 1900, more than in Boston, and many more than in New York, but fewer than in most other large U.S. cities. By the inter-war period, however, 'city of homes' was incompatible with not only 'city of tenements' but also 'city of tenants'. Philadelphia maintained its reputation, its homeownership rate more than doubling to reach 51 per cent in 1930, compared to 45 per cent in Queens, 31 per cent in Chicago and 2.5 per cent in Manhattan.[20]

Toronto, like Philadelphia, saw its homeownership rate double, from 27 per cent in 1901 to 52 per cent in 1931, although the latter figure was a reduction compared to ten years earlier, probably reflecting the major boom in apartment-house construction during the 1920s. In the days before condominiums, apartments were almost all rented, and for this reason in particular were fiercely opposed by many political and social commentators. The most vociferous opponent of apartment housing in inter-war Toronto, Alderman Sam McBride, affirmed that his city 'was a city of homes, not of apartment houses'. But the phrase had been applied to Toronto at least as early as 1909 by Horace Boultbee, writing on 'Toronto: A City of Homes' in the *Canadian Magazine*.[21] One implication was that children needed 'homes' – with gardens – rather than apartments with no private space around the dwelling; another was that homeowners took more pride in their surroundings, demanding sewers, paved roads and sidewalks, maintaining their property by regular painting, and installing modern improvements, all of which contributed to a sense of belonging and civic pride.

Homeowners were unlikely to go on strike, and almost certain not to participate in sudden 'wildcat' industrial protests, for fear that they might lose their homes if they were unable to meet mortgage repayments. This was noted as early as 1872 by Engels, who observed that homeownership would 'stifle all revolutionary spirit in the workers by selling them small dwellings to be paid for in annual instalments', effectively creating a new feudalism.[22] For Engels, homeownership was a form of false consciousness, distracting workers from their class interest as wage-earners. Homeowners were also unlikely to move house very often, thereby functioning as a defence against sudden neighbourhood change: there would be too few housing vacancies to allow a rapid takeover of an area by a new social or ethnic group. Equally, because of their investment in 'bricks and mortar' (more likely, in North America, timber and nails) they would resist anything likely to reduce the value of their investment. Because they paid property taxes directly, unlike tenants whose taxes might be hidden in the rent they paid to their landlord, they also provided a brake on profligate public spending by city councils. In a variety of ways, therefore, they were perceived as a force for conservatism, elevating private interest over class interests and neighbourhood over solidarity in the workplace.

There are other reasons why owner-occupied homes could be seen as 'shaky palaces', offering some double-edged benefits to their owners.[23] Firstly, homeownership is very inflexible; at the best of times, it takes time and money to move between one owner-occupied house and another; in worse times, it stranded owners, making it hard for them to move to places where work might be available. In the absence of demand, they would be unable to sell (or let) their homes, but also unable to keep up mortgage payments and taxes.

Secondly, seduced by the attractions of 'a home of your own' many marginal owner-occupiers had nothing left to spend on anything else. Children might be withdrawn from school at the earliest opportunity to take jobs to help their family repay the loan. Or they might lose out by attending schools poorly funded by local school boards anxious to keep taxes to a minimum. Either way, they could be denied the quality and length of education that might be the passport to a good job and upward social mobility. An empirical test of these ideas in the context of suburban Boston between 1880 and 1910 found that homeowners' sons tended to have lower-income jobs than the sons of tenants of equivalent occupational status and income. The same study also contrasted the development of school systems in two Boston suburbs, each with high rates of homeownership: middle-class Brookline and working-class Somerville. In the latter there was only one teacher for every sixty elementary school pupils in 1890, and little expectation of further education. Local government regularly ignored funding requests from the school committee. But in Brookline there was strong public support to expand the school system. A survey in 1917 showed that a large majority of school pupils expected to go on to high school, and almost half planned on going to college.

Finally, while house purchase was normally presented as a form of investment, which would pay handsomely in the future as house prices and resale values increased, the kinds of poorly serviced, frame houses owned by working-class homeowners were more likely to depreciate in value, at least in relative terms.

Landlords and tenants

Just as the mobile rich saw some advantages in renting, so it may have been more advantageous for the poor to continue renting. Indeed we should not forget that, at some time in their lives, almost everybody was a private tenant, and that, even in most American and Canadian cities, the majority of households were tenants. Even in 1930, before the Depression had made its impact, only three of the twenty largest North American cities had rates of homeownership of 50 per cent or above (Toronto 52 per cent, Philadelphia 51 per cent, Baltimore 50 per cent); and we should treat these figures cautiously since they relate to the percentage of homes owned, not the percentage of households who owned their homes.[24]

While renters were more concentrated in inner cities than in suburbs, and in apartments rather than single-family dwellings, it nonetheless follows that even in the 1920s substantial numbers of suburban dwellings were owned by private landlords of different kinds (and, by the 1920s, many – mainly low-rise, walk-up – apartment buildings were located in suburban districts). There were builders who had chosen to retain ownership of what they had built (like Yates in south London), or who had not yet succeeded in finding buyers (like Love Bros in Toronto[25]). There were also erstwhile owner-occupiers who had moved home but retained ownership of their old home; small-scale landlords who had purchased a short terrace or a semi-detached pair and lived in one dwelling while letting the others; widows and spinsters whose principal source of income was the rents they received from owning a handful of houses, probably managed by the family solicitor; and community landlords, who specialised in letting homes to co-ethnics or co-religionists. Some speculative landlords purchased property when it was cheap (e.g., during the 1890s depression) in anticipation of reselling at a profit when the market revived; others used their investment in property as a means of accumulating capital which could then be employed in some other form of business, or converted via philanthropy into cultural or political capital.[26]

In Toronto, as immigration continued, especially in the decade preceding World War I, landlords of houses downtown found it easy to increase profits by maintaining a scarcity of rented housing. Rather than build more houses for rent, they increased rents. Between 1896, in the trough of a depression, and 1913, at the peak of the following boom, rents trebled, providing another incentive for existing tenants to move out into suburban owner-occupation.[27] The supply of rental housing also suffered because of disinvestment by existing inner-city landlords who decided that, in a rising market, it was easier to make their money by converting rents into mortgages. This is the opposite of what was happening during business depressions when, as we have seen above, existing housing moved from owner-occupied to rented.

In a British context, R. J. Morris identified a property cycle in the eighteenth and nineteenth centuries in which investors switched over the course of their lives from 'enterprise' (investing in business/industry) to 'rentier' (investing in property).[28] This corresponded to a shift from active to passive involvement in their investments, and from a relatively high-risk to a much lower-risk form of business. Letting property was regarded as a safe way of making money, hence the phrase 'as safe as houses'. In North America, we can add a third stage to the cycle – the shift from rentier to mortgagee (investing in money). Rather than rent out housing to tenants on monthly terms, with all the attendant worries – that tenants might default, that the property might remain empty between tenancies, that there might be unforeseen decorating or maintenance costs, that rising property taxes might not be recouped from rising rental income should there be an economic recession or decline in demand – it seemed more attractive to convert rents into vendor-take-back mortgages, selling either with vacant possession to an incoming owner-occupier or to a sitting tenant, whose rent would be converted into a mortgage repayment. The burden of risk was thereby shifted onto the shoulders of the erstwhile tenant. If they managed to maintain repayments they would, in time, own their home outright. If they defaulted, they would sink back into the ranks of tenants or boarders while the property generally reverted to the mortgagee who could begin the process over again. Meanwhile, income from mortgage repayments could be reinvested by the mortgagee, either in the stock market (e.g., by investing in railroad, steamship or mining companies) or in land speculation, either 'out west' or on the new urban fringe.

A switch by landlords from investing in property to investing in stocks and shares, or the less risky options of local authority bonds or a building society savings account, was also evident in Britain but, prior to World War I, there does not seem to have been as much active disinvestment – selling existing rental property – as in North America.[29] However, there were additional disincentives to the construction of *new* housing to rent, including rising levels of municipal taxation associated with local spending on welfare, health, education and other amenities. At the cheaper end of the market, where tenants moved house frequently, local authorities collected rates (property taxes) direct from landlords, who were expected but not always able to recoup them by raising rents. Slum clearance schemes were also significant, targeting areas where housing was owned by private landlords. But the new houses and flats erected in their place were usually owned either by limited-dividend companies or philanthropic trusts, rather atypical kinds of private landlords, or, after 1890, by local authorities.[30]

The introduction of rent control in 1915, initially as a wartime emergency measure, compounded landlords' perceived disadvantage, as did the institutionalisation of the mortgage market. As noted in Chapter 7, private mortgages had to be renegotiated every few years but, because the only payments were of interest, they appeared cheaper in the short term than amortised building society mortgages. The former were fine for landlords who could continue making repayments indefinitely provided that monthly rental income always exceeded monthly interest payments; the latter increased the level of monthly repayments, but were ideal for owner-occupiers who ended up with outright ownership of their homes. To maintain profits while repaying amortised loans, landlords needed to increase rents which, if permitted at all, might prove counterproductive, pushing prospective tenants into other tenures. Promotion of homeownership by government and building societies also challenged the 'years purchase' method of valuing property as a multiple of expected annual income. Under this system, trustworthy sitting tenants added value: they provided the assurance of steady profits into the future. But with rent control, and competition from state-subsidised council housing and cheap mortgages, those profits were no longer guaranteed. With vacant possession, however, hitherto rental housing could make the leap into the enhanced values that characterised the owner-occupied sector. Self-interested, rational landlords would be foolish to ignore the opportunities presented by obtaining vacant possession. Hamnett and Randolph estimate that the number of privately rented dwellings across England and Wales was reduced by about 15 per cent between 1914 and 1938 by transfers into owner-occupation.[31]

To summarise the argument of the preceding sections, there was nothing 'natural' about homeownership or about its association with suburbanisation, and some, at least, of the growth of suburban homeownership resulted from a 'push' caused by crises in other systems of housing provision or from a promise of property-owning bliss that was at least part mirage. Suburbia was, however, vital as a 'spatial fix' for the investment of capital, especially as a site for the consumption of domestic technologies and commodities.

The experience of suburbia

What was everyday life like in modern suburbs? Focusing on middle-class suburbs in nineteenth-century American cities, Roger Miller intriguingly speculated on the consequences of moving from downtown to suburbia for patterns of sociability and particularly for the 'discretionary time' enjoyed by middle-class housewives. Living at a distance from downtown meant that longer periods of uninterrupted free time were required to visit downtown stores or even to engage in philanthropic activities as 'lady visitors', settlement-house workers, or other charitable functionaries working in poorer parts of the city. But, in any case, the professionalisation of social work – its conversion into a career for college-educated single women, and the associated proliferation of certificates and diplomas testifying to their competence – restricted opportunities for volunteers to engage in good works.[32]

More critically, suburbanisation coincided with (and perhaps reinforced) a crisis in the supply of domestic servants. Nineteenth-century middle-class housewives had been domestic managers, directing the labour of resident domestic servants. Quite modest households would employ at least a maid of all work; truly middle-class families required a housekeeper, cook, maid(s) and nurse, and probably some non-resident staff such as gardeners. At the best of times finding suitable domestic staff was a never-ending problem, equivalent to the obsession of today's double-income professional households with finding and keeping the right au pair or nanny. The Marches in William Dean Howells' *A Hazard of New Fortunes* agonise over how they are going to retain their trusted servants when they move from Boston to New York. George Gissing's stories are full of dishonest or slovenly servants, or of housewives in perpetual warfare with their maids. The Grossmiths' *Diary of a Nobody* also features a servant with less than total respect for her employers. But the 'servant problem' intensified at the end of the nineteenth century with the growth of alternative employment opportunities for young women, as teachers, nurses, shop assistants, office workers and telephone switchboard operators, mostly jobs which offered free time in the evenings and at weekends and a sense of independence. This new freedom created a new set of 'girl problems' – how to protect the virtue and sobriety of young women living away from their parents and prey to all the vices of city life. But the immediate consequence was to reduce the numbers of potential domestic servants (and probably the quality, since it would be those with less initiative and ambition who would be left). In a situation where demand exceeded supply, it was also likely that servants would prefer to work for households who still lived downtown, where they had access to shops and entertainment facilities, rather than in remote, inaccessible suburbs where the density of housing was such that it was hard even to converse with neighbouring servants over the garden fence.

Despite the shortage of live-in servants in suburbia, it was still possible to recruit daily helps, charwomen or laundresses to work for a few hours each day. The Pooters' young live-in maid, Sarah, is supplemented by a loud and seemingly common charwoman, Mrs Birrell. Women willing to undertake these jobs were generally older than live-in servants, married with their own families, and living in the suburbs (though not in the same suburbs as their employers). Miller quotes from a *Handbook of Housekeeping* (1912) which advised housewives how they could drive hard bargains with charwomen, asking them to work 'split shifts' for a few hours in the morning and again late in the afternoon, and only paying them for the hours worked, although it would clearly be expensive or impracticable for their employees to go home or do any other paid work in the middle of the day. Yet a 1920 advertisement for an electric washing machine, depicting a delicate, smartly dressed, middle-class housewife in negotiation with a coarse-featured older woman, presumably her charlady, was captioned '$4.00 a Day – and Lunch – and Car Fare?' The implication was that the charwoman was exploiting her employer, who would be better off dispensing with her services altogether and doing the washing herself using the latest technology.[33]

So, suburban, middle-class housewives were transformed from managers into domestic workers. The introduction of new domestic technologies – vacuum cleaners, washing machines, refrigerators – admittedly made domestic work less demanding physically, but also prompted new expectations about cleanliness, neatly summed up by Ruth Schwartz Cowan as 'more work for mother'.[34] Another consequence was that housewives became the targets for advertising of domestic appliances in magazines such as *Saturday Evening Post* in the United States and *Good Housekeeping* in Britain. Instead of illustrations showing servants operating the cumbersome appliances that were available to aid washing and cleaning before World War I, advertisements from the 1920s were more likely to show elegantly dressed housewives, apparently vacuuming the lounge carpet and furniture in preparation for a dinner party; or they concentrated on mothers caring for their children by keeping the house free from dust and, by using the latest refrigerator, their food free from contamination. Previously, this too would have been a job for nursemaid or kitchen staff. Now it was middle-class women's work to care for their home and their children themselves, not simply by supervising servants.[35] But if it was work, it was modern, scientifically informed, work: domestic science. Rational planning underlay the internal layout of new homes, for example, the relationship between kitchen and dining room in the servantless home, ideally connected by a hatch which could be closed to keep cooking smells and steam out of the dining room, but opened so that food and crockery could be passed effortlessly between the two rooms.[36]

In pre-industrial homes, and even in nineteenth-century working-class houses where a kitchen range was the main source of domestic heating, the kitchen had been a multi-purpose room where domestic duties were combined with socialising and entertaining close friends. But the twentieth-century kitchen became a unifunctional laboratory. Women might not spend so much time there, but when they did, their attention was concentrated on matters of home economics and domestic science. The social isolation of middle-class suburban housewives was not just a matter of geographical distance from neighbours or communal social and recreational activities; it was also a matter of functional segregation *within* the home.

Technological improvements which made heating and lighting safer and more efficient also promoted the dispersal of family members to their own private spaces within the home: children could safely be left, and then would choose to work or play, in rooms on their own, free from the fear that they would knock over candles or oil lamps or dislodge coal- or wood-fires. Comfort and privacy were substituted for constant togetherness. Whether the gain in personal space made for a higher quality of sociability when family members continued to gather – around dinner table, piano or wireless – is debatable.

For men commuting to work by public transport, their suburban home may have been a retreat from the business world (though the owners and managers of businesses would often install an electric telegraph or, later, telephone, in their home to keep in touch with their workplace), but it also became a site for male domesticity: painting, decorating and gardening (or, at least, lawn-mowing) which allowed non-manual workers to engage in some modest manual labour, and to demonstrate their status by displaying a neat and respectable façade to their neighbours.[37] Mr Pooter begins his diary by recording some gentle domestic pleasures:

There is always something to be done: a tin-tack here, a Venetian blind to put straight, a fan to nail up, or part of a carpet to nail down – all of which I can do with my pipe in my mouth; while Carrie is not above putting a button on a shirt, mending a pillow-case, or practising the 'Sylvia Gavotte' on our new cottage piano (on the three years' system), manufactured by W. Bilkson (in small letters) from Collard and Collard (in very large letters).[38]

This simple passage neatly connects the dual role of the suburban home as a place of domestic work and as a new market for mass-produced goods, at the same time highlighting the pre-eminence of consumption over production: it is more important that the piano has been bought from Collard and Collard than that it was made by W. Bilkson.

Very soon, Mr Pooter is at work in their garden, planting mustard-and-cress and radishes and then, with the guidance of a 'capital little book' on *Gardening*, 'some half-hardy annuals' to make a 'warm, sunny border'.[39] The boldest of Pooter's home improvements involves his obsession with Pinkford's red enamel paint, which he applies to flower-pots, wash-stand, towel-horse, chest of drawers, coal-scuttle and bath with predictably disastrous consequences.

The Pooters have a few good friends in the immediate neighbourhood of their Holloway home – Gowing, who lives within walking distance, and Mr and Mrs Cummings, who live across the road – but they are not even on speaking terms with the disruptive Griffin family next door. They attend the local parish church, and there are occasional references to other members of the congregation, but none of them is more than an acquaintance. They exchange visits with Mr Franching, who lives in Peckham, in south-east London, and they make one-off trips to new acquaintances and social events in Muswell Hill, East Acton, Islington, and the City, where Mr Pooter works as a clerk; but Mrs Pooter's most intimate friend, dating back at least twenty years to before their marriages, is Mrs James of Sutton, a free-standing outer suburb south of London (Figure 8.3). They make day trips by train to visit her family, and the two women also stay with one another several times during the diary's fifteen months. Mrs James is better-off and moves in grander social circles than Mrs Pooter, who looks to her for advice over what to wear on the rare occasions when the Pooters are invited out. From Mr Pooter's perspective, Mrs James is pretentious and in thrall to every passing fashion, a dangerously expensive influence on his wife!

All this may appear trivial or irrelevant – after all, the Pooters are fictional characters constructed as a parody of lower middle-class suburban life by two brothers who lived in central London and moved in bohemian theatrical circles. But the reason for the enduring popularity of *The Diary* is its evident faithfulness to real life: it is a lampoon and an exaggeration, but not by much. The Pooters stand for hundreds of thousands of real suburban Londoners, whose friendships and movements around the metropolis were much like those described in *The Diary*. The Pooters' strongest allegiance is to their *home*, but their social network reflects their past histories – an

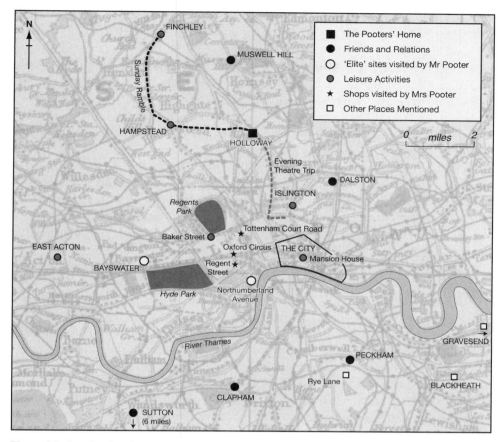

Figure 8.3. London in *The Diary of a Nobody* (1892).

aunt in Clapham, a mother-in-law somewhere west of London, friends made in child-hood or at work, a local community based on conflict or irritation (with neighbours, with local tradesmen) as much as on friendship. In a more serious novel, George Gissing's *The Whirlpool*, set higher up the social spectrum, Harvey Rolfe reflects on his life in Pinner (the north-west London equivalent of Sutton), while on a visit to his childhood home in 'Greystone', a sleepy town in the English Midlands:

'We know a hundred people or so, but have no intimates. Is there such a thing as intimacy of families in London? I'm inclined to think not. Here [in Greystone], you go into each other's houses without fuss and sham; you know each other, and trust each other. In London there's no such comfort, at all events for educated people. If you have a friend, he lives miles away; before his children and yours can meet, they must travel for an hour and a half by 'bus and underground.'[40]

The Rolfes are in the process of moving from Pinner to Gunnersbury, still suburban but slightly closer to central London, primarily so that their young son can go to the right kindergarten, run by Harvey's friend Mrs Abbott. Harvey explains to his wife that 'if one lives in London, it's in the nature of things to change houses once a year or so'; but the consequence of this suburban rootlessness is a lack of identity. As his wife observes after their move, 'Nobody's ancestors ever lived in a semi-detached villa'.[41]

In working-class, owner-built suburbs, like those around Toronto, everybody was a newcomer and everybody had to work hard, to make their community, both physically and socially.[42] Women in Earlscourt were geographically isolated, a mile or more beyond the streetcar terminus, on unmade streets that turned into quagmires every time it rained. In the face of adversity and isolation residents collaborated to construct a sense of community. This was also true among the residents of LCC 'out-county' estates in the 1920s, negotiating the provision of community facilities and united in resistance to the antagonistic attitudes of nearby middle-class homeowners, who labelled the estates as 'little Moscows', supposed hotbeds of socialism that had no place in privatised suburbia, threatening private property values and stimulating increases in rates to pay for all the additional local services that the newcomers required. In these circumstances, it is unsurprising that working-class suburbanites banded together. But 'community' rarely outlived the initial teething problems. Once streets were paved, and other services installed, once local opposition had subsided into cautious avoidance, support for local community associations waned.[43]

In lower middle-class semi-detached London – the inter-war equivalent of Victorian Holloway or Camberwell – church attendance was still an important entry-point into community life, developers reserved sites for the erection of churches, just as they had in nineteenth-century suburbs, and many social institutions – children's uniformed organisations such as guides and scouts and adult amateur dramatic societies – met in church halls. But there were also more secular alternatives – tennis clubs, golf clubs, horticultural societies, cinemas (especially with the introduction of 'talkies' in 1928), or simply staying at home listening to the wireless; or the avowedly apolitical, but implicitly conservative, ratepayers' and residents' associations, another product of the shift from private renting to owner-occupation. Protecting one's property was an ongoing reason for association.[44]

Suburbanite conservatism is central to Morley Callaghan's novel, *It's Never Over* (1930), set in 1920s Toronto, in which John Hughes, an aspiring professional singer, lodges with Mr and Mrs Errington, 'a respectable family' who own their own home, 'on a street not far away from the park, only farther up the hill' and with a distant view from their back sunroom south over the lake. In 1909, when Callaghan was six years old, his parents moved to just such a house on Wolfrey Avenue, Riverdale, where Love Bros were active. Callaghan lived there for the next twenty years, so it is unsurprising that the shadow of the street falls so strongly across *It's Never Over*. On the one hand, this is a suburban idyll: children play on the front lawns, neighbours chat while they tidy their gardens, a local tradesman sells corn cobs from a wagon 'heaped' with fresh produce: 'The street was all of a small, simple, orderly world.' But this cosy exterior conceals a defensive and hypocritical heart. When John is visited by his former girlfriend, whose brother has been hanged for murdering a policeman, he is promptly given notice to quit. As Mrs Errington explains, 'It wouldn't do at all for us, if people got to know about it'. At the church where he is employed as a bass soloist, John finds that his landlord has also informed the minister of the situation, so that he is asked to quit there too. Meanwhile, his current girlfriend has moved into a new apartment building in the northern suburbs of the city, but he cannot stay there either 'for they did not want the caretaker in the apartment-house to think she was a loose woman'. However blissful the suburbs may seem at first sight, they prove to be places of restraint, repression and prohibition, lacking in compassion.[45]

Lodgers and multi-occupancy in cities of homes

John Hughes' status as a suburban lodger was commonplace in 1920s Toronto, where boarding and lodging persisted, even in quite affluent areas, despite the city's reputation as a 'city of homes'.[46] The 1931 Canadian census indicated that 23.2 per cent of Toronto households accommodated one or more lodgers, while another 8.4 per cent comprised more than one family. Using entries for 'roomers' and 'boarders' in city directories for earlier years, when the census did not identify lodgers as such, Richard Harris shows that there were even more lodgers at the peak of the housing boom in the early 1910s, when population growth outstripped rates of housing construction. Beginning in 1890, the only period when there were as few lodgers as in 1930 was during the housing depression and immigration slowdown of the mid-1890s.[47] Taking in lodgers meant that families could pay off their mortgages quickly, a virtue among skilled artisans and clerks unaccustomed to being in debt; and the restrictions imposed on apartment-house construction in suburban areas paradoxically had the effect of increasing the incidence of unplanned multiple occupancy.

American literature on lodgers focuses primarily on large lodging houses, on the occupational and ethnic congruence of landlords and their tenants, and on the switch from 'boarding', whereby hosts provided their boarders with meals, cleaning and laundry service, effectively treating them as part of an extended family, to 'rooming', in which lodgers rented rooms with no provision of meals or other services.[48] The impersonality of the latter was regarded as symptomatic of the breakdown of community life in big cities. From a modernist perspective, 'boarding' constituted an intrusion into the privacy of the nuclear family. 'Rooming' might be anonymous, but at least it implied a clearer demarcation between roomers' and hosts' private space. Yet for many nineteenth-century boarders and their hosts the lack of privacy was a small price to pay for belonging to a community that provided both an introduction to big-city life and a surrogate family.[49]

In London's Victorian suburbs, lower middle-class residents of villas and terraced houses routinely shared their homes with lodgers. In the mid-1870s, it was claimed that 'three-fourths of London houses were lodging-houses – that is to say, houses in which two or more families or groups extemporise residences in a building constructed for the accommodation of a single one'.[50] This particularly applied to multi-storey town houses in parts of the West End, like Bloomsbury and Covent Garden, and to inner suburbs like Camden Town, that had declined in status during the course of the nineteenth century. In 1881, of 46 occupied houses in Gower Place, Bloomsbury, six contained only the members of one family. Another nine houses were occupied by one household each, but the households also accommodated between one and six lodgers. Ten houses accommodated two households each, but in five of these houses there were also lodgers. Fourteen houses were each occupied by three households, again supplemented by lodgers in five houses. Six houses were shared by four households each, also with an assortment of individual lodgers. And one house was occupied by six households. In total, the 46 houses were shared by 107 households and 50 lodgers.[51]

Many two- and three-storey houses farther out into suburbia also accommodated at least two families or one or more lodgers. Among the six-roomed houses in Hollington Street, Camberwell (Figure 7.2), inspected by Charles Booth's school board officers in 1889, no. 21 was occupied by nineteen persons in five separate households: five persons in two rooms on the ground floor, a widow on her own and a three-person family on the floor above, and two families, each five persons, each occupying one room on the top floor.[52]

Hollington Street was part of a notorious speculative development which quickly became a suburban slum; but multi-occupancy was also common in more respectable suburbs such as Camden Town, Kentish Town and Kilburn. By 1881, some Kilburn streets seemed 'specially given over to being sublet in tenements or lodgings'. In Alexandra and Chichester Roads, for example, where whole houses could be rented for about £45 per annum, many were let out in lodgings.[53] When Booth revised his poverty map in 1899, he found lodgers and houses divided up into 'apartments' (rooms, not self-contained, purpose-built apartment suites) throughout the older suburbs. For example, in Camden Town, down the Hampstead Road, 'the houses are generally let in floors', and in Houghton Place, where the residents a few years later included the artist, Spencer Gore, 'lodgers are coming in more and more'. Farther out, in Kentish Town, Ospringe Road contained 'a better class' denoted by 'the absence of lodgers' and Brecknock Park Road was 'mainly in hands of single occupants, without lodgers'; but the three-storey houses on Leverton Street were now 'good working class: 3 or 4 families to a house: let by floors at 8/- to 9/- a week for three rooms', and Leighton Road was 'now much poorer than Brecknock Park Road' with a few houses displaying 'apartment' notices, but most sublet unfurnished to working-class families.[54]

Gissing commented on De Crespigny Park in Denmark Hill, one of the poshest streets in this part of south London, coloured 'gold' on Booth's 1889 poverty map, that 'in this locality lodgings are *not* to let' (Figure 7.2). But by 1899, De Crespigny Park had been reduced from gold to red. Nearby detached villas on Champion Grove were 'getting past their best days, but still in single occupancy'; but in Camberwell Grove lodgers were 'coming in to many of the smaller houses'.[55]

In newer and higher quality suburbs farther out, lodgers were still frowned upon, but they were far from absent.[56] In one of Gissing's rare ventures into comic literature, *The Paying Guest*, set in the outer south London suburb of Sutton, Clarence and Emmeline Mumford, a young married couple, renting a house at the very limit of their means, see an advertisement from 'a young lady' seeking accommodation. Emmeline comments: 'It wouldn't be nice if people said that we were taking in lodgers', but Clarence is keen to set her mind at rest: 'No fear of that. . . . It's a very common arrangement nowadays, you know; they are called "paying guests."'[57]

New inter-war suburbs were less likely to accommodate lodgers, although Alan Jackson alludes to young widows or separated wives obliged to take in 'paying guests', and notes that many marginal owner-occupiers 'resorted to subletting or taking in a lodger, practices which were forbidden on council estates'. Upwardly mobile working-class families, moving out of council housing on the LCC's Watling Estate into nearby private housing, were 'astonished to discover the high incidence of multi-occupation in roads where they had expected to experience a rise in status'.[58] But in suburbs that dated from Victorian times, most houses continued to be occupied by two families: 'the average working family's expectation of a home was two rooms and a kitchen in a shared house'.[59]

The conclusion to be drawn from this survey of the occupancy of 'single-family dwellings' is that they were not quite as private, self-contained and home-like as they were often represented. Some multi-occupancy could be rationalised as the homeowner's choice. Householders could select who should be allowed to infringe on their space, perhaps choosing to exclude 'blacks', 'Jews', 'Irish', 'Chinese' or others unlike themselves. But most lodging and sharing of single-family dwellings was forced on the occupants, by the shortage of adequate housing or the necessity to pay rents or mortgages beyond their means. In the 1850s, Ashpitel and Whichcord noted of middle-class houses in London that 'Planned for one family, they are inhabited by three or four . . . With thin partitions and thinner doors . . . there can be no privacy, no comfort, no home.' In the 1870s William H. White repeated their critique.[60] For each of them, the answer was simple. If people shared dwellings that weren't meant to be shared, why not opt instead for purpose-built blocks of self-contained flats, where each separate household could have its own bathroom, toilet and kitchen?

For all its faults, nineteenth- and early twentieth-century suburbia had (and has) many virtues as I outlined in the introduction to Chapter 7. Nonetheless, as I have suggested in these two chapters, suburbs were home to some significant tensions and contradictions. They may have been populated principally by women and children but, like department stores (to be discussed in Chapter 11) they were, at least initially, women's spaces designed by and for the benefit of men. They were communities of conflict (resisting 'others') and competition (keeping up appearances) as much as neighbourly harmony. They were modern in their nostalgia as well as their orderliness. They were not only 'retreats', where energy for public life was renewed, but escapes from metropolitan taxes, diversity and responsibilities; and while suburbia may have been 'home' for families of homeowners, it was a home shared with lodgers and tenants, even including, as I will discuss in the next chapter, the residents of suburban apartment buildings.

9

Mansion flats and model dwellings

During the second half of the nineteenth century an alternative to the suburban single-family dwelling attracted the attention of housing reformers: the self-contained, purpose-built flat. If the reality was that many houses designed for single-family occupancy were actually occupied by several families, surely it would be preferable to provide purpose-built flats, each with its own sanitary amenities, and a clear distinction between the private space of each flat and 'common parts' such as staircases, yards and gardens, to be maintained communally or by property owners?

Flats lend themselves to discourses of modernity. To contemporaries in England and North America, they were self-evidently 'modern'. They were an easy target for opponents of modernity, for whom flats embodied everything they considered undesirable about modern buildings, modern social relations and modern lifestyles. They were a favourite imagined landscape, disproportionately colonising the pages of realist novels, partly because the novelists themselves had plenty of experience of living in them, and partly because the kinds of people who lived in flats were thought to lead more turbulent, transient, unconventional lives that made for good stories:

Mrs Munt . . . was so interested in the flats that she watched their every mutation with unwearying care. In theory she despised them – they took away that old-world look – they cut off the sun – flats house a flashy type of person. But, if the truth had been known, she found her visits to Wickham place twice as amusing since Wickham Mansions had arisen.[1]

In this chapter, I review some basic chronology, 'home in' on the key issue of whether flats could be 'homes', and then discuss different ways in which flats could be considered 'modern': economically, technologically, socially and geographically. I will discuss not only middle-class 'mansion flats' (or 'apartments' in North American parlance) but also working-class 'block dwellings' and 'tenements'. Indeed, one aim of this chapter is to unsettle the distinction between different types of multiple dwelling, to identify overlaps in personnel, in development practices, and in representations, between 'mansion flats' and 'model dwellings', 'apartments' and 'tenements'. I will pay particular attention to the vocabulary of discourse on either side of the Atlantic, but also to the quantitative record to establish just how distinctive flat-dwellers were compared to the population at large.

The vocabulary of flat-living varied both geographically and temporally. In London, 'apartment' referred to a portion of a house, a set of rooms, not necessarily self-contained, not necessarily all on the same floor. Only recently have Londoners started to employ 'apartment' in imitation of its American usage and to signify an emphatically cosmopolitan, global lifestyle. The word 'flat' was derived from Scots usage to denote a floor of a house and, by extension, a suite of rooms on one floor, although some luxury flats extended over more than one floor.[2] Australian cities adopted and retained the same vocabulary,[3] but in Canada as well as the United States, 'apartment' displaced 'flat' as the term used by architects and real estate dealers to denote a self-contained suite of rooms. 'Apartment' was shorthand for a 'suite of apartments'. Yet 'flat' remained in popular usage into the twentieth century. In late-1880s New York, Howells' protagonists in *A Hazard of New Fortunes* (1890) used 'flat' and 'apartment' interchangeably, as did Howells in his own correspondence.[4] In *Sister Carrie* (1900), Dreiser and his characters invariably referred to 'flats' in New York, with the sole exception of Mrs Vance's 'elegant apartments' in The Chelsea, itself a cross between a hotel and a luxury apartment building; and even here the use of 'apartments' in the plural drew attention to the grandeur of each separate room, not their collective status as 'an apartment'.[5] Edith Wharton, too, in *The House of Mirth* (1905), situated the bachelor, Selden, in a 'flat-house' and his virtuous cousin, Gerty Farish, in a 'little flat'.[6] In 1900s Toronto, *Saturday Night*'s 'Lady Gay' described the adventures of 'Four Girls in a Flat' and discussed 'Flats I Have Known', in which she alluded to the 'new flat on the Belmont property at 81' and 5th Avenue [New York]'.[7] This was 998 Fifth Avenue, one of the most elegant and exclusive luxury apartment houses on New York's Upper East Side, never a 'flat' in estate agent's terminology! In essence, 'flat' was a more homely, familiar name for 'apartment' in early twentieth-century America.

Other commentators labelled buildings according to their social status and architectural form. The *Brooklyn Daily Eagle* differentiated 'a few high toned apartment houses' from 'long rows of flat houses' and 'improved tenements'. Apartment houses normally had passenger elevators. However, some 'very handsome flat houses' also boasted elevators; and the *Eagle*'s reporter confessed that 'the actual difference between the improved tenement and the high class apartment is one of degree rather than reality'.[8]

Evidently, there were different terminologies depending on whether the observer was a novelist, a prospective tenant or a housing professional. Morley Callaghan neatly demonstrated the subtlety of language in writing about inter-war Toronto. At the beginning of *They Shall Inherit the Earth* (1935), Michael Aikenhead lives in one room of what, from his father's perspective, is described as a 'rooming house'. Yet the residents are sufficiently permanent to have their names listed on the wall in the hall. And as the novel progresses, so Callaghan switches to calling the building 'an apartment house'.[9] 'Rooming houses' are where other people – strangers – live (and it is critical that Michael has been almost estranged from his father for some time). Once you have got to know the inmates, and to sympathise with them, their rooms become 'homes' or at least 'apartments', sufficiently private to be apart. So the question of terminology overlaps with sentiment, an issue to which I will return shortly.

Buildings and mansions; tenements and apartments

In mainland Europe and in Scottish cities, living in flats had long been commonplace, but eighteenth- and early nineteenth-century buildings were vertically stratified by social class: the poor lived in the attic, farthest from street-level toilets and water supply; the rich occupied flats on ground and first floors, with higher ceilings, larger windows and fewer stairs to climb. In buildings that were more uniformly middle-class, sleeping quarters for resident servants would be situated in the attic (stiflingly hot in summer, freezing cold in winter) or the basement (dark and damp). But in the course of the nineteenth century, technological advances such as lifts, high-pressure water supplies and improved heating and ventilation systems reduced the disadvantages of living far from the ground and made it feasible to construct entirely middle-class blocks.

At much the same time, purpose-built, multi-storey 'model dwellings' were proposed for the respectable poor, who needed to live centrally to cater for the round-the-clock needs of the rich, but who could not afford to rent whole cottages erected on expensive land in city centres. Model dwellings were to be 'model' in at least two senses of the word: model as ideal, the perfect solution to the problem of housing the working classes sanitarily but also economically, without resorting to charity, which would be de-moralising; and model as exemplary, demonstrating to ordinary investors that it was possible to make a reasonable profit out of housing the poor. The aims of the first model housing agencies in London were evident in their elaborate names: the Society for Improving the Condition of the Labouring Classes (SICLC) and the Metropolitan Association for Improving the Dwellings of the Industrious Classes (MAIDIC), both established in the early 1840s, coinciding with the wave of interest in public health associated with Edwin Chadwick's *Report on the Sanitary Condition of the Labouring Population of Great Britain* (1842). The SICLC developed out of an earlier body, the Labourers' Friend Society, which encouraged the provision of allotments for landless rural labourers. As the rural poor migrated to urban areas, so the Labourers' Friend Society followed them. Both SICLC and MAIDIC experimented with a variety of schemes – including hostels and suburban cottages – before settling on 'block dwellings' as the most efficient way of providing for the poor. It was for others – the Improved Industrial Dwellings Company (IIDCo.) from 1863 and a swathe of new agencies associated with renewed panic about the conditions of the poor in the mid-1880s, such as the East End Dwellings Company (EEDCo.) and the Four Per Cent Industrial Dwellings Company (which particularly catered to Jewish working-class families) – to operate on a much larger scale.[10]

Both SICLC and MAIDIC solicited subscriptions but held out the promise of a modest return on investment, and the following generation of limited companies aimed to pay annual dividends to their shareholders of around 5 per cent. Susannah Morris shows that the average dividend paid by six model dwellings companies in London between 1870 and 1915 ranged between 4 per cent and 6.55 per cent, virtually identical with dividends paid by ordinary (non-philanthropic) commercial property companies. Extending her argument to encompass the 'realised rate of return' to shareholders, which incorporates the changing market value of shares as well as the

Figure 9.1. Farringdon Road Buildings, London (1874): contemporary illustration reproduced as part of a triptych of 'Three Kinds of Metropolitan Slum' in Catherine Bauer, *Modern Housing* (1934).

annual dividend, she notes that model dwellings shares were just as profitable as other forms of domestic shareholding during the 1880s and 1890s, but took a dip during the crisis that affected all landlords in Britain just prior to World War I.[11] The secretary of the IIDCo. assured a select committee in 1881 that his company was 'a commercial association, and in no wise a charitable institution'.[12] In today's parlance, they provided opportunities for 'ethical investment'.

Housing historians have often equated these limited-dividend companies with another set of housing agencies originating in the 1860s, which were much more explicitly 'philanthropic'. The Peabody Trust (1862), the Guinness Trust (1889) and the Sutton Dwellings Trust (1900) all derived their capital from gifts or bequests by prominent businessmen.[13] With no investors to satisfy, the trusts might have been expected to operate more charitably than the limited dividend companies. However, they were just as committed to Victorian liberalism, self-help and the dangers of undermining the private housing market by providing accommodation at less than market rents, aiming at a return of around 3 per cent so that they could continue to build without exhausting their capital. In 1877, for example, the Peabody Trust's net income was $3\frac{1}{4}$ per cent. A 1901 net gain from rents and interest of only 2.44 per cent was reported as the lowest on record, and thereafter net gains fluctuated between 2.0 and 2.7 per cent, apart from a brief dip below 2 per cent between 1919 and 1922 to make up for the backlog of repairs neglected during World War I.[14] The result was that while bodies like the Peabody Trust housed families who were slightly poorer than those in 'five per cent' accommodation – more 'labourers' and fewer policemen or skilled artisans – none of the housing agencies made much room for 'the poorest of the poor'.

The buildings erected by model dwellings trusts and companies were mostly five-storey walk-up blocks, sometimes facing central courtyards (the typical Peabody Trust layout), or in rows separated by narrow playgrounds (e.g., Farringdon Road Buildings (Figure 9.1), erected by MAIDIC in Clerkenwell in 1874), or isolated blocks facing directly onto public streets (e.g., many IIDCo. estates). Individual flats ranged from one-room dwellings intended for widows or childless couples to three- and four-room suites for families with children. The Improved Industrial Dwellings

Company always built self-contained flats, with their own kitchens, toilets and wash basins, but the Peabody Trust provided 'associated flats' where neighbours on the same staircase shared sanitary facilities. Part of the logic for this layout, apart from the financial savings, was to ensure that toilets and kitchens would be kept clean by subjecting them to communal scrutiny of caretakers and fellow tenants. It was also hoped that higher-status tenants, who could afford to occupy three rooms, would set an example to poorer one-room tenants.

Architecture ranged from an overbearing neo-gothic through the ornamented iron balconies that fronted most IIDCo. buildings, to the bare austerity of some MAIDIC and East End Dwellings Company estates. In *The Nether World* (1889), Gissing famously referred to the Farringdon Road Buildings as 'terrible barracks... Vast, sheer walls, unbroken by even an attempt at ornament... millions of tons of brute brick and mortar, crushing the spirit as you gaze. Barracks, in truth...'[15] This description comes at a point in the story when Clara, who had left home to become an actress, has been forced to return to her father and half-siblings, by now sharing a flat in Farringdon Road Buildings. It is unsurprising that she thinks of the buildings so negatively! Yet Gissing's account also remarkably prefigures another reference to Farringdon Road Buildings in the architectural literature. In 1934, in a book advocating garden suburbs, new towns and modern*ist* design, the American housing reformer, Catherine Bauer, included an illustration of 'Three Kinds of Metropolitan Slum', in which Farringdon Road Buildings appears, sandwiched between 'central chaos' (jerry-built courts and cellar dwellings) and 'the chaos of uncontrolled expansion' (shanty towns), and described in terms that Gissing would surely have endorsed: 'a built-in slum'. To Bauer, Farringdon Road Buildings represented a class of buildings 'which were slums from the moment the plans were conceived'.[16]

The association of multi-storey living with working-class block dwellings initially frustrated attempts to extend the lifestyle to the middle classes. Through the late 1840s and early 1850s *The Builder* frequently included articles and letters advocating similar buildings for middle-class families, but the first scheme to be executed was a series of 'houses' erected on newly completed Victoria Street in 1853.[17] Each 'house' comprised six shops at street level, above which were eight suites, two per floor, typically comprising four bedrooms, drawing room, dining room, kitchen, servants' bedroom, store room and two WCs (but no bathrooms). There were separate staircases, one for residents and guests, another for servants and tradesmen, thereby maintaining a proper segregation of servants and served. The flats were thought to be particularly attractive 'to parties who remain only a portion of the year in London... as the porter in their absence takes charge of the apartments'.[18] Rents ranged from £80 to £200 per annum. By contrast, rents for the first Peabody estate, opened in Spitalfields in 1864, ranged between 2/6 and 5/- per week for one to three rooms (a maximum of £13 per annum). Further middle-class flats were erected around 1860 on nearby Carlisle Place and Morpeth Terrace, purely residential streets; but it was not until the late 1870s and 1880s that middle-class mansion flats were built in substantial numbers across London's West End.

There were also several schemes during the 1870s, aimed at lower middle-class tenants. In the 1880s, George Gissing occupied a three-room flat in Cornwall Residences, a series of five- and six-storey blocks backing onto Baker Street Station,

Figure 9.2. Two adjacent Improved Industrial Dwellings Company estates in Chelsea, London: Wellington Buildings (left) and Chelsea Gardens (right) (author's photographs).

erected between 1872 and 1875. There was no lift, just a bare stone staircase in each 'house', and in many respects the building was just a slightly more generous version of model dwellings such as Farringdon Road Buildings. The differences were as much managerial as physical: Gissing signed a lease for three years and paid his rent quarterly, whereas the residents of Farringdon Road Buildings were weekly tenants. Gissing's rent worked out at 15/6 per week (£40 p.a.), roughly twice the rent of a three-room flat at Farringdon Road.[19] *The Builder* also reported on Matthew Allen's lower middle-class flats in Stoke Newington.[20] Allen was building contractor for the Improved Industrial Dwellings Company, and several of that company's schemes were pitched at a superior clientele. For example, facing Chelsea Bridge Road and fronting its working-class Wellington Buildings, the company erected the more elaborate, turreted and mansard-roofed Chelsea Gardens (Figure 9.2).[21] Gissing's contemporary, Jerome K. Jerome (author of *Three Men in a Boat* and editor of popular literary magazines) lived in a flat in Chelsea Gardens, and Gissing situated Will Warburton, a bachelor partner in a firm of sugar importers, in a fourth-floor flat there, in his last novel, *Will Warburton* (1905).[22] There was evidently no clear distinction between 'model dwelling' and 'mansion flat', and it may be argued that this ambiguity served to limit the popularity of the latter among the better-off, fearful that they might be mistaken for living in a block dwelling.

Several commentators observed the ambiguity of language used to describe blocks of flats. Working-class flats were usually situated in 'Buildings' or 'Houses', and the individual blocks were labelled simply 'Block A', 'Block B', etc. In *Howards End*, Leonard Bast lived in the 'semi-basement' of 'Block B', somewhere south of Vauxhall, while Henry Wilcox, the chairman of the Imperial and West African Rubber Company, took a short lease on a flat in 'Wickham Mansions' in the West End, for his family to use as a pied-à-terre away from their home in the country.[23] Over time, however, 'Mansions' was appropriated for less grand residences. Gissing expressed his contempt at the circular he received informing him that, henceforth, Cornwall Residences was to be known as Cornwall Mansions; and Sydney Perks, the author of an Edwardian guide to managing flats, observed that 'the word "Mansion" has long ceased to convey the idea of a mansion, and when "Gardens" are referred to, few people expect to see a garden'.[24]

Critics on both sides of the Atlantic referred to middle-class flats as 'French Flats'.[25] Occasionally, this was intended as a mark of continental sophistication. In Toronto, *Saturday Night* reported on tenants who had hosted 'at homes' and parties in their '*appartements*' in the newly-built St George and Sussex Court apartment buildings; and the owner of the latter explicitly linked his building to the palaces of Fontainebleau and Versailles and the apartments of the Champs Elysées.[26] More frequently, however, references to France implied guilt by association with Parisian apartments where, it was assumed, residents followed an immoral and promiscuous lifestyle, not only sexually but also in their disdain for private virtues such as home cooking, preferring a public life of dining in restaurants, drinking in pavement cafes and sauntering idly through the city's arcades. Edith Wharton parodied the attitudes of 1870s New Yorkers when, in *The Age of Innocence* (1920), she described the domestic arrangements of the elderly matriarch, Mrs Mingott, who lived entirely on the ground floor of her uptown mansion, her bedroom directly connected to her sitting room.

Her visitors were startled and fascinated by the foreignness of this arrangement, which recalled scenes in French fiction, and architectural incentives to immorality such as the simple American had never dreamed of.[27]

An even more serious charge associated middle-class apartments with working-class tenements. Tenements lacked the saving grace of being well managed by philanthropic landlords. In critics' eyes, either they were slums already or they were slums in the making. To New York journalist James McCabe, Parisian apartments were simply 'magnificent tenements', thereby implying a promiscuous mixing of ages, sexes and classes, and a physical density and neglect of maintenance that would facilitate the spread of physical as well as moral disease.[28] In Toronto, where the first middle-class apartment buildings were not completed until 1902 and there were no 'model dwellings' to prove that working-class blocks could be both densely populated and healthy, an anti-apartment campaign played on the association of 'apartments' with 'tenements'. The *Globe* began an editorial in March 1912 by predicting 'a tenement-house boom in Toronto this spring'. Labelling the buildings as 'tuberculosis breeders', the editorial concluded that 'Toronto must look to her building laws or she will be overrun, as San Francisco has been, with a plague of disease-breeding tenements and apartment houses'. The personification of Toronto as a vulnerable female, and the language of 'breeding' aligned the author with racist and eugenic discourses

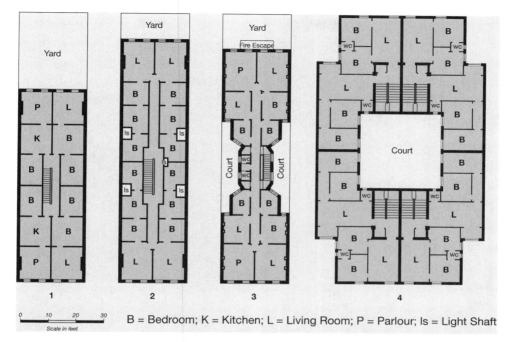

B = Bedroom; K = Kitchen; L = Living Room; P = Parlour; ls = Light Shaft

Figure 9.3. The Evolution of Tenement Housing in New York: (1) Pre-1879 tenement house without light or ventilation, except in outer rooms (2) Pre-1879 railroad flats, with tiny light wells and covering 90 per cent of lot (3) Typical dumb-bell plan, 1879 (4) Proposed plan for New-Law (1901) tenement house on double lot; redrawn from plans in New York State Assembly, Tenement House Committee, *Report of 1895*; R. W. DeForest and L. Veiller, eds, *The Tenement House Problem* (1903); R. Plunz, *A History of Housing in New York City* (1990).

that portrayed (British) Canada 'overrun' by 'foreign' (non-British) immigrants. A follow-up, a month later, more soberly but just as insistently argued that 'many of the more recently built apartment houses . . . are in essence tenements, with all the evil features that the word implies and none of the good ones'. Drawing on evidence from Glasgow, the article claimed that one- and two-room dwellings accommodated shorter, lighter, sicklier children than three- and four-room dwellings. The implication was that children were smaller *because* they lived in flats, not that they were smaller because they came from poor families who could not afford to rent more than a couple of rooms. Other opponents invoked the spectre of New York, as a city not of luxurious apartments but of squalid and overcrowded tenements.[29]

As early as 1865, there were more than 15,000 tenement buildings in Manhattan, occupied by about 480,000 inhabitants. By 1900, 2.3 million of Greater New York's 3.4 million residents lived in 'tenements'.[30] However, it was difficult to determine a precise dividing line between 'tenements' and 'apartments'. The city introduced a Tenement House Act in 1867, revised in 1879, which imposed minimum standards of sanitation and ventilation, leading to the proliferation of so-called 'dumbbell' tenements, deep and narrow, shaped like dumbbells to include air shafts which provided a minimum of light and air to rooms in the middle of buildings (Figure 9.3). Since tenements were defined in law as buildings which contained three or more dwellings with independent cooking facilities, some apartment builders were able to evade the

Figure 9.4. William Dean Howells' New York Homes: The Hampshire, 46 West 9th Street (left) and the Chelsea Hotel, 222 West 23rd Street, Manhattan (right) (author's photographs).

act by providing communal services and calling their buildings 'apartment hotels'. A handful of luxurious cooperative apartment buildings were also exempt, since their residents were technically owner-occupiers and the tenement laws applied only to rented dwellings.[31]

As in London so in New York, purpose-built apartment houses for the middle classes lagged some years behind multi-storey dwellings for the poor, but by the 1880s New York apartments far outnumbered London mansion flats. The earliest purpose-built apartment house, the Stuyvesant, opened in 1869. In 1875, 112 new apartment buildings were erected in Manhattan; in 1880, 516. In 1883, out of 10,174 dwelling units under construction, only 800 were single-family dwellings; 5700 were in apartment buildings and 3674 in tenements. By 1890 nearly 39 per cent of dwellings in Manhattan were in buildings of ten or more units, and 75 per cent in buildings of at least four units.[32] The most spectacular new apartment buildings were around Central Park, beginning with the Central Park Apartments or 'Spanish Flats' at Seventh Avenue and 59th Street, completed in 1883, and the Dakota, facing the park at West 72nd Street, opened in 1884.[33] Farther south were more modest buildings, such as the Hampshire on West 9th Street, a six-storey block where William Dean Howells lived with his family for two months early in 1888;[34] but also the Chelsea on West 23rd, now the Chelsea Hotel, and renowned for its bohemian clientele including Andy Warhol, William Burroughs and Sid Vicious, but built in 1883 as fashionable serviced apartments (Figure 9.4). Howells lived here, too, describing it in a letter to his father in April 1888: 'This is one of the vast caravanseries which are becoming so common in New York, – ten stories high, and housing six hundred people. We take an apartment of four rooms, and eat in the restaurant.'[35]

A new Tenement House Law in 1901 more clearly included middle-income apartments, but by now developers in New York preferred to label all their buildings as 'apartments', perhaps lending credence to the objections of Toronto critics that 'apartments' was just a fancy word for 'tenements'. Between 1914 and 1920, only 5134 'tenements' but 89,356 'apartments' were erected in New York City; and in 1929 introduction of the Multiple Dwellings Law did away with the use of both terms as legal descriptors.[36]

Despite the proliferation of both luxury apartments and speculatively-built tenements, there were few philanthropic or limited-dividend model dwellings in nineteenth-century New York. Alfred T. White, a Brooklyn businessman, built three estates – in 1877, 1879 and 1890 – all in Brooklyn, closely imitating the designs of Sir Sydney Waterlow's Improved Industrial Dwellings Company; and there were several one-off schemes in Manhattan's East Side: the Improved Dwellings Association, founded in 1880 with the support of Cornelius Vanderbilt, and limiting dividends to shareholders to 5 per cent, completed only one estate; so did the Tenement House Building Company, which imposed a 4 per cent limit on its dividends. More impressive, quantitatively, was the City and Suburban Homes Company, founded in 1896, building on a large scale in Manhattan's East Side as well as in the outer boroughs. By 1938 they had promoted fifteen major projects, and generated an average annual return of 4.2 per cent. Internally, their apartments were better equipped than purely commercial tenements, but they filled their Manhattan sites at very high densities: six-storey walk-up apartment buildings occupying 80 per cent of their sites. By comparison, A. T. White's last project, Riverside Buildings (1890), covered only 49 per cent of its site, the remainder devoted to a park, playground and bandstand.[37]

On both sides of the Atlantic, women were actively involved as managers of model dwellings. In London, Angela Burdett-Coutts, heiress to the fortune generated by private bankers, Coutts & Co., financed the development of Columbia Square, four five-storey blocks of high Gothic dwellings in Bethnal Green, completed in 1862. Later in the century, Octavia Hill became famous for her opposition to block dwellings as the solution to the problem of housing the working classes, preferring to take over more conventional cottage property – two or three storeys at most – and renovating it without initially making much in the way of modern improvements, concentrating instead on instilling habits of cleanliness and punctual rent-paying among her tenants. The key to success was firm but sympathetic management, imparted by lady visitors, educated middle-class women like Hill herself, who could advise and encourage the women from whom they collected rent. But Hill's management system was also employed by some of the block dwellings companies, especially the East End Dwellings Company, for whom Beatrice Webb (née Potter) worked at their Katharine Buildings estate in Whitechapel. In North American cities, women were also prominent as investors. In Boston, one-third of stockholders and half of the board of directors of the Boston Cooperative Building Company (founded 1871) were women; and in Toronto, out of fourteen founding directors of the limited-dividend Toronto Housing Company, which built a pair of low-rise estates of flats between 1912 and 1915, four were women.[38]

Could an apartment ever be a *home*?

The involvement of so many women in housing management, building on an earlier form of charitable and missionary endeavour – of well-off women as slum visitors – but also reflecting the professionalisation of social work as an appropriate career for educated single women, drew attention to the objective of converting working-class dwellings into *homes* despite the impracticability of working-class homeownership. This was really the crux of the debate about apartment-living: could an apartment ever be a home – when it was rented, not owned; when it lacked a garden or back yard where children could play in safety and adults could cultivate flowers and vegetables; when privacy was compromised by wafer-thin party walls and shared 'common parts' such as lifts, staircases, roof gardens and courtyards? Moreover, the integrity of 'real' homes – single-family detached houses – was threatened when they might be over-looked and overshadowed, and when their monetary value might be diminished by adjacent blocks of flats.

The editor of *Canadian Architect and Builder*, W. A. Langton, returned from a trip to New York appalled by his observation of hordes of middle-class children playing on the streets of Harlem – the children of apartment-house families who had no other place to play. But if young couples who lived in apartments opted not to have children, that was just as bad, a form of 'race suicide'. Langton was also fearful of the apartment's role in the emancipation of women: 'Not only is pride in their families vanishing but pride in their housekeeping as well; and apartment life will complete the process.' He feared for the moral state of apartment women with 'credit and a telephone' but no children and 'almost no housekeeping . . . nothing to do at home'.[39] Sex and shopping would be their only diversions!

Flat-dwellers' every move might be observed by residents on the same floor in neighbouring blocks, or by passengers looking out from elevated trains, much as John Sloan and Edward Hopper depicted in their respective versions of 'Night Windows' (1910, 1928). Sloan's view portrays working-class tenements, showing their residents face-on: one woman reaching out of the window to a washing line, another washing or combing her hair while she looks out from her lighted room into the night (Figure 4.8). Hopper's pictures offer more furtive glimpses of apartment residents going about their private business – the backside of a woman seen through the window of a sparsely furnished but brightly lit bedroom in 'Night Windows'; a maid or housewife making the bed, also glimpsed unawares, in 'Apartment Houses' (1923).[40] While this invasion of privacy could be countered in real life by the simple expedient of closing the curtains, it was harder not to share sounds with neighbours – voices raised in argument, babies crying, musical instruments and gramophones playing. In Toronto's *Saturday Night*, 'Lady Gay' linked the problem of noise to the desirability of anonymity:

To really enjoy a flat one must live in splendid isolation, one must not be chummy with the lady whose little boy squalls, nor the gentleman who practices on the flute. Then one can freely lodge a protest with the janitor and have the noise kept in a sufficiently subdued state.[41]

In some blocks of flats, where servants from different households shared dormitory accommodation in attics or basements, or whose kitchens looked out on a small central 'area', little wider than an air shaft, or where there was a 'secondary staircase' intended to segregate servants from family and visitors, gossip could spread from flat to flat by way of the servants. There was also the ambiguity of the 'common parts', not-quite-private, not-quite-public spaces such as staircases and flat roofs used as gardens or, more modestly, drying areas for laundry. Already into her second year of living in a flat on 78th Street in New York's Upper West Side, Dreiser's *Sister Carrie* comments that 'I have been in this house with nine other families for over a year and I don't know a soul'. Carrie at last meets her neighbour, Mrs Vance, when they both open the doors to their shared dumb-waiter (a hoist allowing tradesmen to send up groceries and other goods to flats on the upper floors) at the same time to collect their newspapers and milk: 'She was in a night-gown and dressing robe, with her hair very much tousled', clearly not expecting to be observed by somebody she did not yet know.[42] For respectable middle-class Americans this was the wrong kind of intimacy – not community but promiscuity.

A decade earlier the question of 'home' had been central to the opening chapters of Howells' *A Hazard of New Fortunes*, in which Basil and Isabel March move from a dignified Boston townhouse, a family home which they had shared with their two daughters and two domestic servants, to a sub-let flat in a purpose-built New York apartment house. Howells spent several chapters describing their search for a suitable apartment, discussing the dilemmas of moving to a more expensive city, where they quickly had to revise their aspirations in the light of their financial circumstances. Mrs March lay down the ground rules to her husband: 'The *sine qua nons* are an elevator and steam-heat, not above the third floor, to begin with. Then we must each have a room, and you must have your study and I must have my parlour; and the two girls must each have a room.' There must also be a kitchen and a dining-room. 'And the kitchen must be sunny ... And the rooms must *all* have outside light. And the rent must not be over eight hundred for the winter.' The first place they visit turns out to be 'a large, old mansion cut up into five or six dwellings'. The rooms were large, but there was no elevator and no steam heat and the rent was nine hundred, unfurnished.[43]

Their next visit is to Mrs Grosvenor Green's apartment: furnished, (over)heated, served by an elevator summoned by an electric bell, but only six rooms, eight floors up, and the rent was $250 *per month*. It is too small, too expensive, but also vulgarly pretentious. At the entrance from the street, gas lamps engraved with the building's name flanked a 'heavily spiked, aesthetic-hinged black door'. The janitor wears a 'gold-banded cap, like a continental *portier*' and the superintendent treats them disdainfully, while the apartment itself is full of every kind of affectation: dragon candlesticks, Japanese fans and screens, Armenian, Turkish and Persian 'tidies' (antimacassars), China pugs, brass sunflower and brass peacock.[44]

As their search continues, the Marches discuss what constitutes the essence of a *home*. By now Isabel has lost patience with flats, 'denounc[ing] their stupid inadequacy to the purposes of a Christian home'. And Basil joins in the attack:

Think of a baby in a flat! It's a contradiction in terms; the flat is the negation of motherhood ... none of these flats has a living-room. They have drawing-rooms to foster social pretence, and they have dining-rooms and bedrooms; but they have no room where the family can all come together and feel the sweetness of being a family . . . the Anglo-Saxon home, as we know it in the Anglo-Saxon house, is simply impossible in the Franco-American flat, not because it's humble, but because it's false.[45]

Yet, after visiting numerous other, even less suitable, flats over the following days, they end up taking Mrs Grosvenor Green's apartment, at the reduced rent of $175 per month, still more expensive than they had originally planned, and still pretentious in the extreme. They discover that, after all, a flat can be a *home*:

It went far to reconcile Mrs March to the apartment that her children were pleased with its novelty; when this wore off for them, she had herself begun to find it much more easily manageable than a house. After she had put away several barrels of gimcracks, and folded up screens and rugs and skins, and carried them all off to the little dark store-room which the flat developed, she perceived at once a roominess and coziness in it unsuspected before.[46]

The name of the building in which the Marches make their home is the 'Xenophon', one of a trio of buildings, of which the others are the 'Thucydides' and the 'Herodotus': three classical Greek historians, of whom Xenophon is best remembered as author of the *Anabasis*, an autobiographical-historical account of how he accompanied, and then assumed the leadership of, a group of Greek mercenaries who had travelled to what is now Iraq to fight on behalf of Cyrus the Younger in 401 B.C. In the battle of Cunaxa – not far from present-day Baghdad – Cyrus was killed just at the moment of victory. The Greeks attempted to negotiate a safe withdrawal, but in the midst of negotiations the leading Greek generals were murdered. Xenophon took charge and led the survivors *home* a thousand miles across Armenia to the Black Sea and then back to the Aegean.[47] Xenophon, through his *Anabasis*, stands for the struggle to get home.[48]

It may be objected that there is a difference between 'getting home' and 'getting a home' and that Howells' employment of 'Xenophon' in his account of the latter process was just coincidence. Yet in the pages of the *Brooklyn Daily Eagle*, one of New York's leading newspapers, in addition to frequent references to Xenophon in reports of lectures, sermons and the syllabuses of high schools and college entrance examinations, and even to a racehorse named 'Xenophon' – perhaps expected to overcome every obstacle to get home ahead of the field – the name was also used as a pseudonym by people seeking homes to buy or rent. In 1881, for example, 'Xenophon' offered to exchange a three-storey, high-stoop, brick house, 'near Dr Scudder's church', for a double house with 12–15 rooms, located between Pacific Street, Green, Clinton and Marcy Avenues. Three years later, another 'Xenophon' advertised in search of the lower part of a house, not less than six rooms, 'within 15 minutes' ride of Fulton Ferry'.[49]

Howells must have expected his educated middle-class readers to understand his reference to Xenophon as an indication that finding a home would not be easy or straightforward. The Marches are seduced, snubbed, diverted and dismissed by doormen, janitors, agents, landlords and existing tenants. They wander into areas and inspect properties that are obviously inappropriate – in Washington Square (far too expensive), over shops and 'far into old Greenwich Village' (socially ambiguous), in Harlem and 'far up-town' (too remote from Basil's office on West 11th Street) – and, by accident, they look at some apartments more than once. Howells' own experience of the New York housing market was not so different from that of his characters. He had lived in and around Boston for about 25 years before moving to New York in February 1888, where he rented a flat in The Hampshire, a five year old, purpose-built six-storey block at 46 West 9th Street, 'a great comfort after our wanderings to have even this image of a home'.[50] But with the expiry of the lease only two months later, the family moved to The Chelsea. Retreating to New England for the summer, Howells and his wife were back in New York for six days in September, when they 'looked at nearly a hundred flats and houses...Every thing that would suit our complicated family was frightfully dear.' He made another assault on the New York housing market in early October 1888, and by November, they were installed at 330 East 17th, 'an apartment in two floors, in a huge old house overlooking Livingstone Place, where we shall dwell in some rooms of rather a European effect'. It was here that he began writing *A Hazard of New Fortunes*.[51]

To Elizabeth Hawes, Howells' complex residential history, mirrored in the novel, indicates 'his own ambivalence about contemporary values' and 'the disorientation and the deracination of a society on the move'. She finds it surprising, and indicative of 'a rather radical shift in their self-image', that Howells and his wife opted to live in apartments from the late 1880s, when they were already well into middle age with a history of being 'well-bred, tradition-loving people accustomed to and appreciative of private houses'.[52] But Howells was fortunate in that he could afford, and had the flexibility as a writer, to leave the city for part of each year, combining an apartment in the city with a cottage in the country.

The Marches and their creator learn that, for all its disadvantages, an apartment could also be a home. In London, George Gissing followed the opposite trajectory. When Gissing first moved into his own flat in Cornwall Residences, he was overjoyed:

I used to have a prejudice agst. Flats, but I see that it came of insufficient knowledge, like most prejudices. In a wilderness like London, it is vastly better even than a house of one's own. No rates & taxes, one door which shuts in everything, a large, well-lighted common staircase, &, lastly, a location in a neighbourhood where the rent of a house would be extravagant. The privacy is absolute.[53]

Six weeks into his tenancy, he pronounced himself 'admirably quartered here, feeling I have a home for the first time in my life'.[54]

But his enthusiasm was short-lived. Less then eight months after moving in, he complained to his brother: 'I live a very hermit's life; weeks pass & I do not exchange three words with a soul....I pay an enormous rent for the privilege of living in a barracks.'[55] And by 1903, when his semi-autobiographical memoir, *The Private Papers of Henry Ryecroft*, was published, his antipathy to flats had reached fever pitch:

I should like to add to the Litany a new petition: 'For all inhabitants of great towns, and especially for all such as dwell in lodgings, boarding-houses, flats, or any other sordid substitute for Home which need or foolishness may have contrived.'[56]

Gissing's middle-class characters equally discover the barrenness of life in a flat. After attending his friend's wedding, Barfoot 'had no inclination to go home, if the empty flat could be dignified with such a name'.[57] On the downward spiral into poverty, Edwin Reardon denigrates his flat near Regent's Park: 'Compare what we call our home with that of rich people.' Yet later, from the poverty-stricken perspective of rooms in Islington, he concludes their flat had been 'home-like'.[58] And for Ida Starr, a working-class ex-prostitute in her Fulham model dwelling in *The Unclassed* (1884):

> 'It's like having a house of my own. I see nothing of the other people in the building, and feel independent. . . . I pay only three-and-sixpence a week, and so long as I can earn that, I'm sure at all events of a home, where I can be happy or miserable, as I please.'[59]

In essence, for people accustomed to a whole house of their own, a flat was a miserable substitute for home; but for those who had hitherto rented rooms where they had shared cooking and washing facilities, or who had been lodgers or boarders in other people's homes, then a flat to themselves was all that a home should be. Even a New York tenement could qualify as a home: 'Why, those tenements are better and humaner than those flats! There the whole family lives in the kitchen, and has its consciousness of being . . .'[60]

If the homeliness of a flat was a matter for contemporary debate, there could be less argument about its modernity. Flats were associated with new technology, with new financial practices, with new forms of management, with new lifestyles, with modern patterns of residential segregation and modern forms of spatial regulation.

Modern technology

The erection of apartment buildings and model dwellings prompted economies of scale: prefabrication of doors and window frames, use of modern materials such as concrete or a steel frame, and, where new estates comprised several similar blocks, a form of Fordist production line, where teams of specialist craftsmen worked their way from block to block – steel erectors, then bricklayers, carpenters, roofers, glaziers, plumbers, electricians, plasterers, painters and decorators.[61]

The modernity of apartments was even more obviously expressed in their incorporation of modern technology, such as 'dumb waiters', lifts, speaking tubes, electric bells, communal heating and vacuum cleaning systems, electric light and telephones. 'Dumb waiters' not only relieved tradesmen and servants of the physical labour of carrying groceries, coal and other necessities up several flights of stairs but, as critically, eliminated the need for them to use the 'common parts' of the building at all and the associated dilemmas of cross-class encounters between middle-class tenants and working-class servants on the stairs.

Hydraulic and later electric elevators, at first restricted to only the most luxurious flats, led to a reassessment of the value of different floors. F. E. Eales, the architect of Oxford & Cambridge Mansions, luxury flats near Edgware Road that also featured in Gissing's *The Whirlpool*, calculated that the cost of providing an elevator to serve six floors was between £400 and £500. Including the wages of an attendant and the increase in water-rate (for a hydraulic elevator) the annual expense was about £800.[62] This was a substantial sum at a time when the rent for a luxury flat was around £150 per annum. It was clearly not viable where flats were arranged in 'houses' around separate staircases, as at Oxford & Cambridge Mansions. In these circumstances, flats

Figure 9.5. Joseph Pennell (1857–1926), 'Queen Anne's Mansions' (1904), originally in Henry James, *English Hours* (1905), reprinted in J. C. Squire, ed, *A London Reverie* (1928).

on the higher levels were cheaper to rent than those on the first floor; and in some buildings – imitating Parisian practice – servants might be accommodated in the attic rather than within individual flats. On the other hand, at Queen Anne's Mansions, an 11-storey block of flats overlooking St. James's Park, begun in the mid-1870s and massively extended a decade later, there were 'large and convenient lifts' from the beginning; but in this case, suites of rooms were accessed by corridors, so each lift served several suites on each floor (Figure 9.5). The 'fine panoramic view' from the upper storeys meant that higher rents could be charged at these levels, the beginnings of the trend towards penthouse living. This pattern also depended on a high pressure water supply adequate to the needs of tenants on the top floors and also sufficient in case of fire, since fire brigade hoses and ladders would not reach so high. At Queen Anne's Mansions, as in many New York apartment buildings, massive water tanks were positioned on the roof.[63]

Eales was sufficiently confident of internal security in London mansion flats that he thought it unnecessary to lock main entrance-doors or employ resident janitors or concierges at the foot of each staircase, monitoring and directing visitors. The Parisian concierge was widely regarded by British commentators as a busybody intruding on tenants' privacy. Instead, all that was needed was a board in the entrance-hall, with a list of tenants and in/out signs. But by the end of the century, tenants expected more advanced technology such as electric bells, speaking tubes and telephone cabinets. In Carrie Meeber's New York flat on 78th Street, there was a front-door bell for each flat outside the street entrance. In response to this, a button inside each flat 'caused the front door of the general entrance on the ground floor to be electrically unlatched'. Residents who had forgotten their outside keys often pressed their neighbours' bell-push to get them to unlatch the front door.[64]

Adverts for Canadian flats in the early twentieth century stressed the provision of communal heating, an important consideration in harsh winters. No need to get coal in and stoke one's own boiler; the janitor in the basement would look after the communal boiler. Some buildings also advertised vacuum cleaning systems where residents connected hoses in their own flats to wall fittings which in turn linked to a monster vacuum cleaner in the basement, supposedly with enough suction to cope with the whole building's dust. There were also refrigerators 'cooled by a plant in the basement'.[65] As well as these communal facilities, apartment buildings came equipped with the latest domestic appliances in each flat. Westinghouse Electric advertised in trade magazines as 'leaders in apartment installations', noting 'the choice of Westinghouse Electric Ranges' for various luxury apartment buildings in Toronto in the late 1920s, while a full-page advertisement in the *Toronto Globe* in May 1927 announced the completion of 'Four Hundred Avenue Road' – 'Toronto's Beautiful New Apartment on the Hill' – including a list of firms involved in construction: Canadian General Electric had installed 'Hotpoint Hi-Speed Electric Ranges', electric refrigeration was by Kelvinator Toronto Ltd and 'The Snow White Cabinet Clothes Dryer' was a feature of the communal basement laundry.[66]

By comparison, model dwellings might be thought lacking in the latest technology, but even they included up-to-date sanitation, bath-houses, laundries, dust chutes, and gas lighting, still absent from many of the dwellings from which tenants had moved. The earliest purpose-built London block, erected in St Pancras in 1847 by the Metropolitan Association for Improving the Dwellings of the Industrious Classes, included gas lighting on the staircases and separate WCs, slate sinks, galvanised-iron coalboxes and meat safes in each flat.[67] When the same association erected Farringdon Road Buildings in 1874, they guaranteed fireproofing, through the use of reinforced concrete floors, and provided a metered gas supply to each flat.[68] Thereafter, further innovations seem to have been few in the five per cent/philanthropic sector. Wally Harwood, who grew up in the 1920s and 1930s in Darwin Buildings, an Improved Industrial Dwellings Company estate erected in Walworth in south-east London in 1881, recalls washing in a zinc bath in front of the fire and having to use a paraffin lamp to visit the WC after dark, because it had no fixed lighting. Other rooms and the communal staircases continued to be lit by gas until the 1930s when electricity was at last introduced. Harwood notes that at 1/6 per week for a single hanging light – at a time when the rent for a three-room flat was 9/6 – 'most householders settled for a single electric light in the kitchen-cum-living room'.[69]

If nineteenth-century model dwellings were slow to modernise, new working-class flats, such as those erected by the London County Council from the mid-1890s, continued to incorporate new technology and design characteristics. Some LCC buildings differed little from the austere barracks that continued to be erected by philanthropic trusts and five per cent companies, but on flagship estates such as at Boundary Street in Shoreditch, and on the Bourne Estate in Holborn and the Millbank Estate around the new Tate Gallery in Pimlico, all constructed between 1895 and 1903, design standards matched those of middle-class mansion flats.[70]

In inter-war working-class flats, however, modernity sometimes became a casualty of war between rival technologies. The gas industry made vigorous attempts to promote modern flats in which gas heating systems could hold their own against the incursion of electricity and in which technology could come to the aid of the modern housewife. Books, films and exhibitions were deployed to make the case, and Kensal House in North Kensington, a 68-suite estate opened in 1936 by the Gas Light and Coke Company, soon became 'an icon for the Modern Movement in Britain'.[71] It was reported that 84 per cent of new dwellings on London housing estates erected since 1928 still used 'the bad old system of cooking in the living room' using a coal-fired range or 'combination grate' and in 87 per cent hot water was not obtainable automatically. However, it appears that many of these dwellings were lit by electricity, whereas at Kensal House, gas lighting had been installed. The price structures offered by gas and electricity suppliers meant that a combination of the two fuels was too expensive to be affordable by working-class tenants: so, 'the wizard of modernity [electricity] must have at his elbow the smoky spirit of nineteenth century fuel'.[72]

By comparison, by the early 1930s the latest mansion flats, less modernist in external appearance than Vienna-inspired workers' flats, came with 'all reasonable labour-saving devices, including refrigerators, constant hot water and central heating, electric passenger and trade lifts'. London County Freehold & Leasehold Properties Ltd., owners of more than 6000 London mansion flats, acknowledged that 'a flat is a machine for living in', but they balanced Le Corbusier's observation with the assertion that 'it must also be a "home" with all the intimate associations implicit in that very English word'.[73]

Modern ownership

Small blocks of suburban walk-up apartments, such as those which proliferated in Toronto in the early 1910s, could be financed by individual promoters (Figure 9.6). Typically, the building costs of a 6-suite, two storeys plus basement apartment house were only about $10–15,000, little more than the cost of a substantial detached villa. Larger and more luxurious buildings, however, involved the creation of financial syndicates or limited companies to protect individual investors. Five of the six most valuable, purely residential apartment buildings erected in Toronto by 1913 were company-owned. In total, of 186 apartment blocks, only 18 were owned by companies, eight by groups of executors, and 160 by private individuals. But although companies owned only 10 per cent of the total number of buildings, they owned 23 per cent of buildings by assessed value. During the 1920s, the average size of new building increased substantially – from 11.7 units per building completed between 1911 and 1921 to 19.8 units per building completed between 1921 and 1931. Unsurprisingly, the proportion owned by companies also increased. Companies and partnerships

Figure 9.6. Ainger Apartments (1911–12), Bloor Street East, Toronto. City of Toronto Archives, Series 372, Sub-Series 9, Item 9.

accounted for 49 per cent of new apartment building by value in the boom period between 1925 and 1931.[74]

Two related questions follow from this trend: how were these buildings financed, and were they built as speculations, to be sold as soon as they were completed, or as long-term investments? Of 139 Toronto apartment buildings listed in the assessment rolls for 1914 (compiled in mid-1913), 90 were still owned by the person or company listed on the building permit granted up to thirteen years earlier. The remaining 49 (35 per cent) had changed hands at least once. Further analysis of 54 Toronto apartment buildings constructed prior to 1930, whose ownership and financial history was examined in detail using Land Registry records, showed that 18 (33 per cent) changed owners within three years of completion, suggestive that they had been erected on speculation. We might infer, therefore, that up to two-thirds of apartment buildings were built as investments; they could not be financed, as much speculative housing was, by builders building to sell and build again. In fact, the proportion built as investments was probably higher; a close matching of assessment roll and Land Registry data indicates that at least some transfers of ownership, from builders to property companies, were purely notional: the company was the builder by another name. Modernity lay less in the existence of an active property market, more in the array of financial devices designed to protect investors.

In the same sample of 54 buildings, 48 (89 per cent) were subject to institutional mortgages at some stage in their pre-1950 history, involving at least 111 mortgage transactions. In the cases of 24 buildings, transfers of ownership followed mortgage defaults and acquisition of ownership by the mortgagees or their being granted power of sale to a third party. Many of these defaults occurred during the depression years of the 1930s, when vacancy rates increased despite landlords reducing rents so that income fell far short of outgoings. Some of the most luxurious buildings erected during the boom of the late 1920s quickly found themselves in receivership or subject to financial restructuring by bondholders' committees, comprised of representatives of those with the largest financial interests, usually life assurance companies.[75]

There has been no systematic quantitative analysis of the ownership of flats in London, but research on individual developers demonstrates both the increasing sophistication of their financial and managerial arrangements and the lack of any clear distinction between model dwellings and mansion flats. Among companies building mansion flats in London, the Middle Class Dwellings Co. Ltd., registered in 1888 by R. E. Farrant, erected flats along Buckingham Palace Road, near Victoria Station, and in Ridgmount Gardens, Bloomsbury. These were high-class mansion flats, mostly rated in the 1890s at between £70 and £110 per annum. The company subsequently became part of London County Freehold & Leasehold Properties Ltd, a public company formed in 1925 which, by 1933, 'with its five 100% Subsidiary Companies, own[ed] more than 6,000 distinctive Mansion Flats in London valued at more than £7,000,000'. The company claimed not to have sold a single block of flats during its eight years as a public company, emphasising its long-term commitment to its tenants as investors, not dealers.[76]

At the same time as running the Middle Class Dwellings Co., Farrant was also deputy chairman and managing director of the Artizans', Labourers' and General Dwellings Co., famous for its suburban estates of terraced houses (described in Chapter 7), but also – during Farrant's tenure – responsible for nearly 1,500 working-class block dwellings in central London. Morris regards the Artizans' Company as the highest performing model dwellings company between 1887 and 1896 in terms of its average annual realised rates of return on ordinary shares. By 1914 the company had an issued capital of nearly £3,000,000, and since its foundation in 1867 had paid an average annual dividend of 4.89 per cent.[77] Just as the Middle Class Dwellings Co. developed sites on the aristocratic Grosvenor and Bedford estates, so the first Artizans' Company working-class flats were on the Portman estate in Marylebone.[78] In many respects the development and management of mansion flats and block dwellings was the same business. The Artizans' Company and the Middle Class Dwellings Co. operated out of the same offices in Great George Street, close to Whitehall.

Not all the flats owned by London County Freehold & Leasehold Properties Ltd in the 1930s had been built by the company or its five subsidiaries. Corporate control of the luxury end of the market also reflected acquisitions of buildings originally owned independently. For example, in 1879, C. Eales & Son, architects, applied to the Metropolitan Board of Works on behalf of trustees administering the estate of the late John Bond Cabbell, seeking permission to demolish existing houses and workshops and replace them with twelve 'houses' comprising 74 flats, arranged over six storeys but accessed from twelve separate staircases, the whole forming one continuous V-shaped range of buildings. The owner was listed as James Humphress, and his name continued to appear in ratebooks after the completion of the mansions, by now known as Oxford & Cambridge Mansions, in 1882. But by 1890 the ratebooks recorded the owners as George Weston and Samuel Richard Walker (executors), and by 1910 the estate was listed among the holdings of Consolidated London Properties Ltd., a City firm with offices in Cannon Street shared with City & West End Properties Ltd., whose name also appeared on some planning applications for Oxford & Cambridge Mansions in the 1930s.[79] Critical in this story is the role of estate trustees or executors. The site became available following the death of the previous owner, Cabbell, and the decision of his trustees to pursue redevelopment; the completed buildings came under corporate control following the death of their owner, Humphress, and their disposal by his executors. The market was not as open and unfettered as models of laissez-faire capitalism might suggest, but often depended on accidents of death and inheritance.

Among individual entrepreneurs, James Hartnoll (1853–1900) built at least a dozen blocks of flats in central London between 1880 and 1895, some on slum clearance and street improvement sites acquired from the Metropolitan Board of Works (MBW), a source of relatively cheap land also exploited by the Peabody Trust and some model dwellings companies. Hartnoll began as a contractor building to order for other landlords, but by 1885 he was engaged on his own account in a large development of more than 500 flats in Poplar. In the same year, he began work on Devon Mansions on Tooley Street, an area subsequently incorporated into the new layout of streets and institutional buildings at the southern end of Tower Bridge, discussed in Chapter 1. In the late 1880s and early 1890s he acquired further sites in Southwark, Bermondsey, Charing Cross Road, Shaftesbury Avenue, Gray's Inn Road and Rosebery Avenue, mostly on or close to new streets cut through former slum districts by the MBW. Hartnoll's flats bridged the gap between model dwellings and mansion flats, a little more upmarket than those of the Improved Industrial Dwellings Company, but less expensive than the mansion flats going up in Bayswater and Victoria. Isobel Watson notes that the most difficult of his estates to manage was that in Poplar, plagued by high levels of vacancies and, in 1915, a rent strike. In this respect, Hartnoll's experience was identical to that of the model dwellings companies and the London County Council, which also found flats in Poplar and close to the Thames hard to let and constantly troubled by rent arrears.[80]

Hartnoll's developments were all in his own name, but a longer-lived contemporary, Abraham Davis (1857–1924), who progressed from building working-class flats and houses and an 'oriental-style' market in the East End to erecting more than 2,000 flats in St Pancras, St John's Wood and Maida Vale, shifted during his career from one-off partnerships with his brothers into a more modern world of company formation. Once Davis had negotiated a building agreement with a landowner, he would assign the agreement to the Central London Building Company Ltd., which he had founded to act as contractor for his various schemes. On completion, the developed site would be sold on to another associated company, thereby releasing working capital and insulating Davis from any personal financial liability. Among the bodies Davis founded during the 1910s were the London Housing Society, a 'public utility society' entitled to borrow money from the Public Works Loan Commissioners at below-market interest rates for the purpose of erecting working-class housing; the Lady Workers Homes Ltd., to provide accommodation for single working women;

Service Flats Ltd., to manage buildings with communal facilities such as crèches, laundries and restaurants; and the Public Utility Housing Society, responsible for flats in St John's Wood which simultaneously satisfied both the landowners who had supplied the site on condition that Davis erected 'high class residential flats' and the Ministry of Health which assessed the flats as 'working-class' and therefore eligible for subsidy under the Addison Act (1919).[81]

To Watson, Davis's 'use of a complex pattern of companies perhaps anticipates the sophisticated financial arrangements of the building world of the later 20th century'.[82] His Toronto counterpart, John W. Walker (1859–1936), equally spanned the worlds of entrepreneurial and corporate capitalism. When Walker died his obituarists portrayed him as a self-made man who had begun as a horsecar driver, moved into property by chance, and retained personal responsibility for every stage of building and management: 'Although he owned more than 30 apartment houses and homes, he had an intimate knowledge of the details of every one, having built most of them himself.'[83] Yet, if Walker had begun as a small-scale entrepreneur, he soon learnt how to turn methods of corporate financing to his advantage.

In the city's first apartment-house boom, prior to 1913, Walker was listed in building permits as owner and builder of four new apartment buildings, none more than three storeys in height or accommodating even as many as twenty suites. He lived just down the road from one of his buildings, in a house of which he was only the tenant. This was typical of small-scale nineteenth-century builders, sinking all their limited capital into their building projects: his modest walk-up apartments were no different from other builders' rows of single-family houses. After World War I, Walker's name featured only once more in the City permit register, for an apartment building on St Clair Avenue estimated to cost $85,000. Yet, at his death, he owned more than twenty apartment buildings that had been erected during the 1920s boom. Many lay just outside city limits in York County, where there were no geographical restrictions on erecting apartments as there were in the City after 1912, and where regulations on fireproofing were less strict.[84]

Walker's real estate, of which about 90 per cent was in apartment buildings, was valued for probate at $783,000, but this figure represented his equity, after the deduction of outstanding mortgages and interest payments. For example, the Balmoral Apartments were recorded in the city's assessment rolls with a value of $16,404 for the land and $160,000 for the buildings; but Walker's equity in the apartment house was worth only $90,054. Like Jacob Singer, discussed in Chapter 7, Walker was both mortgagor and mortgagee. In the latter capacity, he owned mortgages worth $142,000 and appears to have acquired the Balmoral four years after its completion through his role as mortgagee. Advanced publicity, building permit and legal documents for this most luxurious of blocks recorded the developers as Messrs Wilkie and Delamere, trading as Balmoral Apartments Ltd. There was no mention of Walker. But he was involved from the outset, granting a $100,000 mortgage jointly to Balmoral Apartments Ltd and De Jonckheere Construction Co. Ltd only a few weeks after the permit had been issued, and ensuring that his mortgage was legally the first mortgage (and therefore had prior rights in the event of foreclosure) despite the developers having already contracted a vendor-take-back mortgage for $50,000 from the previous landowner. Three first mortgages later Walker assumed personal ownership, when

Balmoral Apartments Ltd defaulted in August 1933.[85] While Walker may not have used the device of limited liability as extensively as Abraham Davis did, his operations were modern in their sensitivity to modern legal and financial practices and even in the cultivation of his image as 'ideal landlord' and 'father of Toronto apartment houses'.[86]

Not all apartment developers were as astute. In London, E. J. Cave, who erected mansion flats in Maida Vale and West Hampstead in the 1890s, was declared bankrupt in 1900. His flats had been financed by taking individual stakes in advance from prospective investors, who lost all but 6d of each pound they had invested. Yet while his bankruptcy ruined many of his creditors, it did not stop Cave's own activities. Recognising the need for protection through limited liability, his family founded the Middlesex Building Company in 1905, with Cave as managing director and shares owned by family members.[87] Writing in the same year, Sydney Perks observed that it was very difficult to sell blocks of flats, even when vacancy rates were low. Many blocks had fallen into the hands of mortgagees. He advised that flats for rental at less than £70 per annum would not pay *as a speculation*, although they might yield a fair profit if built as a long-term investment.[88] The case studies from London and Toronto described in this section show how apartment developers were learning to exploit modern methods of financing, but also that the business remained a precarious form of enterprise.

Modern marketing for a modern lifestyle

Nineteenth-century flats depended on signboards and small ads to attract potential tenants. When Artillery Mansions opened on Victoria Street, Westminster, small ads were placed in *The Times*, separately advertising 'Family Flats' and 'Bachelors' Rooms and Suites' on at least four occasions during September and October 1895, and 'For Ladies Only – Rooms and Suites' on the last two occasions. No prices were included in the 'Family Flats' advertisements, but bachelors were offered 'single rooms from £20 [per annum]' while ladies were charged 'from £25' for apparently similar rooms and services.[89] Artillery Mansions was also promoted on a postcard depicting the grand entrance archway to the flats. Various details were painted in: in the background, the fountain in the courtyard had been 'improved' by the addition of white-foamed water, while in the foreground, an elegantly dressed lady was depicted reclining in her carriage, drawn by two high-trotting horses, driven by two top-hatted, black-coated coachmen (Figure 9.7). Postcards were a common form of publicity in early twentieth-century Toronto, too.[90]

By the time Artillery Mansions opened, two property registers concentrating on flats were being published in London, both by estate agents based in Victoria Street. *Flats*, which ran from August 1889 until March 1921, included illustrations and 'reviews' of selected blocks. *Flatland* continued publication until 1934, although the early editions, at least, were simply unillustrated listings of flats to let, little different from newspaper small ads.[91] Another innovation was the brochure displaying a company's complete portfolio of residential property. Issued by City and West End Properties Ltd. in about 1911, *Residential Flats* included exterior photographs and brief details, but no prices, of twenty-three estates of mansion flats

Figure 9.7. Artillery Mansions, Victoria Street, Westminster (1895). Postcard (1907): WCA00124 (E138 Victoria Street (078)), City of Westminster Archives Centre.

scattered through the West End and one set of chambers, including office and residential suites, in the City. Word and image together sought to combine modern efficiency and old fashioned elegance. Along with fireproofing, 'perfect sanitation' and electric bells, at Carlisle Mansions 'Additional Bedrooms in Basement can be rented', presumably to accommodate households with too many servants to fit into the 'Double Flats' of '4 Reception Rooms, 7 and 8 Bedrooms and Dressing Room'. Nearby, in Victoria Street, Princes Mansions offered wine cellars in the basement.[92]

Just as London's Artillery Mansions was promoted with an image of stylish mobility, so in publicity for Toronto apartments a generation later, illustrations featured fashionably dressed young men and women standing in the street outside the buildings, often admiring, boarding or alighting from the latest open-topped automobiles.[93]

Figure 9.8. Advertisement for The Claridge, Avenue Road, *Toronto Globe*, 17 October 1928.

A 1928 newspaper advertisement for the Claridge, a 6-storey + basement block near the top of Avenue Road Hill, combined Art Deco typography, a modernist impression of the building, including several speedy automobiles converging on the entrance and a sunburst exploding from behind the building (Figure 9.8), and a message about 'distinction': 'Toronto's Most Distinguished Residential Apartment. Quietly correct, of incomparable excellence in design and finish. Liveried attendants. A gracious home in everything but the responsibility.'[94]

Another indicator of style was the name. Different kinds of name targeted different kinds of tenant. The most homely names, usually for fairly basic 'efficiency' flats, simply drew upon the street name or the names of members of the builder's own family. In Toronto, 'Lillian' stood next to 'Irene', 'Stanley' next to 'Florence'. Other Toronto buildings proclaimed their allegiance to the mother country – 'King Edward', 'Royal George', 'Royal Pembroke' – or to the establishment: the 'Claridge' stood across the street from the 'Clarendon'. But there were also racier, American or continental names: 'Manhattan', 'Waldorf', 'Biltmore', 'Ansonia', all copying names from American cities, appeared, usually in much shrunken versions. And in a city with as puritanical reputation as Toronto's before World War I, it was a form of cosmopolitan defiance to label one's building 'Villa Nova' or 'La Plaza'. By the 1920s, the fashion was to eschew names, and make the number into the name: '400 Avenue Road', '77 Wellesley'. It helped if the number was easily memorable but, because large apartment blocks occupied sites where several houses had previously stood, developers usually had some choice among a variety of numbers.[95]

Modern tenants

In nineteenth-century London it was argued that flats were ideal for bachelors, for childless couples, for people who travelled a lot, and for those who hankered after a simple life. Flats were also appropriate for widows and, by the end of the century, for career-minded single women. All types of people who either had not existed in earlier times or who would have been expected to live with relatives or in lodgings. In contrast, model dwellings were definitely family housing. Reviewing the cast of characters in Gissing's novels, we find Edwin and Amy Reardon beginning married life in a three-room flat on the edge of Regent's Park; the widowed Mrs Frothingham in a flat in Swiss Cottage; another widow, Mrs Luke Widdowson, still in her 30s, in a flat in Victoria Street; two bachelors, Bevis and Barfoot, in separate flats in the same block in Bayswater; the reclusive Lord Polperro, who has abandoned his wife and lives the life of a middle-aged bachelor, in a first-floor flat in 'Lowndes Mansions', Sloane Street; another bachelor, Will Warburton, in a flat by Chelsea Bridge; the 'new woman' Beatrice French in a 'bachelor's flat' in Brixton; and the childless Hugh and Sibyl Carnaby, newly returned from a round-the-world trip, in a flat in Oxford & Cambridge Mansions. At the other end of the social spectrum, Ida Starr lives in a two-room flat in a Fulham model dwelling, while John Hewett and his children share a three-room flat in Farringdon Road Buildings with the elderly Mr and Mrs Eagles.[96] The only families with children in this roll-call are the Hewetts, who are grateful to have been rescued from a 'kitchen' in the basement of a house on King's Cross Road and who are not quite a complete family since John has been twice widowed, and the Reardons who have a baby son and are already uncomfortable at the lack of privacy in their modest flat.

The Carnabys have at least one servant;[97] Lord Polperro has a housekeeper; Mrs Frothingham rejoices in having 'Just one servant, who can't make mistakes, because there's next to nothing to do'. But Bevis has just sacked his maidservant for stealing his tobacco and cigars and notes that good servants are hard to retain because 'they miss the congenial gossip of the area door'. Warburton and the Reardons both depend on non-resident domestic help, but while the comfortably off Warburton employs an older woman, Mrs Hopper, the Reardons make do with a younger, cheaper girl, 'recently emancipated from the Board school'.[98]

So who, in real life, lived in apartments and model dwellings? Gissing's propensity to place his characters in real buildings means that we can compare the novel Oxford & Cambridge Mansions and Farringdon Road Buildings with the real thing.[99] In 1891 only 5 per cent of the inhabitants of Oxford & Cambridge Mansions were aged 0–9, compared to 28 per cent in Farringdon Road Buildings. In the former, 46 per cent of household heads were women in 1891; at Farringdon Road, only 15 per cent. Average household size was 3.3 persons in the mansions (in flats of 6–9 rooms), 5.0 persons in the buildings (in flats of 1–3 rooms). Almost two-thirds of the population of the buildings, and 53 per cent of households, lived at densities of more than two persons per room. The census recorded two households of twelve persons, each living in three rooms, and another four ten-person households, one of which occupied only two rooms. So the Hewett-Eagles household portrayed in *The Nether World* – seven persons crowded into three rooms – was not atypical.

Only 11 households in the mansions had no resident domestic servant, 35 had one, 14 had two, and two households each employed three servants. There were fifteen general servants living in Farringdon Road Buildings, but all had close relationships to the head of household – thirteen were daughters, one sister, one mother-in-law – indicating that either this was part of their family duties or they were employed elsewhere, as non-resident servants, rather like the Reardons' maid. There were also four older women, recorded as charwomen, like Mrs Hopper or Gissing's own daily help, Mrs King, who lived a few minutes' walk from his flat and to whom he paid five shillings per week.

Yet Farringdon Road Buildings was not occupied by a particularly poor population. Of 207 male heads of household whose occupations were recorded in the 1891 census, 20 were 'labourers' and 15 'porters' but there were also 19 printers, 10 carpenters or joiners, 14 metal workers, 9 warehousemen, a host of other skilled trades, and three clerks. Overall, MAIDIC tenants were superior in occupational status to Peabody tenants, but inferior to IIDCo. tenants. Around 1880, about 2.3 per cent of IIDCo. tenants were recorded as 'labourers', compared to 5.3 per cent of MAIDIC tenants and 16.1 per cent of Peabody tenants. At the other end of the social spectrum, there were twice as many clerks in IIDCo. as in MAIDIC flats, and twice as many in MAIDIC as in Peabody flats. Female-headed households were generally poorer than male-headed households. Widows with no occupation, laundresses, charwomen and needlewomen predominated (although some had adult sons in better-paid employment living at home). As with male occupations, so with female: there were more charwomen, dressmakers and needlewomen on Peabody estates, far fewer in IIDCo. flats.[100]

The 'respectable working-class' bias in model dwellings is also illustrated by statistics produced in the course of Charles Booth's poverty survey. Of all the tenants who lived in 'block dwellings', the majority of which were not 'philanthropic or semi-philanthropic', 9.4 per cent were classed as 'very poor' (Booth's Classes A and B) and 29.2 per cent as 'poor' (Classes C and D). But restricting our attention to 'philanthropic and semi-philanthropic' blocks, the proportions were only 3.9 per cent and 19.4 per cent.[101]

Tenants' registers, which survive for many Peabody Trust estates, also record the earnings of new tenants and their places of work. For example, when the trust's estate at Herbrand Street, Bloomsbury, opened in 1885, larger flats were occupied as much by better-off tenants as by larger families. Tenants of one-room flats were not only poorer, but lived at higher densities, nearly 2.2 persons per room compared to 1.7 persons per room in two- and three-room flats. One-room tenants earned on average 18/7 per week compared to £1–5s-10d for two-room tenants and £1–7s-8d for those in three rooms. While the average wages of subsequent cohorts of new tenants increased and their levels of overcrowding decreased, the differentials between one-room and larger flats continued well into the twentieth century (Table 9.1).[102]

In the 1880s most Herbrand Street tenants worked within easy walking distance of their home. Several employers' names recurred: Shoolbred's and Maple's department stores and Meux's Brewery, all on Tottenham Court Road, each employed several tenants, as did the British Museum and Crosse and Blackwell's of Soho Square. The 1900s cohort included tenants employed at Hammersmith and Paddington – farther

Table 9.1. *Characteristics of Peabody Trust Tenants: Herbrand Street Estate,
Bloomsbury, Central London*

(i) Characteristics of Tenants moving into Herbrand Street Estate on opening (1885) and
during two subsequent five-year periods (1900–04 and 1920–24), based on a sample of 100
of the 205 flats on the estate:

Tenants Moving in during: **No. of new tenants**	**1885** **100**	**1900–04** **53**	**1920–24** **20**
Male heads	94	40	12
Female heads	6	13	8
(no. moving into 1-room flats)	12	9	4
(no. moving into 2-room flats)	44	38	12
(no. moving into 3-room flats)	43	6	3
Average income (all new tenants)	**£1–5s-10d**	**£1–4s-0d**	**£2–3s-0d**
(moving into 1-room flats)	18s-7d	17s-11d	£1–2s-6d
(moving into 2-room flats)	£1–5–10d	£1–5s-1d	£2–2s-11d
(moving into 3-room flats)	£1–7–8d	£1–6s-10d	£3–5s-0d
Persons per room (all new tenants)	**1.74**	**1.46**	**1.34**
(moving into 1-room flats)	2.17	1.67	1.75
(moving into 2-room flats)	1.64	1.38	1.38
(moving into 3-room flats)	1.76	1.67	1.33
Average period of residence in flat	**6 yr 8 mo**	**4 yr 1 mo**	**10 yr 4 mo**
(moving into 1-room flats)	4 yr 1 mo	3 yr 9 mo	10 yr 8 mo
(moving into 2-room flats)	3 yr 5 mo	4 yr 1 mo	10 yr 0 mo
(moving into 3-room flats)	10 yr 6 mo	4 yr 8 mo	13 yr 9 mo
Average period of residence in estate	**9 yr 2 mo**	**9 yr 0 mo**	**18 yr 7 mo**

(ii) Turnover rates

Period	Total number of changes of tenant in sample of 100 flats	No. of changes per flat per annum in		
		1-room flats	2-room flats	3-room flats
1885–89	143	0.48	0.41	0.10
1890–94	125	0.28	0.34	0.15
1895–99	131	0.29	0.33	0.18
1900–04	97	0.32	0.24	0.11
1905–09	93	0.17	0.28	0.10
1910–14	87	0.19	0.23	0.12
1915–19	78	0.11	0.24	0.10
1920–24	35	0.09	0.09	0.05
1925–29	43	0.13	0.10	0.06

Source: Peabody Trust Tenants' Registers

afield but easily accessible by Metropolitan Railway – but the majority still worked in
Bloomsbury and the West End. By the 1920s workplaces were more varied, including
Southwark, Westminster and the City. It is likely that this pattern reflected the scarcity
of housing after World War I rather than the choice of employees to live farther from
their work.

The same squeeze on housing is evident when rates of population turnover are
examined. Among the original tenants, the average length of time that they stayed
in their flat was just under seven years. Many tenants moved between flats on the

same estate, from one or two to three rooms as they prospered, or out of necessity as their families increased in size; or they 'downsized' on the death of a partner or as children left home. The average period of residence on the estate was around nine years for tenants who moved in during both the 1880s and the 1900s; and tenants of three-room flats stayed much longer than those in smaller flats, whose financial circumstances were less secure. But there was a dramatic shift after World War I. Tenants moving in during the early 1920s averaged more than ten years in the same flat and nearly twenty years on the estate. In part, this was a response to a post-war housing shortage: there were few vacancies to move to. In addition, with the introduction of rent control in 1915, tenants were disinclined to move for a small improvement in their living conditions or geographical situation since, by doing so, they surrendered their right to a controlled rent. A final indication of decreasing mobility is provided by the total number of tenancy changes in successive five year periods. High levels of turnover in the 1880s and 1890s reflected an initial sorting-out process: some of the original tenants quickly found that the discipline and management style was not to their liking and left within a few months of moving in. There was a gradual decline in turnover rates during the 1900s and 1910s, but then a dramatic decrease in the 1920s. If this pattern was typical of rental housing more generally, if renting no longer offered the flexibility of being able to move whenever family or work circumstances altered, it must have reduced the attractions of renting relative to home-ownership, and provided another stimulus for the move into owner-occupation in the 1930s.

Herbrand Street was a popular estate in a respectable district. Most model dwellings and council flats in the West End and around the fringes of the City of London were oversubscribed. But in the East End flats often proved hard to let. At Katharine Buildings, a minimum-standards East End Dwellings Company estate near St Katharine's Dock, of 238 small flats, more than 30 were vacant at the close of 1886, 1887 and 1888, years associated with especial economic hardship. Even in less poverty-stricken districts in Bethnal Green, Stepney and King's Cross, the EEDCo. never managed to fill its new buildings as quickly and easily as the Peabody Trust, whose only serious problems occurred in Shadwell, near the London Docks, in the late 1860s, and in Herne Hill, a rare venture into the then outer suburbs, in the 1900s. Perhaps the greatest problems with the management of block dwellings, and certainly the most extreme contrasts between West End and East End, were encountered by the London County Council during the 1900s. Rent losses through empties frequently exceeded 25 per cent in blocks of council flats in Poplar, Rotherhithe and Deptford, but rarely reached 1 per cent on estates in Holborn and St Pancras. Eviction rates followed a similar pattern. Rents were too high and earnings too inconsistent for the casual poor to find permanent homes in block dwellings, whether owned by housing trusts, five per cent companies or local authorities.[103]

We might expect the middle-class residents of mansion flats to have been less 'nomadic' than the occupants of working-class buildings. The former often leased their flats on three- or seven-year terms, while the latter rented from week to week. In practice, subletting was common among middle-class lessees so that, within central London, there seems to have been little difference in the residential mobility of different classes in different types of flat. About 13 per cent of males on the electoral roll for Farringdon Road Buildings in 1884 were still at the same address in the 1891 census while as many again had moved flats but remained within the Buildings. By comparison, 19 per cent of household heads in the 1891 census for Oxford & Cambridge Mansions had been there seven years earlier, and only 9 per cent of heads at Cornwall Residences had remained as long.[104] Of course, there was more scope to move flats within a large estate like Farringdon Road Buildings (260 flats in all) than in Cornwall Residences (64 suites) or Oxford & Cambridge Mansions (74 suites). Nonetheless, these statistics confirm the hopes and fears of contemporaries. One objective of model dwellings was to 'fix' their inhabitants, to put an end to 'flitting' from one 'rookery' to another: families in model dwellings were supposed to be less transient than their slum-living neighbours. But the occupants of mansion flats were more transient than middle-class residents of single-family dwellings; flats threatened the geographical as well as the social stability of the West End.

Oxford & Cambridge Mansions was not at the very top of the social hierarchy. According to the 1891 census, blocks in Kensington accommodated many more servants. At Albert Hall Mansions, almost a quarter of households were *headed* by servants, indicating the absence of their employers, perhaps living in a country house or touring the continent on census day. There were also proportionally more children in Oxford & Cambridge Mansions than in flats in Kensington and Victoria (Table 9.2). But all these blocks shared a rich diversity in the birthplaces and geographical experiences of their residents: the empire on furlough or in retirement, the continent come to London. Among birthplaces recorded by the inmates of Oxford & Cambridge Mansions were Jamaica, Tasmania, Calcutta, the Punjab, Cairo, Cape Colony, Buffalo, Niagara, Oporto, Paris, Dresden, Augsburg, Hamburg, Luxembourg, Boulogne, Denmark, Holland and Belgium. In Kensington Court Gardens there was an Indian Army general, a lieutenant-colonel and a major-general (both retired), two young second lieutenants, a retired Indian civil servant and a widow from South Australia. Even the hall attendant was an army pensioner whose wife had been born in India. At Queen Anne's Mansions, which provided dining rooms and other communal facilities for its bachelor clientele, the skilled catering staff was entirely foreign: a German manager presided over a German head waiter, seven German, one Austrian, one Danish and one Italian waiter, a German kitchen clerk and a female French cook. By contrast, at Farringdon Road Buildings, less than one per cent of residents were born outside the British Isles: three skilled male workers – a cigar maker from Brussels, a Swiss looking-glass maker and an Italian cabinet maker; three adult women – from Germany, Poland and New York; and a pipe manufacturer's family from Strasbourg and Paris. There was no evidence of a colonial presence, apart from a handful of Irish-born, at barely one per cent a much lower proportion of Irish than was present elsewhere in central London.

Oxford & Cambridge Mansions were about the same level in the social hierarchy as the apartments that Howells occupied in Manhattan in the late 1880s and in which he placed the Marches in *A Hazard of New Fortunes*. A brief foray into the US Federal Census for 1900 for three small New York apartment houses – the Hampshire on West 9th, where Howells lived in 1888, its neighbour, the Portsmouth, and the Ardea, three blocks to the north – reveals similar social patterns to flats in central London:

Table 9.2. *Comparative Statistics for Characteristics of Mansion-Flat Tenants (Selected London Flats, 1891) and Apartment-House Tenants (New York, 1900)*

Buildings	No. of h'holds	Persons per h'hold	Females per Male	Children (0–15) per household	Servants per household	% Female-headed households*	% Foreign-born**
Farringdon Road Bdgs, Clerkenwell	247	5.0	1.0	2.26	0	15	1
Cornwall Mnsns, nr. Baker Street Stn	51	2.2	2.0	0.12	0.4	40	7
Oxford & Cambridge Mnsns, nr. Edgware Road Stn	62	3.3	2.6	0.27	1.1	45	14
3 Blocks of Kensington flats: Albert Hall Mnsns Kensington Court Gdns Kensington Court Mnsns	101	4.4	3.8	0.21	2.3	40	7
3 Blocks of New York apts: Portsmouth, W9th Hampshire, W9th Ardea, W12th	45	3.6	1.7	0.29	1.0	22	29

*Households apparently headed by servants (presumably because their employers were absent) have been omitted.

**For London flats' includes all persons born outside British Isles; for New York apartments' includes all persons born outside United States.

Sources: 1891 Census enumerators' books (for London); 1900 Federal Census enumerators' returns (for New York).

between three and four persons per household, including one servant, and between five and six per cent of the population aged 0–9; but fewer female-headed households, and a less female population overall (Table 9.2). The male heads of household in the Hampshire, Portsmouth and Ardea were manufacturers, dealers, bankers, company secretaries, accountants, lawyers, physicians and architects, many with offices along Broadway and in Lower Manhattan.[105] They were, perhaps, a less distinctively 'new' population than flat-dwellers in London, where middle-class flats were a more recent and still a less common form of living than in New York. Unlike the foreign and colonial heads of household in London mansion flats, the heads of household in these New York apartments were nearly all American-born; but their servants, contrasting with the mainly rural British-born servants in London, were mostly first-generation immigrants, especially from Ireland and Sweden. Among 46 servants in the three New York buildings, only seven were American-born, five of whom were black.

Evidence from Toronto is more revealing of new social trends during the first third of the twentieth century.[106] As late as 1914, only 20 per cent of heads of household living in Toronto apartments were female; by 1930, 39 per cent of heads were women. Meanwhile, the proportion of female heads in the city as a whole was much lower, and their rate of increase much slower: 10 per cent in 1921, 14 per cent in 1931. Whereas 60 per cent of female apartment heads before World War I were widows, by 1930 single (never married) women accounted for 57 per cent of all female apartment heads; widows comprised only 37 per cent. Apartments were in the vanguard of working women living independently in the twentieth-century city. Unfortunately, while assessment rolls recorded the occupations of male householders, they returned only the marital status of female heads; but of those women who could also be traced in city directories, the most popular occupations were teacher, clerk, stenographer and nurse.

There were few children living in apartments – just 2.8 per cent of apartment residents were aged 5–16 in 1914; and the average size of apartment households declined from 2.6 persons in 1914 to 2.2 in 1930 (when the citywide average for all households was 4.2). As apartments proliferated so they tended to become smaller. The earliest buildings mostly comprised luxury apartments, each large enough for a middle-class family; inter-war apartments were more often 'efficiency' units of just two or three rooms designed for occupancy by only one or two persons.

In 1914 nearly 13 per cent and in 1930 more than 16 per cent of apartment suites were vacant. By comparison, typical vacancy rates among houses on adjacent streets were around 5 per cent. Persistence rates, too, were lower among apartment tenants than among residents of nearby houses. Only 22 per cent of householders living in Toronto apartments in 1909 were still at the same address five years later, whereas 42 per cent of householders in nearby streets were still listed as occupying the same houses. Equivalent persistence rates for 1930–1935 were 15 per cent (apartment tenants) and 38 per cent (nearby householders). By 1930 many of Toronto's apartments, especially low-rent 'efficiency' units, were located in suburban districts – they were more likely to be occupied by male-headed households than apartments downtown, they accommodated slightly larger households, fewer male heads in professional or clerical jobs and proportionally more commercial travellers and skilled working class. But the most marked difference between suburban and downtown apartments lay in the lower vacancy rate for suburban apartments: 7 per cent of suites compared to 20 per cent downtown.

Summarising a mass of statistical data, we may conclude that the characteristics of suburban apartment dwellers were not so different from those of their non-apartment-living neighbours. Yet owners and occupiers of suburban single-family homes continued to treat apartments with suspicion, and to lobby councils to exclude apartment housing from 'residential' neighbourhoods. In the modernist litany of 'a place for everything and everything in its place', the place for apartments continued to be some place else.

Modern geography

Mansion flats and middle-class apartments began as a West End/Midtown phenomenon, where their scale and style matched that of neighbouring buildings; they were part of a modern city of big stores and big office buildings; in smaller cities like Toronto they were evidence of metropolitan status. They were viewed as 'commercial', rather than 'residential', machines for profit as much as for living. So when they spread into middle-class suburbs, whether as street-corner, low-rise, walk-up 'efficiency' apartments or as luxury flats, they met with opposition from local householders, who feared the intrusion of 'commerce' into 'residential' districts. There were some complaints, usually about the loss of light and air, or about being overlooked, in parts of Westminster and Kensington, and even in Manhattan in the 1880s, but opposition was much more intense in Toronto and in cities farther west like Winnipeg and Minneapolis, where rates of suburban homeownership were so much higher than in metropolises like New York and London.[107]

The fear was that apartment buildings, especially those that were too high or occupied too large a proportion of their sites, would cause a reduction in property values, effectively undermining a prime reason for the growth of homeownership. In London or Manhattan, if you disliked what was happening next door to your rented home, you could choose to move elsewhere, probably at relatively short notice, and without incurring legal expenses. It was the housing landlords who suffered if their property became less attractive to potential tenants. But in 'cities of homes', it was less easy and more costly to move, especially if it was plain to prospective purchasers that they would be acquiring a depreciating asset. In practice, it is hard to find evidence that property values did decline in the vicinity of apartment buildings; but there is no doubting some sharp practice among apartment developers that aroused suspicion and antagonism among neighbours. Several cases in pre-1914 Toronto involved developers building or threatening to build out to the sidewalk, contrary to accepted local conventions that builders would set their new buildings back from the street. In some cases, threats to build were sufficient to get local homeowners to club together to buy strips of land to prevent such construction. Apartment developers profited by not building as well as by building. The consequence was a pair of by-laws in Toronto in 1912, the first specifying the amount of space that must be left open around apartment blocks, the second prohibiting the building of apartments on specified streets, in practice almost all the 'residential' parts of the city.

However, the way was open for apartment builders to apply for exemption by-laws granting permission to build on otherwise prohibited streets. By 1939 approximately 500 exemption by-laws had been passed, half for new buildings and half for the conversion of existing dwellings into apartments, perhaps indicating that the interests of local homeowners were only one, and possibly a relatively minor, component in the introduction of legislation. The by-laws were introduced at a time when the market was being flooded with new apartments and in anticipation of the property boom collapsing, which it did in the following year. So the prohibition by-law may be interpreted as a form of safety valve, designed to control but not prohibit construction. When demand increased, more exemptions could be granted. In this way the legislation benefited existing apartment owners, maintaining a degree of scarcity which promised low vacancy rates. The by-law could also be used as a geographical regulator. Initially, exemptions were granted in parts of the city where single-family dwellings were already being converted into rooming houses: better a purpose-built apartment house than a decaying multi-occupied mansion. But exemptions were denied in areas that appeared to be maintaining their middle-class status, such as the Avenue-St Clair corridor north of the city centre. By the mid-1920s, however, this area was in decline: the largest villas were now too large, given the fashion for smaller families and fewer servants. So, despite the protests of surviving homeowners, exemptions were granted to allow the construction of luxury apartment buildings, including 400 Avenue Road, the Balmoral, the Clarendon and the Claridge, all now prized examples of inter-war architecture, but fiercely contested at the time.

The result was a spatial pattern in which some neighbourhoods became 'apartment districts', either because there was never any prohibition on their construction, for example along strips following streetcar routes, or because large numbers of exemptions were granted in the same area over a relatively short period of time (Figure 9.9). Other aspects of the legislation affected the pattern at a more localised scale. Buildings were allowed on street corners where a 'residential' road joined a 'commercial' street, provided that the building lot was deemed to face onto the latter. So an apartment building might extend back down the side street for, perhaps, a hundred feet. But this made it easier for a developer to gain an exemption to build an apartment house farther down the 'residential' street, citing the proximity of the street-corner apartments as justification for a further incursion. Corner sites were also preferred because less open space was required around the apartment building: the two streets were deemed to constitute the open space necessary to guarantee sufficient light and air circulation.

In London there was no specifically geographical restriction, only the need to conform to the London Building Acts which, in the wake of controversy over tall buildings such as Queen Anne's Mansions, overlooking St. James's Park and Buckingham Palace, and Hyde Park Court, backing onto Hyde Park, specified strict limits on the height of new buildings. Nevertheless, spatial concentration followed from the perceptions and experience of developers. Writing in 1905, Sydney Perks observed concentrations of mansion flats in Kensington, spreading eastward into Piccadilly, south to Battersea and Clapham, and north-west from Baker Street and Marylebone Road into West and South Hampstead and Maida Vale.[108]

In *The Suburbans*, published in the same year as Perks' guide, T. W. H. Crosland lampooned the residents of 'naughty St John's Wood', immediately north-east of Maida Vale, another district where flats were becoming popular in the 1900s:

Five rooms up a giddy lift and near the stars, with electric lights let into the ceiling, electric bells throughout, hot and cold water night and day, private restaurant, a gold-laced porter, and no taxes, are luring the sharp-sighted suburban out of his old villas and secluded gardens. . . . 'It comes much cheaper,' says good man Subub. 'Mrs Subub likes it, because it is the thing, don't you know; and, besides, there can be no getting away from the fact that the flat is the proper dwelling-place of a highly complex civilization such as ours.'[109]

Flats were spreading into suburbs hitherto occupied by family houses, such as St John's Wood and Brixton, but, to Perks, suburban flats were not yet as popular as in America. Hamnett and Randolph estimated that, in 1978, there were nearly 22,000 private flats in 600 blocks in central London dating from before 1919, another 16,500

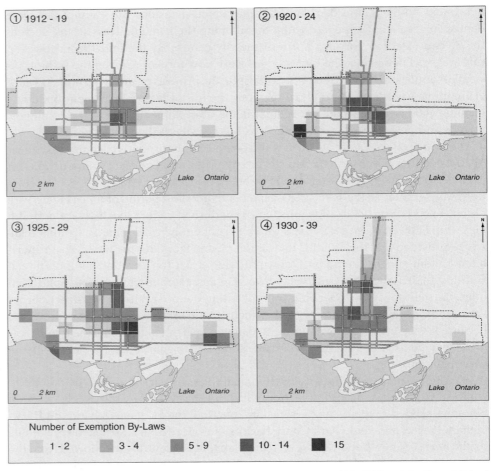

Figure 9.9. The Geography of Exemption By-Laws in Toronto, 1912–1939, originally published in *Planning Perspectives* **15** (2000), 286, reproduced courtesy of Taylor & Francis (http://www. informaworld.com).

pre-1919 flats in 500 blocks in the rest of inner London (much of which would have been regarded as 'suburban' by Perks), and fewer than 2,500 flats in 87 blocks in outer London (outside the boundaries of the London County Council). Allowance should be made for flats demolished between 1919 and 1978, either as a result of redevelopment or because of bomb damage; but these would have been mostly in central and inner London. Between 1919 and 1939, the number of flats in central and inner London approximately doubled, but nearly 17,000 flats in more than 500 blocks were added in outer London. Blocks erected in the 1920s and 1930s were larger (43 flats per block) than pre-1919 blocks (averaging 35 flats), and central London blocks contained on average more flats than outer London blocks (45 compared to 32), but these summary statistics hide the presence of some massive suburban blocks, such as the 780-flat Du Cane Court in Balham, opened in 1936.[110] Among the flats owned by London County Freehold & Leasehold Properties Ltd in 1933, there were blocks in Richmond, Kew, Ealing and Streatham as well as in central and inner London. Some suburban blocks, such as at Hanger Hill in Ealing, were designed in 'Tudor Manor House Style', an inflated version of the mock half-timbering that characterised much of semi-detached suburbia. Tudor-style flats were also built in suburban Toronto, modern interiors behind picturesquely anti-modern façades.[111]

Hamnett and Randolph excluded council flats from their calculations, but they included *all* privately-owned blocks, including some working-class tenements and philanthropic model dwellings, where the number of separate flats will have declined after World War II when buildings were renovated to ensure that every flat had its own bathroom and toilet. As noted earlier, in discussion of the Artizans' and Middle-Class Dwellings Companies, both mansion flats and model dwellings featured in the redevelopment plans of West End aristocratic estates. They were especially useful in providing well-ordered 'cordons sanitaires' where estates abutted on less well regulated property, guarding against the spread of decay which might otherwise infect the margins of areas like Mayfair and Belgravia. Better a block of well-managed model dwellings than a disorderly slum. Other sites that proved attractive to philanthropic trusts and limited-dividend companies were slum clearance sites acquired from the Metropolitan Board of Works at a fraction of their value on the open market. Most of these schemes in the 1870s and 1880s were on the sites of 'black spots' in and around the City and West End, where there was no shortage of demand from respectable artisans. Model dwellings agencies were less inclined to acquire clearance sites in the East End and especially close to the docks where they had learnt from experience in the 1860s that flats would be hard to let. Unlike apartments in suburban North America, which were perceived as threatening property values, British model dwellings were regarded as instruments of improvement, increasing rateable values and local government revenue, both in and of themselves and in their effect on the areas in which they were built.

Geography was also important at the micro-scale in the layout of estates and individual flats to ensure an appropriate partition between public and private space, residents' space and servants' and tradesmen's space, space for sleeping, eating and entertaining. In model dwellings, should flats open directly onto the public staircase, or should there be some intervening space, equivalent to the pocket-sized front gardens found in streets of working-class terraced housing? At Farringdon Road Buildings, the Metropolitan Association provided balconies which functioned as semi-private space between staircase landings and front doors (Figure 4.7). The association claimed tenants could use the balconies to grow flowers in pots or as spaces where small children could safely play without leaving the confines of domestic space. Critics pointed out that because the balconies were shared between adjacent flats they were not properly private and were likely to be the cause of dissent among neighbours unable to agree on their use and upkeep. Moreover, the balconies denied light and air to toilets and sculleries set back under the overhang of the floor above, and therefore might be the cause of unsanitary conditions and disease.[112]

There were also lengthy discussions among designers of mansion flats. Should servants be accommodated inside flats, in rooms opening directly off the kitchen and ideally with their own WC, or should they be housed communally in attic or basement? Should there be separate staircases for servants, which would ensure a proper social segregation, but might allow servants to slip up and down and out, without their employers' knowledge. Perks thought that even the requirement that external iron fire escapes be provided had liberated servants from their mistresses. Previously, it had been difficult to recruit good servants to live in flats, as Gissing's Bevis had observed; but in Edwardian London it appeared that many servants preferred flats.[113]

Plans of apartments in nineteenth-century New York and early twentieth-century Toronto mostly depict long, narrow apartments, a succession of rooms opening off of a corridor running the depth of the building. At the front, a bay-windowed parlour overlooked the street, possibly with a dining room or the best bedroom also enjoying this aspect. Behind them stretched a succession of bedrooms, with bathroom and kitchen bringing up the rear (Figure 4.7). Downmarket versions (Figure 9.3) were often referred to as 'railroad flats'. Trains and flats combined in Isabel March's nightmare, when she awoke with a scream dreaming of a hideous monster 'with two square eyes and a series of sections growing darker and then lighter, till the tail of the monstrous articulate was quite luminous again'. Her husband was quick to interpret: 'nothing but a harmless New York flat – seven rooms and a bath'.[114]

While this arrangement neatly segregated the 'public' rooms at the front from 'private' rooms behind, it meant that food from the kitchen had to be carried down a long corridor past the bedrooms. But if the dining room was placed towards the rear, next to the kitchen, then guests would have to be ushered past the bedrooms. A solution was easier to achieve if flats were L- or U-shaped, arranged around a central courtyard or at least an 'area' or ventilation shaft, adjacent to the kitchen to carry away steam and smells. Then there could be multiple routes from the entrance hall, one leading to the bedrooms, another to the public rooms, and a third to kitchen and servants' rooms (Figure 9.10). But this was an elaborate and expensive layout, and even architects like F. E. Eales, who advocated the segregation of different functions, were seldom able to implement their ideal in practice.[115]

Conclusion

From her top-floor window in Farringdon Road Buildings, Clara Hewett surveyed 'the tract of modern deformity' where London was being restructured – the building of Clerkenwell Road (opened 1878), Smithfield Market (1868, extended 1875), the Metropolitan Railway through Farringdon (1863–5), Holborn Viaduct (1869), all contrasting with the apparently permanent and unchanging 'black majesty' of St Paul's Cathedral.[116] For Clara, it was a depressing and terrifying prospect. In Manhattan, the Marches emerged from their eighth-floor apartment in the Xenophon to enjoy the stimulus of a ride on the elevated railway, threading its way through neighbourhoods of diverse class and ethnicity, allowing them to imagine the lives of residents of tenement flats glimpsed from the passing train. We cannot consider the history or the geography of flats in isolation from all the other new sites and experiences of modern cities. But, in themselves, as I hope to have demonstrated in this chapter, flats provide an ideal distillation of numerous different facets of modernity, mobilising capital through new forms of corporate agencies, embodying the architectural and

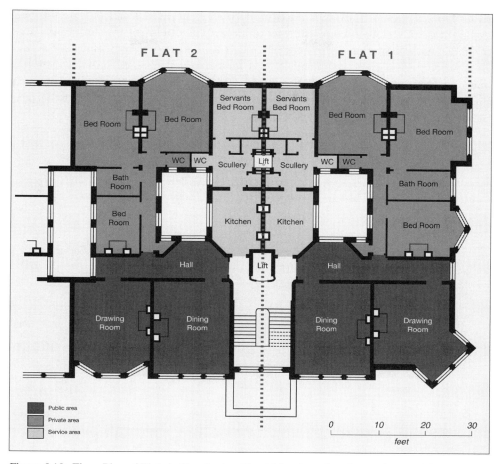

Figure 9.10. Floor Plan of Flats in Kensington Court Mansions, London, redrawn with additional annotations from S. Perks, *Residential Flats of All Classes* (1905), Fig. 95.

technological up-to-date, accommodating new household structures that responded to the 'servant problem' at the same time as providing space for the 'new woman', organising space internally and citywide in ways that expressed the anxieties of a class-conscious but socially mobile society, and employing advertising that was keenly aware of the power of representation. The space of flats was produced by speculators and philanthropists, planners and legislators; it was contested by neighbours and by the residents themselves. If middle-class flats were imagined as spaces of amoral indiscipline or licensed bohemianism, working-class block dwellings were conceptualised as disciplinary spaces, spaces of moral improvement, sites for exercising the liberal rule of freedom.

It might also be argued that flats appeared most obviously 'modern' in environments that were otherwise less modern – in nineteenth-century London and twentieth-century Toronto, rather than in Manhattan where the rapidity of growth and the attractions of downtown meant that the most conventional of middle-class families were prepared or obliged to embrace apartment life. And although we might think of flat-living as primarily a downtown lifestyle, by the early twentieth century suburban flats were acquiring a more 'modern' reputation, perhaps because of their apparent distinctiveness contrasted to suburban villadom. Yet this modernity was often disguised, contained within a shell of half-timbering or neo-Gothic decoration, or it proved a straitjacket that has defied further modernisation: model dwellings and mansion flats for ever locked into the late nineteenth century however much they may be transformed internally; if not quite 'built-in slums', at least the new picturesque of the postmodern metropolis.

10

Geographies of downtown: office spaces

Reflecting in the 1850s on her first visit to London, Lucy Snowe (in Charlotte Brontë's *Villette*) observed:

Since those days I have seen the West End, the parks, the fine squares, but I love the city far better. The city seems so much more in earnest: its business, its rush, its roar, are such serious things, sight, and sounds. The city is getting its living – the West End but enjoying its pleasure. At the West End you may be amused, but in the city you are deeply excited.[1]

In 1842, when Brontë first visited the City of London, it was still 'Georgian' in character, its physical appearance little changed since the post-Fire rebuilding of the late seventeenth century, and it still boasted a substantial night-time population. Although many merchants and bankers had moved with their families to suburban villas and no longer lived above their counting-houses, much of the accommodation they vacated remained residential, occupied by tradesmen, caretakers and junior clerks.[2] But, as Lucy sensed, whatever the similarities in the built environment, the culture of the City was a world away from that of the West End.

Eighty years later, another young female traveller, Elizabeth Dalloway, was equally sensitive to the differences as she rode the bus east from Victoria Street along the Strand: 'It was quite different here from Westminster, she thought, getting off at Chancery Lane. It was so serious; it was so busy.' So far, she had made it only as far as the legal quarter around the Temple, but she edged a little way further towards the City: 'She looked up Fleet Street. She walked just a little way towards St Paul's, shyly, like someone penetrating on tiptoe, exploring a strange house by night with a candle.'[3] Woolf implies that, as a woman of the 1920s, Elizabeth's future lay in the seriousness and business of the City rather than the frivolous consumption of the West End. Taken together, these two passages from each end of my period embody two of the principal themes of this and the following chapter: the increasing differentiation of City and West End or, in North America, different downtowns centred on business and pleasure; and the shifting role of women as consumers and in business.

I will begin this chapter by outlining the principal patterns and trends in the locations of financial and commercial office districts. While offices were mainly concentrated in central business districts – 'downtowns' in North America, City and West End in London – they were not excluded from suburban districts, even prior to World

War I, and I will draw some examples from company headquarters in suburban locations. But my primary focus will be on banks, exchanges and office buildings in the
City of London and in New York's Lower Manhattan. In Toronto, particularly in this
early period of the city's growth towards metropolitan status, 'City' and 'West End'
functions were less differentiated, but the beginnings of a similar pattern to that in
Manhattan are evident – with financial business intensifying in a 'lower downtown'
and stores and places of entertainment migrating slowly northward. There will also
be diversions westwards to Chicago but, in broad outline, this chapter will move from
the City of London in the mid- to late-nineteenth century to late nineteenth- and
early twentieth-century North America and then back to inter-war London, concluding by examining the growth of employment in financial and clerical occupations and
especially the position of women in office-work. This focus on women's work forms a
bridge to the following chapter which concentrates on department stores, discussing
some themes in the history and organisation of high-order retailing, and reflecting
on the role of consumption for modern city people.

In the course of these chapters I want to stress the complexity of the relationship
between finance and commerce in the geography of modern cities as well as the
relationship between the built environment of banks, skyscrapers and department
stores, and its experience by office-workers who were also shoppers, and shoppers
who also included the wives and daughters (and occasionally the sons) of office-
workers. My focus will be primarily with the better-off. While I would not wish to
endorse E. M. Forster's aside early on in *Howards End*, 'We are not concerned with
the very poor. They are unthinkable, and only to be approached by the statistician or
the poet', it remains true that literature on modernity has been primarily concerned
with 'gentlefolk, or with those who are obliged to pretend that they are gentlefolk'.
One of the functions of the office and the department store, as expressions of changing
occupational structure and mass consumption, was to allow people like Leonard
Bast, Forster's insurance clerk, who 'stood at the extreme verge of gentility', to
substantiate that pretence, but to marginalise still further a residuum whose shopping
was undertaken in street markets and who were unlikely to visit offices even as
cleaners.[4]

Geographies of business

In London, both 'City', as the centre of business and finance, and 'West End', as the
focus for consumption, expanded in area during the nineteenth century, but their
core areas remained fixed. 'Downtown' is much harder to define. Robert Fogelson
equates downtown with the public city of business, including shopping, and uptown
with the private city of residence. For Fogelson, therefore, Downtown New York
quickly embraces all of both Lower Manhattan and what is now considered Midtown.
He also argues that use of the term 'central business district' (CBD) as applied to
nineteenth-century American cities is anachronistic because it was only in the 1920s
that suburban business districts developed to rival downtown. Contemporaries did
not bother to use the prefix 'central' until the 1900s.[5] But most urban geographers,
unlike Fogelson, are happy to refer to CBDs in nineteenth- as well as twentieth-
century cities. In maps of New York's urban structure in 1860 and 1900, Michael

Conzen restricts the CBD to the area below Canal Street, even in the latter year, and positions most department stores outside of the CBD, even in 1860. The text accompanying his maps is less precise, using 'downtown' and 'CBD' interchangeably, but the important point is his conclusion that, by the 1920s, 'most major cities had separate downtown sectors for produce markets, wholesaling, retail shopping, finance, and government administration'.[6]

In London, the separation went back to the very origins of the metropolis: the dual centres of London and Westminster. As these two separate centres grew towards one another, a marginal zone developed that became spatially central but socially marginal: the slums of Clare Market, the theatres of Wych Street and the intricate mix of Jewish old clothes stores and radical and pornographic book and print shops on Holywell Street that Lynda Nead explored in *Victorian Babylon*, and that was finally obliterated by the grandiose development of Kingsway and the Aldwych. The marginal zone was also occupied by other activities that mediated between business and parliament and between production and consumption: the legal thicket of Chancery Lane, the Inns of Court and, by 1882, the Royal Courts of Justice; and, to their east, Fleet Street, long associated with printing and publishing, but especially important as the centre of the newspaper industry until the 1980s.

In contrast to London, both New York and Toronto grew from a single main nucleus but, as they did, so there was an equivalent separation of specialist functions. Manhattan's retail district moved rapidly north up Broadway while new office buildings located on ever more intensively redeveloped sites in Lower Manhattan. As in London, courts and offices of major newspapers came to occupy the zone between the two, as did municipal government (which still did not exist in mid-nineteenth-century London), along Park Row and around City Hall Park.[7] In the much smaller city of Toronto, all the activities of a Central Business District were at first concentrated along King Street, then only a couple of blocks north of the waterfront (Front Street). City hall, market and cathedral occupied adjacent sites close to the intersection of King and Church Streets. When more substantial banks and office buildings were erected at the end of the nineteenth century they concentrated on either side of King Street, extending west as far as Bay Street. Meanwhile, from the 1850s, retailing expanded north up Yonge Street, trailing behind the suburbanisation of middle-class customers as they moved up Jarvis Street and into the then peripheral districts of Rosedale and the Annex (Figure 1.6).[8] The intersection of King and Yonge Streets, discussed in Chapter 6, marked the intersection of worlds of business and consumption.

Segregation and suburbanisation

In each city, therefore, the second half of the nineteenth century was characterised by an increasing separation of different 'downtown' functions. But I also want to draw attention to two other significant spatial trends. The first is the increasing degree of segregation *within* business districts, as financiers, merchants, insurers, brokers, commission agents, warehousemen and even the manufacturers of boxes and packaging for the goods that were being traded came to occupy connected, but separate, parts of downtown.

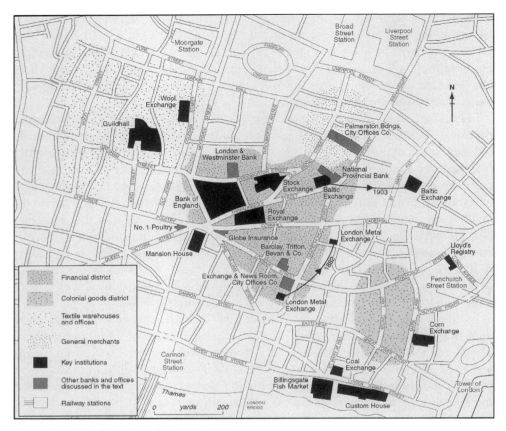

Figure 10.1. The City of London, 1840–1910.

In London, by the 1870s, the financial district was no more than 350 yards across, extending from just west of the Bank of England as far east as Gracechurch Street. Stockbrokers concentrated around the Stock Exchange, insurance brokers along Cornhill, shipping agents, general merchants and company agents in new office blocks on the eastern edge of the district along Gracechurch Street and Bishopsgate. Farther south and east (towards the Custom House), around Mincing Lane, was a district specialising in 'colonial goods'; while to the west, around Wood Street, were warehouses and offices of dealers in textiles; and to the north-east, in Old Broad Street, were 'general merchants' (Figure 10.1).[9]

In New York, until about 1850, dry-goods merchants concentrated along the East River waterfront. Jobbers (who bought the merchandise and immediately sold it on at a profit) located on Pearl Street, a couple of blocks inland, and commission merchants (who charged a commission to move other people's goods) on Front and Water Streets, between Pearl and the waterfront. Packing-box makers also located a block or two inland from the East River. Wholesale grocers were concentrated on Front Street, especially near Coenties Slip and Fulton Market, but also at Washington Market on the Hudson riverfront. Commercial banks and the offices of daily newspapers were on lower Broadway from Wall Street to City Hall Park.[10]

By the 1870s, dry-goods merchants had their financial offices near Wall Street, their wholesale warehouses on the west side of Broadway extending as far north as Canal Street. They stored bulk commodities in other warehouses closer to the Hudson waterfront, and maintained retail outlets on Ladies' Mile (Broadway north of Union Square). Commission merchants had also moved west of Broadway and north of City Hall, positioning themselves between the importers' warehouses and a chain of commercial hotels that had developed along Broadway. Scobey notes that nearly 90 per cent of commission merchants were located 'in a five-block stretch between Thomas and White streets'. Packing-box makers had also moved to be close to this new wholesaling district. Newspapers had been displaced from Broadway into Park Row and Printing-House Square by the expansion of commercial banking, which could no longer be contained within the confines of a few blocks around Wall Street. Nevertheless, they retained their strategic relative location, sandwiched between business, government and the courts. Yet this sorting-out still accommodated considerable local diversity. Newspapers shared Printing-House Square with all kinds of printing and publishing, with stationers supplying one kind of raw material for the trade, and news agencies supplying another. Different financial agencies – bankers, brokers, insurers – required constant contact with one another and occupied offices in the same buildings.[11]

We can gain some idea of the situation in the financial district by the early 1890s by plotting the addresses of prominent insurance companies, banks and trust companies recorded in the 1892 edition of Moses King's *Handbook of New York City* (Figure 10.2).[12] Of seventeen leading fire and marine insurance companies, nine were located on lower Broadway, all between 115 and 168 Broadway, three were on Pine Street, two on Nassau Street, and one at the corner of Wall and William Streets. Only two companies whose addresses were given – the New York Bowery and the Rutgers Fire Insurance Companies, at Bowery and Grand, and at Chatham Square – were located outside the core financial district. The head offices of eighteen other insurance companies, the majority involved in life assurance, were less concentrated, extending from 29 Broadway (well south of Wall Street) as far north as Broadway and Leonard (346–348 Broadway). Trust companies were almost all on or within two blocks of Wall Street. The most famous national banks were all on Wall Street, but King's Handbook also recorded some apparently more specialised banks with head offices outside the financial district – such as the Chemical National Bank (270 Broadway, near Chambers), the National Butchers' and Drovers' Bank (Bowery and Grand), and the National Shoe and Leather Bank (Broadway and Chambers) – and some neighbourhood banks, including the Eleventh Ward Bank (Avenue D and East 10th), the Madison Square Bank and the Mount Morris Bank (Park Avenue and East 125th in East Harlem).

The second trend that merits attention is the suburbanisation of all kinds of business activity. Some large-scale office activities moved out of the most expensive parts of CBDs, especially life insurance companies that did not depend on frequent face-to-face contact with high-status professionals and businessmen (*sic*), and that employed large numbers of relatively low-grade clerical staff engaged in routine filing and typing. In London, the Prudential Assurance Company, founded in 1848, moved to a massive block of Gothic Revival offices in Holborn in 1879.[13] While

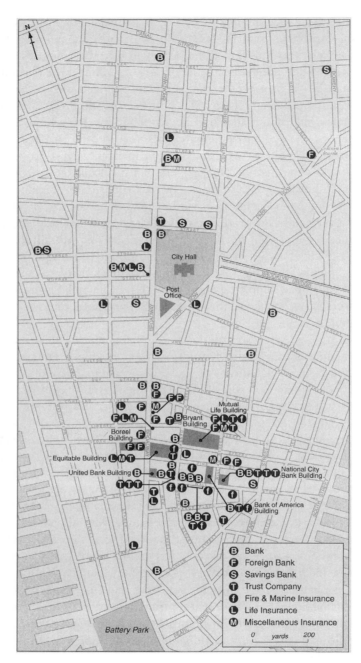

Figure 10.2. Lower Manhattan in 1892: Banks and Insurance Companies listed in Moses King's *Handbook of New York City* (Boston, 1892).

certainly not 'suburban', it was well away from the main concentration of insurance business on streets surrounding the Bank of England in the heart of the City[14]. In New York, Metropolitan Life moved in 1893 from Park Place, already towards the northern edge of Lower Manhattan, to a 10-storey 'Early Italian Renaissance' building facing Madison Square (23rd Street), forty blocks north. Domosh notes that at the time the decision was made to move, there were no major office buildings north of 14th Street. In 1909, a 50-storey tower was added so that, for a few years, until the completion of the Woolworth Building in Lower Manhattan, it was the tallest building in the world.[15] Evidently, height was not simply correlated with land value, since the cost of land around Madison Square was a fraction of the cost in Lower Manhattan. But Madison Square was convenient for Metropolitan Life's huge army of clerks and typists – by 1914, 2371 female white-collar, 1288 male white-collar and 600 blue-collar workers (such as printers and chefs) were employed in the building – and also for the 15,000 people who visited the offices each day on business.[16] Other office buildings in what was then 'uptown' Manhattan were popular with engineers and agencies connected with the entertainment business, and with architects, squeezed out of downtown by high rents.[17] Such enterprises remind us that most office-work was not connected with high finance and had no need to occupy high-rent locations close to Wall Street or the Bank of England. In London, there were not only the offices of government departments along Whitehall but also, on nearby streets, large numbers of 'chambers' occupied by professional firms and philanthropic agencies dependent on government contracts or hoping to influence government policy.[18]

In Toronto, a generation behind London and New York, reflecting the city's smaller size, the Manufacturers Life Insurance Company moved through a succession of rented office spaces downtown before commissioning a brand-new 6-storey office building close to the intersection of Bloor and Jarvis Streets, still suburban when the building opened in 1925 (Figure 1.6). The Canada Life Assurance company erected a four-storey building on King Street in 1874, then a seven-storey building (75,000 square feet) next door on the corner of King and Bay Streets in 1891. In 1931, the company moved to new headquarters on University Avenue, hardly suburban, but located several blocks to the west on much cheaper land where there was scope to erect a distinctive 11-storey building (300,000 square feet) with a 17-storey tower that stood head and shoulders above neighbouring structures.[19]

Not all life insurance companies chose to suburbanise, but a 'suburban solution' was more attractive to this form of business than to other financial enterprises which still depended on frequent face-to-face contact among the executives of different companies. Moreover, locating a building well away from other large structures meant that quite modest 'skyscrapers' appeared taller and more distinguished than if they were incorporated into a downtown cityscape where all the buildings were high-rise. Office buildings were not anonymous containers of economic activity; they also embodied meanings and symbolised values as much as more obviously spiritual or cultural buildings. No wonder they were often touted as 'cathedrals' of commerce.

Banks and offices in the City of London

Why did the nineteenth century witness such an explosion in office-building? One origin of modern offices lies in the coffeehouses and exchanges in which merchants and brokers conducted business in the seventeenth and eighteenth centuries. The Victorian successors to brokers who held court in named coffeehouses at specified hours required their own permanent offices and heavy ledgers in place of a

pocketbook. Likewise, groups of brokers who discussed business in the informal setting of a coffeehouse eventually found it necessary to establish formal institutions in
their own premises. In this way, a Stock Exchange was opened in London's Threadneedle Street in 1773. Following a dispute among the members, a purpose-built Stock
Exchange was erected in Capel Court in 1802, comprising 'a large high rectangular
room where the brokers congregated' and a gallery equipped with desks for clerks.[20]
Lloyd's of London, the society of insurance underwriters, and the associated Lloyd's
Register, initially restricted to classifying ships according to their seaworthiness and
level of risk, originated in Lloyd's Coffeehouse in the late seventeenth century, subsequently taking rooms in the Royal Exchange. Successive Royal Exchanges of 1570
and 1669, destroyed in fires in 1666 and 1838, each comprised a central courtyard
bounded by cloisters, with shops (later, offices) at first-floor level. Different parts of
the courtyard and cloisters were associated with different 'walks' where groups of
merchants engaged in the same trade – either the same commodity or trade with a
particular part of the world – would congregate to transact business.

By the time a third Royal Exchange was erected in 1844, many of its trading
functions had been usurped by more specialised exchanges. The standard form of
these buildings comprised a square or round trading floor, invariably top-lit by a central dome, with individual offices around the edges. A new cast-iron-framed Coal
Exchange, erected in 1849, was particularly impressive, with offices both on the
ground floor and opening off of three tiers of balconies around a central rotunda
(Figure 10.3). The London Metal Exchange began in 1877 in a rented room over
a hat shop in Lombard Court, but within five years, its membership exceeded 300
brokers and it moved to a purpose-built exchange in Whittington Avenue (just east
of Gracechurch Street). The Baltic Exchange met in coffeehouses until 1858 when it
acquired South Sea House in Threadneedle Street, where there was a glazed rectangular courtyard. Rivalled by, and soon merged with, a short-lived London Shipping
Exchange, established in 1893, the Baltic Exchange moved in 1903 to a new 'free
renaissance' building on St Mary Axe, where a 20,000 square-feet trading floor was
lit by a central dome 40 feet in diameter.[21]

Another source of modern office-work lay in 'counting-houses' where individual
merchants and manufacturers recorded their business, the kinds of offices in which
Dickensian clerks like Bob Cratchit were employed. Counting-houses were usually
attached to the warehouse or the workshop in which commodities were stored or
made, or they occupied rooms in merchants' private residences. In fact, in the early
nineteenth century the word 'office' was reserved for spaces visited by the public,
occupied by banks, brokers, agents and lawyers.[22] But whatever term we use, and
here I will employ 'office' in its modern usage, to refer to any kind of space set apart
for business, the growth in economic activities of all kinds necessitated bigger offices
to accommodate more staff, and more offices for more separate businesses. More
business implied more traffic, more noise, more congestion, and also higher land
values. All of which was an incentive for merchants to move their families to quieter,
pleasanter homes on less valuable land. In the short term, their places were taken
by live-in clerks and caretakers. But in the long term, business districts lost their
resident populations. The population of the City of London fell from 129,000 in 1851
to 20,000 in 1911, while the numbers employed in or visiting the City on business

Figure 10.3. William Luker, Jr (1867–1951), 'The Interior of the London Coal Exchange' (c.1900). Wash ink on paper (23.2 × 15.9 cm). Guildhall Library, City of London W.156/COA(1).

rose dramatically. In 1866, 170,000 persons were employed in the City, while 549,613 were counted as entering over a 12-hour day. By 1911, the number in employment had more than doubled, though most still worked in very small businesses: 364,000 workers were divided among 40,000 firms.[23]

An expanding economy stimulated demand for capital, for new forms of credit and for ways to use capital more efficiently, by speeding up its circulation. The authorisation of joint-stock companies, facilitating the raising of capital from a wide range of investors, in turn led to legislation on limited liability and the establishment of limited companies to protect investors' personal wealth in the event of business failure. Banking was also liberalised, to allow joint-stock banks as well as private banks, to permit banks in London to offer the same services as had hitherto been reserved for the Bank of England, and to establish clearing banks with multiple branches.

In 1708, the Bank of England had secured a monopoly of joint-stock banking in England and Wales which it retained until 1833 as far as London was concerned. Until then, all other banks in London were restricted to private partnerships with a maximum of six partners. The reform of 1833 allowed joint-stock banks in the capital to receive funds for deposit, but not to issue notes. The London and Westminster was the first joint-stock bank to be established in London, opening for business in March 1834, with offices in both the City (38 Throgmorton Street) and the West End (9 Waterloo Place), the latter to tap the market for deposit facilities among the growing middle classes, hitherto the preserve of private banks. By 1836, there were three London joint-stock banks and by 1857 eight. Joint-stock banking, even without limited liability, allowed a much wider capital base to be tapped through share subscriptions. But some provincially-based banks continued to be excluded from the London area, because they wished to issue their own banknotes. Thus, the National Provincial Bank, established in 1833, developed a network of more than 120 branches across England and Wales, all outside London, though administered from a head office in Bishopsgate where the bank could not engage in business with the public. It was not until the early 1860s that the National Provincial gave up issuing notes, whereupon it was permitted to open branches in London and promptly erected a spectacular new head office. Among other provincial banks, Lloyds moved its head office to London in 1884; the Midland Bank followed suit in 1891.[24]

Through the second half of the nineteenth century, the number of private and joint-stock banks declined, as smaller and provincial banks were taken over by London-based banks. The number of private banks in the London Clearing House (the method of authorising the clearance at one bank of cheques drawn on another) decreased from thirteen in 1870 to only five by 1891. But at the same time international banking increased in importance. From the mid-nineteenth century there were joint-stock banks reflecting Britain's colonial and trading interests in the Mediterranean (for example, the Ionian Bank, Bank of Egypt, Ottoman Bank), in Latin America (London & Brazilian Bank), and in settler-colonies such as Australia. American connections were typified by George Peabody, whose philanthropic interests, built on the profits of his merchant bank, were discussed in the previous chapter. Peabody's partner, J. S. Morgan, was the father of the New York banker, J. P. Morgan, and by 1910 the London business had been transformed into Morgan Grenfell. In total, by the early twentieth century there were more than forty British-owned overseas banks and around thirty foreign banks in the City.[25]

Associated with the growth in credit and the circulation of capital was a proliferation of all kinds of insurance: marine insurance, covering ships and their cargoes from risks of shipwreck and piracy; fire insurance, protecting buildings and their contents; and personal insurance, extending from sick and burial clubs – to provide artisans with a privatised form of poor relief and especially to ensure funds for a respectable burial – to life insurance to provide pensions and benefits to dependants. All these forms of insurance became more necessary, not only because the sums involved were increasing as buildings, ships and levels of factory production all got bigger, but also because so much business depended on credit. What if your warehouse burnt down when you still owed money on both the building and its contents? Who would lend you the money in the first place if they stood to lose in case of failure or disaster?

The number of Lloyd's underwriters increased from 257 to 621 between 1853 and 1913, by which date approximately two-thirds of world marine insurance was handled in the City of London. By 1938, Lloyd's membership had reached 1,882. Life insurance was less concentrated in the metropolis, and in the early nineteenth century was still restricted to the better-off. In the 1840s, there were only an estimated 100,000 policies contracted with life insurance companies, yet by 1875 one London-based company, Prudential Assurance, had more than two million 'industrial' assurance policies, for which premiums were paid by workingmen in weekly instalments. By the beginning of the twentieth century, London boasted nearly fifty fire insurance companies, eighteen involved in marine insurance and more than eighty life insurance companies.[26]

Finally in this review of new business, and hence new demands for space, we should note various ancillary activities – what today would be called business services – such as accountancy, legal services, printing, advertising and telegraph offices. Michie comments that 'Whereas clerks and book-keepers could be left with maintaining the accounts reflecting everyday business, events such as bankruptcy, merger or public flotation all required specialist advice and expertise'.[27] From 1900 the auditing of joint-stock companies was compulsory. By 1880, there were already 500 accountants and fifty auditors in the City; by 1891, 701 accountancy firms and more than two thousand solicitors.[28] Gissing's Luckworth Crewe was the archetype City advertising agent, taking three rooms in 'a huge building in Farringdon Street' where he employed three clerks. Among his business, he handled the advertising for Beatrice French's South London Fashionable Dress Supply Association, the placing of hoardings visible from passing trains, and the promotion of a new seaside resort. He had also written a 'Guide to Advertising': 'It advertises *me* . . . Costs nothing to print; the advertisements more than pay for that.'[29]

Less incestuous and more useful information came through the medium of the electric telegraph. Among telegraph offices in the City, a 'Central Telegraph Station' was erected behind the Bank of England in 1848, Julius Reuter set up his 'Submarine Telegraph' office in Royal Exchange Buildings (next to the Royal Exchange) in 1851, a month before the opening of the cross-channel cable, and in 1859, the English and Irish Magnetic Telegraph opened offices in Threadneedle Street. New office blocks, such as the City Offices Company building on the corner of Lombard and Gracechurch Streets, contained their own 'Exchange and News Room'. Financial newspapers exploited the availability of up-to-date, telegraphically derived, information: *Financial News* was founded in 1884. The *Financial Times* followed in 1888.[30]

So what were the physical expressions of all this new activity in the built environment of modern cities? Apart from offices in exchanges, already discussed, we can identify three sources of new office space: the conversion of residences into offices; the commissioning of new headquarters buildings for banks, insurance companies and other businesses; and the erection on speculation of 'stacks of office buildings' to be let, room by room, or floor by floor, to a variety of business tenants. I will concentrate here on the second and third of these.

From the 1830s to the 1870s there was a plethora of new bank buildings, mostly erected by fast-growing joint-stock banks eager to establish their public image. The newly-formed London and Westminster Bank developed a site in Lothbury, immediately behind the Bank of England, opening its building in December 1838. Unlike previous private banking 'houses' – which operated out of buildings little different from residential London town houses, usually three storeys, only one plot wide, and with, at most, a hint of security provided by rusticated stone on the ground-floor façade – the London and Westminster's bank was designed as an Italian 'palazzo'. The building was organised around an impressive public banking hall, behind and above which were smaller offices. Iain Black suggests that there was a notion of architecture as 'symbolic capital' in which discourses of aesthetics and economics were combined. The design of the bank was intended to promote confidence and underline its honesty, openness and trustworthiness. By contrast, for private bankers, 'architectural ostentation would have seemed both reckless and impulsive, not a form of advertising by which to attract business'.[31] Private banks were 'houses'; everyday business would be transacted at a counter, but personal discussions took place in the parlour, a more intimate space, assuring clients of privacy and discretion.

In practice, buildings like the London and Westminster's exaggerated the scale of their owners' activities. The bank initially let the offices on the top floor to other businesses, which gained a prestigious address and a share in an impressive corporate image. In return, the bank gained a useful additional source of income. Other joint-stock banks followed the London and Westminster's example, as did some private banks. Barclay, Tritton, Bevan & Co. erected a new four-storey bank on Lombard Street in 1864. A 22-feet high banking hall on the ground floor was backed by private spaces, including a parlour for private business and partners' rooms. Most of the upper floors were let to a variety of tenants, though Dalgety & Co., colonial wool brokers, were the sole tenants by the 1890s. The new building also included living rooms, kitchen and bedrooms for caretakers and watchmen, indicating both continuity and change with older traditions of private banking.[32] Of course, in letting space to tenants, these banks were also anticipating future growth, delaying the time when they would have to move again or redevelop the site to keep up with their own needs for more new space.

Image also depended on the adoption of an appropriate architectural style and in the middle decades of the nineteenth century – in New York as well as London – that style was Italianate. It conjured up memories of renaissance merchant princes and

Figure 10.4. The National Provincial Bank of England, Bishopsgate, London. *Illustrated London News*, 20 January 1866, p. 57. Senate House Library, University of London.

aligned the cities with Venice and Florence as the centres of far-reaching commercial empires. It was more ornate than the Greek revival style which was considered suitable for invoking the spirit of classical democracy appropriate to public buildings such as city halls. The most spectacular product of the new age of joint-stock banking was also the most explicitly symbolic. The new headquarters of the National Provincial Bank, opened in Bishopsgate in 1866, appears profligate in its disdain for the economic principles that had guided other banks (Figure 10.4). There was no lettable space here, merely a huge, single-storey building faced with Corinthian columns and capped by statuary symbolic of Manchester, England, Wales, Birmingham, Newcastle, Dover and London, indicative that this was a truly *national* bank. Beneath the cornice were panels representing the arts, commerce, science, manufactures, agriculture and navigation, suggestive of the bank's involvement in every aspect of national life. The interior was equally lavish, mainly given over to a banking hall claimed to be the largest in the metropolis, decorated with panels depicting the riches of land and water, the production of gold, and its smelting, coining and banking. Like the exchanges I discussed earlier, the banking hall was top-lit through a series of rotundas, a practice also shared with many department stores, intended to impart a sense of the openness of public space and discourse in a building which was, of course, privately owned and regulated.[33]

'Symbolic capital' was not confined to new banks or to the mid-Victorian boom. Architectural historian John Summerson argued that, initially, insurance companies were more competitive and more ambitious than joint-stock banks in bidding for the most conspicuous sites. Among numerous insurance companies building new offices between 1838, when the Globe opened on the prestigious angled corner of Cornhill and Lombard Street (just across from the Royal Exchange and the Bank of England), and 1858, when the collapse of a dozen companies brought the boom to an end, Summerson records ten by name, variously located on Cornhill, Lombard Street, Cheapside, Bartholomew Lane, Lothbury and Threadneedle Street. Their buildings were richly adorned with allegorical sculpture: 'Navigation' and 'Hope' on the façade of the Marine Assurance Company, 'Atlas' over the door of the Atlas, whose building was 'inspired by Inigo Jones'.[34]

Half a century later, when Lloyd's Register, founded in 1760 to examine merchant ships and classify them as a basis for determining insurance premiums, required new offices in Fenchurch Street in the east of the City, the brief to the architect, Thomas Collcutt, was 'sketchy with little emphasis on office needs. It appears to have been more concerned with making a fine architectural show.' Collcutt's initial designs were rejected as too understated. As built in 1901, the offices took the form of a sixteenth-century Italian stone palazzo, utilising the finest materials: Portland stone and carved Hopton Wood limestone on the façades; corner tourelles and cupolas reminiscent of the French renaissance and a loggia at second-floor level; and a variety of sculptural groups of maidens carrying ships and plans, of Mercury and Hermes, of sea nymphs, sea monsters and dolphins. The interior was equally elaborate, with marble floors and staircases, a library with richly decorated barrel-vaulted ceiling and a General Committee Room with painted ceiling and side panels by Gerald Moira, 'largely inspired by Michelangelo's Sistine Chapel ceiling in the Vatican', depicting the elements, the signs of the zodiac, the seasons, the sun, the moon, day and night.[35] All designed to elevate the necessary but mundane business of risk appraisal to the status of high culture worthy of a permanent place in history.

Yet for all these grand statements, the fact remains that most businesses in the City were tenants renting a few rooms in a speculatively-built office block. 'Stacks of offices' became common in the 1840s. In 1845, Sir Francis Moon, a Threadneedle Street printseller, developed a site at the back of the Royal Exchange, for which his architect, Edward I'Anson designed a 4-storey building, thirteen bays long. By 1848, there were 38 tenants in occupation.[36] Speculators particularly favoured small frontages on high-value main streets which could be combined with lower-value back plots. In this way, they could boast a prestigious address at minimum expense. In the 1860s, as schemes increased in size and therefore in their capital requirements, limited companies began to exploit what had hitherto been the preserve of individuals and private partnerships. Both the City of London Real Property Company and the City Offices Company were founded in 1864. The former took over a private partnership of the rum importers, James and John Innes, who had invested the profits from the sale of their Jamaican properties in purchasing twelve buildings near their own head office in Mincing Lane. One, on Mark Lane, was a 4-storey block of counting-houses with an arcaded façade screening a self-supporting iron frame. The City Offices Company had five buildings by the end of 1864, including a block of about 200 rooms between Old Broad Street and Bishopsgate (Palmerston Buildings), in which they installed a hydraulically powered lift in 1873. By 1895, more than two hundred passenger lifts were operational in City offices. The company's most prominent building was

Figure 10.5. Offices, Exchange and News Room erected by the City Offices Company, Gracechurch Street and Lombard Street, London. *Illustrated London News*, 1 August 1868, p. 105. Senate House Library, University of London.

erected in 1868 at the junction of Lombard and Gracechurch Streets. By 1875, tenants included a bank and 28 other firms plus an Exchange and News Room (Figure 10.5). In a City where most building lots were long and narrow, where landownership was fragmented, and where tenure arrangements might vary between adjacent lots, it could be a difficult and lengthy process acquiring sites sufficiently large for such a block. The City Offices Company had to acquire 23 separate properties, freehold and leasehold, at a cost of £70,000 down and £653,000 over 99 years, before spending £70,000 on building one new office block.[37]

The overall consequence was that, over time, there were fewer separate 'buildings' but just as many separate occupiers. In four different parts of the central financial district, the number of separately rated properties in 1871 was between a third and a half of what it had been at the end of the seventeenth century, and even between 1851 and 1871, the number of properties declined by about a third. In 1881, 26 buildings, each listed as a single building in the census, contained a total of 1,320 lettings, an average of 51 occupiers per building. Meanwhile, the assessed value of property roughly trebled between 1851 and 1871. This created an enormous incentive for redevelopment with more intensive occupancy, but also, by the early twentieth century, led to overbuilding. Of every five buildings standing in 1855, only one remained 50 years later. Only seven per cent of buildings in the City in 1911 were primarily residential in function, and of buildings erected between 1907 and

1912, more than sixty per cent were offices or offices combined with shops or ware-houses.[38]

Skyscrapers in North American cities

I have discussed the Victorian City of London in some detail because it foreshadows in so many ways the fashion for skyscrapers that developed in Chicago and New York from the 1880s and in Toronto a generation later. Just like the London buildings I have described, skyscrapers were built to impress as much as out of economic necessity; prestigious buildings were particularly favoured by institutions like banks, insurance companies and newspapers that wanted to make a public statement of their virtues; and most buildings owned by or named after major institutions were actually occupied by a wide variety of tenants. On both sides of the Atlantic developers attempted to assemble sites large enough to permit substantial buildings – in London extending from front street to back street, in America occupying a whole city block – but the fragmentation in property ownership often led to L-shape developments built around property that could not be acquired. And on both sides of the Atlantic it may be argued that the rise in land values was as much the consequence as the cause of 'densification'. Building technology was more obviously important in allowing the construction of very tall buildings in North American cities, but even in this case, there were examples from the City of London in the 1860s and 1870s of iron-framed buildings and buildings with lifts.

Like London, New York was replete with new commercial exchanges. In the 1880s alone, these included the New York Produce Exchange at the foot of Broadway, completed in 1884, where a massive trading hall was supported and surrounded by 190 rented offices; the seven-storey Cotton Exchange at Hanover Square (1885); and the more modest five-storey Mercantile Exchange at Hudson and Harrison Streets (1886), with fifty rented offices, and Consolidated Stock and Petroleum Exchange, Exchange Place (1887–1888). There was also the 'immense and imposing', eight-storey Coal and Iron Exchange, at the south-east corner of Cortlandt and Church Streets (1873–1876), but this was an exchange in name only, since its primary function was as the head office of the Delaware & Hudson Canal Company. All these buildings were palazzo-type structures, between five and ten storeys high, sometimes surmounted by towers which added another couple of storeys. They were larger than the equivalent buildings in London, but essentially similar in layout.[39]

A new generation of newspaper offices, erected around City Hall Park during the 1870s and 1880s, could lay claim to being the first explicitly tall buildings in New York. The Tribune Building (11 storeys, 260 feet high), erected between 1873 and 1875, was designed by Richard Morris Hunt, the same architect as for the Coal and Iron Exchange, and advertised itself with the words, 'THE TRIBUNE', cut in granite blocks on each side of its central tower. The New York World Building (16 storeys) (1889–1890) was more of a vertically elongated shrine, topped with a dome in a style that Domosh calls 'French Renaissance Revival'. As Scobey argues, attitudes towards Second Empire Paris were ambivalent in New York in the 1860s – admiration of Haussmann's imperial planning tempered by anxiety about its undemocratic, imperious imposition – but one consequence was the adoption of French architectural styles, not only for the Tribune and World buildings but also for their near neighbours, the Federal Post Office, begun in 1869 on the southern half of City Hall Park, and the Western Union Telegraph Building, on Broadway two blocks south of the park, completed in 1875.[40]

Although these buildings were heavy with symbolism, they were still not particularly innovative: they were still referred to as 'palaces', not 'towers', and they still had solid masonry walls which carried all the weight of the upper floors, and which limited their maximum height. Load-bearing walls had to be thicker at the base, and this meant that there was less 'lettable space' on the lower floors, the levels which would still have been expected to fetch the highest rents. By the time the World Building was being erected, the critical technological breakthrough – the development of the steel frame on which non-load-bearing 'curtain walls' were hung – had been made, not in New York but in Chicago. The Home Insurance Building erected by William Le Baron Jenney in 1884 was a fairly modest structure – 10 storeys in all – but the top four storeys were built around a steel frame. The Home Insurance Building was demolished in 1931 but another Chicago office building, the Monadnock, survives to demonstrate the difference between old and new technologies. The Monadnock was begun in 1891, but still using load-bearing masonry, so that the walls – 15 feet thick at the base – appear concave in profile; when it was extended laterally two years later, the use of a steel frame meant that the walls could be vertical. In New York the first complete steel-frame skyscraper was the 20-storey American Surety Building, erected on lower Broadway in 1895.[41]

The technology of the steel frame was complemented by other new technologies: the elevator, at first hydraulic (the Otis Safety Elevator dates from 1854), later (in the 1880s) electrically powered; the typewriter (1868); the telephone (1876); Edison's incandescent electric light (1879); all of which were exploited within the high-rise office building; and improved transportation technologies – elevated trains, streetcars and subways – which were vital if thousands of staff were to be conveyed to and from a single building during morning and evening rush hours. By the 1890s, therefore, it was technologically feasible to build skyscrapers, and organisationally desirable to concentrate large numbers of office workers in close proximity; but it is still necessary to ask why developers preferred to expand upwards rather than sideways, and also why skyscraper design differed between New York and Chicago, the two cities in which high-rise buildings were most dominant.

Carol Willis argues persuasively that we need to integrate the 'vernaculars of capitalism' – the local circumstances which produced slender, very tall towers in New York compared to squat, but bulkier office buildings in Chicago – with the economics of skyscraper financing, construction and letting. She acknowledges that in some cases very tall or elaborately decorated buildings were erected in part for their symbolic impact. The campanile-style tower of the Metropolitan Life building on Madison Square (1909) aligned the company with the spirit of the Italian renaissance and was instantly recognisable as a company logo; the rich gothic of the Woolworth Building (1913) evoked the *hôtels de ville* of medieval Flanders, where virtuous trade enriched civic culture. But she thinks that, in abandoning economic determinism, historians have placed too much emphasis on issues of corporate identity and iconography.[42]

Despite all the technological advances of the late nineteenth century, an important limiting factor prior to the development of fluorescent lighting was the need for natural light to complement the modest power of incandescent electric light bulbs. Office space that was more than about twenty-five feet from a window was hard to let at rents that repaid the costs of land and construction – hence the need either to build relatively slender towers around a central core of elevators and essential services or to incorporate light wells into the interior of buildings and to ensure that natural light really did reach the windows, that buildings were not overshadowed by other tall buildings nearby.[43]

The implication is that skyscrapers were designed from the inside out, starting with the basic building block of the individual office.[44] But the ability of architects to design the ideal office building was also circumscribed by local circumstances. In Lower Manhattan, where land had been traded and subdivided since the seventeenth century, plot sizes were smaller than in more recently platted Chicago. It was difficult to assemble sites large enough to accommodate structures that spread laterally. In New York, prior to 1916, there were no height restrictions; in Chicago there were, as early as 1893. So a different form – lower but broader, often around a central courtyard – was developed to maximise profits in Chicago.[45]

What then was the relationship between building height and land values? The traditional argument is that the scarcity of land in Lower Manhattan, or within the Loop in Chicago, drove up land values and hence necessitated high-rise building. Certainly, land values did rise very rapidly – sevenfold – in Chicago in the 1880s. Even so, and perhaps reflecting the greater severity of the 1890s slump in Chicago, by 1903 land values in New York were four times those in Chicago. Both cities had steep land value gradients, but New York's was steeper than Chicago's. In New York, in 1903, land was valued at $400 per square foot in the vicinity of the Stock Exchange (Wall and Broad Streets), $250–350 per square foot on Broadway north from Rector Street to Liberty Street, but only $10 per square foot, three blocks to the west, at the intersection of Rector and Washington Streets. Using the more customary measure of value per foot of street frontage, land was valued as high as $24,750 per front-foot on Wall Street in 1910, but less than half a mile away, at only $1000 per foot. In Chicago, in the same year, values varied between $31,000 per front-foot on part of State Street and $3,000–5,000 per foot along the western and northern margins of the Loop. So in either city developers could have opted for cheaper land within comfortable walking distance of the core of the existing CBD. Rather than high land values resulting in the construction of skyscrapers, it might be argued that it was the desire of developers to build high, increasing the income that could be derived per unit area, and their reluctance in venturing into new districts, that made it possible for landowners to raise land values. Building skyscrapers led to higher land values, rather than the other way around.[46]

The history of high-rise building in Chicago illustrates that the relationship between land value and building height was far from simple. The erection of so many high-rise buildings in the late 1880s and early 1890s, quickly followed by a downturn in the economy, led to an oversupply of office space. In 1893, the city council introduced a law limiting new buildings to no more than 130 feet (approx. 10 storeys). This served the interests of owners of property outside the current CBD, who wanted any future expansion to be lateral, so that they could share in at least modest increases in property values. It also served the interests of owners of still undeveloped sites in the CBD, who did not want to be assessed for property tax on land values inflated by the assumption that their land *could* accommodate a skyscraper. If new skyscrapers were banned, land values would fall, and so would their property taxes (and the effect of this relationship is evident in the less extreme peak of values in the centre of the Loop – about ten times values on the periphery of the CBD – compared to Lower Manhattan where values around Wall Street were more than twenty times those a few blocks away). Moreover, owners of existing, possibly half-empty, skyscrapers, wanted to maintain scarcity, so that any recovery in demand would first of all benefit them.[47]

In Chicago, after 1893, planning, and height regulation in particular, was used as a kind of tap which could be turned on and off to control the supply of new office space. When the market revived, as it had done by 1902, height restrictions could be relaxed; a new law allowed buildings of up to 260 feet in height. When there was a recession, as occurred in the early 1910s, restrictions were tightened again, limiting new buildings to 200 feet. Municipal regulations also responded to safety issues: in 1896, reacting to claims that owners were simply modifying unsafe old buildings to cater for the beginnings of a post-slump revival, the council raised the limit to 155 feet in order to encourage *new* building, but two years later, following a serious fire, the lower limit was reintroduced. Whatever the limit, the council could always agree to an exemption in individual cases.[48] These forms of control were equivalent to the regulation of apartment building in Toronto, discussed in Chapter 9, where the introduction of a ban on new apartments in 'residential' areas, followed by the discretionary granting of exemptions from the ban, allowed the city council to regulate supply, both as demand fluctuated and as the social character and economic prosperity of different neighbourhoods changed over time.

New York had to wait until 1916 before height restrictions were implemented, and in this case there was an explicitly spatial component to regulation in the introduction of zoning. Zoning specified both the types of land use that were permitted in each part of the city and the height to which buildings were allowed to rise. One stimulus for zoning was the fear of non-conforming land uses: Fifth Avenue retailers were concerned that high-status shoppers were deterred from visiting their stores by the presence, especially during lunch-breaks, of large numbers of poorly dressed and poorly spoken factory workers such as the girls employed as sewing-machine operatives in lofts over and behind the retail stores where the shirts, blouses and dresses they made were subsequently sold. Far better if producers and consumers could be spatially separated. More generally, it was argued that single-use districts would maximise property values.[49]

Other stimuli for height regulations were fears of downtown gridlock as streets and public transport systems designed to serve low-rise buildings were now expected to cater for the thousands of workers employed in each and every skyscraper, and disputes over access to light and air. When the American Surety Building was completed in 1895, the Astor estate, which owned an adjacent, but much lower T-shaped building, threatened to erect a 21-storey skyscraper (one storey higher than American Surety) which would deny light and air, and therefore rental income from tenants, to two sides of the American Surety Building. The American Surety Company was forced to sign a 99-year lease to rent the Astor estate building in order to prevent its redevelopment. Farther up Broadway, the view of the 47-storey Singer Tower was obscured from the north, even before it was completed, by the massive bulk of the 43-storey City Investing Building. More critically, since the bulk of the Singer Building was not 47 storeys but a much more modest 14-storey slab, most of its occupants were denied natural light by the City Investing Building next door.[50]

Both of these disputes were between *private* property owners over their rights to light and air; but the case of the Equitable Building, completed in 1915 on an entire block – Broadway–Pine–Nassau–Cedar – raised problems of access to light in the public street. The H-shaped Equitable rose 40 storeys vertically from the sidewalk. Apart from two vertical light wells facing onto Broadway and Nassau Street, it filled every inch of the block with 40-storey high building, potentially turning Pine and Cedar Streets into deep, dark canyons if owners of land on the other side of those streets chose to erect similar buildings (Figure 10.6).[51]

Yet, for all these individual disputes about light, air, congestion and the niceties of social distinctions, the catalyst for zoning was economic. Following a downturn in the economy in 1913, office vacancy rates increased sharply – to 12.5 per cent across Lower Manhattan, and to 15–17 per cent for offices located on the second to sixth floors, the offices most likely to suffer from the shadows cast by very tall buildings. In a renters' market, tenants moved to the newest, best equipped offices, like those in the Equitable Building: the Equitable stole 'tenants as well as sunlight from surrounding buildings'.[52]

The city council's response was to include regulations in the 1916 Act specifying a 'zoning envelope' within which new buildings had to fit, with different limitations in different city zoning districts. For example, in a '2 times district' no new building could be more than twice as high as the width of the street, *except* that for each foot that the building was set back it could add an extra four feet to its height. The consequence was for upper storeys of post-1916 skyscrapers to be stepped back, producing the 'wedding cake' shape that characterised classic skyscrapers of the inter-war period, such as the Chrysler Building (77 storeys, 1048 feet, completed in 1930) and the Empire State Building (102 storeys, 1250 feet, completed in 1931).[53]

Yet, as Carol Willis has noted, the precise dimensions of these step-back skyscrapers were a consequence of financial considerations as much as planning law: 'form follows finance'. Going beyond Gad and Holdsworth's analysis of the modern skyscraper as a product of *corporate* capitalism, she shows how, for *speculative* projects such as the Empire State Building, their form was a consequence of calculating the returns on lettable space for buildings of different heights, and balancing the number of elevator shafts that would be needed for efficient access at higher levels against the space that would be occupied by those shafts and other vital services, thereby reducing the amount of lettable space at lower levels. Early plans for the site occupied by the Empire State Building envisaged a 55-storey building costing $45 million. At rents anticipated at the time of planning (the summer of 1929), this would have yielded a gross return of 11.4 per cent. But an 80-storey building, adding a 25-storey tower to the original plan, would have increased income proportionally more than the increase in costs, producing a gross return of 12.6 per cent. Once the

Figure 10.6. Equitable Building, New York, from *New York Illustrated* (c.1919) (Author's collection).

argument for a *very* high building had been won, then it was worth making it the *tallest* building in the world since that, in itself, would attract tenants and also provide a source of income from sightseers visiting the building's observation decks.[54]

In practice, the financial estimates proved far from correct. While the building was completed under budget and ahead of schedule, in time for letting on May 1, New

York's traditional annual letting day, 1931, the Wall Street Crash and the onset of the Great Depression had conspired to reduce rent levels and raise vacancy rates so that through the 1930s the building was known as the 'Empty State'. In total, more than 100 buildings of at least 20 storeys had been erected in Manhattan during the 1920s. In 1932, the city boasted 29 office buildings more than 500 feet high, all of which – even those ostensibly associated with a named corporation – offered space to let. The total amount of office space in New York increased from 74 million square feet in 1920, to 112 million in 1930 and 138 million by 1935: oversupply on a massive scale.[55]

Nonetheless, it was the anticipation of profit levels that shaped post-1916 skyscrapers as much as the zoning regulations. The Empire State Building was actually smaller than regulations allowed, because the developers calculated that less space, with a good supply of natural light and air, would command higher rents than more space, much of it deep inside the building, far from natural light, and with no envelope of 'private airspace' that could not be violated whatever neighbouring developers chose to erect.

Through her analysis of skyscrapers such as the Woolworth Building and the Empire State Building, Willis concludes that 'Skyscrapers should be understood not simply as containers expanding to accommodate corporate needs, but as businesses themselves'.[56] She emphasises that even supposedly non-speculative buildings, named after a major corporation, rented out much of their space, and this point has also been demonstrated most forcibly by Fenske and Holdsworth. The New York Tribune initially occupied only two of its nine floors; the Singer Company let out all the space in its tower other than one floor where the company president had his office; Metropolitan Life let about forty per cent of its building to tenants and continued to do so despite complaining that it needed to take over adjacent blocks around Madison Square to accommodate its own expansion; and Woolworth's occupied less than two storeys out of fifty in the Woolworth Building.[57] There were about 600 named individuals or companies on a tenants' list in 1913, including 'manufacturing, engineering, railroad, and publishing concerns, but also a vast number of lawyers'.[58] Most rented only a few rooms each. So-called 'corporate' buildings with distinctive profiles had enormous publicity value for small businesses who could claim status and security by association with the famous names whose property they occupied, but the most critical advantages of co-location with hundreds of other businesses also applied to 'speculative' buildings whose owners sought out 'anchor' tenants to rent just as much space as corporate owners occupied in their own buildings. Despite its name, the Equitable Building was a speculative development, in which the Equitable Life Insurance Company rented about ten per cent of the space.[59] But all these buildings, whether 'corporate' or 'speculative', facilitated linkages among the agents, lawyers, accountants, advertising agencies and small businesses who occupied them. It could even be claimed that large skyscrapers *reduced* congestion on the surrounding streets because their inmates could satisfy *all* their needs without leaving the building: 'in downtown New York a business man consults his broker, eats his lunch, sees his lawyer, buys his wife a box of candy, gets a shave, all in the same building'.[60] Each building was 'a city in itself'.

It is sometimes possible to identify interlocking directorships, where the directors of different companies overlapped, and also cases where the same 'establishment' (the same address within a building) functioned as the office for several companies. For example, in Toronto's Royal Bank Building in 1922, directories and assessment rolls recorded 162 separate companies but only 108 'establishments'. The tenants' list for the Woolworth Building contained more than 400 names in 1924, yet only five years later the city directory recorded 1,025 businesses in the building.[61] Presumably, there had not been a dramatic fragmentation in occupancy; rather, many tenants carried on several businesses from the same offices. *How* tenants came to occupy particular buildings, and *how* they interacted, is mainly a matter of inference at this remove in time; whether interacting firms deliberately co-located in the same building or developed their interaction as a result of their co-location is difficult to judge short of researching their full business histories.

As their business expanded, companies that owned named buildings usually expected to take over more of the space for themselves.[62] The Toronto city directory for 1892 recorded 51 different businesses in 73,000 square feet of office space in the Canada Life Building. By 1907, the number of businesses had been reduced to 28 and by 1927, shortly before Canada Life's move to its new building on University Avenue, there were only seven. In their new building, which could accommodate around 1400 workers, the company initially employed 626 of their own staff, occupying about half the space. The most prestigious skyscraper in inter-war Toronto was the new headquarters of the Canadian Bank of Commerce, completed in 1931 (Figure 10.7). Its previous, 7-storey, building had accommodated 15 tenants in the 1890s, but was fully occupied by the Bank's own employees by 1915. In the new 32-storey building, 'tallest in the British Empire', the Bank occupied all nine storeys beneath the tower, which was let to more than 50 tenants, including bond-dealers, brokers, lawyers and companies such as Brazilian Traction and Mexican Light, Heat and Power.[63]

Inter-War London

Despite superficial differences in the architectural form of office buildings, there were broad similarities in the organisation of office districts, including the functioning of individual buildings, and the interaction of economics, technology, planning and culture in each of the cities from which I have drawn examples. These similarities were reinforced by the Americanisation of office-building in inter-war London. David Scobey has emphasised New York's role in the American imagination as 'Empire City', integrating commerce and culture into 'a center of capitalist energy and civilizational progress'.[64] Londoners in the first half of the twentieth century sought reassurance from the built environment that theirs was not only still an imperial capital but one characterised by energy and continuing progress.

Several commentators have used Neils Lund's painting of *The Heart of the Empire* (1904) as evidence of the uneasy role of an imperial city in an increasingly post-imperial world.[65] The painting – imperial in its size (roughly 6 feet by 4½ feet) and panoramic detail, and owned by the City Corporation – depicts the commercial

Figure 10.7. Canadian Bank of Commerce, King Street, Toronto (c.1931). City of Toronto Archives, Series 1057, Item 409.

heart, Bank Junction, abutted by the Bank of England, the Royal Exchange (from the roof of which the painting was made), the Mansion House, and the Italianate Victorian offices at No. 1, Poultry, all overseen by the looming spiritual presence of St Paul's Cathedral. In debates in the 1980s, prior to the demolition of No. 1, Poultry, critics implied that the removal of this particular building would sever the connections between Lund's imperial capital and today's postcolonial city, and that the view of St Paul's from the Royal Exchange had assumed such an iconic status that it must be preserved in perpetuity. Iain Black points out, however, that much of the foreground in Lund's painting had already been swept away by rebuilding during the 1920s and 1930s. The Bank of England itself, the National Provincial Bank and the Midland Bank, all erected new buildings within the space depicted by Lund, and these structures were complemented by new headquarters for Lloyds Bank on Lombard Street and the National Westminster Bank on Lothbury.[66] Of the 'temple-like character of the banking hall' in the new Lloyds Bank, Black comments that 'Contemporary American models clearly influenced the architects here', and he quotes C. H. Reilly, a British professor of architecture at the time, on the difficulties facing London architects in designing buildings to vie with those in New York. To Reilly, the form of monumentalism espoused by the new London banks failed to reflect the steel-frame construction that underlay them. It was an argument about sham modernity, similar to the criticisms levelled at Tower Bridge forty years earlier, which I discussed at the very beginning of this book. To Black, 'the late-imperial rebuilding of the City of London seemed to reflect the uncertainties of empire in its very fabric'.[67]

Elsewhere in inter-war London, the influence of American modernism was more evident, sometimes bullishly coupled to a continuing celebration of Empire. The Daily Express Building on Fleet Street was described on its opening in 1932 as 'Britain's most modern building for Britain's most modern newspaper'.[68] A supremely modernist building, with a concrete structure sheathed in glossy black glass and vitriolite, its entrance foyer was inspired by American cinemas and New York skyscraper lobbies. But the global and at least partially imperial dimension to Lord Beaverbrook (the owner of the *Daily Express*)'s vision was also evident in Byzantine-style silver and gilt relief panels on either side of the foyer, one depicting 'east' (elephants, snake charmers, turbaned sitar players), the other 'west' (trains, boats, planes and industry).

London was still bound by a Building Act which limited the height of new buildings to a mere 80 feet (exclusive of two storeys in the roof and of ornamental towers) unless the special consent of the London County Council was forthcoming, and this tended to be given only where buildings overlooked open space – on Park Lane facing Hyde Park or along the Thames Embankment, for example. The Victorian solution to the height provisions was to include two substantial storeys of flats or offices in steeply pitched roofs, thereby raising the actual height of buildings to 100 feet or more, but in the late 1920s Charles Holden adopted an American style of set-back to elicit permission from the LCC for the new headquarters for the London Underground Group (subsequently the headquarters for London Transport) at 55 Broadway, between Victoria Street and St. James's Park (Figure 10.8). Its central tower is 175 feet high, but Holden was careful to make it easy for the LCC to grant permission. Each wing of the building has a set-back at the seventh floor exactly 80 feet above the street. Above that are additional storeys surmounted by a parapet whose coping lies on a line drawn from the outer edge of the set-back at 75 degrees to the horizontal, 75 degrees being the highest pitch of roof surface allowed in the interpretation of the phrase 'two storeys in the roof'. In this way, Holden and other inter-war architects were able to build modernist buildings within the framework of regulations designed for buildings with traditional pitched roofs.[69]

Figure 10.8. London Transport Headquarters, 55 Broadway (June 1937). London Transport Museum, 1998/75702. Photo by Dell & Wainwright, 6399-DW.

The London Underground Group required a building that expressed its status as the foremost public transport undertaking in London, if not in the world. Their 'flagship' was to be 55 Broadway, and on an acute-angled corner, with set-backs and a tower that could be interpreted as the captain's bridge or even as a liner's funnel, it symbolised the progress the company was making in improving and extending public transport: a 1920s version of the acute-angled 'flatiron' buildings that had represented progress a generation earlier. Just as flashing beacons and observation decks atop the Metropolitan Life and New York World towers symbolised their businesses' intent to reach out in all directions in the gathering of news or the spreading of civilisation, so the sculptures of 'Day' and 'Night' and of the four winds by the most eminent young artists – Jacob Epstein, Eric Gill, Henry Moore – that adorn the exterior walls of 55 Broadway indicated the company's mission to provide round-the-clock service to the four quarters of the metropolis: 'city as empire' as much as 'empire city'.[70]

Office workers

Directories and tax rolls can indicate what kinds of businesses went on in modern office buildings, but they provide few clues to the everyday life of the office. Not that all offices were alike. The rhythm of work would have been very different in a broker's office in an exchange building from an administrator's office in 55 Broadway or the filing department of Metropolitan Life. 'Here everyone seems to run rather than to walk', commented one observer of life in the City of London at the end of the nineteenth century. At the same time City clerks were extremely conservative in their dress – 'bobbing silk hats' in winter, 'supplanted by straw' in summer – and in their reluctance to accept the typewriter or the telephone.[71] Mr Pooter, who has worked for the same City firm for twenty-one years, even has trouble mastering a new stylographic pen, and is horrified at the risky share speculation in which his son engages on obtaining a job with Job Cleanands and Co., a firm of stock and share brokers. Pooter is portrayed as extremely deferential in his relations with his employer, Mr Perkupp. He is rewarded by promotion to senior clerk and a salary increase of £100 per annum, beyond his wildest dreams, but less than his son earns in a day's speculation. Following the brokers' collapse, Pooter's son reluctantly takes a job as a junior clerk with his father's employer but is dismissed after only a few weeks when he recommends the services of a rival firm to one of Mr Perkupp's most valued clients. The rivals first pay him a commission of £25 for directing new business in their direction, then engage him as a clerk at £200 per annum. The Grossmiths' gentle lampoon depends on the credibility – the recognition by their first readers – of the contrast between two kinds of firm and two kinds of employee. On the one hand, firms that were hierarchical, conservative, 'regular-downright-respectable-funereal-first-class-City' firms; on the other, risk-taking, willing to countenance sharp practice, 'the firm of the future!' On the one hand, employees who were deferential, loyal, conventional in their dress and habits; on the other, regularly changing jobs, preferring cosmopolitan Bayswater and a pony-and-trap to commuting by bus from suburban Holloway, snappy dressers who bought their suits from Sewell & Cross, Howell & James or Waterloo House.[72]

Gissing too describes the City as a place for masculine competitiveness, but his sour pessimism conceives it also as a machine for grinding down the uncompetitive. In *The Crown of Life*, Piers Otway sets up in business in Fenchurch Street as a merchant in the Russian trade. At first:

He felt the joy of combat; sped to the City like any other man, intent on holding his own amid the furious welter, seeing a delight in the computation of his chances; at once a fighter and a gambler, like those with whom he rubbed shoulders in the roaring ways.

But the next paragraph exposes the inhumanity of business:

The shiny-hatted figure who rushed or sauntered, gloomed by himself at corners or made one of a talking group, might elsewhere be found a reasonable and kindly person, with traits, peculiarities; here one could see in him nothing but a money-maker of this or that class, ground to a certain pattern.[73]

Novelists had much less experience of City life than of domestic tensions, shopping or recreational activities, and we may suspect that Gissing was less assiduous in his research into the City than in his earlier novels set in slums and suburbs he knew all too well.[74] The same lack of both knowledge and sympathy characterised artists' engagement with the world of finance. Artists were enthusiastic in depicting street life and cityscapes around the Royal Exchange and the Bank of England, City Hall Park, Broadway and Wall Street.[75] Robert Gagen's 'Temples of Commerce' dramatically portrayed Toronto's ascent to metropolitan status, showing the stepped profile of three skyscrapers at the intersection of King and Yonge Streets, each in its turn the 'tallest building in the British Empire', towering over the old trading city, represented in the painting's foreground by boats in the harbour and the flattened rotunda of the Board of Trade building.[76]

But painters were even less likely than novelists to venture inside the skyscrapers. Ashcan artists in New York mostly ignored big business, concentrating instead on scenes of working-class labour and trade, though John Sloan did produce a charcoal sketch and an oil painting depicting the inside of a savings bank. Even here, however, his focus was on the 'poor thrifty' reduced to a huddled, dark-coated mass beneath the opulent, gold-painted walls, columns and domed ceiling which their savings had helped to build.[77] A similar contrast appeared fifty years earlier in George Elgar Hicks' paintings of 'Dividend Day at the Bank of England,' showing a palatial, gold-painted banking hall, filled with a throng of widows and pensioners jostling to reach the counter where bank clerks were patiently dispensing funds.[78]

Trading activities in exchanges also attracted the attention of artists, from representations in popular magazines to Nevinson's drypoint depiction of the floor of the New York Stock Exchange.[79] Degas' painting of 'A Cotton Office in New Orleans' (1873) also represents a more public space than a private office, focusing on merchants feeling the cotton spread out on table and chair while a visitor reads a newspaper and other merchants and office staff look on.[80] But I know of no major painting of an 'ordinary' office prior to Edward Hopper's 'Office at Night' (1940). Hopper recalled that the painting derived from frequent glimpses of office interiors from passing elevated trains but, after experimenting with viewpoints looking in through the office window, he settled on a fly-on-the-wall perspective. A man seated at his desk, telephone at his elbow, is reading a document by the light of a table lamp. His secretary stands with her hands in a half-opened filing cabinet. Various papers are lying on a chair, beside a typewriter on a desk in the opposite corner of the room to the man's, and on the floor beside his desk. Both the window and the door to the outer office are open, and the billowing cord on the window blind indicates that there is at least a slight breeze, perhaps drawing attention to the intrusion of the public realm into a private relationship. As in so many Hopper paintings we are left to make up our own story from the clues he provides, but there is an undoubted sexual tension in the play of different sources of light and the enigmatic relationship between the two figures.[81]

By 1940, men and women had been working together in offices for at least half a century, invariably in the situations of relative power and status depicted in Hopper's painting. We can ascertain both the aggregate numbers and the gender balance from decennial censuses. In the United States, the number of clerical workers increased from 82,000 in 1870 (out of a total employed population of nearly 13 million) to more than 737,000 in 1900 (out of 29 million employed). On the eve of the Depression, there were nearly four million Americans in clerical occupations. Geographically, they were concentrated in major urban areas: by 1890 clerical workers comprised 11–12 per cent of the total workforce in New York, Brooklyn and Chicago. In Canada there were only 33,000 clerical workers (2% of the total labour force) as late as 1891, but by 1931 there were 260,000 (6.7%). In the whole of London, employees in financial and business services made up 0.1 per cent of the workforce in 1851, 0.7 per cent in 1891, and 1.3 per cent by 1911.[82]

Especially from the turn of the century, an increasing proportion of clerical workers and bank employees were female. In London and the Home Counties there were 179,000 clerks in 1891 of whom only 8 per cent were women; twenty years later the number of clerks had doubled, but women now made up 21 per cent of them. In Chicago, women made up barely 21 per cent out of a total of 41,000 clerical workers in 1890. By 1930, their numbers had increased almost fifteen-fold, to comprise 53 per cent out of 238,000, a proportion replicated in the United States as a whole, with Britain only a few percentage points behind. In Canada, women made up only 14 per cent of all clerical workers in 1891. By 1931, their numbers had increased by 2500 per cent to 45 per cent of the clerical workforce.[83] Part of the shift reflected the increasing acceptability for married women to seek paid employment.

In the province of Quebec, the 1891 census recorded 343 female filing clerks and copyists and 125 stenographers and typists. By 1911, there were more than eight times as many, just in the city of Montreal. The city's Sun Life Assurance Company hired its first woman in 1894. The Bank of Montreal's first female employee started work in 1902; by 1910 there were 23, and by 1918, replacing male clerks who had enlisted in the armed forces, there were 262 women employed by the bank.[84] In fact, banks tended to lag behind other businesses in employing women, particularly as cashiers dealing directly with the general public. It was thought that women cashiers would not inspire as much confidence in prospective borrowers or investors as male bank clerks. In one Canadian bank discussed by Graham Lowe, there were 350 female stenographers, 273 female general clerks, but only seven female tellers in 1916.[85] In downtown Toronto in 1914, there were eighteen women whose wages were sufficiently high for them to be listed in the tax assessment rolls as employees in the Head Office of the Canadian Bank of Commerce on King Street. Another nine women worked in the Toronto branch of the bank in the same building. In the Imperial Bank of Canada on Wellington Street the equivalent numbers were fourteen and three. In both cases, almost all of them were recorded as 'stenographer' or 'clerk' rather than as bank tellers.[86] Interestingly, the colonial periphery here lagged behind the supposedly conservative imperial centre. At Baring's Bank in Bishopsgate in the City of London, the first female member of staff had been employed as early as 1873 and by a decade later there were ten women on the staff.[87]

The mechanisation and routinisation of work associated with the typewriter favoured the employment of women. Typewriters had been invented in 1868 but not until the 1890s were they in widespread use. Rather like telephone switchboards they were thought to require the 'nimble fingers' which women were assumed to use in dressmaking. Previous experience of piano-playing, another middle-class female pastime, was also thought advantageous, making the fingers 'light and supple and quick'.[88] Male clerks saw the repetition, standardisation and precision needed in typing to be demeaning. Business schools were established to train women in secretarial skills. In Gissing's *The Odd Women* (1893), two feminist-minded women, Mary Barfoot and Rhoda Nunn, run a school in Great Portland Street in the West End of London, where they 'train young girls for work in offices', including typewriting at 'fifty words a minute at least'. Their target students are not 'the lower classes' but 'the daughters of educated people', single women such as Monica Madden and Mildred Vesper, living in lodgings. [89] In another Gissing novel, *Eve's Ransom* (1895, but set in 1884), Eve Madeley moves to London from the West Midlands to take up work as a pound-a-week bookkeeper.[90]

In North America, women like Eve Madeley were commonly referred to as 'women adrift', living apart from parents or other relatives. In 1900, one in five adult wage-earning women lived 'adrift' in American cities: 13 per cent in Brooklyn, 20 per cent in Manhattan, 21 per cent in Chicago, more than 30 per cent in Minneapolis-St Paul. In general, 'women adrift' were more likely to be employed in service work (e.g. as shop assistants) and in manufacturing than in clerical work. In the late nineteenth century, they were unlikely to live *alone*, more likely to share lodgings or live in a hostel with other women like themselves; but by 1930 an increasing proportion could afford a small apartment of their own.[91]

In Sinclair Lewis's *The Job* (1916), Una Golden, who is first a copy typist and then a stenographer with a succession of New York firms – in trade publishing, architectural practice, toiletries, and real estate – lives with her mother in a walk-up tenement flat on 148th Street. When her mother dies, Una finds accommodation in a Lexington Avenue 'railroad flat' whose tenants let out their spare rooms to a motley collection of lonely boarders. Next she discovers the more luxurious, but fearsomely disciplined Temperance and Protection Home Club for Girls, on Madison Avenue, just above 34th Street, from which she moves again into a three-room flat which she shares with another woman from the Home Club. Just as Upton Sinclair's *The Jungle* critiqued a succession of jobs and spaces through which its working-class immigrant hero was required to pass, so Lewis's novel depicts the range of workplaces and living spaces available to women office workers adrift in 1910s New York.[92]

Employers generally preferred young women who lived with their parents or other relatives, especially in clerical or retailing occupations where 'respectability' was paramount: 'A girl who boards out cannot support herself on a low wage. We have to enforce the rule as to living with the family or with friends to insure the moral character of our employe[e]s.'[93] Of course, the underlying problem was employers' expectations that they could pay women lower wages than men, and deny them any career progression. In multi-branch businesses such as banks, men could expect to be promoted as they were transferred from one branch or department to another. Men were suspect (for lacking sufficient masculine ambition) if they didn't apply to move; women were suspect (for being unstable) if they did. By the 1920s, popular magazines portrayed domestic life as a form of bondage – shackled to the home; in practice, female workers in typing pools were much more constrained, socially and spatially, engaged in repetitive work in open-plan offices where they were under the constant gaze of a supervisor, little different from the discipline of a nineteenth-century textile mill.[94] By comparison with these very un-domestic working conditions, male managers worked in a domesticated environment of comfortable furniture and decorations on the walls of their private offices.[95] They also, of course, had the equivalent of an 'office wife' (their secretary).

In Toronto, of nineteen female bank employees listed in city assessment rolls in 1914 whose names and addresses were also recorded in the city directory, only four were boarders, but generally living closer to their downtown workplaces than the thirteen who lived with their families or the two who were householders in their own right. Comparing the addresses of all forty-four female employees of the Canadian and Imperial Banks of Commerce listed in the assessment with the names of householders listed in the directory for those addresses, nineteen lived in houses where the household head shared their surname, twenty in houses where the head's surname was different, and five in apartment buildings, from which we might infer that as many as half may have been 'women adrift'.[96] Unfortunately, city assessment records usually record only one name as the 'occupier' of a house or apartment, but it is unlikely that many single women, even in office work, earned enough to afford a whole apartment for themselves, and we know from popular magazine articles that three or four girls sharing a flat was common enough, even in the early 1900s.[97] In the Midmaples Apartments, a new block of purpose-built apartments on Huron Street, Toronto, which had evaded the anti-apartment regulations by claiming to be a 'ladies' residence' rather than an apartment block, most suites were occupied by female householders in 1914. Among sharers were three sisters (two stenographers and a shop assistant in a milliner's) and two stenographers, one working for a real estate business, the other for an insurance company, both in Bay Street. Among twenty-six female residents whose occupations were listed in the city directory, twelve were stenographers, two were clerks, and seven were teachers.[98]

The relations between men and women working together in offices were a cause of continuing concern. Una Golden, summoned to take dictation from a young desk-editor in the *Motor and Gas Gazette* office, soon finds herself staying late to help him get an article finished, and before long is romantically involved.[99] When the office marriage-market worked smoothly, it met with official approval. Kate Boyer calculates that more than a quarter of the marriages reported in a Bank of Montreal employee journal between 1929 and 1932 were to other Bank of Montreal employees. The expectation was that, within a few years, most female employees would marry and leave employment, a self-fulfilling confirmation to employers that it was pointless to promote women to positions of responsibility they would soon abandon. But when flirtation misfired, it was invariably the woman who was blamed (and fired or forced to resign) for distracting the male employee from his work.[100] Employers therefore preferred to allow mixing of the sexes only in controlled situations. Their attempts to segregate employees at work ranged from a separate entrance for women in the redesigned Baring's Bank in London in 1880, to separate cafeterias, lounges and recreational facilities for male and female bank and insurance company staff in Montreal head offices forty years later.[101] By the early 1930s, the Sun Life Insurance Company also ran a 'Club House' offering evening classes and meals for all female employees, and residence for some.[102]

In the Metropolitan Life Building in New York there were rigorous efforts to keep the sexes apart. Entire divisions of the business were single-sex: the mail room was male; the telephone switchboard was entirely female. Where men and women did work together, women were confined to routine tasks such as filing and copy-typing while men worked calculating machines. Women sat at tables, men at desks. Men made phone calls; women operated the switchboard connecting them to other men. There were separate entrances, elevators and dining rooms for each sex. Men were allowed out into the city during their lunch-hour; women were expected to stay in the building and gain their fresh air on the rooftop promenade. Yet, as Olivier Zunz notes, 'Sexual mores in the society itself were changing, and the skyscraper proved to be a locus for change rather than a fortress against it'. Men were permitted on the roof at the same time as women. The company arranged out-of-hours dancing classes for women: they learnt to dance with other women, but were thereby prepared for the dance halls of Manhattan and Coney Island.[103]

As important, women who worked in downtown or midtown offices were conveniently positioned for patronising department stores, movie houses and other city centre entertainments; and women who lived on their own in lodgings or apartments, while they paid a substantial proportion of their earnings in rent, also had control over their income to spend as they saw fit. A survey of women workers in Chicago in 1892 found that stenographers and typists averaged $11.98 per week, bookkeepers $11.48, clerks $7.49, cashiers $6.41 and non-office employees only $5.71. Whereas factory operatives spent only $63 per annum on clothing and still ended up $15 in debt at the end of the year, stenographers could spend $140 on clothing and save $77 during the year.[104] Women continued to earn less than men in equivalent occupations, and continued to be concentrated in lower-paid jobs. Nevertheless, the increasing number of women in the workforce reinforced their growing purchasing power as consumers.

In this chapter I have discussed the changing geography of downtowns and the interaction of technological, economic, symbolic and regulatory factors in shaping office buildings in different cities. I have continued to waltz between documentary and fictional accounts of office development and office life, coming to rest on the increasing presence of working women downtown. I have argued that the development of financial and other office districts exemplified classic modernist tendencies to segregation and specialisation, both spatially and organisationally. I have also indicated commonalities between Britain and North America, as British mercantile activities were replicated in American cities in the nineteenth century and American modernism was imitated in inter-war Britain.

In 1907 Una Golden's workplace was on the eighth floor of the 'Septimus Building', 'a lean, jerry-built, flashingly pretentious cement structure with cracking walls and dirty, tiled passages' which Lewis situated on Nassau Street, in the heart of Lower Manhattan, the kind of building likely to have been cast into shadow, physically and economically, by new skyscrapers like the Equitable Building. Five years later Una is working in the 'Zodiac Building', an 18-storey, 12-elevator, 200-tenant, marble-floored confection on 34th Street between Fifth Avenue and Broadway. But for its more modest scale, the 'Zodiac' accurately predicts the Empire State Building which rose in just this district a decade and a half later. The 'Septimus' was not quite respectable, '"run up" by a speculative builder for a "quick turn-over"' and mostly occupied by 'fly-by-night companies – shifty promoters, mining-concerns, beauty-parlours for petty brokers, sample-shoe shops, discreet lawyers, and advertising dentists. Seven desks in one large room make up the entire headquarters of eleven international corporations.' By contrast, the 'Zodiac' was not only stylish but its hallway functioned as 'Main Street' for all who worked there. Watching these 'village people' Una 'found such settled existence as made her feel at home'.[105] In its midtown location, and in incorporating a range of retail services, the 'Zodiac' represented the reaction against absolute geographical and functional segregation, demonstrating that the modern office building could also be a source of personal identity, less a remote cathedral of commerce than a parish church at the heart of everyday life, albeit one dedicated, however benignly, to Mammon.

11

Geographies of downtown: the place of shopping

When Una Golden left work in the 'Septimus Building' one summer Saturday in 1907, and wanted to cheer herself up, she 'skipped across to the Sixth Avenue Elevated and went up to the department-store district. She made elaborate plans for the great adventure of shopping.' She also visited a new Sixth Avenue restaurant – one with a modern décor that shouted 'Personality' but proved to have the same old food as every other downtown café – and a motion-picture show. Both were lonely experiences for a single woman on her own. But in the department store she chatted first with the shop-walker who directed her to the appropriate counter and then with a sales assistant.[1] Shopping was about social interaction as much as economic transaction.

The origins and development of department stores

Most nineteenth-century department stores originated as drapers' (dry-goods) stores or, occasionally, as grocers', often as private partnerships – such as Swan & Edgar, Debenham & Freebody, Derry & Toms, Bourne & Hollingsworth in London, or Abraham & Straus and Lord & Taylor in New York. Typically, they would expand either by removing to larger premises or by taking over neighbouring shops, meanwhile extending the range of goods they stocked, diversifying from textile materials and ready-made clothes into soft furnishings, millinery, 'notions' or 'novelties', toys, perfume, jewellery, luggage, kitchen hardware, furniture, carpets and, in the twentieth century, electrical goods, and also providing an increasing range of services, such as tea rooms, restaurants, hairdressers, travel and real estate agencies.[2]

The retailers who preceded department stores might run neighbourhood stores in middle-class suburbs, such as Harrod's in Knightsbridge, or they were located in business districts that still mixed financial, office and retail functions. As outlined at the beginning of Chapter 10, the nineteenth century generally witnessed the physical separation of 'City' and 'West End' activities. In London, department stores pulled the commercial West End westward from its origins on Holborn and the Strand. Along Tottenham Court Road, a string of drapers and furniture retailers, marketing the products of local manufacturers, evolved into department stores such as Shoolbred's (1817), Heal's (1840) and Maple's (1842). On and around Oxford Street and

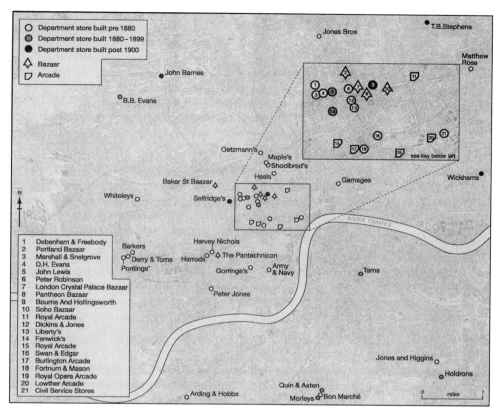

Figure 11.1. Locations of Department Stores, Arcades and Bazaars in Central and Inner Suburban London, 1820–1920.

Regent Street, family firms and partnerships, often originating on side streets, moved sites and developed into multi-department businesses: Swan & Edgar evolved from market stall to shop in Ludgate, in the City, moved to Piccadilly in 1812 and then to Regent Street; Debenham & Freebody began as a draper's near Cavendish Square, moving to Wigmore Street in 1851; Dickins & Jones began as Dickins & Smith on Oxford Street in 1790, moving to Regent Street in 1835, acquiring their new name in 1890, before being absorbed into Harrod's in 1914, and rebuilding their store in 1922 (Figure 11.1).[3]

The boldest developments took high-class retailing much farther west: Harrod's began as a grocery store in Knightsbridge in 1849, extended first by acquiring adjacent stores and developing both the back yards and the forecourts of each store, then rebuilt following a fire in 1883, and converted into a limited liability company in 1889. Whiteley's, opened in Bayswater in 1863, also expanded by taking over adjacent shops, rebuilding after fire, and moving to a new purpose-built store in Queensway in 1911. A string of stores lined Kensington High Street: Derry & Toms (1862), Barker's (1870), Pontings' (1893), and at Sloane Square, Peter Jones (1877).[4] At the time of their establishment we may think of these stores as having escaped the bounds of the CBD for high-class suburbia, the equivalent of New York's Upper East and, later, Upper West Sides. Just as the latter was at last opened up for development first by the building of the elevated railway up Ninth Avenue in 1878 and then by the opening of the subway in 1904, so Bayswater and Kensington were made newly accessible by the construction of the west side of the Circle Line by the Metropolitan and Metropolitan District Railways between 1863 and 1871. While these outliers of fashion developed, the core of the West End consolidated, notably with the establishment of Selfridge's in its own purpose-built store from the outset (1909), and then with the construction of new stores to house existing businesses, such as Bourne & Hollingsworth (originally 1902, new store 1922–1928), D. H. Evans (originally 1879, new store 1937) and Liberty's (originally 1875, new store 1925).[5]

Geographical shifts in fashionable retailing were even more dramatically signified in New York by the migration of particular businesses. A. T. Stewart's store, at Broadway and Chambers (at the north end of City Hall Park), was considered too far north when it opened in 1846. But the store lasted only sixteen years before it was superseded by a replacement, more than twenty blocks farther north, on Broadway between 9th and 10th Streets. The old store, originally feted as a 'marble palace' was converted to serve as a wholesale establishment. By the 1890s, it had been remodelled again, as the Stewart Building, offering office space to businesses such as the Washington Trust Company and the F. W. Woolworth Company. Another leading New York department store, Lord & Taylor, moved from Catherine Street to Grand and Chrystie by the early 1850s and then to Broadway and 20th in 1869, ending up on Fifth Avenue between 38th and 39th in 1914. Macy's, situated at Herald Square (the intersection of Sixth Avenue, Broadway and 34th Street) since 1902, originated twenty blocks south at Sixth and 14th in 1858. But, like Harrod's and Whiteley's in London, there are also department stores that have always been located uptown: Bloomingdale's was founded in 1872, only three blocks south of the site at Third Avenue and 59th Street that it has continued to occupy into the twenty-first century despite frequent remodellings of the store (Figure 11.2).[6]

The migration of fashion is poignantly charted in Howells' *A Hazard of New Fortunes* (1890). When Basil and Isabel March arrive in New York in the mid-1880s, they find the lower reaches of Broadway, south of Union Square, to be much less frenetic than they remember from their first visit, on their honeymoon, two decades earlier. They 'stood for a moment before Grace Church [at Broadway and 10th – adjacent to Stewart's second store], and looked down the stately thoroughfare, and found it no longer impressive, no longer characteristic. It is still Broadway in name, but now it is like any other street. You do not now take your life in your hand when you attempt to cross it . . . all that certain processional, barbaric gaiety of the place is gone.'[7] Farther south, below Canal Street, lower Broadway would still have been busy with bankers, brokers and merchants. Farther north, above Union Square, Ladies' Mile would have been full, at least in the afternoons, of women and their consorts engaged in a 'showy parade'.[8] But the space between, although still respectably occupied by wholesalers, small businesses and traders servicing middle-class neighbourhoods such as Washington Square, was 'in transition', no longer fashionable.

Less often discussed than the migration of stores in pursuit of their fashionable customers but just as significant was the establishment of new department stores in less affluent suburban areas. The claim to be London's first *purpose-built* department store (in contrast to stores that grew by taking over neighbouring premises and

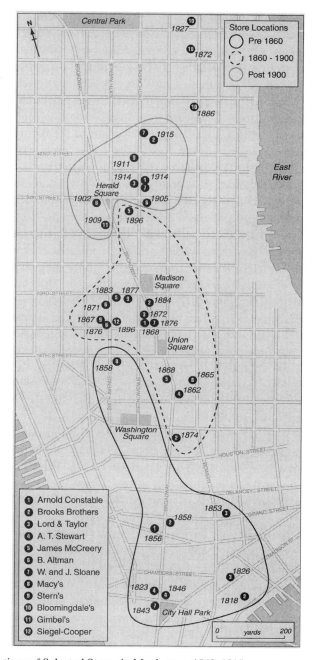

Figure 11.2. Locations of Selected Stores in Manhattan, 1840–1915.

knocking through to create internal connections between them) was made by the Brixton Bon Marché, which opened in 1877, stealing its name from the already established store in Paris. Another prominent suburban store was Jones Brothers in Holloway (the north London lower middle-class suburb inhabited by the Pooters in

The Diary of a Nobody), opened as a draper's in 1867, expanding to comprise four adjacent shops by 1877, and rebuilt as a purpose-built store in 1895.[9]

Lower middle-class suburbanites might patronise both suburban and city-centre stores: Mrs Pooter visited the local 'Bon Marché' in Holloway but also made purchases from Shoolbred's (Tottenham Court Road), Liberty's (Regent Street) and Peter Robinson's (Oxford Circus).[10] Women in south-west London told the *Evening News* in 1907 that their local shops were 'up-to-date' and fine for minor purchases, but they preferred to travel to the West End stores if at all possible.[11] In Gissing's *In The Year of Jubilee*, Beatrice French, with the advice of her friend, the up and coming advertising agent, Luckworth Crewe, establishes the South London Fashionable Dress Supply Association, in 'a handsome shop' with club-room and refreshment bar, 'its windows cunningly laid out to allure the female eye' and a commissionaire distributing newly printed handbills to passers-by. Its target customers were 'the servant-keeping females in Brixton, Camberwell, and Peckham', so lacking in refinement that they 'could not, with any confidence, buy a chemise or a pair of stockings; and when it came to garments visible, they were lost indeed'.[12] Gissing himself recorded in his diary a visit to the Brixton Bon Marché to buy furniture for the rooms he rented in Brixton in 1893, but he also made a trip back to Oetzmann's on Hampstead Road to buy carpet, curtains, and linoleum; and when the Gissings moved again – to their own unfurnished villa in Epsom – he returned to Oetzmann's to buy bedroom furniture, while his wife 'made a lot of purchases' at Shoolbred's.[13]

As stores expanded and diversified, each new line of business would constitute a separate 'department', assigned its own share of the store's running costs and expected to prove its own profitability. In a few cases, especially in American stores, some new and risky ventures would initially be franchised to independent retailers with previous experience of that form of business. At Macy's in New York, new lines such as silverware, china and shoes were introduced in this way but, as Joy Santink notes with a hint of Canadian moral superiority, the leading store owner in Toronto, Timothy Eaton, never leased space and always took the risks himself.[14] The reintroduction of franchising in department stores more recently not only recovers this early history, but also points to an alternative genealogy for the department store, connected to the bazaars and arcades that characterised retailing in the late eighteenth and early nineteenth centuries.

In London, there were at least ten bazaars by 1850, mostly along Oxford Street and the Strand, specialising in the sale of items of female dress, jewellery and 'toys' (trinkets, luxuries). As late as 1880, the Soho Bazaar, Oxford Street, accommodated 21 businesses trading in toys, books, millinery, jewellery, hardware, and Chinese and Japanese goods.[15] Irrespective of the geographical origins of the commodities, bazaars conjured up the exoticism of the East, the Orientalist fascination with 'other' ways of doing business by barter and making shopping into a social as well as an economic activity. Later in the nineteenth century, the word 'bazaar' went down-market, adopted by retailers such as Marks and Spencer, whose 'penny bazaars', originating in a Leeds market stall in 1884, blossomed as cut-price stores in suburban London in the 1890s and 1900s. By 1915, there were about thirty Marks and Spencer stores in London, but only one, on Edgware Road, was remotely near the West End, and it was not until 1930, by which time they had moved up-market and long abandoned the terminology of the bazaar, that they opened a store at the Marble Arch end of Oxford Street. Coincidentally, the company's second Oxford Street store, opened in 1938, was erected on the site of the Pantheon, another of Oxford Street's nineteenth-century bazaars, described by George Sala in the 1860s as a 'Hampton Court-like maze of stalls, laden with pretty gimcracks'.[16]

The term 'bazaar' also survived in department-store advertising, but referred to seasonal promotions and sales usually aimed at less well-off customers. From its opening, the Brixton Bon Marché advertised an annual 'Grand Christmas Bazaar'.[17] The spirit of the oriental bazaar was also invoked by businesses such as Liberty's, which specialised in fabrics and designs imported from or imitative of Asia, and Selfridge's, especially in advertising which portrayed the store 'where East meets West' and in displays linked to the visit of the Russian Ballet to London in 1911. In New York, the Siegel-Cooper department store staged a six-week 'Carnival of Nations' in 1903, culminating in 'Oriental Week'.[18] Mica Nava seeks to distinguish between the authoritarian, colonising imagination of orientalism, a power relationship between the occidental (usually male) explorer/appropriator and the (feminised if not female) orient, and the exoticising imagination associated with commercial transactions in places like Selfridge's, where cultural difference was produced as something attractive and non-threatening: a commodity to be purchased. She prefers to align the latter with the idea of cosmopolitanism, a positive and explicitly modernist transcendence of national identities, perhaps easier to accept in the case of Selfridge himself, who had migrated from Chicago to London, or in the United States, which was experiencing its peak rates of immigration in the years preceding World War I, than among Selfridge's or Liberty's customers who were still overwhelmingly white, middle-class and British imperialist.[19]

Like bazaars, arcades offered a variety of stores under one roof, but in the form of a private street that could also be used as a pedestrian route through the city. So, while they preceded department stores chronologically, they also continued as an alternative shopping experience, especially in English provincial cities such as Leeds and Birmingham, which had relatively few department stores at the beginning of the twentieth century. In Manhattan, the New York Arcade, laid out in 1827, accommodated forty stores in 'a skylight-covered corridor', just east of Broadway, between Maiden Lane and John Street.[20] In London, at the beginning of the twentieth century, the Royal Arcade, built in 1879, off New Bond Street, was renowned for 'dainty shops, bright with flowers or with the most artistically coquettish creations of the milliner's art', whereas arcades farther east, at Ludgate Circus, catered for 'the requirements of the homely rather than of the luxurious'.[21] Small shops lining London's Lowther Arcade (1830–1904), on the north side of the Strand, originally sold a range of luxury and novelty items, much like the Oxford Street bazaars, but by the middle of the nineteenth century nearly all its shops concentrated on selling children's toys. It was a safe public place where the commercial traveller, Mr Gammon, could meet with his volatile young lady friend, Polly Sparkes, from whom he was trying to detach himself, in Gissing's comic novel, *The Town Traveller* (1898).[22] By contrast, the Burlington Arcade (1819) early on had a reputation for dandyism and prostitution, a combination of attributes also associated with the Parisian arcades explored in Walter Benjamin's fragmentary but voluminous writings.[23]

A few department stores were born fully-formed: the Bon Marché in Brixton in south London, also unusual in being the brainchild of a lone individual, James Smith, a printer and racehorse owner with no previous experience in retailing; and, most famously, Selfridge's, opened in 1909 by Harry Gordon Selfridge who had previously been retail manager and junior partner in Marshall Field, Chicago's most prestigious store. Moving to London in 1906, he planned a store on American principles: fixed prices, no pressure on people who entered the store to make a purchase, regular sales – not just at the end of season to shift dead stock but also at the beginning to stimulate interest – and an all-the-year-round bargain basement. Plate-glass windows fronting the street would not simply be packed full of stock but would be 'dressed' artistically by skilled window-dressers, to form an aesthetic attraction in their own right, even when the store was closed. At the Brixton Bon Marché an extension was added to the frontage in 1908, so that pedestrians could walk through a covered arcade with window displays on both sides, as close as it was possible to come to the ideal of having the public street run through the middle of the store, one of the many ways in which real department stores matched Zola's 'Ladies' Paradise' (Bonheur des Dames), itself derived from its author's study of the Paris Bon Marché.[24]

The emphasis on window display meant that even for stores that had grown by accretion, the ideal was to obtain an 'island site', an entire city block, with entrances and plate-glass windows on all sides. After their move from Bayswater to Oxford Street in 1902, Bourne & Hollingsworth set about acquiring the rest of the block in which their store was situated, removing two residential tenants, thirteen retailers, three wholesalers, four offices, seven workshops and a chapel before erecting a new block-sized store in the 1920s.[25] This kind of redevelopment was obviously intended to connote both modernisation, in creating a more efficient and technologically up-to-date store, and modernity, marketing a cosmopolitan lifestyle behind a 'moderne' or Art Deco façade. On Kensington High Street, the rebuilding of Derry & Toms replaced a motley collection of stores and workshops, gradually acquired over the previous half-century, with open-plan floors maximising flexibility in the arrangement of different departments (Figure 11.3). This was a form common in America, but still unusual in London in 1929 when the plans were finalised. It should come as no surprise that a Chicago architect, C. A. Wheeler, was employed as consulting architect for the interior layout and equipment (such as the bank of eight lifts at the back of the retailing space). In the mid-1930s, an elaborate roof garden was added, including a 'Sun Pavilion', reflecting inter-war enthusiasm for sunbathing as the key to health, and a 'Spanish Garden' with Moorish features, a style replicated in numerous Spanish-style Odeon and Granada cinemas in the 1930s.[26] In Toronto, Eaton's sought to modernise its image by constructing an Art Deco store on a new site on the south-west corner of Yonge and College Streets, half-a-mile north of the business's existing site near the intersection of Yonge and Queen Streets. On land acquired in 1914 but not developed until the late 1920s, a 40-storey skyscraper was planned but only the first stage of the project, a 7-storey store, had been completed when the Great Depression brought an end to further expansion.[27]

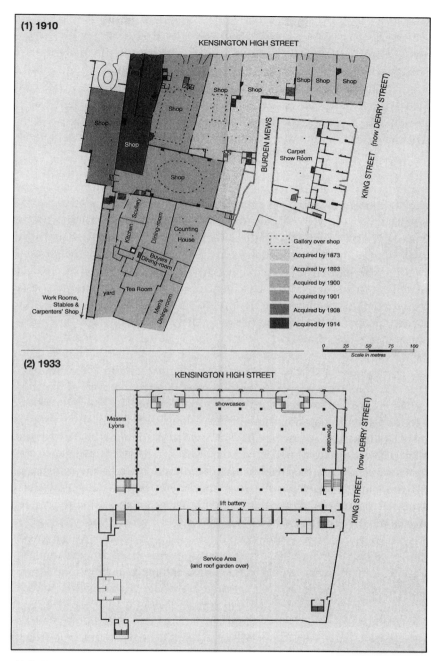

Figure 11.3. Derry & Toms Department Store, Kensington, before and after rebuilding (adapted from plans in *Survey of London, Volume 42, Kensington Square to Earl's Court* (1986), Figs. 31 and 32, with additional information).

Eaton's

The case of Eaton's illustrates so many aspects of department-store history that it merits further discussion.[28] Timothy Eaton first established a dry-goods business on Yonge Street, just south of its intersection with Queen Street, in 1869. By 1881, he employed 36 sales clerks in his store, and 12 seamstresses in adjacent workrooms. The city assessment rolls only listed a handful of male clerks as employees whose incomes exceeded the taxable minimum, so the vast majority of his workforce must have been low-paid youths and girls, although there were also a few women in supervisory positions. By 1882, the business had burst the bounds of the original store and its mid-1870s extension, but there was no further scope for expansion on the site south of Queen. With the aid of a 90 per cent mortgage from the Union Loan and Savings Company, Eaton acquired a row of stores a little farther north, just across the junction with Queen Street. To the horror of local interests, he proceeded to demolish his new property, even though the stores were only twenty-six years old and still regarded as among the city's finest retail buildings. In their place he erected a single store with a frontage of 51 feet, with a basement displaying bulky items such as trunks, topped by three floors selling different kinds of dry goods. Several light wells topped by skylights maximised the amount of natural light, complemented by electric light. There were also two hydraulic elevators. Other facilities included a 'Ladies Gallery and Waiting Room', later supplemented by a coffee room and a small restaurant.

Even this purpose-built store soon proved inadequate. From 1885 onwards, Eaton acquired more and more property abutting or across the street from the store (Figure 11.4). Some premises were leased at first, then bought outright when they became available for purchase or when the business's finances allowed; some property was purchased in advance of requirements and rented out for a few years to other users; some was adapted to Eaton's needs, but most was demolished and built anew as additional sales space, manufacturing lofts or to accommodate a fast growing mail-order business. From at least the late 1870s, the store had offered to deliver goods by train to outlying customers, but mail-order began in earnest in 1884 with the production of a 32-page catalogue distributed free to visitors to the annual Toronto Industrial Exhibition. By 1896, Eaton's were sending out more than 200,000 parcels annually. The 1899 catalogue had grown to 250 pages, profusely illustrated on high-quality paper; and by 1904, circulation had grown to 1.3 million catalogues per annum, some sent to Canadians living in Europe, Asia, Jamaica and Mexico, as well as the United States. Volume manufacturing, as opposed to workshop alterations and special orders, began seriously in 1889, with 12 sewing machines in a workroom next door to the store. Initially, production concentrated on men's shirts and women's underwear. By the turn of the century, Eaton factories employed more than 700 workers using nearly 500 sewing machines, in addition to 115 dressmakers producing items to order. By 1909, when the business covered 22 acres of downtown Toronto, there were 2156 sales staff, 1260 'expense staff' employed in maintenance, delivery and other ancillary roles, 449 mail-order staff and more than 4000 employed in the firm's factories. But by now, Eaton's had expanded outside Toronto – there was another huge store in Winnipeg, and factories in Oshawa, just east of Toronto, and in Montreal: over 11,000 employees in the Eaton's empire.

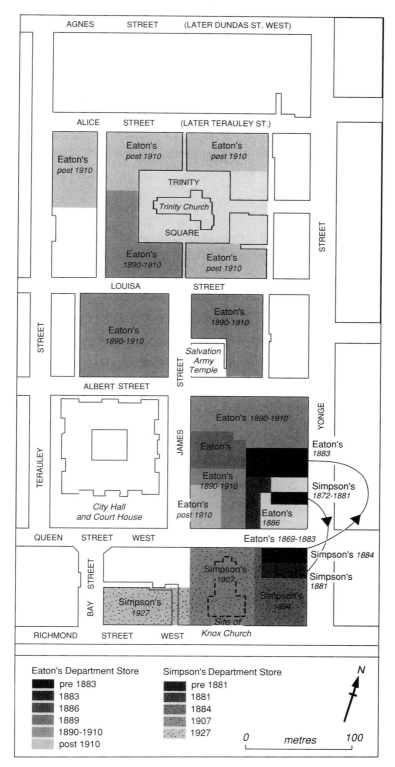

Figure 11.4. The Expansion of Eaton's and Simpson's Department Stores in Downtown Toronto, 1869–1927 (modified from map in M. Kluckner, *Toronto: The Way It Was* (1988), with additional information).

Women workers in department stores

Drapers' stores, hardware stores and the other single-specialisation stores that pre-ceded multi-department enterprises had not usually priced goods with clearly marked labels, nor had they displayed much of their stock. It was assumed that a customer entering a store was making a commitment to buy, that they would entrust themselves to a male assistant who would recommend and demonstrate products appropriate to the customer's needs, and who would have the authority to negotiate the price with the customer. Regular customers would be entitled to credit. But department stores welcomed shoppers, insisting that they were under no obligation to buy. While there might still be a male shopwalker who would meet customers at the door and direct them to the appropriate department, they were free to wander around the store on their own. Goods would be clearly marked with a fixed price and customers were at first expected to pay cash. With this simplification of the transaction, it was thought that the business of selling could be entrusted to female sales assistants. Many stores also had workshops or factories where women were employed as seamstresses, either making or altering clothes to the orders of individual clients or, increasingly, engaged in mass production of ready-to-wear branded goods such as shirts, blouses, underwear, skirts and trousers.

In 1906, the City of Toronto assessment rolls listed 514 male and 170 female Eaton employees on sufficiently high incomes to be paying tax, out of a then total workforce of around 3000. But the majority of the untaxed were female: for example, in Decem-ber 1896 there were 308 male and 463 female sales staff.[29] In general, it appears that the feminisation of department store workforces proceeded most rapidly in North America, more slowly in continental Europe, with Britain somewhere in between. Yet in mid-nineteenth-century New York, A. T. Stewart had preferred to employ men, noticing that ladies who visited his store engaged in gossiping and flirting with male sales assistants.[30] While this interaction may have boosted sales, it appalled moral-ists. George Ellington, in *The Women of New York or the Underworld of the Great City* (1869), a critique of the new class of idle, irresponsible, bourgeois women who spent their time in shopping and frivolous leisure, condemned the married women of New York who formed 'very indiscreet acquaintances' with sales clerks in stores where 'shopkeepers make it a rule to employ the finest-looking young men they can find to draw custom'.[31] In their history of New York, Burrows and Wallace suggest that it was the shortage of male labour during the American Civil War that led to the employment of women on the sales floors of Stewart's store (much as women entered the labour force in huge numbers in Britain during World War I), though a few pages later they date their appearance a little later – to the same year as the publication of Ellington's book (1869).[32] Whatever the precise chronology or the cat-alyst, in the long run, women were cheaper to employ, and a different form of social intercourse developed between female sales staff and female customers – the confi-dential advice of one woman to another; although this could backfire on employers when discontented staff advised potential customers where they could find cheaper or better quality goods!

Feminisation continued apace through the twentieth century. At Gordon Self-ridge's purpose-built department store in London's Oxford Street, there were 3500 employees in 1914, five years after opening, of whom only 950 were men. In the two London stores owned by the John Lewis Partnership in 1931 (John Lewis on Oxford Street and Peter Jones in Sloane Square), there were 650 male employees, average age 34, and 1663 women, average age 27. Sixty (9%) of the men but only thirty-six (2%) of the women earned more than £8 per week; 65 per cent of men but only 32 per cent of women earned £3–£8; 2 per cent of men and 4 per cent of women earned less than £1, leaving fewer than one-quarter of male employees but more than 60 per cent of females earning between £1 and £3.[33]

Although most women shop-workers, like women office-workers, held relatively menial and low-paid jobs, some quickly assumed more powerful roles in the employment hierarchy. In a 1902 essay on 'London's drapers', Mrs Belloc-Lowndes used the male pronoun to refer to buyers in general, but she singled out 'the important lady whose business it is to superintend the millinery department. It is she who decides of what materials the hat or toque is to be made, and what price is to be asked for it.'[34] By World War I, women made up at least a third of department store buyers in the United States, with their own budgets and in a position to control trends in fashion.[35] Mrs Belloc-Lowndes also differentiated between 'squadders', young men responsible for cleaning, dusting and unpacking the goods each morning, and young ladies who took charge of window-dressing. Reacting to the assertion 'that women cannot be taught the business side of life' she observed that 'in the great drapery establishments the cash desk is almost always occupied by a girl clerk'.[36] A generation later, in 1932, 28 out of 47 senior staff included in a group photograph at Fenwick's in Newcastle-upon-Tyne were women. Nevertheless, the usual expectation was that women would leave employment once they were married. Hence, the younger age profile of John Lewis's female employees, and high rates of staff turnover.[37]

Despite their unequal treatment, most young women regarded working in a department store as preferable to either factory work or domestic service. As with women office workers, those who lived with their parents were preferred by employers, but among the ranks of sales assistants there were inevitably many 'women adrift', living in lodgings and hostels apart from their families. When Carrie Meeber first arrives in Chicago at the beginning of *Sister Carrie*, her family's expectation is that she will lodge with her sister and her husband. Carrie seeks work in a succession of businesses. At a wholesale dry-goods firm, she is turned down when she confesses she has no experience of stenography/typewriting, and is advised to try the department stores; but at 'The Fair', one of Chicago's leading stores, her inexperience in retailing counts against her again. She eventually finds tiring and tiresome work as a machine operator in a shoe factory, where her companions are coarse in both looks and behaviour. By contrast, the shop assistants in 'The Fair' were 'pretty in the main, some even handsome, with a certain independence and toss of indifference which added, in the case of the more favored, a certain piquancy. Their clothes were neat, in many instances fine' and only served to emphasise her own inferiority.[38]

In Chicago and New York, few store owners provided any accommodation for their workers. 'Living in' had been associated with many small dry-goods stores. For a short time in the early 1870s, several of Eaton's young male clerks had occupied rooms on the top floor of his Yonge Street store, but they had soon been displaced as the business expanded.[39] In Gissing's *The Odd Women*, before she goes to secretarial college,

Monica shares a room with five other shopgirls in the employ of Messrs Scotcher and Co., drapers, Walworth Road (in the inner suburbs of south-east London). The living-in system was suited to long opening hours and the need for stock to be put away after trading and set out again before opening next morning, and Monica's hours were typically long. Gissing exaggerates only slightly in describing her working day: thirteen hours and a half every weekday, and sixteen hours on Saturday, with no more than twenty minutes' break for dinner and tea and no sitting down behind the counter.[40] But stores of this kind did much of their business late on Saturday nights, after the working week had ended for most of their working-class clientele and male breadwinners had handed over a share of their wages to their wives to spend on food and clothing. City-centre department stores, dependent on a middle-class clientele of women with leisure to spend shopping during the day, kept much shorter hours, especially on Saturdays, and were often vocal in support of the Early Closing Movement, a humanitarian stance they could easily afford since they stood to lose so little business by closing early.[41]

When Eaton's was still just a dry-goods store and Toronto a town of only 50–100,000, the store stayed open until 9 p.m. on Saturdays; but in 1877, both Eaton's and the rival proto-department store, Simpson's, opted to close at 6 p.m. By the mid-1880s, Eaton's was closing at 2 p.m. on Saturdays in summer, copying the practice of leading New York stores (though, to compensate, they stayed open later on weekdays during the warm summer evenings).[42] Typical opening hours in central London in the mid-1880s were from 8 a.m. to 6 p.m. or 6:30 p.m. in winter, 7 p.m. or 8 p.m. in summer, but closing around 2 p.m. on Saturdays. Suburban stores stayed open along with local convenience stores on Saturday afternoons. The Brixton Bon Marché made a special effort to attract rich American visitors, especially from the Cecil Hotel in the Strand (Europe's largest hotel when it opened, with 600 rooms, in 1886), who were left with money to burn but nothing much to do once the West End stores had closed at lunchtime.[43]

Nonetheless some London department stores did provide housing for some of their staff. Whiteley's staff accommodation was separate from the store, not over the shop; the Brixton Bon Marché also included a block to accommodate employees; and John Barnes & Co., opened in Finchley Road in north-west inner suburbia in 1900, provided on-site accommodation for 400 employees, with three separate staff dining rooms: for male assistants, for female assistants and for buyers.[44] All these examples indicate a continuing paternalistic concern for the health and morals of employees, which might be thought of as pre-modern. Surely a modern approach was to separate housing provision from commercial activity, to leave housing to a specialist class of developers and landlords? On the other hand, there was also a very modern concern to nurture company loyalty, through physical provisions such as staff sports clubs and financial devices such as share issues and, eventually, in the case of the John Lewis Partnership, by converting employees into partners.

A more common financial device was to convert privately owned stores into public companies, usually to raise capital for major expansion. When Charles Digby Harrod, the son of the original owner, decided to withdraw from the business, Harrod's was floated as a limited liability company in 1889. In the same year, Eaton's became the

T. Eaton Co. Ltd., though it remained in the control of the Eaton family. Ownership of the Brixton Bon Marché was assumed by a public company in 1892 when the original owner went bankrupt. In America, Marshall Field's was incorporated in 1901 and Macy's in 1922.[45] Stores also faced merger or take-over as individual entrepreneurship gave way to corporate capitalism, partly in response to competition from retailers who, from the outset, operated as 'multiples', like Marks and Spencer, British Home Stores, Freeman, Hardy & Willis (shoes) and Montague Burton (men's outfitters). In 1919–1920 the Brixton Bon Marché absorbed its local rivals – Pratt's of Streatham and Quin & Axten's in Brixton – but by 1927 it, in turn, had been swallowed up into Selfridge's, which took over a large number of suburban and provincial stores during the 1920s, also including Whiteley's, by now stranded in no longer fashionable Bayswater.[46]

Culture and commerce

The interiors of purpose-built stores had at least two sources of inspiration, both grounded in the idea of spectacle: the theatre and the international exhibition. In the days before electric light (and even afterwards, given the need for customers to match colours, ideally in 'natural' light), it was important to introduce as much natural light as possible through the use of light wells topped by skylights or, more impressively, glass domes. Consequently, sales floors could not run continuously across the length and breadth of buildings, but this could be turned to advantage by constructing balconies and galleries so that customers could look across and up and down the light wells, much as they would from the front row of a theatre balcony. They could orientate themselves more easily in a large and potentially labyrinthine building: they might be able to see the department which they wished to visit next.[47] But the balcony was also the ideal vehicle for display – of customers as much as merchandise. Just as at the theatre, the department store was the place to see and be seen.

One of the first stores of this kind was the 'Marble Palace' erected by A. T. Stewart at Broadway and Chambers Street in 1846. The five-storey building, faced in white marble, centred on a rotunda with a domed skylight. The rotunda was decorated with frescoes, chandeliers and mirrors. A gallery 'for the ladies to promenade upon' ran around the base of the dome.[48] Stewart's next store, at Broadway and 10th Street, an 'Iron Palace' completed in 1862, had an even more elaborate central court, again top-lit, with five tiers of encircling balconies which 'contributed to the spectacle atmosphere of the store' (Figure 11.5). However, the fourth and fifth floors, which gave access to the topmost balconies, affording a truly bird's eye view of the sales floors below, were devoted to the *manufacture* of ladies wear, furs and upholstery, and to a laundry and storeroom.[49] Production and consumption had not yet been geographically segregated, but the consequence was an even more theatrical distribution of different social classes, akin to the working classes in the cheap seats in 'The Gods' looking down on the bourgeoisie in the stalls and dress circle.

Initially, there were no displays in Stewart's ground-floor windows; rather, the display was the crowd of shoppers already inside the store, tempting those outside

Figure 11.5. The Interior of Stewart's Astor Place Store ('Iron Palace') (1862) in the 1880s. Bella C. Landauer Collection, negative number 70132. Collection of The New-York Historical Society.

to enter to see what all the fuss was about.[50] Compare this strategy with Mouret's intentions in Zola's *Au Bonheur des Dames*:

He laid it down as a law that not a corner of the Bonheur des Dames was to remain unfrequented; everywhere he insisted upon noise, crowds, life . . . First of all there should be a crush at the entrance, it should seem to people in the street as if there was a riot in the shop . . . [51]

Parallels with the theatre or the opera house were enhanced by the practice of many department stores of staging concerts. The opening of Eaton's new store in 1883 was marked by two open evenings, when no goods were on sale but visitors were invited to inspect the new premises, on the second of which there was also a 'Grand Promenade Concert'. On another occasion, Easter was marked by an 8-piece orchestra playing in the store inside the shell of a giant Easter egg![52] At the Brixton Bon Marché, the Christmas Bazaar in 1920, although primarily a children's event, also featured 'live orchestral music for adults'.[53] In New York, Siegel-Cooper, a Sixth Avenue store renowned for 'spectacular extravaganzas', hosted a succession of stage shows during the 1900s and even advertised an all-women orchestra in the grocery department. Far more serious musical occasions were two performances in 1904 of Richard Strauss' appropriately home-and-family related *Symphonia Domestica*, conducted by the composer in Wanamaker's, the retail business which had taken over Stewart's 'Iron Palace'.[54]

Between the openings of Stewart's first and second stores, New York had witnessed the erection of a 'Crystal Palace' in 1853, emulating Paxton's Great Exhibition building constructed in London's Hyde Park two years earlier. The New York version, topped by a 123-feet-high glass dome, housed an 'Exhibition of the Industry of All Nations' supported by more than 4000 American and international exhibitors.[55] In London, the young William Whiteley was reputedly inspired by the Hyde Park Great Exhibition to create a store which would provide an equivalent commercial as well as cultural experience. In the 1880s, his store was described as 'an immense symposium of the arts and industries of the nation and of the world', language almost identical to that ascribed to international exhibitions.[56] The iron and glass arcades of Paxton's Crystal Palace were also imitated in shops such as Osler's in Oxford Street, built with a barrel-vaulted, coloured-glass roof in 1858. Its architect, Owen Jones, had worked extensively on the interior decoration of the real Crystal Palace, including a spectacular crystal fountain, which was reinstalled as a central feature when the Crystal Palace was rebuilt on an even grander scale – with Jones playing an even more prominent part in its design – to function as a permanent exhibition building in the south London suburb of Sydenham.[57] A contemporary account of the Oxford Street version described it as a rationalised, demystified, sanitised bazaar – a bazaar devoid of the shadows and assumed duplicity of its oriental(ist) origins, a quintessentially modern shopping experience: 'From the galleries, we look down upon the ground floor and find it arranged with counters in a very systematical order, loaded with uncountable trinkets.'[58]

Department store proprietors such as A. T. Stewart in New York, Marshall Field in Chicago, William Whiteley and Gordon Selfridge in London were not only offering a safe, controlled version of the new and exotic, more romantic than erotic – encapsulated in the title of Selfridge's own book, *The Romance of Commerce* – but they also attempted to align their businesses with high culture and civic values. They presented their stores as public, not private, institutions, committed to public service. Selfridge thought of his London store as a 'social centre'. Whiteley even proposed to the painter, William Powell Frith, who lived nearby in Pembridge Villas, that he follow his spectacular scenes of public display and social interaction – 'Ramsgate Sands', 'Derby Day' and 'The Railway Station' – by depicting the scene outside his Bayswater store, thereby claiming his business as a national institution and leisure activity, on a par with a day at the races or a holiday excursion.[59]

Domosh notes that there were two types of public space in New York in the 1860s – those displaying cultural status, like parks and museums, and those serving consumer demands, like shops and restaurants. But Stewart, and others like him, designed their stores in styles previously reserved for public buildings – ennobled by murals and frescoes, literally en-lightened, flooded with light to emphasise the honesty and transparency of their business. In these ways, a visit to a department store would be as much of an educational and cultural experience as a visit to the Metropolitan Museum. The store and, by implication, the part of downtown in which it was situated, became domesticated by the provision of lounges, libraries, toilet facilities and restaurants in which women dining alone or in the company of other women could feel comfortable.[60] In the mid-nineteenth-century world of 'separate spheres', this was less a case of undermining that ideology, more a way of redefining its geographical boundaries. None of this was intended to hide the stores' commercial functions. Rather, the point was to ally commerce and culture, to legitimise the former by demonstrating its compatibility with the latter.[61]

Women consumers

Alignment with fine art, architecture and civil engineering was not enough to ensure the success of department stores or the consumer boom upon which they relied. We normally think about the mid-to-late nineteenth century as a period of high-minded sobriety in which the occasional scandals of politicians and businessmen who succumbed to alcohol or extra-marital sex were the exceptions that proved the rule of temperance and modesty. Yet department stores were about promoting consumption beyond the bare necessities of life, about shopping as a leisure activity when respectable middle-class women might otherwise have been supervising their servants, ensuring their children were educated aright and engaging in 'good works' – attending prayer meetings or volunteering for philanthropic service. The *production* of more and more goods was to be applauded, a sign of the ingenuity and hard work of the 'captains of industry'; but conspicuous and unrestrained *consumption*, which was necessary if there was to be a market for all these new products, was not such an obvious *good*. There was a tension between the virtue of self-control, undoubtedly modern, associated with order, rationality and discipline, and the necessity of desire, envy and impulsiveness, attributes of a more individualistic modernity. So middle-class women in Victorian society were assigned the role of saintly consumers. As saints they were expected to preserve family values; and one way to do this was to consume correctly: to buy clothes and upholstery, fabrics and furnishings which would enhance the family and its home. Correct consumption was women's *work*. It could be rationalised as another form of production; where, previously, women had produced the home by their own sewing and dressmaking, cooking and gardening, or at least by personally supervising their own staff in doing these things, now they did so by selecting and arranging appropriate commodities. Moreover, because of their presumed 'natural' morality, they could be trusted not to over-indulge, not to consume beyond their means.[62]

There was even a religious dimension to all this. The terms 'temples of commerce' and 'cathedrals of consumption' in some hands had a critical edge: had the worship of goods replaced the worship of God? But they also indicated the sacramental nature of shopping: 'By turning shoppers into "worshippers" in "cathedrals" of commerce, the store owners hoped to portray consumption as a moral act, a kind of religious duty of women.'[63] At least one commentator drew attention to the juxtaposition of Stewart's 'Iron Palace', 'erected...to the worship of dry-goods', and Grace Episcopalian Church, side-by-side at Broadway and 10th.[64] There was also an uneasy alliance between religion and shopping as stores highlighted the festivals of Christmas, Easter and Thanksgiving as special opportunities for consumption. William Leach concludes that 'The department stores, and the fashion industry that underlay them, penetrated into and contaminated the life of established religion, creating a paradoxical marriage between commodity capitalism and religious life that has persisted into our own time'.[65] We should also note the changing contents of diary entries among female New Yorkers. The 1848 diary of a dry-goods merchant's wife never mentions shopping but expresses her anxiety about her religious duty; in 1879, the diary of a minister's wife records her visits to Macy's, Stewart's, Altman's, Tiffany's and various bazaars on Ladies' Mile *alongside* prayer meetings and missionary work; and by the early twentieth century, for one upstate New Jersey woman, shopping in Manhattan was at least a weekly experience: her diary 'has virtually nothing in it but shopping dates and excursions'.[66]

Lead Us Not Into Temptation

In practice, not all women managed to exercise the self-control associated with their supposed natural morality. Especially prior to reform of law concerning married women's right to own property (and therefore to have any assets which could be forfeited to pay debts), numerous court cases on both sides of the Atlantic hinged on judges' interpretation of what constituted 'necessaries', goods that husbands were obliged to provide for their wives, and which wives could therefore reasonably purchase on credit, confident that their husbands would settle the bill. Were husbands liable for luxury items such as bonnets and sealskin jackets purchased on credit by their wives contrary to their instructions? Originally, department stores had insisted on purchases being made with cash. The refusal of credit had enabled them to charge lower prices than ordinary drapers' shops. But as stores competed with one another, and as they sought to attract customers who were either too poor to pay outright for expensive items such as pianos and suites of furniture or too rich to bother with carrying cash, so they reintroduced payment on credit or 'easy terms', with the consequence of more bad debts, mostly incurred by women for the simple reason that most shopping was undertaken by women.[67] For those women who did pay up, doubts might be cast on how they got the money: might they succumb to prostitution or gambling to pay for their shopping habits? For the poor, regular window-shopping was at best a distraction from their duties as industrious daughters and housewives, at worst a temptation leading them into shoplifting or prostitution.[68]

On Carrie Meeber's first visit to 'The Fair' – in search of work – she walked through the store, looking at the goods for sale and seeing 'nothing which she did not long to own'. Before long, she was back in the store with 'two soft, green, handsome ten-dollar bills' courtesy of her friend, Charles Drouet, hesitantly embarking on her new role as a kept woman.[69] In *The House of Mirth*, Lily Bart is already in debt to her dressmaker and jeweller when she also begins to accumulate gambling debts. The rich, and married, Gus Trenor lends her the money to settle her debts, turning her too, in Gus's expectations and in the eyes of other members of their set, into a kept woman.[70]

A generation later, in several short stories, the Toronto novelist Morley Callaghan was more interested in the dilemmas of being poor in an affluent society, the awkward relationships between men and women without money, and the more-than-economic consequences of falling prey to the temptations of fashion. In 'Day by Day', the young Mrs Winslow spends her day wandering through department stores and looking in shop windows. As a result she isn't home in time to prepare dinner for her husband. When she tells him there is no harm in window-shopping, he takes it as a personal attack, as if she is reminding him that they have no money to spend on real shopping, and then he jumps to the conclusion that she is late home because she was doing something more, and worse, than window-shopping. In 'The Red Hat', Frances stops every night on her way home from work to look in the hat-shop window where a particularly fetching red felt hat is displayed. Her husband has been out of work for four months, she knows she cannot afford the hat and that her husband will disapprove, but when she sees two more smartly dressed women enter the shop to try some of the hats on, she decides to follow, convincing herself that if she is careful, she can always wear the hat for an evening out and take it back to the shop the next day. She is intimidated by the 'deep-bosomed saleswoman, splendidly corseted, and wearing black silk' who realises that Frances cannot really afford the hat. Inevitably, she buys it and her husband loses his temper, tearing the hat as he snatches it off her head, so that she cannot even return it to the shop to get her money back.[71]

The most poignant of Callaghan's shopping stories dating from the mid-1920s concerns Lena Schwartz, thirty-two and plain, at last about to be married after a fifteen-year wait for her fiancé to get a better job. The day before she is due to leave Toronto to join him, she goes shopping in one of the city's department stores. She loves the romance of the store – gliding up the escalators, looking down over the counters and the white electric lighting globes. She plans to spend about $25 on a new dress, but the dresses she is shown fail to fulfil her fantasies; she wants 'something special'. So she steals a $75 dress (which proves not to suit her), is promptly apprehended, and spends the night in a police cell. Fortunately her fiancé is prepared to pay for the dress on her behalf, and the magistrate merely orders her to 'keep out of the department stores for a year', an injunction which might reasonably have been applied to all the fictional and real characters I have discussed over the last couple of pages.[72]

Advertising

Window- and counter-displays were one form of advertising, but advanced information of what to expect also circulated through the medium of newspaper and magazine advertisements, most of which were directed at women. In Britain, the abolition of advertising duty in 1853, newspaper stamp duty in 1855, and paper duty in 1861 all facilitated the growth of advertising. The most basic advertising concentrated on enumerating specific items for sale, much like today's full-page newspaper ads or inserts from supermarkets and chain stores illustrating their current bargains and special offers. Jones Brothers placed adverts in national newspapers like the *Daily Mirror* and the *Daily Mail* where, under a slogan announcing 'The Shopping Centre of North London', there were illustrations of the latest stock. On July 15, 1905, this included a 'becoming Wash Frock', 'Cream Ribbed Chemise Vests', an 'Extremely Smart White Mackintosh "exact to sketch"', and many other items, all clearly priced, including the cost of postage for those who preferred to shop by mail order. A more elaborate form of advertising, with much higher quality artwork, was the catalogue produced to show off new season fashions. Jones Brothers' 1914 Spring/Summer catalogue pandered to its readers' assumed enthusiasm for things continental, noting the popular colours being worn in Paris and the variety of French styles on offer, and reporting that the millinery manageress had recently returned from Paris 'where she has been busy noting the spring styles'. Women's costumes were given French names, 'Lucrèce', 'Franchette', 'Cretienne', 'Cyprien', 'Angelique' as well as the more homely 'Nellie' and 'Irene'. Other French affectations in the catalogue were the description of one outfit as 'absolutely the *dernier cri*' and a reference to a new hat's 'floral *cache-peigne*'. The store's appeal to a well-off clientele was also evident in references to 'Lady motorists' and 'the speciality of the motor department . . . smart new under-coats of leather in colors to match any car'. Whereas adverts in the *Daily Mirror* referred to 'colours', burgeoning Americanisation was reflected in the use of 'color' in the more upmarket (and slightly later in date) catalogue. By the mid-1920s more outfits were advertised with American names, such as 'Fay', 'Lena' and 'Letty'.[73]

Stores also advertised themselves by distributing flyers, postcards and balloons. The Brixton Bon Marché's first Christmas bazaar saw the store decorated in 'the latest Parisian style' and the distribution of 50,000 balloons. Zola describes the 'free gift of a balloon to each customer' at the opening of the Bonheur des Dames's new premises as 'a stroke of genius: they were red balloons, made of fine Indian rubber and with the name of the shop written on them in big letters; when held on the end of a string they travelled through the air, parading a living advertisement through the streets!' And Beatrice French's South London Fashionable Dress Supply Association was advertised 'through the medium of hand-bills, leaflets, nicely printed little pamphlets, gorgeously designed placards', while its owner herself was 'attired as a walking advertisement'.[74]

Much of this publicity advertised the stores rather than the goods they sold. Beginning in 1886, three years after the opening of new premises, newspaper advertising for Eaton's Toronto store changed from informing readers of prices to extolling the virtues of the store, printed to look more like ordinary news articles than advertisements.[75] But the most lavish – and most fully documented – advertising campaign was undoubtedly that marking the opening of Selfridge's in 1909. One illustration depicted 'London receiving her newest institution' with the metropolis cast in the role of an idealised woman – in Rappaport's words 'a statuesque goddess . . . no ordinary British matron, but rather a combination of Nike and her secularized version, Fame' – wearing the arms of the city as a necklace and a generic city skyline as her headband. In her hands she held a model of the store, 'a natural object for her protective regard'.[76] Another illustration, 'The Dedication of a Great House', had Selfridge himself on bended knee presenting the store as an offering to woman, who was seated royally two steps above him (Figure 11.6). Both advertisements emphasised that Selfridge's was 'Dedicated to Woman's Service', and the ritualistic nature of the presentation and the receipt of the gift confirmed its pseudo-religious character. Although advertisements also described the store as 'devoted to the Children's needs' and 'the Man's Best Buying Place', the imagery suggested that the success of the store lay firmly in women's hands.

Leach observes that in modern economies commodities 'circulate freely and have no binding power' with no commitment between buyer and seller beyond a financial transaction. Yet good business practice also involves the cultivation of customer loyalty – to the place of purchase as much as to the brand name. So department stores 'attempted to endow the goods with transformative messages'.[77] Commodities acquired new meanings through their association with particular stores, and the same commodity was imbued with different meanings dependent on where it had been bought. Customers attempted to construct new identities for themselves, based not only on what they wore or what they owned, but also on where they did their shopping. Along with 'branded' goods went the 'brand' – the mix of ingredients and the identity they implied – associated with different places of purchase. Hence the concern of every store proprietor – from the sober, teetotal Methodist Timothy Eaton to the flamboyant, cosmopolitan Gordon Selfridge – to emphasise the identity of his *(sic)* store.

Feminist or feminised?

However 'feminised' the department store, as a place numerically dominated by women employees and women shoppers, it was still essentially a male-run institution. For Zola's Mouret, his 'sole passion was the conquest of Woman', an elision of erotics and economics. Blomley argues that 'the geographies of the store [*Bonheur des Dames*] are powerfully masculine'. Domosh concludes that gender relations were resituated but not fundamentally changed: 'it seems likely that women's participation in the new public life of the city helped to maintain the existing social order'.[78]

Yet there were exceptions to this affirmation of a patriarchal social order, in which separate spheres had merely been relocated to accommodate all the other spatial changes in residence, work and leisure associated with urban expansion, suburbanisation, segregation and specialisation. The department store was not just a space in which women could continue to perform domestic roles, an extension of the domestic into downtown. As well as the increasing presence of women in the middle ranks of stores' occupational hierarchies, as buyers and department managers, they were also significant as investors. Rappaport reports the disclosure by the *Financial News*

Figure 11.6. 'Selfridge's: The Dedication of a Great House'. Reproduced by permission of Selfridges and the History of Advertising Trust.

in April 1909 that 'between 12 and 15 percent of all the shareholders in the leading drapery and furnishing establishments were women'. Almost half of private investors in Selfridge's were women.[79] The fact that many of them were women of very modest socio-economic status – domestic servants, teachers, nurses – can be read in at least two ways. It demonstrates the incorporation of countless ordinary people into the project of corporate capitalism, paralleling the rise of a property-owning democracy of homeowners that I charted in an earlier chapter; but should they be interpreted as 'pawns' in the same way that the extension of homeownership was read by Marxist historians as 'lawns for pawns'? The modest assets of most female investors mean that even if they constituted a large proportion of investors, they accounted for only a small proportion of investment.

Department stores' support for women's suffrage provided another challenge to the existing order. On the one hand, the new consumption culture caused a rethink of the aims of the women's movement; on the other, department stores had to pay attention to the movement's demands if they were not to be the subject of boycotts or window-smashing protests. Leach refers to 'the clear merger of feminism, marked by a secular, internationalist perspective, with the cosmopolitan, heterogeneous culture of consumption' in early twentieth-century America, and Rapppaport notes the convergence of 'women's emancipation and consumer pleasures' in Edwardian London.[80]

Thirdly, there is the empirical point that men were also consumers, to a greater extent than journalists and copywriters were prepared to acknowledge. Male departments might be positioned near the entrance to make it as easy as possible for men to use the store, as they were at Eaton's in the 1890s; or there might be a completely separate 'men's shop'.[81] In his discussion of 'the hidden consumer', Christopher Breward focuses principally on tailors and outfitters that provided specialist services for male shoppers. In *The Practical Retail Draper* (1912), Fred Burgess advised outfitters that business would increase 'when men's outfitting is kept quite separate, especially when men are not required to pass through women's departments to reach the men's department'; but department stores, such as Arding & Hobbs (in Clapham, south London) and Marshall & Snelgrove (Oxford Street) also ensured that men's departments were strategically located on ground-floor corners. Breward concludes that this 'discreet, though central, placing of menswear provision' may be read 'as an attempt to retain the integrity of a specific masculine mode of consumption within the broader sphere of a consumer activity more usually defined as feminine'.[82]

Department stores and intra-urban communications

I have focused on the department store as a 'cathedral of consumption', but stores were also associated with distribution, through burgeoning mail-order departments, and manufacturing, through the production of brand-name goods, especially ready-to-wear clothing. In some cases – including the Army & Navy Stores in London, discussed in Chapter 5, and Eaton's in Toronto and Derry & Toms in London, discussed earlier in this chapter – workshops and warehouses were situated on back streets adjacent to retail stores. In others, manufacturing lofts and mail-order warehouses were located in less central districts where rents and land values were lower. In Toronto, Eaton's rivals, Simpson's, erected a new mail-order warehouse in 1916 on Mutual Street, a few blocks east of the CBD. Harrod's Furniture Depository was located beside the Thames at Barnes in south-west London; and Whiteley's owned two farms and a food processing factory at Hanworth, twelve miles south-west of the Bayswater store.[83]

Like office blocks, department stores depended on improved intra-urban communications. Selfridge's advertised its location over the 'tuppenny tube' – the Central London Electric Railway, now the Central Line. More generally, advertising for the London Underground emphasised the attractions of the system for access to shops and theatres. One category of poster featured the convenience of the underground for visiting winter or summer sales or for Christmas shopping; another promoted off-peak travel, advising shoppers to 'Shop Between Ten & Four: The Quiet Hours'. The Central London Railway even offered special season tickets for women passengers during the January sales. Illustrations were often accompanied by verses, sometimes doggerel but often invoking literary classics. 'Winter's Discontent Made Glorious' (1909) depicted an underground train about to enter a tunnel to escape from a heavy rainstorm. Through the windows of the train we can see scenes from the theatre, a fashionable restaurant and a West End store. 'The Sales' (1930) featured a quotation from Boswell's *Life of Johnson* – 'And there is no place where economy can be so well practised as in London: more can be had here for the money, even by ladies, than anywhere else' – beneath an illustration of a mainly female crowd emerging from an underground station beside plate-glass windows full of brightly patterned and artfully displayed 'Fabrics'. Even in public transport advertising, therefore, there was an attempt to align commerce with culture, as well as to stress the pleasurable, relaxing character of shopping, at least for the knowledgeable shopper who avoids the rush-hour and doesn't wait until the last minute to do her Christmas shopping.[84]

But other forms of communications were also important, especially the electric telegraph and, later, the telephone. For offices, they allowed connections between businesses; for department stores, they facilitated the decentralisation of functions such as warehousing, mail-order and factories, which could be located on the fringe of the city, or at least on cheaper land outside the centre, and yet remain in close contact with the sales floor.

Conclusions

I began the previous chapter by laying out a modernist argument about the increasing differentiation of City and West End, finance and consumption, and about the growing presence of women both in employment in offices and stores and as consumers in public space, apparently undermining a rigid early to mid nineteenth-century ideology of separate spheres. But this does not imply a total separation of different functions, nor the complete dismantling of separate spheres. There *was* increasing geographical segregation of the worlds of finance and consumption, *but*, firstly, the former was still associated with a material world of real commodities being imported, stored in warehouses, traded and distributed. Secondly, most office workers were not employed in banking and insurance, but in commercial businesses, many of which located outside of the City of London or Lower Manhattan. Plenty of offices were located in the West End or in Midtown Manhattan. The workforce of a store like Eaton's included manufacturing operatives, typists and filing clerks as well as sales assistants. Thirdly, workers in the City or on Wall Street needed services, too; if not the grandest department stores, they required cafes, convenience stores, men's and women's outfitters. Rather than conceive of a functional break between one area and another, we need to imagine different *combinations of functions* in each part of the modern city.

The department store, while maintaining its geographical distinctiveness in West End or midtown and middle-class suburban or uptown locations, deliberately blurred the functional differentiation of modern cities. Shopping was both work and leisure; stores were also museums and exhibitions and theatres and clubs and restaurants. Likewise, skyscraper offices contained a range of public retail and catering services at ground level. Zoning may have implied 'a place for everything and everything in its place' but 'everything' was shorthand for 'every combinations of functions', not 'every separate thing'. Nonetheless, the one distinction that seemed to be sacrosanct was that between 'home' and 'not-home'. Apart from artists and writers, whose homes incorporated studios and studies, few middle-class city dwellers worked (in the sense of paid, non-domestic employment) at home. Department stores may have reproduced 'ideal homes' in room settings and flat displays showing how to combine the furniture, fabrics and china they sold, and they may have created outliers of the domestic sphere within public space, but they were only inhabited during store hours.

We also need to revisit debates about differences between Britain and North America, and about the chronology of modernity. Zigzagging my way between London, Toronto, New York and occasionally Chicago, I have implied the fundamental similarities between these cities. At different times, the current of influence flows more strongly in one direction than the other – from Britain to America in the nineteenth century, from America to Britain in the 1900s and especially the 1920s. Toronto shifts from being a British city on North American soil to an American city in the British Empire. Stores in late nineteenth-century New York were contained in more modern structures than stores in London because the relentless migration of population uptown required businesses to relocate at frequent intervals to keep in touch with their clientele. But they were less obviously different in their business practices. By comparison with Selfridge's, A. T. Stewart's in the 1860s and even Eaton's in the 1890s were really just inflated dry-goods stores, whose customers were, mostly, sober-minded Victorian housewives. However, it was in Selfridge's interests to exaggerate the differences between American and British retailing in the 1900s, to imply that his store was truly revolutionary. The likelihood is that most American stores were less innovative than they were portrayed, and less 'modern' in promoting cosmopolitan or unconventional values and lifestyles, while most British stores were not quite as old-fashioned as Selfridge implied.

From the middle until the end of the nineteenth century, stores could be labelled 'department stores' in that they comprised multiple departments, spatially and financially distinct, but most of the departments were still concerned with fabrics or some aspect of female dress, and most draper-proprietors did not explicitly encourage irresponsible consumerism. For the most part, the expansion of their businesses depended upon the expansion and increasing affluence of the middle classes. Shopping was women's domestic *work*. The fact that some women spent beyond their means, succumbed to shoplifting, or became so enamoured with shopping as to neglect their domestic and religious duties, was blamed on store-owners by moralists who clung to the idea of the innate goodness of woman. By the 1890s and 1900s leisure was no longer considered sinful and shopping could be promoted as leisure without much fear of moral condemnation. The fact that an increasing proportion of potential consumers now lived in suburbs beyond walking-distance of shops meant that non-food shopping was no longer a matter of 'popping out' to shop on a daily basis, maybe visiting a different specialist shop each day – yesterday the milliner, today the dressmaker, tomorrow the soft furnishing store. Instead, shopping became an expedition, a whole-day excursion, requiring the provision of toilets and cafes, and encouraging store-owners to provide as much as possible under one roof. By the 1920s, increasing secularisation and the fluidity of social mobility meant that shopping had become firmly established as a source of individual identity, and the logic of advanced capitalism, the paradox of 'built-in obsolescence' for 'consumer durables' and the necessity of promoting ever-changing fashions in the mass market, also required a modernist built environment which could comfortably accommodate the vagaries of changing styles.

Vital to all these developments were the communications articulating the different sites of modernity that I have discussed in this and the preceding chapters and, indeed, many related sites – warehouses, workshops, factories, markets, restaurants, bars, museums, theatres, music-halls, picture houses, government buildings, docks, railway termini, police stations, fire stations, waterworks, gasworks, and many more – that I have not addressed in detail. So it is to the connections between sites, the idea of the 'networked city' that I turn in my final chapter.

12

Networked cities

I began this book with the stories of three bridges spanning physical barriers to urban development. But the modern city was one in which social and financial divides were often more difficult to bridge. Social segregation and land-use specialisation depended on communications linking home and work, office, warehouse and store, home and shops or places of entertainment. The viability of big cities made up of distinctive areas of wealth and poverty also involved citywide governments which facilitated the transfer of resources – from West End to East End, from suburbs to inner cities, from rich to poor. Hence the creation of the London County Council and of Greater New York, and the annexation of suburban districts into the City of Toronto. Hence, unsurprisingly, the resistance of rich, low-tax suburbs to annexation or amalgamation. More practically, the growth of cities required other forms of interconnection – water pipes and sewers, gas mains and electricity grids.

This chapter will look at three networks of connections: the building of sewers; the creation of telegraph and telephone networks; and the development of intra-urban railway systems, and especially the elevated railway in New York. Each of these networks functioned both literally and symbolically. An efficient sewage disposal system implied a city that was also morally cleansed, where the subterranean no longer threatened civilisation in contrast to images where seeds of revolution and catastrophe were nurtured underground. Telegraph and telephone wires were evidence of a highly charged, 'electric' atmosphere; they were the nerves of the city, indicative of its sensitivity to react instantaneously to new stimuli. The elevated railway, threading its way effortlessly between buildings, signified the efficiency of circulation long after the real circulation was mostly undertaken by subway or automobile.

In each case, new networks reinforced existing patterns of land use and residential segregation. The areas which were first connected to main sewers included relatively prosperous streets where sewerage constituted an investment in the future value of property; streets which continued to rely on cesspits were mostly those where rack-renting property owners and house farmers declined to invest in improvements. The first telephone exchanges were established in central business districts and in upmarket residential areas where downtown businessmen had their homes. Streetcars and railways initially served middle-class suburbs, thereby reinforcing their advantage, and the level of rents, relative to places farther from public transport routes. Elevated railways and subways connected suburbs and downtown, leapfrogging over or burrowing under poorer inner-city districts.

But networks also threatened the discomforts of too intimate a connection between rich and poor. Passengers of different social classes and ethnicities rubbed up against one another on one-class electric trams and subway trains. The thrill of transgression enjoyed by Nancy Lord or Elizabeth Dalloway on a London bus was felt more anxiously by less adventurous passengers, especially at night or underground. Sewers accommodated a rich stew, promiscuously and indiscriminately mixing waste products of rich and poor alike. It was feared they might spread disease at the same time as they appeared to cleanse the city. Messages between male, middle-class merchants, bankers and brokers depended on the good offices of female, working-class switchboard operators and occasionally succumbed to the diversions of crossed or party lines. There were risks as well as opportunities in a networked city.

I should emphasise that my concern is with the networking rather than the technology per se. Harold Platt notes of Chicago, where the 1893 World Fair had demonstrated the potential for an electric city, that it took another two decades before the city could boast a networked system of electricity supply.[1] Until the mid-1890s, central power stations comprised numerous identical, small-scale generators; direct current could be transmitted only over short distances, no more than half a mile from the generating station, while alternating current could not yet be applied to the principal potential user, the streetcar. Consequently, many of the earliest commercial users, such as hotels, theatres and office buildings, installed their own generators rather than rely on a central supply. The only residential users – in luxury apartment buildings or elite suburbs – also relied on their own private generators. In no sense did this pattern of supply and usage constitute a network. The same was true of London where an early, modest attempt at central generation, in Holborn, lasted only four years, and some lighting installations, such as that along the Victoria Embankment, reverted from electricity to gas during the 1880s. It was not until 1894 that even as limited an area as the City of London was supplied by a single electricity company, operating through two generating stations.[2]

What was true of electricity in the 1890s had been true of waste disposal earlier in the century. 'Sewer drains' to deal with storm run off or to drain areas of standing water in order to prevent miasmas were rarely connected to form a *system* of sewers and, in American cities, they were usually privately owned, funded by those well-off residents and property owners who directly benefited. To make a network that extended across both public and private property and connected everybody depended on a degree of municipal intervention that contradicted the prevailing belief in liberal individualism.[3] Matthew Gandy notes of New York's first great public network, the supply of water through the Croton Aqueduct, that 'almost all the opposition to the new water system came from uptown residents and property owners whose wells were not yet polluted', individuals who saw no immediate personal benefit to themselves.[4] Yet the logic of governmentality was that improvements in sanitation – water supply and sewerage, as well as regulation of sanitary behaviour, such as urination and spitting in public places – and in lighting would produce self-disciplined citizens whose behaviour would benefit the civic economy. Inhabitants who experienced well-lit schools, stores and public spaces would prioritise improvements in the lighting of their own homes; individuals who were shielded from 'natural' processes in the public city would expect an equal prurience in their domestic ablutions.[5]

Networks, as opposed to local improvements, required either highly capitalised private corporations or public ownership, often supported by the issue of municipal bonds. Most public utilities – water, gas, electricity – were first supplied by private companies. Likewise, urban transport and telecommunications generally started out as private sector operations. But during the late nineteenth or early twentieth centuries many utility companies were taken into public ownership – the reverse of the process that has characterised recent decades when buses, railways, telephone services and the supply of water, gas and electricity have all been privatised and deregulated. Maureen Ogle observed that in great cities, like New York, it was easier for citizens to accept increasing government involvement. Population growth had 'all but destroyed local ground water supplies' and commerce and industry stood to benefit from better public services. In smaller cities there was more resistance to municipal ownership.[6] In 1880, about 49 per cent of American city waterworks were publicly owned; by 1924 the proportion had increased to 70 per cent; but of the 50 largest American cities, 41 had public waterworks as early as 1897.[7] London's water supply remained in the control of private companies throughout the nineteenth century, despite frequent recommendations by central and local government commissions in favour of creating a public water authority. There was, however, increasing regulation of the city's eight private water companies and in 1903 the Metropolitan Water Board was at last created to take them over. By 1914, two-thirds of Britain's population received water from a publicly owned waterworks.[8]

The rationale for public ownership was not simple. The term 'municipal socialism' has often been used to describe the activities of councils like the London County Council and Glasgow Corporation in taking control of a whole range of activities at the end of the nineteenth century. But as Philip Waller has argued, 'If there was a distinct ideology about it, it was rather municipal capitalism than municipal socialism'. It was 'in the nature of social investment capital to maximize the product of private enterprise',[9] similar to more recent investments in improving infrastructure, so-called 'pump priming', which is claimed to benefit the efficiency and profitability of (and, therefore, the tax revenue to be derived from) private businesses. American businessmen, too, accepted that at least some public control was necessary, not to redistribute resources and costs between rich and poor, but to provide the infrastructure for continuing economic growth.

In a British context, John Kellett drew a threefold distinction between 'municipal socialism', 'municipal enterprise' and 'municipal trading'.[10] Municipal socialism involved subsidies, for socially desirable ends, benefiting some groups or areas more than others, as in the provision of subsidised council housing. One of the key arguments for the creation of metropolitan government, the ability to redistribute income from rich to poor, implied redistribution from rich areas to poor areas. In London in the 1880s, West End vestries resisted the creation of the LCC while East End vestries supported the idea. London-wide government meant that taxes raised in the West End could be spent in the East End, or that the problems of the East End, or of inner London, could be solved, not in situ, but by building in West End districts, or in outer London. It meant suburban districts recognising their responsibility for many of the costs incurred in central districts, such as congestion, pollution and waste disposal charges.

Municipal enterprise typically involved services that were unattractive to private enterprise, but from which everybody benefited – sewers, asylums, infectious disease hospitals, law and order, parks, public libraries. Finally, municipal trading included activities where councils behaved like private corporations, competing with and out-performing private enterprise, for example in the supply of gas or electricity. Often, the rationale was that the most efficient system of supply was a monopoly – it was absurd to have competing gas mains laid down the same street – and if the public was to be protected from private exploitation of monopoly power, it was preferable for the monopoly enterprise to be in public control.

Sewers

In contrast to the money to be made out of collecting 'nightsoil', emptying private cesspits and selling the contents to suburban market gardeners, there was less scope to make profits out of sewer systems. The costs of installing and maintaining sewers could rarely be recouped by suburban sewage farms. Sewers became a local government responsibility. In London, the first stage in the establishment of citywide government was the creation of the Metropolitan Commission of Sewers (1847), and its failure prompted the Metropolis Management Act (1855), setting up the Metropolitan Board of Works, one of whose earliest actions was to appoint Joseph Bazalgette to design a sewer network with the capacity to cope with the increasing waste generated by a population increasing not only in numbers but also in affluence and thereby in effluence.[11]

When flush toilets were first introduced, it was illegal to connect them to public sewers intended primarily as conduits for rainwater. But cesspits, designed for a limited supply of solid waste, could not cope with the increasing volumes of flushed water and faeces. As they overflowed, so they polluted water supplies drawn from nearby wells.[12] From 1815, householders were permitted to connect their cesspools and water closets to public sewers, and from 1847 they were obliged to do so, but all this achieved was overflowing sewers and waste discharged straight into the Thames, often close to sites of extraction of drinking-water. Successive cholera epidemics and the 'Great Stink' of 1858, when the stench from the Thames caused the adjournment of Parliament, bore testimony to the consequences. Bazalgette's solution was a series of intercepting sewers running roughly parallel to the river, diverting waste out of existing sewers to enter the Thames at outfall stations sufficiently far downstream that the sewage would not be carried back into the city by incoming tides. Given the gradualness of the river's fall through London, sewers with the same lack of gradient would have been prone to solid waste separating out as sediment on sewer bottoms. Hence the need to raise the level of the sewers at successive pumping stations across London, increasing the gradient of the downstream sewers. Between 1858 and 1875, 82 miles of intercepting sewers, 1100 miles of subsidiary sewers and four pumping stations were completed.

A notable feature of some sewer maps depicting the new network was their annotation with the time that it was estimated to take sewage to flow from west to east

across the capital: nine hours from Hammersmith to Barking, six and a half hours
from Chelsea, just over four hours from the City of London, two hours from Abbey
Mills (Figure 12.1).[13] Congestion underground was just as threatening to the health of
the city as the traffic delays above ground, so graphically portrayed by Gustave Doré
and which gave rise to the cutting of new streets enumerated in Chapter 5. In aggregate, middle-class sewage from the West End was being joined on its journey east
by working-class waste from the East End. But London's class geography was not so
neat as to exclude cases of working-class sewage passing beneath middle-class areas,
a violation that, it was feared, would undermine the safety of the well-to-do. In 1862,
the journalist John Hollingshead followed up his exposure of *Ragged London* with
an exploration of *Underground London*, including a 'saunter' through the sewers of
the West End. From under Berkeley Square, he noted that 'there was nothing . . . in
the quality of our black flood, to tell us that we were so near the abodes of the blest'.
A little farther on, the same black flood passed beneath Buckingham Palace where
Hollingshead patriotically sang the National Anthem.[14]

The implication that even the royal family might be threatened by lesser folks'
sewage assumed a more sinister form when, in 1871, the Prince of Wales (the future
Edward VII) contracted typhoid, his illness widely attributed to breathing in sewer
gas, generated by waste accumulating in the sewers, which escaped up the drains
designed to carry liquid waste in the opposite direction.[15] It seemed that the rich,
with indoor plumbing, were at greater risk than the poor, whose water closets and
waste pipes were mostly outdoors. And women, confined to the supposed safety of
the home, seemed to be more at risk than men who went out into the fresh air of the
streets on their way to and from work. The underworld of sewers was perceived as
threatening the sanctity of the private home.

Privacy was also undermined by the complexity of the sewer network. Cesspools
had been located under backyards; they were the responsibility of the landlord or
householder, part of a closed system which entailed no outside intervention. Sewers,
like gas and electricity, involved the intrusion of an external institution into the private
home. They enforced connections between public and private space, the surrender of
local control. A *Punch* cartoon depicted a 'fastidious host' entertaining an 'inquisitive
guest' to dinner. Over and across the dinner table winds a network of pipes. When
the guest inquires what they are for, his host replies: 'O, it's the *drains*! I like to have
'em where I can look after 'em myself.'[16]

The fear of sewers built upon and contributed to an apocalyptic language of underworld that goes back to religious images of the descent into hell and forward through
H. G. Wells's *The Time Machine* and Fritz Lang's *Metropolis* to more recent films set
in the Paris, London and New York subway systems, whether human dystopias or stories involving the disturbance of long forgotten 'natural' monsters from their subterranean habitats.[17] It is no coincidence that John Martin, the early nineteenth-century
artist whose massive canvases included 'Belshazzar's Feast', 'The Fall of Babylon'
and 'The Last Judgement', was also an early advocate for sewers and embanking
the Thames. Richard Humphreys refers to his 'unique apocalyptic imagination that
eventually inspired early epic cinema sets' and Stuart Oliver to his 'belief in manure
as excrement-redeemed'.[18]

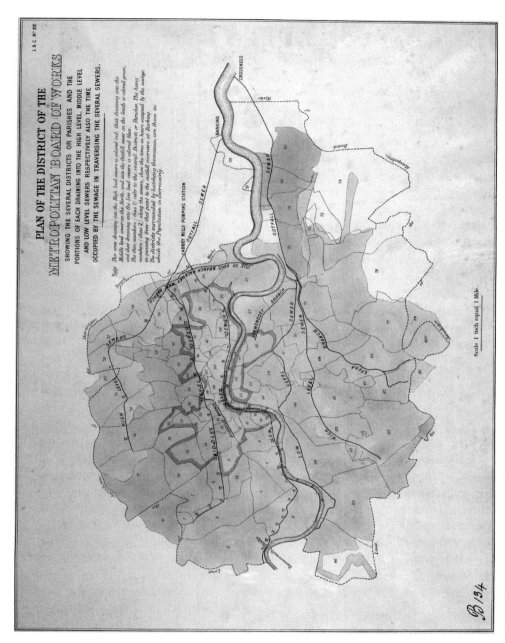

Figure 12.1. Plan of the District of the Metropolitan Board of Works: Sewer Map of London (c.1883). Museum of London L323/4. Reproduced by permission of Thames Water. Note in particular the annotation of sewers north of the Thames showing the time in hours for sewage to reach the outfall at Barking.

Hollingshead alluded to visions of London's sewers as 'volcanoes of filth; gorged veins of putridity; ready to explode at any moment in a whirlwind of foul gas, and poison all those whom they fail to smother'.[19] The year that Hollingshead published these words – 1862 – also witnessed the bursting of the Fleet Sewer, disturbed by the excavations for another venture underground – the building of London's first underground railway. A contemporary local historian sensationalised the sewer's collapse as if it was an uncontrollable apocalyptic disaster: the earth shook 'as if under the influence of an earthquake'; immense piers of brickwork took on a life of their own, 'slowly moving from the bottom', and finally a 'dark foetid liquid covered all, and rolled its way towards the mouth of the tunnel, tearing down, as it went, all obstructions, and snapping like straws the strongest piles of massive timber'.[20] *The Times* noted two additional problems: at high tide, water from the Thames flowed back up the sewer causing flooding as far up the railway tunnel as King's Cross; and the force of water also destroyed gas mains under several streets, prompting fears of either an explosion or 'the alternative of midnight darkness for several hours throughout the densely populated district'.[21]

The interdependence of different networks – in this case sewers, railways and gas pipes – is also observed by Christopher Otter in his discussion of the positive and negative uses of technology in nineteenth-century London. Otter contrasts 'negative' technologies, such as new forms of sanitation, which excluded what were now deemed unwholesome practices, including defecating and spitting in public, the noise and stench of muddy streets, and the sight of blood in slaughterhouses and meat markets, with 'positive' technologies, such as electric lighting, intended 'to stimulate and seduce the senses, to maximize human ocular or aural capacities'.[22] But he also emphasises their interdependence: new, closely regulated abattoirs had to be close to railways and waterways, and they should be bathed in electric light to demonstrate their cleanliness.

The dangers of sewers to public health could be countered privately by installing drain traps, re-establishing the boundary between public and private, 'a private sphere freed from the engulfing, alienating mechanisms of the modern city'.[23] But they could also be minimised by careful design of public sewer networks. Bazalgette emphasised the need for a steady fall – of at least two feet per mile – to keep the sewage flowing and prevent the build-up of sewer gas, while an American sanitary engineer, George E. Waring, Jr, proposed separating storm-water sewers from household waste sewers.[24] With 'combined sewers' the movement of household waste into the main sewers might be delayed every time there was heavy rain which would pour into the sewers causing waste in the tributary drains to back up. With 'separate sewers' human faeces would always reach the public sewers rapidly, still 'fresh', while storm water was allowed to run off, either through drains reserved only for rainwater or in gutters at the side of the road. In practice, while separate sewers were adopted by many small American cities, almost all large cities, starting with Brooklyn and Chicago in the late 1850s, opted for combined sewers. In cities with heavy traffic, all of it still horse-drawn, run-off from the streets was as much polluted – with animal excrement – as household sewage. There was little point in trying to separate them.

The connection of local sewers onto a city system might depend on local property owners, whether they were prepared to petition city authorities to be connected, and to pay the improvement rate the council would charge. Resident owners, or responsible absentee landlords, would see this as money well spent, not only because it improved public health but also because it would enhance property values. In the case of Toronto, Catherine Brace has shown how the sewer network expanded after 1859, as residents petitioned the city council to provide sewers under their streets.[25]

Brace contrasts this steady expansion of the local sewer network with the enormous problems the city council encountered when they proposed raising taxes to build a trunk sewer. This was envisaged as Toronto's version of Bazalgette's intercepting sewers. Sewage was being discharged into Lake Ontario from outfalls downtown, where the presence of Toronto Island only a few hundred yards offshore acted as a barrier, preventing the rapid dissipation of waste products into the body of the lake. But although the council first raised the matter in the 1870s, it took until 1908 before the city's taxpayers approved a by-law raising money to pay for intercepting sewers and a sewage disposal plant. Evidently, the good of the city as a whole was too remote or too abstract a good to warrant expenditure. Taxpayers could see the need for a sewer on their street, but they were less worried about what happened to the sewage once it had left their neighbourhood. Out of scent, out of mind.

I suggested at the outset that patterns of service provision tended to reinforce existing inequalities. However, there were exceptions to the rule. In New York, some of the wealthiest householders saw no advantage in subscribing to either new water supplies or new sewerage systems, since they had already made satisfactory private arrangements for both water supply and waste disposal. When the Croton Aqueduct was opened, a new law permitted householders to flush their waste into the city sewers, but only if they also subscribed to the new water supply. Since many wealthy residents still had their own water supply from wells, and did not want to pay for Croton water, they were denied access to the sewers.[26] Of course, like the Londoners whose views were explored by Michelle Allen, they may have preferred to keep control of their own waste, at least until it was evident that their overflowing cesspools were polluting their own water supply. Nonetheless, they had to learn that citizen autonomy and the culture of privatism came at a cost: 'The inevitable tension between the public and private evident in public provision for intimate, private functions went right to the heart of liberal governmentality.'[27]

New York sewerage was improved during the 1850s, strongly influenced first by the ongoing sanitary debate in Britain, and subsequently by Bazalgette's plans for intercepting sewers. Yet it was estimated in the late 1850s that three-quarters of the city's streets still lacked any sewers. Melosi argues that the wealthiest areas were not always the first to obtain new sewers because their drainage problems were not perceived as warranting them, but a more sceptical interpretation would follow Gandy's argument about the extension of water supply which, he suggests, was firmly economic in motivation, not socially redistributive: 'If impoverished Irish and German wards had received water before the wealthy residents of the Upper West Side, this was simply an anomalous outcome of the speed with which new pipes were constructed under the more densely populated parts of lower Manhattan.'[28] Even when the whole city had been connected to a sewerage network, the sewers discharged straight into New York Harbour and it was not until 1937 that the first sewage treatment plant opened.[29]

Telegraphy and telephony

If the class relations inherent in sewer systems were ambiguous, the same could not be said about the telegraph and the telephone, whose use was more clearly concentrated among the elite and business classes. And if innovations in sewerage spread from Britain to America, they flowed in the opposite direction in the case of telephony. The electric telegraph had been invented by Samuel Morse in 1837, but it was first used commercially in 1844. On both sides of the Atlantic, private telegraph companies initially focused on inter-urban links, transmitting information of a factual and financial nature, especially commodity and stock market prices. Commodity exchanges in major American cities fixed prices across extensive hinterlands, and Wall Street was setting prices for the securities market all over the United States by the 1860s. In effect, the telegraph facilitated a speeding-up in the circulation of capital, much as David Harvey discussed in his essays on the urbanisation of capital.[30]

However, once a message arrived at a city telegraph office, it had to be decoded and then distributed to individual brokers and agents by messenger boys; local trans-mission of information took longer and cost more than long-distance transmission. One solution to this problem lay in the production of specialist devices for displaying and printing out financial information: ticker-tape and telex machines, for example. Companies set up their own private telegraph lines, linking factory to warehouse to shop to counting house. Downtown department stores could check instantly on the availability of stock in their warehouses. In theory, therefore, the telegraph facilitated the decentralisation of production and warehousing, another stage in the geograph-ical separation of different land uses within cities.

District telegraph companies also started to cultivate residential as well as com-mercial clients. Usage was still primarily commercial, for example allowing business-men to send messages between home and office, but in this way an organisational framework was created which facilitated the rapid adoption of the telephone after its invention in 1876.

Joel Tarr also discusses the municipal uses of the telegraph – to assist fire brigades in fire-fighting and police forces in riot-fighting. Writing in 1855, William Channing, a Boston doctor, likened the municipal telegraph to the human nervous system:

> Its function is . . . to organize a single city or town so as to bring every subordinate part into relation with its centre of government and direction. Its purpose is to multiply points of communication, to cover the surface of the municipal body as thickly . . . with telegraphic signalizing points as the surface of the human body is covered with nervous extremities or papillae, the whole being intelligently connected into a system by which the municipal body shall understand itself in every part . . . [31]

The same imagery linking the nervous system to telegraphy and, by now, telephony, is evident seventy-five years later in Nevinson's painting of London's Fleet Street, 'Amongst the Nerves of the World' (1930), discussed in Chapter 6 (Figure 6.7).

Responding to Channing's vision, first Boston and by 1880 more than a hundred American cities had established fire-alarm telegraph systems, connecting district fire stations to a central station and to alarm boxes across their cities. In a similar way, police telegraph systems linked police stations to one another. They were not in contact with individual police officers on their beat, nor did they allow the public to contact the police, so the systems were not used to fight particular crimes. They were more useful in moving reserve officers around the city from one district to another in anticipation of crime or disorder. Fighting disorder was equivalent to fighting fire. But when the system was extended in the 1880s to encompass policemen on the beat, it involved the telephone rather than the telegraph.[32]

Legally and functionally, the telephone was regarded as a superior telegraph. Although there were some novelty uses of the telephone as a means of entertainment, transmitting concerts and sermons from city-centre halls and churches to listeners sitting in the comfort of their own homes, or as a source of factual information (nineteenth-century forerunners of more recent teletext and web subscription services), its primary use was, as the telegraph had been, as an aid to business and government. In London, the first two exchanges, opened in 1879 by different private companies, were both in the City. In Britain, where the Post Office had monopoly rights to collect and distribute mail and thereby had acquired control of telegraph services in 1870, it was soon established that a telephone conversation was equivalent to an exchange of letters or telegrams and therefore the Post Office could impose conditions on telephone companies. Perhaps as a result of this central regulation, use of the telephone spread much more slowly in Britain than in North America. The Post Office refused to co-operate with the National Telephone Company, the principal private company, denying them rights to lay wires under public streets or to connect their customers with users of the Post Office's own telephone service. But there were other reasons for the sluggish adoption of the innovation in Britain: the problems of obtaining powers of 'wayleave' (the right to erect poles on and stretch wires across other people's land) and the dislike of overhead wires, especially in historic city centres, necessitating the burying of wires underground on densely built-up streets where there was already a maze of water pipes, gas pipes and sewers. Eventually, government resolved to buy out the NTC when its 31-year lease expired in 1912.[33] But by then, Britain was far behind America in telephone usage. In 1882, London had only 1600 subscribers compared to 4060 in New York and 10325 in Boston, where Alexander Bell, who had patented the invention, was based. By 1929, there were 29 telephones for every one hundred residents of Chicago, 27 in both New York and Toronto, but only 8 in London and fewer than 5 in Glasgow and Birmingham.[34]

The telephone's social and geographical consequences were considerable. Much more complex information could be transmitted than by telegraph, not only facts and figures but emotions and subtleties of language. Tone of voice could convey trust or suspicion in business deals, deepen or cool personal relationships among residential users. In time, the phone's use was promoted, not only for business but as a potential saviour in emergencies and an aid to shopping as well as a means of conversation. NTC advertisements from around 1900 promoted the telephone as a way to save money and increase business at the same time, but also to summon help in crises. One advert soberly announced that 'ACCIDENTS WILL HAPPEN. Then minutes, yes seconds may save LIFE PROPERTY MONEY'; another more dramatically depicted a woman rushing to the phone in the downstairs study while flames engulfed the hall and stairs of her home. But by now the telephone also had more mundane domestic uses. An advertisement proclaiming 'the most modern service at the most moderate cost' depicted a modern housewife, telephone in one hand (again positioned in the entrance hall with the stairs behind), telephone directory in the other; yet another showed an elegantly dressed young woman, telephone in one hand, passing a message on to her almost identical companion: 'How charming! Shall we accept?'[35] An American etiquette guide explained in 1922 that 'The telephone has come more and more into use as a medium for giving invitations, even for elaborate entertainments. For a dinner dance last winter, to which hundreds of guests were asked, Mrs Cornelius Vanderbilt gave most of the invitations by telephone. Mrs Vincent Astor recently used it for a smaller dance, which however, was formal in all other respects.'[36] If the Vanderbilts and the Astors could use the phone for such important functions, who could deny its social acceptability?

These and similar advertisements and illustrations indicate at least two other critical issues. Whereas the unemotional, statistics-imparting telegraph was perceived as a masculine device, the telephone was increasingly gendered female. Switchboard operators, connecting callers manually through exchange switchboards, were almost always female, partly because women were thought to be more patient and polite, intoning 'Hello, Central!' and 'Number, Please' far more winningly than any male operator, and partly because the physical act of connecting wires to sockets was associated with the 'nimble fingers' dexterity of female knitting and piano-playing. Switchboard operators were in a privileged position: as working-class intermediaries who could listen in to middle-class conversations, they could act as censors – 'pulling the plug' on any call of which they disapproved – or as sources for gossip, roles that were also available to anybody who shared a 'party line' with another user.[37]

A second theme of illustrations relates to the placement of the phone within the private home. Should it be in the intimate, private space of the master bedroom or study, where only the head of the household could use it without asking permission; or in the semi-public space of the hall, where all could use it but all could listen in; or should there be a 'telephone cabinet', equivalent to the private space of the public call box? Should servants answer the phone as they were expected to answer the doorbell, or would this encourage them to abuse their situation and make personal calls of their own?

Initially, few families had phones in their own homes. They depended on public phones. The first public phones, often located in drugstores in the United States and pharmacies in England, were supervised by uniformed attendants, denying their users any privacy. But in 1890 ten coin-operated phones were installed in New York, and in London the first public telephone kiosks (forerunners of the red phone box) were introduced later in the 1890s. People unfamiliar with how to use the phone had to be educated in telephone etiquette: an NTC advertisement from 1893 portrayed a brief two-act 'play' set in 'Mr Higgs' Pharmacy', where an innocent customer was initiated in use of the phone.[38]

In a scene in *The Job* (1916), set in Upper Manhattan in 1907, Una Golden has to walk four blocks to find an all-night drugstore from which she can phone to summon a doctor to visit her dying mother. Lewis highlights the irony of living in a modern networked city, with subway, asphalt streets, and even 'a wireless message winging overhead', with the practical inaccessibility of modern communications for ordinary people at home. The denial of modernity's effectiveness is reinforced by the city's inability to deal with the forces of nature: it is pouring with rain. Unregulated water 'did not belong to the city . . . It was violent here, shocking and terrible.'[39]

More than a decade earlier, in *Sister Carrie* (1900), the geographical hinge in the novel, when the action shifts from Chicago to New York, occurs when Hurstwood, working late and alone, removes $10,000 from his employer's safe, panics, and decides to flee the city. It is half past one at night as Hurstwood leaves his office: 'At the first drug store he stopped, seeing a long-distance telephone booth inside. It was a famous drug store and contained one of the first private telephone booths ever erected.'[40] It is critical that the booth is *private*, so that he can phone the railway station without being overheard by the night clerk in the store.

So Hurstwood discovers that there is just time to collect Carrie and catch the three o'clock mail train to Detroit, hoping to cross the border into Canada by the time his theft is discovered. Yet he knows he cannot escape detection for ever: the same telephone network that aids his escape can also be used by the police to alert forces in Montreal ahead of his arrival there.

Dreiser is relatively unusual in making the telephone so critical in his narrative. Novelists prior to World War I make frequent use of the electric telegraph; the telegram as a kind of speeded-up letter is useful for accelerating the plot and increasing dramatic tension but, as Stein observes, the form of the nineteenth-century novel 'relies on misunderstandings and missed communications to generate plot movement'[41] and these are difficult to contrive if characters can speak directly to one another by phone. Only in the 1920s do references to the telephone become common in fiction.

Meanwhile, the use of the telephone in the real world was expanding rapidly. In 1880, there were fewer than 250 telephone subscribers in Montreal, fewer than 10 percent of whom were purely residential. Until the 1900s, the telephone was adopted principally by centrally located businesses which already used the electric telegraph. In the affluent Anglophone suburb of Westmount, the first exchange was opened in 1887 yet within twenty years more than 90 per cent of households were connected. At the luxurious Linton Apartments, close to downtown, 75 per cent of residents were telephone subscribers in 1910, when the citywide rate was only 6 per cent. There were fewer subscribers among the Francophone population in the east of the city, except among lawyers and managers. Not until 1920 did the rate approach 50 per cent among households in the industrial suburb of Maisonneuve, while in a working-class district close to the Lachine Canal, only 18 per cent of households had phones as late as 1930. Claire Poitras concludes that between 1900 and 1930, the diffusion of the telephone in Montreal varied according to socio-economic group, language and housing type, as well as location.[42] Yet even in skilled working-class areas like Maisonneuve more people had access to a phone than in middle-class Hampstead in north London, where the number of subscribers increased from only 0.23 per cent of the borough's population in 1902–1903 to 9.25 per cent in 1921. Assuming an average household size of four persons, this meant that less than 40 per cent of all residents had access to a phone even in 1921, nearly all among the higher socio-economic groups.[43] In London, the divide between rich and poor was continuing to widen during the early decades of the twentieth century, whereas in North American cities, where the middle-class market for the telephone was almost saturated by the 1910s, the 1920s witnessed a reduction in class differences in access to the telephone.

Public transport

Many of the mainline railways built into London from the late 1830s were obliged to penetrate the city by way of tunnels, cuttings, embankments and viaducts. In east and south-east London, the approaches of the London and Greenwich Railway (1836) into London Bridge, the Eastern Counties Railway (1840) into Bishopsgate, and the London and Blackwall Railway (1841) into Fenchurch Street all involved lengthy brick viaducts. When the South Eastern Railway extended westwards from London Bridge to Charing Cross and the London, Chatham and Dover Railway pushed north to Blackfriars and Ludgate Hill, both in the mid-1860s, they too resorted to brick viaducts to minimise demolition of existing buildings (and, of course, the amount of compensation paid to property owners). Early hopes that the arches could accommodate middle-class homes and businesses, and that roads flanking the viaducts would develop into fashionable promenades, soon yielded to the reality that viaducts acted as barriers between adjacent neighbourhoods, creating liminal spaces blighted by noise, soot and vibration, fit only for the most marginal businesses.[44] Perhaps in response to this experience, London's *intra-urban* rapid transit was diverted underground wherever possible, beginning with the cut-and-cover construction of the Metropolitan Railway between Paddington and Farringdon, opened in 1863, gradually extended until what became known as the Circle Line was completed in 1884.[45]

Meanwhile, the railway viaduct offered a new way of seeing inner-city districts. As early as 1845, the author of *The Mysteries of London* noted the voyeuristic possibilities of the view from the Eastern Counties Railway as it passed through Spitalfields and Bethnal Green:

The traveller upon this line may catch, from the windows of the carriage in which he journeys, a hasty but alas! too comprehensive glance of the wretchedness and squalor of that portion of London. He may actually obtain a view of the interior and domestic misery peculiar to the neighbourhood; he may penetrate with his eyes into the secrets of those abodes of sorrow, vice and destitution. In summertime the poor always have their windows open, and thus the hideous poverty of their rooms can be readily descried from the summit of the arches on which the railroad is constructed.[46]

Claims to observe women 'half naked . . . ironing the linen of a more wealthy neighbour' or 'preparing the sorry meal', often 'scolding, swearing and quarrelling' suggest more a fertile imagination than a 'hasty glance'. Nevertheless, the same opportunity to look into the lives of the poor was also apparent a quarter-century later in Gustave Doré's illustration, 'Over London By Rail' (Figure 12.2).[47] Contrary to some interpretations, I read Doré's picture not as evidence of terrible slums, more as a warning of the dehumanising consequences of 'progress'. The houses he depicted were not slums by the standards of the 1870s – although overcrowded to our eyes, each house was self-contained with its own backyard and outdoor toilet – but en masse they constituted a soulless, regimented cityscape in comparison to more distant, lower density

Figure 12.2. Gustave Doré (1832–1883), 'Over London By Rail', from G. Doré and B. Jerrold, *London: A Pilgrimage* (London, 1872).

suburbs, hinted at by the speeding train, then enjoyed only by the comfortably well-off. But at least the well-off would find it hard to remain ignorant of the conditions of the working classes, in stark contrast to the situation described by Engels in 1840s Manchester where, because the major radial streets were all lined with shops, hiding the poor residential districts that lay behind them, wealthy suburbanites could 'go in and out daily without coming into contact with a working-people's quarter or even with workers'.[48] So the viaduct offered de Certeau's view from above, a personalised version of Booth's poverty map.

Of course, by leapfrogging the inner city, the above-ground railway protected suburbanites from *direct* contact with the poor. On the underground railway, things were arranged differently. Here, the evidence of what conditions were like above ground was limited to the characteristics of passengers boarding and alighting at successive stations. A degree of social segregation was maintained by providing separate compartments for different classes of passenger, a system that was abandoned on the deep-underground 'tube' lines that opened from the 1890s, where carriages were not only one-class but 'open-plan', not divided into individual compartments.[49]

As noted in Chapter 6, and as illustrated in paintings such as W. M. Egley's 'Omnibus Life in London' (1859) and G. W. Joy's 'The Bayswater Omnibus' (1895) (Figure 12.3), London buses and horse-trams could accommodate a diverse range of passengers squeezed into a confined space where it was impossible to avoid physical

Figure 12.3. George W. Joy (1844–1925), 'The Bayswater Omnibus' (1895). Reproduced by permission of Museum of London.

contact and difficult to avoid eye contact.[50] On a bus, or an above-ground train, at least one could look out of the window at the passing cityscape; underground, there was nowhere to look. Advertising panels offered one excuse to avoid other passengers (and they feature prominently in Joy's painting); but it remained harder to escape the unwelcome attentions of fellow passengers on a fast-moving, infrequently-stopping train than on a bus, and still more difficult in the semi-darkness of a minimally gas-lit underground compartment. George Sims speculated on the day-time thrill but night-time threat of travelling in the same compartment as notorious criminals.[51] And, whereas novelists were reluctant to employ the telephone, they enthusiastically sent their characters on trips by underground train. Trollope's Hetta (*The Way We Live Now*, 1875) and Gissing's Helen Norman (*Workers in the Dawn*, 1880), Monica Widdowson (*The Odd Women*, 1893) and Eve Madeley (*Eve's Ransom*, 1895) all ride the Underground alone. Henry James (*A London Life*, 1898), John Galsworthy (*The Man of Property*, 1906) and H. G. Wells (*Tono-Bungay*, 1909) also set scenes on the Underground. Often, the setting was one of sexual electricity (on a Circle Line that was steam-operated until 1905).

In *Eve's Ransom* Maurice Hilliard, infatuated with a photograph of Eve Madeley, whom he has never met, tracks her down to lodgings in Gower Place and then sits opposite her on the train one evening all the way from Gower Street (today's Euston Square) to Earl's Court, eventually getting to talk to her under the electric illuminations of the International Health Exhibition.[52] In *Tono-Bungay*, George and Marion travel alone first-class by underground when he first declares his love for her.[53] David

Pike comments that 'The first-class Underground could be simultaneously a space of propriety and one of transgression, by turn private and public'.[54]

As long as the Metropolitan and Metropolitan District were the only components of the underground, the system needed little unravelling. The trains were only a flight of stairs below ground, and at most stations and often between stations, there was a brief glimpse of daylight and an occasional opportunity to fix one's bearings. But the proliferation of deep-level tubes, starting in 1890 with the City and South London (subsequently incorporated into the Northern Line), but soon including the Central London (now the Central Line) (1900), the Bakerloo and the Piccadilly (both 1906), stimulated the need for more imaginative, colour-coded cartography, culminating in Harry Beck's geometric map, first published in 1933 and variously claimed to be inspired by either electrical wiring diagrams or sewer maps.[55] The very inflexibility of the different underground lines, the paucity of track connections between different lines, made it easier to produce a topological map of the network, by comparison with the New York subway system, where different services use the same tracks, and routes can easily be changed to accommodate changes in demand or engineering works.

Even before Beck created his map, London Underground posters had represented the underground as an orderly, well-regulated and democratic space. The Central London Railway exhorted travellers to 'TAKE THE TUPPENNY TUBE AND AVOID ALL ANXIETY' (1905). Another early poster advertised the underground as 'The Way for All' (1911). Yet nearly all the passengers depicted on these posters were smartly dressed, middle-class, never crowded and always allowed plenty of personal space to maintain a polite distance from one another.[56]

By contrast, Reginald Marsh's paintings and etchings of travellers on the New York subway in the 1920s and 1930s depict the awkwardness of encounters across gender, class and ethnicity, updating and relocating the nineteenth-century scenes of omnibus passengers I alluded to above. His most famous painting depicts a black labourer, asleep, slumped across two seats, a nervous woman perched next to him, and another woman, forced to stand, with her back to the scene as she studies a fashion magazine. Under the seat beneath the sleeping labourer is a discarded newspaper, its headline asking 'Does the Sex Urge Explain Judge Crater's Strange Disappearance' (Figure 12.4). The painting is entitled 'Why Not Use the "L"?' and features a contemporary advertising campaign designed to woo passengers back to the ailing but less crowded elevated train services:

> The Subway is fast – Certainly
> But the *Open Air Elevated*
> Gets you there quickly, too
> – and with *more comfort*
> **Why not use the 'L'?**[57]

Marsh was evidently directing this message at all three characters: the standing woman would get a seat, the man would stay awake in the fresh air, and there would be less likelihood of having to sit next to somebody with 'sex urges' if you travelled on the 'open air elevated'!

Figure 12.4. Reginald Marsh (1898–1954), 'Why Not Use the "L"?' (1930). Egg tempera on canvas (91.4 × 121.9 cm). Whitney Museum of American Art, New York; Purchase 31.293. © ARS, NY and DACS, London 2007.

The El

Elevated railway systems in New York and Chicago were a curious mixture of the ungainly antiquated and the technologically modern, the efficient and the disruptive. In retrospect, it is extraordinary that the unwieldy el was *ever* tolerated, certainly in its original New York form, steam-operated, dispensing sparks, soot and ashes on the street below. Now, after its erasure from most of Manhattan, surviving stretches of original el or el-like formations where the subway emerges above ground are treasured – iconically inserted into nostalgia-tinged films like Woody Allen's *Manhattan* (1979) and Wayne Wang's adaptation of Paul Auster's stories, *Smoke* (1995); and the elevated Loop in Chicago is an integral part of that city's downtown heritage.[58]

My discussion of the New York elevated is intended to serve not only as an illustration of another form of network in the city, but as a conclusion to the whole book. By considering different themes – the trains, the superstructure, life over and under the el, the view of and from the el, we can see how the el functioned as both an icon of modernity and modernity's other. Its dismantling in lower and midtown Manhattan, extending from the mid-1920s to the mid-1950s, serves as an extended wake for the kind of modern city that I have surveyed (and celebrated) in this book.

The first proposals for an elevated railway in Manhattan date from the 1830s and 1840s. In the 1860s, hard on the heels of London's first underground railway, there were proposals for a subway under parts of Broadway and Fifth Avenue. But the

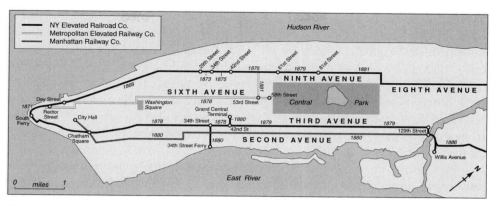

Figure 12.5. Elevated Railways in Manhattan.

impossibility of including open sections (as on London's Metropolitan Railway) in an already built-up Manhattan would have made it difficult (and certainly expensive) to accommodate steam traction underground. The plans were opposed both by the operators of existing street railways and by Broadway property owners unhappy at the disruption to street life and trade, and to utilities such as water and gas supply, which the building of a subway would involve. But elevated railway proposals fared no better: nobody believed artists' fanciful impressions of light, ornamental, airy elevated structures; rather, they feared living in the physical and the economic shadow of the el – the beginning of a long-running debate on whether the el would raise property values by improving access or reduce them through the negative externalities of noise, pollution, and strangers.[59]

It was easier to gain approval for an el away from Broadway, on streets lined by warehouses and manufacturing lofts, where the access argument outweighed any social costs, although the money-making potential for promoters was correspondingly less. So New York's first el was a single-track, cable-operated railway precariously balanced above Ninth Avenue, opened in 1867 but bankrupt by 1870. The company had one valuable asset – a 999-year franchise to operate on Ninth Avenue – so it is unsurprising that it was promptly resurrected and reopened in 1872 as the steam-operated New York Elevated Railroad Company.

Once one line was up and running there were proposals galore. By 1878, the Ninth Avenue el had been extended south to South Ferry (Battery Park) and north to 61st Street; the Metropolitan Elevated had opened on 6th Avenue; and the New York Elevated Railway Company had reached all the way up 3rd Avenue to 129th Street. In 1879, all these lines were acquired by the Manhattan Railway Company, which by 1880 had also opened the length of 2nd Avenue. A few spurs and connecting lines were quickly added but, apart from extensions into the suburban boroughs, the system on Manhattan was effectively complete by 1880 (Figure 12.5).[60] In much the same way, once the first line had been authorised in Chicago – in 1888 – all the other elevated routes in the city followed within a decade.

The New York lines were all steam-operated, and the inevitable problems – noise, dirt, the danger of operating high-pressure steam locomotives in congested surroundings, and the limited acceleration of steam locomotives, which forced a choice between low speeds and inconveniently distant stations – were soon recognised. Cheape notes that traffic on the elevated lines grew to 86 million fare-paying passengers in 1882, and 200 million by 1893; but during the rest of the 1890s elevated traffic stagnated and even declined in some years, while streetcar traffic doubled as track mileage was extended, some lines were converted to cable operation and, from 1895, others were electrified.[61] It was not until 1902 that the elevated lines were at last electrified, fourteen years after Frank Sprague had first developed the electric trolley, nine years after the first successful use of electrification for elevated railways (at the Chicago 1893 Exposition and, more permanently, on the Liverpool Overhead Railway), and seven years after the electrification of the first sections of the elevated railway in Chicago. Electrification increased passenger capacity by allowing faster, longer trains, and ridership increased correspondingly, reaching a peak of 384 million in 1921.

But the first subway line had opened in 1904, by which time the Manhattan Railway Company had been absorbed into the subway company, the Interborough Rapid Transit Company (IRT). By 1905, all surface streetcar lines, elevated railways and subways in Manhattan and the Bronx were controlled by one company, the IRT. In other words, the electrified el was the most up-to-date transport technology in New York for barely two years, 1902–1904. After 1904 the el was yesterday's transport. Abandonment began in 1923, although it was not until the late 1930s and early 1940s that most of Manhattan's els – on 2nd, 6th and 9th Avenues – were dismantled. The last to go was the 3rd Avenue el in 1955.

Yet it is from the 1910s and 1920s that some of the most 'modern' images of the el date. As Michael Brooks has noted, there is often a time lag between the introduction of an innovation and its adoption in realist art and literature.[62] Then, there may be a brief period when an innovation's modernity is emphasised in a fairly unambiguous way; but then a longer period of more complex and nuanced interpretation.

Compare, for example, the treatment of the el in Howells' *A Hazard of New Fortunes* (1890), Wharton's *The House of Mirth* (1905) and Dos Passos' *Manhattan Transfer* (1925). As I have already discussed, much of the first part of Howells' book is occupied with the Marches' anxious search for somewhere to live. But in visiting apartments and, subsequently, friends and business colleagues, they also make extensive use of the elevated railway:

At Third Avenue they took the Elevated, for which [Isabel] confessed an infatuation. She declared it the most ideal way of getting about in the world, and was not ashamed when he reminded her of how she used to say that nothing under the sun could induce her to travel on it.[63]

But, as much as the el was modern and efficient, it was also picturesque, a combination of 'curving tracks and châlet-stations':[64]

'Those bends in the L that you get in the corner of Washington Square, or just below the Cooper Institute – they're the gayest things in the world. Perfectly atrocious, of course, but incomparably picturesque!'[65]

The Marches' most rhapsodic enthusiasm for the elevated comes when they are travelling at night:

They leaned over the track, and looked up at the next station, where the train, just starting, throbbed out the flame-shot steam into the white moonlight.

'The most beautiful thing in New York – the one always and certainly beautiful thing here,' said March.[66]

If 'the night transit was even more interesting than the day', it was also because of the opportunities it offered to survey the lives of others:

... the fleeting intimacy you formed with people in second and third floor interiors, while all the usual street life went on underneath, had a domestic intensity mixed with a perfect repose that was the last effect of good society with all its security and exclusiveness. He said it was better than the theatre, of which it reminded him, to see those people through their windows: a family party of work-folk at a late tea, some of the men in their shirt sleeves; a woman sewing by a lamp; a mother laying her child in its cradle; a man with his head fallen on his hands upon a table; a girl and her lover leaning over the window-sill together. What suggestion! what drama! what infinite interest![67]

The elevated was not an unmitigated blessing: 'They kill the streets and avenues, but at least they partially hide them, and that is some comfort; and they do triumph over their prostrate forms with a savage exultation that is intoxicating.'[68] This was most evident along the Bowery, already on the way down socially by the time the elevated line was built; but the unpleasantness of the noise and smuts from steam locomotives accelerated the street's transformation into the city's skid row. Howells wrote of 'the gay ugliness – the shapeless, graceless, reckless picturesqueness of the Bowery ... the prevailing hideousness ... that uproar to the eye':

He [March] was interested in the insolence with which the railway had drawn its erasing line across the Corinthian front of an old theatre, almost grazing its fluted pillars, and flouting its dishonoured pediment.[69]

The overall effect was of a struggle for the survival of the fittest played out among the components of the built environment: 'The whole at moments seemed to him lawless, godless; the absence of intelligent, comprehensive purpose in the huge disorder...' Or, to draw a parallel with Berman's discussion of traffic on Paris boulevards, individual acts of rationality generating an apparent chaos in the aggregate.[70]

Riding the elevated also allowed one to experience the city's differentiated social geography. On the 6th Avenue line, the passengers were mainly, 'according to the hour, American husbands going to and from business, and American wives going to and from shopping', but March 'rather preferred the east side to the west side lines, because they offered more nationalities, conditions, and characters to his inspection'. On the east side, 'March never entered a car without encountering some interesting shape of shabby adversity, which was almost always adversity of foreign birth'.[71]

Howells lamented the lack of attention that artists had paid to the picturesque el. Yet when they did eventually start to portray the el, they settled on many of the same locations and images that Howells described: the Bowery, Chatham Square, the sharp bends south of Washington Square. Like Howells they depicted the el as a scene of ambiguous modernity, picturesque, best seen at night (or at least, at twilight), a viewpoint *from which* to observe the life of the city, and a frame *within which* to situate life on the streets.[72]

In the New York sections of Dreiser's *Sister Carrie* (1900), the el is strangely absent, perhaps indicative of how the system had stagnated since the heady days of expansion preceding Howells' novel. Yet Edith Wharton's much more moneyed characters in *The House of Mirth* at least register the existence of the 'rumble' and 'shriek' of the trains, even if Simon Rosedale, the Jewish financier, is the only one who is recorded as travelling on the el. For most of Wharton's characters, the el is for other people.[73]

Where Howells was writing about modern New York but using a nineteenth-century narrative form, *Manhattan Transfer* is, as I discussed in Chapter 4, a moder*nist* novel, in which the text itself is a kind of city, made up of different rhythms, languages, segregations, juxtapositions, collisions and uncertainties.[74] It also spans a longer time period, from the 1890s to the 1920s. In the first part of the book, the el is a regular presence, a city sight to be pointed out to children and new immigrants. It is part of characters' routine, by turns both threatening and revelatory.

Dos Passos naturalised the el as part of the landscape/soundscape. On Allen Street, its 'annihilating clatter'[75] was no more likely to distract local residents than the yells of their children playing. Years later (despite electrification), 'Morning clatters with the first L train down Allen Street. Daylight rattles through the windows, shaking the old brick houses, splatters the girders of the L structure with bright confetti.'[76] But when Joe Harland was evicted from his lodgings, and stomped off in a rage, 'Jagged oblongs of harsh sound broke one after another over his head as an elevated past *(sic)* over'.[77] When Bud was newly arrived and still optimistic that he could make it in New York, 'the sun shines through the Elevated striping the blue street with warm seething yellow stripes'. When he was broke and unemployed, 'The Elevated thundered overhead. Dustmotes danced before his eyes in the girderstriped sunlight'. On 6th Avenue, the L train left 'a humming rattle to fade among the girders'.[78]

The el might be taken-for-granted, part of the scenery on Allen Street and Third Avenue, but in the touristy parts of town, it was a 'sight'. When the young Jimmy Herf arrived back in New York on 4th July by boat with his mother, she pointed out the sights including 'A funny little train with a green engine [which] clatters overhead'. And another newly-arrived Irish boy-immigrant was met by his uncle: 'And this here's the L station, South Ferry . . . Come along Padraic your uncle Timothy's goin to take ye on th' Ninth Avenoo L.'[79]

Later in the book the principal characters, admittedly also now older and, mostly, better-off, were much more likely to ride the subway or hail a cab. Finally, the el is established as the stage scenery for film noir: 'Jimmy Herf [now girl-less, job-less and out of place] stepped out from in front of the truck; the mudguard just grazed the skirt of his raincoat. He stood a moment behind an L stanchion while the icicle thawed out of his spine.'[80] The el is for the poor, and it defines an underworld of the marginalised.

The noise of the el was also highlighted in King Vidor's *silent* film, 'The Crowd' (1928), where el trains pass outside the window of the newlywed John and Mary Sims. John works as a clerk in a Wall Street office. He proposes to Mary after a night out in Coney Island. On the subway home, his eye is caught by an advertisement: 'You furnish the girl. We'll furnish the home.' But the nearest he gets to the all-American suburban home is later in the film when he is going door-to-door selling vacuum cleaners. Meanwhile they make do with a tiny tenement flat with a bed that folds up into the wall and space-saving cupboards that also fold into the wall around the kitchen basin. As the caption to John's banjo-strumming tells us:

> Wife and I are happy
> And everything is swell
> It's heavenly inside our flat
> But outside it is El!

Before long, the interior isn't so heavenly, either – the doors constantly swing open, the bed won't stay locked into the wall, the cistern breaks, and John and Mary are quarrelling. How much of this is attributable to the vibration and the noise of the el outside the window?[81]

'The Crowd' also included shots of Lower Manhattan where the prominence of el trains winding their way above and around teeming crowds indicated the circulation of the city. Seven years before 'The Crowd', in 'Manhatta', Charles Sheeler and Paul Strand, too, had used shots tracking elevated trains from above, emphasising both the magisterial scale and the mechanistic functioning of the modern city.[82] But the city could also be an aggressive and alienating environment. Another of King Vidor's shots – of double-deck elevated lines over a 'herd' of black saloon automobiles, all filmed side-on – was replicated in a lithograph by Louis Lozowick, entitled simply 'Traffic' (1930).[83] Yet the real circulation by this time was going on unseen, underground.

The el's serpentine modernity, threading its way between skyscrapers towards the Valhalla of Lower Manhattan, featured in another of Lozowick's lithographs, 'Third Avenue' (1929).[84] But several years before Lozowick, the English artist, C. R. W. Nevinson depicted a similar view in his painting 'The Soul of the Soulless City' (1920) which also exists in print and pastel versions entitled, less judgmentally, 'New York: An Abstraction' and 'Railway Skyscrapers' (Figure 12.6). One contemporary critic commented on the print that 'It was a criticism-picture, yet its final effect was not depressing. For one could see from the beams of light that fell across the railroad track where it traversed the cross-streets that the sun was shining on New York.'[85] While this may have been an absurdly optimistic interpretation of Nevinson's art, it could certainly be conceded that the alienation of the skyscraper city was tempered by the freedom offered by new modes of mobility.

Another Nevinson oil painting of the el takes us back to Dos Passos: 'Third Avenue, Elevated Railway' (1920) explored the light and shadow of the sun shining through the superstructure, creating a model of the grid that structured the whole city, a pattern also reproduced in Lozowick's lithograph, 'Allen Street (Under the El)' (1929).[86] A purer modernist exploration of the same abstract geometry was evident in some of Paul Strand's photographs, such as 'From the El' (1915), where Strand looked down from an el platform onto a latticework of supporting girders and mottled stripes of sunlight on the street below.[87]

Yet life under the el could also be much more animated. Allen Street, which was spanned by the 2nd Avenue El, lay at the heart of the Jewish quarter of the Lower East Side and was the location of several markets, for household items such as bed-linen and antiques, some of which were hung from poles underneath the elevated superstructure. Philip Reisman depicted a chaotic scene of mothers, babies and their

Figure 12.6. C. R. W. Nevinson (1889–1946), 'Railway Skyscrapers' (c.1920). Charcoal & crayon on paper. Private Collection/The Bridgeman Art Library.

children in his 'Under the "L"' (1928) (Figure 12.7). His drawing appeared in the socialist magazine, *New Masses*, with the caption, 'The Working-Class Mother: The busy street is the only summer resort she and her children ever visit'.[88] In the heat of a New York summer, the shadow of the el provided relief from the overcrowding and stifling atmosphere of a Lower East Side tenement block. In his autobiographical novel, *Jews Without Money* (1930), Michael Gold confirmed this experience of summer in the Lower East Side:

In the maelstrom of wagons, men, pushcarts, street cars, dogs and East Side garbage, the mothers calmly wheeled their baby carriages. They stopped in the shade of the Elevated trains, to suckle their babies with big sweaty breasts.[89]

Figure 12.7. Philip Reisman, 'Under the "L"' (1928) (17.5 × 12.6 cm). EPC 4866. UCL Art Collections, University College London.

A few blocks farther west, the 3rd Avenue El straddled the Bowery, by the inter-war years a street turned over almost exclusively to hostels, missions, brothels and secondhand clothes stores. Reginald Marsh made numerous paintings and drawings that included the elevated framing the Bowery's low life. 'The Bowery' (1930) features a variety of hopeless or no-good cases beneath signs that announce the 'Marathon Hotel' (for those for whom life was a painful struggle?) and the 'Onward Hotel – Rooms 30 cents' (only onward in the sense of ever-transient?).[90]

The artist who, in both style and subject matter, best encapsulated the ambiguous modernity of the elevated railway was John Sloan. His paintings and etchings of ordinary people, cooking, washing or relaxing in backyards and on rooftops, were mostly based on scenes glimpsed from the window of his Greenwich Village studio, yet they could equally well have been inspired by views *from* the el, much as Howells described. But Sloan also made several paintings over a period of more than twenty years that focused *on* the el.[91] His most explicit hymn to the modernity of the el, 'Six

O'Clock, Winter' (1912), illustrates the ability of the commuting classes to escape the congestion and discomfort of downtown, hinting at the el's capacity to leapfrog over the slums, much like Doré's 'Over London By Rail'. The progressive thrust of the not-yet-old technology is evident in the contrast between the purposeful take-off of the train crossing the picture diagonally compared to the chaos of the rush-hour crowd on the street below, where nobody is getting anywhere very quickly. The el will take you away from all this, in a flash. To cannibalise the epigram of Forster's *Howards End*, Sloan's painting might reasonably have been called 'Only Dis-connect'. Douglas Tallack calls this 'a scene of excess', to indicate not only the intensity of activity depicted by Sloan but also his concern to represent both the individuality and the collectivity of the crowd.[92]

Sloan continued to paint the el through the 1920s. And herein lies the dilemma of an 'old' artist continuing to paint what was by now an 'old' technology. His most famous el painting, 'The City from Greenwich Village' (1922), includes a modern city of skyscrapers and bright lights, but only as a fantasy on the horizon. The line of the el leads us from old-style New York (Sixth Avenue) in the right foreground towards the fairyland in the left background. But it is diverted to the left along 3rd Street and there is a middle ground that is mostly low-rise and relatively gloomy. This reflected a topographical truth of New York – that, for geological reasons, there were few tall buildings between City Hall and Madison Square – but Sloan used this void to emphasise the gap between the values of Greenwich Village and those of Lower Manhattan.[93]

In 'Sixth Avenue Elevated at Third Street' (1928) (Figure 12.8) Sloan depicted the same curve as painted from above in 'The City from Greenwich Village', but now looking up Sixth Avenue towards the Jefferson Market Courthouse. If this had been painted twenty, or even ten years earlier, I don't think we could doubt the modernity of the scene. But by 1928 the Sixth Avenue El was barely a decade away from closure and the picture may be considered an exercise in nostalgia for a more innocent modernity. Far from the grim struggle for existence in the nether worlds of Allen Street and the Bowery, life under *this* el features a Laurel-and-Hardyesque couple of businessmen lurching down the sidewalk, slightly worse for wear, and two gaggles of working girls out on the town after work, one group being scattered by the driver of an open-top car, the other clearly determined to have a good time. Howells' protagonists preferred the el at night when the steam trains were at their most spectacular. Twenty to forty years on, each of these three Sloan paintings also shows the el, if not late at night, then in the early evening. The el may facilitate the journey to work, but it is what happens after work that really counts in a city of modern consumption.

In summary, the el lent itself to images of progress; especially once it was not only elevated but electric. When the sun shone, the grid of the city streets was replicated on the pavement beneath the el. It provided evidence of the city of circulation, the 'networked city' (even though most circulation went on out of sight). It could masquerade as the great liberator and democratiser, opening the length and breadth of the city to anybody who could afford the 5 cent fare. At the same time as it provided transportation for all classes and races, it also facilitated segregation: residential segregation of rich and poor, and traffic segregation of local traffic on the streets and

Figure 12.8. John Sloan (1871–1951), 'Sixth Avenue Elevated at Third Street' (1928). Oil on canvas (76.2 × 101.6 cm). Whitney Museum of American Art, New York; Purchase 36.154.

'rapid transit' above and below. And at the same time as it facilitated segregation, it allowed surveillance. In these ways, it was far from liberalising: it hemmed in the poor, subject to constant observation; and it hemmed in the poor, in the darkness and thunder underneath the el. If it began as the bright hope of modernity, it soon became picturesque: modernity's comfortable 'other'.

Postlude

The 'de-construction' of the el is an appropriate theme on which to end this exploration of the spaces of modern cities. The substitution of telephony and the automobile, two individual modes of communication, for mass transit and mass media, is a process that is still ongoing. From the perspective of the early twenty-first century, we can also chart the gradual dismantling of mass consumption, the mergers and closures of chain stores and the franchising of separate retail outlets within department stores, almost a return to the bazaars and arcades of the early nineteenth century. Likewise, we can see the end of routine employment in offices and on production lines that first made space for women's paid work, the breaking of the connection between economic growth and employment growth, and the end of the 'career for life', which facilitated the growth of both homeownership and secure private renting which, in turn, made for relatively predictable and simple patterns of mass commuting to work from suburban homes.

The el is also an appropriate point to end because it embodies the contradictions and multiple points of view that characterise modernity and that have characterised this book. My method has been partly that of the realist novel – the view from above – interweaving different stories and locations with the aim of making a convincing narrative; but the nature of the interweaving has also resembled the modernist novel of the streets, passing the baton from character to character or, in my case, from city to city, as their stories intersected. My hope is that, as with a newspaper or a panoramic painting, each incident has gained significance from its position among its neighbours. In adopting this structure, I hope to have emphasised the kaleidoscopic, contingent nature of modern urbanism, the diversity of spatial practices in cities conceptualised in the representations made by government, planners, reformers and ideologues but challenged in the representational spaces appropriated by novelists, artists and a variety of marginalised or subaltern urban populations.

One objection to Marshall Berman's vision of modernity was that he denied the diversity of modernities and imposed a teleological framework in which different cities stood for different phases in a unified whole – from Baudelaire's Paris to Dostoevsky's St Petersburg to Moses' New York. The method is not so different from Asa Briggs' less explicitly theoretical *Victorian Cities* which moved from Birmingham through Manchester to Leeds to London, each typifying successive decades of the nineteenth century. By interweaving historical geographies of London with those of other cities, especially New York and Toronto, I have tried to avoid the association of each city with its own unique period, but I *am* implying that their different histories all belong in the same book.

In *City People* Gunther Barth argued that new metropolitan values and practices, and their embodiment in apartment buildings, department stores, ball parks, vaudeville theatres and a modern press, were means of unifying culturally diverse populations in late nineteenth-century American cities.[94] To Barth, less diverse European cities had less need of the glue of new, universalising cultural institutions. An essay published in the London-based *Harmsworth's Magazine* in 1902 would seem to confirm popular impressions of transatlantic differences. In 'If London Were Like New York', an expatriate Briton returns from Africa to find London 'Yankeefied'.[95] Beyond the superficial name changes – Victoria Station is now Victoria Depot, Buckingham Palace Road has become Fifth Avenue – the city is characterised by a more frenetic, service-oriented and money-centred lifestyle: ability to pay trumps breeding, young women lead independent, unchaperoned public lives, everywhere there is aggressive touting for business, all is hurry and scurry and nervous anxiety. A political machine (Mansion House is now Tammany Hall) and a hardened Irish police force ensure order and efficiency. Illustrations depict Park Row skyscrapers bordering Trafalgar Square and elevated trains slicing through Piccadilly Circus and crossing Tower Bridge. Yet the ease with which changes could be made (e.g., the City-West End line of Cheapside-Holborn-Oxford Street effortlessly becomes Broadway), the fact that the transformation is placed, not in the distant future but in 1907, only five years hence, and the parallels with serious critiques – Gissing's abhorrence of advertising culture, Forster's anxieties about the architecture and language of 'hurry' – indicate how similar the cities were in practice, and how quickly they were converging.

Barth concluded that metropolitan culture spread out to permeate the whole nation – department stores distributed their goods nationwide, vaudeville artists toured the country, major-league baseball became a national spectator sport. So diversity gave birth to sameness. But writing in 2007, there seem greater differences, certainly in political culture, between major American metropolises and the small-town and rural heartland than between 'global cities' on either side of the Atlantic.

Contrary to the current enthusiasm for different modernities – and without wanting to deny those differences in processes of modernisation in today's developing world – it seems to me that the cities on which I have focused had more in common with one another than they had different from one another. Differences in architectural form (vertical or horizontal expressions of status and identity), in housing tenure (private ownership or renting on terms that translated dwelling into home), and even in the role of the state (and this is the period when Canadian cities were most American, ceasing to be 'colonial' but not yet consciously 'postcolonial' or 'multicultural') were less significant than common beliefs in technological progress, the efficacy of the market, the ability of hard work and education to facilitate social mobility, and the common power of mass production, mass media and mass consumption.

It may also be objected that modernity focuses on the experience and opportunities available to the middle classes, further marginalising the already marginalised. While I have tried to consider female agency as well as experience, I have paid less attention to the agency of children or the elderly, the poor, the sick and the 'alien'. But the marginalisation of the marginalised is a problem for theoretical perspectives other than modernity. Governmentality still writes history from above, the *rule* of freedom, however much it explores its acting out by the subjects of government. Postmodernism celebrates diversity, but often by turning a blind eye to injustice and inequality. As studies of those other modernities – in Latin America, Asia and Africa – have demonstrated, poverty is as much a part of the modern as affluence, new belief systems as much a part of the modern as secularisation.[96]

Whether or not a category of 'modern cities' is theoretically sustainable, the places and, within them, the spaces on which I have concentrated all helped to shape as much as they were shaped by global processes of modernisation and identity formation. And, while eschewing a 'lessons from history' justification for this book, the situations and representations I have discussed not only have innate interest (to me at least!) but also bear contemplation in our even more self-conscious times. In contrast to our own postmodern – or hyper-modern – cities, where individuation triumphs over a mostly hypocritical rhetoric of compassion and common interest, the cities in this book continued to hold in tension the contradictory impulses to segregate and to integrate, the paradoxes of order and diversity, rationalism and pluralism, modernisation and modernism, representations of space and spatial practice.

Notes

Chapter 1. Building bridges

1. M. Berman, *All That Is Solid Melts Into Air* (London, 1982), pp. 35, 132.
2. D. Harvey, *The Condition of Postmodernity* (Oxford, 1989); for an especially convincing expression of these themes, see L. Nead, *Victorian Babylon* (New Haven CT, 2000).
3. J. House, 'From realism to the "impression"' in K. Lochnan, ed, *Turner Whistler Monet* (London, 2004), pp. 109–111.
4. For the same argument applied to the rise of the modern novel, see M. Bradbury, 'The cities of modernism' in M. Bradbury and J. McFarlane, eds, *Modernism* (Harmondsworth, 1991), pp. 96–104.
5. P. J. Taylor, *Modernities* (Cambridge, 1999).
6. D. Ward and O. Zunz, 'Between rationalism and pluralism: creating the modern city' in D. Ward and O. Zunz, eds, *The Landscape of Modernity* (New York, 1992), pp. 3–15.
7. H. Lefebvre, *The Production of Space* (Oxford, 1991); M. de Certeau, *The Practice of Everyday Life* (Berkeley, 1984). Useful introductions to Lefebvre include A. Merrifield, 'Henri Lefebvre: a socialist in space' in M. Crang and N. Thrift, eds, *Thinking Space* (London, 2000), pp. 167–182; R. Shields, *Lefebvre, Love, and Struggle* (London, 1999); R. J. Johnston et al, *The Dictionary of Human Geography, 4th Edition* (Oxford, 2000), pp. 644–647.
8. De Certeau, *Everyday Life*, pp. 91–93, 117–122; A. Thacker, *Moving through Modernity* (Manchester, 2003), pp. 29–36.
9. P. Joyce, *The Rule of Freedom* (London, 2003), p. 6.
10. N. Thrift, '"Not a straight line but a curve", or, Cities are not mirrors of modernity' in D. Bell and A. Haddour, eds, *City Visions* (Harlow, 2000), pp. 233–263. On the irrational in modernity, see also B. Rieger and M. Daunton, 'Introduction' in M. Daunton and B. Rieger, eds, *Meanings of Modernity: Britain from the Late Victorian Era to World War II* (Oxford, 2001), p. 6.
11. Thrift, 'Not a straight line', p. 234.
12. D. Harvey, *Consciousness and the Urban Experience* (Oxford, 1985) and *Paris, Capital of Modernity* (London, 2003).
13. *New York Illustrated* (New York, n.d.); K. Jackson, ed, *The Encyclopedia of New York City* (New Haven CT, 1995), p. 1228.
14. M. D. Alexander, 'Posed to Unposed: encounters with the camera' in J. Elderfield et al, eds, *Modern Starts: People, Places, Things* (New York, 1999), pp. 153, 156–157.
15. By this time Roebling had also completed the Covington and Cincinnati Suspension Bridge over the Ohio, with a central span of 1057 feet, and had rebuilt another suspension bridge, at Wheeling.
16. A. Trachtenberg, *Brooklyn Bridge: Fact and Symbol* (Chicago, 1979); E. Homberger, *The Historical Atlas of New York City* (New York, 1994), pp. 82–83, 108–109.
17. *Harper's Weekly*, quoted in H. Godfrey, *Tower Bridge* (London, 1988), p. 6.

18. *Brooklyn Daily Eagle*, 23 May 1883, p. 2, quoted in R. Haw, *The Brooklyn Bridge: A Cultural History* (New Brunswick NJ, 2005), p. 35.

19. Trachtenberg, *Brooklyn Bridge*; Jackson, *Encyclopedia of NYC*, pp. 154–155.

20. P. B. Hales, *Silver Cities: The Photography of American Urbanization, 1839–1915* (Philadelphia, 1984), p. 83.

21. Quoted in Trachtenberg, *Brooklyn Bridge*, pp. 85–88. See also the discussion of Vladimir Mayakovsky's poem, 'The Brooklyn Bridge' (1925), in Haw, *The Brooklyn Bridge*, p. 47. Mayakovsky contrasted the 'rooted conservatism' of the stone archways with the 'radical uplift' of the steel cables.

22. For example, see W. H. Gerdts, *Impressionist New York* (New York, 1994), pp. 164–172; and illustrations in E. Sussman et al, *City of Ambition: Artists and New York* (New York, 1996), pp. 12–23.

23. Joseph Stella's numerous depictions of the bridge, from 'New York Interpreted' (1922) to 'The Brooklyn Bridge: Variation on an Old Theme' (1939), may be interpreted in this way, as may prints by C. R. W. Nevinson (1919–1920) and Louis Lozowick (1930–1938). See R. Ingleby et al, *C. R. W. Nevinson: The Twentieth Century* (London, 1999) and J. Flint, *The Prints of Louis Lozowick* (New York, 1982).

24. Trachtenberg, *Brooklyn Bridge*, pp. 123, 169.

25. T. S. Eliot, *The Waste Land and Other Poems* (London, 1971), p. 29, line 62; L. Mumford, interviewed in 'Brooklyn Bridge', documentary film by Ken Burns (Florentine Films, 1981); Trachtenberg, *Brooklyn Bridge*, p. 170.

26. All illustrated in Burns' film. See also Haw, *The Brooklyn Bridge*, pp. 3–4.

27. Gerdts, *Impressionist New York*, pp. 118–120; The Singer Tower featured twice in *New York Illustrated*; it was also at the centre of iconic photographs by Alfred Stieglitz ('The City of Ambition', 1910) and Alvin Langdon Coburn ('Brooklyn Bridge, New York', 1911).

28. 'The Bridge: Its History Reviewed and its Future Foreshadowed', *Brooklyn Daily Eagle*, 9 May 1883, p. 2.

29. 'Delight all round', *Brooklyn Daily Eagle*, 24 May 1883, p. 12. The Tsar's coronation actually took place on 27 May (15 May according to the Russian calendar).

30. *New York Tribune*, 25 May 1883, p. 1, quoted in Haw, *The Brooklyn Bridge*, p. 43.

31. Haw, *The Brooklyn Bridge*, p. 41.

32. G. Doré and B. Jerrold, *London: A Pilgrimage* (London, 1872), p. 11; E. de Maré, *The London Doré Saw* (London, 1973), pp. 68–69.

33. Godfrey, *Tower Bridge*, pp. 11–12; R. Trench and E. Hillman, *London Under London: A Subterranean Guide* (London, 1984); D. L. Pike, '"The greatest wonder of the world": Brunel's tunnel and the meanings of underground London', *Victorian Literature and Culture* **33** (2005), 341–367.

34. B. Weinreb and C. Hibbert, eds, *The London Encyclopaedia* (London, 1983), p. 869.

35. A. Nevins, *Abram S. Hewitt* (New York, 1935), p. 57, quoted in Trachtenberg, *Brooklyn Bridge*, p. 123.

36. Godfrey, *Tower Bridge*, pp. 24, 56–58. Godfrey, pp. 66–68, notes that in 1943, following some minor war damage, one modernist architect proposed encasing the superstructure in glass, streamlining the design and incorporating commercial office space around the towers!

37. Weinreb and Hibbert, *London Encyclopaedia*, pp. 447–448, 576–577, 623, 754.

38. P. J. Waller, *Town, City and Nation* (Oxford, 1983), pp. 24–28; J. Schneer, *London 1900: The Imperial Metropolis* (New Haven CT, 1999), pp. 37–63, 70.

39. Nead, *Victorian Babylon*, pp. 13–56; J. Summerson, *The London Building World of the Eighteen-Sixties* (London, 1973); D. Owen, *The Government of Victorian London* (Cambridge MA, 1982); D. H. Porter, *The Thames Embankment* (Akron OH, 1998).

40. J. Winter, *London's Teeming Streets, 1830–1914* (London, 1993); P. J. Edwards, *History of London Street Improvements, 1855–1897* (London, 1898).

41. Weinreb and Hibbert, *London Encyclopaedia*, p. 909.

42. H. Clout, ed, *The Times London History Atlas* (London, 1997), p. 92; Godfrey, *Tower Bridge*, p. 59; by comparison, Brooklyn Bridge was used by 100,000 people per day in the 1890s and 200,000 per day in the 1900s: Gerdts, *Impressionist New York*, p. 165.

43. Godfrey, *Tower Bridge*, pp. 60–61, 75–76.

44. P. J. Atkins, 'How the West End was won: the struggle to remove street barriers in Victorian London', *Journal of Historical Geography* **19** (1993), 265–277.

45. This section is based on a comparison of successive editions of the 1:2500 Ordnance Survey map. Reprints published by Alan Godfrey Maps (London Sheet 77 Bermondsey & Wapping, dated 1872, 1894, 1914; published in 1995, 1986, 1983) also include excerpts from street directories for Tooley Street.

46. For example, Patrick Keiller, 'London' (Connoisseur, 1993). Keiller's film opens with a long shot of a cruiseship moving slowly upstream through the bridge. His use of this scene implies London's postcolonial identity. Other, older depictions of Tower Bridge on film are more innocent. C. Sorensen, *London on Film: 100 Years of Filmmaking in London* (London, 1996), pp. 80, 145, includes the trademark frame for 'A Two Cities Film', which shows a view of Tower Bridge superimposed on a background of the New York skyline, and a still from 'The Fugitive Futurist: A Q-riosity by "Q"' (Gaston Quiribet, 1924) depicting a future London in which the Thames has been drained, a railway line passes under Tower Bridge and a monorail utilises the high-level walkway as a station!

47. Illustrated in Godfrey, *Tower Bridge*, pp. 6, 56.

48. J. M. S. Careless, *Toronto to 1918* (Toronto, 1984), pp. 96, 136.

49. J. Lemon, 'Plans for early 20th-century Toronto: lost in management', *Urban History Review* **18** (1) (1989), 11–31.

50. H. Werner, 'Bridging politics: a political history of the Bloor Street Viaduct' (1989), typescript in City of Toronto Archives.

51. *Toronto World*, 19 Oct 1918.

52. J. Lemon, *Toronto since 1918* (Toronto, 1985), pp. 142, 199; B. West, *Toronto* (Toronto, 1967), pp. 211–212.

53. *Toronto Daily Star* and *Toronto World*, 18 Oct 1918.

54. Ibid, 21 Oct 1918.

55. *The Canadian Engineer* **31** (28 Sep 1916), 244; *Toronto Daily Star*, 3 Sep 1919.

56. *Toronto World*, 18 Oct 1918; *Toronto Daily Star*, 16 Dec 1918, and 1, 7 and 11 Feb and 20 Nov 1919.

57. Two exceptions are Stanley F. Turner, 'Construction of the Bloor Street Viaduct' (etching in collection of Art Gallery of Ontario), reproduced in E. G. Firth, *Toronto in Art* (Toronto, 1983), p. 112, and a 1918 poster advertising 'Victory Bonds', which exaggerated the height of the viaduct to convert the piers into tall pillars (victory columns?), reproduced in R. Stacey, *The Canadian Poster Book: 100 Years of the Poster in Canada* (Toronto, 1979), p. 15.

58. H. Hood, *The Governor's Bridge is Closed* (Toronto, 1973); M. Atwood, *Cat's Eye* (London, 1990) and *The Blind Assassin* (London, 2000).

59. M. Ondaatje, *In The Skin of a Lion* (Toronto, 1987).

60. D. Duffy, 'Furnishing the pictures: Arthur S. Goss, Michael Ondaatje and the imag(in)ing of Toronto', *Journal of Canadian Studies* **36** (2001), 106–129.

61. Ondaatje, *Skin*, pp. 26–27 (references are to the Penguin edition, 1988).

62. *Toronto World*, 16 Oct 1918; Duffy, 'Furnishing the pictures', 120; Ondaatje, *Skin*, p. 30; City of Toronto Archives RG8, Series 10, Item 818.

63. Ondaatje, *Skin*, pp. 35, 41, 43.

64. Haw, *The Brooklyn Bridge*, p. 69.

65. I am grateful to my student, Joshua Holmes, for introducing me to this theme through his coursework, now published as 'Building bridges and breaking boundaries: modernity and agoraphobia', *Opticon* **1** (1) (Autumn 2006), online at http://www.ucl.ac.uk/ics/opticon1826/VfPModernityAgoraphobiaPDF.pdf; see also A. Vidler, *Warped Space: Art, Architecture and Anxiety in Modern Culture* (Cambridge MA, 2000).

66. C. Arscott, 'The representation of the city in the visual arts' in M. Daunton, ed, *The Cambridge Urban History of Britain Volume III, 1840–1950* (Cambridge, 2000), p. 822 and Plate 41; O. Anderson, *Suicide in Victorian and Edwardian England* (Oxford, 1987) claimed around 30 suicides a year in the 1840s, just from Waterloo Bridge, supposedly the most popular site for the act in nineteenth-century London; quoted in L. J. Nicoletti, 'Downward mobility:

Victorian women, suicide and London's "Bridge of Sighs"', *Literary London* **2** (2004), online at http://www.literarylondon.org/london-journal/march2004/nicoletti.html; J. Dos Passos, *Manhattan Transfer* [1925] (London, 1987), pp. 118–120; D. Duffy, 'Suicide bridge 1918–2003', *Toronto Life* **37** (Feb 2003), 114.

67. Ondaatje, *Skin*, pp. 26, 143.

68. For general histories of nineteenth- and early twentieth-century London, see R. Porter, *London: A Social History* (London, 1994); F. Sheppard, *London: A History* (Oxford, 1998); S. Inwood, *A History of London* (London, 1998). For factual details, see Weinreb and Hibbert, *London Encyclopaedia*.

69. For population data on New York, see Jackson, *Encyclopedia of NYC*, pp. 920–923.

70. Careless, *Toronto to 1918*, p. 149.

71. Lemon, *Toronto since 1918*; see also J. Lemon, 'Toronto among North American cities' in V. L. Russell, ed, *Forging a Consensus: Historical Essays on Toronto* (Toronto, 1984), pp. 323–351.

72. H. Mayer and R. C. Wade, *Chicago: Growth of a Metropolis* (Chicago, 1969); J. Lemon, *Liberal Dreams and Nature's Limits: Great Cities of North America Since 1600* (Toronto, 1996), pp. 140–190; D. Smith, *The Chicago School* (Basingstoke, 1988); M. Girouard, *Cities and People* (New Haven CT, 1985), Chapter 15.

73. J. Saywell, *Canada: Pathways to the Present* (Toronto, 1994), p. 90; A. Germain and D. Rose, *Montréal: The Quest for a Metropolis* (Chichester, 2000), pp. 19–33.

74. L. D. McCann and P. J. Smith, 'Canada becomes urban: cities and urbanization in historical perspective' in T. Bunting and P. Filion, eds, *Canadian Cities in Transition* (Toronto, 1991), pp. 69–99, esp. 84–89. See also G. Gad and D. W. Holdsworth, 'Building for city, region, and nation' in Russell, *Forging a Consensus*, p. 301; D. Kerr and D. W. Holdsworth, eds, *Historical Atlas of Canada Volume III: Addressing the Twentieth Century 1891–1961* (Toronto, 1990), Plate 9 'Financial Institutions' and Plate 15 'The Emergence of Corporate Toronto'.

75. A. Briggs, *Victorian Cities* (Harmondsworth, 1968), pp. 277–310; G. Davison, *The Rise and Fall of Marvellous Melbourne* (Melbourne, 1978).

76. See, for example, A. Mayne, *The Imagined Slum: Newspaper Representation in Three Cities 1870–1914* (Leicester, 1993); S. O'Hanlon, *Together Apart: Boarding house, hostel and flat life in pre-war Melbourne* (Melbourne, 2002); A. Brown-May, *Melbourne Street Life* (Melbourne, 1998).

77. Davison, *Marvellous Melbourne*, p. 7.

78. P. Greenhalgh, 'The art and industry of mammon: international exhibitions, 1851–1901' in J. M. MacKenzie, ed, *The Victorian Vision: Inventing New Britain* (London, 2001), pp. 265–279; P. Greenhalgh, *Ephemeral Vistas: The Expositions Universelles, Great Exhibitions and World's Fairs, 1851–1939* (Manchester, 1988); K. Walden, *Becoming Modern in Toronto: The Industrial Exhibition and the Shaping of a Late Victorian Culture* (Toronto, 1997); H. Kalman, *A History of Canadian Architecture Volume 2* (Toronto, 1994), p. 566.

79. By comparison, in the 1880s the proportion was just under 30 per cent, and in 1980, only 24 per cent: Jackson, *Encyclopedia of NYC*, pp. 581–586.

80. Ibid, pp. 112–115, 598–602, 604–606.

81. Careless, *Toronto to 1918*, pp. 201–202; Lemon, *Toronto since 1918*, pp. 195–197; Jackson, *Encyclopedia of NYC*, pp. 620–622.

82. Schneer, *London 1900*, pp. 7–8.

83. Ward and Zunz, 'Between rationalism and pluralism'.

84. Rieger and Daunton, 'Introduction'.

85. Berman, *All That Is Solid Melts Into Air*, pp. 16–17; D. Frisby, *Cityscapes of Modernity* (Cambridge, 2001), p. 3.

86. Frisby, *Cityscapes*, p. 9.

87. F. Driver and D. Gilbert, 'Heart of empire? Landscape, space and performance in imperial London', *Environment and Planning D: Society and Space* **16** (1998), 11–28; F. Driver and D. Gilbert, eds, *Imperial Cities: Landscape, Display and Identity* (Manchester, 1999).

88. P. Goheen, 'The ritual of the streets in mid-19th-century Toronto', *Environment and Planning D: Society and Space* **11** (1993), 127–145.

89. Careless, *Toronto to 1918*, pp. 147, 209.

90. D. M. Scobey, *Empire City: The Making and Meaning of the New York City Landscape* (Philadelphia, 2002), pp. 43–47; C. H. Voorsanger and J. K. Howat, eds, *Art and the Empire City: New York 1825–1861* (New Haven CT, 2000).

91. J. Schneer, 'Anti-imperial London: the Pan-African Conference of 1900' in Driver and Gilbert, *Imperial Cities*, pp. 254–267; I. S. Black, 'Rebuilding 'The Heart of the Empire': bank head-quarters in the City of London, 1919–1939' in D. Arnold, ed, *The Metropolis and its Image* (Oxford, 1999), pp. 127–152; C. Ross, *Twenties London* (London, 2003), pp. 67–82; Scobey, *Empire City*, pp. 44–45.

92. J. Donald, *Imagining the Modern City* (London, 1999), pp. 95–96.

Chapter 2. The idea of progress

1. P. Boyer, *Urban Masses and Moral Order in America, 1820–1920* (Cambridge MA, 1978); P. Boyer et al, *The Enduring Vision* (Lexington MA, 1996); A. Lees, *Cities Perceived: Urban Society in European and American Thought, 1820–1940* (Manchester, 1985); D. Ward, *Poverty, Ethnicity and the American City, 1840–1925* (Cambridge, 1989).

2. D. Owen, *The Government of Victorian London* (Cambridge MA, 1982); K. Young and P. Garside, *Metropolitan London: Politics and Urban Change 1837–1981* (London, 1982).

3. T. Hunt, *Building Jerusalem: The Rise and Fall of the Victorian City* (London, 2004), p. 361.

4. D. J. Taylor, in 'Thursday Review', *The Independent*, 4 Jan 2001.

5. http://www.metrovsa.org/about.htm – the website of the Metropolitan Chapter of the Victorian Society in America refers to 'fostering the appreciation and preservation of our nineteenth-century heritage' and advertises activities centred on visits to (elite) private homes and campaigns to preserve 'the incomparable wealth of nineteenth- and early twentieth-century historic districts'.

6. T. J. Schlereth, *Victorian America: Transformations in Everyday Life 1876–1915* (New York, 1992).

7. Ibid, pp. 304–305.

8. M. Berman, *All That Is Solid Melts Into Air* (London, 1982), p. 13.

9. On the picturesque and 'creative destruction' in modern cities, see L. Nead, *Victorian Babylon* (New Haven CT, 2000); M. Page, *The Creative Destruction of Manhattan, 1900–1940* (Chicago, 1999).

10. Taylor, 'Thursday Review'.

11. D. Ward, 'The place of Victorian cities in developmental approaches to urbanization' in J. Patten, ed, *The Expanding City* (London, 1983), pp. 355–379; D. Ward and J. Radford, *North American Cities in the Victorian Age* (Norwich, 1983).

12. B. Disraeli, *Sybil* (London, 1845); J. London, *The People of the Abyss* [1903] (London, 1978); C. F. G. Masterman, *From the Abyss* (London, 1902).

13. Boyer, *Urban Masses*, Chapters 6 and 10; Ward, *Poverty, Ethnicity, and the American City*, Chapter 3; C. Bauer, *Modern Housing* (Boston MA, 1934).

14. T. Sharp, *Town Planning* [1940] (Harmondsworth, 1945), pp. 12, 15, 17.

15. L. Mumford, *The City in History* (Harmondsworth, 1961); quotations from pp. 494, 508, 509, 656.

16. R. Vaughan, *The Age of Great Cities* (London, 1843).

17. There are elements of such a view in Hunt's *Building Jerusalem* and in planning histories, from W. Ashworth, *The Genesis of Town Planning* (London, 1954) to P. Hall, *Cities in Civilization* (London, 1999).

18. Ward, *Poverty, Ethnicity and the American City*, Chapters 2–4.

19. D. Spain, *How Women Saved the City* (Minneapolis, 2001); K. K. Sklar, 'Hull-House Maps and Papers: social science as women's work in the 1890s' in M. Bulmer, K. Bales and K. K. Sklar, eds, *The Social Survey in Historical Perspective, 1880–1940* (Cambridge, 1992), pp. 111–147; J. S. Woodsworth, *My Neighbor* [1911] (Toronto, 1972); R. Allen, *The Social Passion: Religion and Social Reform in Canada* (Toronto, 1971).

20. D. Ward, 'Social reform, social surveys, and the discovery of the modern city', *Annals of the Association of American Geographers* **80** (1990), 491–503; D. Englander and R. O'Day, eds, *Retrieved Riches: Social Investigations in Britain 1840–1914* (Aldershot, 1995); J. C. Weaver, 'The modern city realized: Toronto civic affairs, 1880–1915' in A. F. J. Artibise and G. Stelter, eds, *The Usable Urban Past* (Toronto, 1979), pp. 39–72.

21. G. Best, *Mid-Victorian Britain 1851–75* (London, 1971), pp. 25–26. I am indebted to Philip Howell for drawing my attention to the illustration in *Reynolds's Miscellany* (21 Jan 1865), 72. There are similar illustrations in *Illustrated Times* (12 Mar 1864), 169, and *The British Workman* (1 Feb 1866), 56.

22. *The Builder*, **44** (3 Feb 1883), 140; *Residential Flats and Chambers to Let* (undated pamphlet, c. 1910, Westminster Archives Centre); both illustrations are reproduced in R. Dennis, 'Reconciling geographies, representing modernities' in I. Black and R. Butlin, eds, *Place, Culture and Identity* (Laval, 2001), pp. 17–43.

23. All quotations cited in W. H. Gerdts, *Impressionist New York* (New York, 1994), pp. 112–118.

24. For examples of the former, see *New York Illustrated* (New York, n.d., c. 1919); but perhaps the most celebratory images are combined on the covers of *New York, New York: The City in Art and Literature* (New York, 2000), an illustrated anthology of literature produced by the Metropolitan Museum of Art: front and back covers of a photograph and painting of the Flatiron are complemented by endpapers featuring rival chromolithographs of fireworks at the opening of Brooklyn Bridge. For the latter, see Douglas Tallack's close reading of the composition of photographs of the Flatiron Building by Stieglitz, Coburn and Steichen in D. Tallack, *New York Sights: Visualizing Old and New New York* (Oxford, 2005), pp. 25–30.

25. Lees, *Cities Perceived*, p. 307.

26. G. Davison, 'The city as a natural system: theories of urban society in early nineteenth-century Britain' in D. Fraser and A. Sutcliffe, eds, *The Pursuit of Urban History* (London, 1983), p. 349.

27. Quoted in Lees, *Cities Perceived*, p. 56.

28. Quoted in R. Allen, *The Moving Pageant: A Literary Sourcebook on London Street-Life, 1700–1914* (London, 1998), p. 170.

29. H. James, *English Hours* [1905] (London, 1960), p. 17.

30. Ibid, pp. 20, 30. Note, however that James also thought 'A small London would be an abomination' (p. 6) and that, despite the 'tremendous list of reasons why it should be insupportable . . . London is on the whole the most possible form of life' (in F. O. Matthiessen and K. B. Murdock, eds, *The Notebooks of Henry James* (New York, 1947), pp. 27–28).

31. H. James, *The American Scene* (London, 1907), pp. 74–75.

32. On Lang's 'Metropolis' see M. Minden, 'The city in early cinema: *Metropolis*, *Berlin* and *October*' in E. Timms and D. Kelley, eds, *Unreal City: Urban Experience in Modern European Literature and Art* (Manchester, 1985), pp. 193–213; J. R. Gold, 'From "Metropolis" to "The City": film visions of the future city' in J. A. Burgess and J. R. Gold, eds, *Geography, the media and popular culture* (London, 1985), pp. 123–143. 'Moloch' was a Canaanite god who could be placated only by offerings of blood from child sacrifice. Andrew Lees notes use of 'moloch' by Rousseau (1762), to describe Paris, and by the American commentator, E. H. Gruening (1922), to describe New York. See Lees, *Cities Perceived*, pp. 9, 290.

33. For example, W. J. Loftie, *In and Out of London* (London, 1875), pp. 15, 23, quoted in J. Winter, *London's Teeming Streets* (London, 1993), p. 2. See also W. J. Loftie, *History of London Volume I* (London, 1884), p. 1, for another reference to 'the restless tide of building'.

34. E. M. Forster, *Howards End* [1910] (London, 1983), pp. 115, 329.

35. Ford Madox Ford, *The Soul of London* [1905] (London, 1995), pp. 23, 26.

36. G. Cunningham, 'Houses in between: navigating suburbia in late Victorian writing', *Victorian Literature and Culture* **32** (2004), 423. She particularly refers to Conan Doyle's *Beyond the City* (1912) and H. G. Wells' *Ann Veronica* (1909), *The New Machiavelli* (1911) and, later in her essay, *The War of the Worlds* (1898).

37. 1 Cor. 12, 12-27; B. I. Coleman, ed, *The Idea of the City in Nineteenth-Century Britain* (London, 1973), pp. 55–56, 87–94, 97–101; Lees, *Cities Perceived*, pp. 29–31, 45–47, 92–94.

38. R. Sennett, *Flesh and Stone: The Body and the City in Western Civilization* (London, 1994).
39. Quoted in Coleman, *The Idea of the City*, p. 101.
40. W. C. Conant, 'Will New York Be the Final World Metropolis', *Century* **26** (1883), 687, quoted in R. Haw, *The Brooklyn Bridge: A Cultural History* (New Brunswick NJ, 2005), p. 29. Transferring his allegiance from the heart to the stomach, Conant continued: 'It [the metropolis] is the alimentary center where the national wealth is digested, mobilized, and infused into the circulation to nourish every fiber of the system.'
41. Masterman, *From the Abyss*, p. 6.
42. Davison, 'The city as a natural system', p. 362.
43. Quoted in E. G. Burrows and M. Wallace, *Gotham: A History of New York City to 1898* (New York, 1999), p. 774.
44. J. Strong, *The Twentieth-Century City* (New York, 1898), pp. 124–125, quoted in Boyer, *Urban Masses*, p. 255.
45. D. Trotter, *Circulation* (Basingstoke, 1988), pp. 61, 106–110.
46. Winter, *London's Teeming Streets*, pp. 5–7.
47. W. Cobbett, *Rural Rides* [1830] (Harmondsworth, 1967); Lees, *Cities Perceived*, Chapter 6; J. G. Williamson, *Coping with city growth during the British Industrial Revolution* (Cambridge, 1990).
48. For example, in proposing a 'People's Park' in New York in 1848 (several years before Central Park was authorised), the landscape architect Andrew Jackson Downing argued that it would constitute the 'lungs of the city': Burrows and Wallace, *Gotham*, pp. 790–791.
49. London, *People of the Abyss*, pp. 31–32.
50. M. Foucault, *The Birth of the Clinic* (London, 1974); Davison, 'The city as a natural system', pp. 357–359; C. Philo, '*The Birth of the Clinic*: an unknown work of medical geography', *Area* **32** (2000), 11–19; F. Driver, 'Moral geographies: social science and the urban environment in mid-nineteenth century England', *Transactions Institute of British Geographers* **13** (1988), 275–287.
51. F. Driver, *Power and pauperism: the workhouse system 1834–1884* (Cambridge, 1993); M. Ogborn, 'Discipline, government and law: separate confinement in the prisons of England and Wales, 1830–1877', *Transactions Institute of British Geographers* **20** (1995), 295–311, and 'Law and discipline in nineteenth-century English state formation: the Contagious Diseases Acts of 1864, 1866 and 1869', *Journal of Historical Sociology* **6** (1993), 28–55; C. Philo, '"Fit localities for an asylum": the historical geography of the nineteenth-century "mad business" in England as viewed through the pages of the *Asylum Journal*', *Journal of Historical Geography* **13** (1987), 398–415.
52. A. Mearns, 'The Bitter Cry of Outcast London', reprinted in P. Keating, ed, *Into Unknown England 1866–1913: Selections from the Social Explorers* (London, 1976), p. 97; G. Stedman Jones, *Outcast London* (Oxford, 1971), pp. 222–223.
53. London County Council, *The Housing Question in London* (London, 1900), pp. 191–192.
54. G. Godwin, *Town Swamps and Social Bridges* [1859] (Leicester, 1972). For a parallel discussion about physical and moral contagion and environmental influences in New York, see Ward, *Poverty, Ethnicity, and the American City*, Chapters 2–4.
55. London, *People of the Abyss*, p. 114.
56. Ibid.
57. U. Sinclair, *The Jungle* [1906] (New York, 1981).
58. 'The Jago', the setting for Morrison's novel, was the real-life 'Nichol' swept away for the LCC's Boundary Street scheme mentioned earlier in this chapter.
59. Lees, *Cities Perceived*, pp. 200–201.
60. Compare, for example, James Greenwood, famous for 'A Night in a Workhouse' (1866); Olive Malvery, who adopted numerous disguises in order to undertake a succession of menial jobs which she reported in *Pearson's Magazine* (1904–05); and George Orwell, who reported his experiences in *Down and Out in Paris and London* (1933). On Greenwood, see Keating, *Into Unknown England*, pp. 15–18, 33–54; on Malvery, see Allen, *The Moving Pageant*, pp. 19–21, 215–217, Winter, *London's Teeming Streets*, pp. 103–107 and J. R. Walkowitz, 'The Indian

woman, the flower girl, and the Jew: photojournalism in Edwardian London', *Victorian Studies* **42** (1998), 3–46.

61. A phrase made famous by the New York social explorer, Jacob Riis in *How the Other Half Lives* (1890): see below, Chapter 3.

62. Quoted in Lees, *Cities Perceived*, p. 28.

63. W. Rauschenbusch, *Christianity and the Social Crisis* (New York, 1907), pp. 251–252, quoted in Boyer, *Urban Masses*, p. 127.

64. A. Mayne, 'Representing the slum', *Urban History Yearbook* **17** (1990), 71. See also A. Mayne, *The Imagined Slum: Newspaper Representations in Three Cities, 1870–1914* (Leicester, 1993).

65. London, *People of the Abyss*, p. 11.

66. H. G. Wells, *The Time Machine* [1895] (London, 1995), pp. 43–44.

67. J. Lawton, 'Introduction' in Wells, *Time Machine*, p. xxxix.

68. London, *People of the Abyss*, p. 88.

69. C. F. G. Masterman, *From the Abyss*, pp. 4, 2, 18. On the uncanny in modernity, see J. Donald, *Imagining the Modern City* (London, 1999), Chapter 3.

70. Masterman, *From the Abyss*, pp. 16–17.

71. Wells, *Time Machine*, Chapter 11.

72. F. Driver, *Geography Militant: Cultures of Exploration and Empire* (Oxford, 2000), esp. Chapter 8, 'Exploring "Darkest England": Mapping the Heart of Empire'.

73. Boyer, *Urban Masses*, pp. 140–141; Burrows and Wallace, *Gotham*, pp. 1156–1158.

74. W. Booth, *In Darkest England and the Way Out* (London, 1890), Part I, Chapter I.

75. Ibid.

76. R. Williams, *The Country and the City* (London, 1973); J. R. Short, *Imagined Country: Society, Culture and Environment* (London, 1991).

77. H. Mayhew, *London Labour and the London Poor* (4 volumes) (London, 1861); D. E. Nord, 'The social explorer as anthropologist: Victorian travellers among the urban poor' in W. Sharpe and L. Wallock, eds, *Visions of the Modern City* (Baltimore, 1987), pp. 122–134.

78. Acceptance of evolution implied a future very different from the present; hence Wells' alternative futures: in *The Time Machine*, set far in the future, humankind has evolved into two separate and specialised species, a logical result of 'Darwinism at its purest' (Lawton, 'Introduction', p. xxxiii); in *The War of the Worlds* (1898), set in the present, London is destroyed by invading Martians, who have evolved technologically and genetically far beyond the inhabitants of Earth.

79. E. Bellamy, *Looking Backward: 2000–1887* (New York, 1888), Chapter XXVIII. Another sepulchral metaphor had been used nearly twenty years earlier by Sir Charles Trevelyan, describing London as a 'whited sepulchre', beautiful on the outside but 'full of dead men's bones': 'while it aspires to Christianise the heathen, it exercises a far more direct and effectual influence in heathenising Christians': quoted in Hunt, *Building Jerusalem*, p. 289.

80. Quoted in Boyer, *Urban Masses*, pp. 170, 176.

81. J. W. and D. B. Shepp, *Shepp's New York City Illustrated* (Philadelphia, 1894), Chapter XII.

82. *Oxford English Dictionary Online* (2005).

83. Matthew 7, v. 13.

84. Mark 15, v. 34.

85. A. Sawyer, 'Notes' in H. G. Wells, *War of the Worlds* (London, 2005), pp. 187–199.

86. Genesis 11, vv. 1–9.

87. Revelation 18, vv. 12–13.

88. Daniel 5, vv. 1–4.

89. Daniel 5, vv. 5, 26–30.

90. Revelation 18, v. 2.

91. Both quoted in Coleman, *The Idea of the City*, pp. 25, 39.

92. M. Girouard, *Cities and People: A Social and Architectural History* (New Haven CT, 1985), pp. 344–345; R. Hyde, *Panoramania!: The Art and Entertainment of the 'All Embracing' View* (London, 1988), pp. 105, 123.

93. L. Nead, *Victorian Babylon* (New Haven CT, 2000), p. 215; G. Doré and B. Jerrold, *London: A Pilgrimage* (London, 1872). As well as regular new editions of Doré's and Jerrold's book,

the illustrations are constantly recycled, e.g. in E. de Maré, *The London Doré Saw* (London, 1973), itself reissued as *Victorian London Revealed: Gustave Doré's Metropolis* (London, 2001). Doré's illustrations have sometimes been used as inspiration for television or film adaptations of Dickens' novels, effectively creating a monopoly on present-day perceptions of Victorian London. For one especially striking image, from David Lean's *Oliver Twist* (1948), see C. Sorensen, *London on Film* (London, 1996), pp. 100–101.

94. W. Morris, *News from Nowhere* [1890] (London, 1918), p. 76.

95. Lees, *Cities Perceived*, pp. 6–7; J. Ellul, *The Meaning of the City* (Grand Rapids MI, 1970).

96. Psalm 137, vv. 1, 4.

97. In a letter to Augustus John (5 Nov 1942), Lewis described Toronto as 'this sanctimonious bush-babylon': W. K. Rose, ed., *The Letters of Wyndham Lewis* (Norfolk CT, 1963), p. 339. See also Lewis' novel, based on his experiences in Toronto: *Self Condemned* (London, 1954).

98. C. Brontë, *Villette* [1853] (London, 1970), p. 54.

99. James, *English Hours*, p. 1; H. James, *The Ambassadors* (1903), Book II, Chapter 2, quoted in Girouard, *Cities and People*, p. 348.

100. M. Callaghan, *That Summer in Paris* [1963] (Toronto, 1976), p. 116. Note however, that Callaghan enfolded several layers of meaning into the term 'Babylonian': Paris was to be praised for 'its open beauty, its elegance' but also for the non-judgmental attitude of its citizens towards their neighbours' private lives, except in terms of money. And Callaghan considered that North Americans in Paris, like his friends Ernest Hemingway and Scott Fitzgerald, who had made little attempt to become French, were living in a kind of exile. Moreover, French writers who had rejected 'the stuff of daily life' had 'exiled themselves in their own dreams' (pp. 229–230).

101. Forster, *Howards End*, p. 117.

102. M. Brosseau, 'The city in textual form: *Manhattan Transfer*'s New York', *Ecumene* **2** (1995), 104.

103. J. Dos Passos, *Manhattan Transfer* [1925] (London, 1987), p. 340.

104. Revelation 21, v. 2.

105. P. Hall, *Cities of Tomorrow* (Oxford, 1988), Chapters 4 and 7; Girouard, *Cities and People*, pp. 348–360; Coleman, *The Idea of the City*, pp. 162–164.

106. Hall, *Cities of Tomorrow*, Chapter 6; James, *American Scene*, pp. 130, 133.

107. Short, *Imagined Country*, p. 81.

108. R. Dennis, 'Morley Callaghan and the moral geography of Toronto', *British Journal of Canadian Studies* **14** (1999), 35–51.

Chapter 3. Surveying the city

1. M. G. Hannah, *Governmentality and the Mastery of Territory in Nineteenth-Century America* (Cambridge, 2000), esp. pp. 39, 56–59, 114–117, 189, 226–227; P. Joyce, *The Rule of Freedom* (London, 2003), p. 25.

2. F. Driver, *Geography Militant: Cultures of Exploration and Empire* (Oxford, 2000); J. A. Riis, *How the Other Half Lives* (New York, 1890).

3. T. Owen and E. Pilbeam, *Ordnance Survey: Map Makers to Britain since 1791* (Southampton, 1992).

4. M. Bulmer, K. Bales and K. K. Sklar, *The Social Survey in Historical Perspective, 1880–1940* (Cambridge, 1992), p. 34; B. P. Hindle, *Maps for Local History* (London, 1988), p. 92; S. Donnelly, 'Mapping Rich and Poor: Putting Charles Booth's *Enquiry into London Life and Labour* Online', *Cartographic Journal*, **39** (1) (2002), 83.

5. R. Hyde, 'Edward Stanford and his library map of London', notes accompanying a 24-sheet facsimile of *Stanford's Library Map of London and its Suburbs* (London, 1980); on the 'skeleton survey', see also L. Nead, *Victorian Babylon* (New Haven CT, 2000), pp. 19–22.

6. R. Hyde, *Panoramania! The art and entertainment of the all-embracing view* (London, 1988), pp. 58–61, 79–83.

7. Ibid, pp. 83–85, 109–114.

8. R. Waddell, *Moving Uptown: Nineteenth-century Views of Manhattan*, online exhibition of prints from the collections of the New York Public Library, includes numerous examples from mid-1830s to mid-1860s: http://www.nypl.org/research/chss/spe/art/print/exhibits/movingup/opening.htm; E. G. Burrows and M. Wallace, *Gotham: A History of New York City to 1898* (New York, 1999), pp. 672–673.

9. Hyde, *Panoramania!*, p. 84.

10. J. M. Schwartz, 'Photographs from the edge of Empire' in A. Blunt et al, eds, *Cultural Geography In Practice* (London, 2003), pp. 154–171. The panoramas proved a two-edged sword: what seemed sophisticated and developed viewed from Toronto appeared like a frontier settlement viewed from London!

11. P. B. Hales, *Silver Cities: The Photography of American Urbanization, 1839–1915* (Philadelphia, 1984), pp. 73–87; R. Haw, *The Brooklyn Bridge: A Cultural History* (New Brunswick NJ, 2005), pp. 93–101.

12. M. King, *Handbook of New York City* (Boston, 1892); *New York Illustrated* (New York, 1919).

13. M. de Certeau, *The Practice of Everyday Life* (Berkeley, 1984).

14. Hyde, *Panoramania!*, pp. 45–49, 76–77, 100–101; Nead, *Victorian Babylon*, pp. 21–22, 79–80, 84–85.

15. In *Moving Uptown*, http://www.nypl.org/research/chss/spe/art/print/exhibits/movingup/opening.htm

16. Hales, *Silver Cities*, pp. 48–49.

17. V. M. Welter, *Biopolis: Patrick Geddes and the City of Life* (Cambridge MA, 2002); H. Meller, *Patrick Geddes: Social Evolutionist and City Planner* (London, 1990).

18. J. Donald, *Imagining the Modern City* (London, 1999), p. 14.

19. Reproduced in Nead, *Victorian Babylon*, p. 21. See also F. Barker and P. Jackson, *The History of London in Maps* (London, 1990), pp. 138–139, for a revised version of the same view issued nearly thirty years later.

20. Nead, *Victorian Babylon*, p. 22, drawing on the insights of Louis Marin, *Utopics* (London, 1984).

21. E. W. Gilbert, 'Pioneer maps of health and disease in England', *Geographical Journal* **124** (1958), 172–183; House of Lords 1842 XXVII, *Local reports on the sanitary condition of the labouring population in England*; H. Gavin, *Sanitary Ramblings* (London, 1848); P. K. Gilbert, 'The Victorian social body and urban cartography' in P. K. Gilbert, ed, *Imagined Londons* (Albany NY, 2002), pp. 11–30; R. Hyde, *Printed Maps of Victorian London 1851–1900* (Folkestone, 1975), p. 24.

22. W. A. Seymour, ed, *A History of the Ordnance Survey* (Folkestone, 1980), pp. 113–114; Owen and Pilbeam, *Ordnance Survey*, pp. 46–56.

23. Owen and Pilbeam, *Ordnance Survey*, p. 76.

24. Joyce, *The Rule of Freedom*, pp. 41–45, 52–56.

25. G. Rowley, 'British fire insurance plans: cartography at work', *Bulletin, Society of University Cartographers* **18** (1) (1984), 1–8, and 'British fire insurance plans: the Goad productions, c.1885 – c.1970', *Archives* **17** (74) (1985), 67–78; E. N. Moody, 'Urban history in fire insurance maps: Nevada as a case study', *Information Bulletin, Western Association of Map Libraries* **10** (2) (1979), 129–139; R. J. Hayward, 'Chas. E. Goad and Fire Insurance Cartography' in B. Farrell and A. Desbarats, eds, *Explorations in the History of Canadian Mapping* (Ottawa, 1988), pp. 179–193; C. Nehls, 'Sanborn Fire Insurance Maps': http://fisher.lib.virginia.edu/sanborn/about.html.

26. K. Arlitsch, 'Digitizing Sanborn fire insurance maps for a full color, publicly accessible collection', *D-Lib Magazine* **8** (7/8) (July/August 2002): http://www.dlib.org/dlib/july02/arlitsch/07arlitsch.html.

27. D. W. Holdsworth, 'Morphological change in Lower Manhattan, New York, 1893–1920' in J. Whitehand and P. Larkham, eds, *Urban Landscapes: International Perspectives* (London, 1992), pp. 114–129.

28. P. Jackson, *John Tallis's London Street Views 1838–1840* (London, 1969); Barker and Jackson, *The History of London in Maps*, pp. 116–119, 126–127.

29. A real *left* glove, with the reverse orientation – Great Exhibition in the palm and City at the fingertips – is attached to a register of designs in the National Archives; see R. Hyde, 'A "handy" map', *Map Collector* (June 1986), 47.

30. Joyce, *The Rule of Freedom*, pp. 191–193; Hyde, *Printed Maps*, pp. 43–44, and 'Edward Stanford'.

31. J. B. Harley, 'Maps, knowledge and power' in D. Cosgrove and S. Daniels, eds, *The Iconography of Landscape* (Cambridge, 1988), pp. 277–312, and 'Deconstructing the map', *Cartographica* **26** (1989), 1–20.

32. Barker and Jackson, *The History of London in Maps*, pp. 140–141; Hyde, *Printed Maps*, p. 27; B. Harrison, 'Pubs' in H. J. Dyos and M. Wolff, eds, *The Victorian City: Images and Realities* (London, 1973), pp. 161–190.

33. Bureau of Municipal Research, *What is 'The Ward' Going to Do with Toronto?* (Toronto, 1918), pp. 56–65.

34. D. L. Pike, 'Modernist space and the transformation of Underground London' in Gilbert, *Imagined Londons*, pp. 101–119; K. Garland, *Mr Beck's Underground Map* (Harrow, 1994).

35. J. Tagg, *The Burden of Representation: Essays on Photographies and Histories* (London, 1988), pp. 149, 129.

36. D. Duffy, 'Furnishing the pictures: Arthur S. Goss, Michael Ondaatje and the imag(in)ing of Toronto', *Journal of Canadian Studies* **36** (2001), 106–129. Goss's photographs illustrated Hastings' *Report of the Medical Health Officer Dealing with the Recent Investigation of Slum Conditions in Toronto* (Toronto, 1911), in which two out of eight illustrations of 'slum conditions' prominently featured people, in both cases mostly children.

37. Hales, *Silver Cities*, pp. 179–184; J. Thomson and A. Smith, *Street Life in London* (London, 1877).

38. Hales, *Silver Cities*, pp. 233–242.

39. Ibid, Chapter 4; M. Stange, *Symbols of Ideal Life: Social Documentary Photography in America 1890–1950* (New York, 1989), pp. 1–10; D. Leviatin, 'Preface' and 'Introduction' to J. A. Riis, *How the Other Half Lives* (Boston, 1996), pp. x–xi, 3–5.

40. Leviatin, 'Introduction', pp. 38–40.

41. Hales, *Silver Cities*, pp. 171–173.

42. Stange, *Symbols of Ideal Life*, pp. 10–12; Leviatin, 'Introduction', pp. 37–38.

43. Riis, *How the Other Half Lives* (1996 edn), p. 98.

44. Stange, *Symbols of Ideal Life*, p. 13.

45. D. Tallack, *New York Sights: Visualizing Old and New New York* (Oxford, 2005), pp. 95, 91; see also D. Tallack, 'The rhetoric of space: Jacob Riis and New York City's Lower East Side' in *City Sites: an electronic book, multimedia essays on New York and Chicago, 1870–1939*: http://artsweb.bham.ac.uk/citysites/.

46. M. M. Hambourg, *Paul Strand Circa 1916* (New York, 1998), p. 34.

47. L. Nead, 'Animating the everyday: London on camera circa 1900', *Journal of British Studies* **43** (2004), 74; 'Spirit of the Times', *Photography* (30 July 1891), 480, quoted in Nead, 'Animating', 74.

48. See, for example, the films made in the 1900s by Mitchell and Kenyon in industrial towns in northern England, and which were shown in marquees and church halls where workers and their families paid to see themselves on the screen: V. Toulmin, S. Popple and P. Russell, eds, *The Lost World of Mitchell and Kenyon* (London, 2004).

49. Hambourg, *Paul Strand*, p. 38.

50. Hales, *Silver Cities*, p. 278. On the Pittsburgh Survey, see M. W. Greenwald and M. Anderson, eds, *Pittsburgh Surveyed: Social Science and Social Reform in the Early Twentieth Century* (Pittsburgh, 1996); Stange, *Symbols of Ideal Life*, Chapter 2, 'The Pittsburgh Survey: Lewis Hine and the establishment of documentary style', pp. 47–87.

51. M. J. Anderson, *The American Census: A Social History* (New Haven CT, 1988).

52. Malthus had published the first edition of his *Essay on the Principle of Population* in 1798 during the same crisis. For an introduction to the British census, see E. Higgs, *Making Sense of the Census Revisited* (London, 2005).

53. Bulmer et al, *The Social Survey in Historical Perspective*, p. 7; Joyce, *The Rule of Freedom*, pp. 26–34; Hannah, *Governmentality*, pp. 54–55.
54. Higgs, *Making Sense*, pp. 6–14, 32–36.
55. *Illustrated Times*, 13 Apr 1861, 235, 239–246 and 20 Apr 1861, 255, 259. In addition to the illustrations discussed, all reproduced in Dyos and Wolff, *The Victorian City: Images and Realities* Volume 2, illns. 396–400, the articles showed the discipline and efficiency of recording and indexing processes inside the Census Office, and included some smaller sketches, one of a woman's body lying prone in shallow water, labelled 'One who escaped the census', as if the only way to evade the gaze of the state was to commit suicide.
56. The American census asked for the 'profession, occupation or trade' of 'each male person over 15 years of age' in 1850; by 1860, 'each person, male and female, over 15 years of age' merited an occupational entry; and by 1870, the age limit had been removed, so that 'at school' or 'at home' also appeared in the occupation column.
57. Hannah, *Governmentality*, p. 57.
58. Lynn Lees, for example, translated an Irish-born population of 109,000 in London in 1851 into a minimum Irish population of 156,000 (including the English-born children of Irish-born parents): L. H. Lees, *Exiles of Erin* (Manchester, 1979), p. 46.
59. C. Bressey, 'Looking for blackness: a researcher's paradox', *Ethics, Place and Environment* **6** (2003), 215–226, and 'Forgotten histories: three stories of black girls from Barnardo's Victorian archive', *Women's History Review* **11** (2002), 351–375.
60. Hannah, *Governmentality*, pp. 109, 142–149, 209.
61. Higgs, *Making Sense*, pp. 15–16, 37–42.
62. R. S. Holmes, 'Identifying nineteenth-century properties', *Area* **6** (1974), 273–277. This assumes that enumerators followed a logical route and that the schedules they collected from house-holders were copied into enumerators' books in the order in which they had been collected. At the very least, as is evident where full addresses *were* recorded, there are often several out-of-order schedules transcribed at the end of each enumerator's book, presumably households that were absent on his first visit or whose existence only came to light late in the process of enumeration.
63. Higgs, *Making Sense*, pp. 37–39, 117–118.
64. Hannah, *Governmentality*, pp. 123–127; Anderson, *The American Census*, p. 89; F. F. Furstenberg et al, 'What happened when the census was redone', *Sociology and Social Research* **63** (1979), 475–505, cited in R. H. Steckel, 'The quality of census data for historical enquiry: a research agenda', *Social Science History* **15** (1991), 585–586; B. Curtis, *The Politics of Population: State Formation, Statistics and the Census of Canada, 1840–1875* (Toronto, 2001).
65. D. H. Parkerson, 'Comments on the underenumeration of the US census, 1850–1880'; P. R. Knights, 'Potholes in the road of improvement? Estimating census underenumeration by longi-tudinal tracing: US censuses, 1850–1880'; and Steckel, 'The quality of census data for historical enquiry', all in *Social Science History* **15** (1991), 509–515, 517–526, 579–599.
66. For a survey of literature up to the 1980s see my *English Industrial Cities of the Nineteenth Century* (Cambridge, 1984).
67. Higgs, *Making Sense*, pp. 69–70; R. Harris and C. Hamnett, 'The myth of the promised land: the social diffusion of home ownership in Britain and North America', *Annals of the Association of American Geographers* **77** (1987), 173–190.
68. M. Daunton, 'House-ownership from rate books', *Urban History Yearbook* (1976), 21–27.
69. D. M. Thompson, 'The religious census of 1851' in R. Lawton, ed, *The Census and Social Structure* (London, 1978), pp. 241–286.
70. Joyce, *The Rule of Freedom*, pp. 13, 21.
71. D. Englander and R. O'Day, *Retrieved Riches: Social Investigation in Britain 1840–1914* (Aldershot, 1995); Bulmer et al, *The Social Survey in Historical Perspective 1880–1940*.
72. C. Topalov, 'The city as *terra incognita*: Charles Booth's poverty survey and the people of London, 1886–1891', *Planning Perspectives* **8** (1993), 411.
73. C. Booth, *Life and Labour of the People in London*, 17 volumes (London, 1902–1903). Selected excerpts are included in H. W. Pfautz, ed, *Charles Booth on the City* (Chicago, 1967) and A. Fried and R. Elman, eds, *Charles Booth's London* (Harmondsworth, 1969).

74. H. L. Smith, *New Survey of London Life and Labour*, 9 volumes (London, 1930–1935).

75. R. O'Day, 'Women and social investigation: Clara Collet and Beatrice Potter' in Englander and O'Day, *Retrieved Riches*, pp. 165–200; B. Webb, *My Apprenticeship* (Harmondsworth, 1971); N. and J. Mackenzie, *The Diary of Beatrice Webb*, 4 volumes (London, 1982–1986); D. McDonald, *Clara Collet 1860–1948: An Educated Working Woman* (London, 2004).

76. C. Booth, *Life and Labour of the People*, volume 1 (London, 1889), p. 157; P. F. Matthiesen, A. C. Young and P. Coustillas, eds, *The Collected Letters of George Gissing Volume Four 1889–1891* (Athens OH, 1993), pp. 249, 307; P. Coustillas, ed, *London and the Life of Literature in Late Victorian England: The Diary of George Gissing, Novelist* (Hassocks, 1978), pp. 232, 313.

77. Topalov, 'The city as *terra incognita*', 400.

78. Ibid, 410.

79. S. B. Warner, 'The management of multiple urban images' in D. Fraser and A. Sutcliffe, eds, *The Pursuit of Urban History* (London, 1983), p. 387.

80. J. A. Yelling, *Slums and Slum Clearance in Victorian London* (London, 1986).

81. Topalov, 'The city as *terra incognita*', 412.

82. The first edition of the poverty map is available in a modern reprint: D. Reeder, *Charles Booth's Descriptive Map of London Poverty 1889* (London, 1987). The revised edition and accompanying notebooks can be studied online at http://booth.lse.ac.uk/.

83. C. Russell and H. S. Lewis, *The Jew in London* (London, 1900).

84. Topalov, 'The city as *terra incognita*', 418.

85. K. K. Sklar, '*Hull-House Maps and Papers*: social science as women's work in the 1890s' in Bulmer et al, *The Social Survey in Historical Perspective*, pp. 121–129.

86. M. Bulmer, 'W. E. B. Du Bois as a social investigator: *The Philadelphia Negro*, 1899' in Bulmer et al, *The Social Survey in Historical Perspective*, pp. 170–188.

87. J. Addams, *Twenty Years at Hull House* (New York, 1910), p. 112.

88. J. Addams, 'Prefatory note' in *Hull-House Maps and Papers* (Boston, 1895), pp. vii–viii, quoted in Sklar, '*Hull-House Maps and Papers*', p. 123.

89. Mackenzie King was the author of four long articles on slum housing, immigrants and sweated labour in Toronto, all in *Toronto Mail and Empire*, 18 and 25 September, 2 and 9 October 1897. See R. Dennis, '"Foreigners who live in Toronto": attitudes towards immigrants in a Canadian city, 1890–1918' in B. Messamore, ed, *Canadian Migration Patterns from Britain and North America* (Ottawa, 2004), pp. 183–199.

90. P. G. Mackintosh, 'Scrutiny in the modern city: the domestic public and the Toronto Local Council of Women at the turn of the twentieth century', *Gender, Place and Culture* **12** (2005), 29–48.

91. H. B. Ames, *The City Below the Hill* [1897] (Toronto, 1972).

92. We can only speculate whether Ames also had in mind the image of the 'city upon a hill' – the city that should be *A Modell of Christian Charity* in the words of John Winthrop's sermon to the founders of the Massachusetts Bay Colony (1630) – or, more generally, Jesus' allusion to 'a city set on a hill' that 'cannot be hid' (Matthew 5 v. 14). Ames led an anti-corruption campaign against boss politics in Montreal and had been strongly influenced by the 'social gospel' movement while a student at Amherst College in the United States, but he made no explicit reference to religious ideas in *The City Below the Hill*.

93. P. F. W. Rutherford, 'Introduction' to Ames, *The City Below the Hill*, p. xiii. See also T. Copp, *The Anatomy of Poverty: The condition of the working class in Montreal, 1897–1929* (Toronto, 1974).

94. Bulmer et al, *The Social Survey in Historical Perspective*, esp. pp. 25–27, 35–38.

95. R. Plunz, *A History of Housing in New York City* (New York, 1990), pp. 44–46; Stange, *Symbols of Ideal Life*, pp. 28–45.

96. Stange, *Symbols of Ideal Life*, p. 46; S. Turner, 'The Pittsburgh Survey and the Survey Movement' in Greenwald and Anderson, *Pittsburgh Surveyed*, pp. 39–40.

97. S. M. Harrison, *Community Action through Surveys* (New York, 1916), p. 27, quoted in D. Ward, 'Social reform, social surveys, and the discovery of the modern city', *Annals of the Association of American Geographers* **80** (1990), 495.

98. D. Harvey, *Social Justice and the City* (London, 1973), p. 144.

99. L. Symes, 'The great American fact finding farce', *Harpers Magazine* **164**, 354, quoted in Ward, 'Social reform', 500.
100. Hannah, *Governmentality*, pp. 10–11.
101. City of Toronto, *Report of Housing Commission* (Dec 1918) included tables recording annual rates of housing vacancies, building permits, homeownership and tenancy. Annual *Municipal Handbooks* recorded numbers of building permits and the approximate value of buildings erected each year. More elaborate tables of ward data were published annually in the Assessment Commissioner's *Report*, included each December in Appendix C of the printed council minutes. The same Appendix also published ward data from a roughly annual *Police Census* of buildings and population. Many of these statistics were then reprinted in the city press, especially the *Toronto Daily Star* and the *Toronto Evening Telegram*, and in Might's Directory Co., *Toronto City Directories*.
102. Bureau of Municipal Research, *What is 'The Ward' Going to Do with Toronto?*, pp. 14–22.
103. For example, the Canadian journal, *Contract Record and Engineering Review* published annual building statistics under titles such as 'Our Annual Inventory! What Story Does It Tell?', vol. **36** (1922), 1216–1230, and 'The Greatest Year in the History of Canadian Construction', **42** (1928), 1313–1321.
104. R. Dennis, 'The social geography of Victorian Huddersfield' in E. A. H. Haigh, ed, *Huddersfield: A Most Handsome Town* (Huddersfield, 1992), pp. 423–448.
105. See, for example, D. R. Green and A. G. Parton, 'Slums and slum life in Victorian England: London and Birmingham at mid-century' in M. Gaskell, ed, *Slums* (Leicester, 1990), pp. 67–68.
106. G. Tulchinsky, '"Said to be a very honest Jew": the R. G. Dun credit reports and Jewish business activity in mid-19th century Montreal', *Urban History Review* **18** (1990), 200–209.
107. P. J. Atkins, *The Directories of London, 1677–1977* (London, 1990), Chapter 3.
108. C. Wall, '"At *Shakespear's-Head*, Over-Against *Catharine-Street* in the *Strand*": Forms of address in London streets' in T. Hitchcock and H. Shore, eds, *The Streets of London: From the Great Fire to the Great Exhibition* (London, 2003), pp. 10–26.
109. Atkins, *The Directories of London*, Chapters 3 and 4; Joyce, *The Rule of Freedom*, pp. 197–198.
110. See, for example, A. V. Bloomfield and R. Harris, 'The journey to work: a historical methodology', *Historical Methods* **30** (1997), 97–109.

Chapter 4. Writing and picturing the city

1. On Callaghan, see M. Callaghan, *That Summer in Paris* [1963] (Toronto, 1976); on Gissing, see J. Halperin, *Gissing: A Life in Books* (Oxford, 1982); B. Postmus, 'George Gissing's *Scrapbook*: A Storehouse of "Elements of Drama to be Fused and Minted in his Brain"' in J. Spiers, ed, *Gissing and the City* (Basingstoke, 2006), pp. 199–211.
2. R. Zurier, R. W. Snyder and V. M. Mecklenburg, *Metropolitan Lives: The Ashcan Artists and Their New York* (New York, 1995); G. Levin, *Edward Hopper as Illustrator* (New York, 1979); M. W. Greenwald, 'Visualizing Pittsburgh in the 1900s: Art and Photography in the Service of Social Reform' in M. W. Greenwald and M. Anderson, eds, *Pittsburgh Surveyed* (Pittsburgh, 1996), pp. 124–152.
3. For example, T. Shapiro, 'The metropolis in the visual arts: Paris, Berlin, New York, 1890–1940' and P. Keating, 'The metropolis in literature', both in A. Sutcliffe, ed, *Metropolis 1890–1940* (London, 1984), pp. 95–127 and 129–145.
4. Keating, 'The metropolis in literature', pp. 133–134, 141.
5. E. Timms, 'Introduction: Unreal city – theme and variations' in E. Timms and D. Kelley, eds, *Unreal City: Urban Experience in Modern European Literature and Art* (Manchester, 1985), p. 3.
6. E. Gilbert, 'Naturalist metaphors in the literature of Chicago, 1893–1925', *Journal of Historical Geography* **20** (1994), 288.
7. On the London artists, see M. Galinou and J. Hayes, *London in Paint: Oil Paintings in the Collection at the Museum of London* (London, 1996), esp. pp. 283–337; C. Wood, *Victorian Panorama* (London, 1976).

8. R. Williams, *The Country and the City* (London, 1973), pp. 292–293.

9. M. Bradbury, 'The cities of modernism' in M. Bradbury and J. McFarlane, eds, *Modernism: A Guide to European Literature* (Harmondsworth, 1976, 1991), p. 99.

10. A. Thacker, *Moving through Modernity* (Manchester, 2003), esp. Chapters 3–5; R. Hughes, *American Visions* (London, 1997), Chapter 6; F. Whitford, 'The city in painting' in Timms and Kelley, *Unreal City*, pp. 45–64. The phrase 'unreal city' derives from T. S. Eliot's *The Waste Land* (1922).

11. Williams, *The Country and the City*, p. 282.

12. Ibid, pp. 202, 259.

13. P. Preston and P. Simpson-Housley, eds, *Writing the City* (London, 1994), p. 6.

14. Bradbury, 'The cities of modernism', p. 97.

15. E. James, 'An insight into the management of railway bookstalls in the eighteen fifties', *Publishing History* **10** (1981), 65–69; T. Davies, 'Transports of pleasure' in Formations Collective, eds, *Formations of Pleasure* (London, 1983), p. 49. For other commentaries on reading and rail travel, see W. Schivelbusch, *The Railway Journey* (Leamington Spa, 1977), pp. 64–69; P. Bailey, 'Adventures in space: Victorian railway erotics, or taking alienation for a ride', *Journal of Victorian Culture* **9** (2004), 1–21.

16. Bradbury, 'The cities of modernism', p. 99.

17. J. Loughery, *John Sloan: Painter and Rebel* (New York, 1995), pp. 120, 154–155; Hughes, *American Visions*, pp. 353–357; R. Rosenblum et al, *1900: Art at the Crossroads* (London, 2000).

18. V. Knight, 'The private life of William Powell Frith' in M. Bills and V. Knight, eds, *William Powell Frith: Painting the Victorian Age* (New Haven CT, 2006), p. 19.

19. Gagen's picture is reproduced on the dust jacket and pp. 94–95 of E. G. Firth, *Toronto in Art* (Toronto, 1983) and critically interpreted by J. Caulfield, 'The imagined cities of three Canadian painters', *Urban History Review* **20** (1) (1991), 3–14.

20. Bell-Smith's painting is included in Firth, *Toronto in Art*, p. 66, and discussed by R. Fleming, 'The trolley takes command, 1892 to 1894', *Urban History Review* **19** (1991), 218–225, and E. L. Ramsay, 'Modernity and post-colonialism: *The Heart of the Empire* (1909) by F. M. Bell-Smith', *Labour/Le Travail* **52** (2003).

21. M. Wolff and C. Fox, 'Pictures from the magazines' in H. J. Dyos and M. Wolff, eds, *The Victorian City: Images and Realities* (London, 1973), pp. 559–582. On New York, see F. L. Mott, *A History of American Magazines* (Cambridge MA, 1938); K. Jackson, ed, *The Encyclopedia of New York City* (New Haven CT, 1995), pp. 528–529, 666; D. M. Scobey, *Empire City* (Philadelphia, 2002), pp. 26–28.

22. *The Graphic*, 4 Dec 1869, 10; E. D. H. Johnson, 'Victorian artists and the urban milieu' in Dyos and Wolff, *The Victorian City*, p. 459.

23. M. Cowling, *Victorian Figurative Painting: Domestic Life and the Contemporary Social Scene* (London, 2000), pp. 188–190.

24. Loughery, *John Sloan*, p. 38.

25. Zurier, *Metropolitan Lives*, pp. 59–68.

26. A. Poole, *Gissing in Context* (Totowa NJ, 1975), p. 143.

27. M. New, ed, *The Complete Novels and Selected Writings of Amy Levy 1861–1889* (Gainesville FL, 1993): *The Romance of a Shop* (1888) occupies pp. 59–196, and the quotations are from pp. 95, 116, 109 and 195. On St John's Wood as an artists' quarter, see K. Wedd et al, *Creative Quarters: The Art World in London from 1700 to 2000* (London, 2001), pp. 86–90.

28. R. Labrusse and J. Munck, 'André Derain in London (1906–07)' in Courtauld Institute, *André Derain: The London Paintings* (London, 2005), p. 13.

29. P. Ackroyd, *Dickens* (London, 1990); P. Collins, 'Dickens and London' in Dyos and Wolff, *The Victorian City*, pp. 537–557.

30. J. Johnson, 'Introduction' to J. Joyce, *Ulysses* (Oxford, 1993), pp. ix–xxxvii.

31. S. Patin, 'The return of Whistler and Monet to the Thames' in K. Lochnan, ed, *TurnerWhistlerMonet* (London, 2004), pp. 179–183; Courtauld Institute, *André Derain*, pp. 14, 45–47.

32. A. G. Robins, 'The greatest artist the world has ever seen' in A. G. Robins and R. Thomson, *Degas, Sickert and Toulouse-Lautrec: London and Paris 1870–1910* (London, 2005), pp. 66–69.

33. M. Brosseau, 'Geography's literature', *Progress in Human Geography* **18** (1994), 347.

34. C. L. Salter and W. L. Lloyd, *Landscape in Literature* (Washington, 1977), cited in Brosseau, 'Geography's literature', 336.

35. M. Brosseau, 'The city in textual form: *Manhattan Transfer*'s New York', *Ecumene* **2** (1995), 90.

36. Ibid, 93.

37. S. Daniels, 'Images of the railway in nineteenth century paintings and prints' in *Train Spotting: Images of the Railway in Art* (Nottingham, 1985), p. 18. Mary Cowling provides a detailed analysis of both 'Derby Day' and 'The Railway Station' in *Victorian Figurative Painting*, Chapter 2.

38. M. Cowling, 'Frith and his followers' in Bills and Knight, *William Powell Frith*, p. 73.

39. E. Ehrman, 'Frith and fashion', pp. 120–121, and C. Arscott, 'William Powell Frith's *The Railway Station*: classification and the crowd', pp. 79–93, both in Bills and Knight, *William Powell Frith*. Quotation from p. 81.

40. Cowling, *Victorian Figurative Painting*, pp. 140–143; Galinou and Hayes, *London in Paint*, pp. 302–304.

41. Cowling, *Victorian Figurative Painting*, pp. 146, 150; Galinou and Hayes, *London in Paint*, pp. 253–255.

42. Johnson, 'Victorian artists and the urban milieu', p. 456; Cowling, *Victorian Figurative Painting*, pp. 170–179.

43. H. Mayhew, *London Labour and the London Poor* (London, 1861–1862).

44. D. Tallack, 'City Sights: Mapping and Representing New York City' in M. Balshaw and L. Kennedy, eds, *Urban Space and Representation* (London, 2000), p. 29. Tallack repeats this observation in an extended discussion of Bellows' 'New York' in *New York Sights: Visualizing Old and New New York* (Oxford, 2005), Chapter 4.

45. J. M. Whistler, *The Gentle Art of Making Enemies* (New York, 1967), p. 136, quoted in K. Lochnan, 'Turner, Whistler, Monet: An Artistic Dialogue' in Lochnan, *TurnerWhistlerMonet*, p. 29.

46. P. Fisher, 'The novel as newspaper and gallery of voices: the American novel in New York City: 1890–1930' in T. Bender and C. E. Schorske, eds, *Budapest and New York: Studies in Metropolitan Transformation: 1870–1930* (New York, 1994), pp. 332–351.

47. Ibid, p. 337.

48. D. Bindman, *Industry and Idleness: The Moral Geography of Hogarth's London* (London, 1997).

49. R. W. Snyder and R. Zurier, 'Picturing the city' in Zurier, *Metropolitan Lives*, p. 110.

50. Shapiro, 'The metropolis in the visual arts', p. 101. See also M. Doezema, *George Bellows and Urban America* (New Haven CT, 1992), pp. 188–195.

51. T. Tanner, 'Introduction' to W. D. Howells, *A Hazard of New Fortunes* (Oxford, 1990), p. ix.

52. G. Woodcock, *'Moral Predicament': Morley Callaghan's* More Joy in Heaven (Toronto, 1993), p. 45; G. Boire, *Morley Callaghan: Literary Anarchist* (Toronto, 1994).

53. R. Dennis, 'Morley Callaghan and the moral geography of Toronto', *British Journal of Canadian Studies* **14** (1) (1999), 35–51.

54. Keating, 'The metropolis in literature', p. 133.

55. Cowling, 'Frith and his followers', p. 75.

56. R. Thomson, 'Modernity, figure, metropolis' in Robins and Thomson, *Degas, Sickert and Toulouse-Lautrec*, p. 42.

57. Tallack, *New York Sights*, p. 51.

58. Tallack, 'City sights', p. 37; see also Tallack, *New York Sights*, pp. 51–55; Doezema, *George Bellows and Urban America*, Chapter 1.

59. J. Dos Passos, *Manhattan Transfer* [1925] (London, 1987), pp. 23, 54–55.

60. Ibid, p. 68.

61. Brosseau, 'The city in textual form', 97–98.

62. On the other hand, fire in shared, multi-storied premises was a real and constant hazard in New York. R. W. DeForest and L. Veiller devote a whole chapter in *The Tenement House Problem* (New York, 1903) to enumerating newspaper reports of tenement fires.

63. Fisher, 'The novel as newspaper'.

64. Ibid.

65. Quoted in Brosseau, 'The city in textual form', 96.

66. Ibid, 96.

67. Ibid, 102.

68. Dos Passos, *Manhattan Transfer*, p. 207.

69. Ibid, pp. 84, 49, 336, 346, 300, 113, 143, 309.

70. Keating, 'The metropolis in literature', p. 130.

71. J. Goode, 'Introduction' to G. Gissing, *The Nether World* (Brighton, 1974), p. xi.

72. Williams, *The Country and the City*, p. 131.

73. J. Caulfield, 'Augurs of "gentrification": city houses of four Canadian painters' in P. Simpson-Housley and G. Norcliffe, eds, *A Few Acres of Snow* (Toronto, 1992), p. 193.

74. P. Larisey, *Light for a Cold Land: Lawren Harris's Work and Life* (Toronto, 1993), p. 20.

75. Caulfield, 'Augurs', p. 195.

76. On Hopper, see G. Levin, *Edward Hopper: The Art and the Artist* (New York, 1980), and *Edward Hopper: An Intimate Biography* (New York, 1995); T. Slater, 'Fear of the city 1882–1967: Edward Hopper and the discourse of anti-urbanism', *Social & Cultural Geography* **3** (2002), 135–154.

77. J. Hardin et al, *Monet's London: Artists' Reflections on the Thames 1859–1914* (St Petersburg FL, 2005).

78. E. Shanes, *Impressionist London* (New York, 1994), p. 31.

79. W. Corn, 'The artist's New York: 1900–1930' in Bender and Schorske, *Budapest and New York*, pp. 284–286.

80. H. B. Weinberg et al, *American Impressionism and Realism: The Painting of Modern Life, 1885–1915* (New York, 1994), pp. 183–188; Tallack, *New York Sights*, pp. 124, 142–143, and 'New York, New York', http://www.nottingham.ac.uk/3cities/tallack2.htm.

81. Shapiro, 'The metropolis in the visual arts', p. 101.

82. K. Adler et al, *Americans in Paris 1860–1900* (London, 2006), pp. 15, 110, 253.

83. Weinberg, *American Impressionism and Realism*, pp. 155–162; Tallack, *New York Sights*, p. 34; Gerdts, *Impressionist New York*, pp. 134–138. Weinberg suggests that Prendergast's 'Central Park' may date from 1903, since the absence of automobiles and the fashions of female park-goers indicate a date before 1908; but the artist's technique implies a reworking as late as 1914–1915.

84. J. Baudrillard, *America* (London, 1988), p. 56, quoted in D. B. Clarke, 'Introduction: previewing the cinematic city' in D. B. Clarke, ed, *The Cinematic City* (London, 1997), p. 1.

85. N. AlSayyad, *Cinematic Urbanism: A History of the Modern from Reel to Real* (New York, 2006).

86. C. McArthur, 'Chinese boxes and Russian dolls: tracking the elusive cinematic city' in Clarke, *The Cinematic City*, pp. 19–45.

87. A. Sutcliffe, 'The metropolis in the cinema' in Sutcliffe, *Metropolis 1890–1940*, pp. 147–171.

88. McArthur, 'Chinese boxes', pp. 28–31.

89. J. R. Gold, 'From 'Metropolis' to 'The City': film visions of the future city, 1919–39' in J. A. Burgess and J. R. Gold, eds, *Geography, the Media and Popular Culture* (London, 1985), pp. 123–143; Hughes, *American Visions*, pp. 382–384; 'Manhatta' is available online at http://www.metmuseum.org/explore/artists_view/manhatta_main.html.

90. L. Charney, 'In order: fragmentation in film and vaudeville' in P. McDonnell, ed, *On the Edge of Your Seat: Popular Theater and Film in Early Twentieth-Century American Art* (New Haven CT, 2002), p. 108.

91. S. Kern, *The Culture of Time and Space 1880–1918* (Cambridge MA, 1983), p. 117.

92. R. Zurier, 'City, stage, and screen: John Sloan's urban theater', pp. 175–187, and R. Silberman, 'Edward Hopper and the theatre of the mind: vision, spectacle, and the spectator', pp. 137–155, both in McDonnell, *On the Edge of Your Seat*.

93. F. Moretti, *Atlas of the European Novel 1800–1900* (London, 1998), pp. 40–47.

94. Ibid, pp. 70, 18.

95. G. Gissing, *Workers in the Dawn* [1880] (Brighton, 1985), pp. 9, 17.

96. G. Gissing, *The Whirlpool* [1897] (London, 1984), p. 2.

97. G. Gissing, *In The Year of Jubilee* [1894] (London, 1994), p. 351.

98. A. Thacker, *Moving through Modernity: Space and Geography in Modernism* (Manchester, 2003).

99. M. de Certeau, *The Practice of Everyday Life* (Berkeley CA, 1984), p. 117.

100. Thacker, *Moving through Modernity*, p. 33.

101. H. G. Wells, *Tono-Bungay* [1909] (London, 1994), p. 7.

102. 'Walk with me, reader, into Whitecross Street': Gissing, *Workers in the Dawn*, p. 3; 'Journey on the top of a tram-car from King's Cross to Holloway': G. Gissing, *Thyrza* [1887] (Brighton, 1984), p. 319.

103. Dos Passos, *Manhattan Transfer*, p. 55.

104. Gissing, *Jubilee*, p. 334.

105. A. D. King, *The Bungalow: the production of a global culture* (London, 1984).

106. Gissing, *Whirlpool*, pp. 196–204, 278–291.

107. L. Hapgood, 'The literature of the suburbs: versions of repression in the novels of George Gissing, Arthur Conan Doyle and William Pett Ridge, 1890–1899', *Journal of Victorian Culture* **5** (2000), 303–305.

108. On space syntax as a method to analyse the complexity of urban form including measures of network and geometry, see B. Hillier and J. Hanson, *The Social Logic of Space* (Cambridge, 1984); and for a recent application of space syntax to Booth's poverty maps, see L. Vaughan et al, 'Space and exclusion: does urban morphology play a part in social deprivation?', *Area* **37** (2005), 402–412.

109. W. D. Howells, *A Hazard of New Fortunes* [1890] (Oxford, 1990), pp. 380–381, 384, 403.

110. G. Gissing, *The Nether World* [1889] (London, 1973), pp. 219–221, 260, 331–332.

111. Ibid, p. 271.

112. Howells, *Hazard*, p. 38; E. C. Cromley, *Alone Together: A History of New York's Early Apartments* (Ithaca NY, 1990).

113. Gissing, *Whirlpool*, p. 285.

114. G. Gissing, *New Grub Street* [1891] (Harmondsworth, 1968), p. 165.

115. Gissing, *Nether World*, pp. 241, 244, 273.

116. Ibid, p. 280.

117. D. Dewing, ed, *Home and Garden: Paintings and Drawings of English, Middle-Class, Urban Domestic Spaces 1675 to 1914* (London, 2003), pp. 142–145; W. Baron, *The Painters of Camden Town 1905–1920* (London, 1988).

118. Baron, *Camden Town*, pp. 82–4; A. G. Robins, 'Sickert and the Paris art world' in Robins and Thomson, *Degas, Sickert and Toulouse-Lautrec*, pp. 155–201.

119. Zurier, *Metropolitan Lives*, pp. 112–115, 175–178, 201.

120. Loughery, *John Sloan*, p. 153.

Chapter 5. Improving streets

1. M. de Certeau, *The Practice of Everyday Life* (Berkeley, 1984); M. Domosh, 'Those "Gorgeous Incongruities": polite politics and public space on the streets of nineteenth-century New York City', *Annals of the Association of American Geographers* **88** (1998), 209–226.

2. P. Joyce, *The Rule of Freedom: Liberalism and the Modern City* (London, 2003).

3. C. Otter, 'Making liberalism durable: vision and civility in the late Victorian city', *Social History* **27** (2002), 1–15. Quotations are from pp. 3, 6, 11, 12. See also C. Otter, 'Streets' in S. Pile, S. Harrison and N. Thrift, eds, *Patterned Ground* (London, 2004), pp. 238–240, and for a more empirical discussion, R. Turvey, 'Street mud, dust and noise', *London Journal* **21** (1996), 131–148.

4. E. Blackmar and R. Rosenzweig, 'The park and the people: Central Park and its publics: 1850–1910' in T. Bender and C. E. Schorske, eds, *Budapest and New York: Studies in Metropolitan Transformation* (New York, 1994), pp. 108–134.

5. Jurgen Habermas, quoted in P. Goheen, 'Negotiating access to public space in mid-nineteenth century Toronto', *Journal of Historical Geography* **20** (1994), 430–449.

6. Ibid.

7. M. Daunton, 'Public place and private space: the Victorian city and the working-class household' in D. Fraser and A. Sutcliffe, eds, *The Pursuit of Urban History* (London, 1983), pp. 212–233.

8. W. Schivelbusch, *Disenchanted Night: The Industrialisation of Light in the Nineteenth Century* (Oxford, 1988), pp. 185–186.

9. P. Goheen, 'Public space and the geography of the modern city', *Progress in Human Geography* **22** (1998), 479–496.

10. J. Winter, *London's Teeming Streets 1830–1914* (London, 1993). For information on particular streets, B. Weinreb and C. Hibbert, eds, *The London Encyclopaedia* (London, 1983); G. Tyack, 'James Pennethorne and London street improvements, 1838–1855', *London Journal* **15** (1990), 38–56; D. Schubert and A. Sutcliffe, 'The "Haussmannization" of London?: the planning and construction of Kingsway-Aldwych, 1889–1935', *Planning Perspectives* **11** (1996), 115–144.

11. P. J. Edwards, *History of London Street Improvements, 1855–1897* (London, 1898); D. Owen, *The Government of Victorian London* (Cambridge MA, 1982), Chapters 4 and 5.

12. A classic example of this is discussed in A. Pred, *Lost Words and Lost Worlds: Modernity and the Language of Everyday Life in Late Nineteenth-Century Stockholm* (Cambridge, 1990), Chapter 4. See also A. Pred, 'Languages of everyday practice and resistance: Stockholm at the end of the nineteenth century' in A. Pred and M. J. Watts, *Reworking Modernity* (New Brunswick NJ, 1992), pp. 118–154. In London between 1855 and 1873 the MBW had renamed 1500 streets and named 2400 new streets: Owen, *Government*, p. 116.

13. Dundas was the name of a colonial administrator at the time of Toronto's founding (as York) in 1784. He also gave his name to the town of Dundas, west of Toronto.

14. J. Lemon, 'Plans for early 20th-century Toronto: lost in management', *Urban History Review* **18** (1) (1989), 11–31.

15. M. Page, *The Creative Destruction of Manhattan 1900–1940* (Chicago, 1999); M. Gandy, *Concrete and Clay: Reworking Nature in New York City* (Cambridge MA, 2002), Chapter 3; K. Jackson, ed, *The Encyclopedia of New York City* (New Haven CT, 1995), p. 508.

16. For a general historical background, see I. Watson, *Westminster and Pimlico Past* (London, 1993) and S. Bradley and N. Pevsner, *Buildings of England, London 6: Westminster* (London, 2003).

17. G. Gissing, *The Odd Women* [1893] (London, 1980), p. 118.

18. G. Bernard Shaw, *Plays Pleasant and Unpleasant* (1898), quoted in V. Kingman, 'The world of the new: the first ten years' in Ashley Gardens Residents Association, *Ashley Gardens: Backward Glances* (1990), pp. 14–25.

19. Charles Booth Police Notebooks B360, pp. 204–205, 214–215 (Booth Archive, LSE)

20. A. Goodman, *Gilbert and Sullivan's London* (London, 2000), pp. 95–97.

21. St. James's Court is now St. James's Hotel and Apartments; Artillery Mansions has also been renovated and partially redeveloped as The Artilleries.

22. Charles Booth Police Notebooks B360, pp. 204–205.

23. Goodman, *Gilbert and Sullivan's London*, p. 95.

24. T. H. S. Escott, *England: its People, Polity and Pursuits* (London, 1891), p. 230.

25. Ibid, pp. 221–222.

26. V. Woolf, *Mrs Dalloway* [1925] (London, 1992), p. 174.

27. Watson, *Westminster*, p. 100.

28. G. Doré and B. Jerrold, *London: A Pilgrimage* (London, 1872), p. 95.

29. *The Builder* **19** (1861), quoted in D. J. Olsen, *The City as a Work of Art* (New Haven CT, 1986), p. 202.

30. Charles Booth Police Notebooks B360, pp. 202–203.
31. It is interesting to note that this exchange follows a more obvious joke on the same theme only a few lines earlier. Mr Worthing tells Lady Bracknell that he owns a house in Belgrave Square – no. 149. Lady Bracknell comments, 'The unfashionable side', but adds that that could be changed, either the side or the fashion. Evidently Lady Bracknell has the power to set and change society fashions, but she has neither the knowledge about nor the interest in changing the fortunes of railway companies: O. Wilde, *The Importance of Being Earnest* [1895] (Cambridge, 1999), pp. 29–31.
32. *Residential Flats and Chambers to Let*, undated pamphlet, c. 1912, Westminster Archives Centre.
33. See some of the paintings illustrated in R. R. Brettell and J. Pissarro, *The Impressionist and the City: Pissarro's Series Paintings* (New Haven CT, 1992) and A. Distel et al, *Gustave Caillebotte: The Unknown Impressionist* (London, 1996), pp. 82–97.
34. R. Sennett, *Flesh and Stone: The Body and the City in Western Civilization* (London, 1994); W. Schivelbusch, *The Railway Journey* (Leamington Spa, 1986), Chapter 4.
35. M. Berman, *All That is Solid Melts into Air* (London, 1982), pp. 159–160.
36. Both films are included in Museum of London, *Journeys through Victorian London* (CD) (2001).
37. Winter, *London's Teeming Streets*, p. 48; J. White, *London in the Twentieth Century* (London, 2001), p. 14. White also notes that in the more-trafficked but far more regulated conditions of 1997, there were 276 deaths.
38. E. M. Forster, *Howards End* [1910] (London, 1983), pp. 115–116.
39. Woolf, *Mrs Dalloway*, p. 182.
40. Ibid, pp. 176–177.
41. Ibid, p. 178.
42. D. E. Nord, *Walking the Victorian Streets: Women, Representation, and the City* (Ithaca NY, 1995), pp. 247–248.
43. White, *London in the Twentieth Century*, p. 31. Note, however, that formal bus stops were still rare. The LGOC first introduced fixed bus stops in 1913, but buses still had to stop wherever requested, and it was not until the 1930s that fixed stops became commonplace. See J. Reed, *London Buses: A Brief History* (Harrow, 2000).
44. T. Barker and M. Robbins, *A History of London Transport Volume 2* (London, 1974), pp. 215–225.
45. J. Joyce, *London's Trams* (London, 1990).
46. J. P. McKay, *Tramways and Trolleys: The Rise of Mass Urban Transport in Europe* (Princeton, 1976).
47. R. J. Harley, *LCC Electric Tramways* (London, 2002), p. 7.
48. R. Fleming, 'The trolley takes command, 1892 to 1894', *Urban History Review* **19** (1991), 218–225; R. M. Stamp, *Bright Lights, Big City: The History of Electricity in Toronto* (Toronto, 1991), pp. 34–37.
49. Fleming, 'The trolley', 218.
50. C. McShane, 'The origins and globalization of traffic control signals', *Journal of Urban History* **25** (1999), 379–404.
51. Winter, *London's Teeming Streets*, pp. 35–36, 48; C. Ross, *Twenties London: A City in the Jazz Age* (London, 2003), p. 127.
52. McShane, 'Traffic control signals', 382–385.
53. Stamp, *Bright Lights, Big City*, p. 33; *Toronto Globe*, 11 Mar and 18 Mar 1927.
54. Winter, *London's Teeming Streets*, p. 10.
55. McShane, 'Traffic control signals', 387, 386.
56. L. Nead, *Victorian Babylon* (New Haven CT, 2000), p. 85.
57. Ibid, pp. 98–100.
58. Ibid, p. 83.
59. D. Nye, 'The electric sublime in the American city, 1870–1931', paper presented at University of Nottingham, May 1998, http://www.nottingham.ac.uk/3cities/nye.htm.

60. D. Nye, *Electrifying America: Social Meanings of a New Technology, 1880–1940* (Cambridge MA, 1990), p. 66; W. R. Taylor, *In Pursuit of Gotham: Culture and Commerce in New York* (New York, 1992), p. 48; J. A. Jakle, *City Lights: Illuminating the American Night* (Baltimore, 2001), p. 185. Nye (p. 391) notes a similar trick being played in 1898 when President McKinley pushed a button in Washington to turn on the lights at the New York Electric Show.

61. Taylor, *Gotham*, Chapter 4 (written with T. Bender).

62. Nead, *Victorian Babylon*, pp. 89, 97.

63. Schivelbusch, *Disenchanted Night*, p. 51.

64. Jakle, *City Lights*, esp. pp. 52–54, 76, 171. The quotation is from William Archer (1900), cited in Jakle, p. 171. See also W. Louis Sonntag Jr's painting, 'The Bowery at Night' (1895) in the collection of the Museum of the City of New York.

65. Weinreb and Hibbert, *London Encyclopaedia*, p. 304; Jackson, *Encyclopedia of NYC*, p. 673.

66. Nead, *Victorian Babylon*, pp. 94–96; Schivelbusch, *Disenchanted Night*, pp. 33–37.

67. Ibid, p. 88; Weinreb and Hibbert, *London Encyclopaedia*, pp. 837–838.

68. Jakle, *City Lights*, p. 24; M. King, *Handbook of New York City 1892* (Boston, 1892), pp. 49, 185.

69. Weinreb and Hibbert, *London Encyclopaedia*, p. 838.

70. Jakle, *City Lights*, p. 45, citing Wetzler (1892).

71. Schivelbusch, *Disenchanted Night*, pp. 40, 115, 127.

72. C. Newall, *The Grosvenor Gallery Exhibitions: Change and Continuity in the Victorian Art World* (Cambridge, 1995); Weinreb and Hibbert, *London Encyclopaedia*, pp. 255–256, 838.

73. Jakle, *City Lights*, p. 71; Jackson, *Encyclopedia of NYC*, pp. 673–675.

74. Stamp, *Bright Lights, Big City*, pp. 11–13; K. Walden, *Becoming Modern in Toronto: the Industrial Exhibition and the Shaping of a Late Victorian Culture* (Toronto, 1997), pp. 304–310.

75. D. Nasaw, 'Cities of light, landscapes of pleasure' in D. Ward and O. Zunz, eds, *The Landscape of Modernity* (New York, 1992), p. 274; Jakle, *City Lights*, p. 45; Stamp, *Bright Lights, Big City*, p. 31.

76. F. Goodall, 'Gas in London: a divided city', *London Journal* **27** (2002), 37.

77. Quoted in Stamp, *Bright Lights, Big City*, p. 13.

78. Nasaw, 'Cities of light', p. 276.

79. Quoted in Jakle, *City Lights*, p. 174.

80. Ibid, p. 194.

81. Nye, *Electrifying America*, p. 60.

82. Stamp, *Bright Lights, Big City*, pp. 15, 46.

83. Jakle, *City Lights*, pp. 152–154, 172–174.

84. Nasaw, 'Cities of light', p. 274; E. Rappaport, *Shopping for Pleasure: Women in the Making of London's West End* (Princeton, 2000), pp. 162–164. Note, however, Schivelbusch's observation (*Disenchanted Night*, p. 148) that after 1850 gas lights with reflectors were fixed on the *outside* of shops in London, allowing them to shine brightly and safely on commodities *inside*.

85. For some early examples of electric crosses outside New York churches, see Nye, *Electrifying America*, pp. 51–52.

86. Weinreb and Hibbert, *London Encyclopaedia*, p. 598; D. Oxford, *Piccadilly Circus* (Stroud, Glos, 1995), illustrations on pp. 39, 47, 54, 57.

87. Jakle, *City Lights*, pp. 199–204; Nye, 'The electric sublime'; E. Sandeen, 'Signs of the times: waiting for the millennium in Times Square', paper presented at University of Nottingham, May 1998, http://www.nottingham.ac.uk/3cities/sandeen.htm; on Fifth Avenue, see Page, *Creative Destruction*, Chapter 2, esp. p. 60.

88. Nasaw, 'Cities of light', pp. 273–274.

89. T. Dreiser, *Sister Carrie* [1900] (London, 1986), p. 331.

90. Ibid, p. 330.

91. Ibid, p. 478.

92. Ibid, p. 485.

93. Ibid, pp. 493–494.

94. Nasaw, 'Cities of light', p. 276; Taylor, *Gotham*, p. 48.

95. Schivelbusch, *Disenchanted Night*, pp. 148, 149.

96. Taylor, *Gotham*, pp. 48–49, notes the first certain use of ticker-tape, thrown from the windows of Wall Street skyscrapers to celebrate the re-election of Theodore Roosevelt in 1910.

97. Ibid, pp. 42–44.

98. Ibid, pp. 43–45. In 1890 the population of Philadelphia was 1,047,000; in 1891 the population of Merseyside (Greater Liverpool including Birkenhead on the opposite bank of the Mersey) was 860,000.

99. A. Brown-May, *Melbourne Street Life* (Melbourne, 1998), pp. 95–107.

100. Winter, *London's Teeming Streets*, p. 127.

101. B. Penner, 'A world of unmentionable suffering: women's public conveniences in Victorian London', *Journal of Design History* **14** (2001), 35–51.

102. Rappaport, *Shopping for Pleasure*, pp. 83–85.

103. PP, 1845 (348), XVII, Second Report, RC on Metropolis Improvements, QQ 31, 40, quoted in H. J. Dyos, 'The objects of street improvement in Regency and early Victorian London' in D. Cannadine and D. Reeder, eds, *Exploring the Urban Past: Essays in Urban History by H. J. Dyos* (Cambridge, 1982), pp. 81–86.

104. T. Beames, *The Rookeries of London* [1852] (London, 1970), p. 119.

105. F. Engels, *The Housing Question* (1887).

106. J. Hollingshead, *Ragged London in 1861* [1861] (London, 1986), pp. 53–54.

107. Ibid, pp. 56–57.

108. Doré and Jerrold, *Pilgrimage*, p. 43.

109. Census enumerators' books for 1851 and 1891. I am grateful to Jill Barber for uncovering this comparison.

110. F. Engels, *The Condition of the Working Class in England* [1845] (London, 1969), pp. 79–80.

111. D. Reeder, *Charles Booth's Descriptive Map of London Poverty 1889* (London, 1987).

112. Charles Booth Police Notebooks B360, pp. 216–219, 248–249.

113. Hollingshead, *Ragged London*, pp. 56–57.

114. R. F. Harney and H. Troper, *Immigrants: A Portrait of the Urban Experience 1890–1930* (Toronto, 1975), p. 40.

115. W. D. Howells, *A Hazard of New Fortunes* [1890] (Oxford, 1990), pp. 52–53 (my emphases).

116. Jackson, *Encyclopedia of NYC*, p. 1129.

117. D. R. Green, 'Street trading in London: a case study of casual labour 1830–60' in J. H. Johnson and C. Pooley, eds, *The Structure of Nineteenth Century Cities* (London, 1982), pp. 129–151.

118. A. Bridle, 'Etchings in the Ward', *Toronto Saturday Night*, 23 Dec 1905, 7.

119. E. Ross, 'Slum journeys: ladies and London poverty 1860–1940' in A. Mayne and T. Murray, eds, *The Archaeology of Urban Landscapes: Explorations in Slumland* (Cambridge, 2001), p. 11. See also Nord, *Walking the Victorian Streets*, Chapter 7.

120. J. R. Walkowitz, 'The Indian Woman, the Flower Girl, and the Jew: photojournalism in Edwardian London', *Victorian Studies* **42** (1998), 3–46; see also Winter, *London's Teeming Streets*, pp. 103–107, 180, 182. Walkowitz concentrates on the theatricality of Malvery's self-presentation while Winter offers a straightforward account of what she reported.

Chapter 6. Public spaces – practised places

1. P. J. Atkins, 'How the West End was won: the struggle to remove street barriers in Victorian London', *Journal of Historical Geography* **19** (1993), 265–277.

2. G. Crossick, *An Artisan Elite in Victorian Society: Kentish London, 1840–1880* (London, 1978).

3. Atkins, 'How the West End was won'.

4. H. Mayhew, *London Labour and the London Poor Volume I* (London, 1861), pp. 11–13.

5. Charles Booth Police Notebooks B360, pp. 238–239 (Booth Archive, LSE).

6. A. Brown-May, 'A charitable indulgence: street stalls and the transformation of public space in Melbourne, c.1850–1920', *Urban History* **23** (1996), 48–71; quotation from p. 68.

7. E. Rappaport, *Shopping for Pleasure: Women in the Making of London's West End* (Princeton NJ, 2000), p. 45.

8. D. Bluestone, 'The pushcart evil' in D. Ward and O. Zunz, eds, *The Landscape of Modernity* (New York, 1992), pp. 287–312.

9. Mayor's Pushcart Commission, 'The New York pushcart: recommendations of the mayor's commission', *Charities and the Commons* **16** (22 Sep 1906), 615–618.

10. Report of the Mayor's Pushcart Commission, The City of New York, 1906, cited in Bluestone, 'Pushcart evil', p. 301.

11. L. Nead, 'From alleys to courts: obscenity and the mapping of mid-Victorian London', *New Formations* **37** (1999), 33–46.

12. Brown-May, 'A charitable indulgence', 69–70.

13. C. Stansell, *City of Women: Sex and Class in New York, 1789–1860* (New York, 1986); T. Gilfoyle, *City of Eros: New York City, Prostitution, and the Commercialization of Sex, 1790–1920* (New York, 1992).

14. Gilfoyle, *City of Eros*, p. 205.

15. Ibid, quotations from contemporary observers, cited on pp. 207, 209 and 206.

16. Ibid, p. 211.

17. J. Winter, *London's Teeming Streets 1830–1914* (London 1993), pp. 11–12, 173–179; but see L. Nead, *Victorian Babylon* (New Haven CT, 2000), p. 65, for evidence that in the 1860s Regent Street was associated with 'smart, daytime prostitution'.

18. Albert Smith, in *Household Words* (12 Sep 1857), quoted in W. Acton, *Prostitution, Considered in its Moral, Social & Sanitary Aspects, in London and Other Large Cities*, 2nd edn (London, 1870), p. 21.

19. Nead, *Victorian Babylon*, esp. pp. 109–46; Acton, *Prostitution*, pp. 16–19.

20. P. Howell, 'Victorian sexuality and the moralization of Cremorne Gardens' in J. P. Sharp, P. Routledge, C. Philo and R. Paddison, eds, *Entanglements of Power: Geographies of Domination/Resistance* (London, 2000), pp. 43–66; quotations on pp. 60, 57.

21. P. Howell, 'A private Contagious Diseases Act: prostitution and public space in Victorian Cambridge', *Journal of Historical Geography* **26** (2000), 377.

22. Ibid, emphasis added.

23. M. Cook, *London and the Culture of Homosexuality, 1885–1914* (Cambridge, 2003), pp. 39, 40. See also G. Chauncey, *Gay New York: Gender, Urban Culture and the Making of the Gay Male World 1890–1940* (New York, 1994) for an especially insightful discussion of the definition and language associated with gay identities at the beginning of the twentieth century.

24. M. Houlbrook, *Queer London: Perils and Pleasures in the Sexual Metropolis, 1918–1957* (Chicago, 2005), pp. 67, 52.

25. Chauncey, *Gay New York*, p. 28.

26. Houlbrook, *Queer London*, p. 3.

27. Quoted in S. Maynard, '"Without working?" Capitalism, urban culture and gay history', *Journal of Urban History* **30** (2004), 378–398.

28. Maynard, 'Without working', 378–379, 384–385.

29. H. Garner, *Cabbagetown* (Toronto, 1968), pp. 89–99, 286–294.

30. Maynard, 'Without working', 385–386.

31. S. Buck-Morss, *The Dialectics of Seeing: Walter Benjamin and the Arcades Project* (Cambridge, MA, 1989); J. Wolff, 'The invisible *flâneuse*: women and the literature of modernity', *Theory, Culture and Society* **2** (1985), 37–46; G. Pollock, 'Modernity and the spaces of femininity' in *Vision and Difference: Femininity, Feminism and Histories of Art* (London, 1988), pp. 50–90.

32. D. Parsons, 'Flâneur or flâneuse? Mythologies of modernity', *New Formations* **38** (1999), 96.

33. E. Wilson, 'The invisible flâneur', *New Left Review* **191** (1992), 109.

34. Parsons, 'Flâneur or flâneuse?', 92.

35. G. Gilloch, '"The return of the flâneur": the afterlife of an allegory', *New Formations* **38** (1999), 105.

36. Parsons, 'Flâneur or flâneuse?', 98.

37. D. Parsons, *Streetwalking the Metropolis: Women, the City and Modernity* (Oxford, 2000): pp. 17–18 provide a brief review of the dictionary history of 'flâneur', while 'Introduction'

and Chapter 1, 'Mythologies of Modernity' complement and further contextualise her essay in *New Formations*.

38. Nead, *Victorian Babylon*, p. 69.
39. E. Wilson, *The Sphinx in the City: Urban Life, the Control of Disorder, and Women* (London, 1991).
40. C. Brontë, *Villette* [1853] (London, 1970), pp. 54–60.
41. Nead, *Victorian Babylon*, pp. 63–64.
42. M. Domosh, 'Those "Gorgeous Incongruities": Polite Politics and Public Space on the Streets of Nineteenth-Century New York City', *Annals of the Association of American Geographers* **88** (1998), 221.
43. Ibid, 222.
44. Nead, *Victorian Babylon*, pp. 71–73.
45. Ibid, p. 78.
46. Rappaport, *Shopping for Pleasure*, p. 94.
47. Ibid, p. 106.
48. Domosh, 'Those "gorgeous incongruities"', 209; E. Wharton, *The House of Mirth* [1905] (London, 1993) and *The Age of Innocence* [1920] (London, 1974).
49. Dreiser, *Sister Carrie*, pp. 322–324.
50. Rappaport, *Shopping for Pleasure*, p. 111.
51. Ibid, p. 117.
52. Ibid, p. 123.
53. V. Woolf, *Mrs Dalloway* [1925] (London, 1992), pp. 176–177.
54. Sidney Starr's painting, 'The City Atlas' (1889), depicts a young woman riding alone on the top deck front seat of the horse bus of that name, which ran between Trafalgar Square and St John's Wood. In her almost contemporaneous *The Romance of a Shop* (1888), Amy Levy twice sends Gertrude Lorimer riding on the top deck of the same 'Atlas' omnibus. See A. G. Robins and R. Thomson, *Degas, Sickert and Toulouse-Lautrec: London and Paris 1870–1910* (London, 2005), pp. 66–67; M. New, ed, *The Complete Novels and Selected Writings of Amy Levy 1861–1889* (Gainesville FL, 1993), pp. 86, 105; A. P. Vadillo, *Women Poets and Urban Aestheticism: Passengers of Modernity* (Basingstoke, 2005), Introduction and Chapter 1.
55. E. Rappaport, 'Travelling in the Lady Guides' London: consumption, modernity, and the *fin-de-siècle* metropolis' in M. Daunton and B. Rieger, eds, *Meanings of modernity: Britain from the late-Victorian era to World War II* (Oxford, 2001), pp. 25–43.
56. G. Gissing, *The Odd Women* [1893] (London, 1980), pp. 193, 127.
57. Ibid, pp. 17–18; for Gissing's own interest in Holywell Street, see P. F. Mattheisen, A. C. Young and P. Coustillas, eds, *The Collected Letters of George Gissing Volume Three 1886–1888* (Athens OH, 1992), p. 113.
58. Gissing, *Odd Women*, p. 149.
59. M. Harvey, 'From *passante* to *flâneuse*: encountering the prostitute in Dorothy Richardson's *Pilgrimage*', *Journal of Urban History* **27** (2001), 750.
60. For further discussion of the place of 'new women' and 'shopgirls' in late nineteenth-century cities, see S. Ledger, *The New Woman: Fiction and Feminism at the Fin de Siècle* (Manchester, 1997), Chapter 6, 'The New Woman in the modern city'. An earlier version of much of this chapter, specifically focused on Gissing's 'odd women' is S. Ledger, 'Gissing, the Shopgirl and the New Woman', *Women: A Cultural Review* **6** (1995), 261–274.
61. Mattheisen et al., *Gissing Letters Volume Three*, pp. 125, 127.
62. G. Gissing, *In The Year of Jubilee* [1894] (London, 1994), pp. 21–22.
63. Ibid, pp. 52–53.
64. Ibid, pp. 54–58.
65. Nead, *Victorian Babylon*, p. 78.
66. G. Simmel, 'The metropolis and mental life' (1903), reprinted in G. Bridge and S. Watson, eds, *The Blackwell City Reader* (Oxford, 2002), pp. 15, 16.
67. Gissing, *Jubilee*, pp. 58, 54, 60.
68. Harvey, 'From *passante* to *flâneuse*', 748.

69. Parsons, *Streetwalking the Metropolis*, p. 83.

70. D. E. Nord, *Walking the Victorian Streets: Women, Representation, and the City* (Ithaca NY, 1995), esp. Chapter 6.

71. Ledger, *New Woman*, pp. 157–162; Nord, *Walking the Victorian Streets*, pp. 183–206; Parsons, *Streetwalking the Metropolis*, pp. 86–97.

72. Parsons, *Streetwalking the Metropolis*, p. 87.

73. New, *The Complete Novels*, pp. 86, 105, 168–169, 110.

74. Ibid, pp. 124, 149, 169.

75. Parsons, *Streetwalking the Metropolis*, p. 93.

76. New, *The Complete Novels*, p. 536; St. James's Street lay at the heart of *masculine* clubland. For further discussion of Levy's own life as a 'new woman' in 1880s London, see L. H. Beckman, *Amy Levy: Her Life and Letters* (Athens OH, 2000). Tragically, Levy committed suicide in 1889, aged only 27.

77. J. Law (Margaret Harkness), *A City Girl* (London, 1887); *Out of Work* [1888] (London, 1990).

78. Woolf, *Mrs Dalloway*, pp. 4, 5.

79. Ibid, p. 4.

80. Ibid. Quotations are, in order, from pp. 51, 71, 62, 65, 65 and 67.

81. B. Penner, 'The construction of identity: Virginia Woolf's city' in I. Borden and J. Rendell, eds, *InterSections: Architectural Histories and Critical Theories* (London, 2000), p. 274.

82. Woolf, *Mrs Dalloway*, p. 70.

83. Parsons, *Streetwalking the Metropolis*, p. 74.

84. Penner, 'The construction of identity', p. 275.

85. R. Mace, *Trafalgar Square: Emblem of Empire* (London, 1976), p. 15.

86. Quoted in Mace, *Trafalgar Square*, p. 87.

87. Ibid, pp. 210–211.

88. P. A. Jackson, *Maps of Meaning* (London, 1989), Chapter 4.

89. J. M. Roberts, 'Spatial governance and working class public spheres: the case of a Chartist demonstration at Hyde Park', *Journal of Historical Sociology* **14** (2001), 308–336; Mace, *Trafalgar Square*, p. 157.

90. Quoted in Mace, *Trafalgar Square*, p. 165. See also G. Stedman Jones, *Outcast London* (Oxford, 1971) and G. Weightman and S. Humphries, *The Making of Modern London 1815–1914* (London, 1983).

91. But note the juxtaposition of the themes of Jubilee and unemployment in Law (Harkness), *Out of Work*, where Jos Coney descends from out-of-work carpenter to unskilled dock labourer to down-and-out, camping in Trafalgar Square in the autumn of 1887. At the time of the Jubilee, however, he is still living in the East End, and the only references to the public celebrations surrounding the Jubilee relate to the Queen's visit to the East End to open the People's Palace in Mile End Road.

92. Mace, *Trafalgar Square*, pp. 160–189; in *Out of Work* Harkness has Coney caught up in the events of 'Bloody Sunday'. She concisely describes the aims of the 'Radicals and Socialists': 'to show that the square belonged to the public' (pp. 196–197).

93. Mace, *Trafalgar Square*, pp. 192–197.

94. Ibid, pp. 204–218, 200.

95. On Paris, see D. Harvey, *Consciousness and the Urban Experience* (Oxford, 1985); on New York, E. Homberger, *The Historical Atlas of New York City* (New York, 1994): pp. 96–97 include maps depicting the progress of the Draft Riots.

96. P. Goheen, 'The ritual of the streets in mid-19th-century Toronto', *Environment and Planning D: Society and Space* **11** (1993), 127–145

97. P. Goheen, 'Symbols in the streets: parades in Victorian urban Canada', *Urban History Review* **18** (1990), 237–243.

98. Goheen, 'The ritual of the streets', 132.

99. Quoted in Goheen, 'Symbols in the streets', 239.

100. H. Mah, 'Phantasies of the public sphere: rethinking the Habermas of historians', *Journal of Modern History* **72** (2000), 168, quoted in Roberts, 'Spatial governance', 315.

101. Ibid.
102. P. Goheen, 'The assertion of middle-class claims to public space in late Victorian Toronto', *Journal of Historical Geography* **29** (2003), 79.
103. Goheen, 'The ritual of the streets', 127.
104. Ibid, 133–134.
105. Goheen, 'Symbols'; P. Goheen, 'Honouring "one of the great forces of the dominion": the Canadian public mourns McGee', *Canadian Geographer* **41** (1997), 350–362.
106. 'Her Majesty's Jubilee', *The Times*, 22 Jun 1887, 5–8.
107. 'The Diamond Jubilee', *The Times*, 21 Jun 1897, 17.
108. Ibid; W. L. Arnstein, 'Queen Victoria's diamond jubilee', *The American Scholar* **66** (1997), 591–597.
109. 'Her Majesty's Jubilee', 7.
110. Goheen, 'Symbols'. Similarly, the procession in Toronto in 1860 attracted an estimated 50,000 spectators at a time when the city's total population was only about 44,000.
111. T. Richards, 'The image of Victoria in the year of jubilee', *Victorian Studies* **31** (1987), 12.
112. See, for example, *Daily Chronicle*, 23 Jun 1897; *Daily Mail*, 23 Jun 1897; *Illustrated London News*, 26 Jun 1897; *Daily Graphic* 28 Jun 1897. I am grateful to Ting Cheung for her research on these illustrations. 'Who's Who of Victorian Cinema' www.victorian-cinema.net/victoria.htm lists twelve cinematographers 'amongst others' who each recorded the procession.
113. G. Gissing, *The Nether World* [1889] (London, 1973), pp. 104–113.
114. Mattheisen et al., *Gissing Letters Volume Three*, p. 198.
115. K. Adler, *Pissarro in London* (London, 2003).
116. Ibid, p. 7.
117. This part of Gissing's novel is set in 1879.
118. For an example of discomfort in church, see Harkness, *Out of Work*, Chapter 1.
119. C. Poulsen, *Victoria Park* (London, 1976).
120. Harkness, *Out of Work*. Quotations are, in order, from pp. 16, 45, 47, 42–43, 44.
121. E. Blackmar and R. Rosenzweig, 'The park and the people: Central Park and its publics: 1850–1910' in T. Bender and C. E. Schorske, eds, *Budapest and New York: Studies in Metropolitan Transformation: 1870–1930* (New York, 1994), p. 116; M. Gandy, *Concrete and Clay: Reworking Nature in New York City* (Cambridge MA, 2002), p. 99.
122. Blackmar and Rosenzweig, 'The park and the people', p. 114.
123. Quoted in Ibid, p. 122.
124. H. James, *The American Scene* (London, 1907), pp. 176, 117–118.
125. G. Gad and D. W. Holdsworth, 'Streetscape and society: the changing built environment of King Street, Toronto' in R. Hall, W. Westfall and L. S. MacDowell, eds, *Patterns of the Past: Interpreting Ontario's History* (Toronto, 1988), pp. 174–205.
126. Ibid, pp. 186–190. Neither the Janes Building nor the Dominion Bank Chambers survived more than a generation before another round of creative destruction. The Dominion Bank erected a ten-storey replacement on the same site, and the Janes Building was replaced by the twenty-storey Royal Bank, both in 1914. For further details, see G. Gad and D. W. Holdsworth, 'Building for city, region and nation: office development in Toronto 1834–1984' in V. L. Russell, ed, *Forging a Consensus: Historical Essays on Toronto* (Toronto, 1984), esp. pp. 290–301.
127. R. M. Stamp, *Bright Lights, Big City: The History of Electricity in Toronto* (Toronto, 1991), pp. 12–15.
128. Ibid, p. 31.
129. G. Norcliffe, *The Ride to Modernity: The Bicycle in Canada, 1869–1900* (Toronto, 2001), p. 74; P. G. Mackintosh and G. Norcliffe, 'Flâneurie on bicycles: acquiescence to women in public in the 1890s', *Canadian Geographer* **50** (2006), 17–37.
130. Note, though, that in some cities today diagonal crossing is acceptable behaviour at intersections with pedestrian traffic lights (e.g. Auckland, New Zealand); possibly the same applied in the nineteenth century at intersections regulated by traffic police.
131. R. Fleming, 'The trolley takes command, 1892 to 1894', *Urban History Review* **19** (1991), 223.

132. There are very similar figures in Paris and Boston street scenes by Gustave Caillebotte and Childe Hassam. Bell-Smith painted an equally busy watercolour of traffic and pedestrians in front of London's Royal Exchange in his version of 'The Heart of the Empire': see E. L. Ramsay, 'Modernity and post-colonialism: *The Heart of the Empire* (1909) by F. M. Bell-Smith', *Labour/Le Travail* **52** (2003).

133. Gad and Holdsworth, 'Streetscape and society', p. 186.

134. Stamp, *Bright Lights, Big City*, p. 24.

135. For other illustrations that juxtapose animals with modern streets and buildings, see Winter, *London's Teeming Streets*, p. 87, Figure 8 (reproduced from *The Graphic*, 1877) and 'The New City Dwellings for the Labouring Classes, Farringdon Road,' *The Illustrated Times*, 14 Jan 1865.

136. For example, see 'A City Thoroughfare', also in Doré and Jerrold, *Pilgrimage*, facing p. 22. An illustration of 'The Railway-Bridge about to be erected across Ludgate-Hill' (*Illustrated London News*, 14 Nov 1863) depicted a much more leisurely, uncongested scene, but hinted at busier times ahead, noting that the span of the new bridge made provision for widening the street from 42 feet to 60 feet.

137. D. Cohen, 'The rising city: urban themes in the art and writings of C. R. W. Nevinson' in R. Ingleby et al, *C. R. W. Nevinson: The Twentieth Century* (London, 1999), p. 49.

138. There is no sign of traffic lights, though H. P. Clunn, *The Face of London* (London, 1964), p. 7, notes that automatic traffic signals were installed at Ludgate Circus in 1930.

139. M. Galinou and J. Hayes, *London in Paint: Oil Paintings in the Collection at the Museum of London* (London, 1996), pp. 412–413.

Chapter 7. Building suburbia

1. Oxford English Dictionary (2nd Edition, 1989) Online (2005).

2. J. Archer, 'Colonial suburbs in south Asia, 1700–1850, and the spaces of modernity' in R. Silverstone, ed, *Visions of Suburbia* (London, 1997), pp. 26–54.

3. A leading article, 'The formation of London suburbs', in *The Times*, 25 Jun 1904, 8, indicated some anxieties associated with the change: 'The habit of living at a distance from the scene of work has spread from the merchant and the clerk to the artisan . . . the suburb is now mainly the residence of the family of small means – say, from £100 to £300 per annum. . . . And every suburban extension makes existing suburbs less desirable. . . . It is no longer possible to escape from the dull suburb into unspoiled country. It is the more necessary, if possible, to redeem the suburb from meanness and squalor.'

4. H. G. Wells, *The War of the Worlds* [1898] (London, 2005). The quotation is from H. G. Wells, *Experiment in Autobiography Volume I* (London, 1934), p. 542, quoted in G. Cunningham, 'Houses in between: navigating suburbia in late Victorian writing', *Victorian Literature and Culture* **32** (2004), 432.

5. Cunningham, 'Houses in between', 429.

6. Wells, *War*, p. 145; E. M. Forster, *Howards End* [1910] (London, 1983), p. 329.

7. Wells, *War*, p. 155.

8. A. D. King, *The Bungalow: the production of a global culture* (London, 1984), esp. Chapter 5; A. D. King, 'Excavating the multicultural suburb: hidden histories of the bungalow' in Silverstone, *Visions*, pp. 55–85; P. Oliver, I. Davis and I. Bentley, *Dunroamin: the suburban semi and its enemies* (London, 1981); F. M. L. Thompson, 'Introduction' in F. M. L. Thompson, ed, *The Rise of Suburbia* (Leicester, 1982), pp. 2–25.

9. L. Hapgood, 'The literature of the suburbs: versions of repression in the novels of George Gissing, Arthur Conan Doyle and William Pett Ridge, 1890–1899', *Journal of Victorian Culture* **5** (2000), 287–310. See also Cunningham, 'Houses in between', 423; K. Flint, 'Fictional suburbia', *Literature and History* **8** (1982), 67–81; L. Hapgood, *Margins of Desire: The Suburbs in Fiction and Culture 1880–1925* (Manchester, 2005).

10. Writing as a suburban novelist, e.g., in *Beyond the City: the Idyll of a Suburb* (1893), rather than as author of Sherlock Holmes' stories.

11. Hapgood, 'The literature of the suburbs', 290–291.

12. J. Hartley, 'The sexualization of suburbia' in Silverstone, *Visions*, p. 184. For an American interpretation of suburbia as imperial expansion, see C. Jurca, *White Diaspora: The Suburb and the Twentieth-Century American Novel* (Princeton NJ, 2001).

13. Oliver et al, *Dunroamin*, p. 14.

14. G. and W. Grossmith, *The Diary of a Nobody* [1892] (London, 1965).

15. Ibid, p. 19.

16. L. Hapgood, '"The New Suburbanites" and contested class identities in the London suburbs, 1880–1900' in R. Webster, ed, *Expanding Suburbia* (Oxford, 2000), p. 48.

17. E. W. Burgess, 'The growth of the city' in R. E. Park et al, eds, *The City* (Chicago, 1925), pp. 47–62.

18. D. Hayden, *Building Suburbia* (New York, 2003), pp. 91–92.

19. U. Sinclair, *The Jungle* [1906] (New York, 1981).

20. M. Marsh, *Suburban Lives* (New Brunswick NJ, 1990), pp. 148–149; Jurca, *White Diaspora*, p. 68.

21. S. B. Warner, *Streetcar Suburbs* (Cambridge MA, 1962); M. A. Weiss, *The Rise of the Community Builders* (New York, 1987).

22. A. A. Jackson, *Semi-Detached London* (London, 1973), p. 44; J. W. R. Whitehand and C. M. H. Carr, *Twentieth-Century Suburbs: A Morphological Approach* (London, 2001), Chapter 3.

23. Important comparative studies include D. Cannadine, 'Urban development in England and America in the nineteenth century: some comparisons and contrasts', *Economic History Review* **33** (1980), 309–325; M. Daunton, ed, *Housing the Workers: A Comparative History, 1850–1914* (London, 1990); R. Harris and C. Hamnett, 'The myth of the promised land: the social diffusion of home ownership in Britain and North America', *Annals of the Association of American Geographers* **77** (1987), 173–190.

24. D. Harvey, *The Urbanization of Capital* (Oxford, 1985).

25. The phrase is from J. M. Richards, *The Castles on the Ground: The Anatomy of Suburbia* (London, 1946).

26. R. Fishman, *Bourgeois Utopias* (New York, 1987). Fishman defines the bourgeoisie as 'those most prosperous members of the middle class whose businesses and capital accumulation . . . gave them an income comparable to the rural squirearchy and even to some of the aristocracy, yet who maintained the living and working habits of the urban middle class' (p. 27).

27. Ibid, p. 32.

28. Ibid, p. 9.

29. See also C. Miele, 'From aristocratic ideal to middle-class idyll: 1690–1840' in A. Saint et al, *London Suburbs* (London, 1999), pp. 31–59; R. Fishman, 'The origins of the suburban idea in England', *Chicago History* **13** (2) (1984), 26–35; H. Binford, *The First Suburbs: Residential Communities on the Boston Periphery, 1815–1860* (Chicago, 1984).

30. K. Jackson, *Crabgrass Frontier* (New York, 1985), pp. 76–86; Fishman, *Bourgeois Utopias*, pp. 125–133; Hayden, *Building Suburbia*, Chapter 4; J. R. Stilgoe, *Borderland* (New Haven CT, 1988), pp. 52–55; Saint, *London Suburbs*, pp. 85–99, 190.

31. H. J. Dyos, *Victorian Suburb* (Leicester, 1961); Warner, *Streetcar Suburbs*. See also D. Reeder, 'A theatre of suburbs' in H. J. Dyos, ed, *The Study of Urban History* (London, 1968), pp. 253–271; Thompson, *The Rise of Suburbia*.

32. D. Dash Moore, 'On the fringes of the city' in D. Ward and O. Zunz, eds, *The Landscape of Modernity* (New York, 1992), p. 254; K. Jackson, ed, *The Encyclopedia of New York City* (New Haven CT, 1995), pp. 150–152, 416–418, 945–946, 969.

33. Saint, *London Suburbs*, pp. 19–21.

34. G. Gissing, *In The Year of Jubilee* [1894] (London, 1994), pp. 5, 15–16, 42, 44, 177. See also G. Cunningham, 'The riddle of suburbia: suburban fictions at the Victorian *fin de siècle*' in Webster, *Expanding Suburbia*, pp. 63–66; R. Dennis, 'Modern London' in M. Daunton, ed, *Cambridge Urban History of Britain Volume III, 1840–1950* (Cambridge, 2000), pp. 104–109.

35. Gissing, *Jubilee*, pp. 183–184.

36. Saint, *London Suburbs*, pp. 216, 218.

37. P. G. Scott, *The London & Birmingham Railway Through Harrow 1837–1987* (Harrow, 1987).

38. J. R. Kellett, *Railways and Victorian Cities* (London, 1969), pp. 260, 277, 377.

39. Ibid, pp. 409–411.

40. D. J. Olsen, *The Growth of Victorian London* (London, 1976), esp. pp. 142–150. See also D. J. Olsen, *Town Planning in London: The Eighteenth and Nineteenth Centuries* (New Haven CT, 1982); H. Hobhouse, *Thomas Cubitt: Master Builder* (London, 1971).

41. On early nineteenth-century New York, see E. Blackmar, *Manhattan for Rent, 1785–1850* (Ithaca NY, 1989); on twentieth-century American and Canadian cities, see Marsh, *Suburban Lives*, pp. 169–171; R. Harris, *Creeping Conformity: How Canada Became Suburban, 1900–1960* (Toronto, 2004) , pp. 85–90.

42. R. Dennis, '"Every advantage of an apartment is here": middle-class housing to rent in twentieth-century Toronto', unpublished typescript.

43. P. W. Moore, 'Zoning and planning: the Toronto experience, 1904–1970' in A. F. J. Artibise and G. Stelter, eds, *The Usable Urban Past* (Toronto, 1979), pp. 316–341; R. Dennis '"Zoning" before zoning: the regulation of apartment housing in early twentieth-century Winnipeg and Toronto', *Planning Perspectives* **15** (2000), 267–299.

44. J. White, *London in the Twentieth Century* (London, 2001), p. 36; A. Rubinstein, ed, *Just Like the Country: Memories of London Families Who Settled the New Cottage Estates 1919–1939* (London, 1991), pp. 53–54; for American examples, see Hayden, *Building Suburbia*, pp. 66–70, 111–113.

45. Dyos, *Victorian Suburb*, pp. 124–127.

46. H. J. Dyos, 'The speculative builders and developers of Victorian London', in D. Cannadine and D. Reeder, eds, *Exploring the Urban Past* (Cambridge, 1982), pp. 154–78.

47. Dyos, *Victorian Suburb*, pp. 82, 127–137; H. J. Dyos, 'A Victorian speculative builder: Edward Yates', in Cannadine and Reeder, *Exploring*, pp. 179–189.

48. Jackson, *Semi-Detached London*, Chapter 6; Whitehand and Carr, *Twentieth-Century Suburbs*, pp. 87–90.

49. E. Cooper, *Pinner Streets Yesterday and Today* (Pinner, 1976), pp. 29–36.

50. Jackson, *Semi-Detached London*, pp. 136–141.

51. R. Harris, 'The making of American suburbs, 1900–1950s: a reconstruction' in R. Harris and P. Larkham, eds, *Changing Suburbs: Foundation, Form and Function* (London, 1999), p. 100.

52. R. Harris, *Unplanned Suburbs* (Baltimore, 1996), pp. 180–185, 192–196.

53. G. Wright, *Building the Dream: A Social History of Housing in America* (Cambridge MA, 1981), p. 113.

54. M. Doucet and J. Weaver, *Housing the North American City* (Montreal, 1991), p. 62; Warner, *Streetcar Suburbs*, pp. 37–38, 126–129, 184–185.

55. Doucet and Weaver, *Housing*, pp. 61, 69–70, 103; Warner, *Streetcar Suburbs*, p. 117.

56. Doucet and Weaver, *Housing*, pp. 112–126; Weiss, *Community Builders*.

57. Not all of these dwellings would have been built; and there are two identifiable cases (where the exact addresses of houses to be built were recorded) of two permits being issued for the same address.

58. Building permits and assessment rolls in City of Toronto Archives; see also *Toronto Globe*, 30 May 1907, 14; 7 Dec 1907, 17; 10 Sep 1908, 11.

59. E. Clark and P. Ashley, 'The merchant prince of Cornville', *Chicago History* **21** (3) (1992), 4–19.

60. Hayden, *Building Suburbia*, pp. 79–88.

61. Sinclair, *The Jungle*, pp. 44–52, 64–69, 175–177; see also E. H. Monkkonen, *America Becomes Urban* (Berkeley, 1988), pp. 183–185.

62. Harris, *Unplanned Suburbs*; R. D. Simon, *The City-Building Process: Housing and Services in New Milwaukee Neighborhoods* (Philadelphia, 1978); O. Zunz, *The Changing Face of Inequality* (Chicago, 1982).

63. R. Harris, 'A working-class suburb for immigrants, Toronto 1909–1913', *Geographical Review* **81** (1991), 318–332, and 'The impact of building controls on residential development in Toronto, 1900–1940', *Planning Perspectives* **6** (1991), 269–296.

64. Harris, *Unplanned Suburbs*, pp. 34–40; M. Doucet, 'Mass transit and the failure of private ownership: the case of Toronto in the early twentieth century', *Urban History Review* **3** (1977), 3–33; D. F. Davis, 'Mass transit and private ownership: an alternative perspective on the case of Toronto', *Urban History Review* **3** (1978), 60–98. See also C. Armstrong and H. V. Nelles, 'Suburban street railway strategies in Montreal, Toronto, and Vancouver, 1896–1930' in G. Stelter and A. Artibise, eds, *Power and Place* (Vancouver, 1986), pp. 187–218. For press reaction connecting the lack of suburban public transport to congestion, see 'Intensifying congestion', *Toronto World*, 28 Mar 1912, 10.

65. J. W. Hood, *The Toronto Civic Railways* (Toronto, 1986).

66. Harris, *Unplanned Suburbs*, pp. 2–3, 123–130; 'Working-class suburb', 326; 'Self-building in the urban housing market', *Economic Geography* **67** (1991), 1–21.

67. Note, too, that values on building permits generally exceeded assessed values, which deliberately underestimated market values to allow for maintenance and management costs. On kit-built housing, see A. Gowans, *The Comfortable House: North American Suburban Architecture 1890–1930* (Cambridge MA, 1986); Hayden, *Building Suburbia*, Chapter 6; P. Ennals and D. W. Holdsworth, *Homeplace: the making of the Canadian dwelling over three centuries* (Toronto, 1998), Chapter 8.

68. Harris, *Unplanned Suburbs*, pp. 49–50, 79.

69. R. Harris and R. Lewis, 'Constructing a fault(y) zone: misrepresentations of American cities and suburbs, 1900–1950', *Annals of the Association of American Geographers* **88** (1998), 622–639; T. Gardner, 'The slow wave: the changing residential status of cities and suburbs in the United States, 1850–1940', *Journal of Urban History* **27** (2001), 293–312.

70. Jackson, *Crabgrass Frontier*, Chapter 8.

71. J. M. S. Careless, *Toronto to 1918* (Toronto, 1984); J. Lemon, *Toronto since 1918* (Toronto, 1985).

72. R. Lewis, *Manufacturing Montreal* (Baltimore, 2000); Harris, *Unplanned Suburbs*; R. Lewis, ed, 'Special issue: Industrial suburbanization of Canadian and American cities, 1850–1950', *Journal of Historical Geography* **27** (2001), 1–92; R. Harris and R. Lewis, 'The geography of North American cities and suburbs, 1900–1950', *Journal of Urban History* **27** (2001), 262–292.

73. Harris, *Unplanned Suburbs*, pp. 32–34, 40–85; J. Miles, ed, *West Toronto Junction Revisited* (Erin ON, 1986).

74. But see D. Hardy and C. Ward, *Arcadia for All: the legacy of a makeshift landscape* (London, 1984).

75. F. Driver, *Geography Militant: Cultures of Exploration and Empire* (Oxford, 2001), pp. 170–198.

76. J. N. Tarn, *Five Per Cent Philanthropy* (Cambridge, 1973), p. 27; C. Gatliff, 'On improved dwellings and their beneficial effects on health and morals', *Journal of the Statistical Society of London* **38** (1875), 33–63; H. J. Dyos, 'Workmen's fares in south London, 1860–1914' in Cannadine and Reeder, *Exploring*, p. 90.

77. Artizans' & General Properties Company Limited, *Artizans' Centenary 1867–1967* (London, 1967); E. McDonald and D. J. Smith, *Artizans and Avenues: A History of the Queen's Park Estate* (London, 1990).

78. R. J. Harley, *LCC Electric Tramways* (London, 2002), pp. 18, 44; Jackson, *Semi-Detached London*, Chapter 3; R. Thorne, 'The White Hart Lane Estate: An LCC venture in suburban development', *London Journal* **12** (1986), 80–88.

79. K. Young and P. Garside, *Metropolitan London* (London, 1982); Jackson, *Semi-Detached London*, Chapters 9 and 16.

80. S. Spragge, 'A confluence of interests: housing reform in Toronto, 1900–1920', in Artibise and Stelter, *Usable Urban Past*, pp. 247–267; L. F. Hurl, 'The Toronto Housing Company, 1912–1923: the pitfalls of painless philanthropy', *Canadian Historical Review* **45** (1984), 28–53.

81. P. Johnson, *Saving and Spending: The Working-Class Economy in Britain, 1870–1939* (Oxford, 1985), cited in M. Daunton, 'Home loans versus council houses: the formation of British and American housing policy, 1900–1920', *Housing Studies* **3** (1988), 233.

82. The Liberator was part of the financial empire controlled by nonconformist Liberal MP, J. S. Balfour. The collapse of the society, and with it the ruin of countless modest, temperance-minded, nonconformist savers, was associated with the failure of the building firm of J. W. Hobbs & Co. Ltd. Balfour and Hobbs were responsible for two of London's grandest surviving Victorian apartment buildings: Whitehall Court and Hyde Park Court (now the Mandarin Oriental Hotel). Balfour's story has been told most engagingly by D. McKie, *Jabez: The Rise and Fall of a Victorian Rogue* (London, 2004).

83. Dyos, 'Speculative builders', pp. 165–173; 'A Victorian speculative builder', pp. 178–187.

84. On aspirations to homeownership in 'Kentish London', see G. Crossick, *An Artisan Elite in Victorian Society: Kentish London, 1840–1880* (London, 1978), pp. 144–149.

85. S. J. Price, *Building Societies, Their Origin and History* (London, 1958), pp. 53, 129.

86. Grossmith, *Diary*, p. 233.

87. R. Dennis, 'Landlords and housing in depression', *Housing Studies* **10** (1995), 305–324; M. Swenarton and S. Taylor, 'The scale and nature of the growth of owner-occupation in Britain between the wars', *Economic History Review* **38** (1985), 373–392.

88. Jackson, *Crabgrass Frontier*, pp. 130, 348 (note 31), and *Encyclopedia of NYC*, pp. 1044–1045. See also M. Daunton, 'Cities of homes and cities of tenements', *Journal of Urban History* **14** (1988), 309–311, and 'Rows and tenements: American cities, 1880–1914' in Daunton, *Housing the Workers*, pp. 249–286; Hayden, *Building Suburbia*, p. 78.

89. Daunton, 'Home loans', 238.

90. Whitehand and Carr, *Twentieth-Century Suburbs*, p. 28; Jackson, *Semi-Detached London*, pp. 190–194; Doucet and Weaver, *Housing*, pp. 87, 253.

91. R. Paterson, 'Housing finance in early 20th century suburban Toronto', *Urban History Review* **20** (1991), 63–71.

92. Doucet and Weaver, *Housing*, pp. 253, 275, 277. The same prohibition applied to US banks between 1864 and 1913.

93. Paterson, 'Housing finance', 68–69.

94. R. Dennis, 'Property and propriety: Jewish landlords in early twentieth-century Toronto', *Transactions of the Institute of British Geographers* **22** (1997), 377–397.

95. Dennis, 'Depression', 316–318.

96. Doucet and Weaver, *Housing*, p. 252. For redlining practices by US and Canadian governments in insuring mortgages during the Depression, see Jackson *Crabgrass Frontier*, Chapter 11; J. Belec, 'The Dominion Housing Act', *Urban History Review* **25** (2) (1997), 53–69.

Chapter 8. Consuming suburbia

1. W. S. Clarke, *The Suburban Homes of London* (London, 1881).

2. A. A. Jackson includes several such postcards as illustrations in *Semi-Detached London* (London, 1973).

3. Jackson, *Semi-Detached London*, pp. 201–203.

4. P. Oliver, I. Davis and I. Bentley, *Dunroamin* (London, 1981), pp. 93–99; *Metro-Land* [1932] (Harpenden, 1987).

5. Jackson, *Semi-Detached London*, p. 207; Laing and Nash brochures in housing files A1–2, Museum of London.

6. *Metro-Land*, p. 137; M. Cassell, *Inside Nationwide: One hundred years of co-operation* (London, 1984), p. 59.

7. Phrase used by W. Harris to describe his 1930s houses in Hounslow.

8. D. Hayden, *Building Suburbia* (New York, 2003), pp. 6–8.

9. R. Paterson, 'Creating the packaged suburb: the evolution of planning and business practices in the early Canadian land development industry, 1900–1914' in B. M. Kelly, ed, *Suburbia Re-examined* (Westport CT, 1989), pp. 119–132.

10. '200 Happy Families Live Here Now', *Toronto Sunday World*, 24 May 1914.

11. On this theme, see R. Dennis, '"Foreigners who live in Toronto": Attitudes towards immigrants in a Canadian city, 1890–1918' in B. Messamore, ed, *Canadian Migration Patterns from Britain and North America* (Ottawa, 2004), pp. 183–199.

12. *Toronto Globe*, 15 Jun 1907, 15; 7 Dec 1907, 17; 10 Sep 1908, 11.

13. Clarke, *The Suburban Homes of London*, pp. 44–45, 383.

14. M. Marsh, *Suburban Lives* (New Brunswick NJ, 1990), pp. 1–18; R. Fishman, *Bourgeois Utopias* (New York, 1987).

15. R. Dennis, '"Every advantage of an apartment is here": middle-class housing to rent in twentieth-century Toronto', unpublished typescript. Ancroft Place was designated as a historic site in 1973 and converted to a condominium in 1982.

16. R. G. Barrows, 'Beyond the tenement: patterns of American urban housing, 1870–1930', *Journal of Urban History* **9** (1983), 395–420; M. Swenarton and S. Taylor, 'The scale and nature of the growth of owner-occupation in Britain between the wars', *Economic History Review* **38** (1985), 373–392.

17. R. Dennis, 'Landlords and rented housing in Toronto, 1885–1914', *University of Toronto Centre for Urban and Community Studies Research Paper* **162** (1987). Although the homeownership rate recovered to reach 39 per cent in 1910, this was substantially below the rate of 47 per cent claimed for the city as a whole.

18. V. G. Lewis, 'Earlscourt, Toronto. A descriptive, historical and interpretative study in urban class development', unpublished M. A. thesis, University of Toronto (1920). Note that Lewis's 'Earlscourt' was the area south of 'North Earlscourt' discussed by Harris.

19. R. Dennis, 'Landlords and housing in depression', *Housing Studies* **10** (1995), 305–324; R. Harris and C. Hamnett, 'The myth of the promised land: the social diffusion of home ownership in Britain and North America', *Annals of the Association of American Geographers* **77** (1987), 173–190.

20. M. Daunton, 'Cities of homes and cities of tenements', *Journal of Urban History* **14** (1988), 285; Barrows, 'Beyond the tenement', 413–416.

21. *Toronto Globe*, 6 Dec 1923, 12; R. Dennis '"Zoning" before zoning: the regulation of apartment housing in early twentieth-century Winnipeg and Toronto', *Planning Perspectives* **15** (2000), 286–287; R. Harris, *Unplanned Suburbs* (Baltimore, 1996), pp. 86, 138.

22. Quoted in M. Edel, E. D. Sclar and D. Luria, *Shaky Palaces* (New York, 1984), p. 173.

23. The following paragraphs draw on Edel et al., *Shaky Palaces*, esp. Chapter 5.

24. Harris, *Unplanned Suburbs*, pp. 135–139; Barrows, 'Beyond the tenement', 415–416.

25. On Wolfrey Avenue, in May 1909, in the middle of their programme of development, Love Bros had fourteen houses at various stages of construction; most of those they had already completed had been sold to owner-occupiers, but they retained ownership of four vacant houses and also of four houses occupied by tenants. The City Directory, compiled a few months later, records one of the newly finished houses occupied by the company's president, another common device among builders, occupying one of their own homes until a buyer was forthcoming. By 1914, three of Love Bros' four vacant houses had been sold to owner-occupiers and one to a private landlord; two of their previously tenanted houses were now owner-occupied; two remained tenanted but now owned privately.

26. On types of landlords in pre-World War I Toronto, see Dennis, 'Landlords and rented housing'.

27. E. J. Chambers, 'A new measure of the rental cost of housing in the Toronto market 1890–1914', *Histoire sociale/Social History* **17** (1984), 165–174; James Mavor Papers, University of Toronto, MS Collection 119, Box 70, file Are, 'Rents and Housing in Toronto'.

28. R. J. Morris, 'The middle class and the property cycle during the Industrial Revolution' in T. C. Smout, ed, *The Search for Wealth and Stability* (London, 1979), pp. 91–113.

29. A. Offer, *Property and Politics 1870–1914* (Cambridge, 1981); M. Daunton, *A Property Owning Democracy? Housing in Britain* (London, 1987).

30. A. S. Wohl, *The Eternal Slum* (London, 1977); J. A. Yelling, *Slums and Slum Clearance in Victorian London* (London, 1986), and *Slums and Redevelopment: Policy and Practice in England, 1918–45* (London, 1992).

31. C. Hamnett and B. Randolph, *Cities, Housing and Profits* (London, 1988), Chapters 3 and 4.

32. R. Miller, 'The Hoover in the garden: middle-class women and suburbanization, 1850–1920', *Environment and Planning D: Society and Space* **1** (1983), 73–87.

33. R. Miller, 'Selling Mrs Consumer: advertising and the creation of suburban socio-spatial relations, 1910–1930', *Antipode* **23** (1991), 263–301.

34. R. S. Cowan, *More Work for Mother* (London, 1989).

35. Miller, 'Selling Mrs Consumer'; B. Braithwaite and N. Walsh, *Home Sweet Home: The Best of Good Housekeeping 1922–1939* (London, 1995).

36. P. Ward, *A History of Domestic Space: Privacy and the Canadian Home* (Vancouver, 1999); G. Wright, *Building the Dream: A Social History of Housing in America* (Cambridge MA, 1981), pp. 111–112, 169–172.

37. Marsh, *Suburban Lives*.

38. G. and W. Grossmith, *The Diary of a Nobody* [1892] (London, 1965), pp. 19–20.

39. Ibid, p. 30.

40. G. Gissing, *The Whirlpool* [1897] (London, 1984), p. 344.

41. Ibid, pp. 207, 368. Perhaps this concern explains why *The Suburban Homes of London* was so anxious to demonstrate how many notable ancestors had endowed what were now suburban schools and churches, and lay buried in suburban churchyards.

42. R. Harris, 'Household work strategies and suburban homeownership in Toronto, 1899–1913', *Environment and Planning D: Society and Space* **8** (1990), 97–121.

43. R. Durant, 'Community and association in a London housing estate' in R. E. Pahl, ed, *Readings in Urban Sociology* (Oxford, 1968), pp. 159–185; G. Weightman and S. Humphries, *The Making of Modern London 1914–1939* (London, 1984), pp. 102–111; A. Olechnowicz, *Working-Class Housing in England Between the Wars* (Oxford, 1997); for a more positive view of local community life, see D. Bayliss, 'Building better communities: social life on London's cottage council estates, 1919–1939', *Journal of Historical Geography* **29** (2003), 376–395.

44. Jackson, *Semi-Detached London*, Chapter 10.

45. M. Callaghan, *It's Never Over* [1930] (Toronto, 1972). Quotations are from pp. 8, 36, 81 and 48. The novel is set in the 1920s when Ontario was subject to alcohol prohibition, but the description of Mr Errington as 'a prohibitionist' (p. 81) evidently applies to more than just alcohol, just as his name indicates Callaghan's own views of his character's stance.

46. R. Harris, 'The end justified the means: boarding and rooming in a city of homes, 1890–1951', *Journal of Social History* **26** (1992), 331–358.

47. R. Harris, 'The flexible house: the housing backlog and the persistence of lodging, 1891–1951', *Social Science History* **18** (1994), 31–53.

48. J. Modell and T. K. Hareven, 'Urbanization and the malleable household: an examination of boarding and lodging in American families', *Journal of Marriage and the Family* **35** (1973), 467–479; M. Peel, 'On the margins: lodgers and boarders in Boston, 1860–1900', *Journal of American History* **72** (1986), 813–834.

49. W. Gamber, 'Away from home: middle-class boarders in the nineteenth-century city', *Journal of Urban History* **31** (2005), 289–305.

50. T. R. Smith and W. H. White, 'Model dwellings for the rich', *The British Architect and Northern Engineer* **5** (31 Mar 1876), 156. Walt Whitman made a similar estimate for New York City: Gamber, 'Away from home', 289.

51. 1881 Census enumerators' books, RG11/188/75–85. Gissing lodged on the north side of Gower Place during 1878, paying 6/6 per week for a single room; he returned three years later to occupy three rooms on the south side. The north-side lodging house features in his first novel, *Workers in the Dawn* (1880), while both sets of lodgings worked their way into *Eve's Ransom* (1895).

52. H. J. Dyos, *Victorian Suburb* (Leicester, 1961), p. 113.

53. Clarke, *Suburban Homes*, pp. 532–533.

54. Charles Booth Police Notebooks B356, 357 (Booth Archive, LSE).

55. G. Gissing, *In The Year of Jubilee* [1894] (London, 1994), p. 5; Booth Notebooks B373.

56. H. Long, *The Edwardian House* (Manchester, 1993), pp. 55–61.

57. G. Gissing, *The Paying Guest* (London, 1896), p. 2.

58. Jackson, *Semi-Detached London*, pp. 169, 191.

59. J. White, *London in the Twentieth Century* (London, 2001), p. 124.

60. A. Ashpitel and J. Whichcord, *Town Dwellings* (London, 1855), p. 14, quoted in S. Marcus, *Apartment Stories* (Berkeley, 1999), p. 115; W. H. White, 'Middle-class houses in Paris and central London', *The Builder* **35** (24 Nov 1877), 1166–1170.

Chapter 9. Mansion flats and model dwellings

1. E. M. Forster, *Howards End* [1910] (London, 1983), p. 68.
2. For example, Albert Hall Mansions (1880–1887): see F. Sheppard, ed, *Survey of London Volume XXXVIII* (London, 1975), pp. 342–345.
3. S. O'Hanlon, *Together Apart: Boarding house, hostel and flat life in pre-war Melbourne* (Melbourne, 2002), pp. 101–102.
4. W. D. Howells, *A Hazard of New Fortunes* [1890] (Oxford, 1990); Robert C. Leitz III et al, eds, *William Dean Howells: Selected Letters Volume 3: 1882–1891* (Boston, 1980).
5. T. Dreiser, *Sister Carrie* [1900] (London, 1986): for The Chelsea, see p. 456.
6. E. Wharton, *The House of Mirth* [1905] (London, 1993), pp. 5, 157.
7. *Toronto Saturday Night*, 14 Apr 1900, 30 Jul 1910.
8. 'Flats and apartments', *Brooklyn Daily Eagle*, 17 Sep 1893, 8.
9. M. Callaghan, *They Shall Inherit the Earth* [1935] (Toronto, 1992), pp. 7–9, 107, 119.
10. The standard histories of model dwellings in London are J. N. Tarn, *Five Per Cent Philanthropy: An Account of Housing in Urban Areas Between 1840 and 1914* (Cambridge, 1973); A. S. Wohl, *The Eternal Slum: Housing and Social Policy in Victorian London* (London, 1977). For a discussion of the origins of SICLC, see D. Fitz-Gibbon, 'Spaces of moral improvement: allotment gardens, philanthropic housing and moral geography in early-Victorian England, 1830–1850', unpublished MSc dissertation, UCL Department of Geography (2003).
11. S. Morris, 'Market solutions for social problems: working-class housing in nineteenth-century London', *Economic History Review* **54** (2001), 525–545.
12. Report of the Select Committee on Artizans' and Labourers' Dwellings Improvement (SCALDI), PP 1881 VII, p. 178.
13. On Guinness, see P. Malpass, 'Continuity and change in philanthropic housing organisations: the Octavia Hill Housing Trust and the Guinness Trust', *London Journal* **24** (1999), 38–57; on Sutton, see P. Garside, 'The impact of philanthropy: housing provision and the Sutton Model Dwellings Trust, 1900–1939', *Economic History Review* **53** (2000), 742–766, and *The Conduct of Philanthropy: William Sutton Trust 1900–2000* (London, 2000).
14. Peabody Trust Annual Reports (London Metropolitan Archives).
15. G. Gissing, *The Nether World* [1889] (London, 1973), p. 274.
16. C. Bauer, *Modern Housing* (1934), Plate 4 and pp. 14, 19.
17. *The Builder* **5** (1 May 1847), 209; **6** (28 Oct 1848), 524–525; **7** (12 May 1849), 220–221; **7** (1 Dec 1849), 566–569; **9** (Feb 1851), 79; **10** (April 1852), 245.
18. *The Builder* **11** (3 Dec 1853), 721–722; S. Perks, *Residential Flats of All Classes* (London, 1905), pp. 21–22.
19. R. Dennis, 'Buildings, Residences and Mansions: George Gissing's "Prejudice Against Flats"' in J. Spiers, ed, *Gissing and the City* (Basingstoke, 2006), pp. 41–62.
20. *The Builder* **37** (29 Nov 1879), 1327.
21. Both erected in 1878. See Improved Industrial Dwellings Company Ltd., Half-Yearly Reports; J. N. Tarn, 'The Improved Industrial Dwellings Company', *Transactions of the London and Middlesex Archaeological Society* **22** (1968), 43–59.
22. G. Gissing, *Will Warburton* [1905] (London, 1985), p. 5.
23. Forster, *Howards End*, pp. 59–61, 67–68.
24. P. F. Mattheisen, A. C. Young and P. Coustillas, eds, *The Collected Letters of George Gissing Volume Three 1886–1888* (Athens OH, 1992), p. 228; Perks, *Residential Flats*, p. 204.
25. E. C. Cromley, *Alone Together: A History of New York's Early Apartments* (Ithaca NY, 1990); J. N. Tarn, 'French flats for the English in nineteenth-century London' in A. Sutcliffe, ed, *Multi-Storey Living* (London, 1974), pp. 19–40.
26. *Toronto Saturday Night*, 25 Feb 1905, 3; 1 Apr 1905, 8; 8 Apr 1905, 4; 22 Apr 1905, 3; 17 Jun 1905, 3; 'Apartment house', 18 Nov 1905, 9.
27. E. Wharton, *The Age of Innocence* [1920] (London, 1974), p. 27. For a superior example of the kind of French fiction she had in mind, see E. Zola, *Pot-Bouille* (1882), translated as *Restless*

House (1953) and *Pot Luck* (1999); and for a commentary, see S. Marcus, *Apartment Stories: City and Home in Nineteenth-Century Paris and London* (Berkeley, 1999).

28. Cromley, *Alone Together*, p. 39.
29. For detailed references, see R. Dennis, 'Interpreting the apartment house: modernity and metropolitanism in Toronto, 1900–1930', *Journal of Historical Geography* **20** (1994), 305–322.
30. R. Plunz, *A History of Housing in New York City* (New York, 1990), pp. 11, 22, 30.
31. Ibid, pp. 22, 24, 84.
32. Cromley, *Alone Together*, pp. 69–70, 101, 128–129; K. Baar, 'The national movement to halt the spread of multifamily housing, 1890–1926', *Journal of the American Planning Association* **58** (1) (1992), 40.
33. E. Hawes, *New York, New York: How the Apartment House Transformed the Life of the City* (New York, 1993), pp. 60–61, 93–104.
34. N. White and E. Willensky, *AIA Guide to New York City, 4th Edition* (New York, 2000), p. 129; Leitz, *Howells Letters*, pp. 218–223.
35. Leitz, *Howells Letters*, p. 225. On the Chelsea, see also Hawes, *New York*, pp. 57–59; A. Alpern, *New York's Fabulous Luxury Apartments* (New York, 1987), pp. 18–19.
36. Plunz, *Housing*, pp. 84–85, 123.
37. E. L. Birch and D. S. Gardner, 'The seven-percent solution: a review of philanthropic housing, 1870–1910', *Journal of Urban History* **7** (1981), 403–438; Plunz, *Housing*, Chapter 4.
38. Birch and Gardner, 'The seven-percent solution', 406, 409, 412–417; S. Spragge, 'A confluence of interests: housing reform in Toronto, 1900–1920' in A. Artibise and G. Stelter, eds, *The Usable Urban Past* (Toronto, 1979), pp. 247–267; L. F. Hurl, 'The Toronto Housing Company, 1912–1923: the pitfalls of painless philanthropy', *Canadian Historical Review* **45** (1984), 28–53; S. Purdy, '"This is not a company; it is a cause": class, gender and the Toronto Housing Company, 1912–1920', *Urban History Review* **21** (1993), 75–91.
39. W. A. Langton, 'Apartment life', *Canadian Architect and Builder* **16** (1903), 77–78.
40. R. Zurier et al., *Metropolitan Lives: The Ashcan Artists and Their New York* (Washington DC, 1995), p. 201; G. Levin, *The Complete Oil Paintings of Edward Hopper* (New York, 2001), pp. 158, 188–189.
41. 'Lady Gay's Column', *Toronto Saturday Night*, 29 Aug 1903, 8.
42. Dreiser, *Sister Carrie*, p. 318.
43. Howells, *Hazard*, pp. 34–37.
44. Ibid, pp. 37–39.
45. Ibid, pp. 54–55.
46. Ibid, pp. 84–85.
47. Xenophon, *The Persian Expedition* (translated by R. Warner) (Harmondsworth, 1949).
48. Xenophon's *Anabasis* also provided the inspiration for a more recent saga of getting home in New York, Sol Yurick's 1965 novel, *The Warriors*, turned into a cult film of the same name by Walter Hill (1979), in which the members of a Coney Island gang fight and thread their way home through the subway from a gang convention in Van Cortlandt Park in the Bronx, where they have been accused of assassinating the self-styled leader of gang leaders, Cyrus. For twentieth-century teenage New Yorkers, the Bronx to Coney Island could be as epic a journey as Boston to New York in the 1880s for Howells and the Marches, as Persia to Greece for Xenophon in 400 B.C., a curious inversion of time–space compression and reductions over time in the friction of distance. To late twentieth-century as well as late nineteenth-century New Yorkers, Xenophon implies homecoming. See also M. W. Brooks, *Subway City: Riding the Trains, Reading New York* (New Brunswick NJ, 1997), pp. 210–211.
49. http://eagle.brooklynpubliclibrary.org/ References in the racing columns were on 4 Jan 1891, 18 Jan 1891, 29 Mar 1891, 23 Oct 1892, 26 Feb 1893, 5 Mar 1893, 17 Sep 1893. Real estate advertisements appeared on 17 Nov 1881, 11 Apr 1884. Dr Scudder was pastor of the Central Congregational Church, Hancock Street, Brooklyn, from 1871 to 1882, during which time the church's membership increased from 368 to 1342, making it the denomination's second largest congregation. Pacific Street lay farther west in Brooklyn Heights. Fulton Ferry was a principal means of getting from Brooklyn to lower Manhattan prior to the opening of Brooklyn Bridge.

Note that this advertisement appeared almost a year after the bridge had opened; although the number of passengers declined, the ferry continued to operate until 1924.

50. Leitz, *Howells Letters*, p. 218.
51. Ibid, pp. 230–239.
52. Hawes, *New York*, p. 119.
53. P. F. Mattheisen, A. C. Young and P. Coustillas, eds, *The Collected Letters of George Gissing Volume Two 1881–1885* (Athens OH, 1991), p. 279.
54. Ibid, p. 291.
55. Ibid, p. 337.
56. G. Gissing, *The Private Papers of Henry Ryecroft* [1903] (London, 1912), p. 8.
57. G. Gissing, *The Odd Women* [1893] (London, 1980), p. 125.
58. G. Gissing, *New Grub Street* [1891] (Harmondsworth, 1968), pp. 232, 282.
59. G. Gissing, *The Unclassed* [1884] (London, 1930), p. 151.
60. Howells, *Hazard*, p. 55.
61. See, for example, an illustration of 'a row of eight apartment blocks in various stages of construction' erected by the Toronto developer, John W. Walker: *Contract Record* **36** (17 May 1922), 437.
62. 'Houses in flats', *The Builder* **46** (8 Mar 1884), 351–353.
63. *The Builder* **35** (2 Jun 1877), 556; *The Builder* **54** (18 Feb 1888), 128.
64. Dreiser, *Sister Carrie*, p. 319.
65. *Toronto World*, 21 Feb 1912; *'Midmaples Group' and 'Allan Gardens'*, advertising brochure, May 1914, copy in Dinnick Papers, MU904, Ontario Archives, Toronto.
66. *Contract Record* **40** (29 Dec 1926), 185; *Toronto Globe*, 3 May 1927.
67. S. Denford, 'Luxury living for the lower classes', *Camden History Review* **20** (1996), 9–13.
68. 'The new dwellings for the industrial classes in Farringdon-road', *The Builder* **32** (9 May 1874), 393.
69. W. Harwood, 'A Walworth Boy: Looking back on growing up 1922–1939', unpublished typescript (1977), Southwark Local Studies Library. I am grateful to Colin Evans for alerting me to this source.
70. S. Beattie, *A Revolution in London Housing: The LCC Architects and Their Work, 1893–1914* (London, 1980).
71. M. Llewellyn, '"Urban village" or "white house": envisioned spaces, experienced places, and everyday life at Kensal House, London in the 1930's', *Environment and Planning D: Society and Space* **22** (2004), 237.
72. S. C. Leslie, 'The case for gas – Kensal House', in *Flats: Municipal and Private Enterprise* (Ascot Gas Water Heaters Ltd., London, 1938), pp. 279–286.
73. London County Freehold & Leasehold Properties Ltd., *The Illustrated Index to London's Most Attractive Mansion Flats* (1932), and *The Ideal London Home* (1933).
74. Further details can be found in my papers: 'Toronto's first apartment-house boom: an historical geography, 1900–1920', *University of Toronto Centre for Urban & Community Studies Research Paper* **177** (1989); 'Interpreting the apartment house'; and 'Apartment housing in Canadian cities, 1900–1940', *Urban History Review* **26** (2) (1998), 17–31.
75. Based on Land Registry records and a detailed study of Ancroft Place Ltd, from company records in City of Toronto Archives. Ancroft Place was high-status rental housing managed in the same way as luxury apartment houses and marketed as having 'all the advantages of apartments and none of the disadvantages'. The company's records frequently referred to the plight of 'rival' apartment buildings.
76. C. Hamnett and B. Randolph, 'The rise and fall of London's purpose-built blocks of privately rented flats: 1853–1983', *London Journal* **11** (1985), 160–175; London County Freehold & Leasehold Properties Ltd, *The Ideal London Home*; Middle Class Dwellings Co. Ltd, Ledger, 1888– (Museum of London).
77. Morris, 'Market solutions', 536–539.
78. Artizans' & General Properties Company Limited, *Artizans Centenary 1867–1967* (London, 1967), p. 19.

79. Marylebone ratebooks and drainage plans (Westminster Archives Centre); MBW/BA/27686 and MBW/1700, 1709 (District Surveyor's Returns, St Marylebone North) (London Metropolitan Archives).

80. I. Watson, 'The buildings of James Hartnoll', *Camden History Society Newsletter* **58** (Mar 1980); R. Dennis, '"Hard to let" in Edwardian London', *Urban Studies* **26** (1989), 77–89.

81. I. Watson, 'Rebuilding London: Abraham Davis and his Brothers, 1881–1924', *London Journal* **29** (1) (2004), 62–84.

82. Ibid, 79.

83. *Toronto Daily Star*, 3 Apr 1936. See also obituaries in the *Globe* and *Evening Telegram*, 3 Apr 1936.

84. R. Harris, 'The impact of building controls on residential development in Toronto, 1900–1940', *Planning Perspectives* **6** (1991), 269–296.

85. Probate records in Archives of Ontario; City Property Committee records in City of Toronto Archives; Land records in Ontario Land Registry. It seems likely that Walker had a prior connection with the construction company, which had been listed a few years earlier as 'owner' on the building permit for another large apartment building which soon became part of his empire.

86. Two phrases used in his obituary, *Toronto Daily Star*, 3 Apr 1936.

87. I. Watson, '"A very large speculator in building": the double life of EJ Cave', *Camden History Review* **24** (2000), 26–31.

88. Perks, *Residential Flats*, pp. 214–218.

89. *The Times*, 14, 17 and 28 Sep and 25 Oct 1895.

90. For example, postcards of the Alexandra and La Plaza Apartments, both in the photographic collection of the Baldwin Room, Toronto Reference Library.

91. Runs of both *Flats* and *Flatland* are held in the British Library Newspaper Library, Colindale.

92. *Residential Flats*, undated pamphlet, c. 1911, pp. 3, 9; copies in Kensington Local Studies Library and Westminster Archives Centre.

93. For example, illustrations of the Athelma Apartments in *Contract Record*, 30 Oct 1912, and Allan Gardens in '*Midmaples Group*' and '*Allan Gardens*' .

94. *Toronto Globe*, 17 Oct 1928, 9.

95. Apartment names listed in Might's *Directory of the City of Toronto*, various years.

96. The Reardons are in *New Grub Street*, Mrs Frothingham and the Carnabys in *The Whirlpool*, Mrs Widdowson, Bevis and Barfoot in *The Odd Women*, Lord Polperro in *The Town Traveller*, Will Warburton in *Will Warburton*, Beatrice French in *In The Year of Jubilee*, Ida Starr in *The Unclassed* and the Hewetts in *The Nether World*. Curiously, another fictional 'Lowndes Mansions' appears in *Moth and Rust* by Mary Cholmondeley (1912).

97. There are references to 'a small page', 'the servant', 'the maid-servant', 'the housemaid' and 'the same servant'.

98. Quotations from *The Whirlpool*, p. 107; *The Odd Women*, p. 206; *New Grub Street*, p. 77.

99. Except where indicated otherwise, sources for the following paragraphs are the 1891 census enumerators' books, RG12/225, 71–94 (Farringdon Road Buildings), RG12/99, 94–98 (Oxford & Cambridge Mansions).

100. R. Dennis, 'The geography of Victorian values: philanthropic housing in London, 1840–1900', *Journal of Historical Geography* **15** (1989), 43–44.

101. C. Booth, ed, *Labour and Life of the People. Volume II* (London, 1891), pp. 236–262.

102. The registers, including those for Herbrand Street, are now held at the London Metropolitan Archives: ACC/3445/PT/07. At the time of research they were still in the possession of the Peabody Trust.

103. This paragraph is based on records of the Peabody Trust and the London County Council, held in London Metropolitan Archives, and of the East End Dwellings Company, deposited in Tower Hamlet Archives. For further details, see Dennis, 'Hard to let'.

104. Based on linking census records to electoral registers (in London Borough of Islington Archives, Finsbury) and to Post Office Directories (in London Metropolitan Archives and Westminster Archives Centre).

105. Based on a linkage of the 1900 Federal Census with Trow's *General Directory for year ending July 1 1901* (copy in New York Public Library). The 1890 Census no longer exists.
106. The following paragraphs summarise results reported in R. Dennis and C. Giles, *Modernity and multi-storey living: apartment tenants in Canadian cities, 1900–39*, End of Award Report to ESRC (Mar 1999).
107. This section draws on three of my papers: 'Apartment housing in Canadian cities'; '"Zoning" before zoning: the regulation of apartment housing in early twentieth century Winnipeg and Toronto', *Planning Perspectives* **15** (2000), 267–299; and 'La regolamentazione degli edifice per appartamenti a Toronto e Londra: una preistoria', *Storia Urbana* **108** (2005), 15–37.
108. Perks, *Residential Flats*, p. 212.
109. T. W. H. Crosland, *The Suburbans* (London, 1905), pp. 117–118.
110. Hamnett and Randolph, 'Rise and fall', 161–163.
111. *Modern Flats in Tudor Manor House Style*, advertising brochure, n.d. (1932?), housing file A2, Museum of London; A. Saint et al., *London Suburbs* (London, 1999) illustrates half-timbered flats in Ealing and Cricklewood (pp. 119, 124), but also ultra-modernist 1930s flats in 'Ealing Village' (p. 192).
112. 'New buildings, Farringdon Road', *The Builder* **32** (1874), 1003; F. Butler, 'The new dwellings in Farringdon Road', *The Builder* **32** (1874), 1056; F. Chancellor, 'Improved dwellings for the working classes', *The Builder* **34** (1876), 583–584.
113. Perks, *Residential Flats*, pp. 44, 48, 176; W. Shaw Sparrow, *Flats, Urban Houses and Cottage Homes* (London, 1907).
114. Howells, *Hazard*, p. 51.
115. Compare Eales' comments in *The Builder* **46** (8 Mar 1884), 351–353 with the subsequent discussion in *The Builder* **46** (15 Mar 1884), 386 and his plans for Oxford & Cambridge Mansions in *The Builder* **44** (3 Feb 1883), 149.
116. Gissing, *Nether World*, p. 280.

Chapter 10. Geographies of downtown: office spaces

1. C. Brontë, *Villette* [1853] (London, 1970), pp. 57–58.
2. D. Kynaston, 'A changing workscape: the City of London since the 1840s', *London Journal* **13** (1988), 99–105.
3. V. Woolf, *Mrs Dalloway* [1925] (London, 1992), pp. 178–180.
4. E. M. Forster, *Howards End* [1910] (London, 1983), p. 58.
5. R. M. Fogelson, *Downtown: Its Rise and Fall, 1880–1950* (New Haven CT, 2001), Chapters 1 and 4.
6. M. P. Conzen, 'The impact of industrialism and modernity on American cities, 1860–1930', in T. F. McIlwraith and E. K. Muller, eds, *North America: The Historical Geography of a Changing Continent, Second Edition* (Lanham MD, 2001), pp. 346–348.
7. Three very different perspectives on this sorting-out process – detailed narrative, cartographic, and interpretative – are E. G. Burrows and M. Wallace, *Gotham: A History of New York City to 1898* (New York, 1999); E. Homberger, *The Historical Atlas of New York City* (New York, 1994); and D. M. Scobey, *Empire City: The Making and Meaning of the New York City Landscape* (Philadelphia, 2002).
8. J. M. S. Careless, *Toronto to 1918: An Illustrated History* (Toronto, 1984); J. L. Santink, *Timothy Eaton and the Rise of His Department Store* (Toronto, 1990), pp. 54–55; G. Gad and D. W. Holdsworth, 'Streetscape and society: the changing built environment of King Street, Toronto' in R. Hall, W. Westfall and L. S. MacDowell, eds, *Patterns of the Past: Interpreting Ontario's History* (Toronto, 1988), pp. 174–205.
9. D. Keene, 'The setting of the Royal Exchange: continuity and change in the financial district of the City of London, 1300–1871' in A. Saunders, ed, *The Royal Exchange* (London, 1997), pp. 253–271.
10. M. Domosh, *Invented Cities: The Creation of Landscape in Nineteenth-Century New York and Boston* (New Haven CT, 1996), p. 16; Scobey, *Empire City*, p. 99.

11. Ibid, pp. 94–107. The quotation is from p. 99.

12. M. King, *King's Handbook of New York City 1892* (Boston, 1892), pp. 593–730.

13. B. Weinreb and C. Hibbert, eds, *The London Encyclopaedia* (London, 1983), p. 623.

14. Although there was a specialist cluster of smaller legal insurance firms near Holborn on Chancery Lane: see J. Summerson, 'The Victorian rebuilding of the City of London', *London Journal* **3** (1977), 163–185.

15. King, *Handbook*, p. 630; Domosh, *Invented Cities*, pp. 89–93. See also G. Fenske and D. W. Holdsworth, 'Corporate identity and the New York office building: 1895–1915' in D. Ward and O. Zunz, eds, *The Landscape of Modernity: New York City 1900–1940* (New York, 1992), pp. 139–143; S. B. Landau and C. W. Condit, *Rise of the New York Skyscraper 1865–1913* (New Haven CT, 1996), pp. 361–366.

16. O. Zunz, *Making America Corporate 1870–1920* (Chicago, 1990), p. 116.

17. Landau and Condit, *Rise*, pp. 263–265.

18. For example, at the Parliament Square end of Victoria Street, Westminster Chambers (1861–1863), comprising almost one hundred office suites, each four or five rooms, was mainly occupied by civil engineers: J. Summerson, *The Architecture of Victorian London* (Charlottesville VA, 1976), p. 40.

19. G. Gad and D. W. Holdsworth, 'Corporate capitalism and the emergence of the high-rise office building', *Urban Geography* **8** (1987), 212–231; and 'Looking inside the skyscraper: size and occupancy of Toronto office buildings, 1890–1950', *Urban History Review* **16** (1987), 176–189; J. Tyrwhitt, *Small Things Grow Great: The First 150 Years of the Canada Life Assurance Company* (Toronto, 1996).

20. Weinreb and Hibbert, *London Encyclopaedia*, pp. 825–826.

21. Keene, 'The setting of the Royal Exchange'; D. Kynaston, *The City of London Volume II: Golden Years 1890–1914* (London, 1995), pp. 17–18, 259–261; H. Barty-King, *The Baltic Exchange* (London, 1977). The last of these specialist exchanges to survive, the Baltic Exchange was fatally damaged by an IRA bomb in 1992 and eventually demolished to be replaced by the Swiss Re Building (better known as the 'Gherkin'), completed in 2004.

22. W. Anderson, *The London Commercial Directory and Sea-Port Gazetteer* (London, 1826), p. 521. I am grateful to Deryck Holdsworth for this reference.

23. D. Kynaston, *The City of London Volume I: A World of Its Own 1815–1890* (London, 1994), pp. 244, 287; *City Volume II*, pp. 242, 596; and 'A changing workspace', 100–101; R. C. Michie, *The City of London: Continuity and Change, 1850–1990* (London, 1992), p. 13; Keene, 'The setting of the Royal Exchange', pp. 253–254.

24. I. S. Black, 'Private banking in London's West End, 1750–1830', *London Journal* **28** (2003), 29–59; 'Symbolic capital: the London and Westminster Bank headquarters, 1836–38', *Landscape Research* **21** (1996), 55–72; and 'Spaces of capital: bank office building in the City of London, 1830–1870', *Journal of Historical Geography* **26** (2000), 351–375; Michie, *City*, p. 71; Kynaston, *City Volume I*, p. 333.

25. M. Ball and D. Sunderland, *An Economic History of London, 1800–1914* (London, 2001), p. 345; A. D. King, *Global Cities: Post-Imperialism and the Internationalization of London* (London, 1990), p. 89; Michie, *City*, p. 73; Kynaston, *City Volume I*, pp. 225–226; Weinreb and Hibbert, *London Encyclopaedia*, p. 527.

26. Michie, *City*, pp. 150–163; F. Sheppard, *London 1808–1870: The Infernal Wen* (London, 1971), pp. 196–201; and *London: A History* (Oxford, 1998), pp. 229, 313; J. Schneer, *London 1900: The Imperial Metropolis* (New Haven CT, 1999), p. 67.

27. Michie, *City*, p. 176.

28. Ibid, p. 177; Kynaston, *City Volume II*, p. 21.

29. G. Gissing, *In the Year of Jubilee* [1894] (London, 1994), pp. 84–90, 212, 349–352.

30. Kynaston, *City Volume I*, pp. 362, 397; Keene, 'The setting of the Royal Exchange', p. 261; R. Thorne, 'Office building in the City of London 1830–1880', paper to Urban History Group Colloquium, London (1984).

31. Black, 'Spaces of capital', 356.

32. Ibid, 358–367.

33. Ibid, 367–370.
34. Summerson, *Architecture*, pp. 16–18, and 'The Victorian rebuilding', 165–168.
35. Lloyd's Register, *Building for the Future* (London, n.d.), pp. 17, 28.
36. Keene, 'The setting of the Royal Exchange', p. 265; Thorne, 'Office building', p. 7.
37. Thorne, 'Office building', pp. 8–10, 12; Keene, 'The setting of the Royal Exchange', p. 270; R. Turvey, 'City of London office rents', *LSE Geography Research Papers in Environmental & Spatial Analysis* **38** (1996). See also R. Turvey, 'Office rents in the City of London, 1867–1910', *London Journal* **23** (2) (1998), 53–67, and 'London lifts and hydraulic power', *Transactions of the Newcomen Society* **65** (1993–1994), 149–164.
38. Keene, 'The setting of the Royal Exchange', p. 268; Thorne, 'Office building', p. 11; Kynaston, *City Volume II*, p. 245; Turvey, 'City of London office rents', 6–7.
39. D. W. Holdsworth, 'Re-dressing the mercantile city: the emergence of office buildings in the transition to industrial capitalism', paper to 9th International Conference of Historical Geographers, Singapore (1995); Landau and Condit, *Rise*, pp. 90–94, 116–131; King, *Handbook*, pp. 740–752, 774–775.
40. M. Domosh, 'The symbolism of the skyscraper: case studies of New York's first tall buildings', *Journal of Urban History* **14** (1988), 320–345, and 'Imagining New York's first skyscrapers, 1875–1910', *Journal of Historical Geography* **13** (1987), 233–248; Scobey, *Empire City*, pp. 170–174, 189–192.
41. D. Bluestone, *Constructing Chicago* (New Haven CT, 1991), Chapter 4; E. Relph, *The Modern Urban Landscape* (Baltimore, 1987), pp. 35–36; Landau and Condit, *Rise*, pp. 231–235; Fenske and Holdsworth, 'Corporate identity', pp. 132–133.
42. C. Willis, *Form Follows Finance: Skyscrapers and Skylines in New York and Chicago* (New York, 1995), pp. 7, 10–11, 42–43; Fenske and Holdsworth, 'Corporate identity', pp. 139–146.
43. Willis, *Form Follows Finance*, pp. 24–33.
44. Ibid, p. 24; see also F. Duffy, 'Office buildings and organisational change' in A. D. King, ed, *Buildings and Society* (London, 1980), pp. 255–280.
45. Willis, *Form Follows Finance*, pp. 34–37, 49–50.
46. M. Girouard, *Cities and People: A Social and Architectural History* (New Haven CT, 1985), p. 324; Willis, *Form Follows Finance*, pp. 88, 171–176. See also Fogelson, *Downtown*, pp. 23, 114.
47. Girouard, *Cities and People*, pp. 319–324; Willis, *Form Follows Finance*, p. 50.
48. Fogelson, *Downtown*, pp. 141–144.
49. K. D. Revell, 'Regulating the landscape: real estate values, city planning and the 1916 zoning ordinance' in Ward and Zunz, *Landscape*, pp. 19–45; M. A. Weiss, 'Density and intervention: New York's planning traditions' in Ward and Zunz, *Landscape*, pp. 46–75.
50. Fenske and Holdsworth, 'Corporate identity', pp. 132–139.
51. Ibid, pp. 151–2; Landau and Condit, *Rise*, pp. 392–395.
52. Willis, *Form Follows Finance*, pp. 68–71.
53. Ibid, pp. 67–79; Relph, *Modern Urban Landscape*, pp. 39–42; Fogelson, *Downtown*, pp. 160–166.
54. C. Willis, 'Form follows finance: the Empire State Building' in Ward and Zunz, *Landscape*, pp. 160–187.
55. Ibid, pp. 160–163, 166, 180–181.
56. Ibid, p. 163.
57. Fenske and Holdsworth, 'Corporate identity', pp. 132–143; Willis, *Form Follows Finance*, p. 44.
58. Fenske and Holdsworth, 'Corporate identity', p. 146; Willis, *Form Follows Finance*, p. 148.
59. Fenske and Holdsworth, 'Corporate identity', pp. 151–153; Willis, *Form Follows Finance*, p. 45.
60. H. W. Corbett in 1927, quoted in Fogelson, *Downtown*, p. 176.
61. Gad and Holdsworth, 'Corporate capitalism', 218, and 'Looking inside the skyscraper', 182–183. Willis, *Form Follows Finance*, pp. 148, 199.
62. But note the exception of New York's Metropolitan Life, which preferred to retain rental income from reliable tenants while renting extra accommodation for its own expanding workforce in nearby buildings. There is a parallel with the activities of housing landlords who owned

hundreds of properties which they let to others, but preferred to rent their own homes from another landlord.

63. Gad and Holdsworth, 'Corporate capitalism', 220–225; 'Pinnacle of the city', *Toronto Star Weekly*, 29 Nov 1930.

64. Scobey, *Empire City*, p. 187.

65. See especially J. M. Jacobs, *Edge of Empire* (London, 1996), pp. 38–69.

66. I. S. Black, 'Rebuilding "The Heart of the Empire": bank headquarters in the City of London, 1919–1939' in D. Arnold, ed, *The Metropolis and its Image* (Oxford, 1999), pp. 127–152.

67. Ibid, pp. 136–137, 149.

68. Quoted in 120 Fleet Street (ex Daily Express), London Open House Fact Sheet (2002).

69. T. Ruddock, 'Charles Holden and the issue of high buildings in London, 1927–47', *Construction History* **12** (1996), 83–99.

70. C. Ross, *Twenties London: A City in the Jazz Age* (London, 2003), pp. 132–135.

71. Kynaston, *City Volume II*, pp. 26–31.

72. G. and W. Grossmith, *The Diary of a Nobody* [1892] (London, 1965), esp. pp. 170, 208; A. Goodman, *Gilbert and Sullivan's London* (London, 2000), pp. 64, 81 notes that Sewell & Cross, Howell & James and Waterloo House were all fashionable drapers and costumiers in the West End. They all feature in W. S. Gilbert's lyrics in 'Patience (1881), Act II', in *The Savoy Operas* (London, 1967), p. 204.

73. G. Gissing, *The Crown of Life* [1899] (Hassocks, 1978), pp. 163–164.

74. Gissing records visiting a friend's brother-in-law in the City who gave him information about the business of a Russian corn merchant, but this was only when he had almost finished writing *The Crown of Life*: see P. Coustillas, ed, *London and the Life of Literature in Late Victorian England: The Diary of George Gissing, Novelist* (Hassocks, 1978), p. 508. Popular journalism also provides insights into City business: see C. C. Turner, 'Scenes from exchange and office London', in G. R. Sims, ed, *Living London* (1902), reprinted as *Edwardian London Volume 4* (London, 1990), pp. 198–204.

75. For example, William Logsdail's 'The Bank and Royal Exchange in London' (1887) (see http://cgfa.sunsite.dk/l/p-logsdail1.htm), Fritz Werner's 'The Royal Exchange from Queen Victoria Street' (1904) (illustrated in M. Galinou and J. Hayes, *London in Paint: Oil Paintings in the Collection at the Museum of London* (London, 1996), p. 234), impressionist paintings of lower Manhattan by Colin Campbell Cooper and Childe Hassam (illustrated in W. H. Gerdts, *Impressionist New York* (New York, 1994)), and photographs and paintings by Alfred Stieglitz, Alvin Langdon Coburn, Paul Strand, John Marin and Louis Lozowick (illustrated in E. Sussman et al, *City of Ambition* (New York, 1996)).

76. J. Caulfield, 'The imagined cities of three Canadian painters', *Urban History Review* **20** (1991), 3–14; E. G. Firth, *Toronto in Art* (Toronto, 1983), pp. 94–95.

77. R. W. Snyder and R. Zurier, 'Picturing the city' in R. Zurier et al, *Metropolitan Lives: The Ashcan Artists and Their New York* (New York, 1995), pp. 135–137.

78. There are at least two versions of Hicks' picture: an oil on millboard, at Wimpole Hall, Cambridgeshire (http://cgfa.sunsite.dk/h/p-ghicks1.htm), and the finished oil, exhibited at the Royal Academy in 1859 and owned by the Bank of England (http://www.bankofengland.co.uk/museum/collections/pictures3.asp).

79. The Guildhall Library Print Room holds a number of illustrations – of the interiors of the Coal Exchange, Royal Exchange, Baltic Exchange and Stock Exchange – all by William Luker Jnr and dated 'c.1900'. For Nevinson, see R. Ingleby et al, *C. R. W. Nevinson: The Twentieth Century* (London, 1999), p. 146.

80. Degas' painting hangs in the Musée des Beaux-Arts in Pau, France. For an illustration and brief discussion, see D. C. Rich, *Degas* (London, 1985), pp. 70–71. Several of the people in the painting were Degas' own relatives, who were engaged in the cotton business.

81. 'Office at Night' is part of the Walker Art Collection, Minneapolis, but associated sketches are in the Whitney Museum of American Art, New York. G. Levin, *The Complete Oil Paintings of Edward Hopper* (New York, 2001), pp. 270–273. Levin points out that Hopper was very familiar with Degas' painting; and also that as early as 1913 Hopper had produced a series of

illustrations of office scenes for the trade journal, *The System*. See G. Levin, *Edward Hopper as Illustrator* (New York, 1979), pp. 19–20.

82. J. Bonshek, 'The skyscraper: a catalyst of change in the Chicago construction industries, 1882–1892', *Construction History* **4** (1988), 54, 56; A. Kwolek-Folland, *Engendering Business: Men and Women in the Corporate Office, 1870–1930* (Baltimore, 1994), p. 4; G. S. Lowe, 'Women, work, and the office: the feminization of clerical occupations in Canada, 1901–1931' in V. Strong-Boag and A. C. Fellman, eds, *Rethinking Canada: The Promise of Women's History (3rd edn)* (Toronto, 1997), p. 256; Ball and Sunderland, *Economic History*, p. 64.

83. G. Anderson, 'The white-blouse revolution' in G. Anderson, ed, *The White-Blouse Revolution: Female Office Workers Since 1870* (Manchester, 1988), pp. 1–26; Ball and Sunderland, *Economic History*, p. 326; L. M. Fine, *The Souls of the Skyscraper: Female Clerical Workers in Chicago, 1870–1930* (Philadelphia, 1990), p. 30; Lowe, 'Women, work, and the office', p. 256.

84. K. Boyer, '"Neither forget nor remember your sex": sexual politics in the early twentieth-century Canadian office', *Journal of Historical Geography* **29** (2003), 213–218.

85. Lowe, 'Women, work, and the office', p. 259.

86. R. Dennis, 'Working women downtown: Toronto 1900–1930', *London Journal of Canadian Studies* **22** (2006–2007), 35–57, online at http://www.canadian-studies.info/lccs/LJCS/index.html.

87. Kynaston, *City Volume I*, p. 289.

88. G. Gissing, *The Odd Women* [1893] (London, 1980), p. 36.

89. Ibid, pp. 22, 36.

90. G. Gissing, *Eve's Ransom* (London, 1895), Chapter Four.

91. J. Meyerowitz, *Women Adrift: Independent Wage Earners in Chicago, 1880–1930* (Chicago, 1988). See also C. Strange, *Toronto's Girl Problem: The Perils and Pleasures of the City, 1880–1930* (Toronto, 1995).

92. S. Lewis, *The Job* [1916] (London, 1926).

93. E. Hillman, 1894, quoted in Meyerowitz, *Women Adrift*, p. 28.

94. K. Boyer, '"Miss Remington" goes to work: gender, space, and technology at the dawn of the information age', *Professional Geographer* **56** (2004), 201–212.

95. Kwolek-Folland, *Engendering Business*, esp. pp. 114–119.

96. This is obviously an imperfect measure of whether employees were living with family or not; it could be coincidence that they shared the same surname as their landlord; on the other hand, they might have been married or widowed women who would have a different surname from their parents, or they might be living with other relatives with a different surname from their own. But it is at least suggestive of the extent of 'women adrift'. Compared to bank employees, female schoolteachers were *more* likely to be living apart from their families according to this measure; the employees of Eaton's department store and clothing factories were *less* likely. Of course this was also a function of earnings. Female factory workers and shop assistants at Eaton's were financially less able to afford to live apart from their families than bank clerks and schoolteachers.

97. See, for example, Lady Gay, 'Some sensible sermons: four girls in a flat', *Toronto Saturday Night*, 14 Apr 1900, 8.

98. Dennis, 'Working women downtown'; '*Midmaples Group*' and '*Allan Gardens*', advertising brochure, May 1914, copy in Dinnick Papers, MU 904, Ontario Archives, Toronto.

99. Lewis, *The Job*, Chapters V–VII.

100. Boyer, 'Sexual politics', 218–223.

101. Kynaston, *City Volume II*, pp. 288–289; Boyer, 'Sexual politics', 220.

102. K. Boyer, 'Place and the politics of virtue: clerical work, corporate anxiety, and changing meanings of public womanhood in early twentieth-century Montreal', *Gender, Place and Culture* **5** (1998), 271.

103. Zunz, *Making America Corporate*, pp. 116–121; quotation from p. 120.

104. Fine, *Souls*, pp. 42–44. Note, however, that a survey in 1929, found very little difference between the amounts spent on clothing and recreation by better-paid and low-paid business girls. The

big differences were in room and board ($232 p.a. for women earning $918 p.a.; $705 p.a. for those earning $1650 p.a.), in savings, and in money for vacations. See Fine, pp. 168–170.
105. Lewis, *The Job*, pp. 114–115, 280.

Chapter 11. Geographies of downtown: the place of shopping

1. S. Lewis, *The Job* [1916] (London, 1926), pp. 118–121.
2. A. Adburgham, *Shops and Shopping 1800–1914* (London, 1981); B. Lancaster, *The Department Store: A Social History* (London, 1995); G. Shaw, 'The evolution and impact of large-scale retailing in Britain' in J. Benson and G. Shaw, eds, *The Evolution of Retail Systems, c.1800– 1914* (Leicester, 1992), pp. 135–165.
3. Adburgham, *Shops and Shopping*; Lancaster, *Department Store*, Chapters 2 and 5.
4. Ibid.
5. G. Honeycombe, *Selfridges* (London, 1984); B. Weinreb and C. Hibbert, eds, *The London Encyclopaedia* (London, 1983), pp. 80, 266, 455–456.
6. M. Domosh, *Invented Cities: The Creation of Landscape in Nineteenth-Century New York and Boston* (New Haven CT, 1996), pp. 44–52; K. Jackson, ed, *The Encyclopedia of New York City* (New Haven CT, 1995), pp. 120, 694, 1002–1003, 1123–1124; M. King, *King's Handbook of New York City 1892* (Boston, 1892), p. 715; G. Fenske and D. Holdsworth, 'Corporate identity and the New York office building: 1895–1915' in D. Ward and O. Zunz, eds, *The Landscape of Modernity: New York City 1900–1940* (New York, 1992), p. 145.
7. W. D. Howells, *A Hazard of New Fortunes* [1890] (Oxford, 1990), p. 43.
8. T. Dreiser, *Sister Carrie* [1900] (London, 1981), p. 323.
9. S. Haddrell, 'A Study of London's Suburban Department Stores', unpublished MSc dissertation, UCL Department of Geography (2003), 26–27.
10. G. and W. Grossmith, *The Diary of A Nobody* [1892] (London, 1965), pp. 52, 104, 146, 216.
11. E. Rappaport, *Shopping for Pleasure: Women in the Making of London's West End* (Princeton NJ, 2000), p. 146.
12. G. Gissing, *In The Year of Jubilee* [1894] (London, 1994), pp. 200–201, 273–274.
13. P. Coustillas, ed., *London and the Life of Literature in Late Victorian England: The Diary of George Gissing, Novelist* (Hassocks, 1978), pp. 308, 347–348, 390. In the late 1870s and early 1880s Gissing had lived in a succession of cheap lodgings in Bloomsbury and near Hampstead Road, and would have been familiar with Oetzmann's and Shoolbred's, two not-quite-West End stores.
14. J. L. Santink, *Timothy Eaton and the Rise of His Department Store* (Toronto, 1990), p. 172.
15. Shaw, 'The evolution', p. 138.
16. Weinreb and Hibbert, *The London Encyclopaedia*, p. 498; A. Adburgham, *Shopping in Style* (London, 1979); H. Clout, ed, *The Times London History Atlas* (London, 1997), pp. 106–107; G. Sala, *Twice Round the Clock* (1857), pp. 175–182, quoted in C. Breward, *Fashioning London: Clothing and the Modern Metropolis* (Oxford, 2004), p. 61.
17. Haddrell, 'A Study of London's Suburban Department Stores', 41.
18. M. Nava, 'The cosmopolitanism of commerce and the allure of difference: Selfridges, the Russian Ballet and the tango 1911–1914', *International Journal of Cultural Studies* **1** (1998), 163–196; W. R. Leach, 'Transformations in a culture of consumption: women and department stores, 1890–1925', *Journal of American History* **71** (1984), 330.
19. Nava, 'Cosmopolitanism'.
20. E. G. Burrows and M. Wallace, *Gotham: A History of New York City to 1898* (New York, 1999), p. 437.
21. P. F. William Ryan, 'Scenes from shop and store London' in G. R. Sims, ed, *Living London* (1902), reprinted as *Edwardian London Volume 4* (London, 1990), p. 55.
22. Weinreb and Hibbert, *London Encyclopaedia*, p. 486; G. Gissing, *The Town Traveller* (London, 1898), Chapter XXIV.
23. J. Rendell, '"Industrious females" and "professional beauties"', in I. Borden et al, eds, *Strangely Familiar* (London, 1996), p. 36; W. Benjamin, *The Arcades Project* (Cambridge MA,

1999); S. Buck-Morss, *The Dialectics of Seeing: Walter Benjamin and the Arcades Project* (Cambridge MA, 1989); P. Buse et al, *Benjamin's* Arcades: *An unGuided Tour* (Manchester, 2005).

24. Haddrell, 'London's Suburban Department Stores'; Honeycombe, *Selfridges*; E. Zola, *Au Bonheur des Dames* (1883), translated as *The Ladies' Paradise* (Berkeley CA, 1992); for the Paris Bon Marché, see M. B. Miller, *The Bon Marché: Bourgeois Culture and the Department Store, 1869–1920* (Princeton NJ, 1981); and for the creation of a 'street' through the middle of the Paris Bon Marché, see the illustration of 'La Galerie de la rue de Babylone' in E. Wilson, *Adorned in Dreams: Fashion and Modernity* (London, 1985), p. 148; for a cultural geographer's reading of *Au Bonheur des Dames*, see N. Blomley, ' "I'd like to dress her all over": masculinity, power and retail space' in N. Wrigley and M. Lowe, eds, *Retailing, Consumption and Capital: Towards the New Retail Geography* (London, 1996), pp. 238–256.

25. G. Shaw and T. Wild, 'Retail patterns in the Victorian city', *Transactions Institute of British Geographers* **NS 4** (1979), 279–291. Weinreb and Hibbert's entry in *The London Encyclopaedia*, p. 80, notes that the displaced occupants included 'a brothel, a "nest of Polish tailors", and Savory's cigarette factory'. Bourne & Hollingsworth closed in 1983, and the store was converted into 'The Plaza', a multi-store shopping mall. A similar fate befell Whiteley's, closed in 1981 and reopened as a shopping centre and multiplex cinema complex in 1989.

26. *Survey of London Volume XLII: Southern Kensington: Kensington Square to Earl's Court* (London, 1986), pp. 87–98.

27. R. White, *Too Good to be True: Toronto in the 1920s* (Toronto, 1993), pp. 135–136; P. McHugh, *Toronto Architecture: A City Guide* (Toronto, 1985), p. 72.

28. The following paragraphs draw on Santink, *Timothy Eaton*, Chapters 4–11. See also M. Kluckner, *Toronto: The Way It Was* (Toronto, 1988), pp. 45–48; 'Before e-commerce: a history of Canadian mail-order catalogues', online at http://www.civilization.ca/cpm/catalog/cat0000e.html .

29. Santink, *Timothy Eaton*, pp. 190–191, 233.

30. Lancaster, *Department Store*, p. 188.

31. Quoted in M. Domosh, 'The "Women of New York": a fashionable moral geography', *Environment and Planning D: Society and Space* **19** (2001), 587.

32. Burrows and Wallace, *Gotham*, pp. 878, 970.

33. Honeycombe, *Selfridges*; Lancaster, *Department Store*, pp. 148–152.

34. Mrs Belloc-Lowndes, 'London's drapers', in Sims, *Living London*, reprinted as *Edwardian London Volume 3* (London, 1990), pp. 40–41.

35. Leach, 'Transformations', 332.

36. Belloc-Lowndes, 'London's drapers', pp. 41, 44–46.

37. Lancaster, *Department Store*, pp. 150–151, 176.

38. Dreiser, *Sister Carrie*, p. 23.

39. Lancaster, *Department Store*, p. 69; Santink, *Timothy Eaton*, p. 65.

40. G. Gissing, *The Odd Women* [1893] (London, 1980), pp. 25, 34–35.

41. Lancaster, *Department Store*, p. 133.

42. Santink, *Timothy Eaton*, pp. 86–87, 115–116.

43. Lancaster, *Department Store*, pp. 132–133; Adburgham, *Shopping in Style*; Haddrell, 'London's Suburban Department Stores', 43; Weinreb and Hibbert, *London Encyclopaedia*, p. 830.

44. Lancaster, *Department Store*, p. 127; Adburgham, *Shops and Shopping*.

45. Lancaster, *Department Store*, pp. 23, 68; Santink, *Timothy Eaton*, pp. 140–141; Haddrell, 'London's Suburban Department Stores', 28; Jackson, *Encyclopedia of New York City*, p. 1003.

46. Lancaster, *Department Store*, pp. 85–86, 91; Haddrell, 'London's Suburban Department Stores', 30; M. Winstanley, 'Temples of Commerce: Revolutions in Shopping and Banking' in P. Waller, ed, *The English Urban Landscape* (Oxford, 2000), pp. 167–170.

47. This was a mixed blessing; another strategy, advocated by the proprietor of the Paris Bon Marché, as well as by Zola's Mouret, was to encourage customers to get lost so that they stumbled upon departments and commodities previously unknown to them. In pursuit of this strategy, managers were advised to change the layout of departments periodically. See R. Bowlby, *Just Looking: Consumer Culture in Dreiser, Gissing and Zola* (New York, 1985), pp. 74–75; Blomley, ' "I'd like to dress her all over" ', p. 244.

48. Burrows and Wallace, *Gotham*, pp. 667–668; M. Domosh, 'The feminized retail landscape: gender ideology and consumer culture in nineteenth-century New York City', in Wrigley and Lowe, *Retailing, Consumption and Capital*, pp. 264–266; the quotation is from the [New York] *Evening Post*, 1846.

49. Domosh, 'The feminized retail landscape', p. 267; Burrows and Wallace, *Gotham*, p. 878; E. Homberger, *The Historical Atlas of New York City* (New York, 1994), p. 103.

50. Domosh, 'The feminized retail landscape', p. 267; Burrows and Wallace, *Gotham*, p. 878.

51. Zola, *The Ladies' Paradise*, p. 210; S. Bayley, ed, *Commerce and Culture* (London, 1989), pp. 45–59.

52. Santink, *Timothy Eaton*, pp. 98, 225.

53. Haddrell, 'London's Suburban Department Stores', 43.

54. Leach, 'Transformations', 329–330, 326; the world premiere was in Carnegie Hall, not in Wanamaker's (as claimed by Leach). Wanamaker's original store in Philadelphia also hosted symphony concerts.

55. Burrows and Wallace, *Gotham*, pp. 669–670; Jackson, *Encyclopedia of NYC*, p. 302. Both Crystal Palaces were destroyed by fire: the London version, re-erected in the south London suburb of Sydenham in 1854, survived until 1936; but New York's Crystal Palace lasted only five years.

56. Weinreb and Hibbert, *London Encyclopaedia*, p. 960; Lancaster, *Department Store*, p. 20; D. Olsen, *The Growth of Victorian London* (Harmondsworth, 1979), pp. 123–124.

57. In Paris, Gustave Eiffel, responsible for not only the Eiffel Tower but also buildings at the Paris International Exhibition of 1867, also designed parts of the Bon Marché. For Eiffel and Osler's, see Bayley, *Commerce and Culture*, pp. 45–46, 48; J. Styles, 'Victorian Britain, 1837–1901: Introduction' in M. Snodin and J. Styles, *Design and the Decorative Arts: Britain 1500–1900* (London, 2001), p. 335. For Owen Jones, see J. R. Piggott, *Palace of the People: The Crystal Palace at Sydenham 1854–1936* (London, 2004).

58. Quoted in Breward, *Fashioning London*, p. 61.

59. Nava, 'The cosmopolitanism of commerce', 164; idem, 'Modernity's disavowal: women, the city and the department store', in M. Nava and A. O'Shea, eds, *Modern Times: Reflections on a Century of English Modernity* (London, 1996), pp. 38–76; Leach, 'Transformations', 330–331; C. Wood, *Victorian Panorama* (London, 1976), p. 13; G. Barth, *City People* (New York, 1980), p. 120; Rappaport, *Shopping for Pleasure*, p. 238.

60. On the accessibility to women of restaurants and tea-shops outside of department stores, see R. Thorne, 'Places of refreshment in the nineteenth-century city' in A. D. King, ed, *Buildings and Society* (London, 1980), pp. 228–253. Rappaport, *Shopping for Pleasure*, pp. 102–107, discusses female-owned and managed tea-shops on New Bond Street and the proliferation of ABC and Lyons' tea-shops in the 1890s and 1900s, but S. McCracken, 'Voyages by teashop: an urban geography of modernism' in P. Brooker and A. Thacker, eds, *Geographies of Modernism: Literatures, Cultures, Spaces* (London, 2005), pp. 86–98, intriguingly notes that most ABCs and Lyons' in this period were located in the City, not the West End, implying that they were used more by (female) office workers than by shoppers.

61. Domosh, 'The "Women of New York"', 577, 585, and 'The feminized retail landscape'.

62. Domosh, 'The feminized retail landscape', pp. 259–263.

63. Domosh, *Invented Cities*, p. 63; see also Domosh,'The feminized retail landscape', pp. 267–269, and Bowlby, *Just Looking*, p. 71.

64. Quoted in Domosh, *Invented Cities*, p. 62.

65. W. Leach, *True Love and Perfect Union: The Feminist Reform of Sex and Society* (New York, 1980), p. 232, in Domosh, *Invented Cities*, pp. 62–63.

66. Leach, 'Transformations', p. 333–335 (quotation from p. 334); L. Bondi and M. Domosh, 'On the contours of public space: a tale of three women', *Antipode* **30** (1998), 270–271, 278–281.

67. Rappaport, *Shopping for Pleasure*, Chapter Two; Leach, 'Transformations', 330, 333–334.

68. On shoplifting, see E. Abelson, *When Ladies Go A-Thieving* (New York, 1989); Lancaster, *Department Store*, pp. 184–187; Belloc-Lowndes, 'London's drapers', p. 46.

69. Dreiser, *Sister Carrie*, pp. 22, 62.

70. E. Wharton, *The House of Mirth* [1905] (London, 1993), pp. 25–26, 118–119, 137–138.

71. M. Callaghan, *Morley Callaghan's Stories* (Toronto, 1986), pp. 199–202, 263–269.
72. Ibid, pp. 56–61.
73. Haddrell, 'London's Suburban Department Stores', 44–49.
74. Ibid, 41; Zola, *Ladies' Paradise*, pp. 208–209; Gissing, *Jubilee*, pp. 201, 212.
75. Santink, *Timothy Eaton*, p. 121.
76. Bowlby, *Just Looking*, pp. 20–21; Rappaport, *Shopping for Pleasure*, p. 160.
77. Leach, 'Transformations', 326, 327.
78. Zola, *Ladies' Paradise*, p. 208; Blomley, '"I'd like to dress her all over"', p. 249; Domosh, 'The feminized retail landscape', p. 259.
79. Rappaport, *Shopping for Pleasure*, p. 170.
80. Leach, 'Transformations', p. 339; Rappaport, *Shopping for Pleasure*, p. 220.
81. Santink, *Timothy Eaton*, p. 128; Lancaster, *Department Store*, p. 182.
82. C. Breward, *The Hidden Consumer: Masculinities, Fashion and City Life 1860–1914* (Manchester, 1999), pp. 110, 145–146.
83. Shaw, 'The evolution and impact of large-scale retailing', pp. 146–147; J. Benson, 'Large-scale retailing in Canada' in Benson and Shaw, *Evolution*, pp. 193–196; McHugh, *Toronto Architecture*, pp. 162–163.
84. J. Riddell, *Pleasure Trips By Underground* (London, 1998), pp. 6–15. See also posters for 'Christmas Purchases' (1909; a snowy street scene with the exhortation to 'Travel Underground and Make Your Xmas Purchases in Comfort'), 'Winter Sales' (1913; combining a list of twenty-five West End stores with a nursery rhyme and an illustration of a crowd waiting for a 'winter sale' to open – including 12 women, 3 children, 1 dog, and 1 top hat!) and 'Summer Sales' (1926; a brightly coloured, modernist design of cloche-hatted women picking over garments and materials), all illustrated in M. F. Levey, *London Transport Posters* (Oxford, 1976).

Chapter 12. Networked cities

1. H. L. Platt, 'City lights: the electrification of the Chicago region, 1890–1930' in J. A. Tarr and G. Dupuy, eds, *Technology and the Rise of the Networked City in Europe and America* (Philadelphia, 1988), pp. 246–281.
2. C. Otter, 'Cleansing and clarifying: technology and perception in nineteenth-century London', *Journal of British Studies* **43** (2004), 58–59.
3. M. Ogle, 'Water supply, waste disposal, and the culture of privatism in the mid-nineteenth-century city', *Journal of Urban History* **25** (1999), 321–347. See also P. Joyce, *The Rule of Freedom: Liberalism and the Modern City* (London, 2003), esp. Chapter 2.
4. M. Gandy, *Concrete and Clay: Reworking Nature in New York City* (Cambridge MA, 2002), p. 30.
5. Platt, 'City lights', p. 267; M. H. Rose, 'Urban gas and electric systems and social change, 1900–1940' in Tarr and Dupuy, *Technology*, pp. 229–245; Otter, 'Cleansing', 42–43.
6. Ogle, 'Water supply', 330.
7. M. V. Melosi, *The Sanitary City: Urban Infrastructure in America from Colonial Times to the Present* (Baltimore, 2000), pp. 74, 120.
8. B. Weinreb and C. Hibbert, eds, *The London Encyclopaedia* (London, 1983), pp. 930–932; D. Owen, *The Government of Victorian London* (Cambridge MA, 1982), pp. 27–30, 134–140; P. J. Waller, *Town, City, and Nation: England 1850–1914* (Oxford, 1983), p. 302.
9. Waller, *Town, City, and Nation*, p. 300.
10. J. R. Kellett, 'Municipal socialism, enterprise and trading in the Victorian city', *Urban History Yearbook* (1978), 36–45.
11. S. Halliday, *The Great Stink of London: Sir Joseph Bazalgette and the Cleansing of the Victorian Metropolis* (Stroud, Glos, 1999); Owen, *Government*, Chapters 3 and 4.
12. For an equivalent account of American experience, see J. A. Tarr, 'Sewerage and the development of the networked city in the United States, 1850–1930' in Tarr and Dupuy, *Technology*, pp. 159–185, and *The Search for the Ultimate Sink: Urban Pollution in Historical Perspective* (Akron OH, 1996), Part II.

13. Plan of the District of the Metropolitan Board of Works, c. 1883, map on display in Museum of London.
14. J. Hollingshead, *Underground London* (London, 1862), pp. 67–69. See also M. Allen, 'From cesspool to sewer: sanitary reform and the rhetoric of resistance, 1848–1880', *Victorian Literature and Culture* **30** (2002), 387; L. Nead, *Victorian Babylon* (New Haven CT, 2000), pp. 24–26.
15. Allen, 'From cesspool to sewer', 392–393.
16. Ibid, 396–398.
17. D. L. Pike, *Subterranean Cities: The World Beneath Paris and London, 1800–1945* (Ithaca NY, 2005).
18. R. Humphreys, *The Tate Britain Companion to British Art* (London, 2001), p. 122; S. Oliver, '"Rich earth below the sand" and the origins of the Thames Embankments', *Reconstruction: Studies in Contemporary Culture* **2** (3) (2002), <34>, http://www.reconstruction.ws/023/oliver.htm. See also S. Oliver, *"Chains on the River": The Thames Embankments and the Construction of Nature* (Historical Geography Research Series **37** (2002)), pp. 49–55.
19. Hollingshead, *Underground London*, p. 99.
20. W. J. Pinks, *The History of Clerkenwell* (London, 1865), quoted in A. Emmerson, *The Underground Pioneers: Victorian London and Its First Underground Railways* (Harrow, 2000), p. 25.
21. 'The accident to the underground railway', *The Times*, 20 Jun 1862, 12.
22. Otter, 'Cleansing', 42.
23. Allen, 'From cesspool to sewer', 396.
24. J. A. Tarr, 'The separate vs. combined sewer problem: a case study in urban technology design choice', *Journal of Urban History* **5** (1979), 308–339.
25. C. Brace, 'Public works in the Canadian city: the provision of sewers in Toronto 1870–1913', *Urban History Review* **23** (2) (1995), 33–43.
26. Ogle, 'Water supply', 338.
27. Joyce, *Rule*, p. 74.
28. Melosi, *The Sanitary City*, p. 98; Gandy, *Concrete and Clay*, p. 37.
29. K. Jackson, ed., *The Encyclopedia of New York City* (New Haven CT, 1995), p. 1062.
30. J. A. Tarr, T. Finholt and D. Goodman, 'The city and the telegraph: urban telecommunications in the pre-telephone era', *Journal of Urban History* **14** (1987), 38–80; D. Harvey, *The Urbanization of Capital* (Oxford, 1985).
31. Quoted in Tarr et al, 'The city and the telegraph', 55.
32. Ibid, 60–68.
33. J. Stein, 'The telephone: its social shaping and public negotiation in late nineteenth- and early twentieth-century London' in M. Crang, P. Crang and J. May, eds, *Virtual Geographies* (London, 1999), pp. 44–62, and 'Ideology and the telephone: the social reception of a technology, London 1876–1920', unpublished PhD dissertation, University of London, 1996.
34. C. Poitras, 'Le téléphone dans une grande ville industrielle nord-américaine: Montréal 1880–1930', *Les Cahiers, Télécommunications, Histoire et Société* **5** (1997), 11, and *La Cité Au Bout Du Fil: Le Téléphone à Montréal de 1879 à 1930* (Montreal, 2000).
35. All illustrations reproduced in Stein, 'Ideology and the telephone', pp. 94–100.
36. Quoted in E. Stern and E. Gwathmey, *Once Upon a Telephone: An Illustrated Social History* (New York, 1994), p. 62.
37. Stern and Gwathmey, *Once Upon a Telephone*, Chapter 2; M. Martin, *Hello Central? Gender, Technology, and Culture in the Formation of Telephone Systems* (Montreal, 1991).
38. Stern and Gwathmey, *Once Upon a Telephone*, pp. 117–121; Stein, 'Ideology and the telephone', pp. 80–81, 191–195.
39. S. Lewis, *The Job* [1916] (London, 1926), p. 127.
40. T. Dreiser, *Sister Carrie* [1900] (London, 1981), p. 271.
41. Stein, 'Ideology and the telephone', p. 102.
42. Poitras, 'Le téléphone', 14–30, 35.
43. Stein, 'Ideology and the telephone', Chapter 6.

44. J. R. Kellett, *Railways and Victorian Cities* (London, 1969), p. 345; E. de Maré, *The London Doré Saw* (London, 1973), pp. 56–59; A. R. Bennett, *The First Railway in London* [1912] (London, 1971), pp. 2–7.
45. Emmerson, *The Underground Pioneers*.
46. G. W. M. Reynolds, *The Mysteries of London* (1845), Chapter 42, quoted in R. Allen, *The Moving Pageant: A Literary Sourcebook on London Street-life, 1700–1914* (London, 1998), p. 120.
47. G. Doré and B. Jerrold, *London: A Pilgrimage* (London, 1872), p. 120.
48. F. Engels, *The Condition of the Working Class in England* [1845] (London, 1969), p. 79.
49. For details of early rolling stock, see S. Halliday, *Underground to Everywhere* (Stroud, 2001); O. Green, *The London Underground: An illustrated history* (Shepperton, 1987).
50. Humphreys, *Tate Britain Companion*, p. 139; M. Galinou and J. Hayes, *London in Paint: Oil Paintings in the Collection at the Museum of London* (London, 1996), pp. 333–335.
51. Pike, *Subterranean Cities*, pp. 40–41.
52. G. Gissing, *Eve's Ransom* (London, 1895), Chapter VI.
53. H. G. Wells, *Tono-Bungay* [1909] (London, 1994), p. 107.
54. Pike, *Subterranean Cities*, p. 46.
55. Halliday, *Underground to Everywhere*, pp. 143–145; D. L. Pike, 'Modernist space and the transformation of underground London' in P. K. Gilbert, ed., *Imagined Londons* (Albany, NY, 2002), pp. 101–119; C. Wilk, ed, *Modernism: Designing a New World 1914–1939* (London, 2006), p. 407.
56. I am grateful to UCL student Guanming Low, whose coursepaper on 'Mapping the tube' (UCL, 2006) made me look at these posters afresh. See also C. Wolmar, *The Subterranean Railway: How the London Underground was Built and How it Changed the City Forever* (London, 2004).
57. M. Cohen, *Reginald Marsh's New York* (New York, 1983), pp. 27, 33, 76–81.
58. S. Chan, 'The spell of the El', *New York Times*, 1 May 2005; B. G. Moffat, *The 'L': The Development of Chicago's Rapid Transit System, 1888–1932* (Chicago, 1995).
59. M. W. Brooks, *Subway City: Riding the Trains, Reading New York* (New Brunswick, NJ, 1997); C. Hood, *722 Miles: The Building of the Subways and How They Transformed New York* (New York, 1994).
60. E. Homberger, *The Historical Atlas of New York City* (New York, 1994), pp. 106–107.
61. C. W. Cheape, *Moving the Masses: Urban Public Transit in New York, Boston and Philadelphia, 1880–1912* (Cambridge, MA, 1980), p. 36.
62. Brooks, *Subway City*, p. 4.
63. W. D. Howells, *A Hazard of New Fortunes* [1890] (Oxford, 1990), p. 63.
64. Ibid, p. 272.
65. Ibid, pp. 50–51.
66. Ibid, p. 145.
67. Ibid, p. 63.
68. Ibid, p. 50.
69. Ibid, p. 163. A painting which perfectly captures this scene is W. Louis Sontag, Jr's watercolour, 'The Bowery At Night' (c.1895), in the Museum of the City of New York, reproduced in Homberger, *Historical Atlas of New York City*, p. 114.
70. Howells, *Hazard*, p. 163; M. Berman, *All That Is Solid Melts Into Air* (London, 1982), pp. 159–160.
71. Howells, *Hazard*, pp. 161–162.
72. For an extensive discussion of 'the visual discourse of elevated transit', drawing on guidebook photographs as well as modernist art, see D. Tallack, *New York Sights: Visualizing Old and New New York* (Oxford, 2005), Chapter 3.
73. E. Wharton, *The House of Mirth* [1905] (London, 1993), pp. 273, 303.
74. M. Brosseau, 'The city in textual form: *Manhattan Transfer*'s New York', *Ecumene* **2** (1995), 89–114.
75. J. Dos Passos, *Manhattan Transfer* [1925] (London, 1987), p. 21.
76. Ibid, p. 123.

77. Ibid, p. 148.

78. Ibid, pp. 28, 64, 46.

79. Ibid, pp. 72, 77.

80. Ibid, p. 341. The el is also restricted to the role of scenery in F. S. Fitzgerald, *The Great Gatsby* [1926] (Harmondsworth, 1950), set in 1922. Two scenes depict driving from Long Island through Astoria, 'twist[ing] among the pillars of the elevated' and 'among the spidery girders of the elevated' but 'the tumult of the elevated overhead' is as meaningless as 'the foreign clamour on the sidewalk': merely *noise*. Quotations from pp. 74, 131, 142.

81. Catherine Lavender, Department of History, CSI-CUNY, provides a very useful plot summary of *The Crowd* at http://www.library.csi.cuny.edu/dept/history/lavender/crowdanalysis.html

82. For an analysis of the tension between narrative and abstraction in 'Manhatta' see Tallack, *New York Sights*, pp. 76–78, 146–148.

83. J. Flint, *The Prints of Louis Lozowick: A Catalogue Raisonné* (New York, 1982), p. 89.

84. Ibid, p. 75.

85. Quoted in D. Cohen, 'The rising city: urban themes in the art and writings of C. R. W. Nevinson' in R. Ingleby et al, *C. R. W. Nevinson: The Twentieth Century* (London, 1999), p. 49.

86. Ingleby, *C. R. W. Nevinson*, p. 142; Flint, *The Prints of Louis Lozowick*, p. 60.

87. M. M. Hambourg, *Paul Strand circa 1916* (New York, 1998), Plate 13.

88. A. Hemingway, *Philip Reisman's Etchings: Printmaking and Politics in New York 1926–33* (London, 1996).

89. M. Gold, *Jews Without Money* (New York, 1984), p. 57.

90. Marsh's painting, in the collection of the Metropolitan Museum of Art, New York, is reproduced in M. Robinson, *The American Vision: Landscape Paintings of the United States* (New York, 1988), p. 125; a photograph by Marsh of 'The Bowery' (1938), reproduced in Cohen, *Reginald Marsh's New York*, p. 69, confirms the existence of a real 'Marathon Hotel'.

91. J. Loughery, *John Sloan: Painter and Rebel* (New York, 1995); R. Eleza, *John Sloan's Oil Paintings: A Catalogue Raisonné* (2 vols) (Newark NJ, 1991); R. Zurier et al, *Metropolitan Lives: The Ashcan Artists and Their New York* (New York, 1995).

92. Tallack, *New York Sights*, pp. 70–74.

93. 'The City in Greenwich Village' is in the National Gallery of Art, Washington DC. It can be viewed online and is widely reproduced, e.g. in Eleza, *John Sloan's Oil Paintings*, no. 677 (pp. 257–258).

94. G. Barth, *City People: The Rise of Modern City Culture in Nineteenth-Century America* (New York, 1980).

95. Anon, 'If London were like New York', *Harmsworth's Magazine (The London Magazine)* (Feb 1902), online at http://www.forgottenfutures.com/library/newyork/new_york.htm

96. See, for example, J. Robinson, *Ordinary Cities: Between Modernity and Development* (London, 2005); S. Pile, *Real Cities: Modernity, Space and the Phantasmagorias of City Life* (London, 2005).

Select bibliography

(1) Contemporary sources

Acton, W., *Prostitution, Considered in its Moral, Social & Sanitary Aspects, in London and Other Large Cities*, 2nd edn (London, 1870)

Addams, J., *Twenty Years at Hull House* (New York, 1910)

Ames, H. B., *The City Below the Hill* [1897] (Toronto, 1972)

Anon, 'If London were like New York', *Harmsworth's Magazine (The London Magazine)* (Feb 1902), online at http://www.forgottenfutures.com/library/newyork/new_york.htm

Bauer, C., *Modern Housing* (Boston MA, 1934)

Beames, T., *The Rookeries of London* [1852] (London, 1970)

Belloc-Lowndes, Mrs, 'London's drapers' in G. R. Sims, ed, *Living London* (1902), reprinted as *Edwardian London Volume 3* (London, 1990), pp. 40–46

Booth, C., ed, *Labour and Life of the People. Volume II* (London, 1891)

Booth, C., ed, *Life and Labour of the People in London*, 17 volumes (London, 1902–1903)

Booth, W., *In Darkest England and the Way Out* (London, 1890)

Bureau of Municipal Research, *What is "The Ward" Going to Do with Toronto?* (Toronto, 1918)

Burgess, E. W., 'The growth of the city' in R. E. Park et al, eds, *The City* (Chicago, 1925), pp. 47–62

Clarke, W. S., *The Suburban Homes of London* (London, 1881)

Coustillas, P., ed, *London and the Life of Literature in Late Victorian England: The Diary of George Gissing, Novelist* (Hassocks, 1978)

Crosland, T. W. H., *The Suburbans* (London, 1905)

DeForest, R. W. and Veiller, L., *The Tenement House Problem* (New York, 1903)

Doré, G. and Jerrold, B., *London: A Pilgrimage* (London, 1872)

Edwards, P. J., *History of London Street Improvements, 1855–1897* (London, 1898)

Engels, F., *The Condition of the Working class in England* [1845] (London, 1969)

Engels, F., *The Housing Question* (1887)

Escott, T. H. S., *England: its People, Polity and Pursuits* (London, 1891)

Ford, Ford Madox, *The Soul of London* [1905] (London, 1995)

Gatliff, C., 'On improved dwellings and their beneficial effects on health and morals', *Journal of the Statistical Society of London* **38** (1875), 33–63

Gavin, H., *Sanitary Ramblings* (London, 1848)

Godwin, G., *Town Swamps and Social Bridges* [1859] (Leicester, 1972)

Hollingshead, J., *Ragged London in 1861* [1861] (London, 1986)

Hollingshead, J., *Underground London* (London, 1862)

James, H., *The American Scene* (London, 1907)

James, H., *English Hours* [1905] (London, 1960)

King, M., *Handbook of New York City* (Boston, 1892)

Langton, W. A., 'Apartment life', *Canadian Architect and Builder* **16** (1903), 77–78

Leitz, R. C. III et al, eds, *William Dean Howells: Selected Letters Volume 3: 1882–1891* (Boston, 1980)

Leslie, S. C., 'The case for gas – Kensal House', in *Flats: Municipal and Private Enterprise* (Ascot Gas Water Heaters Ltd., London, 1938), pp. 279–286

London County Council, *The Housing Question in London* (London, 1900)

London, J., *The People of the Abyss* [1903] (London, 1978)

Masterman, C. F. G., *From the Abyss* (London, 1902)

Mattheisen, P. F., Young, A. C. and Coustillas, P., eds, *The Collected Letters of George Gissing Volume Two 1881–1885* (Athens OH, 1991)

Mattheisen, P. F., Young, A. C. and Coustillas, P., eds, *The Collected Letters of George Gissing Volume Three 1886–1888* (Athens OH, 1992)

Matthiesen, P. F., Young, A. C. and Coustillas, P., eds, *The Collected Letters of George Gissing Volume Four 1889–1891* (Athens OH, 1993)

Matthiessen, F. O. and Murdock, K. B., eds, *The Notebooks of Henry James* (New York, 1947)

Mayhew, H., *London Labour and the London Poor* (4 volumes) (London, 1861)

Mayor's Pushcart Commission, 'The New York pushcart: recommendations of the mayor's commission', *Charities and the Commons* **16** (22 Sep 1906), 615–618

Mearns, A., *The Bitter Cry of Outcast London* (London, 1883)

Perks, S., *Residential Flats of All Classes* (London, 1905)

Riis, J. A., *How the Other Half Lives* [1890] (Boston, 1996)

Russell, C. and Lewis, H. S., *The Jew in London* (London, 1900)

Ryan, P. F. W., 'Scenes from shop and store London' in Sims, *Living London* (1902), reprinted as *Edwardian London Volume 4* (London, 1990), pp. 53–59

Shaw Sparrow, W., *Flats, Urban Houses and Cottage Homes* (London, 1907)

Shepp, J. W. and D. B., *Shepp's New York City Illustrated* (Philadelphia, 1894)

Simmel, G., 'The metropolis and mental life' (1903), reprinted in G. Bridge and S. Watson, eds, *The Blackwell City Reader* (Oxford, 2002), pp. 11–20

Smith, H. L., *New Survey of London Life and Labour*, 9 volumes (London, 1930–1935)

Smith, T. R. and White, W. H., 'Model dwellings for the rich', *The British Architect and Northern Engineer* **5** (31 Mar 1876), 156

Thomson, J. and Smith, A., *Street Life in London* (London, 1877)

Turner, C. C., 'Scenes from exchange and office London', in Sims, *Living London* (1902), reprinted as *Edwardian London Volume 4* (London, 1990), pp. 198–204

Webb, B., *My Apprenticeship* [1926] (Harmondsworth, 1971)

White, W. H., 'Middle-class houses in Paris and central London', *The Builder* **35** (24 Nov 1877), 1166–1170

Woodsworth, J. S., *My Neighbor* [1911] (Toronto, 1972)

Xenophon, *The Persian Expedition* (translated by R. Warner) (Harmondsworth, 1949)

(2) Fiction

Atwood, Margaret, *Cat's Eye* (London, 1990)

Atwood, Margaret, *The Blind Assassin* (London, 2000)

Bellamy, Edward, *Looking Backward: 2000–1887* (New York, 1888)

Bennett, Arnold, *Riceyman Steps* (1923)

Bennett, Arnold, *Imperial Palace* (1930)

Brontë, Charlotte, *Villette* [1853] (London, 1970)

Callaghan, Morley, *It's Never Over* [1930] (Toronto, 1972)

Callaghan, Morley, *Such Is My Beloved* (1934)

Callaghan, Morley, *They Shall Inherit the Earth* [1935] (Toronto, 1992)

Callaghan, Morley, *More Joy in Heaven* (1937)

Callaghan, Morley, *Morley Callaghan's Stories* (Toronto, 1986)

Disraeli, Benjamin, *Sybil* (London, 1845)

Dos Passos, John, *Manhattan Transfer* [1925] (London, 1987)
Dreiser, Theodore, *Sister Carrie* [1900] (London, 1986)
Eliot, T. S., *The Waste Land and Other Poems* (London, 1971)
Fitzgerald, F. Scott, *The Great Gatsby* [1926] (Harmondsworth, 1950)
Forster, E. M., *Howards End* [1910] (London, 1983)
Garner, Hugh, *Cabbagetown* (Toronto, 1968)
Gissing, George, *Workers in the Dawn* [1880] (Brighton, 1985)
Gissing, George, *The Unclassed* [1884] (London, 1930)
Gissing, George, *Demos* [1886] (Brighton, 1972)
Gissing, George, *Thyrza* [1887] (Brighton, 1984)
Gissing, George, *The Nether World* [1889] (London, 1973)
Gissing, George, *New Grub Street* [1891] (Harmondsworth, 1968)
Gissing, George, *The Odd Women* [1893] (London, 1980)
Gissing, George, *In The Year of Jubilee* [1894] (London, 1994)
Gissing, George, *Eve's Ransom* (London, 1895)
Gissing, George, *The Paying Guest* (London, 1896)
Gissing, George, *The Whirlpool* [1897] (London, 1984)
Gissing, George, *The Town Traveller* (London, 1898)
Gissing, George, *The Crown of Life* [1899] (Hassocks, 1978)
Gissing, George, *The Private Papers of Henry Ryecroft* [1903] (London, 1912)
Gissing, George, *Will Warburton* [1905] (London, 1985)
Gold, Michael, *Jews Without Money* [1930] (New York, 1984)
Grossmith, George and Weedon, *The Diary of a Nobody* [1892] (London, 1965)
Hood, Hugh, *The Governor's Bridge is Closed* (Toronto, 1973)
Howells, William Dean, *A Hazard of New Fortunes* [1890] (Oxford, 1990)
Law, John (Margaret Harkness), *A City Girl* (London, 1887)
Law, John (Margaret Harkness), *Out of Work* [1888] (London, 1990)
Levy, Amy, *The Romance of a Shop* (London, 1888)
Lewis, Sinclair, *The Job* [1916] (London, 1926)
Lewis, Wyndham, *Self Condemned* (London, 1954)
Morris, William, *News from Nowhere* [1890] (London, 1918)
Morrison, Arthur, *A Child of the Jago* (London, 1896)
Ondaatje, Michael, *In The Skin of a Lion* (Toronto, 1987)
Sinclair, Upton, *The Jungle* [1906] (New York, 1981)
Weill, Kurt, *Streetscene* (New York, 1947)
Wells, H. G., *The Time Machine* [1895] (London, 1995)
Wells, H. G., *The War of the Worlds* [1898] (London, 2005)
Wells, H. G., *Tono-Bungay* [1909] (London, 1994)
Wharton, Edith, *The House of Mirth* [1905] (London, 1993)
Wharton, Edith, *The Age of Innocence* [1920] (London, 1974)
Wilde, Oscar, *The Importance of Being Earnest* [1895] (Cambridge, 1999)
Woolf, Virginia, *Mrs Dalloway* [1925] (London, 1992)
Zola, Émile, *Au Bonheur des Dames* (1883), translated as *The Ladies' Paradise* (Berkeley, 1992)

(3) Secondary sources

Abelson, E., *When Ladies Go A-Thieving* (New York, 1989)
Adburgham, A., *Shopping in Style* (London, 1979)
Adburgham, A., *Shops and Shopping 1800–1914* (London, 1981)
Adler, K., *Pissarro in London* (London, 2003)
Adler, K., Hirshler, E. E. and Weinberg, H. B., *Americans in Paris 1860–1900* (London, 2006)
Alexander, M. D., 'Posed to Unposed: encounters with the camera' in J. Elderfield et al, eds, *Modern Starts: People, Places, Things* (New York, 1999), pp. 147–163

Allen, M., 'From cesspool to sewer: sanitary reform and the rhetoric of resistance, 1848–1880', *Victorian Literature and Culture* **30** (2002), 383–402

Allen, R., *The Social Passion: Religion and Social Reform in Canada* (Toronto, 1971)

Allen, R., *The Moving Pageant: A Literary Sourcebook on London Street-Life, 1700–1914* (London, 1998)

Alpern, A., *New York's Fabulous Luxury Apartments* (New York, 1987)

AlSayyad, N., *Cinematic Urbanism: A History of the Modern from Reel to Real* (New York, 2006)

Anderson, G., 'The white-blouse revolution' in G. Anderson, ed, *The White-Blouse Revolution: Female Office Workers Since 1870* (Manchester, 1988), pp. 1–26

Anderson, M. J., *The American Census: A Social History* (New Haven CT, 1988)

Archer, J., 'Colonial suburbs in south Asia, 1700–1850, and the spaces of modernity' in Silverstone, ed, *Visions of Suburbia* (1997), pp. 26–54

Arlitsch, K., 'Digitizing Sanborn fire insurance maps for a full color, publicly accessible collection', *D-Lib Magazine* **8** (7/8) (July/August 2002): http://www.dlib.org/dlib/july02/arlitsch/07arlitsch.html

Armstrong, C. and Nelles, H. V., 'Suburban street railway strategies in Montreal, Toronto, and Vancouver, 1896–1930' in G. Stelter and A. Artibise, eds, *Power and Place* (Vancouver, 1986), pp. 187–218

Arnstein, W. L., 'Queen Victoria's diamond jubilee', *The American Scholar* **66** (1997), 591–597

Arscott, C., 'The representation of the city in the visual arts' in Daunton, ed, *The Cambridge Urban History of Britain Volume III, 1840–1950* (2000), pp. 811–831

Arscott, C., 'William Powell Frith's *The Railway Station*: classification and the crowd' in Bills and Knight, eds, *William Powell Frith* (2006), pp. 79–93

Artibise, A. F. J. and Stelter, G., eds, *The Usable Urban Past* (Toronto, 1979)

Artizans' & General Properties Company Limited, *Artizans' Centenary 1867–1967* (London, 1967)

Ashworth, W., *The Genesis of Town Planning* (London, 1954)

Atkins, P. J., *The Directories of London, 1677–1977* (London, 1990)

Atkins, P. J., 'How the West End was won: the struggle to remove street barriers in Victorian London', *Journal of Historical Geography* **19** (1993), 265–277

Baar, K., 'The national movement to halt the spread of multifamily housing, 1890–1926', *Journal of the American Planning Association* **58** (1) (1992), 39–48

Bailey, P., 'Adventures in space: Victorian railway erotics, or taking alienation for a ride', *Journal of Victorian Culture* **9** (2004), 1–21

Ball, M. and Sunderland, D., *An Economic History of London, 1800–1914* (London, 2001)

Barker, F. and Jackson, P., *The History of London in Maps* (London, 1990)

Barker, T. and Robbins, M., *A History of London Transport Volume 2* (London, 1974)

Baron, W., *The Painters of Camden Town 1905–1920* (London, 1988)

Barrows, R. G., 'Beyond the tenement: patterns of American urban housing, 1870–1930', *Journal of Urban History* **9** (1983), 395–420

Barth, G., *City People: The Rise of Modern City Culture in Nineteenth-Century America* (New York, 1980)

Bayley, S., ed, *Commerce and Culture* (London, 1989)

Bayliss, D., 'Building better communities: social life on London's cottage council estates, 1919–1939', *Journal of Historical Geography* **29** (2003), 376–395

Beattie, S., *A Revolution in London Housing: The LCC Architects and Their Work, 1893–1914* (London, 1980)

Beckman, L. H., *Amy Levy: Her Life and Letters* (Athens OH, 2000)

Belec, J., 'The Dominion Housing Act', *Urban History Review* **25** (2) (1997), 53–69

Bender, T. and Schorske, C. E., eds, *Budapest and New York: Studies in Metropolitan Transformation* (New York, 1994)

Benjamin, W., *The Arcades Project* (Cambridge MA, 1999)

Bennett, A. R., *The First Railway in London* [1912] (London, 1971)

Benson, J., 'Large-scale retailing in Canada' in Benson and Shaw, eds, *The Evolution of Retail Systems* (1992), pp. 186–198

Benson, J. and Shaw, G., eds, *The Evolution of Retail Systems, c.1800–1914* (Leicester, 1992)

Berman, M., *All That Is Solid Melts Into Air* (London, 1982)

Best, G., *Mid-Victorian Britain 1851–75* (London, 1971)

Bills, M. and Knight, V., eds, *William Powell Frith: Painting the Victorian Age* (New Haven CT, 2006)

Bindman, D., *Industry and Idleness: The Moral Geography of Hogarth's London* (London, 1997)

Binford, H., *The First Suburbs: Residential Communities on the Boston Periphery, 1815–1860* (Chicago, 1984)

Birch, E. L. and Gardner, D. S., 'The seven-percent solution: a review of philanthropic housing, 1870–1910', *Journal of Urban History* **7** (1981), 403–438

Black, I. S., 'Symbolic capital: the London and Westminster Bank headquarters, 1836–38', *Landscape Research* **21** (1996), 55–72

Black, I. S., 'Rebuilding "The Heart of the Empire": bank headquarters in the City of London, 1919–1939' in D. Arnold, ed, *The Metropolis and its Image* (Oxford, 1999), pp. 127–152

Black, I. S., 'Spaces of capital: bank office building in the City of London, 1830–1870', *Journal of Historical Geography* **26** (2000), 351–375

Black, I. S., 'Private banking in London's West End, 1750–1830', *London Journal* **28** (2003), 29–59

Blackmar, E., *Manhattan for Rent, 1785–1850* (Ithaca NY, 1989)

Blackmar, E. and Rosenzweig, R., 'The park and the people: Central Park and its publics: 1850–1910' in Bender and Schorske, eds, *Budapest and New York: Studies in Metropolitan Transformation* (1994), pp. 108–134

Blomley, N., '"I'd like to dress her all over": masculinity, power and retail space' in Wrigley and Lowe, eds, *Retailing, Consumption and Capital: Towards the New Retail Geography* (1996), pp. 238–256

Bloomfield, A. V. and Harris, R., 'The journey to work: a historical methodology', *Historical Methods* **30** (1997), 97–109

Bluestone, D., *Constructing Chicago* (New Haven CT, 1991)

Bluestone, D., 'The pushcart evil' in Ward and Zunz, eds, *The Landscape of Modernity* (1992), pp. 287–312

Boire, G., *Morley Callaghan: Literary Anarchist* (Toronto, 1994)

Bondi, L. and Domosh, M., 'On the contours of public space: a tale of three women', *Antipode* **30** (1998), 270–289

Bonshek, J., 'The skyscraper: a catalyst of change in the Chicago construction industries, 1882–1892', *Construction History* **4** (1988), 53–74

Bowlby, R., *Just Looking: Consumer Culture in Dreiser, Gissing and Zola* (New York, 1985)

Boyer, K., 'Place and the politics of virtue: clerical work, corporate anxiety, and changing meanings of public womanhood in early twentieth-century Montreal', *Gender, Place and Culture* **5** (1998), 261–276

Boyer, K., '"Neither forget nor remember your sex": sexual politics in the early twentieth-century Canadian office', *Journal of Historical Geography* **29** (2003), 212–229

Boyer, K., '"Miss Remington" goes to work: gender, space, and technology at the dawn of the information age', *Professional Geographer* **56** (2004), 201–212

Boyer, P., *Urban Masses and Moral Order in America, 1820–1920* (Cambridge MA, 1978)

Boyer, P., Clark, C. E., Kett, J. F., Salisbury, N., Sitkoff, H. and Woloch, N., *The Enduring Vision: A History of the American People Volume Two: From 1865* (Lexington MA, 1996)

Brace, C., 'Public works in the Canadian city: the provision of sewers in Toronto 1870–1913', *Urban History Review* **23** (2) (1995), 33–43

Bradbury, M., 'The cities of modernism' in M. Bradbury and J. McFarlane, eds, *Modernism* (Harmondsworth, 1991), pp. 96–104

Bradley, S. and Pevsner, N., *Buildings of England, London 6: Westminster* (London, 2003)

Braithwaite, B. and Walsh, N., *Home Sweet Home: The Best of Good Housekeeping 1922–1939* (London, 1995)

Bressey, C., 'Forgotten histories: three stories of black girls from Barnardo's Victorian archive', *Women's History Review* **11** (2002), 351–375

Bressey, C., 'Looking for blackness: a researcher's paradox', *Ethics, Place and Environment* **6** (2003), 215–226

Brettell, R. R. and Pissarro, J., *The Impressionist and the City: Pissarro's Series Paintings* (New Haven CT, 1992)

Breward, C., *The Hidden Consumer: Masculinities, Fashion and City Life 1860–1914* (Manchester, 1999)

Breward, C., *Fashioning London: Clothing and the Modern Metropolis* (Oxford, 2004)

Briggs, A., *Victorian Cities* (Harmondsworth, 1968)

Brooks, M. W., *Subway City: Riding the Trains, Reading New York* (New Brunswick NJ, 1997)

Brosseau, M., 'Geography's literature', *Progress in Human Geography* **18** (1994), 333–353

Brosseau, M., 'The city in textual form: *Manhattan Transfer*'s New York', *Ecumene* **2** (1995), 89–114

Brown-May, A., 'A charitable indulgence: street stalls and the transformation of public space in Melbourne, c.1850–1920', *Urban History* **23** (1996), 48–71

Brown-May, A., *Melbourne Street Life* (Melbourne, 1998)

Buck-Morss, S., *The Dialectics of Seeing: Walter Benjamin and the Arcades Project* (Cambridge MA, 1989)

Bulmer, M., 'W. E. B. Du Bois as a social investigator:*The Philadelphia Negro*, 1899' in Bulmer et al, *The Social Survey in Historical Perspective* (1992), pp. 170–188

Bulmer, M., Bales, K., and Sklar, K. K., *The Social Survey in Historical Perspective, 1880–1940* (Cambridge, 1992)

Burrows, E. G. and Wallace, M., *Gotham: A History of New York City to 1898* (New York, 1999)

Buse, P., Hirschkop, K., McCracken, S. and Taithe, B., *Benjamin's Arcades: An UnGuided Tour* (Manchester, 2005)

Callaghan, M., *That Summer in Paris* [1963] (Toronto, 1976)

Cannadine, D., 'Urban development in England and America in the nineteenth century: some comparisons and contrasts', *Economic History Review* **33** (1980), 309–325

Cannadine, D. and Reeder, D., eds, *Exploring the Urban Past: Essays in Urban History by H. J. Dyos* (Cambridge, 1982)

Careless, J. M. S., *Toronto to 1918* (Toronto, 1984)

Cassell, M., *Inside Nationwide: One hundred years of co-operation* (London, 1984)

Caulfield, J., 'The imagined cities of three Canadian painters', *Urban History Review* **20** (1) (1991), 3–14

Caulfield, J., 'Augurs of "gentrification": city houses of four Canadian painters' in P. Simpson-Housley and G. Norcliffe, eds, *A Few Acres of Snow* (Toronto, 1992), pp. 189–202

Chambers, E. J., 'A new measure of the rental cost of housing in the Toronto market 1890–1914', *Histoire sociale/Social History* **17** (1984), 165–174

Charney, L., 'In order: fragmentation in film and vaudeville' in McDonnell, ed, *On the Edge of Your Seat: Popular Theater and Film in Early Twentieth-Century American Art* (2002), pp. 107–121

Chauncey, G., *Gay New York: Gender, Urban Culture and the Making of the Gay Male World 1890–1940* (New York, 1994)

Cheape, C. W., *Moving the Masses: Urban Public Transit in New York, Boston and Philadelphia, 1880–1912* (Cambridge MA, 1980)

Clark, E. and Ashley, P., 'The merchant prince of Cornville', *Chicago History* **21** (3) (1992), 4–19

Clarke, D. B., 'Introduction: previewing the cinematic city' in Clarke, ed, *The Cinematic City* (1997), pp. 1–18

Clarke, D. B., ed, *The Cinematic City* (London, 1997)

Clout, H., ed, *The Times London History Atlas* (London, 1997)

Cohen, D., 'The rising city: urban themes in the art and writings of C. R. W. Nevinson' in Ingleby et al, *C. R. W. Nevinson: The Twentieth Century* (1999), pp. 39–53

Cohen, M., *Reginald Marsh's New York* (New York, 1983)

Coleman, B. I., ed, *The Idea of the City in Nineteenth-Century Britain* (London, 1973)

Collins, P., 'Dickens and London' in Dyos and Wolff, eds, *The Victorian City* (1973), pp. 537–557.

Conzen, M. P., 'The impact of industrialism and modernity on American cities, 1860–1930', in T. F. McIlwraith and E. K. Muller, eds, *North America: The historical geography of a changing continent, Second Edition* (Lanham MD, 2001), pp. 333–355

Cook, M., *London and the Culture of Homosexuality, 1885–1914* (Cambridge, 2003)

Copp, T., *The Anatomy of Poverty: The Condition of the Working Class in Montreal, 1897–1929* (Toronto, 1974)

Corn, W., 'The artist's New York: 1900–1930' in Bender and Schorske, eds, *Budapest and New York* (1994), pp. 275–308

Cowan, R. S., *More Work for Mother* (London, 1989)

Cowling, M., *Victorian Figurative Painting: Domestic Life and the Contemporary Social Scene* (London, 2000)

Cowling, M., 'Frith and his followers' in Bills and Knight, eds, *William Powell Frith* (2006), pp. 57–77

Cromley, E. C., *Alone Together: A History of New York's Early Apartments* (Ithaca NY, 1990)

Crossick, G., *An Artisan Elite in Victorian Society: Kentish London, 1840–1880* (London, 1978).

Cunningham, G., 'The riddle of suburbia: suburban fictions at the Victorian *fin de siècle*' in Webster, ed, *Expanding Suburbia* (2000), pp. 51–70

Cunningham, G., 'Houses in between: navigating suburbia in late Victorian writing', *Victorian Literature and Culture* **32** (2004), 421–434

Curtis, B., *The Politics of Population: State Formation, Statistics and the Census of Canada, 1840–1875* (Toronto, 2001)

Daniels, S., 'Images of the railway in nineteenth century paintings and prints' in *Train Spotting: Images of the Railway in Art* (Nottingham, 1985)

Dash Moore, D., 'On the fringes of the city' in Ward and Zunz, eds, *The Landscape of Modernity* (1992), pp. 252–272

Daunton, M., 'House-ownership from rate books', *Urban History Yearbook* (1976), 21–27

Daunton, M., 'Public place and private space: the Victorian city and the working-class household' in Fraser and Sutcliffe, eds, *The Pursuit of Urban History* (1983), pp. 212–233

Daunton, M., *A Property Owning Democracy? Housing in Britain* (London, 1987)

Daunton, M., 'Home loans versus council houses: the formation of British and American housing policy, 1900–20', *Housing Studies* **3** (1988), 232–246

Daunton, M., 'Cities of homes and cities of tenements', *Journal of Urban History* **14** (1988), 283–319

Daunton, M. 'Rows and tenements: American cities, 1880–1914' in Daunton, ed, *Housing the Workers* (1990), pp. 249–286

Daunton, M., ed, *Housing the Workers: A Comparative History, 1850–1914* (London, 1990)

Daunton, M., ed, *The Cambridge Urban History of Britain Volume III, 1840–1950* (Cambridge, 2000)

Daunton, M. and Rieger, B., eds, *Meanings of Modernity: Britain from the Late Victorian Era to World War II* (Oxford, 2001)

Davies, T., 'Transports of pleasure' in Formations Collective, eds, *Formations of Pleasure* (London, 1983), pp. 46–58

Davis, D. F., 'Mass transit and private ownership: an alternative perspective on the case of Toronto', *Urban History Review* **3** (1978), 60–98

Davison, G., *The Rise and Fall of Marvellous Melbourne* (Melbourne, 1978)

Davison, G., 'The city as a natural system: theories of urban society in early nineteenth-century Britain' in Fraser and Sutcliffe, eds, *The Pursuit of Urban History* (1983), pp. 349–370

De Certeau, M., *The Practice of Everyday Life* (Berkeley, 1984)

De Maré, E., *The London Doré Saw* (London, 1973)

Denford, S., 'Luxury living for the lower classes', *Camden History Review* **20** (1996), 9–13

Dennis, R., *English Industrial Cities of the Nineteenth Century: A Social Geography* (Cambridge, 1984)

Dennis, R., 'Landlords and rented housing in Toronto, 1885–1914', *University of Toronto Centre for Urban and Community Studies Research Paper* **162** (1987)

Dennis, R., 'Toronto's first apartment-house boom: an historical geography, 1900–1920', *University of Toronto Centre for Urban & Community Studies Research Paper* **177** (1989)

Dennis, R., 'The geography of Victorian values: philanthropic housing in London, 1840–1900', *Journal of Historical Geography* **15** (1989), 40–54

Dennis, R., '"Hard to let" in Edwardian London', *Urban Studies* **26** (1989), 77–89

Dennis, R., 'The Social Geography of Victorian Huddersfield' in E. A. H. Haigh, ed, *Huddersfield: A Most Handsome Town* (Huddersfield, 1992), pp. 423–448

Dennis, R., 'Interpreting the apartment house: modernity and metropolitanism in Toronto, 1900–1930', *Journal of Historical Geography* **20** (1994), 305–322

Dennis, R., 'Landlords and housing in depression', *Housing Studies* **10** (1995), 305–324

Dennis, R., 'Property and propriety: Jewish landlords in early twentieth-century Toronto', *Transactions of the Institute of British Geographers* **22** (1997), 377–397

Dennis, R., 'Apartment housing in Canadian cities, 1900–1940', *Urban History Review* **26** (2) (1998), 17–31

Dennis, R., 'Morley Callaghan and the moral geography of Toronto', *British Journal of Canadian Studies* **14** (1999), 35–51

Dennis, R., 'Modern London' in Daunton, ed, *Cambridge Urban History of Britain Volume III, 1840–1950* (2000), pp. 95–131

Dennis, R., '"Zoning" before zoning: the regulation of apartment housing in early twentieth-century Winnipeg and Toronto', *Planning Perspectives* **15** (2000), 267–299

Dennis, R., 'Reconciling geographies, representing modernities' in I. Black and R. Butlin, eds, *Place, Culture and Identity* (Laval, 2001), pp. 17–43

Dennis, R., '"Foreigners who live in Toronto": attitudes towards immigrants in a Canadian city, 1890–1918' in B. Messamore, ed, *Canadian Migration Patterns from Britain and North America* (Ottawa, 2004), pp. 183–199

Dennis, R., 'La regolamentazione degli edifice per appartamenti a Toronto e Londra: una preistoria', *Storia Urbana* **108** (2005), 15–37

Dennis, R., 'Buildings, Residences and Mansions: George Gissing's "Prejudice Against Flats"' in Spiers, ed, *Gissing and the City* (2006), pp. 41–62

Dennis, R., 'Working women downtown: Toronto 1900–1930', *London Journal of Canadian Studies* **22** (2006–2007), 35–57, online at http://www.canadian-studies.info/lccs/LJCS/index.html

Dewing, D., ed, *Home and Garden: Paintings and Drawings of English, Middle-Class, Urban Domestic Spaces 1675 to 1914* (London, 2003)

Distel, A., Druick, D. W., Groom, G. and Rapetti, R., *Gustave Caillebotte: The Unknown Impressionist* (London, 1996)

Doezema, M., *George Bellows and Urban America* (New Haven CT, 1992)

Domosh, M., 'Imagining New York's first skyscrapers, 1875–1910', *Journal of Historical Geography* **13** (1987), 233–248

Domosh, M., 'The symbolism of the skyscraper: case studies of New York's first tall buildings', *Journal of Urban History* **14** (1988), 320–345

Domosh, M., *Invented Cities: The Creation of Landscape in Nineteenth-Century New York and Boston* (New Haven CT, 1996)

Domosh, M., 'The feminized retail landscape: gender ideology and consumer culture in nineteenth-century New York City', in Wrigley and Lowe, eds, *Retailing, Consumption and Capital* (1996), pp. 257–270

Domosh, M., 'Those "Gorgeous Incongruities": polite politics and public space on the streets of nineteenth-century New York City', *Annals of the Association of American Geographers* **88** (1998), 209–226

Domosh, M., 'The "Women of New York": a fashionable moral geography', *Environment and Planning D: Society and Space* **19** (2001), 573–592

Donald, J., *Imagining the Modern City* (London, 1999)

Donnelly, S., 'Mapping Rich and Poor: Putting Charles Booth's *Enquiry into London Life and Labour* Online', *Cartographic Journal*, **39** (1) (2002), 81–85

Doucet, M., 'Mass transit and the failure of private ownership: the case of Toronto in the early twentieth century', *Urban History Review* **3** (1977), 3–33

Doucet, M. and Weaver, J., *Housing the North American City* (Montreal, 1991)

Driver, F., 'Moral geographies: social science and the urban environment in mid-nineteenth century England', *Transactions Institute of British Geographers* **13** (1988), 275–287

Driver, F., *Power and Pauperism: The Workhouse System 1834–1884* (Cambridge, 1993)

Driver, F., *Geography Militant: Cultures of Exploration and Empire* (Oxford, 2000)

Driver, F. and Gilbert, D., 'Heart of empire? Landscape, space and performance in imperial London', *Environment and Planning D: Society and Space* **16** (1998), 11–28

Driver, F. and Gilbert, D., eds, *Imperial Cities: Landscape, Display and Identity* (Manchester, 1999)

Duffy, D., 'Furnishing the pictures: Arthur S. Goss, Michael Ondaatje and the imag(in)ing of Toronto', *Journal of Canadian Studies* **36** (2001), 106–129

Duffy, F., 'Office buildings and organisational change' in King, ed, *Buildings and Society* (1980), pp. 255–280

Durant, R., 'Community and association in a London housing estate' in R. E. Pahl, ed, *Readings in Urban Sociology* (Oxford, 1968), pp. 159–185

Dyos, H. J., *Victorian Suburb: A Study of the Growth of Camberwell* (Leicester, 1961)

Dyos, H. J., 'The objects of street improvement in Regency and early Victorian London' in Cannadine and Reeder, eds, *Exploring the Urban Past* (1982), pp. 81–86

Dyos, H. J., 'Workmen's fares in south London, 1860–1914' in Cannadine and Reeder, eds, *Exploring the Urban Past* (1982), pp. 87–100

Dyos, H. J., 'The speculative builders and developers of Victorian London' in Cannadine and Reeder, eds, *Exploring the Urban Past* (1982), pp. 154–178

Dyos, H. J., 'A Victorian speculative builder: Edward Yates' in Cannadine and Reeder, eds, *Exploring the Urban Past* (1982), pp. 179–189.

Dyos, H. J. and Wolff, M., eds, *The Victorian City: Images and Realities* 2 volumes (London, 1973)

Edel, M., Sclar, E. D. and Luria, D., *Shaky Palaces: Homeownership and Social Mobility in Boston's Suburbanization* (New York, 1984)

Ehrman, E., 'Frith and fashion' in Bills and Knight, eds, *William Powell Frith* (2006), pp. 111–129

Eleza, R., *John Sloan's Oil Paintings: A Catalogue Raisonné* 2 volumes (Newark NJ, 1991)

Ellul, J., *The Meaning of the City* (Grand Rapids MI, 1970)

Emmerson, A., *The Underground Pioneers: Victorian London and Its First Underground Railways* (Harrow, 2000)

Englander, D. and O'Day, R., eds, *Retrieved Riches: Social Investigations in Britain 1840–1914* (Aldershot, 1995)

Ennals, P. and Holdsworth, D. W., *Homeplace: The Making of the Canadian Dwelling over Three Centuries* (Toronto, 1998)

Fenske, G. and Holdsworth, D. W., 'Corporate identity and the New York office building: 1895–1915' in Ward and Zunz, eds, *The Landscape of Modernity: New York City 1900–1940* (1992), pp. 129–159

Fine, L. M., *The Souls of the Skyscraper: Female Clerical Workers in Chicago, 1870–1930* (Philadelphia, 1990)

Firth, E. G., *Toronto in Art* (Toronto, 1983)

Fisher, P., 'The novel as newspaper and gallery of voices: the American novel in New York City: 1890–1930' in Bender and Schorske, eds, *Budapest and New York: Studies in Metropolitan Transformation: 1870–1930* (1994), pp. 332–351

Fishman, R., 'The origins of the suburban idea in England', *Chicago History* **13** (2) (1984), 26–35

Fishman, R., *Bourgeois Utopias: The Rise and Fall of Suburbia* (New York, 1987)

Fitz-Gibbon, D., 'Spaces of moral improvement: allotment gardens, philanthropic housing and moral geography in early-Victorian England, 1830–1850', unpublished MSc dissertation, UCL Department of Geography (2003)

Fleming, R., 'The trolley takes command, 1892 to 1894', *Urban History Review* **19** (1991), 218–225

Flint, J., *The Prints of Louis Lozowick: A Catalogue Raisonné* (New York, 1982)

Flint, K., 'Fictional suburbia', *Literature and History* **8** (1982), 67–81

Fogelson, R. M., *Downtown: Its Rise and Fall, 1880–1950* (New Haven CT, 2001)

Foucault, M., *The Birth of the Clinic* (London, 1974)

Fraser, D. and Sutcliffe, A., eds, *The Pursuit of Urban History* (London, 1983)

Fried, A. and Elman, R., eds, *Charles Booth's London* (Harmondsworth, 1969)

Frisby, D., *Cityscapes of Modernity* (Cambridge, 2001)

Gad, G. and Holdsworth, D. W., 'Building for city, region and nation: office development in Toronto 1834–1984' in Russell, ed, *Forging a Consensus: Historical Essays on Toronto* (1984), pp. 272–319

Gad, G. and Holdsworth, D. W., 'Corporate capitalism and the emergence of the high-rise office building', *Urban Geography* **8** (1987), 212–231

Gad, G. and Holdsworth, D. W., 'Looking inside the skyscraper: size and occupancy of Toronto office buildings, 1890–1950', *Urban History Review* **16** (1987), 176–189

Gad, G. and Holdsworth, D. W., 'Streetscape and society: the changing built environment of King Street, Toronto', in R. Hall, W. Westfall and L. S. MacDowell, eds, *Patterns of the Past: Interpreting Ontario's History* (Toronto, 1988), pp. 174–205

Galinou, M. and Hayes, J., *London in Paint: Oil Paintings in the Collection at the Museum of London* (London, 1996)

Gamber, W., 'Away from home: middle-class boarders in the nineteenth-century city', *Journal of Urban History* **31** (2005), 289–305

Gandy, M., *Concrete and Clay: Reworking Nature in New York City* (Cambridge MA, 2002)

Gardner, T., 'The slow wave: the changing residential status of cities and suburbs in the United States, 1850–1940', *Journal of Urban History* **27** (2001), 293–312

Garland, K., *Mr Beck's Underground Map* (Harrow, 1994)

Garside, P., 'The impact of philanthropy: housing provision and the Sutton Model Dwellings Trust, 1900–1939', *Economic History Review* **53** (2000), 742–766

Garside, P., *The Conduct of Philanthropy: William Sutton Trust 1900–2000* (London, 2000)

Gerdts, W. H., *Impressionist New York* (New York, 1994)

Germain, A. and Rose, D., *Montréal: The Quest for a Metropolis* (Chichester, 2000)

Gilbert, E., 'Naturalist metaphors in the literature of Chicago, 1893–1925', *Journal of Historical Geography* **20** (1994), 283–304

Gilbert, E. W., 'Pioneer maps of health and disease in England', *Geographical Journal* **124** (1958), 172–183

Gilbert, P. K., 'The Victorian social body and urban cartography' in Gilbert, ed, *Imagined Londons* (2002), pp. 11–30

Gilbert, P. K., ed, *Imagined Londons* (Albany NY, 2002)

Gilfoyle, T., *City of Eros: New York City, Prostitution, and the Commercialization of Sex, 1790–1920* (New York, 1992)

Gilloch, G., '"The return of the flâneur": the afterlife of an allegory', *New Formations* **38** (1999), 101–109

Girouard, M., *Cities and People: A Social and Architectural History* (New Haven CT, 1985)

Godfrey, H., *Tower Bridge* (London, 1988)

Goheen, P., 'Symbols in the streets: parades in Victorian urban Canada', *Urban History Review* **18** (1990), 237–243

Goheen, P., 'The ritual of the streets in mid–19th-century Toronto', *Environment and Planning D: Society and Space* **11** (1993), 127–145

Goheen, P., 'Negotiating access to public space in mid-nineteenth century Toronto', *Journal of Historical Geography* **20** (1994), 430–449

Goheen, P., 'Honouring "one of the great forces of the dominion": the Canadian public mourns McGee', *Canadian Geographer* **41** (1997), 350–362

Goheen, P., 'Public space and the geography of the modern city', *Progress in Human Geography* **22** (1998), 479–496

Goheen, P., 'The assertion of middle-class claims to public space in late Victorian Toronto', *Journal of Historical Geography* **29** (2003), 73–92

Gold, J. R., 'From "Metropolis" to "The City": film visions of the future city, 1919–39' in J. A. Burgess and J. R. Gold, eds, *Geography, the Media and Popular Culture* (London, 1985), pp. 123–143

Goodall, F., 'Gas in London: a divided city', *London Journal* **27** (2002), 34–50

Goode, J., 'Introduction' to G. Gissing, *The Nether World* (Brighton, 1974), pp. v–xv

Goodman, A., *Gilbert and Sullivan's London* (London, 2000)

Gowans, A., *The Comfortable House: North American Suburban Architecture 1890–1930* (Cambridge MA, 1986)

Green, D. R., 'Street trading in London: a case study of casual labour 1830–60' in J. H. Johnson and C. Pooley, eds, *The Structure of Nineteenth Century Cities* (London, 1982), pp. 129–151

Green, D. R. and Parton, A. G., 'Slums and slum life in Victorian England: London and Birmingham at mid-century' in M. Gaskell, ed, *Slums* (Leicester, 1990), pp. 17–91

Green, O., *The London Underground: An Illustrated History* (Shepperton, 1987)

Greenhalgh, P., *Ephemeral Vistas: The Expositions Universelles, Great Exhibitions and World's Fairs, 1851–1939* (Manchester, 1988)

Greenhalgh, P., 'The art and industry of mammon: international exhibitions, 1851–1901' in J. M. MacKenzie, ed, *The Victorian Vision: Inventing New Britain* (London, 2001), pp. 265–279

Greenwald, M. W., 'Visualizing Pittsburgh in the 1900s: Art and Photography in the Service of Social Reform' in Greenwald and Anderson, eds, *Pittsburgh Surveyed* (1996), pp. 124–152

Greenwald, M. W. and Anderson, M., eds, *Pittsburgh Surveyed: Social Science and Social Reform in the Early Twentieth Century* (Pittsburgh, 1996)

Haddrell, S., 'A Study of London's Suburban Department Stores', unpublished MSc dissertation, UCL Department of Geography (2003)

Hales, P. B., *Silver Cities: The Photography of American Urbanization, 1839–1915* (Philadelphia, 1984)

Hall, P., *Cities of Tomorrow* (Oxford, 1988)

Hall, P., *Cities in Civilization* (London, 1999)

Halliday, S., *The Great Stink of London: Sir Joseph Bazalgette and the Cleansing of the Victorian Metropolis* (Stroud, Glos, 1999)

Halliday, S., *Underground to Everywhere* (Stroud, Glos, 2001)

Halperin, J., *Gissing: A Life in Books* (Oxford, 1982)

Hambourg, M. M., *Paul Strand Circa 1916* (New York, 1998)

Hamnett, C. and Randolph, B., 'The rise and fall of London's purpose-built blocks of privately rented flats: 1853–1983', *London Journal* **11** (1985), 160–175

Hamnett, C. and Randolph, B., *Cities, Housing and Profits: Flat Break-Up and the Decline of Private Renting* (London, 1988)

Hannah, M. G., *Governmentality and the Mastery of Territory in Nineteenth-Century America* (Cambridge, 2000)

Hapgood, L., 'The literature of the suburbs: versions of repression in the novels of George Gissing, Arthur Conan Doyle and William Pett Ridge, 1890–1899', *Journal of Victorian Culture* **5** (2000), 287–310

Hapgood, L., '"The New Suburbanites" and contested class identities in the London suburbs, 1880–1900' in Webster, ed, *Expanding Suburbia* (2000), pp. 31–49

Hapgood, L., *Margins of Desire: The Suburbs in Fiction and Culture 1880–1925* (Manchester, 2005)

Hardin, J., House, J. and Chu, P.T-D., *Monet's London: Artists' Reflections on the Thames 1859–1914* (St Petersburg FL, 2005)

Hardy, D. and Ward, C., *Arcadia for All: The Legacy of a Makeshift Landscape* (London, 1984)

Harley, J. B., 'Maps, knowledge and power' in D. Cosgrove and S. Daniels, eds, *The Iconography of Landscape* (Cambridge, 1988), pp. 277–312

Harley, J. B., 'Deconstructing the map', *Cartographica* **26** (1989), 1–20

Harley, R. J., *LCC Electric Tramways* (London, 2002)

Harney, R. F. and Troper, H., *Immigrants: A Portrait of the Urban Experience 1890–1930* (Toronto, 1975)

Harris, R., 'Household work strategies and suburban homeownership in Toronto, 1899–1913', *Environment and Planning D: Society and Space* **8** (1990), 97–121

Harris, R., 'A working-class suburb for immigrants, Toronto 1909–1913', *Geographical Review* **81** (1991), 318–332

Harris, R., 'The impact of building controls on residential development in Toronto, 1900–40, *Planning Perspectives* **6** (1991), 269–296

Harris, R., 'Self-building in the urban housing market', *Economic Geography* **67** (1991), 1–21

Harris, R., 'The end justified the means: boarding and rooming in a city of homes, 1890–1951', *Journal of Social History* **26** (1992), 331–358

Harris, R., 'The flexible house: the housing backlog and the persistence of lodging, 1891–1951', *Social Science History* **18** (1994), 31–53

Harris, R., *Unplanned Suburbs: Toronto's American Tragedy, 1900 to 1950* (Baltimore, 1996)

Harris, R., 'The making of American suburbs, 1900–1950s: a reconstruction' in R. Harris and P. Larkham, eds, *Changing Suburbs: Foundation, Form and Function* (London, 1999), pp. 91–110

Harris, R., *Creeping Conformity: How Canada Became Suburban, 1900–1960* (Toronto, 2004)

Harris, R. and Hamnett, C., 'The myth of the promised land: the social diffusion of home ownership in Britain and North America', *Annals of the Association of American Geographers* **77** (1987), 173–190

Harris, R. and Lewis, R., 'Constructing a fault(y) zone: misrepresentations of American cities and suburbs, 1900–1950', *Annals of the Association of American Geographers* **88** (1998), 622–639

Harris, R. and Lewis, R., 'The geography of North American cities and suburbs, 1900–1950', *Journal of Urban History* **27** (2001), 262–292

Harrison, B., 'Pubs' in Dyos and Wolff, eds, *The Victorian City: Images and Realities* (1973), pp. 161–190

Hartley, J., 'The sexualization of suburbia' in Silverstone, ed, *Visions of Suburbia* (1997), pp. 180–216

Harvey, D., *Social Justice and the City* (London, 1973)

Harvey, D., *The Urbanization of Capital* (Oxford, 1985)

Harvey, D., *Consciousness and the Urban Experience* (Oxford, 1985)

Harvey, D., *The Condition of Postmodernity* (Oxford, 1989)

Harvey, D., *Paris, Capital of Modernity* (London, 2003)

Harvey, M., 'From *passante* to *flâneuse*: encountering the prostitute in Dorothy Richardson's *Pilgrimage*', *Journal of Urban History* **27** (2001), 746–764

Haw, R., *The Brooklyn Bridge: A Cultural History* (New Brunswick NJ, 2005)

Hawes, E., *New York, New York: How the Apartment House Transformed the Life of the City* (New York, 1993)

Hayden, D., *Building Suburbia: Green Fields and Urban Growth, 1820–2000* (New York, 2003)

Hayward, R. J., 'Chas. E. Goad and Fire Insurance Cartography' in B. Farrell and A. Desbarats, eds, *Explorations in the History of Canadian Mapping* (Ottawa, 1988), pp. 179–93

Hemingway, A., *Philip Reisman's Etchings: Printmaking and Politics in New York 1926–33* (London, 1996)

Higgs, E., *Making Sense of the Census Revisited* (London, 2005)

Hillier, B. and Hanson, J., *The Social Logic of Space* (Cambridge, 1984)

Hindle, B. P., *Maps for Local History* (London, 1988)

Hobhouse, H., *Thomas Cubitt: Master Builder* (London, 1971)

Holdsworth, D. W., 'Morphological change in Lower Manhattan, New York, 1893–1920' in J. Whitehand and P. Larkham, eds, *Urban Landscapes: International Perspectives* (London, 1992), pp. 114–129

Holmes, J., 'Building bridges and breaking boundaries: modernity and agoraphobia', *Opticon* **1** (1) (Autumn 2006), online at http://www.ucl.ac.uk/ics/opticon1826/VfPModernityAgoraphobiaPDF.pdf

Holmes, R. S., 'Identifying nineteenth-century properties', *Area* **6** (1974), 273–277

Homberger, E., *The Historical Atlas of New York City* (New York, 1994)

Hood, C., *722 Miles: The Building of the Subways and How They Transformed New York* (New York, 1994)

Hood, J. W., *The Toronto Civic Railways* (Toronto, 1986)

Houlbrook, M., *Queer London: Perils and Pleasures in the Sexual Metropolis, 1918–1957* (Chicago, 2005)

House, J., 'From realism to the "impression"' in Lochnan, ed, *TurnerWhistlerMonet* (2004), pp. 109–111

Howell, P., 'Victorian sexuality and the moralization of Cremorne Gardens' in J. P. Sharp, P. Routledge, C. Philo and R. Paddison, eds, *Entanglements of Power: Geographies of Domination/Resistance* (London, 2000), pp. 43–66

Howell, P., 'A private Contagious Diseases Act: prostitution and public space in Victorian Cambridge', *Journal of Historical Geography* **26** (2000), 376–402

Hughes, R., *American Visions* (London, 1997)

Humphreys, R., *The Tate Britain Companion to British Art* (London, 2001)

Hunt, T., *Building Jerusalem: The Rise and Fall of the Victorian City* (London, 2004)

Hurl, L. F., 'The Toronto Housing Company, 1912–1923: the pitfalls of painless philanthropy', *Canadian Historical Review* **45** (1984), 28–53

Hyde, R., *Printed Maps of Victorian London 1851–1900* (Folkestone, 1975)

Hyde, R., '*Edward Stanford and his library map of London*', notes accompanying a 24-sheet facsimile of *Stanford's Library Map of London and its Suburbs* (London, 1980)

Hyde, R., 'A "handy" map', *Map Collector* (June 1986), 47

Hyde, R., *Panoramania!: The Art and Entertainment of the 'All Embracing' View* (London, 1988)

Ingleby, R., Black, J., Cohen, D. and Cooke, G., *C. R. W. Nevinson: The Twentieth Century* (London, 1999)

Inwood, S., *A History of London* (London, 1998)

Jackson, A. A., *Semi-Detached London: Suburban Development, Life and Transport, 1900–39* (London, 1973)

Jackson, K., *Crabgrass Frontier: The Suburbanization of the United States* (New York, 1985)

Jackson, K., ed, *The Encyclopedia of New York City* (New Haven CT, 1995)

Jackson, P., *John Tallis's London Street Views 1838–1840* (London, 1969)

Jackson, P. A., *Maps of Meaning: An Introduction to Cultural Geography* (London, 1989)

Jacobs, J. M., *Edge of Empire: Postcolonialism and the City* (London, 1996)

Jakle, J. A., *City Lights: Illuminating the American Night* (Baltimore, 2001)

James, E., 'An insight into the management of railway bookstalls in the eighteen fifties', *Publishing History* **10** (1981), 65–69

Johnson, E. D. H., 'Victorian artists and the urban milieu' in Dyos and Wolff, eds, *The Victorian City: Images and Realities* (1973), pp. 449–474

Johnson, J., 'Introduction' to J. Joyce, *Ulysses* (Oxford, 1993), pp. ix–xxxvii

Johnston, R. J., Gregory, D., Pratt, G. and Watts, M., eds, *The Dictionary of Human Geography, 4th Edition* (Oxford, 2000)

Joyce, P., *The Rule of Freedom: Liberalism and the Modern City* (London, 2003)

Jurca, C., *White Diaspora: The Suburb and the Twentieth-Century American Novel* (Princeton NJ, 2001)

Kalman, H., *A History of Canadian Architecture Volume 2* (Toronto, 1994)

Keating, P., ed, *Into Unknown England 1866–1913: Selections from the Social Explorers* (London, 1976)

Keating, P., 'The metropolis in literature' in Sutcliffe, ed, *Metropolis 1890–1940* (1984), pp. 129–145

Keene, D., 'The setting of the Royal Exchange: continuity and change in the financial district of the City of London, 1300–1871' in A. Saunders, ed, *The Royal Exchange* (London, 1997), pp. 253–271

Kellett, J. R., *Railways and Victorian Cities* (London, 1969)

Kellett, J. R., 'Municipal socialism, enterprise and trading in the Victorian city', *Urban History Yearbook* (1978), 36–45

Kern, S., *The Culture of Time and Space 1880–1918* (Cambridge MA, 1983)

Kerr, D. and Holdsworth, D. W., eds, *Historical Atlas of Canada Volume III: Addressing the Twentieth Century 1891–1961* (Toronto, 1990)

King, A. D., ed, *Buildings and Society: Essays on the Social Development of the Built Environment* (London, 1980)

King, A. D., *The Bungalow: The Production of a Global Culture* (London, 1984)

King, A. D., *Global Cities: Post–Imperialism and the Internationalization of London* (London, 1990)

King, A. D., 'Excavating the multicultural suburb: hidden histories of the bungalow' in Silverstone, ed, *Visions of Suburbia* (1997), pp. 55–85

Kingman, V., 'The world of the new: the first ten years', in Ashley Gardens Residents Association, *Ashley Gardens: Backward Glances* (London, 1990), pp. 14–25

Kluckner, M., *Toronto: The Way It Was* (Toronto, 1988)

Knight, V., 'The private life of William Powell Frith' in Bills and Knight, eds, *William Powell Frith: Painting the Victorian Age* (2006), pp. 1–27

Knights, P. R., 'Potholes in the road of improvement? Estimating census underenumeration by longitudinal tracing: US censuses, 1850–1880', *Social Science History* 15 (1991), 517–526

Kwolek-Folland, A., *Engendering Business: Men and Women in the Corporate Office, 1870–1930* (Baltimore, 1994)

Kynaston, D., 'A changing workscape: the City of London since the 1840s', *London Journal* 13 (1988), 99–105

Kynaston, D., *The City of London Volume I: A World of Its Own 1815–1890* (London, 1994)

Kynaston, D., *The City of London Volume II: Golden Years 1890–1914* (London, 1995)

Labrusse, R. and Munck, J., 'André Derain in London (1906–07)' in Courtauld Institute, *André Derain: The London Paintings* (London, 2005), pp. 13–29

Lancaster, B., *The Department Store: A Social History* (London, 1995)

Landau, S. B. and Condit, C. W., *Rise of the New York Skyscraper 1865–1913* (New Haven CT, 1996)

Larisey, P., *Light for a Cold Land: Lawren Harris's Work and Life* (Toronto, 1993)

Lawton, J., 'Introduction' in Wells, *The Time Machine* (1995), pp. xxvii–xlix

Leach, W. R., 'Transformations in a culture of consumption: women and department stores, 1890–1925', *Journal of American History* 71 (1984), 319–342

Ledger, S., 'Gissing, the Shopgirl and the New Woman', *Women: A Cultural Review* 6 (1995), 261–274

Ledger, S., *The New Woman: Fiction and Feminism at the Fin de Siècle* (Manchester, 1997)

Lees, A., *Cities Perceived: Urban Society in European and American Thought, 1820–1940* (Manchester, 1985)

Lees, L. H., *Exiles of Erin: Irish Migrants in Victorian London* (Manchester, 1979)

Lefebvre, H. *The Production of Space* (tr. D. Nicholson-Smith) (Oxford, 1991)

Lemon, J., 'Toronto among North American cities' in Russell, ed, *Forging a Consensus: Historical Essays on Toronto* (1984), pp. 323–351

Lemon, J., *Toronto since 1918* (Toronto, 1985)

Lemon, J., 'Plans for early 20th-century Toronto: lost in management', *Urban History Review* 18 (1) (1989), 11–31

Lemon, J., *Liberal Dreams and Nature's Limits: Great Cities of North America Since 1600* (Toronto, 1996)

Levey, M. F., *London Transport Posters* (Oxford, 1976)

Leviatin, D., 'Preface' and 'Introduction' to J. A. Riis, *How the Other Half Lives* (Boston, 1996), pp. 1–50

Levin, G., *Edward Hopper as Illustrator* (New York, 1979)

Levin, G., *Edward Hopper: The Art and the Artist* (New York, 1980)

Levin, G., *Edward Hopper: An Intimate Biography* (New York, 1995)

Levin, G., *The Complete Oil Paintings of Edward Hopper* (New York, 2001)

Lewis, R., *Manufacturing Montreal: The Making of an Industrial Landscape, 1850 to 1930* (Baltimore, 2000)

Lewis, R., ed, 'Special issue: Industrial suburbanization of Canadian and American cities, 1850–1950', *Journal of Historical Geography* 27 (2001), 1–92

Lewis, V. G., 'Earlscourt, Toronto. A descriptive, historical and interpretative study in urban class development', unpublished M. A. thesis, University of Toronto (1920)

Llewellyn, M., '"Urban village" or "white house": envisioned spaces, experienced places, and everyday life at Kensal House, London in the 1930s', *Environment and Planning D: Society and Space* 22 (2004), 229–249

Lochnan, K., 'Turner, Whistler, Monet: An Artistic Dialogue' in Lochnan, ed, *TurnerWhistlerMonet* (2004), pp. 15–35

Lochnan, K., ed, *TurnerWhistlerMonet* (London, 2004)

Long, H., *The Edwardian House* (Manchester, 1993)

Loughery, J., *John Sloan: Painter and Rebel* (New York, 1995)

Lowe, G. S., 'Women, work, and the office: the feminization of clerical occupations in Canada, 1901–1931' in V. Strong-Boag and A. C. Fellman, eds, *Rethinking Canada: The Promise of Women's History (3rd edn)* (Toronto, 1997), pp. 253–270

Mace, R., *Trafalgar Square: Emblem of Empire* (London, 1976)

Mackenzie, N. and J., *The Diary of Beatrice Webb*, 4 volumes (London, 1982–86)

Mackintosh, P. G., 'Scrutiny in the modern city: the domestic public and the Toronto Local Council of Women at the turn of the twentieth century', *Gender, Place and Culture* **12** (2005), 29–48

Mackintosh, P. G. and Norcliffe, G., 'Flâneurie on bicycles: acquiescence to women in public in the 1890s', *Canadian Geographer* **50** (2006), 17–37

Malpass, P., 'Continuity and change in philanthropic housing organisations: the Octavia Hill Housing Trust and the Guinness Trust', *London Journal* **24** (1999), 38–57

Marcus, S., *Apartment Stories: City and Home in Nineteenth-Century Paris and London* (Berkeley, 1999)

Marsh, M., *Suburban Lives* (New Brunswick NJ, 1990)

Martin, M., *Hello Central? Gender, Technology, and Culture in the Formation of Telephone Systems* (Montreal, 1991)

Mayer, H. and Wade, R. C., *Chicago: Growth of a Metropolis* (Chicago, 1969)

Maynard, S., '"Without working?" Capitalism, urban culture and gay history', *Journal of Urban History* **30** (2004), 378–398

Mayne, A., 'Representing the slum', *Urban History Yearbook* **17** (1990), 66–84

Mayne, A., *The Imagined Slum: Newspaper Representation in Three Cities 1870–1914* (Leicester, 1993)

McArthur, C., 'Chinese boxes and Russian dolls: tracking the elusive cinematic city' in Clarke, ed, *The Cinematic City* (1997), pp. 19–45

McCann, L. D. and Smith, P. J., 'Canada becomes urban: cities and urbanization in historical perspective' in T. Bunting and P. Filion, eds, *Canadian Cities in Transition* (Toronto, 1991), pp. 69–99

McCracken, S., 'Voyages by teashop: an urban geography of modernism' in P. Brooker and A. Thacker, eds, *Geographies of Modernism: Literatures, Cultures, Spaces* (London, 2005), pp. 86–98

McDonald, D., *Clara Collet 1860–1948: An Educated Working Woman* (London, 2004)

McDonald, E. and Smith, D. J., *Artizans and Avenues: A History of the Queen's Park Estate* (London, 1990)

McDonnell, P., ed, *On the Edge of Your Seat: Popular Theater and Film in Early Twentieth-Century American Art* (New Haven CT, 2002)

McHugh, P., *Toronto Architecture: A City Guide* (Toronto, 1985)

McKay, J. P., *Tramways and Trolleys: The Rise of Mass Urban Transport in Europe* (Princeton NJ, 1976)

McKie, D., *Jabez: The Rise and Fall of a Victorian Rogue* (London, 2004)

McShane, C., 'The origins and globalization of traffic control signals', *Journal of Urban History* **25** (1999), 379–404

Meller, H., *Patrick Geddes: Social Evolutionist and City Planner* (London, 1990)

Melosi, M. V., *The Sanitary City: Urban Infrastructure in America from Colonial Times to the Present* (Baltimore, 2000)

Merrifield, A., 'Henri Lefebvre: a socialist in space', in M. Crang and N. Thrift, eds, *Thinking Space* (London, 2000), pp. 167–182

Meyerowitz, J., *Women Adrift: Independent Wage Earners in Chicago, 1880–1930* (Chicago, 1988)

Michie, R. C., *The City of London: Continuity and Change, 1850–1990* (London, 1992)

Miele, C., 'From aristocratic ideal to middle-class idyll: 1690–1840' in A. Saint et al, *London Suburbs* (1999), pp. 31–59

Miller, M. B., *The Bon Marché: Bourgeois Culture and the Department Store, 1869–1920* (Princeton NJ, 1981)

Miller, R., 'The Hoover in the garden: middle-class women and suburbanization, 1850–1920', *Environment and Planning D: Society and Space* **1** (1983), 73–87

Miller, R., 'Selling Mrs Consumer: advertising and the creation of suburban socio-spatial relations, 1910–1930', *Antipode* **23** (1991), 263–301

Minden, M., 'The city in early cinema: *Metropolis, Berlin* and *October*' in Timms and Kelley, eds, *Unreal City: Urban Experience in Modern European Literature and Art* (1985), pp. 193–213

Modell, J. and Hareven, T. K., 'Urbanization and the malleable household: an examination of boarding and lodging in American families', *Journal of Marriage and the Family* **35** (1973), 467–479

Moffat, B. G., *The 'L': The Development of Chicago's Rapid Transit System, 1888–1932* (Chicago, 1995)

Monkkonen, E. H., *America Becomes Urban: The Development of U. S. Cities and Towns, 1780–1980* (Berkeley, 1988)

Moody, E. N., 'Urban history in fire insurance maps: Nevada as a case study', *Information Bulletin, Western Association of Map Libraries* **10** (2) (1979), 129–139

Moore, P. W., 'Zoning and planning: the Toronto experience, 1904–1970' in Artibise and Stelter, eds, *The Usable Urban Past* (1979), pp. 316–341

Moretti, F., *Atlas of the European Novel 1800–1900* (London, 1998)

Morris, R. J., 'The middle class and the property cycle during the Industrial Revolution' in T. C. Smout, ed, *The Search for Wealth and Stability* (London, 1979), pp. 91–113

Morris, S., 'Market solutions for social problems: working-class housing in nineteenth-century London', *Economic History Review* **54** (2001), 525–545

Mumford, L., *The City in History* (Harmondsworth, 1961)

Nasaw, D., 'Cities of light, landscapes of pleasure', in Ward and Zunz, eds, *The Landscape of Modernity* (1992), pp. 273–286

Nava, M., 'Modernity's disavowal: women, the city and the department store', in M. Nava and A. O'Shea, eds, *Modern Times: Reflections on a Century of English Modernity* (London, 1996), pp. 38–76

Nava, M., 'The cosmopolitanism of commerce and the allure of difference: Selfridges, the Russian Ballet and the tango 1911–1914', *International Journal of Cultural Studies* **1** (1998), 163–196

Nead, L., 'From alleys to courts: obscenity and the mapping of mid-Victorian London', *New Formations* **37** (1999), 33–46

Nead, L., *Victorian Babylon: People, Streets and Images in Nineteenth-Century London* (New Haven CT, 2000)

Nead, L., 'Animating the everyday: London on camera circa 1900', *Journal of British Studies* **43** (2004), 65–90

Nehls, C., 'Sanborn Fire Insurance Maps', online at http://fisher.lib.virginia.edu/sanborn/about.html

New, M., ed, *The Complete Novels and Selected Writings of Amy Levy 1861–1889* (Gainesville FL, 1993)

Newall, C., *The Grosvenor Gallery Exhibitions: Change and Continuity in the Victorian Art World* (Cambridge, 1995)

Nicoletti, L. J., 'Downward mobility: Victorian women, suicide and London's "Bridge of Sighs"', *Literary London* **2** (2004), online at http://www.literarylondon.org/london-journal/march2004/nicoletti.html

Norcliffe, G., *The Ride to Modernity: The Bicycle in Canada, 1869–1900* (Toronto, 2001)

Nord, D. E., 'The social explorer as anthropologist: Victorian travellers among the urban poor', in W. Sharpe and L. Wallock, eds, *Visions of the Modern City* (Baltimore, 1987), pp. 122–134

Nord, D. E., *Walking the Victorian Streets: Women, Representation, and the City* (Ithaca NY, 1995)

Nye, D., 'The electric sublime in the American city, 1870–1931', paper presented at University of Nottingham, May 1998, http://www.nottingham.ac.uk/3cities/nye.htm

Nye, D., *Electrifying America: Social Meanings of a New Technology, 1880–1940* (Cambridge MA, 1990)

O'Day, R., 'Women and social investigation: Clara Collet and Beatrice Potter' in Englander and O'Day, eds, *Retrieved Riches* (1995), pp. 165–200

O'Hanlon, S., *Together Apart: Boarding House, Hostel and Flat Life in Pre-War Melbourne* (Melbourne, 2002)

Offer, A., *Property and Politics 1870–1914* (Cambridge, 1981)

Ogborn, M., 'Law and discipline in nineteenth-century English state formation: the Contagious Diseases Acts of 1864, 1866 and 1869', *Journal of Historical Sociology* **6** (1993), 28–55

Ogborn, M., 'Discipline, government and law: separate confinement in the prisons of England and Wales, 1830–1877', *Transactions Institute of British Geographers* **20** (1995), 295–311

Ogle, M., 'Water supply, waste disposal, and the culture of privatism in the mid-nineteenth-century city', *Journal of Urban History* **25** (1999), 321–347

Olechnowicz, A., *Working-Class Housing in England Between the Wars* (Oxford, 1997)

Oliver, P., Davis, I. and Bentley, I., *Dunroamin: The Suburban Semi and Its Enemies* (London, 1981)

Oliver, S., '"Rich earth below the sand" and the origins of the Thames Embankments', *Reconstruction: Studies in Contemporary Culture* **2** (3) (2002), <34>, online at http://www.reconstruction.ws/023/oliver.htm

Oliver, S., '"Chains on the River": The Thames Embankments and the Construction of Nature', *Historical Geography Research Series* **37** (2002)

Olsen, D. J., *The Growth of Victorian London* (London, 1976)

Olsen, D. J., *Town Planning in London: The Eighteenth and Nineteenth Centuries* (New Haven CT, 1982)

Olsen, D. J., *The City as a Work of Art: London, Paris, Vienna* (New Haven CT, 1986)

Otter, C., 'Making liberalism durable: vision and civility in the late Victorian city', *Social History* **27** (2002), 1–15

Otter, C., 'Cleansing and clarifying: technology and perception in nineteenth-century London', *Journal of British Studies* **43** (2004), 40–64

Otter, C., 'Streets', in S. Pile, S. Harrison and N. Thrift, eds, *Patterned Ground: Entanglements of Nature and Culture* (London, 2004), pp. 238–240

Owen, D., *The Government of Victorian London* (Cambridge MA, 1982)

Owen, T. and Pilbeam, E., *Ordnance Survey: Map Makers to Britain since 1791* (Southampton, 1992)

Page, M., *The Creative Destruction of Manhattan, 1900–1940* (Chicago, 1999)

Parkerson, D. H., 'Comments on the underenumeration of the US census, 1850–1880', *Social Science History* **15** (1991), 509–515

Parsons, D., 'Flâneur or flâneuse? Mythologies of modernity', *New Formations* **38** (1999), 91–100

Parsons, D., *Streetwalking the Metropolis: Women, the City and Modernity* (Oxford, 2000)

Paterson, R., 'Creating the packaged suburb: the evolution of planning and business practices in the early Canadian land development industry, 1900–1914' in B. M. Kelly, ed, *Suburbia Re-examined* (Westport CT, 1989), pp. 119–132

Paterson, R., 'Housing finance in early 20th century suburban Toronto', *Urban History Review* **20** (1991), 63–71

Patin, S., 'The return of Whistler and Monet to the Thames' in Lochnan, ed, *TurnerWhistlerMonet* (2004), pp. 179–183

Peel, M., 'On the margins: lodgers and boarders in Boston, 1860–1900', *Journal of American History* **72** (1986), 813–834

Penner, B., 'The construction of identity: Virginia Woolf's city', in I. Borden and J. Rendell, eds, *InterSections: Architectural Histories and Critical Theories* (London, 2000), pp. 269–282

Penner, B., 'A world of unmentionable suffering: women's public conveniences in Victorian London', *Journal of Design History* **14** (2001), 35–51

Pfautz, H. W., ed, *Charles Booth on the City* (Chicago, 1967)

Philo, C., '"Fit localities for an asylum": the historical geography of the nineteenth-century "mad business" in England as viewed through the pages of the *Asylum Journal*', *Journal of Historical Geography* **13** (1987), 398–415

Philo, C., '*The Birth of the Clinic*: an unknown work of medical geography', *Area* **32** (2000), 11–19

Piggott, J. R., *Palace of the People: The Crystal Palace at Sydenham 1854–1936* (London, 2004)

Pike, D. L., 'Modernist space and the transformation of Underground London' in Gilbert, ed, *Imagined Londons* (2002), pp. 101–119

Pike, D. L., '"The greatest wonder of the world": Brunel's tunnel and the meanings of underground London', *Victorian Literature and Culture* **33** (2005), 341–367

Pike, D. L., *Subterranean Cities: The World Beneath Paris and London, 1800–1945* (Ithaca NY, 2005)

Pile, S., *Real Cities: Modernity, Space and the Phantasmagorias of City Life* (London, 2005)

Platt, H. L., 'City lights: the electrification of the Chicago region, 1890–1930' in Tarr and Dupuy, eds, *Technology and the Rise of the Networked City in Europe and America* (1988), pp. 246–281

Plunz, R., *A History of Housing in New York City* (New York, 1990)

Poitras, C., 'Le téléphone dans une grande ville industrielle nord-américaine: Montréal 1880–1930', *Les Cahiers, Télécommunications, Histoire et Société* **5** (1997), 7–37

Poitras, C., *La Cité Au Bout Du Fil: Le Téléphone à Montréal de 1879 à 1930* (Montreal, 2000).

Pollock, G., 'Modernity and the spaces of femininity', in Pollock, G., *Vision and Difference: Femininity, Feminism and Histories of Art* (London, 1988), pp. 50–90

Poole, A., *Gissing in Context* (Totowa NJ, 1975)

Porter, D. H., *The Thames Embankment: Environment, Technology, and Society in Victorian London* (Akron OH, 1998)

Porter, R., *London: A Social History* (London, 1994)

Postmus, B., 'George Gissing's *Scrapbook*: A Storehouse of "Elements of Drama to be Fused and Minted in his Brain"' in Spiers, ed, *Gissing and the City* (2006), pp. 199–211.

Poulsen, C., *Victoria Park* (London, 1976)

Pred, A., *Lost Words and Lost Worlds: Modernity and the Language of Everyday Life in Late Nineteenth-Century Stockholm* (Cambridge, 1990)

Pred, A., 'Languages of everyday practice and resistance: Stockholm at the end of the nineteenth century', in A. Pred and M. J. Watts, *Reworking Modernity* (New Brunswick NJ, 1992), pp. 118–154

Preston, P. and Simpson-Housley, P., eds, *Writing the City: Eden, Babylon, and the New Jerusalem* (London, 1994)

Price, S. J., *Building Societies, Their Origin and History* (London, 1958)

Purdy, S., '"This is not a company; it is a cause": class, gender and the Toronto Housing Company, 1912–1920', *Urban History Review* **21** (1993), 75–91

Ramsay, E. L., 'Modernity and post-colonialism: *The Heart of the Empire* (1909) by F. M. Bell-Smith', *Labour/Le Travail* **52** (2003).

Rappaport, E., *Shopping for Pleasure: Women in the Making of London's West End* (Princeton NJ, 2000)

Rappaport, E., 'Travelling in the Lady Guides' London: consumption, modernity, and the *fin-de-siècle* metropolis' in Daunton and Rieger, eds, *Meanings of Modernity* (Oxford, 2001), pp. 25–43

Reeder, D., 'A theatre of suburbs' in H. J. Dyos, ed, *The Study of Urban History* (London, 1968), pp. 253–271

Reeder, D., *Charles Booth's Descriptive Map of London Poverty 1889* (London, 1987)

Relph, E., *The Modern Urban Landscape* (Baltimore, 1987)

Rendell, J., '"Industrious females" and "professional beauties"' in I. Borden et al, eds, *Strangely Familiar: Narratives of Architecture in the City* (London, 1996), pp. 32–36

Revell, K. D., 'Regulating the landscape: real estate values, city planning and the 1916 zoning ordinance', in Ward and Zunz, eds, *The Landscape of Modernity* (1992), pp. 19–45

Richards, J. M., *The Castles on the Ground: The Anatomy of Suburbia* (London, 1946)

Richards, T., 'The image of Victoria in the year of jubilee', *Victorian Studies* **31** (1987), 8–32

Riddell, J., *Pleasure Trips By Underground* (London, 1998)

Rieger, B. and Daunton, M., 'Introduction' in Daunton and Rieger, eds, *Meanings of Modernity* (2001), pp. 1–21

Roberts, J. M., 'Spatial governance and working class public spheres: the case of a Chartist demonstration at Hyde Park', *Journal of Historical Sociology* **14** (2001), 308–336

Robins, A. G., 'The greatest artist the world has ever seen' in Robins and Thomson, *Degas, Sickert and Toulouse-Lautrec* (2005), pp. 51–92

Robins, A. G., 'Sickert and the Paris art world' in Robins and Thomson, *Degas, Sickert and Toulouse-Lautrec* (2005), pp. 155–201

Robins, A. G. and Thomson, R., *Degas, Sickert and Toulouse-Lautrec: London and Paris 1870–1910* (London, 2005)

Robinson, J., *Ordinary Cities: Between Modernity and Development* (London, 2005)

Robinson, M., *The American Vision: Landscape Paintings of the United States* (New York, 1988)

Rose, M. H., 'Urban gas and electric systems and social change, 1900–1940' in Tarr and Dupuy, eds, *Technology and the Rise of the Networked City in Europe and America* (1988), pp. 229–245

Rose, W. K., ed, *The Letters of Wyndham Lewis* (Norfolk CT, 1963)

Rosenblum, R., Stevens, M., Dumas, A., *1900: Art at the Crossroads* (London, 2000)

Ross, C., *Twenties London: A City in the Jazz Age* (London, 2003)

Ross, E., 'Slum journeys: ladies and London poverty 1860–1940', in A. Mayne and T. Murray, eds, *The Archaeology of Urban Landscapes: Explorations in Slumland* (Cambridge, 2001), pp. 11–21

Rowley, G., 'British fire insurance plans: cartography at work', *Bulletin, Society of University Cartographers* **18** (1) (1984), 1–8

Rowley, G., 'British fire insurance plans: the Goad productions, c.1885 – c.1970', *Archives* **17** (74) (1985), 67–78

Rubinstein, A., ed, *Just Like the Country: Memories of London Families Who Settled the New Cottage Estates 1919–1939* (London, 1991)

Ruddock, T., 'Charles Holden and the issue of high buildings in London, 1927–47', *Construction History* **12** (1996), 83–99

Russell, V. L., ed, *Forging a Consensus: Historical Essays on Toronto* (Toronto, 1984)

Rutherford, P. F. W., 'Introduction' to Ames, *The City Below the Hill* (1972), pp. vii-xviii

Saint, A. et al, *London Suburbs* (London, 1999)

Sandeen, E., 'Signs of the times: waiting for the millennium in Times Square', paper presented at University of Nottingham, May 1998, online at http://www.nottingham.ac.uk/3cities/sandeen.htm

Santink, J. L., *Timothy Eaton and the Rise of His Department Store* (Toronto, 1990)

Sawyer, A., 'Notes' in H. G. Wells, *War of the Worlds* (London, 2005), pp. 187–199

Saywell, J., *Canada: Pathways to the Present* (Toronto, 1994)

Schivelbusch, W., *The Railway Journey* (Leamington Spa, 1977)

Schivelbusch, W., *Disenchanted Night: The Industrialisation of Light in the Nineteenth Century* (Oxford, 1988)

Schlereth, T. J., *Victorian America: Transformations in Everyday Life 1876–1915* (New York, 1992)

Schneer, J., *London 1900: The Imperial Metropolis* (New Haven CT, 1999)

Schneer, J., 'Anti-imperial London: the Pan-African Conference of 1900' in Driver and Gilbert, eds, *Imperial Cities* (1999), pp. 254–267

Schubert, D. and Sutcliffe, A., 'The "Haussmannization" of London?: the planning and construction of Kingsway-Aldwych, 1889–1935', *Planning Perspectives* **11** (1996), 115–144.

Schwartz, J. M., 'Photographs from the edge of Empire' in A. Blunt et al, eds, *Cultural Geography In Practice* (London, 2003), pp. 154–171

Scobey, D. M., *Empire City: The Making and Meaning of the New York City Landscape* (Philadelphia, 2002)

Scott, P. G., *The London & Birmingham Railway Through Harrow 1837–1987* (Harrow, 1987)

Sennett, R., *Flesh and Stone: The Body and the City in Western Civilization* (London, 1994)

Seymour, W. A., ed, *A History of the Ordnance Survey* (Folkestone, 1980)

Shanes, E., *Impressionist London* (New York, 1994)

Shapiro, T., 'The metropolis in the visual arts: Paris, Berlin, New York, 1890–1940' in Sutcliffe, ed, *Metropolis 1890–1940* (1984), pp. 95–127.

Sharp, T., *Town Planning* [1940] (Harmondsworth, 1945)

Shaw, G., 'The evolution and impact of large-scale retailing in Britain' in Benson and Shaw, eds, *The Evolution of Retail Systems* (1992), pp. 135–165

Shaw, G. and Wild, T., 'Retail patterns in the Victorian city', *Transactions Institute of British Geographers* **NS 4** (1979), 279–291

Sheppard, F. *London 1808–1870: The Infernal Wen* (London, 1971)

Sheppard, F., ed, *Survey of London Volume XXXVIII* (London, 1975)

Sheppard, F., *London: A History* (Oxford, 1998)

Shields, R., *Lefebvre, Love, and Struggle* (London, 1999)

Short, J. R., *Imagined Country: Society, Culture and Environment* (London, 1991)

Silberman, R., 'Edward Hopper and the theatre of the mind: vision, spectacle, and the spectator' in McDonnell, ed, *On the Edge of Your Seat* (2002), pp. 137–155

Silverstone, R., ed, *Visions of Suburbia* (London, 1997)

Simon, R. D., *The City–Building Process: Housing and Services in New Milwaukee Neighborhoods* (Philadelphia, 1978)

Sklar, K. K., 'Hull-House Maps and Papers: social science as women's work in the 1890s' in Bulmer, Bales and Sklar, eds, *The Social Survey in Historical Perspective, 1880–1940* (1992), pp. 111–147

Slater, T., 'Fear of the city 1882–1967: Edward Hopper and the discourse of anti-urbanism', *Social & Cultural Geography* **3** (2002), 135–154

Smith, D., *The Chicago School* (Basingstoke, 1988)

Sorensen, C., *London on Film: 100 Years of Filmmaking in London* (London, 1996)

Spain, D., *How Women Saved the City* (Minneapolis, 2001)

Spiers, J., ed., *Gissing and the City: Cultural Crisis and the Making of Books in Late Victorian England* (Basingstoke, 2006)

Spragge, S., 'A confluence of interests: housing reform in Toronto, 1900–1920', in Artibise and Stelter, eds, *Usable Urban Past* (1979), pp. 247–267

Stacey, R., *The Canadian Poster Book: 100 Years of the Poster in Canada* (Toronto, 1979)

Stamp, R. M., *Bright Lights, Big City: The History of Electricity in Toronto* (Toronto, 1991)

Stange, M., *Symbols of Ideal Life: Social Documentary Photography in America 1890–1950* (New York, 1989)

Stansell, C., *City of Women: Sex and Class in New York, 1789–1860* (New York, 1986)

Steckel, R. H., 'The quality of census data for historical enquiry: a research agenda', *Social Science History* **15** (1991), 579–599

Stedman Jones, G., *Outcast London: A Study in the Relationship Between Classes in Victorian Society* (Oxford, 1971)

Stein, J., 'Ideology and the telephone: the social reception of a technology, London 1876–1920', unpublished PhD dissertation, University of London (1996)

Stein, J., 'The telephone: its social shaping and public negotiation in late nineteenth- and early twentieth-century London' in M. Crang, P. Crang and J. May, eds, *Virtual Geographies* (London, 1999), pp. 44–62

Stern, E. and Gwathmey, E., *Once Upon a Telephone: An Illustrated Social History* (New York, 1994)

Stilgoe, J. R., *Borderland: Origins of the American Suburb* (New Haven CT, 1988)

Strange, C., *Toronto's Girl Problem: The Perils and Pleasures of the City, 1880–1930* (Toronto, 1995)

Styles, J., 'Victorian Britain, 1837–1901: Introduction' in M. Snodin and J. Styles, *Design and the Decorative Arts: Britain 1500–1900* (London, 2001), pp. 311–339

Summerson, J., *The London Building World of the Eighteen-Sixties* (London, 1973)

Summerson, J., *The Architecture of Victorian London* (Charlottesville VA, 1976)

Summerson, J., 'The Victorian rebuilding of the City of London', *London Journal* **3** (1977), 163–185

Survey of London Volume XLII: Southern Kensington: Kensington Square to Earl's Court (London, 1986)

Sussman, E. et al, *City of Ambition: Artists and New York* (New York, 1996)

Sutcliffe, A., 'The metropolis in the cinema' in Sutcliffe, ed, *Metropolis 1890–1940* (1984), pp. 147–171

Sutcliffe, A., ed, *Metropolis 1890–1940* (London, 1984)

Swenarton, M. and Taylor, S., 'The scale and nature of the growth of owner-occupation in Britain between the wars', *Economic History Review* **38** (1985), 373–392

Tagg, J., *The Burden of Representation: Essays on Photographies and Histories* (London, 1988)

Tallack, D., 'New York, New York', http://www.nottingham.ac.uk/3cities/tallack2.htm

Tallack, D., 'City Sights: Mapping and Representing New York City' in M. Balshaw and L. Kennedy, eds, *Urban Space and Representation* (London, 2000), pp. 25–38

Tallack, D., 'The rhetoric of space: Jacob Riis and New York City's Lower East Side' in *City Sites: an electronic book, multimedia essays on New York and Chicago, 1870–1939*: http://artsweb.bham.ac.uk/citysites/ (Birmingham, 2000)

Tallack, D., *New York Sights: Visualizing Old and New New York* (Oxford, 2005)

Tanner, T., 'Introduction' to W. D. Howells, *A Hazard of New Fortunes* (Oxford, 1990), pp. vii–xxxv

Tarn, J. N., 'The Improved Industrial Dwellings Company', *Transactions of the London and Middlesex Archaeological Society* **22** (1968), 43–59

Tarn, J. N., *Five Per Cent Philanthropy: An Account of Housing in Urban Areas Between 1840 and 1914* (Cambridge, 1973)

Tarn, J. N., 'French flats for the English in nineteenth-century London' in A. Sutcliffe, ed, *Multi-Storey Living* (London, 1974), pp. 19–40

Tarr, J. A., 'The separate vs. combined sewer problem: a case study in urban technology design choice', *Journal of Urban History* **5** (1979), 308–339

Tarr, J. A., 'Sewerage and the development of the networked city in the United States, 1850–1930' in Tarr and Dupuy, eds, *Technology and the Rise of the Networked City in Europe and America* (1988), pp. 159–185

Tarr, J. A., *The Search for the Ultimate Sink: Urban Pollution in Historical Perspective* (Akron OH, 1996)

Tarr, J. A. and Dupuy, G., eds, *Technology and the Rise of the Networked City in Europe and America* (Philadelphia, 1988)

Tarr, J. A., Finholt, T. and Goodman, D., 'The city and the telegraph: urban telecommunications in the pre-telephone era', *Journal of Urban History* **14** (1987), 38–80

Taylor, P. J., *Modernities: A Geohistorical Interpretation* (Cambridge, 1999)

Taylor, W. R., *In Pursuit of Gotham: Culture and Commerce in New York* (New York, 1992)

Thacker, A., *Moving through Modernity: Space and Geography in Modernism* (Manchester, 2003)

Thompson, D. M., 'The religious census of 1851' in R. Lawton, ed, *The Census and Social Structure* (London, 1978), pp. 241–286

Thompson, F. M. L., 'Introduction' in F. M. L. Thompson, ed, *The Rise of Suburbia* (Leicester, 1982), pp. 2–25

Thomson, R., 'Modernity, figure, metropolis: importing the new painting to Britain in the 1870s' in Robins and Thomson, *Degas, Sickert and Toulouse-Lautrec* (2005), pp. 15–47

Thorne, R., 'Places of refreshment in the nineteenth-century city' in King, ed, *Buildings and Society* (1980), pp. 228–253

Thorne, R., 'Office building in the City of London 1830–1880', paper to Urban History Group Colloquium, London (1984)

Thorne, R., 'The White Hart Lane Estate: An LCC venture in suburban development', *London Journal* **12** (1986), 80–88

Thrift, N., '"Not a straight line but a curve", or, Cities are not mirrors of modernity' in D. Bell and A. Haddour, eds, *City Visions* (Harlow, 2000), pp. 233–263

Timms, E., 'Introduction: Unreal city – theme and variations' in Timms and Kelley, eds, *Unreal City* (1985), pp. 1–12

Timms, E. and Kelley, D., eds, *Unreal City: Urban Experience in Modern European Literature and Art* (Manchester, 1985)

Topalov, C., 'The city as *terra incognita*: Charles Booth's poverty survey and the people of London, 1886–1891', *Planning Perspectives* **8** (1993), 395–425

Toulmin, V., Popple, S. and Russell, P., eds, *The Lost World of Mitchell and Kenyon* (London, 2004)

Trachtenberg, A., *Brooklyn Bridge: Fact and Symbol* (Chicago, 1979)

Trench, R. and Hillman, E., *London Under London: A Subterranean Guide* (London, 1984)

Trotter, D., *Circulation: Defoe, Dickens and the Economies of the Novel* (Basingstoke, 1988)

Tulchinsky, G., '"Said to be a very honest Jew": the R. G. Dun credit reports and Jewish business activity in mid–19th century Montreal', *Urban History Review* **18** (1990), 200–209

Turner, S., 'The Pittsburgh Survey and the Survey Movement' in Greenwald and Anderson, eds, *Pittsburgh Surveyed* (1996), pp. 35–49

Turvey, R., 'London lifts and hydraulic power', *Transactions of the Newcomen Society* **65** (1993–4), 149–164

Turvey, R., 'City of London office rents', *LSE Geography Research Papers in Environmental & Spatial Analysis* **38** (1996)

Turvey, R., 'Street mud, dust and noise', *London Journal* **21** (1996), 131–148

Turvey, R., 'Office rents in the City of London, 1867–1910', *London Journal* **23** (2) (1998), 53–67

Tyack, G., 'James Pennethorne and London street improvements, 1838–1855', *London Journal* **15** (1990), 38–56

Vadillo, A. P., *Women Poets and Urban Aestheticism: Passengers of Modernity* (Basingstoke, 2005)

Vaughan, L. et al, 'Space and exclusion: does urban morphology play a part in social deprivation?', *Area* **37** (2005), 402–412

Vaughan, R., *The Age of Great Cities* (London, 1843)

Vidler, A., *Warped Space: Art, Architecture and Anxiety in Modern Culture* (Cambridge MA, 2000)

Voorsanger, C. H. and Howat, J. K., eds, *Art and the Empire City: New York 1825–1861* (New Haven CT, 2000)

Waddell, R., *Moving Uptown: Nineteenth-century Views of Manhattan*, online exhibition of prints from the collections of the New York Public Library: http://www.nypl.org/research/chss/spe/art/print/exhibits/movingup/opening.htm

Walden, K., *Becoming Modern in Toronto: The Industrial Exhibition and the Shaping of a Late Victorian Culture* (Toronto, 1997)

Walkowitz, J. R., 'The Indian woman, the flower girl, and the Jew: photojournalism in Edwardian London', *Victorian Studies* **42** (1998), 3–46

Wall, C., '"*At Shakespear's-Head*, Over-Against *Catharine-Street* in the *Strand*": Forms of address in London streets' in T. Hitchcock and H. Shore, eds, *The Streets of London: From the Great Fire to the Great Exhibition* (London, 2003), pp. 10–26

Waller, P. J., *Town, City and Nation* (Oxford, 1983)

Ward, D., 'The place of Victorian cities in developmental approaches to urbanization' in J. Patten, ed, *The Expanding City* (London, 1983), pp. 355–379

Ward, D., *Poverty, Ethnicity and the American City, 1840–1925* (Cambridge, 1989)

Ward, D., 'Social reform, social surveys, and the discovery of the modern city', *Annals of the Association of American Geographers* **80** (1990), 491–503

Ward, D. and Radford, J., *North American Cities in the Victorian Age* (Norwich, 1983)

Ward, D. and Zunz, O., 'Between rationalism and pluralism: creating the modern city' in Ward and Zunz, eds, *The Landscape of Modernity* (1992), pp. 3–15

Ward, D. and Zunz, O., eds, *The Landscape of Modernity: Essays on New York City, 1900–1940* (New York, 1992)

Ward, P., *A History of Domestic Space: Privacy and the Canadian Home* (Vancouver, 1999)

Warner, S. B., *Streetcar Suburbs: The Process of Growth in Boston 1870–1900* (Cambridge MA, 1962)

Warner, S. B., 'The management of multiple urban images' in Fraser and Sutcliffe, eds, *The Pursuit of Urban History* (1983), pp. 383–394

Watson, I., 'The buildings of James Hartnoll', *Camden History Society Newsletter* **58** (Mar 1980)

Watson, I., *Westminster and Pimlico Past* (London, 1993)

Watson, I., '"A very large speculator in building": the double life of EJ Cave', *Camden History Review* **24** (2000), 26–31

Watson, I., 'Rebuilding London: Abraham Davis and his Brothers, 1881–1924', *London Journal* **29** (1) (2004), 62–84

Weaver, J. C., 'The modern city realized: Toronto civic affairs, 1880–1915' in Artibise and Stelter, eds, *The Usable Urban Past* (1979), pp. 39–72

Webster, R., ed, *Expanding Suburbia: Reviewing Suburban Narratives* (Oxford, 2000)

Wedd, K. with Peltz, L. and Ross, C., *Creative Quarters: The Art World in London from 1700 to 2000* (London, 2001)

Weightman, G. and Humphries, S., *The Making of Modern London 1815–1914* (London, 1983)

Weightman, G. and Humphries, S., *The Making of Modern London 1914–1939* (London, 1984)

Weinberg, H. B., Bolger, D. and Curry, D. P., *American Impressionism and Realism: The Painting of Modern Life, 1885–1915* (New York, 1994)

Weinreb, B. and Hibbert, C., eds, *The London Encyclopaedia* (London, 1983)

Weiss, M. A., *The Rise of the Community Builders* (New York, 1987)

Weiss, M. A., 'Density and intervention: New York's planning traditions', in Ward and Zunz, eds, *The Landscape of Modernity* (1992), pp. 46–75

Welter, V. M., *Biopolis: Patrick Geddes and the City of Life* (Cambridge MA, 2002)

White, J., *London in the Twentieth Century* (London, 2001)

White, N. and Willensky, E., *AIA Guide to New York City, 4th Edition* (New York, 2000)

White, R., *Too Good to be True: Toronto in the 1920s* (Toronto, 1993)

Whitehand, J. W. R. and Carr, C. M. H., *Twentieth-Century Suburbs: A Morphological Approach* (London, 2001)

Whitford, F., 'The city in painting' in Timms and Kelley, eds, *Unreal City* (1985), pp. 45–64

Wilk, C., ed, *Modernism: Designing a New World 1914–1939* (London, 2006)

Williams, R., *The Country and the City* (London, 1973)

Williamson, J. G., *Coping with City Growth during the British Industrial Revolution* (Cambridge, 1990)

Willis, C., 'Form follows finance: the Empire State Building', in Ward and Zunz, eds, *The Landscape of Modernity*, pp. 160–187

Willis, C., *Form Follows Finance: Skyscrapers and Skylines in New York and Chicago* (New York, 1995)

Wilson, E., *Adorned in Dreams: Fashion and Modernity* (London, 1985)

Wilson, E., *The Sphinx in the City: Urban Life, the Control of Disorder, and Women* (London, 1991)

Wilson, E., 'The invisible flâneur', *New Left Review* **191** (1992), 90–110

Winstanley, M., 'Temples of Commerce: Revolutions in Shopping and Banking', in P. Waller, ed, *The English Urban Landscape* (Oxford, 2000), pp. 151–174

Winter, J., *London's Teeming Streets, 1830–1914* (London, 1993)

Wohl, A. S., *The Eternal Slum: Housing and Social Policy in Victorian London* (London, 1977)

Wolff, J., 'The invisible *flâneuse*: women and the literature of modernity', *Theory, Culture and Society* **2** (1985), 37–46

Wolff, M. and Fox, C., 'Pictures from the magazines' in Dyos and Wolff, eds, *The Victorian City* (1973), pp. 559–582

Wolmar, C., *The Subterranean Railway: How the London Underground was Built and How It Changed the City Forever* (London, 2004)

Wood, C., *Victorian Panorama* (London, 1976)

Woodcock, G., *'Moral Predicament': Morley Callaghan's* More Joy in Heaven (Toronto, 1993)

Wright, G., *Building the Dream: A Social History of Housing in America* (Cambridge MA, 1981)

Wrigley, N. and Lowe, M., eds, *Retailing, Consumption and Capital: Towards the New Retail Geography* (London, 1996)

Yelling, J. A., *Slums and Slum Clearance in Victorian London* (London, 1986)

Yelling, J. A., *Slums and Redevelopment: Policy and Practice in England, 1918–45* (London, 1992)

Young, K. and Garside, P., *Metropolitan London: Politics and Urban Change 1837–1981* (London, 1982)

Zunz, O., *The Changing Face of Inequality: Urbanization, Industrial Development, and Immigrants in Detroit, 1880–1920* (Chicago, 1982)

Zunz, O., *Making America Corporate 1870–1920* (Chicago, 1990)

Zurier, R., Snyder, R. W. and Mecklenburg, V. M., *Metropolitan Lives: The Ashcan Artists and Their New York* (New York, 1995)

Zurier, R., 'City, stage, and screen: John Sloan's urban theater' in McDonnell, ed, *On the Edge of Your Seat* (2002), pp. 175–187.

Index

Page numbers in italics refer to illustrations.

Cambridge Studies in Historical Geography

* Asterisks denote titles available in paperback.